GW01466238

JOHN GIBSON LOCKHART

Born at Cambusnethan, Lanarkshire, in 1794. Contributor to *Blackwood's Magazine* from 1817 to 1846, and to the *Quarterly Review*, of which he became editor in 1826, from 1826 to 1852. In 1820 he married Charlotte Sophia, the elder daughter of Sir Walter Scott, and lived mostly in London from 1825 onwards with frequent sojourns at Abbotsford. After a fruitless visit to Rome to regain health, he returned to Abbotsford, where he died on 25th November 1854.

J. G. LOCKHART

The Life of
Sir Walter Scott

INTRODUCTION BY
W. M. PARKER
M.B.E., HON. M.A. (Edinburgh)

DENT: LONDON
EVERYMAN'S LIBRARY
DUTTON: NEW YORK

NO. *39*

SBN: 460 00039 x

INTRODUCTION

ONE might search in vain through the entire, if somewhat circumscribed, range of literary geniuses for a subject as fit for biography on the large scale as Sir Walter Scott. The friend of all the world, of high and low, rich and poor, one whose habits, characteristics, and interests were well known to his intimates, after Scott's death in 1832 the writing of his life seemed a tempting proposition for the pens of would-be chroniclers of such a universal genius. Indeed, not a few writers had the temerity to rush in where angels might have feared to tread. Scott had not been long in his grave when numerous lives and reminiscences poured forth in periodicals; as Southey commented in 1833: 'The birds of prey are already at work.' But Scott himself had decided that his son-in-law, John Gibson Lockhart, a proved exponent of biography in his *Burns* and *Napoleon*,[1] was the person best fitted to write the *Life*.

When in 1833–4, however, Lockhart was collecting his materials he found himself beset by other writers who wanted to be first in the field with a biography. Scott's son, the second Sir Walter, was displeased at the Scott family's prospect of having to submit to a life by William Laidlaw, the factor of the Abbotsford estate. Laidlaw was not sufficiently competent to do justice to their father's memory nor would his probably mediocre work reap that benefit which the family expected to derive from the Life; the profits on Lockhart's *Life* were to go towards the extinction of Scott's debts. Laidlaw's memoranda did not see the light until 1871.

Further annoyance was caused by two intruders. John McCrone, of James Cochrane & Co., publishers, had secured manuscript material for a life of Scott from his friend James Hogg, 'the Ettrick Shepherd.' Immediately, Lockhart wrote from London to Robert Cadell, who was to publish his (Lockhart's) *Life*, on 11th February 1833: 'One of the Sunday papers (yesterday) announces that one McCrone, partner to Cochrane . . . is in possession of Sir W.'s letters to Constable . . . and that they

---

[1] *See* Everyman's Library edition, No. 3 (1906).

are to appear in a Life already announced by this McCrone. I this day have written to Cochrane signifying that if this sort of thing has been contemplated it must have been in ignorance of the state of the law which requires the consent of Sir W.'s *executors* to any such publication and expressing hope that my warning is in time to save him from incurring any unnecessary expense. If he proceeds, I shall at once hand the affair over to a solicitor to get an injunction. But he, I presume, *won't*.' He wrote to Cadell again, on 13th November 1833, deploring 'how few the incidents of the Life are. Wd. to God we had his letters from Paris in 1815 to give variety, but can't find them.' But by 23rd January 1834 he had managed to secure the Constable letters, and reported to Cadell: 'Really a valuable series & presenting a most pleasing picture of intercourse between a truly great Author & an equally great bookseller.'

Then when Lockhart was on the eve of addressing himself to his *magnum opus*, as he informed Blackwood on 18th August 1834—'I am now about to commence writing my Life of Scott, a heavy and anxious task'—there was published Hogg's *Domestic Manners and Private Life of Sir Walter Scott*, in which, with characteristic self-assertion, Hogg declared: 'Of Lockhart's genius and capabilities, Sir Walter always spoke with the greatest enthusiasm, more than I thought he deserved, for I knew him a great deal better than Sir Walter did, and whatever Lockhart may pretend, I knew Sir Walter a thousand times better than he did.' Both this reference and the publication itself naturally incited Lockhart's wrath, for had he not been the one entrusted to write the authoritative Life?

The progress of Lockhart's composition is reflected in correspondence[1] during 1835-48. By 1836 he was absorbed in his task, for on 1st April his wife Sophia (Scott's elder daughter) reported to her cousin Anne: 'Lockhart is hard at work at the Life and will I think satisfy expectations from what I have heard of it.' On 20th June the hard-wrought biographer was in a quandary about the introduction of Scott's letters, as is shown by what he wrote to Cadell on that date: 'The great thing is to make the Life what it should be & I don't wish you to be making bargains for a pudding out of which it should remain at another's discretion to pluck the plums. . . . The perhaps dismallest thing for *me* (if I were to think of myself at all in this matter) is that very likely, when all his letters are thrown open to an unscrupulous after age, my manipulation may be thrown overboard

[1] All the letters, introduced here, referring to the large *Life* and the abridgment are in the National Library of Scotland.

entirely.' But by 8th December, when a certain amount of the
Life had reached proof stage, a reassuring comment came to him
from the young Sir Walter, who, having perused some sheets,
remarked: 'I am delighted with it.'

The only other person who was privileged to have a preview
of the manuscript was William Scott, sixth laird of Raeburn (a
cousin of Scott), to whom Lockhart wrote from London on 11th
December: 'I am flattered by your anxiety about my Life of
our dear friend Sir Walter which however will well deserve to be
called his own book, not mine, since it opens with a very beautiful sketch of his early history.... The publication however will
not begin for some months as I wish the whole MS. to be
complete before I hazard that step. ... I shall bid the bookseller forward to you the volumes as they are finished at the press,
confiding wholly in your discretion as to the keeping them
entirely to yourself & your own household until they are made
publici juris.... You are the only person to whom the volumes
will come before publication & I beg you will receive them &
their so coming as marks of my regard & respect for Sir Walter's
steady friend & the immediate head of his race.'

The first volume appeared on 18th March 1837, the second
followed on 1st May, the third on 1st June, the fourth on 1st
July, the fifth on 2nd October, the sixth on 30th December, and
the seventh and final volume was published in February 1838,
containing a Preface, in which Lockhart answered some of the
criticisms already passed on the work. In that year he was complimented by Southey on having produced 'the most complete
biography that has yet appeared of a great man.' While still
in the midst of his labours, Lockhart had written to Laidlaw on
19th January 1837 that his sole object was to do Scott justice,
'or rather to let him do himself justice, by so contriving it that
he shall be, as far as possible, from first to last, his own biographer. ... A stern sense of duty—that kind of sense of it
which is combined with the feeling of his actual presence in a
serene state of elevation above all petty terrestrial and temporary
views—will induce me to touch the few darker points in his life
and character as freely as the others which were so predominant;
and my chief anxiety on the appearance of the book will be, not
to hear what is said by the world, but what is thought by you
and the few others who can really compare the representation
of the whole with the facts of the case.'

After a reading of the first volume, Maria Edgeworth conveyed
the impressions of herself and her family to Sophia from Edgeworthstown in Ireland on 7th April 1837. 'The biography is

most interesting. The biographer of Leyden [1] deserved himself
to have such a biographer as he has. Crampton, our Surgeon
General, of whom you know nothing but who is known to Mr
Lockhart as a man of abilities out of his own line, & of real feeling
as I can attest, was the first person in this country whose opinion
of the book I heard. He wrote to me, delighted with it. "That
is biography indeed!" was what he said. . . .

    'Mr Lockhart makes such admirable use of all the letters—they
so unfold to the reader Sir Walter Scott's mind from the earliest
times—these and his own admirable fragment throw as much
light as can be given in confirmation of the Biographer's observations. . . . We have felt obliged to your husband for this
volume of the life of Sir Walter Scott, that beloved, admired
friend.' Lockhart himself acknowledged this epistle on 12th
April: 'Your approbation of my book should it be so fortunate
as to receive it when completed will afford me far greater satisfaction than I cd. draw from all the applauses of all the world
that did not like you know & love Sir Walter Scott.' But by
4th December, when Maria, having evidently read as far as the
fifth volume and expressed her displeasure at certain inaccuracies,
Lockhart, whose wife had died in the interval, conveyed his
apologies on that date. 'I much regret the circumstances which
have given pain to you or to others, but the truth is, the enormous
heaps of letters committed to me were all copied by Ladies &
the originals forthwith returned & I fear besides innumerable
blunders of names & dates which, or the most important of
them, it cost me no small pains to correct, there may have been
on the part of my dear Sophy & her assistants many omissions of
hints about omission which had come to hand on separate papers.
I hope no very serious evil has been occasioned but consider
that she who had been my Secretary for years in preparing
these Memoirs only lived to see not to read my final volume & in
her I lost the only person who could have put & kept me right
as to a thousand little things. I shall bear all you say in mind
when I come, if ever, to a second Edition.' On 2nd July of the
following year Lockhart had also to assure Scott of Raeburn
that 'it shall be my care to attend to your suggestions & corrections whenever the book is to be reprinted.'

    The Life of Scott was, in the main, greeted with enthusiasm and
praise. A reviewer in the Gentleman's Magazine of July 1838,
far from finding inaccuracies in the work, commended Lockhart
for his care. 'Mr Lockhart,' he remarked, 'united to all the

---

[1] Scott had contributed a Memoir of John Leyden, the orientalist, to the
Edinburgh Annual Register of 1811.

familiarity of intimate acquaintance those talents which have enabled him to appreciate and delineate the genius of Scott with accuracy and discrimination.' He then bases the purpose of his review on the work 'to show from the original evidence of his [Scott's] own works, and the attentive observation of his friends, what were the *foundations* on which his genius had built this lofty and extended fabric. . . . So that, however extraordinary, and above all common exertion and ability, were the emanations of Scott's genius; yet we have the satisfaction of understanding and ascertaining their growth, of witnessing the first collection of materials, the choice and disposition of them; and of acknowledging that an originally rich and native genius, united with those resources which well-directed study and laborious research could give, were alone equal to the noble undertakings that he achieved.'

There were many variations of opinion in contemporary criticisms. One main objection raised against it was its inordinate length. Reviewing it, Carlyle maintained that the work 'is not so much a composition as what we may call a compilation well done. . . . To picture forth the Life of Scott according to any rules of art or composition so that a reader, on adequately examining it, might say to himself, "There is Scott, there is the physiognomy and meaning of Scott's appearance and transit on this earth; such was he by nature, so did the world act on him, so he on the world, with such result and significance for us": this was by no manner of means Mr Lockhart's plan. A plan which, it is rashly said, should preside over every biography.' Although Carlyle wrote his review before the final volume appeared, he deprecated the extreme length. This stricture was also voiced by Wordsworth, who, after having received the final volume, wrote to Lockhart on 27th April 1838: 'You allude to the length of the Work as having been objected to, & I hope you will not be hurt when I say that I have been somewhat of the same opinion. The Diary of his Northern Voyage ought, I think, to have been printed apart from the life; & some of the letters also would have been more in their place, if separated from the Narrative.'

It took some time for these expressions of dissatisfaction with regard to the length of the work to have effect on the author and publisher. Meanwhile in 1839 a second edition of the *Life* came out in ten volumes, with some small additions, chiefly of footnotes, and a reprint in one volume, with double columns, was published in 1845, and again in 1850. But evidently as early as 1841 a curtailment was contemplated, for Maria Edgeworth wrote to Lockhart on 22nd December of that year, commending the idea. 'I am glad there is a new edition of Sir Walter's Memoirs compressed into cheap form. If it have the spirit preserved in it as preserved and heightened the spirit of the life of Napoleon as in your powerful compression of Sir Walter Scott's Memoirs of Bonaparte I shall delight in seeing the work. But if any profane vulgar hand has been daring to touch and thinking only of *abridging* may I never see it! I have taken up your Life of Sir Walter Scott at different times and was never able to lay it down without reading on, on, on with insatiable interest and admiration.'

The matter of abridgment was not decided upon until 1847, when, as Lockhart states in the Preface which follows here, Cadell, proposing to take to himself the whole remaining copyright in Scott's Works, stipulated that Lockhart should prepare an abridgment. Lockhart's reluctance to do this was overcome, and, reporting the transaction to Maria Edgeworth on 15th May, he added: 'Being wholly at a loss how to meet demands for interest . . . & really believing that no one else cd. or wd. offer so much for what I had to dispose of, I have signed the agreement.'

Maria's reply of 26th August seems to indicate a changed attitude to the abridgment, and that her fears for the work being tampered with were allayed. 'I hope you received my last letter in reply to that which you so very kindly wrote me giving me an account of the settlement of all your affairs . . . and of your intention to give an Abridgment of the Life. I hope— I trust—that you were not offended if you did receive my letter by the frankness, the boldness with which I spoke of some omissions I should desire in your new Edn. . . . I am sure you would feel my motive was right and that I was urged perhaps beyond propriety by my sincere anxiety for your fame, your moral as well as literary reputation, & *his* [i.e. Scott's].' Lockhart's next communication, on 28th August, shows that far from resenting Maria's proposals he welcomed them. 'As soon as I am well enough to work as usual I must now begin the abridgment of the Life of Sir W. S. Your suggestions on that head are laid by as valuable guidance when I do come to the job and if you can add to the number with the kind frankness that belongs to you most thankfully shall I endeavour to profit by such advice as yours is ever sure to be.' Maria's final letter on the subject was written on 31st August. 'I am not come to thinking about the new Life yet. But I am glad I did not affront you by my presumptuous advising and I shall do the same again as soon as you go to work again which I hope will not be for a great while yet. Very good for your health this Hang sorrow & cast away care.' These extracts from the correspondence are valuable in revealing that Maria Edgeworth contributed so much of the material for the abridgment.

At last, in 1848, it was published in two octavo volumes by Robert Cadell, Edinburgh, and Houlston & Stoneman, London, under the title of *Narrative of the Life of Sir Walter Scott, Bart. Begun by Himself and Continued by J. G. Lockhart, Esq.* The first volume comprised 409 pages, the second 403 pages, and a double-column index ran from page 405 to page 429. The abridgment contained here and there names and details which did not appear in the larger work, even in the subsequently published reprint of 1850. But when A. W. Pollard produced his edition of the large *Life* in five volumes in 1900, he inserted at the end of each volume a note of the alterations and additions which had been introduced into this 1848 abridgment. 'Some of these,' he stated, 'are trifling enough, but those in the first and last volumes are of considerable interest and require to be recorded.' Having bought the copyright of the abridged *Life* at the Cadell sale in 1851, Messrs Adam & Charles Black issued a second edition (1853) in one volume with the shortened title of *Life of Sir Walter Scott*. It consisted of 840-odd pages and 12 plates.

For the later history of the abridgment, after Lockhart's death in 1854, we must turn to another correspondence on the subject, namely, that which passed between James Robert Hope-Scott, Q.C., of Abbotsford (who had married Lockhart's daughter Charlotte), and W. E. Gladstone. On 7th September 1868 Gladstone informed his friend that 'with great delight, and under fascination, I have been treading (in mind) much ground familiar to you, and have been upon a regular perusal of Lockhart's *Life of Scott* from end to end. I am already reflecting with concern how soon I shall probably reach the last page of the last volume. I cannot help fearing it is one of the real vices of the day—at least in the higher & the so-called "educated" classes— to thrust away all prior English literature in favour of that which the hour produces. It can hardly be so however with the more numerous classes.' Evidently unaware that Lockhart himself had abridged the *Life* in 1848, Gladstone wrote again on 1st November: 'I wish I had time to write about the Life of Scott. I may be wrong but I am vaguely under the impression that it has never had a really wide circulation.[1] If so it is the saddest

---

[1] As a fact, between 1837 and 1856 there were sold, of all editions, 38,900 copies. Between 1856 and 1871 only 1,900.

pity: and I should greatly like (without any censure on its present length) to see published an abbreviation of it.' In his reply of 4th November Hope-Scott declared that 'for the present I cannot enlist with you in politics, but I can do so heartily in any attempt to extend a knowledge of Walter Scott.'

More than two years elapsed, and then on 24th March 1871 Hope-Scott informed Gladstone that his wish for a shorter *Life* had not been forgotten in the interval. 'At first,' he wrote, 'I thought that it would require a new work to be written, but, after some attempts to find a qualified writer, I learnt, to my surprise, that Lockhart's own abridgment was scarcely known even among Scott's admirers, and I came to the conclusion that a reprint of it would satisfy all reasonable desires for a shorter biography, and yet leave to Lockhart's wonderful skill the representation of a Character which he so much loved and so well understood.'

Accordingly, Hope-Scott proposed to Messrs Black that they should issue a new edition of the work, which they agreed to do. 'For various reasons,' he explained to Gladstone, 'I propose, if I should feel able, to write a short notice or advertisement to be prefixed to their book,' and he asked Gladstone if this preliminary might be cast 'in the form of a letter or dedication to you, and thus let the public know that you are among those who think that Scott deserves to be still remembered not as an author only but also as a noble and vigorous man.' Acceding to the request, Gladstone, in his reply of 25th March, wrote: 'You offer me a double temptation to which I yield with but too much readiness. I am glad of anything which associates my name with yours; and I feel it a great honour to be marked out in the public view by your selection of me as a loyal admirer of Scott towards whom both as writer and as man I cannot help entertaining feelings perhaps (though this is saying much) even bordering upon excess. Honesty binds me to wish you could do better for your purpose, but if you do not think any other plan desirable I accept your proposal with thanks.'

This reprint of the second edition (1853) of the abridgment, and entitled *The Life of Sir Walter Scott, Bart., Abridged from the Larger Work by J. G. Lockhart, with a Prefatory Letter by James R. Hope-Scott, Q.C.*, appeared appropriately in 1871, the centenary year of Scott's birth. In the course of his long dedicatory epistle Hope-Scott gave his reasons for, and explanations concerning, the work. 'An abridgment by the author himself must necessarily be the best, indeed the only true abridgment of what he has intended in his larger work; and I deem it a very fortunate thing that Cadell's influence overcame Lockhart's repugnance to the task.' Such was one aim in giving the public, 'as the best of all the easier modes of studying the life of Scott, the cheap and convenient reprint.' The reduction of bulk has meant compressing eighty-four chapters into eighteen. 'As regards the preparation of this reprint, I have not been able to do what I had proposed. It was my intention to have revised the text, and to have added notes; but, as the time which I had destined for this work drew near, it pleased God suddenly to stay my hand. . . . With the exception, therefore, of the change of form from two volumes to one, and of the addition of a short and melancholy notice . . . this narrative goes forth as Lockhart left it.'

The importance of this reprint is, that it has become the standard abridged edition, and it is the one of which the present Everyman volume is a reissue. Lord Stanhope, the historian, hailed the book eulogistically in a letter to Messrs Black on 24th June 1871, when acknowledging a copy. It 'seems to me admirably done, & such as no hand but Lockhart's own could have achieved.' Referring to Hope-Scott's having approached an eminent man to undertake the work as mentioned in the Prefatory Letter, Stanhope adds: 'Mr Hope-Scott has great reason to congratulate himself that the overture to another person . . . led to no result since under all the circumstances that result could not possibly have been so satisfactory, or nearly so satisfactory, as is the volume now before me which is compendious at the same time that it is charming.'

Contemporary and later verdicts on Lockhart's supreme literary achievement have been mostly unanimous in its praise. Carlyle hoped that 'all manner of biographies that are written in England will henceforth be written so'; Sir Archibald Alison found the work's charm was due to 'its being so imbued with the spirit of the subject that it may almost be regarded as an autobiography'; and W. H. Prescott concluded that 'fortunate as Sir Walter Scott was in his life, it was not the least of his good fortunes that he left the task of recording it to one so competent as Mr Lockhart, who to a familiarity with the person and habits of his illustrious subject unites such entire sympathy with his pursuits, and such fine tact and discrimination in arranging the materials for publication.'[1] The legal mind of Scott's Whig friend, Lord Cockburn, weighed the pros and cons. Recognizing that 'nothing is kept back or misrepresented' and realizing that Lockhart was blamed for the manner of his performance—a

[1] *Miscellanies* (1855), p. 178.

blame really emanating from Scott idolators who thought 'no imperfection in his character or imprudence in his conduct' should have been revealed—he concludes: 'A son-in-law perhaps ought not to have written the Life. . . . However, upon the whole, I know no biography which gives a truer account of its subject.'[1]

Saintsbury considered that 'the taste and spirit of Lockhart's book are not less admirable than the skill of its arrangement and the competency of its writing; nor would it be easily possible to find a happier adjustment in this respect in the whole annals of biography.'[2] As for Andrew Lang, his Borderer's bias in the work's favour was inevitable. 'Of the literary merits of the *Life of Scott* it is not possible for one whose breviary, as it were, the book has been from boyhood, to speak with impartiality. To a Scot, and a Scot of the Border, the book has the charm of home, and is dear to us as his own grey hills were dear to Sir Walter.'[3] According to Sir Edmund Gosse, this superb *Life* is 'the pre-eminent specimen of early nineteenth-century biography.'[4] Lockhart's biographical style has been praised by Professor Hugh Walker. 'It is simple and unstrained, and wholly free from self-consciousness . . . and the death scene is one of the finest passages in the whole range of English prose.'[5] For that scene the reader of the present volume is referred to page 640. In *English Biography*[6] Professor Waldo H. Dunn gave special commendation to Lockhart's having 'set himself deliberately and firmly against panegyric and dared to tell the story of Sir Walter's life—defects and all—as honestly as it was possible for him to do so.'

Perhaps one of the most searching of later criticisms was that of Sir Harold Nicolson. He subjected the *Life* to tests in literary technique, from which it emerges with flying colours. Remarking that 'Lockhart's success in executing his purpose is beyond praise,' he defended length as necessary for an 'inductive or cumulative method,' and that by massing detail, which is often trivial, Lockhart achieves his effect 'in the exact manner of Balzac.' As proof of Lockhart's constructive powers, he noted how perfectly he fuses 'the indirect with the direct narration' and that in his 'mastery of treatment and of composition conveys

[1] *Journal* (1874) I., pp. 134, 174–5.
[2] *A History of Nineteenth Century Literature* (1896), p. 193.
[3] *The Life and Letters of John Gibson Lockhart* (1897), p. 122.
[4] Article on 'Biography' in the *Encyclopaedia Britannica*, 11th ed. (1910), p. 954.
[5] *The Literature of the Victorian Era* (1910), pp. 923–4.
[6] Dent (1916), p. 165.

all the elucidation that is required.' Again, Lockhart's power of selection is evident in the way 'he secures his effect at the exact moment desired' and in the skill with which he 'places his anecdotes.'[1] Lockhart himself, in the letter to Laidlaw of 1837 already quoted, described the effect for which he had sought in the closing period of the *Life*. 'Out of these confused and painful scraps I think I can continue to put together a picture that will be highly touching of a great mind shattered, but never degraded, and always to the last noble, as his heart continued pure and warm as long as it could beat.'[2]

Every side of Scott's many-sidedness has been included. We see him not only as the prodigious writer, but as the intrepid traveller, keen sportsman, conscientious lawyer, the approachable social host, the presiding genius of the domestic hearth, and so on. The *Life*, of course, has its blemishes due mainly to inaccurate details, the manipulating and telescoping of letters in a deceptive fashion, dramatized episodes, and certain incidents that are imaginative rather than factual. At the same time, Lockhart explicitly rejected the Boswellian practice of introducing transcripts of conversation because there was a danger of misinterpreting the publication of the spoken word.

But far transcending any defects, as a work of art the *Life* remains unchallenged. It celebrates a very great man and a supreme genius so lovingly that it has a universal appeal. It has, with truth, been acknowledged to be one of the two best biographies in our literature, Boswell's *Johnson*, of course, being the other. There are passages which reveal Lockhart's poetic fancy, and others in which, as critic, he excels when epitomizing in cameo form the Waverley Novels; and the general scheme has been wonderfully sustained to the last days and closing scene of Scott's life, the most moving piece of writing in the entire work.

Before concluding this Introduction I should like to advocate to both adult and young readers, who wish to win to the heart of Scott, the man and the writer, that they would do well to read Lockhart's *Life* before embarking on any of the great romancer's works. If, having done so, they then give themselves up to Scott's poems and novels, they will find a relish in, and a comprehension of, these works less likely to be obtained without that prior knowledge of Scott's life, mind, and character. The biography is the more impressive on account of Lockhart's self-effacement. It needed, indeed, 'heaven-sent moments for this skill,' but the inspiration came and Lockhart's literary gifts reached their finest hour in this perennial enshrinement of Scott. The *Life* is Lockhart's own imposing memorial.

W. M. PARKER.

1956.

Select Bibliography xvii

MISCELLANEOUS WORKS. *Peter's Letters to His Kinsfolk*, by Peter Morris (pseudonym), 3 vols., 1819; an abridgment, edited with an Introduction and Notes by C. P. H., 1952. *A Letter to the Right Hon. Lord Byron*, by John Bull (pseudonym), 1821; edited by Alan Lang Strout, 1947. *The History of the Ingenious Gentleman Don Quixote of La Mancha*, translated by Motteux, edited by J. G. Lockhart, 5 vols., 1822. *Janus; or The Edinburgh Literary Almanack* (in collaboration with John Wilson, 'Christopher North'), 1826. *The Ballantyne-Humbug Handled in a Letter to Sir Adam Fergusson*, 1839.

NOVELS. *Valerius: a Roman Story*, 3 vols., 1821; revised ed., 1842. *Some Passages in the Life of Mr Adam Blair, Minister of the Gospel at Cross Meikle: a Novel*, 1822; published with *Matthew Wald*, 1843, 1846. *Reginald Dalton: a Story of English University Life*, 3 vols., 1823; other editions, 1842, 1880. *The History of Matthew Wald: a Novel*, 1824; published with *Adam Blair*, 1843, 1846.

TRANSLATIONS. *Lectures on the History of Literature, Ancient and Modern*, by Friedrich Schlegel, 2 vols., 1818; *Ancient Spanish Ballads, Historical and Romantic*, with Notes, 1823; revised ed., 1841; 5th ed., 1854; revised, with Memoir (New York), 1856; 1870, and numerous later editions and reprints.

BIOGRAPHICAL WORKS. *Life of Robert Burns*, 1828, 1830, 1838, 1847, 1871, 1872, etc. (New York), 1831; edited by W. S. Douglas, 1882 (revised by J. H. Ingram), 1890; Everyman's Library, 1907, 1946. *The History of Napoleon Buonaparte*, 1829; 2 vols. (New York), 1843, 1867, 1889; an abridgment by W. Tegg, 1878; abridged, 1885; Everyman's Library, 1906; Oxford ed. (edited by J. H. Rose), 1916. *The History of the Late War; including Sketches of Buonaparte, Nelson, and Wellington. For Children*, 1832. *Memoirs of the Life of Sir Walter Scott*, 7 vols., 1837–8, 10 vols., 1839, and numerous other editions. *Theodore Hook: a Sketch* (reprinted from *Quarterly Review*, May 1843), 1852.

BOOKS AND ARTICLES ON LOCKHART. *The Life and Letters of John Gibson Lockhart*, by Andrew Lang, 2 vols., 1897; *Lockhart's Literary Criticism* with Introduction and Bibliography by M. Clive Hildyard, 1931; *John Gibson Lockhart: a Critical Study* with Bibliography by Gilbert Macbeth, 1935; 'A Reconsideration of John Gibson Lockhart,' by W. M. Parker, *Quarterly Review*, July 1951; *John Gibson Lockhart*, by Marion Lochhead, 1954; 'John Gibson Lockhart (1794–1854): Editor and Biographer,' by W. M. Parker, *Quarterly Review*, October 1954; *Lockhart as Romantic Biographer*, by Francis Russell Hart, 1969.

BIOGRAPHICAL WORKS ON SCOTT

J. Hogg, *Domestic Manners and Private Life of Sir W. Scott*, 1834; 3rd ed., 1909; G. Saintsbury, *Sir Walter Scott*, 1897; John Buchan, *Sir Walter Scott*, 1932; Dame Una Pope Hennessy, *The Laird of Abbotsford*, 1932; H. J. C. Grierson, *Sir Walter Scott, a new Life*, 1938; Hesketh Pearson, *Walter Scott, His Life and Personality*, 1954; A. Melville Clark, *Sir Walter Scott: The Formative Years*, 1969 (Dr Clark argues that the date of Scott's birth should be 1770 and not 1771 as Scott states in his Autobiography to Lockhart's *Life*).

AUTHOR'S PREFACE

THE closing pages of this book will explain the transaction from which it sprung. When in May 1847 the publisher of Sir Walter Scott's Works proposed to take to himself the whole remaining Copyright in them, he stipulated that I should prepare an abridgement of the Memoirs of the Author, originally comprised in seven volumes, and since reprinted in various forms. If I had been to consult my own feelings, I should have been more willing to produce an enlarged edition; for the interest of Sir Walter's history lies, I think, even peculiarly, in its minute details—especially in the details set down by himself in his Letters and Diaries; and, of course, after the lapse of ten years, more copious use might be made of those materials without offence or indecorum. Mr. Cadell, however, considered that a book of smaller bulk, embracing only what may be called more strictly narrative, might be acceptable to certain classes of readers : and the manner in which this gentleman had throughout conducted himself towards Sir Walter, his family, and his memory—together with other circumstances on which it is not necessary to say more—overcame my reluctance.

It will be understood that whenever the narrative now given at all differs from that of the larger book, I have been endeavouring to profit by letters recently communicated.

J. G. L.

LONDON, 4th August 1848.

CHAPTER I

Ashestiel, April 26th, 1808.

THE present age has discovered a desire, or rather a rage, for literary anecdote and private history, that may be well permitted to alarm one who has engaged in a certain degree the attention of the public. That I have had more than my own share of popularity, my contemporaries will be as ready to admit as I am to confess that its measure has exceeded not only my hopes, but my merits, and even wishes. I may be therefore permitted, without an extraordinary degree of vanity, to take the precaution of recording a few leading circumstances (they do not merit the name of events) of a very quiet and uniform life—that, should my literary reputation survive my temporal existence, the public may know from good authority all that they are entitled to know of an individual who has contributed to their amusement.

From the lives of some poets a most important moral lesson may doubtless be derived, and few sermons can be read with so much profit as the Memoirs of Burns, of Chatterton, or of Savage. Were I conscious of any thing peculiar in my own moral character which could render such development necessary or useful, I would as readily consent to it as I would bequeath my body to dissection, if the operation could tend to point out the nature and the means of curing any peculiar malady. But as my habits of thinking and acting, as well as my rank in society, were fixed long before I had attained, or even pretended to, any poetical reputation,[1] and as it produced, when acquired, no

---

1 I do not mean to say that my success in literature has not led me to mix familiarly in society much above my birth and original pretensions, since I have been readily received in the first circles in Britain. But there is a certain intuitive knowledge of the world, to

remarkable change upon either, it is hardly to be expected
that much information can be derived from minutely inves-
tigating frailties, follies, or vices, not very different in
number or degree from those of other men in my situation.
As I have not been blessed with the talents of Burns or
Chatterton, I have been happily exempted from the influence of their violent passions, exasperated by the
struggle of feelings which rose up against the unjust
decrees of fortune. Yet, although I cannot tell of difficulties vanquished, and distance of rank annihilated by the
strength of genius, those who shall hereafter read this
little Memoir may find in it some hints to be improved, for
the regulation of their own minds, or the training those
of others.

Every Scottishman has a pedigree. It is a national
prerogative, as unalienable as his pride and his poverty.
My birth was neither distinguished nor sordid. According
to the prejudices of my country, it was esteemed *gentle*, as
I was connected, though remotely, with ancient families
both by my father's and mother's side. My father's grandfather was Walter Scott, well known in Teviotdale by the
surname of *Beardie*. He was the second son of Walter
Scott, first Laird of Raeburn, who was third son of Sir
William Scott, and the grandson of Walter Scott, commonly called in tradition *Auld Watt* of Harden. I am
therefore lineally descended from that ancient chieftain,
whose name I have made to ring in many a ditty, and from
his fair dame, the Flower of Yarrow—no bad genealogy
for a Border minstrel.[1] *Beardie*, my great-grandfather
aforesaid, derived his cognomen from a venerable beard,
which most well-educated Scotchmen are early trained, that prevents
them from being much dazzled by this species of elevation. A man
who to good nature adds the general rudiments of good breeding,
provided he rest contented with a simple and unaffected manner of
behaving and expressing himself, will never be ridiculous in the best
society, and, so far as his talents and information permit, may be an
agreeable part of the company. I have therefore never felt much
elevated, nor did I experience any violent change in situation, by the
passport which my poetical character afforded me into higher company than my birth warranted.—1826.

[1] [In whom the male representation of the old Scotts of Buccleuch
is now vested, there is great dispute among heraldic writers,—some
upholding the claim of Lord Napier, the male heir of the Scotts of
Thirlestane,—others that of Lord Polwarth, head of what was always
considered, in point of importance, the second family of the clan, viz.,
the Scotts of Harden, originally designed Scotts of Sinton. Of his
ancestors of this branch, Sir Walter has recorded many anecdotes in

which he wore unblemished by razor or scissors, in token of his regret for the banished dynasty of Stuart. It would have been well that his zeal had stopped there. But he took arms, and intrigued in their cause, until he lost all he had in the world, and, as I have heard, run a narrow risk of being hanged, had it not been for the interference of Anne, Duchess of Buccleuch and Monmouth. Beardie's elder brother, William Scott of Raeburn, my great-granduncle, was killed about the age of twenty-one, in a duel with Pringle of Crichton, grandfather of the present Mark Pringle of Clifton. They fought with swords, as was the fashion of the time, in a field near Selkirk, called from the catastrophe the *Raeburn Meadowspot*. Pringle fled from Scotland to Spain, and was long a captive and slave in Barbary. *Beardie* became, of course, *Tutor of Raeburn*, as the old Scottish phrase called him— that is, guardian to his infant nephew, father of the present Walter Scott of Raeburn. He also managed the estates of Makerstoun, being nearly related to that family by his mother, Isobel MacDougal. I suppose he had some allowance for his care in either case, and subsisted upon that and the fortune which he had by his wife, a Miss Campbell

the notes to the Border Minstrelsy, the Lay of the Last Minstrel, and elsewhere. In conversation he often alluded to the remarkable circumstance of two of them having been lame, and, nevertheless, both especially distinguished by the old rhythmical chronicler of the clan, Scott of Satchells (1688), who says of the first,—

> " It is four hundred winters past in order
> Since that Buccleuch was Warden in the Border
> A son he had at that same tide,
> Which was so lame could neither run nor ride.
> John, this lame, if my author speaks true,
> He sent him to St. Mungo's in Glasgu,
> Where he remained a scholar's time,
> Then he married a wife according to his mind. . .
> And betwixt them twa they did procreat
> Headshaw, Askirk, SINTON, and Glack."

But, if the scholarship of *John the Lamiter* furnished his descendant with many a mirthful allusion, a far greater favourite was the memory of *William the Boltfoot,* who followed him in the sixth generation.

> " The Laird and Lady of Harden
> Betwixt them procreat was a son
> Called William Boltfoot of Harden—
> *He did survive to be* A MAN."

He was, in fact, one of the " prowest knights " of the whole genealogy—a fearless horseman and expert spearsman, renowned and dreaded.—ED.]

of Silvercraigs, in the west, through which connection my
father used to *call cousin*, as they say, with the Campbells
of Blythswood.   Beardie was a man of some learning, and
a friend of Dr. Pitcairn, to whom his politics probably
made him acceptable.   They had a Tory or Jacobite club
in Edinburgh, in which the conversation is said to have
been maintained in Latin.

He left three sons.   The eldest, Walter, had a family,
of which any that now remain have been long settled in
America :—the male heirs are long since extinct.   The
third was William, father of James Scott, well known in
India as one of the original settlers of Prince of Wales
Island.   The second, Robert Scott, was my grandfather.
He was originally bred to the sea; but, being shipwrecked
near Dundee in his trial-voyage, he took such a sincere
dislike to that element, that he could not be persuaded to
a second attempt.   This occasioned a quarrel between him
and his father, who left him to shift for himself.   Robert
was one of those active spirits to whom this was no misfortune.   He turned Whig upon the spot, and fairly abjured
his father's politics, and his learned poverty.   His chief
and relative, Mr. Scott of Harden, gave him a lease of the
farm of Sandy-Knowe, comprehending the rocks in the
centre of which Smailholm or Sandy-Knowe Tower is situated.   He took for his shepherd an old man called Hogg,
who willingly lent him, out of respect to his family, his
whole savings, about £30, to stock the new farm.   With
this sum, which it seems was at the time sufficient for he
purpose, the master and servant set off to purchase a stock
of sheep at Whitsun-Tryste, a fair held on a hill near
Wooler in Northumberland.   The old shepherd went carefully from drove to drove, till he found a *hirsel* likely to
answer their purpose, and then returned to tell his master
to come up and conclude the bargain.   But what was nis
surprise to see him galloping a mettled hunter about the
race-course, and to find he had expended the whole stock
in this extraordinary purchase !—Moses's bargain of green
spectacles did not strike more dismay into the Vicar of
Wakefield's family, than my grandfather's rashness into
the poor old shepherd.   The thing, however, was irretrievable, and they returned without the sheep.   In the
course of a few days, however, my grandfather, who was
one of the best horsemen of his time, attended John Scott
of Harden's hounds on this same horse, and displayed him

to such advantage that he sold him for double the original price. The farm was now stocked in earnest; and the rest of my grandfather's career was that of successful industry. He was one of the first who were active in the cattle trade, afterwards carried to such extent between the Highlands of Scotland and the leading counties in England, and by his droving transactions acquired a considerable sum of money. He was a man of middle stature, extremely active, quick, keen, and fiery in his temper, stubbornly honest, and so distinguished for his skill in country matters that he was the general referee in all points of dispute which occurred in the neighbourhood. His birth, being admitted as *gentle*, gave him access to the best society in the county, and his dexterity in country sports, particularly hunting, made him an acceptable companion in the field as well as at the table.[1]

Robert Scott of Sandy-Knowe married, in 1728, Barbara Haliburton, daughter of Thomas Haliburton of Newmains, an ancient and respectable family in Berwickshire. Among other patrimonial possessions, they enjoyed the part of Dryburgh, now the property of the Earl of Buchan, comprehending the ruins of the Abbey. My granduncle, Robert Haliburton, having no male heirs, this estate, as well as the representation of the family, would have devolved upon my father, and indeed Old Newmains had settled it upon him; but this was prevented by the misfortunes of my granduncle, a weak silly man, who engaged in trade, for which he had neither stock nor talents, and became bankrupt. The ancient patrimony was sold for a trifle (about £3,000), and my father, who might have purchased it with ease, was dissuaded by my grandfather, who at that time believed a more advantageous purchase might have been made of some lands which Raeburn thought of selling. And thus we have nothing left of Dryburgh, although my father's maternal inheritance, but the right of stretching our bones where mine may perhaps be laid ere any eye but my own glances over these pages.

Walter Scott, my father, was born in 1729, and educated to the profession of a Writer to the Signet. He was the eldest of a large family, several of whom I shall have occasion to mention with a tribute of sincere gratitude. My

[1] The present Lord Haddington, and other gentlemen conversant with the south country, remember my grandfather well. He was a fine alert figure, and wore a jockey cap over his grey hair.—1826.

father was a singular instance of a man rising to eminence in a profession for which nature had in some degree unfitted him. He had indeed a turn for labour, and a pleasure in analysing the abstruse feudal doctrines connected with conveyancing, which would probably have rendered him unrivalled in the line of a special pleader, had there been such a profession in Scotland; but in the actual business of the profession which he embraced, in that sharp and intuitive perception which is necessary in driving bargains for himself and others, in availing himself of the wants, necessities, caprices, and follies of some, and guarding against the knavery and malice of others, Uncle Toby himself could not have conducted himself with more simplicity than my father. Most attorneys have been suspected, more or less justly, of making their own fortune at the expense of their clients—my father's fate was to vindicate his calling from the stain in one instance, for in many cases his clients contrived to ease him of considerable sums. Many worshipful and be-knighted names occur to my memory, who did him the honour to run in his debt to the amount of thousands, and to pay him with a lawsuit, or a commission of bankruptcy, as the case happened. But they are gone to a different accounting, and it would be ungenerous to visit their disgrace upon their descendants. My father was wont also to give openings, to those who were pleased to take them, to pick a quarrel with him. He had a zeal for his clients which was almost ludicrous: far from coldly discharging the duties of his employment towards them, he thought for them, felt for their honour as for his own, and rather risked disobliging them than neglecting anything to which he conceived their duty bound them. If there was an old mother or aunt to be maintained, he was, I am afraid, too apt to administer to their necessities from what the young heir had destined exclusively to his pleasures. This ready discharge of obligations which the Civilians tell us are only natural and not legal, did not, I fear, recommend him to his employers. Yet his practice was, at one period of his life, very extensive. He understood his business theoretically, and was early introduced to it by a partnership with George Chalmers, Writer to the Signet, under whom he had served his apprenticeship.

His person and face were uncommonly handsome, with an expression of sweetness of temper, which was not fallacious; his manners were rather formal, but full of genuine kindness, especially when exercising the duties of hospitality. His general habits were not only temperate, but severely abstemious; but upon a festival occasion, there were few whom a moderate glass of wine exhilarated to such a lively degree. His religion, in which he was devoutly sincere, was Calvinism of the strictest kind, and his favourite study related to church history. I suspect the good old man was often engaged with Knox and Spottiswoode's folios, when, immured in his solitary room, he was supposed to be immersed in professional researches. In his political principles he was a steady friend to freedom, with a bias, however, to the monarchical part of our constitution, which he considered as peculiarly exposed to danger during the later years of his life. He had much of ancient Scottish prejudice respecting the forms of marriages, funerals, christenings, and so forth, and was always vexed at any neglect of etiquette upon such occasions. As his education had not been upon an enlarged plan, it could not be expected that he should be an enlightened scholar, but he had not passed through a busy life without observation; and his remarks upon times and manners often exhibited strong traits of practical though untaught philosophy. Let me conclude this sketch, which I am unconscious of having overcharged, with a few lines written by the late Mrs. Cockburn[1] upon the subject. They made one among a set of poetical characters which were given as toasts among a few friends, and we must hold them to contain a striking likeness, since the original was recognised so soon as they were read aloud :—

> " To a thing that's uncommon—a youth of discretion,
>   Who, though vastly handsome, despises flirtation :
>   To the friend in affliction, the heart of affection,
>   Who may hear the last trump without dread of detection."

In April 1758, my father married Anne Rutherford, eldest daughter of Dr. John Rutherford, professor of medicine in the University of Edinburgh. He was one of those pupils of Boerhaave, to whom the school of medicine in our northern metropolis owes its rise, and a man distinguished for professional talent, for lively wit, and for literary acquirements. Dr. Rutherford was twice married. His first

---

[1] Mrs. Cockburn (born Miss Rutherford of Fairnalie) was the authoress of the beautiful song—
> " I have seen the smiling
>   Of fortune beguiling."

wife, of whom my mother is the sole surviving child, was a daughter of Sir John Swinton of Swinton, a family which produced many distinguished warriors during the middle ages, and which, for antiquity and honourable alliances, may rank with any in Britain. My grandfather's second wife was Miss Mackay, by whom he had a second family, of whom are now (1808) alive, Dr. Daniel Rutherford, professor of botany in the University of Edinburgh, and Misses Janet and Christian Rutherford, amiable and accomplished women.

My father and mother had a very numerous family, no fewer, I believe, than twelve children, of whom many were highly promising, though only five survived very early youth. My eldest brother Robert was bred in the King's service, and was in most of Rodney's battles. His temper was bold and haughty, and to me was often checkered with what I felt to be capricious tyranny. In other respects I loved him much, for he had a strong turn for literature, read poetry with taste and judgment, and composed verses himself, which had gained him great applause among his messmates. Witness the following elegy upon the supposed loss of the vessel, composed the night before Rodney's celebrated battle of April the 12th, 1782. It alludes to the various amusements of his mess :—

> " No more the geese shall cackle on the poop,
>   No more the bagpipe through the orlop sound,
> No more the midshipmen, a jovial group,
>   Shall toast the girls and push the bottle round.
> In death's dark road at anchor fast they stay,
>   Till Heaven's loud signal shall in thunder roar ;
> Then starting up, all hands shall quick obey,
>   Sheet home the topsail, and with speed unmoor."

Robert sung agreeably—(a virtue which was never seen in me)—understood the mechanical arts, and when in good humour, could regale us with many a tale of bold adventure and narrow escapes. When in bad humour, however, he gave us a practical taste of what was then man-of-war's discipline, and kicked and cuffed without mercy. I have often thought how he might have distinguished himself had he continued in the navy until the present times, so glorious for nautical exploit. But the peace of 1783 cut off all hopes of promotion for those who had not great interest ; and some disgust which his proud spirit had taken at harsh usage from a superior officer combined to throw poor Robert into the East-India Company's service, for which his habits were ill adapted. He made two voyages to the East, and died a victim to the climate.

John Scott, my second brother, is about three years older than me. He addicted himself to the military service, and is now brevet-major in the 73rd regiment.[1]

I had an only sister, Anne Scott, who seemed to be from her cradle the butt for mischance to shoot arrows at. Her childhood was marked by perilous escapes from the most extraordinary accidents. Among others, I remember an iron-railed door leading into the area in the centre of George's Square being closed by the wind, while her fingers were betwixt the hasp and staple. Her hand was thus locked in, and must have been smashed to pieces, had not the bones of her fingers been remarkably slight and thin. As it was, the hand was cruelly mangled. On another occasion, she was nearly drowned in a pond, or old quarry-hole, in what was then called Brown's Park, on the south side of the square. But the most unfortunate accident, and which, though it happened while she was only six years old, proved the remote cause of her death, was her cap accidentally taking fire. The child was alone in the room, and before assistance could be obtained, her head was dreadfully scorched. After a lingering and dangerous illness, she recovered—but never to enjoy perfect health. The slightest cold occasioned swellings in her face, and other indications of a delicate constitution. At length [in 1801], poor Anne was taken ill, and died after a very short interval. Her temper, like that of her brothers, was peculiar, and in her, perhaps, it shewed more odd, from the habits of indulgence which her nervous illness had formed. But she was at heart an affectionate and kind girl, neither void of talent nor of feeling, though living in an ideal world which she had framed to herself by the force of imagination. Anne was my junior by about a year.

A year lower in the list was my brother Thomas Scott, who is still alive.[2]

[1] He was this year made major of the second battalion by the kind intercession of Mr. Canning at the War Office—1809. He retired from the army, and kept house with my mother. His health was totally broken, and he died, yet a young man, on 8th May 1816.—1826.

[2] Poor Tom, a man of infinite humour and excellent parts, pursued for some time my father's profession; but he was unfortunate, from engaging in speculations respecting farms and matters out of the line of his proper business. He afterwards became paymaster of

Last, and most unfortunate of our family, was my youngest brother, Daniel. With the same aversion to labour, or rather, I should say, the same determined indolence that marked us all, he had neither the vivacity of intellect which supplies the want of diligence, nor the pride which renders the most detested labour better than dependence or contempt. His career was as unfortunate as might be augured from such an unhappy combination; and, after various unsuccessful attempts to establish himself in life, he died on his return from the West Indies, in July 1806.

Having premised so much of my family, I return to my own story. I was born, as I believe, on the 15th August 1771, in a house belonging to my father, at the head of the College Wynd. It was pulled down, with others, to make room for the northern front of the new College. I was an uncommonly healthy child, but had nearly died in consequence of my first nurse being ill of a consumption, a circumstance which she chose to conceal, though to do so was murder to both herself and me. She went privately to consult Dr. Black, the celebrated professor of chemistry, who put my father on his guard. The woman was dismissed, and I was consigned to a healthy peasant, who is still alive to boast of her *laddie* being what she calls a *grand gentleman*. I shewed every sign of health and strength until I was about eighteen months old. One night, I have been often told, I shewed great reluctance to be caught and put to bed; and after being chased about the room, was apprehended and consigned to my dormitory with some difficulty. It was the last time I was to shew such personal agility. In the morning I was discovered to be affected with the fever which often accompanies the cutting of large teeth. It held me three days. On the fourth, when they went to bathe me as usual, they discovered that I had lost the power of my right leg. My grandfather, an excellent anatomist as well as physician, the late worthy Alexander Wood, and many others of the most respectable of the faculty, were consulted. There appeared to be no dislocation or sprain; blisters and other topical remedies were

the 70th regiment, and died in Canada. Tom married Elizabeth, a daughter of the family of M'Culloch of Ardwell, an ancient Galwegian stock, by whom he left a son, Walter Scott, now second lieutenant of Engineers in the East India Company's service, Bombay—and three daughters, Jessie, married to Lieutenant-Colonel Huxley; 2. Anne; 3. Eliza—the two last still unmarried.—1826.

applied in vain. When the efforts of regular physicians had been exhausted, without the slightest success, my anxious parents, during the course of many years, eagerly grasped at every prospect of cure which was held out by the promise of empirics, or of ancient ladies or gentlemen who conceived themselves entitled to recommend various remedies, some of which were of a nature sufficiently singular. But the advice of my grandfather, Dr. Rutherford, that I should be sent to reside in the country, to give the chance of natural exertion, excited by free air and liberty, was first resorted to; and before I have the recollection of the slightest event, I was, agreeably to this friendly counsel, an inmate in the farm-house of Sandy-Knowe.

An odd incident is worth recording. It seems my mother had sent a maid to take charge of me, that I might be no inconvenience in the family. But the damsel sent on that important mission had left her heart behind her, in the keeping of some wild fellow, it is likely, who had done and said more to her than he was like to make good. She became extremely desirous to return to Edinburgh, and as my mother made a point of her remaining where she was, she contracted a sort of hatred at poor me, as the cause of her being detained at Sandy-Knowe. This rose, I suppose, to a sort of delirious affection, for she confessed to old Alison Wilson, the housekeeper, that she had carried me up to the Craigs, meaning, under a strong temptation of the Devil, to cut my throat with her scissors, and bury me in the moss. Alison instantly took possession of my person, and took care that her confidant should not be subject to any farther temptation, so far as I was concerned. She was dismissed, of course, and I have heard became afterwards a lunatic.[1]

---

[1] [The epistle prefixed to the sixth canto of Marmion contains a charming picture of the infant poet's feelings amidst the scenery and associations of Smailholm Tower and Sandy-Knowe.

"It was a barren scene and wild,
Where naked cliffs were rudely piled," &c. &c.

There are still (1836) living in that neighbourhood two old women, who were in the domestic service of Sandy-Knowe, when the lame child was brought thither in the third year of his age. One of them, Tibby Hunter, remembers his coming well; and that " he was a sweet-tempered bairn, a darling with all about the house." The young ewe-milkers delighted, she says, to carry him about on their backs among the crags; and he was " very gleg (quick) at the uptake, and soon kenned every sheep and lamb by head-mark as well as any of them." His great pleasure, however, was in the society of

It is here at Sandy-Knowe, in the residence of my paternal grandfather, already mentioned, that I have the first consciousness of existence; and I recollect distinctly that my situation and appearance were a little whimsical. Among the odd remedies recurred to to aid my lameness, some one had recommended, that so often as a sheep was killed for the use of the family, I should be stripped, and swathed up in the skin, warm as it was flayed from the carcase of the animal. In this Tartar-like habiliment I well remember lying upon the floor of the little parlour in the farm-house, while my grandfather, a venerable old man with white hair, used every excitement to make me try to crawl. I also distinctly remember the late Sir George Mac-Dougal of Mackerstoun, father of the present Sir Henry Hay MacDougal, joining in this kindly attempt. He was, God knows how,[1] a relation of ours, and I still recollect him in his old-fashioned military habit (he had been colonel

the "aged hind" recorded in the epistle to Erskine, "auld Sandy Ormiston," called, from the most dignified part of his function, "the Cow-bailie," who had the chief superintendence of the flocks that browsed upon "the velvet tufts of loveliest green." If the child saw him in the morning, he could not be satisfied unless the old man would set him astride on his shoulder, and take him to keep him company as he lay watching his charge.

> "Here was poetic impulse given
> By the green hill and clear blue heaven."

The Cow-bailie blew a particular note on his whistle, which signified to the maid-servants in the house below when the little boy wished to be carried home again. He told his friend, Mr. Skene of Rubislaw, when spending a summer day in his old age among these well-remembered crags, that he delighted to roll about on the grass all day long in the midst of the flock, and that "the sort of fellowship he thus formed with the sheep and lambs had impressed his mind with a degree of affectionate feeling towards them which had lasted throughout life." There is a story of his having been forgotten one day among the knolls when a thunder storm came on; and his aunt, suddenly recollecting his situation, and running out to bring him home, is said to have found him lying on his back, clapping his hands at the lightning, and crying out, "Bonny! bonny!" at every flash. —Ed.]

[1] He was a second-cousin of my grandfather's. Isobel Mac-Dougal, wife of Walter, the first Laird of Raeburn, and mother of Walter Scott, called Beardie, was grand-aunt, I take it, to the late Sir George MacDougal. There was always great friendship between us and the Makerstoun family. It singularly happened, that at the burial of the late Sir Henry MacDougal, my cousin William Scott, younger of Raeburn, and I myself, were the nearest blood-relations present, although our connection was of so old a date, and ranked as pall-bearers accordingly.—1826.

of the Greys), with a small cocked hat, deeply laced, an embroidered scarlet waistcoat, and a light-coloured coat, with milk-white locks tied in a military fashion, kneeling on the ground before me, and dragging his watch along the carpet to induce me to follow it. The benevolent old soldier and the infant wrapped in his sheepskin would have afforded an odd group to uninterested spectators. This must have happened about my third year, for Sir George MacDougal and my grandfather both died shortly after that period.

My grandmother continued for some years to take charge of the farm, assisted by my father's second brother, Mr. Thomas Scott, who resided at Crailing as factor or land-steward for Mr. Scott of Danesfield, then proprietor of that estate.[1] This was during the heat of the American war, and I remember being as anxious on my uncle's weekly visits (for we heard news at no other time) to hear of the defeat of Washington, as if I had had some deep and personal cause of antipathy to him. I know not how this was combined with a very strong prejudice in favour of the Stuart family, which I had originally imbibed from the songs and tales of the Jacobites. This latter political propensity was deeply confirmed by the stories told in my hearing of the cruelties exercised in the executions at Carlisle, and in the Highlands, after the battle of Culloden. One or two of our own distant relations had fallen on that occasion, and I remember of detesting the name of Cumberland with more than infant hatred. Mr. Curle, farmer at Yetbyre, husband of one of my aunts, had been present at their execution; and it was probably from him that I first heard these tragic tales which made so great an impression on me. The local information, which I conceive had some share in forming my future taste and pursuits, I derived from the old songs and tales which then formed the amusement of a retired country family. My grandmother, in whose youth the old Border depredations were matter of recent tradition, used to tell me many a tale of Watt of Harden, Wight Willie of Aikwood, Jamie Telfer of the fair Dodhead, and other heroes—merrymen all of the persua-

[1] My uncle afterwards resided at Elliston, and then took from Mr. Cornelius Elliot the estate of Woollee. Finally he retired to Monklaw, in the neighbourhood of Jedburgh, where he died, 1823, at the advanced age of ninety years, and in full possession of his faculties. It was a fine thing to hear him talk over the change of the country which he had witnessed.—1826.

sion and calling of Robin Hood and Little John. A more recent hero, but not of less note, was the celebrated *Diel of Littledean,* whom she well remembered, as he had married her mother's sister. Of this extraordinary person I learned many a story, grave and gay, comic and warlike. Two or three old books which lay in the window-seat were explored for my amusement in the tedious winter days. Automathes, and Ramsay's Tea-table Miscellany, were my favourites, although at a later period an odd volume of Josephus's Wars of the Jews divided my partiality.

My kind and affectionate aunt, Miss Janet Scott, whose memory will ever be dear to me, used to read these works to me with admirable patience, until I could repeat long passages by heart. The ballad of Hardyknute I was early master of, to the great annoyance of almost our only visitor, the worthy clergyman of the parish, Dr. Duncan, who had not patience to have a sober chat interrupted by my shouting forth this ditty. Methinks I now see his tall thin emaciated figure, his legs cased in clasped gambadoes, and his face of a length that would have rivalled the Knight of La Mancha's, and hear him exclaiming, " One may as well speak in the mouth of a cannon as where that child is." With this little acidity, which was natural to him, he was a most excellent and benevolent man, a gentleman in every feeling, and altogether different from those of his order who cringe at the tables of the gentry, or domineer and riot at those of the yeomanry. In his youth he had been chaplain in the family of Lord Marchmont—had seen Pope—and could talk familiarly of many characters who had survived the Augustan age of Queen Anne. Though valetudinary, he lived to be nearly ninety, and to welcome to Scotland his son, Colonel William Duncan, who, with the highest character for military and civil merit, had made a considerable fortune in India. In [1795], a few days before his death, I paid him a visit, to inquire after his health. I found him emaciated to the last degree, wrapped in a tartan night-gown, and employed with all the activity of health and youth in correcting a history of the Revolution, which he intended should be given to the public when he was no more. He read me several passages with a voice naturally strong, and which the feelings of an author then raised above the depression of age and declining health. I begged him to spare this fatigue, which could not but injure his health. His answer was remarkable. " I

know," he said, " that I cannot survive a fortnight—and
what signifies an exertion that can at worst only accelerate
my death a few days?" I marvelled at the composure of
this reply, for his appearance sufficiently vouched the truth
of his prophecy, and rode home to my uncle's (then my
abode), musing what there could be in the spirit of authorship that could inspire its votaries with the courage of
martyrs. He died within less than the period he assigned
—with which event I close my digression.

I was in my fourth year when my father was advised that
the Bath waters might be of some advantage to my lameness. My affectionate aunt, although such a journey promised to a person of her retired habits any thing but pleasure or amusement, undertook as readily to accompany me
to the wells of Bladud, as if she had expected all the delight
that ever the prospect of a watering-place held out to its
most impatient visitants. My health was by this time a
good deal confirmed by the country air, and the influence
of that imperceptible and unfatiguing exercise to which the
good sense of my grandfather had subjected me; for when
the day was fine, I was usually carried out and laid down
beside the old shepherd, among the crags or rocks round
which he fed his sheep. The impatience of a child soon
inclined me to struggle with my infirmity, and I began by
degrees to stand, to walk, and to run. Although the
limb affected was much shrunk and contracted, my general
health, which was of more importance, was much strengthened by being frequently in the open air; and, in a word,
I who in a city had probably been condemned to hopeless
and helpless decrepitude, was now a healthy, high-spirited,
and, my lameness apart, a sturdy child—*non sine diis ani-
mosus infans*.

We went to London by sea, and it may gratify the
curiosity of minute biographers to learn that our voyage
was performed in the Duchess of Buccleuch, Captain Beat-
son, master. At London we made a short stay, and saw
some of the common shows exhibited to strangers. When,
twenty-five years afterwards, I visited the Tower of London and Westminster Abbey, I was astonished to find how
accurate my recollections of these celebrated places of visitation proved to be, and I have ever since trusted more
implicitly to my juvenile reminiscences. At Bath, where I
lived about a year, I went through all the usual discipline
of the pump-room and baths, but I believe without the

least advantage to my lameness.   During my residence at
Bath I acquired the rudiments of reading at a day-school,
kept by an old dame near our lodgings, and I had never
a more regular teacher, although I think I did not attend
her a quarter of a year.   An occasional lesson from my
aunt supplied the rest.   Afterwards, when grown a big
boy, I had a few lessons from Mr. Stalker of Edinburgh,
and finally from the Rev. Mr. Cleeve.   But I never acquired a just pronunciation, nor could I read with much
propriety.

In other respects my residence at Bath is marked by
very pleasing recollections.   The venerable John Home,
author of Douglas, was then at the watering-place, and
paid much attention to my aunt and to me.   His wife, who
has survived him, was then an invalid, and used to take he
air in her carriage on the Downs, when I was often invited
to accompany her.   But the most delightful recollections
of Bath are dated after the arrival of my uncle, Captain
Robert Scott, who introduced me to all the little amusements which suited my age, and above all, to the theatre.
The play was As You Like It; and the witchery of the
whole scene is alive in my mind at this moment.   I made,
I believe, noise more than enough, and remember being
so much scandalised at the quarrel between Orlando and
his brother in the first scene, that I screamed out, " A'n't
they brothers ? " [1]   A few weeks' residence at home convinced me, who had till then been an only child in the house
of my grandfather, that a quarrel between brothers was
a very natural event.

The other circumstances I recollect of my residence in
Bath are but trifling, yet I never recall them without a
feeling of pleasure.   The beauties of the parade (which
of them I know not), with the river of Avon winding
around it, and the lowing of the cattle from the opposite
hills, are warm in my recollection, and are only rivalled by
the splendours of a toy-shop somewhere near the Orange
Grove.   I had acquired, I know not by what means, a kind
of superstitious terror for statuary of all kinds.   No ancient
Iconoclast or modern Calvinist could have looked on the
outside of the Abbey church (if I mistake not the principal
church at Bath is so called) with more horror than the image
of Jacob's Ladder, with all its angels, presented to my

[1] [See Scott's Review of the Life of John Kemble, Miscell. Prose,
vol. xx. p. 154.—ED.]

infant eye. My uncle effectually combated my terrors, and formally introduced me to a statue of Neptune, which perhaps still keeps guard at the side of the Avon, where a pleasure boat crosses to Spring Gardens.

After being a year at Bath, I returned first to Edinburgh, and afterwards for a season to Sandy-Knowe;—and thus the time whiled away till about my eighth year, when it was thought sea-bathing might be of service to my lameness.

For this purpose, still under my aunt's protection, I remained some weeks at Prestonpans; a circumstance not worth mentioning, excepting to record my juvenile intimacy with an old military veteran, Dalgetty by name, who had pitched his tent in that little village, after all his campaigns, subsisting upon an ensign's half-pay, though called by courtesy a Captain. As this old gentleman, who had been in all the German wars, found very few to listen to his tales of military feats, he formed a sort of alliance with me, and I used invariably to attend him for the pleasure of hearing those communications. Sometimes our conversation turned on the American war, which was then raging. It was about the time of Burgoyne's unfortunate expedition, to which my Captain and I augured different conclusions. Somebody had shewed me a map of North America, and, struck with the rugged appearance of the country, and the quantity of lakes, I expressed some doubts on the subject of the General's arriving safely at the end of his journey, which were very indignantly refuted by the Captain. The news of the Saratoga disaster, while it gave me a little triumph, rather shook my intimacy with the veteran.[1]

---

[1] Besides this veteran, I found another ally at Prestonpans, in the person of George Constable, an old friend of my father's, educated to the law, but retired upon his independent property, and generally residing near Dundee. He had many of those peculiarities of temper which long afterwards I tried to develop in the character of Jonathan Oldbuck. It is very odd, that though I am unconscious of anything in which I strictly copied the *manners* of my old friend, the resemblance was nevertheless detected by George Chalmers, Esq., solicitor, London, an old friend, both of my father and Mr. Constable, and who affirmed to my late friend, Lord Kinedder, that I must needs be the author of The Antiquary, since he recognised the portrait of George Constable. But my friend George was not so decided an enemy to womankind as his representative Monkbarns. On the contrary, I rather suspect that he had a *tendresse* for my aunt Jenny, who even then was a most beautiful woman, though somewhat advanced in life.

From Prestonpans I was transported back to my father's house in George's Square, which continued to be my most established place of residence, until my marriage in 1797. I felt the change from being a single indulged brat, to becoming a member of a large family, very severely; for under the gentle government of my kind grandmother, who was meekness itself, and of my aunt, who, though of an higher temper, was exceedingly attached to me, I had acquired a degree of licence which could not be permitted in a large family. I had sense enough, however, to bend my temper to my new circumstances; but such was the

To the close of her life, she had the finest eyes and teeth I ever saw, and though she could be sufficiently sharp when she had a mind, her general behaviour was genteel and ladylike. However this might be, I derived a great deal of curious information from George Constable, both at this early period, and afterwards. He was constantly philandering about my aunt, and of course very kind to me. He was the first person who told me about Falstaff and Hotspur, and other characters in Shakespeare. What idea I annexed to them I know not, but I must have annexed some, for I remember quite well being interested on the subject. Indeed, I rather suspect that children derive impulses of a powerful and important kind in hearing things which they cannot entirely comprehend; and therefore, that to write *down* to children's understanding is a mistake; set them on the scent, and let them puzzle it out. To return to George Constable: I knew him well at a much later period. He used always to dine at my father's house of a Sunday, and was authorised to turn the conversation out of the austere and Calvinistic tone, which it usually maintained on that day, upon subjects of history or auld langsyne. He remembered the forty-five, and told many excellent stories, all with a strong dash of a peculiar caustic humour.

George's sworn ally as a brother antiquary was John Davidson, then Keeper of the Signet; and I remember his flattering and compelling me to go to dine there. A writer's apprentice with the Keeper of the Signet, whose least officer kept us in order!—It was an awful event. Thither, however, I went with some secret expectation of a scantling of good claret. Mr. D. had a son whose taste inclined him to the army, to which his father, who had designed him for the Bar, gave a most unwilling consent. He was at this time a young officer, and he and I, leaving the two seniors to proceed in their chat as they pleased, never once opened our mouths either to them or each other. The Pragmatic Sanction happened unfortunately to become the theme of their conversation, when Constable said in jest, " Now, John, I'll wad you a plack that neither of these two lads ever heard of the Pragmatic Sanction."—" Not heard of the Pragmatic Sanction ! " said John Davidson; " I would like to see that;" and with a voice of thunder, he asked his son the fatal question. As young D. modestly allowed he knew nothing about it, his father drove him from the table in a rage, and I absconded during the confusion; nor could Constable ever bring me back again to his friend Davidson's.—1826.

agony which I internally experienced, that I have guarded
against nothing more in the education of my own family,
than against their acquiring habits of self-willed caprice
and domination. I found much consolation during this
period of mortification, in the partiality of my mother. She
joined to a light and happy temper of mind a strong turn
to study poetry and works of imagination. She was
sincerely devout, but her religion was, as became her sex,
of a cast less austere than my father's. Still, the discipline
of the Presbyterian Sabbath was severely strict, and I
think injudiciously so. Although Bunyan's Pilgrim, Ges-
ner's Death of Abel, Rowe's Letters, and one or two
other books, which, for that reason, I still have a favour
for, were admitted to relieve the gloom of one dull sermon succeeding to another—there was far too much
tedium annexed to the duties of the day; and in the end
it did none of us any good.

My week-day tasks were more agreeable. My lameness
and my solitary habits had made me a tolerable reader,
and my hours of leisure were usually spent in reading aloud
to my mother Pope's translation of Homer, which, excepting a few traditionary ballads, and the songs in Allan
Ramsay's Evergreen, was the first poetry which I perused.
My mother had good natural taste and great feeling : she
used to make me pause upon those passages which expressed generous and worthy sentiments, and if she could
not divert me from those which were descriptive of battle
and tumult, she contrived at least to divide my attention between them. My own enthusiasm, however, was
chiefly awakened by the wonderful and the terrible—the
common taste of children, but in which I have remained a
child even unto this day. I got by heart, not as a task,
but almost without intending it, the passages with which
I was most pleased, and used to recite them aloud, both
when alone and to others—more willingly, however, in my
hours of solitude, for I had observed some auditors smile,
and I dreaded ridicule at that time of life more than I
have ever done since.

In [1778] I was sent to the second class of the Gram-
mar School, or High School of Edinburgh, then taught
by Mr. Luke Fraser, a good Latin scholar and a very
worthy man. Though I had received, with my brothers,
in private, lessons of Latin from Mr. James French, now
a minister of the Kirk of Scotland, I was nevertheless

rather behind the class in which I was placed, both in years and in progress. This was a real disadvantage, and one to which a boy of lively temper and talents ought to be as little exposed as one who might be less expected to make up his lee-way, as it is called. The situation has the unfortunate effect of reconciling a boy of the former character (which in a posthumous work I may claim for my own) to holding a subordinate station among his class-fellows—to which he would otherwise affix disgrace. There is also, from the constitution of the High School, a certain danger not sufficiently attended to. The boys take precedence in their *places*, as they are called, according to their merit, and it requires a long while, in general, before even a clever boy, if he falls behind the class, or is put into one for which he is not quite ready, can force his way to the situation which his abilities really entitle him to hold. But, in the meanwhile, he is necessarily led to be the associate and companion of those inferior spirits with whom he is placed; for the system of precedence, though it does not limit the general intercourse among the boys, has nevertheless the effect of throwing them into clubs and coteries, according to the vicinity of the seats they hold. A boy of good talents, therefore, placed even for a time among his inferiors, especially if they be also his elders, learns to participate in their pursuits and objects of ambition, which are usually very distinct from the acquisition of learning; and it will be well if he does not also imitate them in that indifference which is contented with bustling over a lesson so as to avoid punishment, without affecting superiority or aiming at reward. It was probably owing to this circumstance, that, although at a more advanced period of life I have enjoyed considerable facility in acquiring languages, I did not make any great figure at the High School—or, at least, any exertions which I made were desultory and little to be depended on.[1]

Our class contained some very excellent scholars. The first *Dux* was James Buchan, who retained his honoured place, almost without a day's interval, all the while we were at the High School. He was afterwards at the head of the medical staff in Egypt, and in exposing himself to the plague infection, by attending the hospitals there, dis-

[1] [The story of *Green-breeks*, and other passages in the General Preface to the Waverley Novels, afford some curious glimpses of High School life in Scott's days.—Ed.]

played the same well-regulated and gentle, yet determined perseverance, which placed him most worthily at the head of his school-fellows, while many lads of livelier parts and dispositions held an inferior station. The next best scholars (*sed longo intervallo*) were my friend David Douglas, the heir and *élève* of the celebrated Adam Smith, and James Hope, now a Writer to the Signet, both since well known and distinguished in their departments of the law. As for myself, I glanced like a meteor from one end of the class to the other, and commonly disgusted my kind master as much by negligence and frivolity as I occasionally pleased him by flashes of intellect and talent. Among my companions, my good-nature and a flow of ready imagination rendered me very popular. Boys are uncommonly just in their feelings, and at least equally generous. My lameness, and the efforts which I made to supply that disadvantage, by making up in address what I wanted in activity, engaged the latter principle in my favour; and in the winter play-hours, when hard exercise was impossible, my tales used to assemble an admiring audience round Lucky Brown's fireside, and happy was he that could sit next to the inexhaustible narrator. I was also, though often negligent of my own task, always ready to assist my friends; and hence I had a little party of staunch partisans and adherents, stout of hand and heart though somewhat dull of head—the very tools for raising a hero to eminence. So, on the whole, I made a brighter figure in the *yards* than in the class. [1]

My father did not trust our education solely to our High School lessons. We had a tutor at home [Mr. James Mitchell], a young man of an excellent disposition, and a laborious student. He was bred to the Kirk, but unfortunately took such a very strong turn to fanaticism, that he afterwards resigned an excellent living in a seaport town, merely because he could not persuade the mariners

---

[1] I read not long since, in that authentic record called the *Percy Anecdotes*, that I had been educated at Musselburgh school, where I had been distinguished as an absolute dunce; only Dr. Blair, seeing farther into the mill-stone, had pronounced there was fire in it. I never was at Musselburgh school in my life, and though I have met Dr. Blair at my father's and elsewhere, I never had the good fortune to attract his notice, to my knowledge. Lastly, I was never a dunce, nor thought to be so, but an incorrigibly idle imp, who was always longing to do something else than what was enjoined him. —1826.

of the guilt of setting sail of a Sabbath,—in which, by the
by, he was less likely to be successful, as, *cæteris pari-
bus*, sailors, from an opinion that it is a fortunate omen,
always choose to weigh anchor on that day. The calibre
of this young man's understanding may be judged of by
this anecdote; but in other respects, he was a faithful and
active instructor; and from him chiefly I learned writing
and arithmetic. I repeated to him my French lessons, and
studied with him my themes in the classics, but not
classically. I also acquired, by disputing with him (for
this he readily permitted), some knowledge of school-
divinity and church-history, and a great acquaintance in
particular with the old books describing the early history
of the Church of Scotland, the wars and sufferings of the
Covenanters, and so forth. I, with a head on fire for
chivalry, was a Cavalier; my friend was a Roundhead: I
was a Tory, and he was a Whig. I hated Presbyterians,
and admired Montrose with his victorious Highlanders;
he liked the Presbyterian Ulysses, the dark and politic
Argyle: so that we never wanted subjects of dispute; but
our disputes were always amicable. In all these tenets
there was no real conviction on my part, arising out of
acquaintance with the views or principles of either party;
nor had my antagonist address enough to turn the debate
on such topics. I took up my politics at that period, as
King Charles II. did his religion, from an idea that the
Cavalier creed was the more gentlemanlike persuasion of
the two.

After having been three years under Mr. Fraser, our
class was, in the usual routine of the school, turned over to
Dr. Adam, the Rector. It was from this respectable man
that I first learned the value of the knowledge I had
hitherto considered only as a burdensome task. It was
the fashion to remain two years at his class, where we read
Cæsar, and Livy, and Sallust, in prose; Virgil, Horace,
and Terence, in verse. I had by this time mastered, in
some degree, the difficulties of the language, and began to
be sensible of its beauties. This was really gathering
grapes from thistles; nor shall I soon forget the swelling
of my little pride when the Rector pronounced, that though
many of my school-fellows understood the Latin better,
Gualterus Scott was behind few in following and enjoying
the author's meaning. Thus encouraged, I distinguished
myself by some attempts at poetical versions from Horace

and Virgil.[1] Dr. Adam used to invite his scholars to such essays, but never made them tasks. I gained some distinction upon these occasions, and the Rector in future took much notice of me; and his judicious mixture of censure and praise went far to counterbalance my habits of indolence and inattention. I saw I was expected to do well, and I was piqued in honour to vindicate my master's favourable opinion. I climbed, therefore, to the first form; and, though I never made a first-rate Latinist, my school-fellows, and what was of more consequence, I myself, considered that I had a character for learning to maintain. Dr. Adam, to whom I owed so much, never failed to remind me of my obligations when I had made some figure in the literary world. He was, indeed, deeply imbued with that fortunate vanity which alone could induce a man who has arms to pare and burn a muir, to submit to the yet more toilsome task of cultivating youth. As Catholics confide in the imputed righteousness of their saints, so did the good old Doctor plume himself upon the success of his scholars in life, all of which he never failed (and often justly) to claim as the creation, or at least the fruits, of his early instructions. He remembered the fate of every boy at his school during the fifty years he had superintended it, and always traced their success or misfortunes entirely to their attention or negligence when under his care. His "noisy mansion," which to others would have been a melancholy bedlam, was the pride of his heart; and the only fatigues he felt, amidst din and tumult, and the necessity of reading themes, hearing lessons, and maintaining some degree of order at the same time, were relieved by comparing himself to Cæsar, who could dictate to three secretaries at once;—so ready is vanity to lighten the labours of duty.

[1] [One of these little pieces, written in a weak boyish scrawl, within pencil marks still visible, had been carefully preserved by his mother; it was folded up in a cover inscribed by the old lady—" *My Walter's first lines, 1782.*"

> " In awful ruins Ætna thunders nigh,
> And sends in pitchy whirlwinds to the sky
> Black clouds of smoke, which, still as they aspire,
> From their dark sides there bursts the glowing fire:
> At other times huge balls of fire are toss'd,
> That lick the stars, and in the smoke are lost :
> Sometimes the mount, with vast convulsions torn,
> Emits huge rocks, which instantly are borne
> With loud explosions to the starry skies,
> The stones made liquid as the huge mass flies,
> Then back again with greater weight recoils
> While Ætna thundering from the bottom boils."—ED.]

It is a pity that a man so learned, so admirably adapted
for his station, so useful, so simple, so easily contented,
should have had other subjects of mortification.   But the
magistrates of Edinburgh, not knowing the treasure they
possessed in Dr. Adam, encouraged a savage fellow, called
Nicol, one of the undermasters, in insulting his person and
authority.   This man was an excellent classical scholar,
and an admirable convivial humorist (which latter quality
recommended him to the friendship of Burns); but worthless, drunken, and inhumanly cruel to the boys under his
charge.   He carried his feud against the Rector within an
inch of assassination, for he waylaid and knocked him
down in the dark.   The favour which this worthless rival
obtained in the town-council led to other consequences,
which for some time clouded poor Adam's happiness and
fair fame.   When the French Revolution broke out, and
parties ran high in approving or condemning it, the Doctor
incautiously joined the former.   This was very natural,
for as all his ideas of existing governments were derived
from his experience of the town-council of Edinburgh, it
must be admitted they scarce brooked comparison with
the free states of Rome and Greece, from which he borrowed his opinions concerning republics.   His want of
caution in speaking on the political topics of the day lost
him the respect of the boys, most of whom were accustomed to hear very different opinions on those matters in
the bosom of their families.   This, however (which was
long after my time), passed away with other heats of the
period, and the Doctor continued his labours till about a
year since, when he was struck with palsy while teaching
his class.   He survived a few days, but becoming delirious
before his dissolution, conceived he was still in school, and
after some expressions of applause or censure, he said,
" But it grows dark—the boys may dismiss,"—and instantly expired.

From Dr. Adam's class I should, according to the usual
routine, have proceeded immediately to college.   But, fortunately, I was not yet to lose, by a total dismission from
constraint, the acquaintance with the Latin which I had
acquired.   My health had become rather delicate from
rapid growth, and my father was easily persuaded to allow
me to spend half a year at Kelso with my kind aunt, Miss
Janet Scott, whose inmate I again became.   It was hardly

worth mentioning that I had frequently visited her during our short vacations.

At this time she resided in a small house, situated very pleasantly in a large garden, to the eastward of the church-yard of Kelso, which extended down to the Tweed. It was then my father's property, from whom it was after-wards purchased by my uncle. My grandmother was now dead, and my aunt's only companion, besides an old maid-servant, was my cousin, Miss Barbara Scott, now Mrs. Meik. My time was here left entirely to my own disposal, excepting for about four hours in the day, when I was expected to attend the Grammar-school of the village. The teacher, at that time, was Mr. Lancelot Whale, an excellent classical scholar, a humorist, and a worthy man. He had a supreme antipathy to the puns which his very uncommon name frequently gave rise to; inasmuch, that he made his son spell the word *Wale*, which only occasioned the young man being nicknamed *the Prince of Wales* by the military mess to which he belonged. As for Whale senior, the least allusion to Jonah, or the terming him an odd fish, or any similar quibble, was sure to put him beside himself. In point of knowledge and taste, he was far too good for the situation he held, which only required that he should give his scholars a rough founda-tion in the Latin language. My time with him, though short, was spent greatly to my advantage and his gratifi-cation. He was glad to escape to Persius and Tacitus from the eternal Rudiments and Cornelius Nepos; and as perusing these authors with one who began to understand them was to him a labour of love, I made considerable progress under his instructions. I suspect, indeed, that some of the time dedicated to me was withdrawn from the instruction of his more regular scholars; but I was as grateful as I could be. I acted as usher, and heard the inferior classes, and I spouted the speech of Galgacus at the public examination, which did not make the less im-pression on the audience that few of them probably under-stood one word of it.

In the mean while my acquaintance with English litera-ture was gradually extending itself. In the intervals of my school hours I had always perused with avidity such books of history or poetry or voyages and travels as chance presented to me—not forgetting the usual, or rather ten times the usual, quantity of fairy tales, Eastern stories, romances, etc. These studies were totally unregulated and undirected. My tutor thought it almost a sin to open a profane play or poem; and my mother, besides that she might be in some degree trammelled by the religious scruples which he suggested, had no longer the opportunity to hear me read poetry as formerly. I found, however, in her dressing-room (where I slept at one time) some odd volumes of Shakespeare, nor can I easily forget the rapture with which I sat up in my shirt reading them by the light of a fire in her apartment, until the bustle of the family rising from supper warned me it was time to creep back to my bed, where I was supposed to have been safely deposited since nine o'clock. Chance, however, threw in my way a poetical preceptor. This was no other than the excellent and benevolent Dr. Blacklock, well known at that time as a literary character. I know not how I attracted his attention, and that of some of the young men who boarded in his family; but so it was that I became a frequent and favoured guest. The kind old man opened to me the stores of his library, and through his recommendation I became intimate with Ossian and Spenser. I was delighted with both, yet I think chiefly with the latter poet. The tawdry repetitions of the Ossianic phraseology disgusted me rather sooner than might have been expected from my age. But Spenser I could have read for ever. Too young to trouble myself about the allegory, I considered all the knights and ladies and dragons and giants in their outward and exoteric sense, and God only knows how delighted I was to find myself in such society. As I had always a wonderful facility in retaining in my memory whatever verses pleased me, the quantity of Spenser's stanzas which I could repeat was really marvellous. But this memory of mine was a very fickle ally, and has through my whole life acted merely upon its own capricious motion, and might have enabled me to adopt old Beattie of Meikledale's answer, when complimented by a certain reverend divine on the strength of the same faculty :—" No, sir," answered the old Borderer, " I have no command of my memory. It only retains what hits my fancy, and probably, sir, if you were to preach to me for two hours, I would not be able when you finished to remember a word you had been saying." My memory was precisely of the same kind : it seldom failed to preserve most tenaciously a favourite passage of poetry, a playhouse ditty, or, above all, a Border-raid ballad; but names, dates, and the other technicalities of history, escaped me in a most melancholy degree. The philosophy of history, a much more important subject, was also a sealed book at this period of my life; but I gradually assembled much of what was striking and picturesque in historical narrative; and when, in riper years, I attended more to the deduction of general principles, I was furnished with a powerful host of examples in illustration of them. I was, in short, like an ignorant gamester, who kept up a good hand until he knew how to play it.

I left the High School, therefore, with a great quantity of general information, ill arranged, indeed, and collected without system; yet deeply impressed upon my mind; readily assorted by my power of connection and memory, and gilded, if I may be permitted to say so, by a vivid and active imagination. If my studies were not under any direction at Edinburgh, in the country, it may be well imagined, they were less so. A respectable subscription library, a circulating library of ancient standing, and some private book-shelves, were open to my random perusal, and I waded into the stream like a blind man into a ford, without the power of searching my way, unless by groping for it. My appetite for books was as ample and indiscriminating as it was indefatigable, and I since have had too frequently reason to repent that few ever read so much, and to so little purpose.

Among the valuable acquisitions I made about this time, was an acquaintance with Tasso's Jerusalem Delivered, through the flat medium of Mr. Hoole's translation. But, above all, I then first became acquainted with Bishop Percy's Reliques of Ancient Poetry. As I had been from infancy devoted to legendary lore of this nature, and only reluctantly withdrew my attention, from the scarcity of materials and the rudeness of those which I possessed, it may be imagined, but cannot be described, with what delight I saw pieces of the same kind which had amused my childhood, and still continued in secret the Delilahs of my imagination, considered as the subject of sober research, grave commentary, and apt illustration, by an editor who shewed his poetical genius was capable of emulating the best qualities of what his pious labour preserved. I remember well the spot where I read these volumes for the first time. It was beneath a huge plata-

nus-tree, in the ruins of what had been intended for an
old-fashioned arbour in the *garden* I have mentioned. The
summer-day sped onward so fast, that notwithstanding the
sharp appetite of thirteen, I forgot the hour of dinner, was
sought for with anxiety, and was still found entranced
in my intellectual banquet.   To read and to remember was
in this instance the same thing, and henceforth I overwhelmed my school-fellows, and all who would hearken to
me, with tragical recitations from the ballads of Bishop
Percy.   The first time, too, I could scrape a few shillings
together, which were not common occurrences with me,
I bought unto myself a copy of these beloved volumes;
nor do I believe I ever read a book half so frequently, or
with half the enthusiasm.   About this period also I became acquainted with the works of Richardson, and those
of Mackenzie—(whom in later years I became entitled to
call my friend)—with Fielding, Smollett, and some others
of our best novelists.

To this period also I can trace distinctly the awaking of
that delightful feeling for the beauties of natural objects
which has never since deserted me.   The neighbourhood
of Kelso, the most beautiful, if not the most romantic
village in Scotland, is eminently calculated to awaken
these ideas.   It presents objects, not only grand in themselves, but venerable from their association.   The meeting of two superb rivers, the Tweed and the Teviot, both
renowned in song—the ruins of an ancient Abbey—the
more distant vestiges of Roxburgh Castle—the modern
mansion of Fleurs, which is so situated as to combine the
ideas of ancient baronial grandeur with those of modern
taste—are in themselves objects of the first class; yet are
so mixed, united, and melted among a thousand other
beauties of a less prominent description, that they harmonise into one general picture, and please rather by
unison than by concord.   I believe I have written un-
intelligibly upon this subject, but it is fitter for the
pencil than the pen.   The romantic feelings which I have
described as predominating in my mind, naturally rested
upon and associated themselves with these grand features
of the landscape around me; and the historical incidents,
or traditional legends connected with many of them, gave
to my admiration a sort of intense impression of reverence,
which at times made my heart feel too big for its bosom.
From this time the love of natural beauty, more especially

when combined with ancient ruins, or remains of our fathers' piety or splendour, became with me an insatiable passion, which, if circumstances had permitted, I would willingly have gratified by travelling over half the globe.

I was recalled to Edinburgh about the time when the College meets, and put at once to the Humanity class, under Mr. Hill, and the first Greek class, taught by Mr. Dalzell. The former held the reins of discipline very loosely, and though beloved by his students—for he was a good-natured man as well as a good scholar—he had not the art of exciting our attention as well as liking. This was a dangerous character with whom to trust one who relished labour as little as I did; and amid the riot of his class I speedily lost much of what I had learned under Adam and Whale. At the Greek class, I might have made a better figure, for Professor Dalzell maintained a great deal of authority, and was not only himself an admirable scholar, but was always deeply interested in the progress of his students. But here lay the villany. Almost all my companions who had left the High School at the same time with myself had acquired a smattering of Greek before they came to College. I, alas! had none; and finding myself far inferior to all my fellow-students, I could hit upon no better mode of vindicating my equality than by professing my contempt for the language, and my resolution not to learn it. A youth who died early, himself an excellent Greek scholar, saw my negligence and folly with pain, instead of contempt. He came to call on me in George's Square, and pointed out in the strongest terms the silliness of the conduct I had adopted, told me I was distinguished by the name of the *Greek Blockhead*, and exhorted me to redeem my reputation while it was called to-day. My stubborn pride received this advice with sulky civility; the birth of my Mentor (whose name was Archibald, the son of an inn-keeper) did not, as I thought in my folly, authorise him to intrude upon me his advice. The other was not sharp-sighted, or his consciousness of a generous intention overcame his resentment. He offered me his daily and nightly assistance, and pledged himself to bring me forward with the foremost of my class. I felt some twinges of conscience, but they were unable to prevail over my pride and self-conceit. The poor lad left me more in sorrow than in anger, nor did we ever meet again. All hopes of my progress in the

Greek were now over, insomuch that when we were required to write essays on the authors we had studied, I
had the audacity to produce a composition in which I
weighed Homer against Ariosto, and pronounced him
wanting in the balance.   I supported this heresy by a profusion of bad reading and flimsy argument.   The wrath
of the professor was extreme, while at the same time he
could not suppress his surprise at the quantity of out-of-
the-way knowledge which I displayed.   He pronounced
upon me the severe sentence—that dunce I was, and dunce
was to remain—which, however, my excellent and learned
friend lived to revoke over a bottle of Burgundy, at our
literary Club at Fortune's, of which he was a distinguished member.

Meanwhile, as if to eradicate my slightest tincture of
Greek, I fell ill during the middle of Mr. Dalzell's second
class, and migrated a second time to Kelso—where I again
continued a long time reading what and how I pleased, and
of course reading nothing but what afforded me immediate
entertainment.   The only thing which saved my mind from
utter dissipation was that turn for historical pursuit,
which never abandoned me even at the idlest period.   I
had forsworn the Latin classics for no reason I know of,
unless because they were akin to the Greek; but the occasional perusal of Buchanan's history, that of Mathew of
Paris, and other monkish chronicles, kept up a kind of
familiarity with the language even in its rudest state.   But
I forgot the very letters of the Greek alphabet; a loss never
to be repaired, considering what that language is, and
who they were who employed it in their compositions.

About this period—or soon afterwards—my father
judged it proper I should study Mathematics; a study
upon which I entered with all the ardour of novelty.   My
tutor was an aged person, Dr. MacFait, who had in his
time been distinguished as a teacher of this science.   Age,
however, and some domestic inconveniences, had diminished his pupils, and lessened his authority amongst the
few who remained.   I think, that had I been more fortunately placed for instruction, or had I had the spur of
emulation, I might have made some progress in this
science, of which, under the circumstances I have mentioned, I only acquired a very superficial smattering.

In other studies I was rather more fortunate.   I made
some progress in Ethics under Professor John Bruce, and

was selected as one of his students whose progress he approved, to read an essay before Principal Robertson. I was farther instructed in Moral Philosophy at the class of Mr. Dugald Stewart, whose striking and impressive eloquence riveted the attention even of the most volatile students. To sum up my academical studies, I attended the class of History, then taught by the present Lord Woodhouselee, and, as far as I remember, no others, excepting those of the Civil and Municipal Law. So that, if my learning be flimsy and inaccurate, the reader must have some compassion even for an idle workman who had so narrow a foundation to build upon. If, however, it should ever fall to the lot of youth to peruse these pages— let such a reader remember, that it is with the deepest regret that I recollect in my manhood the opportunities of learning which I neglected in my youth; that through every part of my literary career I have felt pinched and hampered by my own ignorance; and that I would at this moment give half the reputation I have had the good fortune to acquire, if by doing so I could rest the remaining part upon a sound foundation of learning and science.

I imagine my father's reason for sending me to so few classes in the College, was a desire that I should apply myself particularly to my legal studies. He had not determined whether I should fill the situation of an Advocate or a Writer; but judiciously considering the technical knowledge of the latter to be useful at least, if not essential, to a barrister, he resolved I should serve the ordinary apprenticeship of five years to his own profession. I accordingly entered into indentures with my father about 1785-6, and entered upon the dry and barren wilderness of forms and conveyances.

I cannot reproach myself with being entirely an idle apprentice—far less, as the reader might reasonably have expected,

"A clerk foredoom'd my father's soul to cross."

The drudgery, indeed, of the office I disliked, and the confinement I altogether detested; but I loved my father, and I felt the rational pride and pleasure of rendering myself useful to him. I was ambitious also; and among my companions in labour, the only way to gratify ambition was to labour hard and well. Other circumstances reconciled me in some measure to the confinement. The allowance for

copy-money furnished a little fund for the *menus plaisirs* of
the circulating library and the Theatre; and this was no
trifling incentive to labour. When actually at oar, no
man could pull it harder than I; and I remember writing
upwards of 120 folio pages with no interval either for food
or rest. Again, the hours of attendance on the office were
lightened by the power of choosing my own books, and
reading them in my own way, which often consisted in
beginning at the middle or the end of a volume. A deceased
friend, who was a fellow-apprentice with me, used often to
express his surprise that, after such a hop-step-and-jump
perusal, I knew as much of the book as he had been able
to acquire from reading it in the usual manner. My desk
usually contained a store of most miscellaneous volumes,
especially works of fiction of every kind, which were my
supreme delight. I might except novels, unless those of
the better and higher class; for though I read many of
them, yet it was with more selection than might have been
expected. The whole Jemmy and Jenny Jessamy tribe I
abhorred; and it required the art of Burney, or the feeling
of Mackenzie, to fix my attention upon a domestic tale.
But all that was adventurous and romantic I devoured
without much discrimination, and I really believe I have
read as much nonsense of this class as any man now living.
Everything which touched on knight-errantry was particularly acceptable to me, and I soon attempted to imitate
what I so greatly admired. My efforts, however, were in
the manner of the tale-teller, not of the bard.

My greatest intimate, from the days of my school-tide,
was Mr. John Irving, now a Writer to the Signet.[1] We
lived near each other, and by joint agreement were wont,
each of us, to compose a romance for the other's amuse-

---

[1] [In speaking of the High School period, Mr. John Irving says :
" He began early to collect old ballads, and as my mother could
repeat a great many, he used to come and learn those she could
recite to him. He used to get all the copies of these ballads he could
and select the best." These, no doubt, were among the germs of a
collection of ballads in six little volumes, which, from the handwriting, had been begun at this early period, and which is still preserved at Abbotsford. And it appears, that at least as early a date
must be ascribed to another collection of little humorous stories in
prose, the *Penny Chap-books,* as they are called, still in high favour
among the lower classes in Scotland, which stands on the same shelf.
In a letter of 1830, he states that he had bound up things of this
kind to the extent of several volumes, before he was ten years old.
—Ed.]

ment. These legends, in which the martial and the miraculous always predominated, we rehearsed to each other
during our walks, which were usually directed to the most
solitary spots about Arthur's Seat and Salisbury Crags.
We naturally sought seclusion, for we were conscious to
small degree of ridicule would have attended our amusement, if the nature of it had become known. Whole holidays were spent in this singular pastime, which continued
for two or three years, and had, I believe, no small effect
in directing the turn of my imagination to the chivalrous
and romantic in poetry and prose.

Meanwhile, the translations of Mr. Hoole having made
me acquainted with Tasso and Ariosto, I learned from his
notes on the latter, that the Italian language contained a
fund of romantic lore. A part of my earnings was dedicated to an Italian class which I attended twice a week,
and rapidly acquired some proficiency. I had previously
renewed and extended my knowledge of the French language, from the same principle of romantic research.
Tressan's romances, the Bibliothèque Bleue, and Bibliothèque de Romans, were already familiar to me; and I
now acquired similar intimacy with the works of Dante,
Boiardo, Pulci, and other eminent Italian authors. I fastened also, like a tiger, upon every collection of old songs
or romances which chance threw in my way, or which my
scrutiny was able to discover on the dusty shelves of James
Sibbald's circulating library in the Parliament Square.
This collection, now dismantled and dispersed, contained at
that time many rare and curious works, seldom found in
such a collection. Mr. Sibbald himself, a man of rough
manners but of some taste and judgment, cultivated music
and poetry, and in his shop I had a distant view of some
literary characters, besides the privilege of ransacking the
stores of old French and Italian books, which were in little
demand among the bulk of his subscribers. Here I saw
the unfortunate Andrew Macdonald, author of Vimonda;
and here, too, I saw at a distance the boast of Scotland,
Robert Burns. Of the latter I shall presently have occasion to speak more fully.[1]

[1] [" As for Burns," he writes, " I may truly say, ' *Virgilium vidi
tantum.*' I was a lad of fifteen in 1786-7, when he came first to
Edinburgh, but had sense and feeling enough to be much interested
in his poetry, and would have given the world to know him; but I
had very little acquaintance with any literary people, and still less
with the gentry of the west country,—the two sets that he most fre-

I am inadvertently led to confound dates while I talk
of this remote period, for, as I have no notes, it is impossible for me to remember with accuracy the progress of
studies, if they deserve the name, so irregular and miscellaneous.

But about the second year of my apprenticeship, my
health, which, from rapid growth and other causes, had
been hitherto rather uncertain and delicate, was affected
by the breaking of a blood-vessel. The regimen I had to
undergo on this occasion was far from agreeable. It was
spring, and the weather raw and cold, yet I was confined
to bed with a single blanket, and bled and blistered till I
scarcely had a pulse left. I had all the appetite of a growing boy, but was prohibited any sustenance beyond what
was absolutely necessary for the support of nature, and that

quented. Mr. Thomas Grierson was at that time a clerk of my
father's. He knew Burns, and promised to ask him to his lodgings
to dinner, but had no opportunity to keep his word, otherwise I
might have seen more of this distinguished man. As it was, I saw
him one day at the late venerable Professor Fergusson's, where there
were several gentlemen of literary reputation, among whom I remember the celebrated Mr. Dugald Stewart. Of course we youngsters sate silent, looked and listened. The only thing I remember
which was remarkable in Burns' manner, was the effect produced
upon him by a print of Bunbury's, representing a soldier lying dead
on the snow, his dog sitting in misery on the one side, on the other
his widow, with a child in her arms. These lines were written
beneath,—

> ' Cold on Canadian hills, or Minden's plain,
>   Perhaps that parent wept her soldier slain :
>   Bent o'er her babe, her eye dissolved in dew,
>   The big drops, mingling with the milk he drew,
>   Gave the sad presage of his future years,
>   The child of misery baptised in tears.'

Burns seemed much affected by the print, or rather the ideas which
it suggested to his mind. He actually shed tears. He asked whose
the lines were, and it chanced that nobody but myself remembered
that they occur in a half-forgotten poem of Langhorne's, called by the
unpromising title of ' The Justice of the Peace.' I whispered my information to a friend present, who mentioned it to Burns, who
rewarded me with a look and a word, which, though of mere
civility, I then received, and still recollect, with very great pleasure.
. . . . . His conversation expressed perfect self-confidence,
without the slightest presumption. Among the men who were the
most learned of their time and country, he expressed himself with
perfect firmness, but without the least intrusive forwardness ; and
when he differed in opinion, he did not hesitate to express it firmly,
yet at the same time with modesty. I do not remember any part of
his conversation distinctly enough to be quoted, nor did I ever see
him again, except in the street, where he did not recognise me, as
I could not expect he should."—*Letter to J. G. L.* 1827.]

in vegetables alone. Above all, with a considerable disposition to talk, I was not permitted to open my lips without one or two old ladies who watched my couch being ready at once to souse upon me, "imposing silence with a stilly sound."[1] My only refuge was reading and playing at chess. To the romances and poetry, which I chiefly delighted in, I had always added the study of history, especially as connected with military events. I was encouraged in this latter study by a tolerable acquaintance with geography, and by the opportunities I had enjoyed while with Mr. MacFait to learn the meaning of the more ordinary terms of fortification. While, therefore, I lay in this dreary and silent solitude, I fell upon the resource of illustrating the battles I read of by the childish expedient of arranging shells, and seeds, and peebles, so as to represent encountering armies. Diminutive cross-bows were contrived to mimic artillery, and with the assistance of a friendly carpenter I contrived to model a fortress, which, like that of Uncle Toby, represented whatever place happened to be uppermost in my imagination. I fought ny way thus through Vertot's Knights of Malta—a book which, as it hovered between history and romance, was exceedingly dear to me; and Orme's interesting and beautiful History of Indostan, whose copious plans, aided by the clear and luminous explanations of the author, rendered my imitative amusement peculiarly easy. Other moments of these weary weeks were spent in looking at the Meadow Walks, by assistance of a combination of mirrors so arranged that, while lying in bed, I could see the troops march out to exercise, or any other incident which occurred on that promenade.

After one or two relapses, my constitution recovered the injury it had sustained, though for several months afterwards I was restricted to a severe vegetable diet. And I must say, in passing, that though I gained health under this necessary restriction, yet it was far from being agreeable to me, and I was affected whilst under its influence with a nervousness which I never felt before or since. A disposition to start upon slight alarms—a want of decision in feeling and acting, which has not usually been my failing—an acute sensibility to trifling inconveniences—and an unnecessary apprehension of contingent misfortunes, rise to my memory as connected with my vegetable diet, although

[1] Home's *Tragedy of Douglas*.

they may very possibly have been entirely the result of the
disorder, and not of the cure. Be this as it may, with this
illness I bade farewell both to disease and medicine; for
since that time, till the hour I am now writing, I have enjoyed a state of the most robust health, having only had
to complain of occasional headaches or stomachic affections
when I have been long without taking exercise, or have
lived too convivially—the latter having been occasionally,
though not habitually, the error of my youth, as the former
has been of my advanced life.

My frame gradually became hardened with my constitution, and being both tall and muscular, I was rather dis-
figured than disabled by my lameness. This personal disadvantage did not prevent me from taking much exercise
on horseback, and making long journeys on foot, in the
course of which I often walked from twenty to thirty miles
a day. A distinct instance occurs to me. I remember
walking with poor James Ramsay, my fellow-apprentice,
now no more, and two other friends, to breakfast at
Prestonpans. We spent the forenoon in visiting the ruins
at Seton and the field of battle at Preston—dined at
Prestonpans on *tiled haddocks* very sumptuously—drank
half a bottle of port each, and returned in the evening.
This could not be less than thirty miles, nor do I remember
being at all fatigued upon the occasion.[1]

[1] [If he is quite accurate in referring (*Preface to Waverley Novels*)
his first acquaintance with the Highlands to his fifteenth year, this
incident belongs to the first season of his apprenticeship. His father
had, among a rather numerous list of Highland clients, Alexander
Stewart of Invernahyle, an enthusiastic Jacobite, who had survived
to recount, in secure and vigorous old age, his active experiences in
the insurrections both of 1715 and 1745. He had, it appears,
attracted Walter's attention and admiration at a very early date; for
he speaks of having " seen him in arms," and heard him " exult in
the prospect of drawing his claymore once more before he died,"
when Paul Jones threatened the descent on Edinburgh; which occurred in September 1779. The eager delight with which the young
apprentice now listened to the tales of this fine old man's early days,
produced an invitation to his residence among the mountains; and
to this excursion he probably devoted the few weeks of an autumnal
vacation—whether in 1786 or 1787, it is of no great consequence to
ascertain. It was, however, to his allotted task of enforcing the
execution of a legal instrument against some Maclarens, refractory
tenants of Stewart of Appin, brother-in-law to Invernahyle, that
Scott owed his introduction to the scenery of the Lady of the Lake.
" An escort of a sergeant and six men," he says, " was obtained
from a Highland regiment lying in Stirling, and the author, then a
writer's apprentice, equivalent to the honourable situation of an

These excursions on foot or horseback formed by far my most favourite amusement. I have all my life delighted in travelling, though I have never enjoyed that pleasure upon a large scale. It was a propensity which I sometimes indulged so unduly as to alarm and vex my parents. Wood, water, wilderness itself, had an inexpressible charm for me, and I had a dreamy way of going much further than I intended, so that unconsciously my return was protracted, and my parents had sometimes serious cause of uneasiness. For example, I once set out with Mr. George Abercromby [1] (the son of the immortal General), Mr. William Clerk, and some others, to fish in the lake above Howgate, and the stream which descends from it into the Esk. We breakfasted at Howgate, and fished the whole day; and while we were on our return next morning, I was easily seduced by William Clerk, then a great intimate, to visit Pennycuik-House, the seat of his family. Here he and John Irving, and I for their sake, were overwhelmed with kindness by the late Sir John Clerk and his lady, the present Dowager Lady Clerk. The pleasure of looking at fine pictures, the beauty of the place, and the flattering hospitality of the owners, drowned all recollection of home for a day or two. Meanwhile our companions, who had walked on without being aware of our digression, returned to Edinburgh without us, and excited no small alarm in my father's household. At length, however, they became accustomed to my escapades. My father used to protest to me on such occasions that he thought I was born to be a strolling pedlar; and though the prediction was intended to mortify my conceit, I am not sure that I altogether disliked it. I was now familiar with Shakespeare, and thought of Autolycus's song—

> " Jog on, jog on, the footpath way,
>   And merrily hent the stile-a ;
>   A merry heart goes all the day,
>   Your sad tires in a mile-a. "

My principal object in these excursions was the pleasure of seeing romantic scenery, or what afforded me at least equal pleasure, the places which had been distinguished by

attorney's clerk, was invested with the superintendence of the expedition. The sergeant was absolutely a Highland Sergeant Kite, full of stories of Rob Roy and of himself, and a very good companion."— *Introduction to Rob Roy.*—Ed.]

[1] Now Lord Abercromby.—1826.

remarkable historical events. The delight with which I
regarded the former, of course, had general approbation,
but I often found it difficult to procure sympathy with the
interest I felt in the latter. Yet to me, the wandering
over the field of Bannockburn was the source of more exquisite pleasure than gazing upon the celebrated landscape
from the battlements of Stirling Castle. I do not by any
means infer that I was dead to the feeling of picturesque
scenery; on the contrary, few delighted more in its general
effect. But I was unable with the eye of a painter to
dissect the various parts of the scene, to comprehend how
the one bore upon the other, to estimate the effect which
various features of the view had in producing its leading
and general effect. I have never, indeed, been capable of
doing this with precision or nicety, though my latter
studies have led me to amend and arrange my original
ideas upon the subject. Even the humble ambition, which
I long cherished, of making sketches of those places which
interested me, from a defect of eye or of hand was totally
ineffectual. After long study and many efforts, I was
unable to apply the elements of perspective or of shade to
the scene before me, and was obliged to relinquish in
despair an art which I was most anxious to practise. But
shew me an old castle or a field of battle, and I was at
home at once, filled it with its combatants in their proper
costume, and overwhelmed my hearers by the enthusiasm
of my description. In crossing Magus Moor, near St.
Andrews, the spirit moved me to give a picture of the
assassination of the Archbishop of St. Andrews to some
fellow-travellers with whom I was accidentally associated,
and one of them, though well acquainted with the story,
protested my narrative had frightened away his night's
sleep. I mention this to shew the distinction between a
sense of the picturesque in action and in scenery. If I
have since been able in poetry to trace with some success
the principles of the latter, it has always been with reference to its general and leading features, or under some
alliance with moral feeling; and even this proficiency has
cost me study.—Meanwhile I endeavoured to make amends
for my ignorance of drawing, by adopting a sort of
technical memory respecting the scenes I visited. Wherever I went I cut a piece of a branch from a tree—these
constituted what I called my log-book; and I intended
to have a set of chessmen out of them, each having refer-

ence to the place where it was cut—as the kings from Falkland and Holy-Rood; the queens from Queen Mary's yew tree at Crookston; the bishops from abbeys or episcopal palaces; the knights from baronial residences; the rooks from royal fortresses; and the pawns generally from places worthy of historical note. But this whimsical design I never carried into execution.

With music it was even worse than with painting. My mother was anxious we should at least learn Psalmody; but the incurable defects of my voice and ear soon drove my teacher to despair.[1] It is only by long practice that I have acquired the power of selecting or distinguishing melodies; and although now few things delight or affect me more than a simple tune sung with feeling, yet I am sensible that even this pitch of musical taste has only been gained by attention and habit, and, as it were, by my feeling of the words being associated with the tune. I have therefore been usually unsuccessful in composing words to a tune, although my friend Dr. Clarke, and other musical composers, have sometimes been able to make a happy union between their music and my poetry.

In other points, however, I began to make some amends for the irregularity of my education. It is well known that in Edinburgh one great spur to emulation among youthful students is in those associations called *literary societies*, formed not only for the purpose of debate, but of composition. These undoubtedly have some disadvantages, where a bold, petulant, and disputatious temper happens to be combined with considerable information and talent. Still, however, in order to such a person being

[1] The late Alexander Campbell, a warm-hearted man, and an enthusiast in Scottish music, which he sang most beautifully, had this ungrateful task imposed on him. He was a man of many accomplishments, but dashed with a *bizarrerie* of temper which made them useless to their proprietor. He wrote several books—as a Tour in Scotland, &c.;—and he made an advantageous marriage, but fell nevertheless into distressed circumstances, which I had the pleasure of relieving, if I could not remove. His sense of gratitude was very strong, and shewed itself oddly in one respect. He would never allow that I had a bad ear; but contended, that if I did not understand music, it was because I did not choose to learn it. But when he attended us in George's Square, our neighbour, Lady Cumming, sent to beg the boys might not be all flogged precisely at the same hour, as, though she had no doubt the punishment was deserved, the noise of the concord was really dreadful. Robert was the only one of our family who could sing, though my father was musical, and a performer on the violoncello at the *gentlemen's concerts.*—1826.

actually spoiled by his mixing in such debates, his talents must be of a very rare nature, or his effrontery must be proof to every species of assault; for there is generally, in a well-selected society of this nature, talent sufficient to meet the forwardest, and satire enough to penetrate the most undaunted.   I am particularly obliged to this sort of club for introducing me about my seventeenth year into the society which at one time I had entirely dropped; for, from the time of my illness at College, I had had little or no intercourse with any of my class-companions, one or two only excepted.   Now, however, about 1788, I began to feel and take my ground in society.   A ready wit, a good deal of enthusiasm, and a perception that soon ripened into tact and observation of character, rendered me an acceptable companion to many young men whose acquisitions in philosophy and science were infinitely superior to any thing I could boast.

In the business of these societies—for I was a member of more than one successively—I cannot boast of having made any great figure.   I never was a good speaker, unless upon some subject which strongly animated my feelings; and, as I was totally unaccustomed to composition, as well as to the art of generalising my ideas upon any subject, my literary essays were but very poor work.   I never attempted them unless when compelled to do so by the regulations of the society, and then I was like the Lord of Castle Rackrent, who was obliged to cut down a tree to get a few faggots to boil the kettle; for the quantity of ponderous and miscellaneous knowledge which I really possessed on many subjects was not easily condensed, or brought to bear upon the object I wished particularly to become master of.   Yet there occurred opportunities when this odd lumber of my brain, especially that which was connected with the recondite parts of history, did me, as Hamlet says, "yeoman's service."   My memory of events was like one of the large, old-fashioned stone-cannons of the Turks—very difficult to load well and discharge, but making a powerful effect when by good chance any object did come within range of its shot.   Such fortunate opportunities of exploding with effect maintained my literary character among my companions, with whom I soon met with great indulgence and regard.   The persons with whom I chiefly lived at this period of my youth were William Clerk, already mentioned; James Edmonstoune,

of Newton; George Abercromby; Adam Fergusson, son of
the celebrated Professor Fergusson, and who combined the
lightest and most airy temper with the best and kindest
disposition; John Irving, already mentioned; the Honourable Thomas Douglas, now Earl of Selkirk; David Boyle,[1]
—and two or three others, who sometimes plunged deeply
into politics and metaphysics, and not unfrequently
" doffed the world aside, and bid it pass."

Looking back on these times, I cannot applaud in all
respects the way in which our days were spent. There
was too much idleness, and sometimes too much conviviality : but our hearts were warm, our minds honourably
bent on knowledge and literary distinction; and if I, certainly the least informed of the party, may be permitted
to bear witness, we were not without the fair and creditable means of attaining the distinction to which we aspired.
In this society I was naturally led to correct my former
useless course of reading; for—feeling myself greatly
inferior to my companions in metaphysical philosophy and
other branches of regular study—I laboured, not without
some success, to acquire at least such a portion of knowledge as might enable me to maintain my rank in conversation. In this I succeeded pretty well; but unfortunately
then, as often since through my life, I incurred the deserved ridicule of my friends from the superficial nature of
my acquisitions, which being, in the mercantile phrase,
got up for society, very often proved flimsy in the texture;
and thus the gifts of an uncommonly retentive memory and
acute powers of perception were sometimes detrimental to
their possessor, by encouraging him to a presumptuous
reliance upon them.[2]

[1] Now Lord Justice-Clerk.—1826.
[2] [Scott was admitted into the most celebrated of the Edinburgh
debating societies, *The Speculative*, in January, 1791. Soon after
he was elected their librarian; and in the November following he
became also their secretary and treasurer :—all which appointments
indicate the reliance placed on his careful habits of business, the
fruit of his chamber education. The minutes kept in his handwriting attest the strict regularity of his attention to the affairs of
the club; but they shew also, as do all his early letters, a strange
carelessness in spelling. His constant good temper softened the
asperities of debate, while his multifarious lore, and the quaint
humour with which he enlivened its display, made him more a
favourite as a speaker than some whose powers of rhetoric were far
above his.

Mr. Francis Jeffrey, on the first night of his attendance at *The*

Amidst these studies, and in this society, the time of my apprenticeship elapsed; and in 1790, or thereabouts, it

Speculative, heard Scott read an essay on ballads, which so much interested the new member, that he requested to be introduced to him. Mr. Jeffrey called on him next evening, and found him " in a small den, on the sunk floor of his father's house in George's Square, surrounded with dingy books," from which they adjourned to a tavern, and supped together. Such was the commencement of an acquaintance, which by degrees ripened into friendship, between the two most distinguished men of letters whom Edinburgh produced in their time. I may add here the description of that early *den,* with which I am favoured by a lady of Scott's family :—" Walter had soon begun to collect out-of-the-way things of all sorts. He had more books than shelves ; a small painted cabinet, with Scotch and Roman coins in it, and so forth. A claymore and Lochaber axe, given him by old Invernahyle, mounted guard on a little print of Prince Charlie ; and *Broughton's Saucer* was hooked up against the wall below it."

But I must explain *Broughton's Saucer.* Mrs. Scott's curiosity was strongly excited one autumn by the regular appearance, at a certain hour every evening, of a sedan chair, to deposit a person carefully muffled up in a mantle, who was immediately ushered into her husband's private room, and commonly remained with him there until long after the usual bed-time of this orderly family. Mr. Scott answered her repeated inquiries with a vagueness which irritated the lady's feelings more and more, until, at last, she could bear the thing no longer ; but one evening, just as she heard the bell ring as for the stranger's chair to carry him off, she made her appearance within the forbidden parlour with a salver in her hand, observing, that she thought the gentlemen had sat so long, they would be the better of a dish of tea, and had ventured accordingly to bring some for their acceptance. The stranger, a person of distinguished appearance, and richly dressed, bowed to the lady, and accepted a cup ; but her husband knit his brows, and refused very coldly to partake the refreshment. A moment afterwards the visitor withdrew—and Mr. Scott lifting up the window-sash, took the cup, which he had left empty on the table, and tossed it out upon the pavement. The lady exclaimed for her china, but was put to silence by her husband's saying, " I can forgive your little curiosity, madam, but you must pay the penalty. I may admit into my house, on a piece of business, persons wholly unworthy to be treated as guests by my wife. Neither lip of me nor of mine comes after Mr. Murray of Broughton's." This was the unhappy man who, after attending Prince Charles Stuart as his secretary throughout the greater part of his expedition, condescended to redeem his own life and fortune by bearing evidence against the noblest of his late master's adherents, when

> " Pitied by gentle hearts Kilmarnock died—
> The brave, Balmerino, were on thy side."

When confronted with Sir John Douglas of Kelhead (ancestor of the Marquis of Queensberry), before the Privy Council in St. James's, the prisoner was asked, " Do you know this witness?" " Not I," became necessary that I should seriously consider to which department of the law I was to attach myself. My father behaved with the most parental kindness. He offered, if I preferred his own profession, immediately to take me into partnership with him, which, though his business was much diminished, still afforded me an immediate prospect of a handsome independence. But he did not disguise his wish that I should relinquish this situation to my younger brother, and embrace the more ambitious profession of the Bar. I had little hesitation in making my choice—for I was never very fond of money; and in no other particular do the professions admit of a comparison. Besides, I knew and felt the inconveniences attached to that of a Writer; and I thought (like a young man) many of them were "ingenio non subeunda meo."[1] The appearance of personal dependence which that profession requires was disagreeable to me; the sort of connection between the client and the attorney seemed to render the latter more subservient than was quite agreeable to my nature; and, besides, I had seen many sad examples, while overlooking my father's business, that the utmost exertions and the best-meant services do not secure the *man of business*, as he is called, from great loss, and most ungracious treatment on the part of his employers. The Bar, though I was conscious of my deficiencies as a public speaker, was the line of ambition and liberty; it was that also for which most of my contemporary friends were destined. And, lastly, although I would willingly have relieved my father of the labours of his business, yet I saw plainly we could not have agreed on some particulars if we had attempted to conduct it together, and that I should disappoint his expectations if I did not turn to the Bar. So to that object my studies were directed with great ardour and perseverance during the years 1789, 1790, 1791, 1792.

In the usual course of study, the Roman or Civil Law was the first object of my attention—the second, the Municipal Law of Scotland. In the course of reading on both subjects, I had the advantage of studying in con-

answered Douglas; "I once knew a person who bore the designation of Murray of Broughton—but that was a gentleman and a man of honour, and one that could hold up his head!" The saucer belonging to Broughton's tea-cup chanced to be preserved; and Walter had made prize of it.—ED.]

[1] Milton, *Eleg. Lib.* **I.**

junction with my friend William Clerk, a man of the most acute intellects and powerful apprehension, and who, should he ever shake loose the fetters of indolence by which he has been hitherto trammelled, cannot fail to be distinguished in the highest degree. We attended the regular classes of both laws in the University of Edinburgh. The Civil Law chair, now worthily filled by Mr. Alexander Irving, might at that time be considered as in *abeyance*, since the person by whom it was occupied had never been fit for the situation, and was then almost in a state of dotage. But the Scotch Law lectures were those of Mr. David Hume, who still continues to occupy that situation with as much honour to himself as advantage to his country. I copied over his lectures twice with my own hand, from notes taken in the class, and when I have had occasion to consult them, I can never sufficiently admire the penetration and clearness of conception which were necessary to the arrangement of the fabric of law, formed originally under the strictest influence of feudal principles, and innovated, altered, and broken in upon by the change of times, of habits, and of manners, until it resembles some ancient castle, partly entire, partly ruinous, partly dilapidated, patched and altered during the succession of ages by a thousand additions and combinations, yet still exhibiting, with the marks of its antiquity, symptoms of the skill and wisdom of its founders, and capable of being analysed and made the subject of a methodical plan by an architect who can understand the various styles of the different ages in which it was subjected to alteration. Such an architect has Mr. Hume been to the law of Scotland, neither wandering into fanciful and abstruse disquisitions, which are the more proper subject of the antiquary, nor satisfied with presenting to his pupils a dry and undigested detail of the laws in their present state, but combining the past state of our legal enactments with the present, and tracing clearly and judiciously the changes which took place, and the causes which led to them.

Under these auspices, I commenced my legal studies. A little parlour was assigned me in my father's house, which was spacious and convenient, and I took the exclusive possession of my new realms with all the feelings of novelty and liberty. Let me do justice to the only years of my life in which I applied to learning with stern, steady, and undeviating industry. The rule of my friend Clerk and myself was, that we should mutually qualify ourselves for undergoing an examination upon certain points of law every morning in the week, Sundays excepted. This was at first to have taken place alternately at each other's houses, but we soon discovered that my friend's resolution was inadequate to severing him from his couch at the early hour fixed for this exercitation. Accordingly, I agreed to go every morning to his house, which, being at the extremity of Prince's Street, New Town, was a walk of two miles. With great punctuality, however, I beat him up to his task every morning before seven o'clock, and in the course of two summers, we went, by way of question and answer, through the whole of Heineccius's Analysis of the Institutes and Pandects, as well as through the smaller copy of Erskine's Institutes of the Law of Scotland. This course of study enabled us to pass with credit the usual trials, which, by the regulations of the Faculty of Advocates, must be undergone by every candidate for admission into their body. My friend William Clerk and I passed these ordeals on the same days—namely, the Civil Law trial on the [30th June 1791], and the Scots Law trial on the [6th July 1792]. On the [11th July 1792] we both assumed the gown with all its duties and honours.

My progress in life during these two or three years had been gradually enlarging my acquaintance, and facilitating my entrance into good company. My father and mother, already advanced in life, saw little society at home, excepting that of near relations, or upon particular occasions, so that I was left to form connections in a great measure for myself. It is not difficult for a youth with a real desire to please and be pleased to make his way into good society in Edinburgh—or indeed anywhere; and my family connections, if they did not greatly further, had nothing to embarrass my progress. I was a gentleman, and so welcome anywhere, if so be I could behave myself, as Tony Lumpkin says, "in a concatenation accordingly."

*   *   *   *   *   *

CHAPTER II

Call to the Bar—Early Friendships and Pursuits—Excursions to the Highlands and Border—Light-Horse Volunteers—Disappointment in Love—Publication of Ballads after Bürger.—1792–1797.

WALTER SCOTT, the eldest son of Robert of Sandy-Knowe, appears to have been the first of the family that ever adopted a town life, or anything claiming to be classed among the learned professions. His branch of the law, however, could not in those days be advantageously prosecuted without extensive connections in the country; his own were too respectable not to be of much service to him in his calling, and they were cultivated accordingly. His professional visits to Roxburghshire and Ettrick Forest were, in the vigour of his life, very frequent; and though he was never supposed to have any tincture either of romance or poetry in his composition, he retained to the last a warm affection for his native district, with a certain reluctant flavour of the old feelings and prejudices of the Borderer. I have little to add to Sir Walter's short and respectful notice of his father, except that I have heard it confirmed by the testimony of many less partial observers. "He passed from the cradle to the grave," says his daughter-in-law, Mrs. Thomas Scott, "without making an enemy or losing a friend. He was a most affectionate parent, and if he discouraged, rather than otherwise, his son's early devotion to the pursuits which led him to the height of literary eminence, it was only because he did not understand what such things meant, and considered it his duty to keep his young man to that path in which good sense and industry might, humanly speaking, be thought sure of success." We have, according to William Clerk, a very accurate representation of the old gentleman in the elder Fairford of Redgauntlet; and there is as little doubt that Walter drew from himself in the younger Fairford, and from his friend Clerk in the Darsie Latimer of that tale.

His mother was short of stature, and by no means comely, at least after the days of her early youth. The physiognomy of the poet bore, if their portraits may be trusted, no resemblance to either of his parents; while, on the other hand, a very strong likeness to him is observable in the pictures both of the shrewd farmer and sports-

man, Robert of Sandy-Knowe, and of the venerable
Jacobite, *Beardie*.   But Scott's mother, there is no doubt,
was, in talents as well as tastes, superior to her husband.
She had strong powers of observation, with a lively relish
for the humorous, and was noted for her skill in story-
telling.   She had, moreover, like Irving's mother, a love
of ancient ballads and Scotch traditions and legends of
all sorts, and her Calvinistic prejudices did not save her
from the worship of Shakespeare.   Her sister, Christian
Rutherford, appears to have been still more accomplished ;
and as she was comparatively young, the intimacy between
her and her nephew was more like what occurs commonly
between a youth and an elder sister.   In the house of his
uncle, Dr. Rutherford, Scott must have had access, from
his earliest days, to a scientific and scholarlike circle of
society.   His own parents, too, were, as we have seen,
personal friends of John Home, the author of Douglas, at
whose villa near Edinburgh young Walter was a frequent
visitor ; but, above all, his intimacy with the son of Dr.
Adam Fergusson, the moralist and historian, who was
then one of the chief ornaments of the University, afforded
easy opportunity of mixing, in as far as his ambition
might gradually aspire, with the most intellectual and
cultivated society of his native place.   It was under that
roof that he conversed with Burns when in his seventeenth
year.

I shall only add to what he sets down on the subject
of his early academical studies, that in this, as in almost
every case, he appears to have underrated his own attainments.   He had, indeed, no pretensions to the name of an
extensive, far less of an accurate, Latin scholar ; but he
could read, I believe, any Latin author, of any age, so as
to catch without difficulty his meaning ; and although his
favourite Latin poet, as well as historian, in later days,
was Buchanan, he had preserved, or subsequently
acquired, a strong relish for some others of more ancient
date.   I may mention, in particular, Lucan and Claudian.
The autobiography has informed us of the early period at
which he enjoyed the real Tasso and Ariosto.   I presume
he had at least as soon as this enabled himself to read Gil
Blas in the original ; and, in all probability, we may refer
to the same time of his life, or one not much later, his
acquisition of as much Spanish as served for the Guerras
Civiles de Grenada, Lazarillo de Tormes, and, above all,

Don Quixote. He read all these languages in after life with about the same facility. I never but once heard him attempt to speak any of them, and that was when some of the courtiers of Charles X. came to Abbotsford, soon after that unfortunate prince took up his residence for the second time at Holyroodhouse. Finding that one or two of these gentlemen could speak no English at all, he made some efforts to amuse them in their own language after the champagne had been passing briskly round the table; and I was amused next morning with the expression of one of the party, who, alluding to the sort of reading in which Sir Walter seemed to have chiefly occupied himself, said— " Mon Dieu ! comme il estropiait, entre deux vins, le Français du bon sire de Joinville ! " Of all these tongues, as of German somewhat later, he acquired as much as was needful for his own purposes, of which a critical study of any foreign language made at no time any part. In them he sought for incidents, and he found images ; but for the treasures of diction he was content to dig on British soil. He had all he wanted in the old wells of " English undefiled," and the still living, though fast shrinking, waters of that sister idiom, which had not always, as he flattered himself, deserved the name of a dialect.

As may be said, I believe, with perfect truth of every really great man, Scott was self-educated in every branch of knowledge which he ever turned to account in the works of his genius—and he has himself told us that his real studies were those lonely and desultory ones of which he has given a copy in the first chapter of Waverley, where the hero is represented as " driving through the sea of books, like a vessel without pilot or rudder ; " that is to say, obeying nothing but the strong breath of native inclination. The *literary* details of that chapter may all be considered as autobiographical.

In all the studies of the two or three years preceding his call to the bar, his chief associate was William Clerk ; and, indeed, of all the connections he formed in life, I now doubt if there was one to whom he owed more. He always continued to say that Clerk was unsurpassed in strength and acuteness of faculties by any man he had ever conversed with familiarly ; and though he has left no literary monument whatever behind him, he was from youth to a good old age indefatigable in study, and rivalled, I believe, by very few of his contemporaries, either in the variety or

the accuracy of his acquired knowledge. He entered
zealously from the first into all Scott's antiquarian pursuits, and he it was who mainly aided and stimulated him
throughout the few years which he did devote to his proper
training for the profession of the bar. But these were not
all the obligations: it was Clerk that first or mainly
awakened his social ambition: it was he that drew him out
of the company of his father's apprentices, and taught him
to rise above their clubs and festivities, and the rough
irregular habits of all their intervals of relaxation. It was
probably very much in consequence of the tacit influence
of this tie that he resolved on following the upper and
more precarious branch of his profession, instead of that
in which his father's eldest son had, if he chose, the certain
prospect of early independence, and every likelihood of a
plentiful fortune in the end.

Yet both in his adoption, soon after that friendship
began, of a somewhat superior tone of manners and habits
generally, and in his ultimate decision for the bar, as well
as in his strenuous preparation during a considerable space
of time for that career, there is little question that another
influence must have powerfully co-operated. Of the few
early letters of Scott that have been preserved, almost all
are addressed to Clerk, who says, "I ascribe my little hand-
ful to a sort of instinctive prophetic sense of his future
greatness;"—but a great mass of letters addressed to
Scott himself, during his early years, are still in being, and
they are important documents in his history, for, as
Southey well remarks, letters often tell more of the
character of the man they are to be read by than of him
who writes them. Throughout all these, then, there
occurs no coarse or even jocular suggestion as to the
conduct of *Scott* in that particular, as to which most
youths of his then age are so apt to lay up stores of self-
reproach. In that season of hot and impetuous blood he
may not have escaped quite blameless; but I have the
concurrent testimony of all the most intimate among his
surviving associates, that he was remarkably free from
such indiscretions; that while his high sense of honour
shielded him from the remotest dream of tampering with
female innocence, he had an instinctive delicacy about him
which made him recoil with utter disgust from low and
vulgar debaucheries. His friends, I have heard more than
one of them confess, used often to rally him on the

coldness of his nature. By degrees they discovered that
he had, from almost the dawn of the passions, cherished a
secret attachment, which continued, through all the most
perilous stage of life, to act as a romantic charm in safe-
guard of virtue. This was the early and innocent affection
to which we owe the tenderest pages, not only of Redgauntlet, but of the Lay of the Last Minstrel, and of
Rokeby. In all of these works the heroine has certain
distinctive features, drawn from one and the same
haunting dream of his manly adolescence.

It was about 1790, according to Mr. William Clerk, that
Scott was observed to lay aside that carelessness, not to
say slovenliness, as to dress, which used to furnish matter
for joking at the beginning of their acquaintance. He
now did himself more justice in these little matters, became
fond of mixing in general female society, and, as his friend
expresses it, " began to set up for a squire of dames."

His personal appearance at this time was not
unengaging. A lady of high rank, who well remembers
him in the Old Assembly Rooms, says, " Young Walter
Scott was a comely creature."[1] He had outgrown the
sallowness of early ill health, and had a fresh brilliant
complexion. His eyes were clear, open, and well set, with
a changeful radiance, to which teeth of the most perfect
regularity and whiteness lent their assistance, while the
noble expanse and elevation of the brow gave to the whole
aspect a dignity far above the charm of mere features.
His smile was always delightful; and I can easily fancy
the peculiar intermixture of tenderness and gravity, with
playful innocent hilarity and humour in the expression, as
being well calculated to fix a fair lady's eye. His figure,
excepting the blemish in one limb, must in those days have
been eminently handsome; tall, much above the usual
standard, it was cast in the very mould of a young
Hercules; the head set on with singular grace, the throat
and chest after the truest model of the antique, the hands
delicately finished; the whole outline that of extraordinary
vigour, without as yet a touch of clumsiness. When he
had acquired a little facility of manner, his conversation
must have been such as could have dispensed with any
exterior advantages, and certainly brought swift forgive-
ness for the one unkindness of nature. I have heard him,
in talking of this part of his life, say, with an arch

[1] The late Duchess Countess of Sutherland.

simplicity of look and tone, which those who were familiar with him can fill in for themselves—" It was a proud night with me when I first found that a pretty young woman could think it worth her while to sit and talk with me, hour after hour, in a corner of the ball-room, while all the world were capering in our view."

I believe, however, that the " pretty young woman " here specially alluded to had occupied his attention before he ever appeared in the Edinburgh Assembly Rooms, or any of his friends took note of him as " setting up for a squire of dames." I have been told that their acquaintance began in the Greyfriars' churchyard, where, rain beginning to fall one Sunday as the congregation were dispersing, Scott happened to offer his umbrella, and the tender being accepted, so escorted *the lady of the green mantle* to her residence, which proved to be at no great distance from his own.[1] To return from church together had, it seems, grown into something like a custom before they met in society, Mrs. Scott being of the party. It then appeared that she and the lady's mother had been companions in their youth, though, both living secludedly, they had scarcely seen each other for many years; and the two matrons now renewed their former intercourse. But no acquaintance appears to have existed between the fathers of the young people, until things had advanced in appearance farther than met the approbation of the good Clerk to the Signet.

Being aware that the young lady—Margaret, daughter of Sir John and Lady Jane Stuart Belches of Invermay, had prospects of fortune far above his son's, Mr. Scott conceived it his duty to give her parents warning that he observed a degree of intimacy which, if allowed to go on, might involve the parties in pain and disappointment. He had heard his son talk of a contemplated excursion to the part of the country in which his neighbour's estates lay, and not doubting that Walter's real object was different from that which he announced, introduced himself with a frank statement that he wished no such affair to proceed, without the express sanction of those most interested in the happiness of persons as yet too young to calculate

---

[1] In one of his latest essays we read—" There have been instances of love-tales being favourably received in England, when told under an umbrella, and in the middle of a shower."—*Miscellaneous Prose Works*, vol. xviii. p. 390.

consequences for themselves.—The northern Baronet had heard nothing of the young apprentice's intended excursion, and appeared to treat the whole business very lightly. He thanked Mr. Scott for his scrupulous attention—but added, that he believed he was mistaken; and this paternal interference, which Walter did not hear of till long afterwards, produced no change in his relations with the object of his growing attachment.

I have neither the power nor the wish to give in detail the sequel of this story. It is sufficient to say, at present, that after he had through several years nourished the dream of an ultimate union with this lady, his hopes terminated in her being married to the late Sir William Forbes, of Pitsligo, Baronet, a gentleman of the highest character, to whom some affectionate allusions occur in one of the greatest of his works, and who lived to act the part of a most generous friend to his early rival throughout the anxieties and distresses of 1826 and 1827. The actual dispersion of the romantic vision and its immediate consequences will be mentioned in due time.

Redgauntlet shadows very distinctly many circumstances connected with the first grand step in the professional history of Alan Fairford. The real *thesis,* however, was on the Title of the Pandects, *Concerning the disposal of the dead bodies of Criminals.* It was dedicated (I doubt not by the careful father's advice) to his friend and neighbour in George's Square, Macqueen of Braxfield, Lord Justice-Clerk (or President of the Supreme Criminal Court) of Scotland. *Darsie* was present at Alan's "bit chack of dinner," and the old Clerk of the Signet was very joyous on the occasion.

I have often heard both *Alan* and *Darsie* laugh over their reminiscences of the important day when they "put on the gown." After the ceremony was completed, and they had mingled for some time with the crowd of barristers in the Outer Court, Scott said to his comrade, mimicking the air and tone of a Highland lass waiting at the Cross of Edinburgh to be hired for the harvest work— "We've stood here an hour by the Tron, hinny, and de'il a ane has speered our price." Some friendly solicitor, however, gave him a guinea fee before the Court rose; and as they walked down the High Street together, he said to Mr. Clerk, in passing a hosier's shop—"This is a sort of a wedding-day, Willie; I think I must go in and

buy me a new night-cap." He did so accordingly; but his
first fee of any consequence was expended on a silver
taper-stand for his mother, which the old lady used to
point to with great satisfaction, as it stood on her
chimney-piece five-and-twenty years afterwards.

The friends had assumed the gown only the day before
the Court of Session rose for the autumn vacation, and
Scott appears to have escaped immediately afterwards
to the familiar scenery of Kelso, where his kind uncle
Robert, the retired East Indian Captain, had acquired the
pretty villa of Rosebank, overhanging the Tweed. He
had on a former occasion made an excursion into
Northumberland as far as Flodden, and given, in a letter
to Mr. Clerk, the results of a close inspection of that
famous battle-field. He now induced his uncle to
accompany him in another Northumbrian expedition,
which extended to Hexham, where the grand Saxon
Cathedral was duly studied. An epistle to Clerk (Sept.
13) gives this picture of his existence after returning from
that trip :—" I am lounging about the country here, to
speak sincerely, as idle as the day is long. Two old
companions of mine, brothers of Mr. Walker of Wooden,
having come to this country, we have renewed a great
intimacy. As they live directly upon the opposite bank of
the river, we have signals agreed upon by which we
concert a plan of operations for the day. They are both
officers, and very intelligent young fellows, and what is
of some consequence, have a brace of fine greyhounds.
Yesterday forenoon we killed seven hares, so you see how
plenty the game is with us. I have turned a keen duck-
shooter, though my success is not very great; and when
wading through the mosses upon this errand, accoutred
with the long gun, a jacket, musquito trousers, and a
rough cap, I might well pass for one of my redoubted
moss-trooper progenitors, Walter Fire-the-Braes, or
rather Willie wi' the Bolt-foot. For about-doors' amusement, I have constructed a seat in a large tree, which
spreads its branches horizontally over the Tweed. This
is a favourite situation of mine for reading, especially in
a day like this, when the west wind rocks the branches on
which I am perched, and the river rolls its waves below
me of a turbid blood colour. I have, moreover, cut an
embrasure, through which I can fire upon the gulls,
herons, and cormorants, as they fly screaming past my

nest.   To crown the whole, I have carved an inscription upon it in the ancient Roman taste."

It was, however, within a few days after Scott's return from his excursion to Hexham, that he made another expedition of more importance to the history of his life. While attending the Michaelmas head-court at Jedburgh, he was introduced to Mr. Robert Shortreed, who spent the greater part of his life in the enjoyment of much respect as Sheriff-substitute of Roxburghshire.   Scott expressed his wish to visit the then wild and inaccessible district of Liddesdale, particularly with a view to examine the ruins of the famous castle of Hermitage, and to pick up some of the ancient *riding ballads,* said to be still preserved among the descendants of the moss-troopers who had followed the banner of the Douglasses, when lords of that grim and remote fastness; and his new acquaintance offered to be his guide.

During seven successive years he made a *raid,* as he called it, into Liddesdale, in company with Mr. Shortreed; exploring every rivulet to its source, and every ruined *peel* from foundation to battlement.   At this time no wheeled carriage had ever been seen in the district—the first, indeed, that ever appeared there was a gig, driven by Scott himself for a part of his way, when on the last of these seven excursions.   There was no inn nor public-house of any kind in the whole valley; the travellers passed from the shepherd's hut to the minister's manse, and again from the cheerful hospitality of the manse to the rough and jolly welcome of the homestead; gathering, wherever they went, songs and tunes, and occasionally more tangible relics of antiquity—even such " a rowth of auld nicknackets " as Burns ascribes to Captain Grose.   To these rambles Scott owed much of the materials of his " Minstrelsy of the Border;" and not less of that intimate acquaintance with the living manners of these unsophisticated regions, which constitutes the chief charm of one of the most charming of his prose works.   But how soon he had any definite object before him in his researches seems very doubtful.   " He was *makin' himsell* a' the time," said Mr. Shortreed; " but he didna ken maybe what he was about till years had passed: At first he thought o' little, I dare say, but the queerness and the fun."

" In those days," says the Memorandum before me, " advocates were not so plenty—at least about Liddesdale;"[1] and the worthy Sheriff-substitute goes on to describe the sort of bustle, not unmixed with alarm, produced at the first farm-house they visited (Willie Elliot's at Millburnholm), when the honest man was informed of the quality of one of his guests. When they dismounted, accordingly, he received the stranger with great ceremony, and insisted upon himself leading his horse to the stable. Shortreed accompanied Willie, however, and the latter, after taking a deliberate peep at Scott, "out by the edge of the door-cheek," whispered, "Weel, Robin, I say, de'il hae me if I's be a bit feared for him now; he's just a chield like ourselves, I think." Half-a-dozen dogs of all degrees had already gathered round "the advocate," and his way of returning their compliments had set Willie at his ease.

According to Mr. Shortreed, this good-man of Milburnholm was the great original of Dandie Dinmont. As he seems to have been the first of these upland sheep-farmers that Scott ever knew, there can be little doubt that he sat for some parts of that inimitable portraiture; and it is certain that the James Davidson, who carried the name of Dandie to his grave with him, and whose thoroughbred deathbed scene is told in the Notes to Guy Mannering, was first pointed out to Scott by Mr. Shortreed himself, several years after the novel had established the man's celebrity all over the Border; some accidental report about his terriers, and their odd names, having alone been turned to account in the tale. But I have the best reason to believe that the kind and manly character of Dandie, the gentle and delicious one of his wife, and some at least of the most picturesque peculiarities of the *menage* at Charlieshope, were filled up from Scott's observation, years after this period, of a family, with one of whose members he had, through the best part of his life, a close and affectionate connection. To those who were familiar with him, I have perhaps already sufficiently indicated the early home of his dear friend William Laidlaw, among " the braes of Yarrow."

They dined at Millburnholm, and after having lingered

[1] I am obliged to Mr. John Elliot Shortreed for some *memoranda* of his father's conversations on this subject. I had, however, many opportunities of hearing Mr. Shortreed's stories from his own lips, having often been under his hospitable roof in company with Sir Walter, who, to the last, was his old friend's guest whenever business took him to Jedburgh.

over Willie Elliot's punch-bowl, until, in Mr. Shortreed's phrase, they were " half glowrin," mounted their steeds again, and proceeded to Dr. Elliot's at Cleughhead, where (" for," says my Memorandum, " folk were na very nice in those days ") the two travellers slept in one bed—as, indeed, seems to have been the case throughout most of their excursions in this district. Dr. Elliot had already a MS. collection of ballads; but he now exerted himself, for several years, with redoubled diligence, in seeking out the living depositaries of such lore among the darker recesses of the mountains. " The Doctor," says Mr. Shortreed, " would have gane through fire and water for Sir Walter, when he ance kenned him."

Next morning they seem to have ridden a long way, for the express purpose of visiting one " auld Thomas o'-Twizzlehope,"—another Elliot, I suppose, who was celebrated for his skill on the Border pipe, and in particular for being in possession of the real *lilt* of *Dick o' the Cow.* Before starting, that is, at six o'clock, the ballad-hunters had, " just to lay the stomach, a devilled duck or twae, and some *London* porter." Auld Thomas found them, nevertheless, well disposed for " breakfast " on their arrival at Twizzlehope; and this being over, he delighted them with one of the most hideous and unearthly of all the specimens of " riding music," and moreover, with considerable libations of whisky-punch, manufactured in a certain wooden vessel, resembling a very small milk-pail, which he called Wisdom, because it " made " only a few spoonfuls of spirits—though he had the art of replenishing it so adroitly, that it had been celebrated for fifty years as more fatal to sobriety than any bowl in the parish. Having done due honour to Wisdom, they again mounted, and proceeded over moss and moor to some other equally hospitable master of the pipe. " Eh me !" says Shortreed, " sic an endless fund o' humour and drollery as he then had wi' him ! Never ten yards but we were either laughing or roaring and singing. Wherever we stopped, how brawlie he suited himsel' to everybody ! He ay did as the lave did; never made himsel' the great man, or took ony airs in the company. I've seen him in a' moods in these jaunts, grave and gay, daft and serious, sober and drunk—(this, however, even in our wildest rambles, was but rare)—but, drunk or sober, he was ay the gentleman. He looked excessively heavy and stupid when he was *fou*, but he was never out o' gude-humour.''

On reaching, one evening, some *Charlieshope* or other (I forget the name) among those wildernesses, they found a kindly reception as usual; but to their agreeable surprise, after some days of hard living, a measured and orderly hospitality as respected liquor. Soon after supper, at which a bottle of elderberry wine alone had been produced, a young student of divinity, who happened to be in the house, was called upon to take the " big ha' Bible,'' in the good old fashion of Burns's Saturday Night; and some progress had been already made in the service, when the goodman of the farm, whose '' tendency was soporific,'' scandalised his wife and the dominie by starting suddenly from his knees, and rubbing his eyes, with a stentorian exclamation of "By ——, here's the keg at last ! '' and in tumbled, as he spake the word, a couple of sturdy herdsmen, whom, on hearing a day before of the advocate's approaching visit, he had dispatched to a certain smuggler's haunt, at some considerable distance, in quest of a supply of *run* brandy from the Solway Firth. The pious "exercise" of the household was hopelessly interrupted. With a thousand apologies for his hitherto shabby entertainment, this jolly Elliot, or Armstrong, had the welcome *keg* mounted on the table without a moment's delay,—and gentle and simple, not forgetting the dominie, continued carousing about it until daylight streamed in upon the party. Sir Walter Scott seldom failed, when I saw him in company with his Liddesdale companion, to mimic the sudden outburst of his old host, on hearing the clatter of horses' feet, which he knew to indicate the arrival of the keg—the consternation of the dame—and the rueful despair with which the young clergyman closed the book.

'' It was in that same season, I think,'' says Mr. Shortreed, '' that Sir Walter got from Dr. Elliot the large old border war-horn, which ye may still see hanging in the armoury at Abbotsford. How *great* he was when he was made master o' *that*! I believe it had been found in Hermitage Castle—and one of the Doctor's servants had used it many a day as a grease-horn for his scythe, before they discovered its history. When cleaned out, it was never a hair the worse—the original chain, hoop, and mouth-piece of steel, were all entire, just as you now see them. Sir Walter carried it home all the way from Liddesdale to

Jedburgh, slung about his neck like Johnny Gilpin's bottle, while I was intrusted with an ancient bridle-bit, which we had likewise picked up.

> ' The feint o' pride—na pride had he . . .
> A lang kail-gully hung down by his side,
> And a great meikle nowt-horn to rout on had he,'

and meikle and sair we routed on't, and ' hotched and blew, wi' micht and main.'   O what pleasant days !   And then a' the nonsense we had cost us naething.   We never put hand in pocket for a week on end.   Toll-bars there were nane—and indeed I think our haill charges were a feed o' corn to our horses in the gangin' and comin' at Riccartoun mill.''

It is a pity that we have no letters of Scott's describing this first *raid* into Liddesdale; but as he must have left Kelso for Edinburgh very soon after its conclusion, he probaby chose to be the bearer of his own tidings.

I have found, however, two note-books, inscribed "Walter Scott, 1792," containing a variety of scraps and hints which may help us to fill up our notion of his private studies during that year.   We have here a most miscellaneous collection, in which there is whatever might have been looked for, with perhaps the single exception of original verse.   One of the books opens with " *Vegtam's Kvitha,* or The Descent of Odin, with the Latin of Thomas Bartholine, and the English poetical version of Mr. Gray; with some account of the death of Balder, both as narrated in the Edda, and as handed down to us by the northern historians—*Auctore   Gualtero   Scott.*"   The Norse original, and the two versions, are then transcribed; and the historical account appended, extending to seven closely written quarto pages, was, I doubt not, read before one or other of his debating societies.   Next comes a page, headed " Pecuniary Distress of Charles the First," and containing a transcript of a receipt for some plate lent to the King in 1643.   He then copies Langhorne's Owen of Carron ; the verses of Canute, on passing Ely ; the lines to a cuckoo, given by Warton as the oldest specimen of English verse; a translation, " by a gentleman in Devonshire," of the death-song of Regner Lodbrog ; and the beautiful quatrain omitted in Gray's elegy,—

> " There scattered oft, the earliest of the year," &c.

After this we have an Italian canzonet on the praises of blue eyes (which were much in favour at this time ;) several

Life of Sir Walter Scott 61

pages of etymologies from Ducange; some more of notes on
the Morte Arthur; extracts from the Books of Adjournal
about Dame Janet Beaton, the Lady of Branxome of the
Lay of the Last Minstrel, and her husband " Sir Walter
Scott of Buccleuch, called *Wicked Watt;*" other extracts
about witches and fairies; various couplets from Hall's
Satires; a passage from *Albania;* notes on the Second
Sight, with extracts from Aubrey and Glanville; a " List
of Ballads to be discovered or recovered;" extracts from
Guerin de Montglave; and after many more similar
entries, a table of the Mæso-Gothic, Anglo-Saxon, and
Runic alphabets;—with a fourth section, headed *German,*
but left blank.

In November, 1792, Scott and Clerk began their regular
attendance at the Parliament House, and Scott, to use Mr.
Clerk's words, " by and by crept into a tolerable share of
such business as may be expected from a writer's connection." By this we are to understand that he was employed from time to time by his father, and probably a few
other solicitors, in that dreary every-day taskwork, chiefly
of long written *informations*, and other papers for the
Court, on which young counsellors of the Scotch Bar were
then expected to bestow a great deal of trouble for very
scanty pecuniary remuneration, and with scarcely a chance
of finding reserved for their hands any matter that could
elicit the display of superior knowledge or understanding.
He had also his part in the cases of persons suing *in forma
pauperis*; but how little important those that came to his
share were, and how slender was the impression they had
left on his mind, we may gather from a note on Redgauntlet, wherein he signifies his doubts whether he really had
ever been engaged in what he has certainly made the *cause
célèbre* of *Poor Peter Peebles*.

But he soon became as famous for his powers of story-
telling among the lawyers of the Outer-House, as he had
been among the companions of his High-School days.
The place where these idlers mostly congregated was
called, it seems, by a name which sufficiently marks the
date—it was *the Mountain*. Here, as Roger North says
of the Court of King's Bench in his early day, " there was
more news than law; "—here hour after hour passed away,
month after month, and year after year, in the interchange
of light-hearted merriment among a circle of young men,
more than one of whom, in after times, attained the highest

honours of the profession. Among the most intimate of
Scott's daily associates from this time, and during all his
subsequent attendance at the Bar, were, besides various
since eminent persons that have been already named, the
first legal antiquary of our time in Scotland, Mr. Thomas
Thomson, and William Erskine, afterwards Lord Kinedder.
Mr. Clerk remembers complaining one morning on finding
the group convulsed with laughter, that *Duns Scotus* had
been forestalling him in a good story, which he had communicated privately the day before—adding, moreover, that
his friend had not only stolen, but disguised it. "Why,"
answered he, skilfully waving the main charge, "this is
always the way with *the Baronet*.[1] He is continually
saying that I change his stories, whereas in fact I only put
a cocked hat on their heads, and stick a cane into their
hands—to make them fit for going into company."

Some interest had been excited in Edinburgh as to the
rising literature of Germany, by an essay of Mackenzie's in
1778, and a subsequent version of *The Robbers,* by Mr.
Tytler (Lord Woodhouselee). About Christmas, 1792, a
German class was formed under a Dr. Willick, which included Scott, Clerk, Thomson, and Erskine; all of whom
soon qualified themselves to taste the beauties of Schiller
and Goethe in the original. This class contributed greatly
to Scott's familiarity with Erskine; a familiarity which
grew into one of the warmest and closest of his friendships. All the others above named, except Erskine, were
by descent and connection Whigs; and though politics
never shook the affection of any of these early companions,
the events and controversies of the immediately ensuing
years could not but disturb, more or less, the social habits
of young barristers who adopted opposite views on the
French Revolution and the policy of Pitt. On such subjects Erskine entirely sympathised with Scott; and though
in many respects, indeed in strength of mind and character,
and in the general turn of opinion and manners, others of
his contemporaries must always have seemed far more
likely to suit Walter Scott, Erskine became, and continued
during the brightest part of his life to be, the nearest and
most confidential of all his Edinburgh associates. Nor

---

[1] *Duns Scotus* was an old college-club nickname for Walter Scott,
a tribute to his love of antiquities. Clerk was with the same set
the Baronet, as belonging to the family of the Baronets of Pennycuick.

can it be doubted that he exercised at the active period we have now reached, a very important influence on his friend's literary tastes, and especially on his German studies.   William Erskine was the son of an Episcopalian clergyman in Perthshire, of a good family, but far from wealthy.   He had received his early education at Glasgow, where he was boarded under the roof of Andrew Macdonald, the author of Vimonda, who then officiated as minister to a small congregation of Episcopalian nonconformists.   From this unfortunate but very ingenious man, Erskine had derived, in boyhood, a strong passion for old English literature, more especially the Elizabethan dramatists ; which, however, he combined with a far livelier relish for the classics of antiquity than either Scott or his master ever possessed.   From the beginning, accordingly, Scott had in Erskine a monitor who, entering most warmly into his taste for national lore—the life of the past—and the bold and picturesque style of the original English school— was constantly urging the advantages to be derived from combining with its varied and masculine breadth of delineation such attention to the minor graces of arrangement and diction as might conciliate the fastidiousness of modern taste.   Directed, as Scott mainly was in the ultimate determination of his literary ambition, by the example of the great founders of the German drama and romance, he appears to have run at first no trivial hazard of adopting the extravagances, both of thought and language, which he found blended in their works with such a captivating display of genius, and genius employed on subjects so much in unison with the deepest of his own juvenile predilections. His friendly critic was just as well as delicate ; and severity as to the mingled absurdities and vulgarities of German detail, commanded deliberate attention from one who admired not less enthusiastically than himself the sublimity and pathos of his new favourites.

In March, 1793, when the Court rose, he proceeded into Galloway, in order to make himself acquainted with the case of a certain Rev. Mr. M'Naught, minister of Girthon, whose trial, on charges of habitual drunkenness, singing of lewd and profane songs, dancing and toying at a penny-wedding with a " sweetie wife " (that is, an iterant vender of gingerbread, etc.), and, moreover, of promoting irregular marriages as a justice of the peace, was about to take place before the General Assembly of the Kirk.

The "case of M'Naught" (fee five guineas) is the earliest of Scott's legal papers that has been discovered; and it is perhaps as plausible a statement as the circumstances could bear. In May he was called on to support it at the bar of the Assembly; and he did so in a speech of considerable length. This was by far the most important business in which any solicitor had as yet employed him, and *The Mountain* mustered strong in the gallery. He began in a low voice, but by degrees gathered more confidence; and when it became necessary for him to analyse the evidence touching the penny-wedding, repeated some coarse specimens of his client's alleged conversation, in a tone so bold and free, that he was called to order with great austerity by one of the leading members of the Venerable Court. This seemed to confuse him not a little; so when, by and by, he had to recite a stanza of one of M'Naught's convivial ditties, he breathed it out in a faint and hesitating style: whereupon, thinking he needed encouragement, the allies in the gallery astounded the Assembly by cordial shouts of *hear! hear!—encore! encore!* They were immediately turned out, and Scott got through the rest of his harangue very little to his own satisfaction.

He believed, in a word, that he had made a complete failure, and issued from the Court in a melancholy mood. At the door he found Adam Fergusson waiting to inform him that the brethren so unceremoniously extruded from the gallery had sought shelter in a neighbouring tavern, where they hoped he would join them. He complied with the invitation, but seemed for a long while incapable of enjoying the merriment of his friends. "Come, *Duns,*" cried *the Baronet;*—"cheer up, man, and fill another tumbler; here's * * * * * going to give us *The Tailor.*"— "Ah!" he answered with a groan—"the tailor was a better man than me, sirs; for he didna venture *ben* until he *kenned the way.*" A certain comical old song, which had, perhaps, been a favourite with the minister of Girthon—

> "The tailor he came here to sew,
> And weel he kenn'd the way o't," etc.

was, however, sung and chorussed; and the evening ended in *High Jinks.*

Mr. M'Naught was deposed from the ministry. It is to be observed, that the research made with a view to pleading this cause, carried Scott for the first, and I believe for the last time, into the scenery of his Guy Mannering; and several of the names of the minor characters of the novel (*M'Guffog,* for example) appear in the list of witnesses.

If the preceding autumn forms a remarkable point in his history, as first introducing him to the manners of the wilder Border country, the summer which followed left traces of equal importance. He then visited some of the finest districts of Stirlingshire and Perthshire; and not in the percursory manner of his more boyish expeditions, but taking up his residence for a week or ten days in succession at the family residences of several of his young allies of *The Mountain,* and from thence familiarising himself at leisure with the country and the people round about. In this way he lingered some time at Tullibody, the seat of the father of Sir Ralph Abercromby, and grandfather of his friend George Abercromby; and heard from the old gentleman's own lips the narrative of a journey which he had been obliged to make to the retreat of Rob Roy. The venerable laird told how he was received by he cateran " with much courtesy," in a cavern exactly such as that of *Bean Lean*; dined on collops cut from some of his own cattle, which he recognised hanging by their heels from the rocky roof beyond; and returned in all safety, after concluding a bargain of *black-mail*—in virtue of which annual payment, Rob Roy guaranteed the future security of his herds against, not his own followers merely, but all freebooters whatever. Scott next visited his friend Edmonstone, at Newton, a beautiful seat close to the ruins of the once magnificent Castle of Doune, and heard another aged gentleman's vivid recollections of all that happened there when John Home, the author of Douglas, and other Hanoverian prisoners, escaped from the Highland garrison in 1745. Proceeding towards the sources of the Teith, he was received for the first time under a roof which, in subsequent years, he regularly revisited, that of another of his associates, Buchanan, the young Laird of Cambusmore. It was thus that the scenery of Loch Katrine came to be so associated with " the recollection of many a dear friend and merry expedition of former days," that to compose the Lady of the Lake was " a labour of love, and no less so to recall the manners and incidents introduced."[1] It was starting from the same house, when the poem itself

[1] Introduction to *The Lady.*

had made some progress, that he put to the test the prac-
ticability of riding from the banks of Loch Vennachar to
the Castle of Stirling within the brief space which he had
assigned to Fitz-James's Grey Bayard, after the duel with
Roderick Dhu; and the principal land-marks in the description of that fiery progress are so many hospitable mansions, all familiar to him at the same period:—Blair-
drummond, the residence of Lord Kaimes; Ochtertyre,
that of John Ramsay, the scholar and antiquary (now best
remembered for his kind and sagacious advice to Burns;)
and "the lofty brow of ancient Kier," the fine seat of
the chief family of the name of Stirling; from which, to
say nothing of remoter objects, the prospect has on one
hand the rock of "Snowdon," and in front the field of
Bannockburn.

Another resting place was Craighall, in Perthshire, the
seat of the Rattrays, a family related to Mr. Clerk, who
accompanied him. From the position of this striking
place, as Mr. Clerk at once perceived, and as the author
afterwards confessed to him, that of *Tully-Veolan* was
faithfully copied; though in the description of the house
itself, and its gardens, many features were adopted from
Bruntsfield and Ravelstone. Mr. Clerk told me that he
went through the first chapters of Waverley without more
than a vague suspicion of the new novelist; but that when
he read the arrival at Tully-Veolan, his suspicion was
converted into certainty, and he handed the book to a
common friend of his and the author's, saying, "This is
Scott's—and I'll lay a bet you'll find such and such things
in the next chapter." I hope to be forgiven for mentioning *the* circumstance that flashed conviction. In the
course of a ride from Craighall, they had both become considerably fagged and heated, and Clerk, seeing the smoke
of a *clachan* a little way before them, ejaculated—" How
agreeable if we should here fall in with one of those sign-
posts where a red lion predominates over a punch-bowl! "
The phrase happened to tickle Scott's fancy—he often
introduced it on similar occasions afterwards—and at the
distance of twenty years Mr. Clerk was at no loss to recognise an old acquaintance in the "huge bear" which "predominates" over the stone basin in the courtyard of Baron
Bradwardine.

I believe the longest stay was at Meigle in Forfarshire,
the seat of Patrick Murray of Simprim, whose passion for

antiquities, especially military antiquities, had peculiarly
endeared him both to Scott and Clerk. Here Adam Fergusson, too, was of the party; and I have often heard
them each and all dwell on the thousand scenes of adventure and merriment which diversified that visit. In the
village churchyard, close beneath Mr. Murray's gardens,
tradition still points out the tomb of Queen Guenever; and
the whole district abounds in objects of historical interest.
Amidst them they spent their wandering days, while their
evenings passed in the joyous festivity of a wealthy young
bachelor's establishment, or sometimes under the roofs of
neighbours less refined than their host, the *Balmawhapples*
of the Braes of Angus. From Meigle they made a trip to
Dunottar Castle, the ruins of the huge old fortress of the
Earls Marischall, and it was in the churchyard of that place
that Scott then saw for the first and last time Robert
Paterson, the living *Old Mortality*. He and Mr. Walker,
the minister of the parish, found the poor man refreshing
the epitaphs on the tombs of certain Cameronians who had
fallen under the oppressions of James the Second's brief
insanity. Being invited into the manse after dinner to
take a glass of whisky punch, " to which he was supposed
to have no objections," he joined the minister's party
accordingly; but " he was in bad humour," says Scott,
" and, to use his own phrase, had no freedom for conversation. His spirit had been sorely vexed by hearing, in a
certain Aberdonian kirk, the psalmody directed by a pitch-
pipe or some similar instrument, which was to Old Mortality the abomination of abominations."

It was also while he had his headquarters at Meigle at
this time, that Scott visited for the first time *Glammis*, the
residence of the Earls of Strathmore, by far the noblest
specimen of the real feudal castle, entire and perfect, that
had as yet come under his inspection. What its aspect
was when he first saw it, and how grievously he lamented
the change it had undergone when he revisited it some
years afterwards, he has recorded in one of the most
striking passages of his *Essay on Landscape Gardening*.

The night he spent at the yet unprofaned Glammis in
1793 was, as he tells us in his *Demonology,* one of he
" *two* periods distant from each other " at which he could
recollect experiencing " that degree of superstitious awe
which his countrymen call *eerie*." " After a *very hospitable* reception from the late Peter Proctor, seneschal of the

castle, I was conducted," he says, " to my apartment in a
distant part of the building. I must own, that when I
heard door after door shut, after my conductor had retired,
I began to consider myself as too far from the living, and
somewhat too near the dead," &c. But one of his notes
on Waverley touches a certain not unimportant part of the
story more distinctly; for we are there informed, that the
silver bear of Tully-Veolan, " the *poculum potatorium* of
the valiant baron," had its prototype at Glammis—a massive beaker of silver, double gilt, moulded into the form
of a *lion,* the name and bearing of the Earls of Strathmore,
and containing about an English pint of wine. " The
author," he says, " ought perhaps to be ashamed of recording that he had the honour of swallowing the contents
of *the lion;* and the recollection of the feat suggested the
story of the Bear of Bradwardine."

From this pleasant tour, so rich in its results, he returned in time to attend the autumnal assizes at Jedburgh,
on which occasion he made his first appearance as counsel
in a criminal court; and had the satisfaction of helping a
veteran poacher and sheep-stealer to escape through some
of the meshes of the law. " You're a lucky scoundrel,"
Scott whispered to his client, when the verdict was pronounced. " I'm just o' your mind," quoth the desperado,
" and I'll send ye a maukin [viz., a hare] the morn, man."
I am not sure whether it was at these assizes or the next
in the same town, that he had less success in the case of a
certain notorious housebreaker. The man, however, was
well aware that no skill could have baffled the clear evidence against him, and was, after his fashion, grateful or
such exertions as had been made in his behalf. He requested the young advocate to visit him once more before
he left the place. Scott's curiosity induced him to accept
this invitation, and his friend, as soon as they were alone
together in the *condemned cell,* said—" I am very sorry,
sir, that I have no fee to offer you—so let me beg your
acceptance of two bits of advice which may be useful perhaps when you come to have a house of your own. I am
done with practice, you see, and here is my legacy. Never
keep a large watchdog out of doors—we can always silence
them cheaply—indeed, if it be a *dog,* 'tis easier than
whistling—but tie a little tight yelping terrier within;
and secondly, put no trust in nice, clever, gimcrack locks—
the only thing that bothers us is a huge old heavy one, no

matter how simple the construction,—and the ruder and
rustier the key, so much the better for the housekeeper."
I remember hearing him tell this story some thirty years
after at a Judges' dinner at Jedburgh, and he summed it
up with a rhyme—" Ay, ay, my lord " (he addressed his
friend Lord Meadowbank)—

> " ' Yelping terrier, rusty key,
> Was Walter Scott's best Jeddart fee.' "

The winter of 1793-4 appears to have been passed like
the preceding one : the German class resumed their sittings ; Scott spoke in his debating club on the questions of
Parliamentary Reform and the Inviolability of the Person
of the First Magistrate; his love affair continued on the
same footing as before;—and for the rest, like the young
heroes in Redgauntlet, he " swept the boards of the Parliament House with the skirts of his gown; laughed, and
made others laugh ; drank claret at Bayle's, Fortune's, and
Walker's, and ate oysters in the Covenant Close." On his
desk " the new novel most in repute lay snugly intrenched
beneath Stair's Institute, or an open volume of Decisions ";
and his dressing-table was littered with " old play-bills,
letters respecting a meeting of the Faculty, Rules of the
Speculative, Syllabus of Lectures—all the miscellaneous
contents of a young advocate's pocket, which contains
everything but briefs and bank-notes." His professional
occupation was still very slender; but he took a lively interest in the proceedings of the criminal court, and more
especially in those arising out of the troubled state of the
public feeling as to politics.

In the spring of 1794 I find him writing to his friends
in Roxburghshire with great exultation about the " good
spirit " manifesting itself among the upper classes of the
citizens of Edinburgh, and above all, the organisation of
a regiment of volunteers, in which his brother Thomas was
enrolled as a grenadier, while, as he remarks, his own
" unfortunate infirmity " condemned him to be " a mere
spectator of the drills." In the course of the same year,
the plan of a corps of volunteer light horse was started ;
and if the recollection of Mr. Skene be accurate, the suggestion originally proceeded from Scott himself, who certainly had a principal share in its subsequent success. He
writes to his uncle at Rosebank, requesting him to be on
the look-out for a " strong gelding, such as would suit a

stalwart dragoon "; and intimating his intention to part
with his collection of Scottish coins, rather than not be
mounted to his mind. The corps, however, was not organised for some time; and in the meanwhile he had
an opportunity of displaying his zeal in a manner
which Captain Scott by no means considered as so respectable.

A party of Irish medical students began, towards the
end of April, to make themselves remarkable in the Edinburgh Theatre, where they mustered in a particular corner
of the pit, and lost no opportunity of insulting the loyalists
of the boxes, by calling for revolutionary tunes, applauding
every speech that could bear a seditious meaning, and
drowning the national anthem in howls and hootings. The
young Tories of the Parliament House resented this licence
warmly, and after a succession of minor disturbances, the
quarrel was put to the issue of a regular trial by combat.
Scott was conspicuous among the juvenile advocates and
solicitors who on this grand night assembled in front of the
pit, armed with stout cudgels, and determined to have *God
save the King* not only played without interruption, but
sung in full chorus by both company and audience. The
Irishmen were ready at the first note of the anthem. They
rose, clapped on their hats, and brandished their shillelahs ;
a stern battle ensued, and after many a head had been
cracked, the lawyers at length found themselves in
possession of the field. In writing to Simprim a few days
afterwards, Scott says : " You will be glad to hear that the
affair of Saturday passed over without any worse consequence to the Loyalists than that five, including your
friend and humble servant *Colonel Grogg*,[1] have been
bound over to the peace, and obliged to give bail for their
good behaviour, which, you may believe, was easily found.
The said Colonel had no less than three broken heads
laid to his charge by as many of the Democrats." Sir
Alexander Wood says : " Walter was certainly our Coryphæus, and signalised himself splendidly in this desperate
fray." After this exhibition of zeal, it will not perhaps
surprise the reader of Scott's letters to find him returning
to Edinburgh from a remote ramble in the Highlands
during the next autumn, on purpose to witness the execu-

---

[1] This was Scott's nickname in a boyish club : derived, it is said,
from a remarkable pair of Grogram breeches—but another etymon
might have its claim.

tion of Watt, who had been tried and condemned for his share in a plot for seizing the Castle, and proclaiming a provisional republican government. He expresses great contempt for the unhappy man's pusillanimous behaviour in his last scene; and soon after, on occasion of another formidable riot, he appears as active among the special constables sworn in by the magistracy.

His rambles continued to give his father considerable vexation. Some sentences in a letter to his aunt, Miss Christian Rutherford, may be worth quoting for certain allusions to this and other domestic matters. Mr. Scott, though on particular occasions he could permit himself, like Saunders Fairford, to play the part of a good Amphytrion, was habitually ascetic in his habits. I have heard his son tell, that it was common with him, if any one observed that the soup was good, to taste it again, and say, "Yes, it is too good, bairns," and dash a tumbler of cold water into his plate. It is easy, therefore, to imagine with what rigidity he must have enforced the ultra-Catholic severities which marked, in those days, the yearly or half-yearly *retreat* of the descendants of John Knox. Walter writes: —" I want the assistance of your eloquence to convince my honoured father that nature did not mean me either for a vagabond or *travelling merchant,* when she honoured me with the wandering propensity lately so conspicuously displayed. I saw Dr. R. yesterday, who is well. I did not choose to intrude upon the little lady, this being sermon week; for the same reason we are looking very religious and very sour at home. However, it is with *some folk selon les règles,* that in proportion as they are pure themselves, they are entitled to render uncomfortable those whom they consider as less perfect."

If his father had some reason to complain of want of ardour as to the weightier matters of the law, it probably gave him little consolation to hear, in June 1795, of his appointment to be one of the curators of the Advocates' Library, an office always reserved for those members of he Faculty who have the reputation of superior zeal in literary affairs. He had for colleagues David Hume, the Professor of Scots Law, and Malcolm Laing, the historian; and his discharge of his functions must have given satisfaction, for I find him further nominated, in March 1796, together with Mr. Robert Cay—an accomplished gentleman, afterwards Judge of the Admiralty Court in Scotland—to " put

the Faculty's cabinet of medals in proper arrangement."
From the first assumption of the gown, he had been accustomed to spend many of his hours in the low gloomy
vaults under the Parliament House, which then formed the
only receptacle for their literary and antiquarian collections. This habit, it may be supposed, grew by what it
fed on. MSS. can only be consulted within the library,
and his highland and border raids were constantly suggesting inquiries as to ancient local history and legends,
which could nowhere else have been pursued with equal
advantage. He became an adept in the deciphering of old
deeds; and whoever examines the rich treasure of the
MacFarlan MSS., and others serviceable for the illustration of Scotch topography and genealogy, will, I am told,
soon become familiar with the marks of his early pencil.
His reputation for skill in such researches reached George
Chalmers, the celebrated antiquary, then engaged in the
preparation of his *Caledonia*. They met at Jedburgh, and
a correspondence ensued which proved very useful to
the veteran author. The border ballads, as they were
gradually collected, and numberless quotations from
MSS. in illustration of them, were eagerly placed at
his disposal.

It must, I think, have been while he was indulging his
vagabond vein, during the autumn of 1795, that Mrs.
Barbauld paid her visit to Edinburgh, and entertained
a party at Mr. Dugald Stewart's, by reading William
Taylor's then unpublished version of Bürger's Lenore. In
the essay on Imitation of Popular Poetry, the reader has a
full account of the interest with which Scott heard, some
weeks afterwards, a friend's imperfect recollections of his
performance; the anxiety with which he sought after a
copy of the original German; the delight with which he at
length perused it; and how, having just been reading the
specimens of ballad poetry introduced into Lewis' Romance
of The Monk, he called to mind the early facility of versification which had lain so long in abeyance, and ventured
to promise his friend a rhymed translation of Lenore from
his own pen. The friend in question was Miss Cranstoun,
afterwards Countess of Purgstall, the sister of George
Cranstoun (Lord Corehouse). He began the task, he tells
us, after supper, and did not retire to bed until he had
finished it, having by that time worked himself into a state
of excitement which set sleep at defiance.

Next morning, before breakfast, he carried his MS. to Miss Cranstoun, who was not only delighted but astonished at it; for I have seen a letter of hers to a friend in the country, in which she says—" Upon my word, Walter Scott is going to turn out a poet—something of a cross I think between Burns and Gray." The same day he read it also to Sir Alexander Wood, who retains a vivid recollection of the high strain of enthusiasm into which he had been exalted by dwelling on the wild unearthly imagery of the German bard. " He read it over to me," says Sir Alexander, " in a very slow and solemn tone, and after we had said a few words about its merits, continued to look at the fire silent and musing for some minutes, until he at length burst out with ' I wish to Heaven I could get a skull and two crossbones.'" Wood said, that if Scott would accompany him to the house of John Bell, the celebrated surgeon, he had no doubt this wish might be easily gratified.[1] They went thither accordingly on the instant. Mr. Bell smiled on hearing the object of their visit, and pointing to a closet, at the corner of his library, bade Walter enter and choose. From a well-furnished museum of mortality, he selected forthwith what seemed to him the handsomest skull and pair of cross-bones it contained, and wrapping them in his handkerchief, carried the formidable bundle home to George's Square. The trophies were immediately mounted on the top of his little bookcase; and when Wood visited him, after many years of absence from this country, he found them in possession of a similar position in his dressing-room at Abbotsford.

All this occurred in the beginning of April 1796. A few days afterwards Scott went to pay a visit at a country house, where he expected to meet the " lady of his love." Jane Anne Cranstoun was in the secret of his attachment, and knew, that however doubtful might be Miss Stuart's feeling on that subject, she had a high admiration of Scott's abilities, and often corresponded with him on literary matters; so, after he had left Edinburgh, it occurred to her that she might perhaps forward his views in this quarter, by presenting him in the character of a printed author. William Erskine being called in to her councils, a few copies of the ballad were forthwith thrown off in the most

[1] Sir A. Wood was himself the son of a distinguished surgeon in Edinburgh. He married one of the daughters of Sir W. Forbes, of Pitsligo—rose in the diplomatic service—and died in 1846.

elegant style, and one, richly bound and blazoned, followed Scott in the course of a few days to the country. The verses were read and approved of, and Miss Cranstoun at least flattered herself that he had not made his first appearance in types to no purpose.[1]

In autumn he saw again his favourite haunts in Perthshire and Forfarshire—among others, the residence of Miss Stuart; and that his reception was not adequate to his expectations, may be gathered from some expressions in a letter addressed to him when at Montrose by his confidante, Miss Cranstoun :—" Dear Scott,"—(she says)— " I bless the gods for conducting your poor dear soul safely to Perth. When I consider the wilds, the forests, the lakes, the rocks—and the spirits in which you must have whispered to their startled echoes, it amazeth me how you escaped. Had you but dismissed your little squire and Earwig [a pony], and spent a few days as Orlando would have done, all posterity might have profited by it; but to trot quietly away, without so much as one stanza to Despair—never talk to me of love again—never, never, never ! I am dying for your collection of exploits. When will you return? In the meantime, Heaven speed you ! Be sober, and hope to the end."

The affair in which Miss Cranstoun took so lively an interest was now approaching its end. It was known, before autumn closed, that the lady of his vows had finally promised her hand to his amiable rival; and, when the fact was announced, some of those who knew Scott the best, appear to have entertained very serious apprehensions as to the effect which the disappointment might have upon his feelings. For example, one of those brothers of *The Mountain* wrote as follows to another of them, on the 12th October 1796 :—" Mr. Forbes marries Miss Stuart. This is not good news. I always dreaded there was some self-deception on the part of our romantic friend, and I now shudder at the violence of his most irritable and ungovernable mind. Who is it that says, ' Men have died, and worms have eaten them, but not for LOVE '? I hope sincerely it may be verified on this occasion."

Scott had, however, in all likelihood, digested his agony during the solitary ride in the Highlands to which Miss Cranstoun's last letter alludes.

---

[1] This story was told by the Countess of Purgstall on her death-bed to Captain Basil Hall. See his *Schloss Hainfeld*, p. 333.

I venture to recall here to the reader's memory the opening of the twelfth chapter of Peveril of the Peak, written twenty-six years after this youthful disappointment :—" The period at which love is formed for the first time, and felt most strongly, is seldom that at which there is much prospect of its being brought to a happy issue. The state of artificial society opposes many complicated obstructions to early marriages; and the chance is very great that such obstacles prove insurmountable. In fine, there are few men who do not look back in secret to some period of their youth, at which a sincere and early affection was repulsed, or betrayed, or became abortive from opposing circumstances. It is these little passages of secret history which leave a tinge of romance in every bosom, scarce permitting us, even in the most busy or the most advanced period of life, to listen with total indifference to a tale of true love."

Rebelling, as usual, against circumstances, Scott seems to have turned with renewed ardour to his literary pursuits; and in that same October, 1796, he was " prevailed on," as he playfully expresses it, " by the *request of friends*, to indulge his own vanity, by publishing the translation of Lenore, with that of the Wild Huntsman, also from Bürger, in a thin quarto." The little volume, which has no author's name on the title-page, was printed for Manners and Miller of Edinburgh. He had owed his copy of Bürger to a young gentlewoman of high German blood, who in 1795 became the wife of his friend and chief, Hugh Scott of Harden. She was daughter of Count Brühl of Martkirchen, long Saxon ambassador at the Court of St. James's, by his wife Almeria, Countess-Dowager of Egremont. The young kinsman was introduced to her soon after her arrival at Mertoun, and his attachment to German studies excited her attention and interest. The ballad of the Wild Huntsman appears to have been executed during the month that preceded his first publication; and he was thenceforth engaged in a succession of versions from the dramas of Meier and Iffland, several of which are still extant in his MS., marked 1796 and 1797. These are all in prose like their originals; but he also versified at the same time some lyrical fragments of Goethe, as, for example, the Morlachian Ballad, " What yonder glimmers so white on the mountain? " and the song from Claudina von Villa Bella. He consulted his friend at Mertoun on all these essays; and I have often heard him say, that among those many "obligations of a distant date which remained impressed on his memory, after a life spent in a constant interchange of friendship and kindness," he counted not as the least the lady's frankness in correcting his Scotticisms, and more especially his Scottish *rhymes*.

His obligations to this lady were indeed various; but I doubt, after all, whether these were the most important. He used to say that she was the first *woman of real fashion* that *took him* up; that she used the privileges of her sex and station in the truest spirit of kindness; set him right as to a thousand little trifles, which no one else would have ventured to notice; and, in short, did for him what no one but an elegant woman can do for a young man, whose early days have been spent in narrow and provincial circles. "When I first saw Sir Walter," she writes to me, "he was about four or five-and-twenty, but looked much younger. He seemed bashful and awkward; but there were from the first such gleams of superior sense and spirit in his conversation, that I was hardly surprised when, after our acquaintance had ripened a little, I felt myself to be talking with a man of genius. He was most modest about himself, and shewed his little pieces apparently without any consciousness that they could possess any claim on particular attention. Nothing so easy and good-humoured as the way in which he received any hints I might offer, when he seemed to be tampering with the King's English. I remember particularly how he laughed at himself, when I made him take notice that ' the little two dogs,' in some of his lines, did not please an English ear accustomed to ' the two little dogs.' "

Nor was this the only person at Mertoun who took a lively interests in his pursuits. Harden entered into all the feelings of his beautiful bride on this subject; and his mother, the Lady Diana Scott, daughter of the last Earl of Marchmont, did so no less. She had conversed, in her early days, with the brightest ornaments of the cycle of Queen Anne, and preserved rich stores of anecdote, well calculated to gratify the curiosity and excite the ambition of a young enthusiast in literature. Lady Diana soon appreciated the minstrel of the clan; and, surviving to a remarkable age, she had the satisfaction of seeing him at the height of his eminence—the solitary person who could give the author of Marmion personal reminiscences of Pope.

With these friends, as well as in his Edinburgh circle, the little anonymous volume found warm favour; Dugald Stewart, Ramsay of Ochtertyre, and George Chalmers, especially prophesied for it great success. The many inaccuracies and awkwardness of rhyme and diction to which Scott alludes in republishing its two ballads towards the close of his life, did not prevent real lovers of poetry from seeing that no one but a poet could have transfused the daring imagery of the German in a style so free, bold, masculine, and full of life; but, wearied as all such readers had been with that succession of flimsy, lackadaisical trash which followed the appearance of the Reliques by Bishop Percy, the opening of such a new vein of popular poetry as these verses revealed, would have been enough to produce lenient critics for inferior translations. Many, as we have seen, sent forth copies of the Lenore about the same time; and some of these might be thought better than Scott's in particular passages; but, on the whole, it seems to have been felt and acknowledged by those best entitled to judge, that he deserved the palm. Meantime, we must not forget that Scotland had lost that very year the great poet Burns—her glory and her shame. It is at least to be hoped that a general sentiment of self-reproach, as well as of sorrow, had been excited by the premature extinction of such a light; and, at all events, it is agreeable to know that they who had watched his career with the most affectionate concern, were among the first to hail the promise of a more fortunate successor.

The anticipations of these gentlemen, that Scott's versions would attract general attention in the south, were not fulfilled. He himself attributes this to the contemporaneous appearance of so many other translations from Lenore. " I was coldly received," he says, " by strangers, but my reputation began rather to increase among my own friends; and on the whole I was more bent to shew the world that it had neglected something worth notice than to be affronted by its indifference; or rather, to speak candidly, I found pleasure in the literary labours in which I had almost by accident become engaged, and laboured less in the hope of pleasing others, though certainly without despair of doing so, than in pursuit of a new and agreeable amusement to myself."

In his German studies, Scott acquired, about this time,
another assistant in Mr. Skene of Rubislaw—a gentleman
considerably his junior, who had just returned to Scotland from a residence of several years in Saxony. Their
fondness for the same literature, with Scott's eagerness to profit by his new acquaintance's superior attainment in it, opened an intercourse which general similarity
of tastes, and I venture to add, in many of the most
important features of character, soon ripened into the
familiarity of a tender friendship—" An intimacy," Mr.
Skene says, in a paper before me, " of which I shall ever
think with so much pride—a friendship so pure and cordial as to have been able to withstand all the vicissitudes
of nearly forty years, without ever having sustained even
a casual chill from unkind thought or word." Mr. Skene
adds—" During the whole progress of his varied life, to
that eminent station which he could not but feel he at
length held in the estimation, not of his countrymen alone,
but of the whole world, I never could perceive the
slightest shade of variance from that simplicity of character with which he impressed me on the first hour of
our meeting."

Among the common tastes which served to knit these
friends together, was their love of horsemanship, in
which, as in all other manly exercises, Skene highly
excelled; and the fears of a French invasion becoming
every day more serious, their thoughts were turned with
corresponding zeal to the project of mounted volunteers.
" The London Light-horse had set the example," says
Mr. Skene; " but in truth it was to Scott's ardour that
this force in the North owed its origin. Unable, by
reason of his lameness, to serve amongst his friends on
foot, he had nothing for it but to rouse the spirit of the
moss-trooper, with which he readily inspired all who
possessed the means of substituting the sabre for the
musket." On the 14th February 1797, these friends and
many more met and drew up an offer to serve as a body
of volunteer cavalry in Scotland; which was accepted by
Government. The organisation of the corps proceeded
rapidly; they extended their offer to serve in any part
of the island in case of invasion; and this also being
accepted, the whole arrangement was shortly completed;
when Charles Maitland of Rankeillor was elected Major-
Commandant; William Rae of St. Catharine's, Captain;

William Forbes of Pitsligo, and James Skene of Rubislaw, Cornets; Walter Scott, Paymaster, Quartermaster,
and Secretary.   But the treble duties thus devolved on
Scott were found to interfere too severely with his other
avocations, and Colin Mackenzie of Portmore relieved
him from those of paymaster.

"The part of quartermaster," says Mr. Skene, "was
purposely selected for him, that he might be spared the
rough usage of the ranks; but, notwithstanding his infirmity, he had a remarkably firm seat on horseback, and
in all situations a fearless one: no fatigue ever seemed
too much for him, and his zeal and animation served
to sustain the enthusiasm of the whole corps, while his
ready 'mot à rire' kept up, in all, a degree of good-
humour and relish for the service, without which the toil
and privations of long *daily* drills would not easily have
been submitted to by such a body of gentlemen.   At
every interval of exercise, the order, *Sit at ease*, was the
signal for the quartermaster to lead the squadron to
merriment; every eye was intuitively turned on 'Earl
Walter,' as he was familiarly called by his associates of
that date, and his ready joke seldom failed to raise the
ready laugh.   He took his full share in all the labours
and duties of the corps, had the highest pride in its progress and proficiency, and was such a trooper himself,
as only a very powerful frame of body and the warmest
zeal in the cause could have enabled any one to be.   But
his habitual good-humour was the great charm, and at
the daily mess (for we all dined together when in quarters)
that reigned supreme."   *Earl Walter's* first charger, by
the way, was a tall and powerful animal, named *Lenore*.
These daily drills appear to have been persisted in during
the spring and summer of 1797; the corps spending moreover some weeks in quarters at Musselburgh.   The
majority of the troop having professional duties to attend
to, the ordinary hour for drill was five in the morning;
and when we reflect, that after some hours of hard work
in this way, Scott had to produce himself regularly in
the Parliament House with gown and wig, for the space
of four or five hours at least, while his chamber practice,
though still humble, was on the increase—and that he
had found a plentiful source of new social engagements
in his troop connections—it certainly could have excited no
surprise had his literary studies been found suffering total

intermission during this busy period. That such was not the case, however, his correspondence and note-books afford ample evidence. His *fee-book* shews that he made by his first year's practice £24 3s.; by the second, £57 15s.; by the third, £84 4s.; by the fourth, £90; and in his fifth year at the Bar—that is, from November, 1796 to July 1797—£144 10s.; of which £50 were fees from his father's chamber. He had no turn, at this time of his life, for early rising; so that the regular attendance at the morning drills was of itself a strong evidence of his military zeal; but he must have, in spite of them, and of all other circumstances, persisted in what was the usual custom of all his earlier life, namely, the devotion of the best hours of the night to solitary study. In general, both as a young man, and in more advanced age, his constitution required a good allowance of sleep, and he, on principle, indulged in it, saying, " he was but half a man if he had not full seven hours of utter unconsciousness "; but his whole mind and temperament were, at this period, in a state of most fervent exaltation, and spirit triumphed over matter.

CHAPTER III

Tour to the English Lakes—Miss Carpenter—Marriage—Lasswade
    Cottage—Original Ballads—Monk Lewis—Goetz of Berlichingen—
    John Leyden—James Hogg—James Ballantyne—Sheriffship of Sel-
    kirk—Publication of the Minstrelsy of the Border. 1797–1803.

After the rising of the Court of Session in July 1797, Scott set out on a tour to the English lakes, accompanied by his brother John and Adam Fergusson. Their first stage was Halyards in Tweeddale, then inhabited by his friend's father, the philosopher and historian; and they stayed there for a day or two, in the course of which he had his first and only interview with David Ritchie, the original of his Black Dwarf. Proceeding southwards, the tourists visited Carlisle, Penrith,—the vale of the Eamont, including Mayburgh and Brougham Castle,—Ulswater and Windermere; and at length fixed their head-quarters at the then peaceful and sequestered little watering place of Gilsland, making excursions from thence to the various

scenes of romantic interest which are commemorated
in The Bridal of Triermain, and otherwise leading very
much the sort of life depicted among the loungers of St.
Ronan's Well.—Scott was, on his first arrival at Gilsland,
not a little engaged with the beauty of one of the young
ladies lodged under the same roof with him; and it was
on occasion of a visit in her company to some part of the
Roman Wall that he indited his lines——

> " Take these flowers which, purple waving,
> On the ruin'd rampart grew," &c.

But this was only a passing glimpse of flirtation. A
week or so afterwards commenced a more serious affair.

Riding one day with Fergusson, they met, some miles
from their quarters, a young lady taking the air on
horseback, whom neither of them had previously remarked, and whose appearance instantly struck both so
much, that they kept her in view until they had satisfied
themselves that she also was one of the party at Gilsland. The same evening there was a ball, at which
Captain Scott produced himself in his regimentals, and
Fergusson also thought proper to be equipped in the
uniform of the Edinburgh Volunteers. There was no
little rivalry among the young travellers as to who should
first get presented to the unknown beauty of the morning's ride; but though both the gentlemen in scarlet had
the advantage of being dancing partners, their friend
succeeded in handing the fair stranger to supper—and
such was his first introduction to Charlotte Margaret
Carpenter.

Without the features of a regular beauty, she was rich
in personal attractions; " a form that was fashioned as
light as a fay's "; a complexion of the clearest and
lightest olive; eyes large, deep-set and dazzling, of the
finest Italian brown; and a profusion of silken tresses,
black as the raven's wing; her address hovering between
the reserve of a pretty young Englishwoman who has
not mingled largely in general society, and a certain
natural archness and gaiety that suited well with the
accompaniment of a French accent. A lovelier vision, as
all who remember her in the bloom of her days have
assured me, could hardly have been imagined; and from
that hour the fate of the young poet was fixed.

She was the daughter of Jean Charpentier, of Lyons,

a devoted royalist, who held an office under Government, and Charlotte Volere, his wife. She and her only brother, Charles Charpentier, had been educated in the Protestant religion of their mother; and when their father died, which occurred in the beginning of the Revolution, Madame Charpentier made her escape with her children first to Paris, and then to England, where they found a warm friend and protector in Arthur, the second Marquis of Downshire, who had, in the course of his travels in France, formed an intimate acquaintance with the family, and, indeed, spent some time under their roof. M. Charpentier had, in his first alarm as to the coming Revolution, invested £4,000 in English securities—part in a mortgage upon Lord Downshire's estates. On the mother's death, which occurred soon after her arrival in London, this nobleman took on himself the character of sole guardian to her children; and Charles Charpentier received in due time, through his interest, an appointment in the service of the East India Company, in which he had by this time risen to the lucrative situation of commercial resident at Salem. His sister was now making a little excursion, under the care of the lady who had superintended her education, Miss Jane Nicholson, a daughter of Dr. Nicholson, Dean of Exeter, and grand-daughter of William Nicholson, Bishop of Carlisle, well known as the editor of "The English Historical Library." To some connections which the learned prelate's family had ever since his time kept up in the diocese of Carlisle, Miss Carpenter owed the direction of her summer tour.

Scott's father was now in a very feeble state of health, which accounts for his first announcement of this affair being made in a letter to his mother; it is undated;—but by this time the young lady had left Gilsland for Carlisle, where she remained until her destiny was settled. He says :—" My dear Mother,—I should very ill deserve the care and affection with which you have ever regarded me, were I to neglect my duty so far as to omit consulting my father and you in the most important step which I can possibly take in life, and upon the success of which my future happiness must depend. It is with pleasure I think that I can avail myself of your advice and instructions in an affair of so great importance as that which I have at present on my hands. You will probably guess from this preamble that I am engaged in a matrimonial plan, which is really the case. Though my acquaintance with the young lady has not been of long standing, this circumstance is in some degree counterbalanced by the intimacy in which we have lived, and by the opportunities which that intimacy has afforded me of remarking her conduct and sentiments on many different occasions, some of which were rather of a delicate nature, so that in fact I have seen more of her during the few weeks we have been together than I could have done after a much longer acquaintance, shackled by the common forms of ordinary life. You will not expect from me a description of her person—for which I refer you to my brother, as also for a fuller account of all the circumstances attending the business than can be comprised in the compass of a letter. Without flying into raptures —for I must assure you that my judgment as well as my affections are consulted upon this occasion—without flying into raptures, then, I may safely assure you, that her temper is sweet and cheerful, her understanding good, and, what I know will give you pleasure, her principles of religion very serious. I have been very explicit with her upon the nature of my expectations, and she thinks she can accommodate herself to the situation which I should wish her to hold in society as my wife, which, you will easily comprehend, I mean should neither be extravagant nor degrading. Her fortune, though partly dependent upon her brother, who is high in office at Madras, is very considerable—at present £500 a-year. This, however, we must, in some degree, regard as precarious—I mean to the full extent; and indeed, when you know her, you will not be surprised that I regard this circumstance chiefly because it removes those prudential considerations which would otherwise render our union impossible for the present. Betwixt her income and my own professional exertions, I have little doubt we will be enabled to hold the rank in society which my family and situation entitle me to fill. Write to me very fully upon this important subject—send me your opinion, your advice, and, above all, your blessing."

Scott remained in Cumberland until the Jedburgh assizes recalled him to his legal duties. On arriving in that town, he immediately sent for his friend Shortreed, whose *Memorandum* records that the evening of the 30th

September 1797 was one of the most joyous he ever spent. "Scott," he says, "was *sair* beside himself about Miss Carpenter;—we toasted her twenty times over—and sat together, he raving about her, until it was one in the morning." He soon returned to Cumberland; and remained there until various difficulties presented by the prudence and prejudices of family connections had been overcome. It appears that at one stage of the business he had seriously contemplated leaving the Bar of Edinburgh, and establishing himself with his bride (I know not in what capacity) in one of the colonies. He attended the Court of Session as usual in November; and was married at Carlisle during the Christmas recess. I extract the following entries from the fly-leaf of his black-letter bible :—

"*Secundum morem majorum hæc de familiâ Gualteri Scott, Jurisconsulti Edinensis, in librum hunc sacrum manu suâ conscripta sunt.*

"*Gualterus Scott, filius Gualteri Scott et Annæ Rutherford, natus erat apud Edinam* 15*mo die Augusti.* A.D. 1771.

"*Socius Facultatis Juridicæ Edinensis receptus erat* 11*mo die Julii,* A.D. 1792.

"*In ecclesiam Sanctæ Mariæ apud Carlisle, uxorem duxit Margaretam Charlottam Carpenter, filiam quondam Joannis Charpentier et Charlottæ Volere, Lugdunensem,* 24*to die Decembris* 1797."[1]

Scott carried his bride to a lodging in George Street, Edinburgh; a house which he had taken, not being quite prepared for her reception. The first fortnight was, I

[1] The account in the text of Miss Carpenter's origin has been, I am aware, both spoken and written of as an uncandid one : it had been expected that even in 1837 I would not pass in silence a rumour of early prevalence, which represented her and her brother as children of Lord Downshire by Madame Charpentier. I did not think it necessary to allude to this story while any of Sir Walter's own children were living; and I presume it will be sufficient for me to say now, that neither I, nor, I firmly believe, any one of them, ever heard either from Sir Walter, or from his wife, or from Miss Nicholson (who survived them both) the slightest hint as to the rumour in question. There is not an expression in the preserved correspondence between Scott, the young lady, and the Marquis, that gives it a shadow of countenance. Lastly, Lady Scott always kept hanging by her bedside, and repeatedly kissed in her dying moments, a miniature of *her father* which is now in my hands; and it is the well painted likeness of a handsome gentleman—but I am assured the features have no resemblance to Lord Downshire or any of the Hill family.

believe, sufficient to convince her husband's family that, however rashly he had formed the connection, she had the sterling qualities of a wife. Notwithstanding some little leaning to the pomps and vanities of the world, she had made up her mind to find her happiness in better things; and so long as their circumstances continued narrow, no woman could have conformed herself to them with more of good feeling and good sense. I cannot fancy that her manners or ideas could ever have amalgamated very well with those of her husband's parents; but the feeble state of the old gentleman's health prevented her from seeing them constantly; and without any affectation of strict intimacy, they soon were, and always continued to be, very good friends. Anne Scott, the delicate sister to whom the Ashestiel Memoir alludes so tenderly, speedily formed a warm and sincere attachment for the stranger; but death, in a short time, carried off that interesting creature, who seems to have had much of her brother's imaginative and romantic temperament, without his power of controlling it.

Mrs. Scott's arrival was welcomed with unmingled delight by the brothers of *The Mountain*. The two ladies who had formerly given life and grace to their society were both recently married. Scott's house in South Castle Street (soon after exchanged for one of the same sort in North Castle Street, which he purchased, and inhabited down to 1826) became now what Cranstoun's and Erskine's had been while their accomplished sisters remained with them. The officers of the Light Horse, too, established a club among themselves, supping once a-week at each other's houses in rotation. The lady thus found two somewhat different, but both highly agreeable circles ready to receive her with cordial kindness; and the evening hours passed in a round of innocent gaiety, all the arrangements being conducted in a simple and inexpensive fashion, suitable to young people whose days were mostly laborious, and very few of their purses heavy. Scott and Erskine had always been fond of the theatre; the pretty bride was passionately so—and I doubt if they ever spent a week in Edinburgh without indulging themselves in this amusement. But regular dinners and crowded assemblies were in those years quite unthought of. Perhaps nowhere else could have been found a society on so small a scale including more of vigorous intellect, varied information, elegant tastes, and real virtue, affection, and mutual confidence. How often have I heard its members, in the midst of the wealth and honours which most of them in due season attained, sigh over the recollection of those humbler days, when love and ambition were young and buoyant—and no difference of opinion was able to bring even a momentary chill over the warmth of friendship.

In the summer of 1798 Scott hired a cottage at Lasswade, on the Esk, about six miles from Edinburgh. It is a small house, but with one room of good dimensions, which Mrs. Scott's taste set off to advantage at very humble cost—a paddock or two—and a garden (commanding a most beautiful view) in which Scott delighted to train his flowers and creepers. Never, I have heard him say, was he prouder of his handiwork than when he had completed the fashioning of a rustic archway, now overgrown with hoary ivy, by way of ornament to the entrance from the Edinburgh road. In this retreat they spent some happy summers, receiving the visits of their few chosen friends from the neighbouring city, and wandering at will amidst some of the most romantic scenery that Scotland can boast—Scott's dearest haunt in the days of his boyish ramblings. They had neighbours, too, who were not slow to cultivate their acquaintance. With the Clerks of Pennycuick, with Mackenzie, the Man of Feeling, who then occupied the charming villa of Auchendinny, and with Lord Woodhouselee, Scott had from an earlier date been familiar; and it was while at Lasswade that he formed intimacies, even more important in their results, with the noble families of Melville and Buccleuch, both of whom have castles in the same valley.

> " Sweet are the paths, O passing sweet,
> By Esk's fair streams that run,
> O'er airy steep, thro' copsewood deep
> Impervious to the sun ;
>
> " From that fair dome where suit is paid
> By blast of bugle free,
> To Auchendinny's hazle shade,
> And haunted Woodhouselee.
>
> " Who knows not Melville's beechy grove,
> And Roslin's rocky glen ;
> Dalkeith, which all the virtues love,
> And classic Hawthornden ? "

Another verse reminds us that

" There the rapt poet's step may rove ; "—

and it was amidst these delicious solitudes that he did produce the pieces which laid the imperishable foundations of
all his fame.   It was here, that when his warm heart was
beating with young and happy love, and his whole mind
and spirit were nerved by new motives for exertion—it was
here, that in the ripened glow of manhood he seems to
have first felt something of his real strength, and poured
himself out in those splendid original ballads which were
at once to fix his name.

I must, however, approach these more leisurely.   When
William Erskine was in London in the spring of this year,
he happened to meet in society with Matthew Gregory
Lewis, M.P. for Hindon, whose romance of The Monk,
with the ballads which it included, had made for him, in
those barren days, a brilliant reputation.   This good-
natured fopling, the pet and plaything of certain fashionable circles, was then busy with that miscellany which at
length came out in 1801, under the name of Tales of
Wonder, and was beating up in all quarters for contributions.   Erskine shewed Lewis the versions of Lenore and
the Wild Huntsman; and when he mentioned that his
friend had other specimens of the German *diablerie* in his
portfolio, the collector anxiously requested that Scott
might be enlisted in his cause;—and he, who was perhaps
at all times rather disposed to hold popular favour as the
surest test of literary merit, and who certainly continued
through life to overestimate all talents except his own,
considered this invitation as a very flattering compliment.
He immediately wrote to Lewis, placing whatever pieces
he had translated and imitated from the German *Volks-
lieder* at his disposal.

In the autumn Lewis made a tour into the north; and
Scott told Allan Cunningham, thirty years afterwards,
that he thought he had never felt such elation as when
the " Monk " invited him to dine with him for the first
time at his hotel.   Since he gazed on Burns in his seventeenth year, he had seen no one enjoying, by general consent, the fame of a poet ; and Lewis, whatever Scott might,
on maturer consideration, think of his title to such fame,
had certainly done him no small service ; for the ballads of
Alonzo the Brave, &c., had rekindled effectually in his

breast the spark of poetical ambition. Lady Charlotte
Campbell (now Bury), always distinguished by her passion
for letters, was ready, "in pride of rank, in beauty's
bloom," to do the honours of Scotland to the Lion of May-
fair; and I believe Scott's first introduction to Lewis took
place at one of her Ladyship's parties. But they met frequently, and, among other places, at Dalkeith—as witness
one of Scott's marginal notes, written in 1825, on Lord
Byron's Diary :—" Lewis was fonder of great people than
he ought to have been, either as a man of talent or as
a man of fashion. He had always dukes and duchesses
in his mouth, and was pathetically fond of any one that
had a title. You would have sworn he had been a *par-
venu* of yesterday, yet he had lived all his life in good
society. His person was extremely small and boyish—he
was indeed the least man I ever saw, to be strictly well and
neatly made. I remember a picture of him by Saunders
being handed round at Dalkeith House. The artist had
ingeniously flung a dark folding-mantle around the form,
under which was half-hid a dagger, a dark lantern, or
some such cut-throat appurtenance; with all this the features were preserved and ennobled. It passed from hand
to hand into that of Henry, Duke of Buccleuch, who, hearing the general voice affirm that it was very like, said
aloud, 'Like Mat Lewis! Why, that picture's like a
MAN!' He looked, and lo, Mat Lewis's head was at his
elbow."

Lewis spent a day or two with Scott at Musselburgh,
where the yeomanry corps were in quarters. Scott received him in his lodgings, under the roof of an ancient
dame, who afforded him much amusement by her daily
colloquies with the fishwomen—the *Mucklebackets* of the
place. His delight in studying the dialect of these people
is well remembered by the survivors of the cavalry, and
must have astonished the stranger dandy. While walking
about before dinner on one of these days, Mr. Skene's recitation of the German *Kriegslied*, " Der Abschied's Tag
ist da " (the day of departure is come), delighted both
Lewis and the Quartermaster; and the latter produced
next morning that spirited little piece in the same measure,
which, embodying the volunteer ardour of the time, was
forthwith adopted as the troop-song of the Edinburgh
Light Horse.

In January 1799, Mr. Lewis appears negotiating with

a bookseller, named Bell, for the publication of Scott's version of Goethe's Tragedy, "Goetz von Berlichingen of the Iron Hand." Bell seems finally to have purchased the copy-right for twenty-five guineas, and twenty-five more to be paid in case of a second edition—which was never called for until long after the copy-right had expired. Lewis writes, "I have made him distinctly understand, that, if you accept so small a sum, it will be only because this is your first publication:"—the tiny adventure in 1796 had been completely forgotten. The *Goetz* appeared accordingly, with Scott's name on the title-page, in the following February.

In March 1799 he carried his wife to London, this being the first time that he had seen the metropolis since the days of his infancy. The acquaintance of Lewis served to introduce him to some literary and fashionable society, with which he was much amused; but his great anxiety was to examine the antiquities of the Tower and Westminster Abbey, and to make some researches among the MSS. of the British Museum. He found his Goetz spoken of favourably, on the whole, by the critics of the time; but it does not appear to have attracted general attention. The truth is, that, to have given Goethe anything like a fair chance with the English public, his first drama ought to have been translated at least ten years before. The imitators had been more fortunate than the master, and this work, which constitutes one of the landmarks in the history of German literature, had not come even into Scott's hands, until he had familiarised himself with the ideas which it first opened, in the puny mimicries of writers already forgotten. He readily discovered the vast gulf which separated Goethe from the German dramatists on whom he had heretofore been employing himself; but the public in general drew no such distinctions, and the English Goetz was soon afterwards condemned to oblivion, through the unsparing ridicule showered on whatever bore the name of *German play,* by the inimitable caricature of The Rovers.

The tragedy of Goethe, however, has in truth nothing in common with the wild absurdities against which Canning and Ellis levelled the arrows of their wit. It is a broad, bold, free, and most picturesque delineation of real characters, manners, and events; the first fruits, in a word, of that passionate admiration for Shakespeare, to which

all that is excellent in the recent imaginative literature of
Germany must be traced.   With what delight must Scott
have found the scope and manner of our Elizabethan
drama revived on a foreign stage at the call of a real
master !—with what double delight must he have seen
Goethe seizing for the noblest purposes of art, men and
modes of life, scenes, incidents, and transactions, all claiming near kindred with those that had from boyhood formed
the chosen theme of his own sympathy and reflection !
In the baronial robbers of the Rhine, stern, bloody, and
rapacious, but frank, generous, and, after their fashion,
courteous—in their forays upon each other's domains, the
besieged castles, the plundered herds, the captive knights,
the browbeaten bishop, and the baffled liege-lord, who
vainly strove to quell all these turbulences—Scott had before him a vivid image of the life of his own and the rival
Border clans, familiarised to him by a hundred nameless
minstrels.   If it be doubtful whether, but for Percy's Reliques, he would ever have thought of editing their Ballads,
I think it not less so, whether, but for the Ironhanded
Goetz, it would ever have flashed upon his mind, that in
the wild traditions which these recorded, he had been unconsciously assembling materials for more works of high
art than the longest life could serve him to elaborate.

He executed about the same time his " House of Aspen,"
rather a *rifacimento* than a translation from one of the
minor dramatists that had crowded to partake the popularity of Goetz.   It also was sent to Lewis in London,
where, having been read and commended by the celebrated
actress, Mrs. Esten, it was taken up by Kemble, and I believe actually put in rehearsal for the stage.   If so, the
trial did not encourage further preparation, and the notion
was abandoned.   Discovering the play thirty years after
among his papers, Scott sent it to the Keepsake of 1829.
In the advertisement he says, " He had lately chanced to
look over these scenes with feelings very different from
those of the adventurous period of his literary life during
which they were written, and yet with such, perhaps, as a
reformed libertine might regard the illegitimate production
of an early amour."   He adds, " there is something to be
ashamed of, certainly; but, after all, paternal vanity whispers that the child has some resemblance to the father."
The scenes are interspersed with some lyrics, the numbers
of which, at least, are worthy of attention.   One has the

metre—and not a little of the spirit—of the boat-song of
Clan-Alpin :—

> " Joy to the victors, the sons of old Aspen,
>   Joy to the race of the battle and scar ! " &c., &c.

His return to Edinburgh was accelerated by the tidings
of his father's death. This worthy man had had a succession of paralytic attacks, under which, mind as well as
body had by degrees been laid quite prostrate. When the
first Chronicles of the Canongate appeared, a near relation
of the family said to me—" I had been out of Scotland for
some time, and did not know of my good friend's illness
until I reached Edinburgh, a few months before his death.
Walter carried me to visit him, and warned me that I
should see a great change. I saw the very scene that is
here painted of the elder Croftangry's sickroom—not a
feature different—poor Anne Scott, the gentlest of creatures, was treated by the fretful patient precisely like this
niece." I have lived to see the curtain rise and fall once
more on a like scene.

Mr. Thomas Scott continued to manage his father's
business. He married early;[1] he was in his circle of
society extremely popular ; and his prospects seemed fair in
all things. The property left by the old gentleman was
less than had been expected, but sufficient to make ample
provision for his widow, and a not inconsiderable addition
to the resources of those among whom the remainder was
divided.

Scott's mother and sister, both much exhausted with
their attendance on a protracted sickbed, and the latter
already in the first stage of the malady which in two years
more carried her also to her grave, spent the greater part
of the following summer and autumn in his cottage at Lasswade. There he was now again labouring assiduously in
the service of Lewis's " hobgoblin repast "; and in an
essay of 1830 he gives us sufficient specimens of the
Monk's Editorial Letters to his contributor—the lectures of
a " martinet in rhymes and numbers—severe enough, but
useful eventually, as forcing on a young and careless ver-
sifier criticisms absolutely necessary to his future success."

---

[1] Mrs. Thomas Scott, born Miss Macculloch of Ardwell, was one
of the best, and wisest, and most agreeable women I have ever
known. She had a motherly affection for all Sir Walter's family
—and she survived them all. She died at Canterbury in April 1848,
aged 72.

As to his imperfect *rhymes* of this period, I have no doubt he owed them to his recent zeal about collecting the ballads of the Border. He had, in his familiarity with compositions so remarkable for merits of a higher order, ceased to be offended, as in the days of his devotion to Langhorne and Mickle he would probably have been, with their loose and vague assonances, which are often, in fact, not rhymes at all; a licence pardonable enough in real minstrelsy, meant to be chanted to moss-troopers with the accompanying tones of the war-pipe, but certainly not worthy of imitation in verses written for the eye of a polished age. Of this carelessness as to rhyme, we see little or nothing in our few specimens of his boyish verse, and it does not occur, to any extent that has ever been thought worth notice, in his great works.

But Lewis's collection did not engross the leisure of this summer. It produced also what Scott justly calls his " first serious attempts in verse "; and of these, the earliest appears to have been the Glenfinlas. Here the scene is laid in the most favourite district of his favourite Perthshire Highlands; and the Gaelic tradition on which it is founded was far more likely to draw out the secret strength of his genius, as well as to arrest the feelings of his countrymen, than any subject with which the stores of German *diablerie* could have supplied him. It has been alleged, however, that the poet makes a German use of his Scottish materials; that the legend, as briefly told in the simple prose of his preface, is more *affecting* than the lofty and sonorous stanzas themselves; that the vague terror of the original dream loses, instead of gaining, by the expanded elaboration of the detail. There may be something in these objections : but no man can pretend to be an impartial critic of the piece which first awoke his own childish ear to the power of poetry and the melody of verse.

The next of these compositions was, I believe, the Eve of St. John, in which Scott re-peoples the tower of Smailholm, the awe-inspiring haunt of his infancy; and here he touches, for the first time, the one superstition which can still be appealed to with full and perfect effect; the only one which lingers in minds long since weaned from all sympathy with the machinery of witches and goblins. And surely this mystery was never touched with more thrilling skill than in that noble ballad. It is the first of his original pieces, too, in which he uses the measure of his own favourite Minstrels; a measure which the monotony of mediocrity had long and successfully been labouring to degrade, but in itself adequate to the expression of the highest thoughts, as well as the gentlest emotions; and capable, in fit hands, of as rich a variety of music as any other of modern times. This was written at Mertoun-house in the autumn of 1799. Some dilapidations had taken place in the tower of Smailholm, and Harden, being informed of the fact, and entreated with needless earnestness by his kinsman to arrest the hand of the spoiler, requested playfully a ballad, of which Smailholm should be the scene, as the price of his assent.

Then came The Grey Brother, founded on another superstition, which seems to have been almost as ancient as the belief in ghosts; namely, that the holiest service of the altar cannot go on in the presence of an unclean person— a heinous sinner unconfessed and unabsolved. The fragmentary form of this poem greatly heightens the awfulness of its impression; and in construction and metre, the verses which really belong to the story appear to me the happiest that have ever been produced expressly in imitation of the ballad of the middle ages. In the stanzas, previously quoted, on the scenery of the Esk, however beautiful in themselves, and however interesting now as marking the locality of the composition, he must be allowed to have lapsed into another strain, and produced a *pannus purpureus* which interferes with and mars the general texture.

He wrote at the same period the fine chivalrous ballad entitled The Fire-King, in which there is more than enough to make us forgive the machinery.

It was in the course of this autumn that he first visited Bothwell Castle, the seat of Archibald Lord Douglas, who had married Lady Frances Scott, sister to Henry Duke of Buccleuch; a woman whose many amiable virtues were combined with extraordinary strength of mind, and who had, from the first introduction of the young poet at Dalkeith, formed high anticipations of his future career. Lady Douglas was one of his dearest friends through life; and now, under her roof, he improved an acquaintance (begun also at Dalkeith) with one whose abilities and accomplishments not less qualified her to estimate him, and who still survives to lament the only event that could have interrupted their cordial confidence—Lady Louisa Stuart, daughter of the celebrated John Earl of Bute. These ladies, who were sisters in mind, feeling, and affection, he visited among scenes the noblest and most interesting that all Scotland can shew—alike famous in history and romance; and he was not unwilling to make Bothwell and Blantyre the subject of another ballad; of which, however, only a first and imperfect draft has been recovered.

One morning, during his visit to Bothwell, was spent on an excursion to the ruins of Craignethan Castle, the seat, in former days, of the great Evandale branch of the house of Hamilton, but now the property of Lord Douglas; and the poet expressed such rapture with the scenery, that his hosts urged him to accept, for his lifetime, the use of a small habitable house, enclosed within the circuit of the ancient walls. This offer was not at once declined; but circumstances occurred before the end of the year which rendered it impossible for him to establish his summer residence in Lanarkshire. The castle of Craignethan is the original of his " Tillietudlem."

His note-book of this year has supplied the recent editions of his poetry with several other ballads in an incomplete state; but notwithstanding all these varied essays, and the charms of the distinguished society into which his reputation had already introduced him, his friends do not appear to have as yet entertained the slightest notion that literature was to be the main business of his life. A letter of one very early correspondent, Mr. Kerr of Abbotrule, congratulates him on his having had more to do at the autumnal assizes of Jedburgh this year than on any former occasion, which intelligence he seems himself to have communicated with no feeble expressions of satisfaction. " I greatly enjoy this," says Kerr. " Go on; and with your strong sense and hourly ripening knowledge, that you must rise to the top of the tree in the Parliament House in due season, I hold as certain as that Murray died Lord Mansfield. But don't let many an Ovid,[1] or rather many a Burns (which is better), be lost in you. I rather think men of business have produced as good poetry in their by-hours as the professed regulars; and I don't see any sufficient reason why Lord President Scott should not be a famous poet (in the vacation time), when we have seen a President Montesquieu step so nobly beyond the trammels

[1] "How sweet an Ovid, Murray was our boast;
How many Martials were in Pult'ney lost."—*Dunciad*, iv. 170.

in the *Esprit des Loix.*   I suspect Dryden would have been
a happier man had he had your profession.   The reasoning
talents visible in his verses assure me that he would have
ruled in Westminster Hall as easily as he did at Button's,
and he might have found time enough besides for everything that one really honours his memory for." This
friend appears to have entertained, in October 1799, the
very opinion as to the *profession of literature* on which
Scott acted through life.

Having again given a week to Liddesdale, in company
with Mr. Shortreed, he spent a few days at Rosebank, and
was preparing to return to Edinburgh for the winter, when
he received a visit which had consequences of importance.

In the early days of Launcelot Whale, he had had for a
classfellow Mr. James Ballantyne, the eldest son of a decent
shopkeeper in Kelso, and their acquaintance had never
been altogether broken off, as Scott's visits to Rosebank
were frequent, and the other had resided for a time in
Edinburgh, when pursuing his education with a view to
the profession of a solicitor.   Mr. Ballantyne had not been
successful in his attempts to establish himself in that
branch of the law, and was now the printer and editor of a
weekly newspaper in his native town.   He called at Rosebank one morning, and requested his old acquaintance to
supply a few paragraphs on some legal question of the
day for his *Kelso Mail.*   Scott complied; and carrying his
article himself to the printing-office, took with him also
some of his recent pieces, designed to appear in Lewis's
Collection.   With these, especially, as his Memorandum
says, the " Morlachian fragment after Goethe," Ballantyne was charmed, and he expressed his regret that
Lewis's book was so long in appearing.   Scott talked of
Lewis with rapture; and, after reciting some of his
stanzas, said—" I ought to apologise to you for having
troubled you with anything of my own when I had things
like this for your ear."—" I felt at once," says Ballantyne, " that his own verses were far above what Lewis
could ever do, and though, when I said this, he dissented,
yet he seemed pleased with the warmth of my approbation."   At parting, Scott threw out a casual observation,
that he wondered his old friend did not try to get some
little booksellers' work, " to keep his types in play during
the rest of the week."   Ballantyne answered, that such an
idea had not before occurred to him—that he had no ac-

quaintance with the Edinburgh "trade"; but, if he had, his types were good, and he thought he could afford to work more cheaply than town-printers. Scott, "with his good-humoured smile," said,—" You had better try what you can do. You have been praising my little ballads; suppose you print off a dozen copies or so of as many as will make a pamphlet, sufficient to let my Edinburgh acquaintances judge of your skill for themselves." Ballantyne assented; and I believe exactly twelve copies of William and Ellen, The Fire-King, The Chase, and a few more of those pieces, were thrown off accordingly, with the title (alluding to the long delay of Lewis's Collection) of "Apology for Tales of Terror—1799." This first specimen of a press, afterwards so celebrated, pleased Scott; and he said to Ballantyne—" I have been for years collecting old Border ballads, and I think I could, with little trouble, put together such a selection from them as might make a neat little volume, to sell for four or five shillings. I will talk to some of the booksellers about it when I get to Edinburgh, and if the thing goes on, you shall be the printer." Ballantyne highly relished the proposal; and the result of this little experiment changed wholly the course of his worldly fortunes, as well as of his friend's.

Mr. Ballantyne, after recounting this conversation, says :—" I do not believe that even at this time he seriously contemplated giving himself much to literature;" but I think a letter addressed to Ballantyne, in the following April, affords considerable reason to doubt the accuracy of this impression. Scott there states, that he and another acquaintance of the printer's had been consulting together as to the feasibility of " no less than a total plan of migration from Kelso to Edinburgh"; and proceeds to say, that, in his opinion, there was then a very favourable opening in Edinburgh for a new printing establishment, conducted by a man of talent and education. He mentions —besides the chance of a share in the printing of law-papers—firstly, a weekly newspaper of the higher class; secondly, a monthly magazine; and thirdly, an annual register, as undertakings all likely to be well received; suggests that the general publishing trade itself was in a very languid condition; and ends with a hint that " pecuniary assistance, if wanted, might (no doubt) be procured on terms of a share, or otherwise." The coincidence of

most of these air-drawn schemes with things afterwards
realised is certainly very striking. At the same time, between October 1799 and April 1800, there had occurred
a change in Scott's personal affairs very likely to have
strengthened, if not originated the design, which Ballantyne did not believe him to have seriously entertained at
the time of their autumnal interview.

Shortly after the commencement of the Winter Session,
the office of Sheriff-depute of Selkirkshire became vacant
by the death of an early ally of Scott's, Andrew Plummer,
of Middlestead, a scholar and antiquary, who had entered
with zeal into his ballad researches, and whose name occurs
accordingly more than once in the notes to the Border
Minstrelsy. Perhaps the community of their tastes may
have had some part in suggesting to the Duke of Buccleuch, that Scott might fitly succeed Mr. Plummer in the
magistrature. Be that as it might, his Grace's influence
was used with Mr. Henry Dundas (afterwards Viscount
Melville), who in those days had the general control of the
Crown patronage in Scotland, and was prepared to look
favourably on Scott's pretensions to some office of this description. Though neither the Duke nor this able Minister
were at all addicted to literature, they had both seen him
frequently under their own roofs, and been pleased with his
manners and conversation; and he had by this time come
to be on terms of affectionate intimacy with some of the
younger members of either family. The Earl of Dalkeith
(afterwards Duke Charles of Buccleuch), and his brother
Lord Montagu, both participating with kindred ardour in
the military patriotism of the period, had been thrown
into his society under circumstances well qualified to ripen
acquaintance into confidence. Robert Dundas, eldest son
of the Minister, had been one of Scott's companions in the
High School; and he, too, had been of late a lively partaker
in the business of the yeomanry cavalry; and, last not
least, Scott always remembered with gratitude the strong
intercession on this occasion of Lord Melville's nephews,
Robert Dundas of Arniston, the Lord Advocate of the
time, and William Dundas, then Secretary to the Board of
Control.

His appointment to the *Sheriffship* bears date 16th December, 1799. It secured him an annual salary of £300;
an addition to his resources which at once relieved his
mind from whatever degree of anxiety he might have felt

in considering the prospect of an increasing family, along with the ever precarious chances of a profession, in the daily drudgery of which it is impossible to suppose that he ever could have found much pleasure. The duties of the office were far from heavy; the territory, small, peaceful, and pastoral, was in great part the property of the Duke of Buccleuch; and he turned with redoubled zeal to his project of editing the ballads, many of the best of which belonged to this very district of his favourite Border— those " tales " which, as the Dedication of the Minstrelsy expresses it, had " in elder times celebrated the prowess and cheered the halls " of his noble patron's ancestors.

Scott found able assistants in the completion of his design. Richard Heber (long Member of Parliament for the University of Oxford) happened to spend this winter in Edinburgh, and was welcomed, as his talents and accomplishments entitled him to be, by the cultivated society of the place. With Scott, his multifarious learning, particularly his profound knowledge of the literary monuments of the middle ages, soon drew him into habits of close alliance; the stores of his library, even then extensive, were freely laid open, and his own oral commentaries were not less valuable. But through him Scott made acquaintance with a person still more qualified to give effectual aid in this undertaking. Few who read these pages can be unacquainted with the leading facts in the history of John Leyden. Few can need to be reminded that this extraordinary man, born in a shepherd's cottage in one of the wildest valleys of Roxburghshire, and of course almost entirely self-educated, had, before he attained his nineteenth year, confounded the doctors of Edinburgh by the portentous mass of his acquisitions in almost every department of learning. He had set the extremest penury at utter defiance, or rather he had never been conscious that it could operate as a bar; for bread and water, and access to books and lectures, comprised all within the bounds of his wishes; and thus he toiled and battled at the gates of science after science, until his unconquerable perseverance carried everything before it; and yet with this monastic abstemiousness and iron hardness of will, perplexing those about him by manners and habits in which it was hard to say whether the moss-trooper or the schoolman of former days most prevailed, he was at heart a poet.

Archibald Constable, in after life one of the most eminent of British publishers, was at this period the keeper of a small book-shop, into which few but the poor students of Leyden's order had hitherto found their way. Heber, in the course of his bibliomaniacal prowlings, discovered that it contained some of

"The small old volumes, dark with tarnished gold,"

which were already the Delilahs of his imagination; and, moreover, that the young bookseller had himself a strong taste for such charmers. Frequenting the place, accordingly, he observed with some curiosity the countenance and gestures of another daily visitant, who came not to purchase, evidently, but to pore over the more recondite articles—often balanced for hours on a ladder with a folio in his hand like Dominie Sampson. The English virtuoso was on the look-out for any books or MSS. that might be of use to the editor of the projected "Minstrelsy," and some casual colloquy led to the discovery that this new stranger was, amidst the endless labyrinth of his lore, a master of legend and tradition—an enthusiastic collector and skilful expounder of these very Border ballads. Scott heard with much interest Heber's account of his odd acquaintance, and found, when introduced, the person whose initials, affixed to a series of pieces in verse, chiefly translations from Greek, Latin, and the northern languages, scattered, during the last three or four years, over the pages of the "Edinburgh Magazine," had often much excited his curiosity, as various indications pointed out the Scotch Border to be the native district of this unknown "J. L."

These new friendships led to a great change in Leyden's position, purposes, and prospects. He was presently received into the best society of Edinburgh, where his uncouthness of demeanour does not seem to have at all interfered with the general appreciation of his genius, his endowments, and amiable virtues. Fixing his ambition on the East, where he hoped to rival the achievements of Sir William Jones, he at length, about the beginning of 1802, obtained the promise of some literary appointment in the East India Company's service; but when the time drew near, it was discovered that the patronage of the season had been exhausted, with the exception of one *surgeon-assistant's* commission—which had been with difficulty secured for him by Mr. William Dundas; who, moreover,

was obliged to inform him, that if he accepted it, he must
be qualified to pass his medical trials within six months.
This news, which would have crushed any other man's
hopes to the dust, was only a welcome fillip to the ardour
of Leyden. He that same hour grappled with a new
science in full confidence that whatever ordinary men could
do in three or four years, his energy could accomplish in as
many months; took his degree accordingly in the beginning
of 1803, having just before published his beautiful poem,
The Scenes of Infancy; sailed to India; raised for himself,
within seven short years, the reputation of the most marvellous of Orientalists; and died, in the midst of the
proudest hopes, at the same age with Burns and Byron,
in 1811.

But to return :—Leyden was enlisted by Scott in the
service of Lewis, and immediately contributed a ballad,
called The Elf-King, to the Tales of Terror. Those
highly-spirited pieces, the Cout of Keeldar, Lord Soulis,
and The Mermaid, were furnished for the original department of Scott's own collection : and the Dissertation of Fairies, prefixed to its second volume, " although
arranged and digested by the editor, abounds with instances of such curious reading as Leyden only had read,
and was originally compiled by him "; but not the least of
his labours was in the collection of the old ballads themselves. When he first conversed with Ballantyne on the
subject of the proposed work, and the printer signified
his belief that a single volume of moderate size would be
sufficient for the materials, Leyden exclaimed—" Dash it !
does Mr. Scott mean another thin thing like Goetz of
Berlichingen? I have more than that in my head myself :
we shall turn out three or four such volumes at least."
He went to work stoutly in the realisation of these wider
views. " In this labour," says Scott, " he was equally
interested by friendship for the editor, and by his own
patriotic zeal for the honour of the Scottish borders; and
both may be judged of from the following circumstance.
An interesting fragment had been obtained of an ancient
historical ballad ; but the remainder, to the great disturbance of the editor and his coadjutor, was not to be
recovered. Two days afterwards, while the editor was
sitting with some company after dinner, a sound was
heard at a distance like that of the whistling of a tem-
pest through the torn rigging of the vessel which scuds

before it. The sounds increased as they approached more near; and Leyden (to the great astonishment of such of the guests as did not know him) burst into the room, chanting the desiderated ballad with the most enthusiastic gesture, and all the energy of what he used to call the *sawtones* of his voice. It turned out that he had walked between forty and fifty miles and back again, for the sole purpose of visiting an old person who possessed this precious remnant of antiquity." [1]

During the years 1800 and 1801, the Minstrelsy formed its editor's chief occupation—a labour of love truly, if ever such there was; but neither this nor his sheriffship interfered with his regular attendance at the Bar, the abandonment of which was all this while as far as it ever had been from his imagination, or that of any of his friends. He continued to have his summer headquarters at Lasswade; and Sir John Stoddart, who visited him there in the course of his Scottish tour (published in 1801), dwells on " the simple unostentatious elegance of the cottage, and the domestic picture which he there contemplated—a man of native kindness and cultivated talent, passing the intervals of a learned profession amidst scenes highly favourable to his poetic inspirations, not in churlish and rustic solitude, but in the daily exercise of the most precious sympathies as a husband, a father, and a friend." His means of hospitality were now much enlarged, and the cottage on a Saturday and Sunday at least was seldom without visitors.

Among other indications of greater ease in his circumstances, which I find in his letter-book, he writes to Heber, after his return to London in May 1800, to request his good offices on behalf of Mrs. Scott, who had " set her heart on a phaeton, at once strong, and low, and handsome, and not to cost more than thirty guineas "; which combination of advantages Heber seems

[1] *Essay on the Life of Leyden*—Miscellaneous Prose. Many tributes to his memory are scattered over his friend's works, both prose and verse; and, above all, Scott did not forget him when exploring, three years after his death, the scenery of The Lord of the Isles :—

> " Scenes sung by him who sings no more:
>   His bright and brief career is o'er,
>   And mute his tuneful strains ;
>   Quench'd is his lamp of varied lore,
>   That loved the light of song to pour;
>   A distant and a deadly shore
>   Has Leyden's cold remains !"

to have found by no means easy of attainment.   The
phaeton was, however, discovered; and its springs must
soon have been put to a sufficient trial, for this was " the
first wheeled carriage that ever penetrated into Liddesdale "—namely, in August 1800.   The friendship of the
Buccleuch family now placed better means of research at
his disposal, and Lord Dalkeith had taken special care
that there should be a band of pioneers in waiting when
he reached Hermitage.

Though he had not given up Lasswade, his sheriffship
now made it necessary for him that he should be frequently in Ettrick Forest.   On such occasions he took
up his lodgings in the little inn at Clovenford, a favourite
fishing station on the road from Edinburgh to Selkirk.
From this place he could ride to the county town whenever business required his presence, and he was also
within a few miles of the vales of Yarrow and Ettrick,
where he obtained large accessions to his store of ballads.
It was in one of these excursions that, penetrating
beyond St. Mary's lake, he found a hospitable reception
at the farm of *Blackhouse*, situated on the Douglas-burn,
then tenanted by a remarkable family, to which I have
already made allusion—that of William Laidlaw.   He
was then a very young man, but the extent of his acquirements was already as noticeable as the vigour and
originality of his mind; and their correspondence, where
" Sir " passes, at a few bounds, through " Dear Sir,"
and " Dear Mr. Laidlaw," to " Dear Willie," shows how
speedily this new acquaintance had warmed into a very
tender affection.   Laidlaw's zeal about the ballads was
repaid by Scott's anxious endeavours to get him removed
from a sphere for which, he writes, " it is no flattery to
say that you are much too good."   It was then, and
always continued to be, his opinion, that his friend was
particularly qualified for entering with advantage on the
study of the medical profession; but such designs, if
Laidlaw himself ever took them up seriously, were not
ultimately persevered in; and I question whether any
worldly success could, after all, have overbalanced the
retrospect of an honourable life spent happily in the open
air of nature, amidst scenes the most captivating to the
eye of genius, and in the intimate confidence of, perhaps,
the greatest of contemporary minds.

James Hogg spent ten years of his life in the service of

Mr. Laidlaw's father, but he had passed into that of another sheep-farmer in a neighbouring valley, before Scott first visited Blackhouse. William Laidlaw and Hogg were, however, most intimate friends, and the former took care that Scott should see, without delay, one whose fondness for the minstrelsy of the Forest was equal to his own, and whose aged mother was celebrated for having by heart several ballads in a more perfect form than any other inhabitant of the vale of Ettrick. The personal history of James Hogg must have interested Scott even more than any acquisition of that sort which he owed to this acquaintance with, perhaps, the most remarkable man that ever wore the *maud* of a shepherd. Under the garb, aspect, and bearing of a rude peasant— and rude enough he was in most of these things, even after no inconsiderable experience of society—Scott found a brother poet, a true son of nature and genius, hardly conscious of his powers. He had taught himself to write by copying the letters of a printed book as he lay watching his flock on the hill-side, and had probably reached the utmost pitch of his ambition, when he first found that his artless rhymes could touch the heart of the ewe-milker who partook the shelter of his mantle during the passing storm. As yet his naturally kind and simple character had not been exposed to any of the dangerous flatteries of the world; his heart was pure, his enthusiasm buoyant as that of a happy child; and well as Scott knew that reflection, sagacity, wit, and wisdom, were scattered abundantly among the humblest rangers of these pastoral solitudes, there was here a depth and a brightness that filled him with wonder, combined with a quaintness of humour, and a thousand little touches of absurdity, which afforded him more entertainment, as I have often heard him say, than the best comedy that ever set the pit in a roar.

Scott opened in the same year a correspondence with the venerable Bishop of Dromore, who seems, however, to have done little more than express a warm interest in an undertaking so nearly resembling that which will ever keep his own name in remembrance. He had more success in his applications to a more unpromising quarter— namely, with Joseph Ritson, the ancient and virulent assailant of Bishop Percy's editorial character. This narrow-minded, sour, and dogmatical little word-catcher had hated the very name of a Scotsman, and was utterly incapable of sympathising with any of the higher views of his new correspondent. Yet the bland courtesy of Scott disarmed even this half-crazy pedant; and he communicated the stores of his really valuable learning in a manner that seems to have greatly surprised all who had hitherto held any intercourse with him on antiquarian topics. It astonished, above all, the amiable and elegant George Ellis, whose acquaintance was at about the same time opened to Scott through their common friend Heber. Mr. Ellis was now busily engaged in collecting the materials for his charming works, entitled Specimens of Ancient English Poetry, and Specimens of Ancient English Romance. The correspondence between him and Scott soon came to be constant. They met personally, before many letters had been exchanged, conceived for each other a cordial respect and affection, and continued on a footing of almost brotherly intimacy ever after. To this alliance, Scott owed, among other advantages, his early and ready admission to the acquaintance and familiarity of Ellis's bosom friend, his coadjutor in the Anti-Jacobin, and the confidant of all his literary schemes, Mr. Canning.

Scott spent the Christmas of 1801 at Hamilton Palace, in Lanarkshire. To Lady Anne Hamilton he had been introduced by her friend, Lady Charlotte Campbell, and both the late and present Dukes of Hamilton appear to have partaken of Lady Anne's admiration for Glenfinlas and the Eve of St. John. A morning's ramble to the majestic ruins of the old baronial castle on the precipitous banks of the Evan, and among the adjoining remains of the primeval Caledonian forest, suggested to him a ballad not inferior in execution to any he had hitherto produced, and especially interesting as the first in which he grapples with the world of picturesque incident unfolded in the authentic annals of Scotland. With the magnificent localities before him he skilfully interwove the daring assassination of the Regent Murray by one of the clansmen of "the princely Hamilton." Had the subject been taken up in after years, we might have had another Marmion or Heart of Mid-Lothian; for in Cadyow Castle we have the materials and outline of more than one of the noblest of ballads.

About two years before this piece began to be handed about in Edinburgh, Thomas Campbell had made his

appearance there, and at once seized a high place in the
literary world by his " Pleasures of Hope." Among the
most eager to welcome him had been Scott; and I find the
brother-bard thus expressing himself concerning the MS.
of Cadyow :—" The verses of Cadyow Castle are perpetually ringing in my imagination—

> ' Where, mightiest of the beasts of chase
>   That roam in woody Caledon,
>   Crashing the forest in his race,
>   The mountain bull comes thundering on '—

and the arrival of Hamilton, when

> ' Reeking from the recent deed,
>   He dashed his carbine on the ground.'

I have repeated these lines so often on the North Bridge,
that the whole fraternity of coachmen know me by tongue
as I pass.   To be sure, to a mind in sober, serious street-
walking humour, it must bear an appearance of lunacy
when one stamps with the hurried pace and fervent shake
of the head, which strong, pithy poetry excites."

According to the original intention, the *Sir Tristrem*,
an imperfect romance, ascribed to Thomas of Ercildoune,
the famous old seer and bard of the border, was to have
had a prominent place in the first *livraison* of the Minstrelsy; but from the rapid accumulation of matter for
notes, as well as of unprinted ballads, this plan was
dropped.   The Cadyow Castle, too, was ready, but " two
volumes," as Ballantyne says, " were already full to overflowing "; so it also was reserved for a third.

Volumes I. and II. appeared in January 1802, from the
respectable house of Cadell and Davies in the Strand;
and, owing to the cold reception of Lewis's Tales of
Wonder, which had come forth a year earlier, these may
be said to have first introduced Scott as an original
writer to the English public.   In his Remarks on the
imitation of Popular Poetry, he says :—" When the book
came out, the imprint, Kelso, was read with wonder by
amateurs of typography, who had never heard of such a
place, and were astonished at the example of handsome
printing which so obscure a town had produced."   One
of the embellishments was a view of Hermitage Castle,
the history of which is rather curious.   Scott executed a
rough sketch of it during the last of his " Liddesdale
raids " with Shortreed, standing for that purpose for an

hour or more up to his middle in the snow. Nothing can
be ruder than the performance; but his friend William
Clerk made a better drawing from it; and from his, a
third and further improved copy was done by Hugh
Williams, the elegant artist, afterwards known as " Greek
Williams." [1]   Scott used to say, the oddest thing of all
was, that the engraving, founded on the labours of three
draughtsmen, one of whom could not draw a straight
line, and the two others had never seen the place meant
to be represented, was nevertheless pronounced by the
natives of Liddesdale to give a very fair notion of the
ruins of Hermitage.   The edition was exhausted in the
course of the year, and the terms of publication having
been that Scott should have half the clear profits, his
share was exactly £78 10s.—a sum which certainly could
not have repaid him for the actual expenditure incurred
in the collection of his materials.

The work was received with very great delight by Ellis;
and I might fill many pages by transcribing applausive
letters from others of acknowledged discernment in this
branch of literature.   John Duke of Roxburgh is among
the number, and he conveys also a complimentary message
from Lord Spencer; Pinkerton issues his decree of approbation as *ex cathedrâ*; Chalmers overflows with heartier
praise; and even Joseph Ritson extols his presentation
copy as " the most valuable literary treasure in his possession."   There follows enough of female admiration to
have been dangerous for another man; a score of fine
ladies contend who shall be the most extravagant in
encomium—and as many professed blue-stockings come
after; among, or rather above the rest, Anna Seward,
" the Swan of Lichfield," who laments that her " bright
luminary," Darwin, does not survive to partake her raptures;—observes, that " in the Border Ballads the first
strong rays of the Delphic orb illuminate Jellon Graeme ";
and concludes with a fact indisputable, but strangely
expressed, viz., that " the Lady Anne Bothwell's Lament,
Cowdenknowes, &c., &c., *climatically* preceded the treasures of Burns, and the consummate Glenfinlas and Eve
of St. John."

The reception of the first volumes elated naturally their
printer, whom George Ellis dubs " the Bulmer of Kelso."
He also went up to London to cultivate acquaintance

[1] His *Travels in Greece* were published in 1820.

with publishers, and on his return writes thus to his employer :—" I shall ever think the printing the Scottish Minstrelsy one of the most fortunate circumstances of my life. I have gained, not lost by it, in a pecuniary light; and the prospects it has been the means of opening to me, may advantageously influence my future destiny. I can never be sufficiently grateful for the interest you unceasingly take in my welfare. One thing is clear—that Kelso cannot be my abiding place for aye." The great bookseller, Longman, repaired to Scotland soon after this, and made an offer for the copyright of the Minstrelsy, the third volume included. This was accepted, and it was at last settled that Sir Tristrem should appear in a separate shape. In July Scott proceeded to the Borders with Leyden. " We have just concluded," he tells Ellis, " an excursion of two or three weeks through my jurisdiction of Selkirkshire, where, in defiance of mountains, rivers, and bogs, damp and dry, we have penetrated the very recesses of Ettrick Forest, to which district, if I ever have the happiness of welcoming you, you will be convinced that I am truly the sheriff of the ' cairn and the scaur.' In the course of our grand tour, besides the risks of swamping and breaking our necks, we encountered the formidable hardships of sleeping upon peatstacks, and eating mutton slain by no common butcher, but deprived of life by the judgment of God, as a coroner's inquest would express themselves. I have, however, not only escaped safe ' per varios casus, per tot discrimina rerum,' but returned *loaded* with the treasures of oral tradition. The principal result of our inquiries has been a complete and perfect copy of Maitland with his Auld Berd Graie, referred to by Douglas in his Palice of Honour. You may guess the surprise of Leyden and myself when this was presented to us, copied down from the recitation of an old shepherd, by a country farmer, and with no greater corruptions than might be supposed to be introduced by the lapse of time, and the ignorance of reciters."

Leyden seems to have spent much of that autumn at the Lasswade cottage, and here he encountered Joseph Ritson. Their host delighted to detail the scene that occurred when his two rough allies first met at dinner. Well knowing Ritson's holy horror of all animal food, Leyden complained that the joint on the table was overdone. "Indeed, for that matter," cried he, "meat can never be too little done, and raw is best of all." He sent to the kitchen accordingly for a plate of literally raw beef, and manfully ate it up, with no sauce but the exquisite ruefulness of the Pythagorean's glances. Mr. R. Gillies, a gentleman of the Scotch Bar (since known for some excellent translations from the German), was present another day when Ritson was in Scotland. "In approaching the cottage," he says, "I was struck with the exceeding air of neatness that prevailed around. The hand of tasteful cultivation had been there, and all methods employed to convert an ordinary thatched cottage into a handsome and comfortable abode. At this early period, Scott was more like the portrait by Saxon, engraved for the Lady of the Lake, than to any subsequent picture. He retained in features and form an impress of that elasticity and youthful vivacity, which he used to complain wore off after he was forty, and by *his own* account was exchanged for the plodding heaviness of an operose student. He had now, indeed, somewhat of a boyish gaiety of look, and in person was tall, slim, and extremely active." He and Erskine were about to start on a walk to Roslin, and Mr. Gillies accompanied them. In the course of their walk, Scott's foot slipped, as he was scrambling towards a cave on the edge of a precipitous bank, and "had there been no trees in the way" (says this writer), "he must have been killed; but midway he was stopped by a large root of hazel, when, instead of struggling, which would have made matters greatly worse, he seemed perfectly resigned to his fate, and slipped through the tangled thicket till he lay flat on the river's brink. He rose in an instant from his recumbent attitude, and with a hearty laugh called out—'Now, let me see who else will do the like.' He scrambled up the cliff with alacrity, and entered the cave, where we had a long dialogue." Even after he was an old and hoary man, he continually encountered such risks with the same recklessness. The extraordinary strength of his hands and arms was his great reliance in all such difficulties, and if he could see anything to lay hold of, he was afraid of no leap, or rather hop, that came in his way. Mr. Gillies adds, that when they drew near the famous chapel of Roslin, Erskine expressed a hope that they might, as habitual visitors, escape hearing the usual endless story of the old woman that shewed the ruins; but Scott answered, "There is a pleasure in the song which none but the songstress knows, and by telling her we know it already, we should make the poor devil unhappy."

On their return to the cottage, Scott inquired for *the learned cabbage-eater*, who had been expected to dinner. "Indeed," answered his wife, "you may be happy he is not here—he is so very disagreeable. Mr. Leyden, I believe, frightened him away." It turned out that it was even so. When Ritson appeared, a round of cold beef was on the luncheon-table, and Mrs. Scott, forgetting his peculiar creed, offered him a slice. "The antiquary, in his indignation, expressed himself in such outrageous terms to the lady, that Leyden first tried to correct him by ridicule, and then, on the madman growing more violent, became angry in his turn, till at last he threatened that if he were not silent, he would *thraw his neck*. Scott shook his head at this recital, which Leyden observing, grew vehement in his own justification. Scott said not a word in reply, but took up a large bunch of feathers fastened to a stick, denominated *a duster*, and shook it about the student's ears till he laughed—then changed the subject." All this is very characteristic of the parties.—Scott's playful aversion to dispute was a trait in his mind and manners that could alone have enabled him to make use at one and the same time, and for the same purpose, of two such persons as Ritson and Leyden.[1]

Shortly after this visit, Leyden went to London, and in the letter that introduced him to Ellis, Scott mentions, among other things to be included in the third volume of the Minstrelsy, "a long poem" from his own pen—"a kind of romance of Border chivalry, in a light-horseman sort of stanza." This refers to the first draught of The Lay of the Last Minstrel; and the author's description of it as being "in a light-horseman sort of stanza," was probably suggested by the circumstances under which the greater part of that draught had been accomplished. He has told us, in his Introduction of 1830, that the poem originated in a request of the young and lovely Countess of Dalkeith, that he would write a ballad on the legend of Gilpin Horner : that he began it at Lasswade, and read

[1] See Gillies's Reminiscences of Sir Walter Scott.

the opening stanzas, as soon as they were written, to
Erskine and Cranstoun : that their reception of these was
apparently so cold as to disgust him with what he had
done; but that finding, a few days afterwards, that the
verses had nevertheless excited their curiosity, and
haunted their memory, he was encouraged to resume the
undertaking. The scene and date of this resumption I
owe to the recollection of the then Cornet of the Light-
horse. While the troop were on permanent duty at
Musselburgh, in the autumnal recess of 1802, the Quartermaster, during a charge on Portobello sands, received a
kick of a horse, which confined him for three days to his
lodgings. Mr. Skene found him busy with his pen; and
he produced before these three days expired the first
canto of the Lay, very nearly, if his friend's memory may
be trusted, in the state in which it was ultimately published. That the whole poem was sketched and filled in
with extraordinary rapidity, there can be no difficulty in
believing. He himself says (in the Introduction of 1830),
that after he had once got fairly into the vein, it proceeded at the rate of about a canto in a week. The Lay,
however, like the Tristrem, soon outgrew the dimensions
which he had originally contemplated; the design of including it in the third volume of the Minstrelsy was of
course abandoned; and it did not appear until nearly three
years after that fortunate mishap on the beach of Portobello.

Next spring, Scott hurried up to London as soon as the
Court rose, in hopes of seeing Leyden once more before
he left England; but he came too late. He thus writes
to Ballantyne, on the 21st April 1803 :—" I have to
thank you for the accuracy with which the Minstrelsy is
thrown off. Longman and Rees are delighted with the
printing. I mean this note to be added, by way of
advertisement :—' In the press, and will speedily be published, the Lay of the Last Minstrel, by Walter Scott,
Esq., Editor of the Minstrelsy of the Scottish Border.
Also Sir Tristrem, a Metrical Romance, by Thomas of
Ercildoune, called the Rhymer, edited from an ancient
MS., with an Introduction and Notes, by Walter Scott,
Esq.' Will you cause such a thing to be appended in
your own way and fashion? "

This letter is dated " No. 15 Piccadilly West,"—he
and Mrs. Scott being there domesticated under the roof of

the late M. Charles Dumergue, a man of superior abilities and excellent education, well known as surgeon-dentist to the royal family—who had been intimately acquainted with the Charpentiers in France, and warmly befriended Mrs. Scott's mother on her first arrival in England. M. Dumergue's house was, throughout the whole period of the emigration, liberally opened to the exiles of his native country; nor did some of the noblest of those unfortunate refugees scruple to make a free use of his purse, as well as of his hospitality. Here Scott met much highly interesting French society, and until a child of his own was established in London, he never thought of taking up his abode anywhere else, as often as he had occasion to be in town.

The letter is addressed to "Mr. James Ballantyne, printer, Abbey-hill, Edinburgh"; which shows, that before the third volume of the Minstrelsy passed through the press, the migration recommended two years earlier had at length taken place. "It was about the end of 1802," says Ballantyne, "that I closed with a plan so congenial to my wishes. I removed, bag and baggage, to Edinburgh, finding accommodation for two presses, and a proof one, in the precincts of Holyrood-house, then deriving new lustre and interest from the recent arrival of the royal exiles of France. In these obscure premises some of the most beautiful productions of what we called *The Border Press* were printed." The Memorandum states, that Scott having renewed his hint as to pecuniary assistance, as soon as the printer found his finances straitened, "a liberal loan was advanced accordingly."

Heber, and Macintosh, then at the height of his reputation as a conversationist, and daily advancing also at the Bar, had been ready to welcome Scott in town as old friends; and Rogers, William Stewart Rose, and several other men of literary eminence, were at the same time added to the list of his acquaintance. His principal object, however—having missed Leyden—was to make extracts from some MSS. in the library of John Duke of Roxburgh, for the illustration of the Tristrem; and he derived no small assistance in other researches of the like kind from the collections which the indefatigable and obliging Douce placed at his disposal. Having completed these labours, he and Mrs. Scott went, with Heber and Douce, to visit Ellis at Sunninghill, where they spent a happy week, and their host and hostess heard the first two or three cantos of the Lay of the Last Minstrel read under an old oak in Windsor Forest.

From thence they proceeded to Oxford, accompanied by Heber; and it was on this occasion that Scott first saw his friend's brother, Reginald, in after days the apostolic Bishop of Calcutta. He had just been declared the successful candidate for that year's poetical prize, and read to Scott at breakfast, in Brazennose College, the MS. of his Palestine. Scott observed that, in the verses on Solomon's Temple, one striking circumstance had escaped him, namely, that no tools were used in its erection. Reginald retired for a few minutes to the corner of the room, and returned with the beautiful lines,—

> " No hammer fell, no ponderous axes rung,
>   Like some tall palm the mystic fabric sprung.
>   Majestic silence," &c.

After inspecting the University and Blenheim, Scott returned to Edinburgh, where the completed Minstrelsy was published in the end of May. The reprint of the first and second volumes went to 1,000 copies— of volume third Messrs. Longman had ordered 1,500. A complete edition of 1,250 copies followed in 1806; a fourth, also of 1,250, in 1810; a fifth, of 1,500, in 1812; a sixth, of 500, in 1820; and since then it has been incorporated in Scott's Collected Poetry. Of the Continental and American editions I can say nothing, except that they have been very numerous. The book was soon translated into German, Danish, and Swedish; and the structure of those languages being very favourable to the undertaking, the Minstrelsy of the Scottish Border has thus become widely naturalised among nations themselves rich in similar treasures of legendary lore.

He speaks, in an Essay of his closing years, as if the first reception of the Minstrelsy on the south of the Tweed had been cold. " The curiosity of the English," he says, " was not much awakened by poems in the rude garb of antiquity, accompanied with notes referring to the obscure feuds of barbarous clans, of whose very names civilised history was ignorant." In writing those beautiful Introductions of 1830, however, he seems to have trusted entirely to his recollection of days long gone by, and he has accordingly let fall many statements which we must take with some allowance. His impressions as to the reception of the Minstrelsy were different, when writing to his brother-in-law, Charles Carpenter, on the 3rd March 1803, for the purpose of introducing Leyden, he said—"I have contrived to turn a very slender portion of literary talents to some account, by a publication of the poetical antiquities of the Border, where the old people had preserved many ballads descriptive of the manners of the country during the wars with England. This trifling collection was so well received by a *discerning public,* that, after receiving about £100 profit for the first edition, which my vanity cannot omit informing you went off in six months, I have sold the copyright for £500 more." This is not the language of disappointment; and though the edition of 1803 did not move off quite so rapidly as the first, and the work did not perhaps attract much notice beyond the more cultivated students of literature, until the Editor's own Lay lent general interest to whatever was connected with his name, I suspect there never was much ground for accusing the English public of regarding the Minstrelsy with more coldness than the Scotch—the population of the Border districts themselves being, of course, excepted. Had the sale of the original edition been chiefly Scotch, I doubt whether Messrs. Longman would have so readily offered £500, in those days of the trade a large sum, for the second. Scott had become habituated, long before 1830, to a scale of bookselling transactions, measured by which the largest editions and copy-monies of his own early days appeared insignificant; but the evidence seems complete that he was well contented at the time.

He certainly had every reason to be so as to the impression which the Minstrelsy made on the minds of those entitled to think for themselves upon such a subject. The ancient ballads in his collection, which had never been printed at all before, were in number forty-three; and of the others—most of which were in fact all but new to the modern reader—it is little to say that his editions were superior in all respects to those that had preceded them. He had, I firmly believe, interpolated hardly a line or even an epithet of his own; but his diligent zeal had put him in possession of a variety of copies in different stages of preservation; and to the task of selecting a standard text among such a diversity of materials, he brought a know-

ledge of old manners and phraseology, and a manly simplicity of taste, such as had never before been united in
the person of a poetical antiquary. From among a hundred
corruptions he seized, with instinctive tact, the primitive
diction and imagery; and produced strains in which
the unbroken energy of half-civilised ages, their stern
and deep passions, their daring adventures and cruel
tragedies, and even their rude wild humour, are reflected
with almost the brightness of a Homeric mirror, interrupted by hardly a blot of what deserves to be called
vulgarity, and totally free from any admixture of artificial
sentimentalism. As a picture of manners, the Scottish
Minstrelsy is not surpassed, if equalled, by any similar
body of poetry preserved in any other country; and it
unquestionably owes its superiority in this respect over
Percy's Reliques, to the Editor's conscientious fidelity, on
the one hand, which prevented the introduction of anything new—to his pure taste, on the other, in the
balancing of discordant recitations. His introductory
essays and notes teemed with curious knowledge, not
hastily grasped for the occasion, but gradually gleaned
and sifted by the patient labour of years, and presented
with an easy, unaffected propriety and elegance of
arrangement and expression, which it may be doubted if he
ever materially surpassed in the happiest of his imaginative narrations. I well remember, when Waverley was a
new book, and all the world were puzzling themselves
about its authorship, to have heard the Poet of " The Isle
of Palms " exclaim impatiently—" I wonder what all
these people are perplexing themselves with : have they
forgotten the *prose* of the Minstrelsy?" Even had the
Editor inserted none of his own verse, the work would
have contained enough, and more than enough, to found
a lasting and graceful reputation.

It is not to be denied, however, that the Minstrelsy of
the Scottish Border has derived a very large accession of
interest from the subsequent career of its Editor. One of
the critics of that day said that the book contained " the
elements of a hundred historical romances ";—and this
critic was a prophetic one. No person who has not gone
through its volumes for the express purpose of comparing
their contents with his great original works, can have
formed a conception of the endless variety of incidents and
images now expanded and emblazoned by his mature art,

of which the first hints may be found either in the text of those primitive ballads, or in the notes, which the happy rambles of his youth had gathered together for their illustration. In the edition of the Minstrelsy published since his death, not a few such instances are pointed out; but the list might have been extended far beyond the limits which such an edition allowed. The taste and fancy of Scott appear to have been formed as early as his moral character; and he had, before he passed the threshold of authorship, assembled about him, in the uncalculating delight of native enthusiasm, almost all the materials on which his genius was destined to be employed for the gratification and instruction of the world.

CHAPTER IV

Contributions to the Edinburgh Review—Wordsworth—Hogg—Sir Tristrem—Removal to Ashestiel—Mungo Park—Publication of the Lay of the Last Minstrel—Partnership with James Ballantyne—Visit to London—Appointment as Clerk of Session. 1804–1806.

SHORTLY after the complete " Minstrelsy " issued from the press, Scott made his first appearance as a reviewer. The Edinburgh Review had been commenced in October 1802, under the superintendence of the Rev. Sydney Smith, with whom, during his short residence in Scotland, he had lived on terms of great kindness and familiarity. Mr. Smith soon resigned the editorship to Mr. Jeffrey, who had by this time been for several years among the most valued of Scott's friends and companions at the Bar; and, the new journal being far from committing itself to violent politics at the outset, he appreciated the brilliant talents regularly engaged in it far too highly, not to be well pleased with the opportunity of occasionally exercising his pen in its service. His first contribution was an article on Southey's Amadis of Gaul. The reader may now trace the sequence of his articles in the Collective edition of his Miscellaneous Prose (1836).

During the summer of 1803, his chief literary work was on the *Sir Tristrem,* but the Lay of the Last Minstrel made progress at intervals—mostly, it would seem, when he was in quarters with his troop of horse, and necessarily without his books of reference. The resumption of the war (after the short peace of Amiens) had given renewed animation to the volunteers, and their spirit was

kept up during two or three years more by the unintermitted threats of invasion. His letters abound in sketches
of the camp-life at Musselburgh. To Miss Seward, for
example, he says, in July:—" We are assuming a very
military appearance. Three regiments of militia, with a
formidable park of artillery, are encamped just by us.
The Edinburgh Troop, to which I have the honour to be
quartermaster, consists entirely of young gentlemen of
family, and is, of course, admirably well mounted and
armed. There are other four troops in the regiment, consisting of yeomanry, whose iron faces and muscular forms
announce the hardness of the climate against which they
wrestle, and the powers which nature has given them
to contend with and subdue it. These corps have been
easily raised in Scotland, the farmers being in general a
high-spirited race of men, fond of active exercises, and
patient in hardship and fatigue. For myself, I must own
that to one who has, like myself, *la tête un peu exaltée*
' the pomp and circumstance of war ' gives, for a time,
a very poignant and pleasing sensation. The imposing
appearance of cavalry, in particular, and the rush which
marks their onset, appear to me to partake highly of the
sublime. Perhaps I am the more attached to this sort of
sport of swords because my health requires much active
exercise, and a lameness contracted in childhood renders
it inconvenient for me to take it otherwise than on horseback. I have, too, a hereditary attachment to the
animal—not, I flatter myself, of the common jockey cast,
but because I regard him as the kindest and most
generous of the subordinate tribes. I hardly even except
the dogs; at least they are usually so much better treated,
that compassion for the steed should be thrown into the
scale when we weigh their comparative merits. My wife
(a foreigner) never sees a horse ill-used without asking
what the poor horse has done in his state of pre-existence?
I would fain hope they have been carters or hackney-
coachmen, and are only experiencing a retort of the ill-
usage they have formerly inflicted. What think you? "

It was in that autumn that Scott first saw Wordsworth. Their common acquaintance, Stoddart, had so
often talked of them to each other, that they met as if
they had not been strangers; and they parted friends.

Mr. and Miss Wordsworth had just completed their
tour in the Highlands, of which so many incidents have

since been immortalised, both in the poet's verse and in the hardly less poetical prose of his sister's Diary. On the morning of the 17th of September, having left their carriage at Roslin, they walked down the valley to Lasswade, and arrived there before Mr. and Mrs. Scott had risen. "We were received," Mr. Wordsworth has told me, "with that frank cordiality which, under whatever circumstances I afterwards met him, always marked his manners; and, indeed, I found him then in every respect— except, perhaps, that his animal spirits were somewhat higher—precisely the same man that you knew him in later life; the same lively, entertaining conversation, full of anecdote, and averse from disquisition; the same unaffected modesty about himself; the same cheerful and benevolent and hopeful views of man and the world. He partly read and partly recited, sometimes in an enthusiastic style of chant, the first four cantos of the Lay of the Last Minstrel; and the novelty of the manners, the clear picturesque descriptions, and the easy glowing energy of much of the verse, greatly delighted me."

After this he walked with the tourists to Roslin, and promised to meet them in two days at Melrose. The night before they reached Melrose they slept at the little quiet inn of Clovenford, where, on mentioning his name, they were received with all sorts of attention and kindness,—the landlady observing that Mr. Scott, "who was a very clever gentleman," was an old friend of the house, and usually spent a good deal of time there during the fishing season; but, indeed, says Mr. Wordsworth, "wherever we named him, we found the word acted as an *open sesamum;* and I believe that, in the character of the *Sheriff's* friends, we might have counted on a hearty welcome under any roof in the Border country."

He met them at Melrose on the 19th, and escorted them through the Abbey, pouring out his rich stores of history and tradition. They then dined together at the inn; but Miss Wordsworth observed that there was some difficulty about arranging matters for the night, "the landlady refusing to settle anything until she had ascertained from *the Sheriff himself* that he had no objection to sleep in the same room with *William.*" Scott was thus far on his way to the Circuit Court at Jedburgh, in his capacity of Sheriff, and there his new friends again joined him; but he begged that they would not enter the court, " for," said he, " I really would not like you to see the sort of figure I cut there." They did see him casually, however, in his cocked hat and sword, marching in the Judge's procession to the sound of one cracked trumpet, and were then not surprised that he should have been a little ashamed of the whole ceremonial. He introduced to them his friend William Laidlaw, who was attending the court as a juryman, and who, having read some of Wordsworth's verses in a newspaper, was exceedingly anxious to be of the party, when they explored at leisure, all the law-business being over, the beautiful valley of the Jed, and the ruins of the Castle of Fernieherst, the original fastness of the noble family of Lothian. The grove of stately ancient elms about and below the ruin was seen to great advantage in a fine, grey, breezy autumnal afternoon; and Mr. Wordsworth happened to say, " What life there is in trees! "—" How different," said Scott, " was the feeling of a very intelligent young lady, born and bred in the Orkney Islands, who lately came to spend a season in this neighbourhood! She told me nothing in the mainland scenery had so much disappointed her as woods and trees. She found them so dead and lifeless, that she could never help pining after the eternal motion and variety of the ocean. And so back she has gone, and I believe nothing will ever tempt her from *the windsweep Orcades* again."

Next day they proceeded up the Teviot to Hawick, Scott entertaining his friends with some legend or ballad connected with every tower or rock they passed. He made them stop to admire particularly a scene of deep and solemn retirement, called *Horne's Pool,* from its having been the daily haunt of a contemplative schoolmaster, known to him in his youth; and at Kirkton he pointed out the little village schoolhouse to which his friend Leyden had walked six or eight miles every day across the moors, " when a poor barefooted boy." From Hawick, where they spent the night, he led them next morning to the brow of a hill, from which they could see a wide range of the Border mountains, Ruberslaw, the Carter, and the Cheviots; and lamented that neither their engagements nor his own would permit them to make at this time an excursion into the wilder glens of Liddesdale, " where," said he, " I have strolled so often and so long, that I may say I have a home in every farm-house."

"And, indeed," adds Mr. Wordsworth, "wherever we went with him, he seemed to know everybody, and everybody to know and like him." Here they parted,—the Wordsworths to pursue their journey homeward by Eskdale—he to return to Lasswade.

The impression on Mr. Wordsworth's mind was, that on the whole he attached much less importance to his literary labours and reputation than to his bodily sports, exercises, and social amusements; and yet he spoke of his profession as if he had already given up almost all hope of rising by it; and some allusion being made to its profits, observed that "he was sure he could, if he chose, get more money than he should ever wish to have from the booksellers." [1]

This confidence in his own literary resources appeared to Mr. Wordsworth remarkable—the more so, from the careless way in which its expression dropt from him. As to his despondence concerning the Bar, I confess his *fee-book* indicates less ground for such a feeling than I should have expected to discover there. His practice brought him, as we have seen, in the session of 1796-7, £144 10s.;—its proceeds fell down, in the first year of his married life, to £79 17s.; but they rose again, in 1798-9, to £135 9s.; amounted, in 1799-1800, to £129 13s.; in 1800-1, to £170; in 1801-2, to £202 12s.; and in the session that had just elapsed (which is the last included in the record before me), to £228 18s.

I have already said something of the beginning of Scott's acquaintance with "the Ettrick Shepherd." Shortly after their first meeting, Hogg, coming into Edinburgh with a flock of sheep, was seized with a sudden ambition of seeing himself in type, and he wrote out that same night a few ballads, already famous in the Forest, which some obscure bookseller gratified him by printing accordingly; but they appear to have attracted no notice beyond their original sphere. Hogg then made an excursion into the Highlands, in quest of employment as overseer of some extensive sheep-farm; but, though Scott had furnished him with strong recommendations to various friends, he returned without success. He printed an account of his travels, however, in a set of letters in the

[1] I have drawn up the account of this meeting from my recollection partly of Mr. Wordsworth's conversation—partly from that of his sister's charming "Diary," which he was so kind as to read over to me on the 16th May 1836.

Scots Magazine, which, though exceedingly rugged and uncouth, had abundant traces of the native shrewdness and genuine poetical feeling of this remarkable man. These also failed to excite attention, but, undeterred by such disappointments, the Shepherd no sooner read the third volume of the " Minstrelsy," than he made up his mind that the Editor's " Imitations of the Ancients " were by no means what they should have been. " Immediately," he says, in one of his many memoirs of himself, " I chose a number of traditional facts, and set about imitating the manner of the ancients myself." These imitations he transmitted to Scott, who warmly praised the many striking beauties scattered over their rough surface. The next time that business carried him to Edinburgh, Scott invited him to dinner, in company with Laidlaw, who happened also to be in town, and some other admirers of the rustic genius. When Hogg entered the drawing-room, Mrs. Scott, being at the time in a delicate state of health, was reclining on a sofa. The Shepherd, after being presented, and making his best bow, took possession of another sofa placed opposite to hers, and stretched himself thereupon at all his length; for, as he said afterwards, " I thought I could never do wrong to copy the lady of the house." As his dress at this period was precisely that in which any ordinary herdsman attends cattle to the market, and his hands, moreover, bore most legible marks of a recent sheep-smearing, the lady of the house did not observe with perfect equanimity the novel usage to which her chintz was exposed. The Shepherd, however, remarked nothing of all this—dined heartily and drank freely, and, by jest, anecdote, and song, afforded plentiful merriment. As the liquor operated, his familiarity increased; from Mr. Scott, he advanced to " Sherra," and thence to " Scott," " Walter," and " Wattie,"—until, at supper, he fairly convulsed the whole party by addressing Mrs. Scott as " Charlotte."

The collection entitled " The Mountain Bard " was eventually published by Constable, in consequence of Scott's recommendation, and this work did at last afford Hogg no slender share of the reputation for which he had so long thirsted. It is not my business, however, to pursue the details of his story.

" Sir Tristrem " was at length published on the 2nd of May 1804, by Constable, who, however, expected so little popularity for the work, that the edition consisted only of 150 copies. These were sold at a high price (two guineas), otherwise they would not have been enough to cover the expenses of paper and printing. Mr. Ellis and other friends were much dissatisfied with these arrangements; but I doubt not that Constable was a better judge than any of them. The work, however, partook in due time of the favour attending its editor's name, and had been twice reprinted before it was included in the collective editions of his poetry. It was not a performance from which he had ever anticipated any pecuniary profit, but it maintained at least, if it did not raise, his reputation in the circle of his fellow-antiquaries; and his own *Conclusion,* in the manner of the original romance, must always be admired as a specimen of skill and dexterity. As to the arguments of the Introduction, I shall not in this place attempt any discussion. Whether the story of Tristrem was first told in Welsh, Armorican, French, or English verse, there can, I think, be no doubt that it had been told in verse, with such success as to obtain very general renown, by Thomas of Ercildoune, and that the copy edited by Scott was either the composition of one who had heard the old Rhymer recite his lay, or the identical lay itself. The introduction of Thomas's name in the third person, as not the author, but the author's authority, appears to have had a great share in convincing Scott that the Auchinleck MS. contained not the original, but the copy of an English admirer and contemporary. This point seems to have been rendered more doubtful by some quotations in the recent edition of Warton's History of English Poetry; but the argument derived from the enthusiastic exclamation, " God help Sir Tristrem the knight—he fought for England," still remains; and stronger perhaps even than that, in the opinion of modern philologists, is the total absence of any Scottish or even Northumbrian peculiarities in the diction. All this controversy may be waived here. Scott's object and delight was to revive the fame of the Rhymer, whose traditional history he had listened to while yet an infant among the crags of Smailholme. He had already celebrated him in a noble ballad;[1] he now devoted a volume to elucidate a fragment supposed to be substantially his work; and we shall find that

[1] See *Poetical Works* (Edition 1841), pp. 572-581.

thirty years after, when the lamp of his own genius was all but spent, it could still revive and throw out at least some glimmerings of its original brightness at the name of Thomas of Ercildoune.[1]

In the course of the preceding summer, the Lord-Lieutenant of Selkirkshire complained of Scott's military zeal as interfering sometimes with the discharge of his shrieval functions, and took occasion to remind him, that the law, requiring every Sheriff to reside at least four months in the year within his own jurisdiction, had not hitherto been complied with. While, in consequence of a renewal of this hint, he was seeking about for some " lodge in the Forest," his kinsman of Harden suggested that the tower of Auld Wat (the *Stammschloss* of their family) might be refitted, so as to serve his purpose; and he received the proposal with enthusiastic delight. On a more careful inspection of the localities, however, he became sensible that he would be practically at a greater distance from county business of all kinds at Harden, than if he were to continue at Lasswade. Just at this time, the house of Ashestiel, situated on the southern bank of the Tweed, a few miles from Selkirk, became vacant by the death of its proprietor, Colonel Russell, who had married a sister of Scott's mother, and the consequent dispersion of the family. The young Laird of Ashestiel, his cousin, was then in India; and the Sheriff took a lease of the house with a small farm adjoining. On the 4th May, two days after the Tristrem had been published, he says to Ellis, who was meditating a northern tour—" I have been engaged in travelling backwards and forwards to Selkirkshire upon little pieces of business, just important enough to prevent my doing anything to purpose. One great matter, however, I have achieved, which is, procuring myself a place of residence, which will save me these teasing migrations in future, so that though I part with my sweet little cottage on the banks of the Esk, you will find me this summer in the very centre of the ancient Reged, in a decent farm-house overhanging the Tweed, and situated in a wild pastoral country." And again, on the 19th, he thus apologises for not having answered a letter of the tenth :—" For more than a month my head was fairly tenanted by ideas, which, though strictly pastoral and rural, were neither

[1] Compare the Fifth Chapter of *Castle Dangerous*.

literary nor poetical. *Long sheep* and *short sheep*, and *tups* and *gimmers*, and *hogs* and *dinmonts*, had made a perfect sheepfold of my understanding, which is hardly yet cleared of them.[1] I hope Mrs. Ellis will clap a bridle on her imagination. Ettrick Forest boasts finely shaped hills and clear romantic streams; but, alas! they are bare to wildness, and denuded of the beautiful natural wood with which they were formerly shaded. It is mortifying to see that, though wherever the sheep are excluded, the copse has immediately sprung up in abundance, so that enclosures only are wanting to restore the wood wherever it might be useful or ornamental, yet hardly a proprietor has attempted to give it fair play for a resurrection."

On the 10th of June 1804, died, at his seat of Rosebank, Captain Robert Scott, the affectionate uncle whose name has often occurred in this narrative. " He was," says his nephew to Ellis, on the 18th, " a man of universal benevolence and great kindness towards his friends, and to me individually. His manners were so much tinged with the habits of celibacy as to render them peculiar, though by no means unpleasingly so, and his profession (that of a seaman) gave a high colouring to the whole. The loss is one which, though the course of nature led me to expect it, did not take place at last without considerable pain to my feelings. The arrangement of his affairs, and the distribution of his small fortune among his relations, will devolve in a great measure upon me. He has distinguished me by leaving me a beautiful little villa on the banks of the Tweed, with every possible convenience annexed to it, and about thirty acres of the finest land in Scotland. Notwithstanding, however, the temptation that this bequest offers, I continue to pursue my Reged plan, and expect to be settled at Ashestiel in the course of a month. Rosebank is situated so near the village of Kelso, as hardly to be sufficiently a country residence; besides, it is hemmed in by hedges and ditches, not to mention Dukes and Lady Dowagers, which are bad things for little people. It is expected to sell to great advantage. I shall buy a moun-

---

[1] Hogg describes the amusement of the Sheriff in 1801, upon hearing a discussion on the meaning of long sheep and short sheep (so called according to the length of the fleece); and adds—" When I saw the very same words repeated near the beginning (p. 4) of the *Black Dwarf,* how could I be mistaken of the author?"—*Autobiography* prefixed to *Altrive Tales.*

tain farm with the purchase-money, and be quite the Laird of the Cairn and the Scaur."

Scott sold Rosebank in the course of the year for £5,000. This bequest made an important change in his pecuniary position, and influenced accordingly the arrangements of his future life. Independently of practice at the Bar, and of literary profits, he was now, with his little patrimony, his Sheriffship, and about £200 per annum arising from the stock ultimately settled on his wife, in possession of a fixed revenue of nearly £1,000 a-year.

Ashestiel will be visited by many for his sake, as long as Waverley and Marmion are remembered. A more beautiful situation for the residence of a poet could not be conceived. The house was then a small one, but, compared with the cottage at Lasswade, its accommodations were amply sufficient. You approached it through an old-fashioned garden, with holly hedges, and broad, green, terrace walks. On one side, close under the windows, is a deep ravine, clothed with venerable trees, down which a mountain rivulet is heard, more than seen, in its progress to the Tweed. The river itself is separated from the high bank on which the house stands only by a narrow meadow of the richest verdure. Opposite, and all around, are the green hills. The valley there is narrow, and the aspect in every direction is that of perfect pastoral repose. The heights immediately behind are those which divide the Tweed from the Yarrow; and the latter celebrated stream lies within an easy ride, in the course of which the traveller passes through a variety of the finest mountain scenery in the south of Scotland. No town is within seven miles but Selkirk, which was then still smaller and quieter than it is now; there was hardly even a gentleman's family within visiting distance, except at Yair, a few miles lower on the Tweed, the ancient seat of the Pringles of Whytbank, and at Bowhill, between the Yarrow and Ettrick, where the Earl of Dalkeith used occasionally to inhabit a small shooting-lodge, which has since grown into a ducal residence. The country all around, with here and there an insignificant exception, belongs to the Buccleuch estate; so that, whichever way he chose to turn, the bard of the clan had ample room and verge enough for every variety of field sport; and being then in the prime vigour of manhood, he was not slow to profit by these advantages. Meantime, the concerns of his own little farm, and the care of his absent relation's woods, gave him healthful occupation in the intervals of the chase; and he had long, solitary evenings for the uninterrupted exercise of his pen; perhaps, on the whole, better opportunities of study than he had ever enjoyed before, or was to meet with elsewhere in later days.

When he first examined Ashestiel, with a view to being his cousin's tenant, he thought of taking home James Hogg to superintend the sheep-farm, and keep watch over the house also during the winter. I am not able to tell exactly in what manner this proposal fell to the ground; but in truth the Sheriff had hardly been a week in possession of his new domains, before he made acquaintance with a character much better suited to his purpose than James Hogg ever could have been. I mean honest Thomas Purdie, his faithful servant—his affectionately devoted humble friend from this time until death parted them. Tom was first brought before him, in his capacity of Sheriff, on a charge of poaching, when the poor fellow gave such a touching account of his circumstances,—a wife, and I know not how many children, depending on his exertions—work scarce and grouse abundant,—and all this with a mixture of odd sly humour, —that the Sheriff's heart was moved. Tom escaped the penalty of the law—was taken into employment as shepherd, and showed such zeal, activity, and shrewdness in that capacity, that Scott never had any occasion to repent of the step he soon afterwards took, in promoting him to the position which had been originally offered to James Hogg.

It was also about the same time that he took into his service as coachman Peter Mathieson, brother-in-law to Thomas Purdie, another faithful servant, who never afterwards left him, and still (1848) survives his kind master. Scott's awkward management of the little phaeton had exposed his wife to more than one perilous overturn, before he agreed to set up a close carriage, and call in the assistance of this steady charioteer.

During this autumn Scott formed the personal acquaintance of Mungo Park, the celebrated victim of African discovery. On his return from his first expedition, Park endeavoured to establish himself as a medical practitioner in the town of Hawick, but the drudgeries of that calling in such a district soon exhausted his ardent temper, and he was now living in seclusion in his native cottage at Fowlsheils on the Yarrow, nearly opposite Newark Castle. His brother, Archibald Park (then tenant of a large farm on the Buccleuch estate), a man remarkable for strength both of mind and body, introduced the traveller to the Sheriff. They soon became much attached to each other; and Scott supplied some interesting anecdotes of their brief intercourse to Mr. Wishaw, the editor of Park's Posthumous Journal, with which I shall blend a few minor circumstances, gathered from him in conversation long afterwards. "On one occasion," he says, "the traveller communicated some very remarkable adventures which had befallen him in Africa, but which he had not recorded in his book." On Scott's asking the cause of this silence, Mungo answered, "That in all cases where he had information to communicate, which he thought of importance to the public, he had stated the facts boldly, leaving it to his readers to give such credit to his statements as they might appear justly to deserve; but that he would not shock their faith, or render his travels more marvellous, by introducing circumstances, which, however true, were of little or no moment, as they related solely to his own personal adventures and escapes." This reply struck Scott as highly characteristic of the man; and though strongly tempted to set down some of these marvels for Mr. Wishaw's use, he on reflection abstained from doing so, holding it unfair to record what the adventurer had deliberately chosen to suppress in his own narrative. He confirms the account given by Park's biographer of his cold and reserved manners to strangers; and, in particular, of his disgust with the *indirect* questions which curious visitors would often put to him upon the subject of his travels. "This practice," said Mungo, "exposes me to two risks; either that I may not understand the questions meant to be put, or that my answers to them may be misconstrued;" and he contrasted such conduct with the frankness of Scott's revered friend, Dr. Adam Ferguson, who, the very first day the traveller dined with him at Hallyards, spread a large map of Africa on the table, and made him trace out his progress thereupon, inch by inch, questioning him minutely as to every step he had taken. "Here, however," says Scott, "Dr. F. was using a privilege to which he was well entitled by his venerable age and high literary character, but which could not have been exercised with propriety by any common stranger."

Calling one day at Fowlsheils, and not finding Park at home, Scott walked in search of him along the banks of the Yarrow, which in that neighbourhood passes over various ledges of rock, forming deep pools and eddies between them. Presently he discovered his friend standing alone on the bank, plunging one stone after another into the water, and watching anxiously the bubbles as they rose to the surface. "This," said Scott, "appears but an idle amusement for one who has seen so much stirring adventure." "Not so idle, perhaps, as you suppose," answered Mungo :—"This was the manner in which I used to ascertain the depth of a river in Africa before I ventured to cross it—judging whether the attempt would be safe, by the time the bubbles of air took to ascend." At this time Park's intention of a second expedition had never been revealed to Scott; but he instantly formed the opinion that these experiments on Yarrow were connected with some such purpose.

His thoughts had always continued to be haunted with Africa. He told Scott, that whenever he awoke suddenly in the night, owing to a nervous disorder with which he was troubled, he fancied himself still a prisoner in the tent of Ali; but when the poet expressed some surprise that he should design again to revisit those scenes, he answered, that he would rather brave Africa and all its horrors, than wear out his life in long and toilsome rides over the hills of Scotland, for which the remuneration was hardly enough to keep soul and body together.

Towards the end of the autumn, when about to quit his country for the last time, Park paid Scott a farewell visit, and slept at Ashestiel. Next morning his host accompanied him homewards over the wild chain of hills between the Tweed and the Yarrow. Park talked much of his new scheme, and mentioned his determination to tell his family that he had some business for a day or two in Edinburgh, and send them his blessing from thence, without returning to take leave. He had married, not long before, a pretty and amiable woman, and when they reached the *William-hope ridge*, "the autumnal mist floating heavily and slowly down the valley of the Yarrow" presented to Scott's imagination "a striking emblem of the troubled and uncertain prospect which his undertaking afforded." He

remained, however, unshaken, and at length they reached
the spot at which they had agreed to separate. A small
ditch divided the moor from the road, and in going over
it, Park's horse stumbled and nearly fell. "I am afraid,
Mungo," said the Sheriff, "that is a bad omen." To
which he answered, smiling, "*Freits* (omens) follow those
who look to them." With this expression Mungo struck
the spurs into his horse, and Scott never saw him again.
His parting proverb, by the way, was probably suggested
by one of the Border ballads, in which species of lore he
was almost as great a proficient as the Sheriff himself;
for we read in "Edom o' Gordon,"—

> "Them look to freits, my master dear,
>   Then freits will follow them."

The brother of Mungo Park remained in Scott's neighbourhood for some years, and was frequently his companion in his mountain rides. Though a man of the most
dauntless temperament, he was often alarmed at Scott's
reckless horsemanship. "The de'il's in ye, Sherra," he
would say: "ye'll never halt till they bring you hame
with your feet foremost." He rose greatly in favour, in
consequence of the gallantry with which he assisted the
Sheriff in seizing a gipsy, accused of murder, from amidst
a group of similar desperadoes, on whom they had come
unexpectedly in a desolate part of the country.

To return to the Lay of the Last Minstrel: Ellis, understanding it to be now nearly ready for the press, writes to
Scott, urging him to set it forth with some engraved illustrations—if possible, after Flaxman, whose splendid designs from Homer had shortly before made their appearance. He answers, August 21—" I should fear Flaxman's
genius is too classic to stoop to body forth my Gothic
Borderers. Would there not be some risk of their resembling the antique of Homer's heroes, rather than the
iron race of Salvator? I should like at least to be at his
elbow when at work. I wish very much I could have sent
you the Lay while in MS., to have had the advantage of
your opinion and corrections. But Ballantyne galled my
kibes so severely during an unusual fit of activity, that I
gave him the whole story in a sort of pet both with him
and with it."

There is a circumstance which must already have struck
such of my readers as knew the author in his latter days,
namely, the readiness with which he seems to have com-

municated this poem, in its progress, not only to his own familiar friends, but to new and casual acquaintances. We shall find him following the same course with his Marmion —but not, I think, with any of his subsequent works. His determination to consult the movements of his own mind alone in the conduct of his pieces was probably taken before he began the Lay; and he soon resolved to trust for the detection of minor inaccuracies to two persons only —James Ballantyne and William Erskine. The printer was himself a man of considerable literary talents : his own style had the incurable faults of pomposity and affectation ; but his eye for more venial errors in the writings of others was quick, and, though his personal address was apt to give a stranger the impression of insincerity, he was in reality an honest man, and conveyed his mind on such matters with equal candour and delicacy during the whole of Scott's brilliant career. In the vast majority of instances he found his friend acquiesce at once in the propriety of his suggestions ; nay, there certainly were cases, though rare, in which his advice to alter things of much more consequence than a word or a rhyme, was frankly tendered, and on deliberation adopted by Scott. Mr. Erskine was the referee whenever the poet hesitated about taking the hints of the zealous typographer ; and his refined taste and gentle manners rendered his critical alliance highly valuable. With two such faithful friends within his reach, the author of the Lay might safely dispense with sending his MS. to be revised even by George Ellis.

In the first week of January 1805, "The Lay" was published ; and its success at once decided that literature should form the main business of Scott's life. I shall not mock the reader with many words as to the merits of a poem which has now kept its place for nearly half a century ; but one or two additional remarks on the history of the composition may be pardoned.

It is curious to trace the small beginnings and gradual development of his design. The lovely Countess of Dalkeith hears a wild rude legend of Border *diablerie*, and sportively asks him to make it the subject of a ballad. He had been already labouring in the elucidation of the " quaint Inglis " ascribed to an ancient seer and bard of the same district, and perhaps completed his own sequel, intending the whole to be included in the third volume of the Minstrelsy. He assents to Lady Dalkeith's request, and casts about for some new variety of diction and rhyme, which might be adopted without impropriety in a closing strain for the same collection. Sir John Stoddart's casual recitation, a year or two before, of Coleridge's unpublished Christabel, had fixed the music of that noble fragment in his memory; and it occurs to him, that by throwing the story of Gilpin Horner into somewhat of a similar cadence, he might produce such an echo of the later metrical romance, as would serve to connect his *Conclusion* of the primitive Sir Tristrem with his imitations of the common popular ballad in the Grey Brother and Eve of St. John. A single scene of feudal festivity in the hall of Branksome, disturbed by some pranks of a nondescript goblin, was probably all that he contemplated; but his accidental confinement in the midst of a volunteer camp gave him leisure to meditate his theme to the sound of the bugle;—and suddenly there flashes on him the idea of extending his simple outline, so as to embrace a vivid panorama of that old Border life of war and tumult, and all earnest passions, with which his researches on the " Minstrelsy " had by degrees fed his imagination, until even the minutest feature had been taken home and realised with unconscious intenseness of sympathy; so that he had won for himself in the past, another world, hardly less complete or familiar than the present. Erskine or Cranstoun suggests that he would do well to divide the poem into cantos, and prefix to each of them a motto explanatory of the action, after the fashion of Spenser in the Faery Queen. He pauses for a moment—and the happiest conception of the framework of a picturesque narrative that ever occurred to any poet— one that Homer might have envied—the creation of the ancient harper, starts to life. By such steps did the Lay of the Last Minstrel grow out of the Minstrelsy of the Scottish Border.

A word more of its felicitous machinery. It was at Bowhill that the Countess of Dalkeith requested a ballad on Gilpin Horner. The ruined castle of Newark closely adjoins that seat, and is now indeed included within its *pleasance*. Newark had been the chosen residence of the first Duchess of Buccleuch, and he accordingly shadows out his own beautiful friend in the person of her lord's ancestress, the last of the original stock of that great house; himself the favoured inmate of Bowhill, introduced certainly to the familiarity of its circle in consequence of his devotion to the poetry of a by-past age, in that of an aged minstrel, "the last of all the race," seeking shelter at the gate of Newark, in days when many an adherent of the fallen cause of Stuart,—his own bearded ancestor, *who had fought at Killiecrankie*, among the rest,—owed their safety to her who

> "In pride of power, in beauty's bloom,
> Had wept o'er Monmouth's bloody tomb."

The arch allusions which run through all these *Introductions*, without in the least interrupting the truth and graceful pathos of their main impression, seem to me exquisitely characteristic of Scott, whose delight and pride was to play with the genius which nevertheless mastered him at will. For, in truth, what is it that gives to all his works their unique and marking charm, except the matchless effect which sudden effusions of the purest heartblood of nature derive from their being poured out, to all appearance involuntarily, amidst diction and sentiment cast equally in the mould of the busy world, and the seemingly habitual desire to dwell on nothing but what might be likely to excite curiosity, without too much disturbing deeper feelings, in the saloons of polished life? Such outbursts come forth dramatically in all his writings; but in the interludes and passionate parentheses of the Lay of the Last Minstrel we have the poet's own inner soul and temperament laid bare and throbbing before us. Even here, indeed, he has a mask, and he trusts it—but fortunately it is a transparent one.

Many minor personal allusions have been explained in the notes to the last edition of the Lay. It was hardly necessary even then to say that the choice of the hero had been dictated by the poet's affection for the living descendants of the Baron of Cranstoun; and now—none who have perused the preceding pages can doubt that he had dressed out his Margaret of Branksome in the form and features of his own first love. This poem may be considered as the "bright consummate flower" in which all the dearest dreams of his youthful fancy had at length found expansion for their strength, spirit, tenderness, and beauty.

In the closing lines—

> "Hush'd is the harp—the Minstrel gone;
> And did he wander forth alone? . . . . .
> No!—close beneath proud Newark's tower
> Arose the Minstrel's humble bower," &c.

—in these charming lines he has embodied what was, at the time when he penned them, the chief day-dream of Ashestiel.   From the moment that his uncle's death placed a considerable sum of ready money at his command, he pleased himself, as we have seen, with the idea of buying a mountain farm, and becoming not only the " sheriff " (as he had in former days delighted to call himself), but " the *laird* of the cairn and the scaur." While he was " labouring *doucement* at the Lay " (as in one of his letters he expresses it), during the recess of 1804, circumstances rendered it next to certain that the small estate of *Broadmeadows*, situated just over against the ruins of Newark, on the northern bank of the Yarrow, would soon be exposed to sale; and many a time did he ride round it in company with Lord and Lady Dalkeith,

> " When summer smiled on sweet Bowhill,"

surveying the beautiful little domain with wistful eyes, and anticipating that

> " *There* would he sing achievement high
> And circumstance of chivalry,
> And Yarrow, as he rolled along,
> Bear burden to the Minstrel's song."

I consider it as, in one point of view, the greatest misfortune of his life that this vision was not realised; but the success of the poem itself changed " the spirit of his dream." The favour which it at once attained had not been equalled in the case of any one poem of considerable length during at least two generations : it certainly had not been approached in the case of any narrative poem since the days of Dryden.   Before it was sent to the press it had received warm commendation from the ablest and most influential critic of the time; but when Mr. Jeffrey's reviewal appeared, a month after publication, laudatory as its language was, it scarcely came up to the opinion which had already taken root in the public mind.   It, however, quite satisfied the author; and I think it just to state, that I have not discovered in any of the letters which he received from brother-poets—no, not even in those of Wordsworth or Campbell—a strain of approbation higher, on the whole, than that of the chief professional reviewer of the period.   When the happy days of youth are over, even the most genial and generous of minds are seldom able to enter into the strains of a new poet with that full and open delight which he awakens in the bosoms of the rising generation about him. Their deep and eager sympathies have already been drawn upon to an extent of which the prosaic part of the species can never have any conception; and when the fit of creative inspiration has subsided, they are apt to be rather cold critics even of their own noblest appeals to the simple primary feelings of their kind.

" It would be great affectation," says the Introduction of 1830, " not to own that the author expected some success from the Lay of the Last Minstrel. The attempt to return to a more simple and natural poetry was likely to be welcomed, at a time when the public had become tired of heroic hexameters, with all the buckram and binding that belong to them in modern days. But whatever might have been his expectations, whether moderate or unreasonable, the result left them far behind; for among those who smiled on the adventurous minstrel were numbered the great names of William Pitt and Charles Fox. Neither was the extent of the sale inferior to the character of the judges who received the poem with approbation. Upwards of 30,000 copies were disposed of by the trade; and the author had to perform a task difficult to human vanity, when called upon to make the necessary deductions from his own merits, in a calm attempt to account for its popularity."

Through what channel or in what terms Fox made known his opinion of the Lay, I have failed to ascertain. Pitt's praise, as expressed to his niece, Lady Hester Stanhope, within a few weeks after the poem appeared, was repeated by her to William Rose, who, of course, communicated it forthwith to the author; and not long after, the Minister, in conversation with Scott's early friend William Dundas, signified that it would give him pleasure to find some opportunity of advancing the fortunes of such a writer. " I remember," writes this gentleman, " at Mr. Pitt's table in 1805, the Chancellor asked me about you and your then situation, and after I had answered him, Mr. Pitt observed—' He can't remain as he is,' and desired me to ' look to it.' He then repeated some lines from the Lay, describing the old harper's embarrassment when asked to play, and said—' This is a sort of thing which I might have expected in painting, but could never have fancied capable of being given in poetry.' " It is agreeable to know that this great statesman and accomplished

scholar awoke at least once from his supposed apathy as
to the elegant literature of his own time.

The poet had under-estimated even the patent and tangible evidence of his success. The first edition of the Lay
was a magnificent quarto, 750 copies; but this was soon
exhausted, and there followed one octavo impression after
another in close succession to the number of fourteen. In
fact, some forty-four thousand copies had been disposed
of in this country, and by the legitimate trade alone, before
he superintended the edition of 1830, to which his biographical introductions were prefixed. In the history of
British Poetry nothing had ever equalled the demand for
the Lay of the Last Minstrel.

The publishers of the first edition were Longman and
Co. of London, and Archibald Constable and Co. of Edinburgh; which last house, however, had but a small share
in the adventure. The profits were to be divided equally
between the author and his publishers, and Scott's moiety
was £169 6s. Messrs. Longman, when a second edition
was called for, offered £500 for the copyright; this was
accepted; but they afterwards, as the Introduction says,
" added £100 in their own unsolicited kindness. It
was handsomely given, to supply the loss of a fine horse
which broke down suddenly while the author was riding
with one of the worthy publishers." The author's
whole share, then, in the profits of the Lay, came
to £769 6s.

Mr. Ballantyne, in his Memorandum, says, that very
shortly after the publication of the Lay, he found himself
obliged to apply to Mr. Scott for an advance of money;
his own capital being inadequate for the business which
had been accumulated on his press, in consequence of the
reputation it had acquired for beauty and correctness of
execution. Already, as we have seen, the printer had received " a liberal loan ";—" and now," says he, " being
compelled, maugre all delicacy, to renew my application,
he candidly answered that he was not quite sure that it
would be prudent for him to comply, but in order to evince
his entire confidence in me, he was willing to make a
suitable advance to be admitted as a third-sharer of my
business." No trace has been discovered of any examination into the state of the business, on the part of Scott, at
this time. However, he now embarked in Ballantyne's
concern almost the whole of the capital which he had a

few months before designed to invest in the purchase of
Broadmeadows. *Dis aliter visum.*

I have hinted my suspicion that he had formed some distant notion of such an alliance, as early as the date of Ballantyne's projected removal from Kelso; and his Introduction to the Lay, in 1830, appears to leave little doubt that the
hope of ultimately succeeding at the Bar had waxed very
faint, before the third volume of the Minstrelsy was brought
out in 1803. When that hope ultimately vanished altogether,
perhaps he himself would not have found it easy to tell.
The most important of men's opinions, views, and projects are sometimes taken up in so very gradual a manner,
and after so many pauses of hesitation and of inward re-
tractation, that they themselves are at a loss to trace in
retrospect all the stages through which their minds have
passed. We see plainly that Scott had never been fond of
his profession, but that, conscious of his own persevering
diligence, he ascribed his scanty success in it mainly to
the prejudices of the Scotch solicitors against employing,
in weighty causes at least, any barrister supposed to be
strongly imbued with the love of literature; instancing the
career of his friend Jeffrey as almost the solitary instance
within his experience of such prejudices being entirely
overcome. Had Scott, to his strong sense and dexterous
ingenuity, his well-grounded knowledge of the jurisprudence of his country, and his admirable industry, added
a brisk and ready talent for debate and declamation, I can
have no doubt that his triumph must have been as complete as Mr. Jeffrey's; nor in truth do I much question
that, had one really great and interesting case been submitted to his sole management, the result would have
been to place his professional character for skill and judgment, and variety of resource, on so firm a basis, that even
his rising celebrity as a man of letters could not have
seriously disturbed it. Nay, I think it quite possible, that
had he been intrusted with one such case after his reputation was established, and he had been compelled to do his
abilities some measure of justice in his own secret estimate,
he might have displayed very considerable powers even as
a forensic speaker. But no opportunities of this engaging kind having ever been presented to him—after he
had persisted for more than ten years in sweeping the
floor of the Parliament House, without meeting with any
employment but what would have suited the dullest drudge,

and seen himself termly and yearly more and more dis-
tanced by contemporaries for whose general capacity he
could have had little respect—while, at the same time, he
already felt his own position in the eyes of society at large
to have been signally elevated in consequence of his extraprofessional exertions—it is not wonderful that disgust
should have gradually gained upon him, and that the
sudden blaze and tumult of renown which surrounded the
author of the Lay should have at last determined him to
concentrate all his ambition on the pursuits which had
alone brought him distinction.

We have seen that, before he formed his contract with
Ballantyne, he was in possession of such a fixed income as
might have satisfied all his desires, had he not found his
family increasing rapidly about him.   Even as that was,
with nearly if not quite £1,000 per annum, he might
perhaps have retired not only from the Bar, but from
Edinburgh, and settled entirely at Ashestiel or Broadmeadows, without encountering what any man of his
station and habits ought to have considered as an imprudent risk.   He had, however, no wish to cut himself off
from the busy and intelligent society to which he had been
hitherto accustomed; and resolved not to leave the Bar
until he should have at least used his best efforts for obtaining, in addition to his Shrievalty, one of those Clerk-
ships of the Supreme Court, which are usually considered
as honourable retirements for advocates who, at a certain
standing, give up all hopes of reaching the Bench.   " I
determined," he says, " that literature should be my
staff but not my crutch, and that the profits of my literary
labour, however convenient otherwise, should not, if I
could help it, become necessary to my ordinary expenses.
Upon such a post an author might hope to retreat, without
any perceptible alteration of circumstances, whenever the
time should arrive that the public grew weary of his endeavours to please, or he himself should tire of the pen.
I possessed so many friends capable of assisting me in this
object of ambition, that I could hardly overrate my own
prospects of obtaining the preferment to which I limited
my wishes; and, in fact, I obtained, in no long period,
the reversion of a situation which completely met them." [1]

The first notice of this affair that occurs in his correspondence, is in a note of Lord Dalkeith's, February 2,

[1] Introduction to the Lay of the Last Minstrel—1830.

1805, in which his noble friend says—" My father desires me to tell you that he has had a communication with Lord Melville within these few days, and that he thinks *your business in a good train, though not certain.*" I consider it as clear, then, that he began his negotiations about a seat at the clerk's table immediately after the Lay was published; and this in the strictest connection with his trading adventure. His design of quitting the Bar was divulged, however, to none but those immediately necessary to his negotiation with the Government; and the nature of his alliance with the printing establishment remained, I believe, not only unknown, but for some years wholly unsuspected, by any of his daily companions except Erskine.

The forming of this commercial tie was one of the most important steps in Scott's life. He continued bound by it during twenty years, and its influence on his literary exertions and his worldly fortunes was productive of much good and not a little evil. Its effects were in truth so mixed and balanced during the vicissitudes of a long and vigorous career, that I at this moment doubt whether it ought, on the whole, to be considered with more of satisfaction or of regret.

With what zeal he proceeded in advancing the views of the new co-partnership, his correspondence bears ample evidence. The brilliant and captivating genius, now acknowledged universally, was soon discovered by the leading booksellers of the time to be united with such abundance of matured information in many departments, and above all, with such indefatigable habits, as to mark him out for the most valuable workman they could engage for the furtherance of their schemes. He had, long before this, cast a shrewd and penetrating eye over the field of literary enterprise, and developed in his own mind the outlines of many extensive plans, which wanted nothing but the command of a sufficient body of able subalterns to be carried into execution with splendid success. Such of these as he grappled with in his own person were, with rare exceptions, carried to a triumphant conclusion; but the alliance with Ballantyne soon infected him with the proverbial rashness of mere mercantile adventure—while, at the same time, his generous feelings for other men of letters, and his characteristic propensity to overrate their talents, combined to hurry him and his friends into a multitude of arrangements, the results of which were often extremely embarrassing, and ultimately, in the aggregate, all but disastrous. It is an old saying, that wherever there is a secret there must be something wrong; and dearly did he pay the penalty for the mystery in which he had chosen to involve this transaction. It was his rule, from the beginning, that whatever he wrote or edited must be printed at that press; and had he catered for it only as author and sole editor, all had been well; but had the booksellers known his direct pecuniary interest in keeping up and extending the occupation of those types, they would have taken into account his lively imagination and sanguine temperament, as well as his taste and judgment, and considered, far more deliberately than they too often did, his multifarious recommendations of new literary schemes, coupled though these were with some dim understanding that, if the Ballantyne press were employed, his own literary skill would be at his friend's disposal for the general superintendence of the undertaking. On the other hand, Scott's suggestions were, in many cases, perhaps in the majority of them, conveyed through Ballantyne, whose habitual deference to his opinion induced him to advocate them with enthusiastic zeal; and the printer, who had thus pledged his personal authority for the merits of the proposed scheme, must have felt himself committed to the bookseller, and could hardly refuse with decency to take a certain share of the pecuniary risk, by allowing the time and method of his own payment to be regulated according to the employer's convenience. Hence, by degrees, was woven a web of entanglement from which neither Ballantyne nor his adviser had any means of escape, except only in that indomitable spirit, the mainspring of personal industry altogether unparalleled, to which, thus set in motion, the world owes its most gigantic monument of literary genius.

In the very first letter that I have found from Scott to his *partner* (April 12, 1805), occur suggestions about new editions of Thomson, Dryden, and Tacitus, and, moreover, of a general edition of the British Poets, in one hundred volumes 8vo, of which last he designed to be himself the editor, and expected that the booksellers would readily give him 30 guineas per volume for his trouble. This gigantic scheme interfered with one of the general body of London publishers, and broke down accordingly; but Constable entered with zeal into the plan of a Dryden, and

Scott without delay busied himself in the collection of materials for its elucidation.

Precisely at the time when his poetical ambition had been stimulated by the first outburst of universal applause, and when he was forming these engagements with Ballantyne, a fresh impetus was given to the volunteer mania, by the appointment of the Earl of Moira (afterwards Marquis of Hastings) to the chief military command in the north. The Earl had married, the year before, a Scottish peeress, the Countess of Loudon, and entered with great zeal into her sympathy with the patriotic enthusiasm of her countrymen. Edinburgh was converted into a camp: besides a large garrison of regular troops, nearly 10,000 fencibles and volunteers were almost constantly under arms. The lawyer wore his uniform under his gown; the shopkeeper measured out his wares in scarlet; in short, the citizens of all classes made more use for several months of the military than of any other dress; and the new commander-in-chief consulted equally his own gratification and theirs, by devising a succession of manœuvres which presented a vivid image of the art of war conducted on a large and scientific scale. In the *sham battles* and *sham sieges* of 1805, Craigmillar, Gilmerton, Braidhills, and other formidable positions in the neighbourhood of Edinburgh, were the scenes of many a dashing assault and resolute defence; and occasionally the spirits of the mock combatants— English and Scotch, or Lowland and Highland—became so much excited, that there was some difficulty in preventing the rough mockery of warfare from passing into its realities. The Highlanders, in particular, were very hard to be dealt with, and once, at least, Lord Moira was forced to alter at the eleventh hour his programme of battle, because a battalion of kilted fencibles could not or would not understand that it was their duty to be beat. Such days as these must have been more nobly spirit-stirring than even the best specimens of the fox-chase. To the end of his life, Scott delighted to recall the details of their counter-marches, ambuscades, charges, and pursuits, and in all of these his associates of the Light Horse agree that none figured more advantageously than himself. Yet such military interludes seem only to have whetted his appetite for closet work. Indeed, nothing but a complete publication of his letters could give an adequate notion of the facility with which he even at this early period combined the conscientious magistrate, the martinet quartermaster, the speculative printer, and the ardent lover of literature for its own sake.

In the course of the summer and autumn of 1805, we find him in correspondence about another gigantic scheme —an uniform series of the Ancient English Chronicles; and there are hints of various minor undertakings in the editorial line. In the same year he contributed to Mr. Jeffrey's journal an admirable article on Todd's edition of Spenser; another on Godwin's Fleetwood; a third, on the Highland Society's Report concerning the poems of Ossian; a fourth, on Johnes's Translation of Froissart; a fifth, on Colonel Thornton's Sporting Tour; and a sixth, on some cookery books—the two last being excellent specimens of his humour. By September, meanwhile, he had made considerable progress with his Dryden : for we find him then writing to Ellis :—" I will not castrate John Dryden. I would as soon castrate my own father, as I believe Jupiter did of yore. What would you say to any man who would castrate Shakespeare, or Massinger, or Beaumont and Fletcher? I don't say but that it may be very proper to select correct passages for the use of boarding schools and colleges, being sensible no improper ideas can be suggested in these seminaries, unless they are intruded or smuggled under the beards and ruffs of our old dramatists. But in making an edition of a man of genius's works for libraries and collections, and such I conceive a complete edition of Dryden to be, I must give my author as I find him, and will not tear out the page, even to get rid of the blot, little as I like it. Are not the pages of Swift, and even of Pope, larded with indecency, and often of the most disgusting kind? and do we not see them upon all shelves and dressing-tables, and in all boudoirs? Is not Prior the most indecent of tale-tellers, not even excepting La Fontaine? and how often do we see his works in female hands ! In fact, it is not passages of ludicrous indelicacy that corrupt the manners of a people—it is the sonnets which a prurient genius like Master Little sings *virginibus puerisque*—it is the sentimental slang, half lewd, half methodistic, that debauches the understanding, inflames the sleeping passions, and prepares the reader to give way as soon as a tempter appears. At the same time, I am not at all happy when I peruse some of Dryden's comedies : they are very stupid, as well as indelicate;

—sometimes, however, there is a considerable vein of liveliness and humour, and all of them present extraordinary pictures of the age in which he lived. My critical notes will not be very numerous, but I hope to illustrate the political poems, as Absalom and Achitophel, the Hind and Panther, &c., with some curious annotations. I have already made a complete search among some hundred pamphlets of that pamphlet-writing age, and with considerable success, as I have found several which throw light on my author."

But there is yet another important item to be included in the list of his literary labours of this year. The General Preface to his Novels informs us, that " about 1805 " he wrote the opening chapters of Waverley; and the second title, *'Tis Sixty Years Since,* selected, as he says, " that the actual date of publication might correspond with the period in which the scene was laid," leaves no doubt that he had begun the work so early in 1805 as to contemplate publishing it before Christmas.[1] He adds, in the same page, that he was induced, by the favourable reception of the Lady of the Lake, to think of giving some of his recollections of Highland Scenery and customs in prose; but this is only one instance of the inaccuracy as to matters of date which pervades all those delightful Prefaces. The Lady of the Lake was not published until five years after the first chapters of Waverley were written; its success, therefore, could have had no share in suggesting the original design of a Highland novel, though no doubt it principally influenced him to take up that design after it had been long suspended, and almost forgotten.

" Having proceeded," he says, " as far as I think the seventh chapter, I shewed my work to a critical friend, whose opinion was unfavourable; and having then some poetical reputation, I was unwilling to risk the loss of it by attempting a new style of composition. I, therefore, then threw aside the work I had commenced, without either reluctance or remonstrance. I ought to add, that though my ingenuous friend's sentence was afterwards reversed, on an appeal to the public, it cannot be considered as any imputation on his good taste; for the specimen subjected to his criticism did not extend beyond the departure of the

[1] I have ascertained, since this page was written, that a small part of the MS. of *Waverley* is on paper bearing the watermark of 1805—the rest on paper of 1813.

hero for Scotland, and consequently had not entered upon the part of the story which was finally found most interesting." It is, I think, evident from a letter of 1810, that the first critic of the opening chapters of Waverley was William Erskine.

His correspondence shows how largely he was exerting himself all this while in the service of authors less fortunate than himself. James Hogg, among others, continued to occupy from time to time his attention; and he assisted regularly and assiduously throughout this and the succeeding year Mr. Robert Jameson, an industrious and intelligent antiquary, who had engaged in editing a collection of ancient popular ballads before the third volume of the Minstrelsy appeared, and who at length published his very curious work in 1807. Meantime, Ashestiel, in place of being less resorted to by literary strangers than Lasswade cottage had been, shared abundantly in the fresh attractions of the Lay, and " booksellers in the plural number " were preceded and followed by an endless variety of tourists, whose main temptation from the south had been the hope of seeing the Borders in company with their Minstrel. One of this year's guests was Mr. Southey— their first meeting, the commencement of much kind intercourse. Scott still writes of himself as " idling away his hours "; he had already learned to appear as if he were doing so to all who had no particular right to confidence respecting the details of his privacy.

Mr. Skene arrived just after a great storm and flood in August; he says in his *Memoranda*—" The ford of Ashestiel was never a good one, and for some time after this it remained not a little perilous. Scott was himself the first to attempt the passage on his favourite black horse *Captain,* who had scarcely entered the river when he plunged beyond his depth, and had to swim to the other side with his burden. It requires a good horseman to swim a deep and rapid stream, but he trusted to the vigour of his steady trooper, and in spite of his lameness kept his seat manfully."

Mr. Skene soon discovered a change which had recently been made in his friend's distribution of his time. Previously it had been his custom, whenever professional business or social engagements occupied the middle part of his day, to seize some hours for study after he was supposed to have retired to bed. His physician suggested that this was very likely to aggravate his nervous headaches, the only malady he was subject to in the prime of his manhood; and, contemplating with steady eye a course not only of unremitting but of increasing industry, he resolved to reverse his plan.   In short he had now adopted the habits in which, with slender variation, he ever after persevered when in the country.   He rose by five o'clock, lit his own fire when the season required one, and shaved and dressed with great deliberation—for he was a very martinet as to all but the mere coxcombries of the toilet, not abhorring effeminate dandyism itself so cordially as the slightest approach to personal slovenliness, or even those " bed-gown and slipper tricks," as he called them, in which literary men are so apt to indulge.   Clad in his shooting-jacket, or whatever dress he meant to use till dinner time, he was seated at his desk by six o'clock, all his papers arranged before him in the most accurate order, and his books of reference marshalled around him on the floor, while at least one favourite dog lay watching his eye, just beyond the line of circumvallation.   Thus, by the time the family assembled for breakfast between nine and ten, he had done enough (in his own language) " *to break the neck of the day's work.*"   After breakfast, a couple of hours more were given to his solitary tasks, and by noon he was, as he used to say, "his own man."   When the weather was bad, he would labour incessantly all the morning; but the general rule was to be out and on horseback by one o'clock at the latest; while, if any more distant excursion had been proposed over night, he was ready to start on it by ten; his occasional rainy days of unintermitted study forming, as he said, a fund in his favour, out of which he was entitled to draw for accommodation whenever the sun shone with special brightness.

It was another rule, that every letter he received should be answered that same day.   Nothing else could have enabled him to keep abreast with the flood of communications that in the sequel put his good nature to the severest test—but already the demands on him in this way also were numerous; and he included attention to them among the necessary business which must be dispatched before he had a right to close his writing-box, or as he phrased it, " to say, *out damned spot,* and be a gentleman.''   In turning over his enormous mass of correspondence, I have almost invariably found some indication that, when a letter had remained more than a day or two unanswered, it was because he found occasion for inquiry.

I ought not to omit, that in those days Scott was far too zealous a dragoon not to take a principal share in the stable duty. Before beginning his desk-work in the morning, he uniformly visited his favourite steed, and neither *Captain* nor *Lieutenant* nor *Brown Adam* (so called after one of the heroes of the Minstrelsy) liked to be fed except by him. The latter charger was indeed altogether intractable in other hands, though in his the most submissive of faithful allies. The moment he was bridled and saddled, it was the custom to open the stable door as a signal that his master expected him, when he immediately trotted to the side of the *leaping-on-stone*, of which Scott from his lameness found it convenient to make use, and stood there, silent and motionless as a rock, until he was fairly in his seat, after which he displayed his joy by neighing triumphantly through a brilliant succession of curvettings. Brown Adam never suffered himself to be backed but by his master. He broke, I believe, one groom's arm and another's leg in the rash attempt to tamper with his dignity.

Camp was at this time the constant parlour dog. He was very handsome, very intelligent, and naturally very fierce, but gentle as a lamb among the children. As for a brace of lighter pets, styled Douglas and Percy, he kept one window of his study open, whatever might be the state of the weather, that they might leap out and in as the fancy moved them. He always talked to Camp as if he understood what was said—and the animal certainly did understand not a little of it; in particular, it seemed as if he perfectly comprehended on all occasions that his master considered him as a sensible and steady friend—the greyhounds as volatile young creatures whose freaks must be borne with.

"Every day," says Mr. Skene, "we had some hours of coursing with the greyhounds, or riding at random over the hills, or of spearing salmon in the Tweed by sunlight: which last sport, moreover, we often renewed at night by the help of torches. This amusement of *burning the water*, as it is called, was not without some hazard, for the large salmon generally lie in the pools, the depths of which it is not easy to estimate with precision by torchlight,—so that not unfrequently, when the

sportsman makes a determined thrust at a fish apparently
within reach, his eye has grossly deceived him, and instead
of the point of the weapon encountering the prey, he
finds himself launched with corresponding vehemence
heels over head into the pool, both spear and salmon
gone, the torch thrown out by the concussion of the
boat, and quenched in the stream, while the boat itself
has of course receded to some distance. I remember
the first time I accompanied our friend, he went right
over the gunwale in this manner, and had I not accidentally been at his side, and made a successful grasp
at the skirt of his jacket as he plunged overboard, he
must at least have had an awkward dive for it. Such
are the contingencies of *burning the water*. The pleasures
consist in being penetrated with cold and wet, having
your shins broken against the stones in the dark, and
perhaps mastering one fish out of every twenty you take
aim at.''

In all these amusements, but particularly in the *burning
of the water*, Scott's most regular companion at this time
was John Lord Somerville, who united with higher qualities an enthusiastic love for such sports, and consummate
address in them. This amiable nobleman then passed
his autumns at Alwyn, some eight or nine miles below
Ashestiel. They interchanged visits almost every week;
and Scott profited largely by his friend's known skill in
every department of rural economy. He always talked
of him as his master in the art of planting.

The laird of Rubislaw seldom failed to spend a part of
the autumn at Ashestiel, as long as Scott remained there;
and during these visits they often gave a wider scope to
their expeditions. '' Indeed,'' says Mr. Skene, '' there
are few scenes at all celebrated either in the history,
tradition, or romance of the Border counties, which we
did not explore together in the course of our rambles.
We traversed the entire vales of the Yarrow and Ettrick,
with all their sweet tributary glens, and never failed to
find a hearty welcome from the farmers at whose houses
we stopped, either for dinner or for the night. He was
their chief-magistrate, extremely popular in that official
capacity; and nothing could be more gratifying than the
frank and hearty reception which everywhere greeted our
arrival, however unexpected. The exhilarating air of the
mountains, and the healthy exercise of the day, secured

our relishing homely fare, and we found inexhaustible
entertainment in the varied display of character which the
affability of *the Sheriff* drew forth on all occasions in
genuine breadth and purity. The beauty of the scenery
gave full employment to my pencil, with the free and
frequent exercise of which he never seemed to feel impatient. He was at all times ready and willing to alight
when any object attracted my notice, and used to seat
himself beside me on the brae, to con over some ballad
appropriate to the occasion, or narrate the tradition of
the glen—sometimes, perhaps, to note a passing idea in
his pocket-book; but this was rare, for in general he
relied with confidence on the great storehouse of his
memory.

" One of our earliest expeditions was to visit the wild
scenery of the mountainous tract above Moffat, including the cascade of the Grey Mare's Tail, and the dark
tarn called Loch Skene. In our ascent to the lake we
got completely bewildered in the thick fog which generally envelopes the rugged features of that lonely region;
and, as we were groping through the maze of bogs, the
ground gave way, and down went horse and horsemen pell-
mell into a slough of peaty mud and black water, out of
which, entangled as we were with our plaids and floundering nags, it was no easy matter to get extricated.
Indeed, unless we had prudently left our gallant steeds at
a farm-house below, and borrowed hill-ponies for the
occasion, the result might have been worse than laugh-
able. As it was, we rose like the spirits of the bog,
covered *cap-à-pie* with slime, to free themselves from
which, our wily ponies took to rolling about on the
heather, and we had nothing for it but following their
example. At length, as we approached the gloomy
loch, a huge eagle heaved himself from the margin and
rose right over us, screaming his scorn of the intruders;
and altogether it would be impossible to picture anything
more desolately savage than the scene which opened, as
if raised by enchantment on purpose to gratify the poet's
eye; thick folds of fog rolling incessantly over the face
of the inky waters, but rent asunder now in one direction, and then in another—so as to afford us a glimpse
of some projecting rock or naked point of land, or island
bearing a few scraggy stumps of pine—and then closing
again in universal darkness upon the cheerless waste.

Much of the scenery of Old Mortality was drawn from that day's ride. It was also in the course of this excursion that we encountered that amusing personage introduced into Guy Mannering as 'Tod Gabbie.' He was one of those itinerants who gain a subsistence among the moorland farmers by relieving them of foxes, polecats, and the like depredators—a half-witted, stuttering, and most original creature.

"Having explored all the wonders of Moffatdale, we turned ourselves towards *Blackhouse Tower*, to visit Scott's worthy acquaintances the Laidlaws, and reached it after a long and intricate ride, having been again led off our course by the greyhounds, who had been seduced by a strange dog that joined company to engage in full pursuit upon the track of what we presumed to be either a fox or a roe-deer. The chase was protracted and perplexing, from the mist that skirted the hill tops; but at length we reached the scene of slaughter, and were much distressed to find that a stately old he-goat had been the victim. He seemed to have fought a stout battle for his life, but now lay mangled in the midst of his panting enemies, who betrayed, on our approach, strong consciousness of delinquency and apprehension of the lash, which was administered accordingly to soothe the manes of the luckless Capricorn—though, after all, the dogs were not so much to blame in mistaking his game flavour, since the fogs must have kept him out of view till the last moment. Our visit to Blackhouse was highly interesting; the excellent old tenant being still in life, and the whole family group presenting a perfect picture of innocent and simple happiness, while the animated, intelligent, and original conversation of our friend William was quite charming.

"Sir Adam Fergusson and the Ettrick Shepherd were of the party that explored Loch Skene and hunted the unfortunate he-goat.

"I need not tell you that Saint Mary's Loch, and the Loch of the Lowes, were among the most favourite scenes of our excursions, as his fondness for them continued to his last days, and we have both visited them many times together in his company. I may say the same of the Teviot and the Aill, Borthwick water, and the lonely towers of Buccleuch and Harden, Minto, Roxburgh, Gilnockie, etc. I think it was either in 1805 or 1806 that I first explored the Borthwick with him, when on our way to pass a week at Langholm with Lord and Lady Dalkeith, upon which occasion the otter-hunt, so well described in Guy Mannering, was got up by our noble host; and I can never forget the delight with which Scott observed the enthusiasm of the high-spirited yeomen, who had assembled in multitudes to partake the sport of their dear young chief, well mounted, and dashing about from rock to rock with a reckless ardour which recalled the alacrity of their forefathers in following the Buccleuchs of former days through adventures of a more serious order.

"Whatever the banks of the Tweed, from its source to its termination, presented of interest, we frequently visited; and I do verily believe there is not a single ford in the whole course of that river which we have not traversed together. He had an amazing fondness for fords, and was not a little adventurous in plunging through, whatever might be the state of the flood, and this even though there happened to be a bridge in view. If it seemed possible to scramble through, he scorned to go ten yards about, and in fact preferred the ford; and it is to be remarked, that most of the heroes of his tales seem to have been endued with similar propensities—even the White Lady of Avenel delights in the ford. He sometimes even attempted them on foot, though his lameness interfered considerably with his progress among the slippery stones. Upon one occasion of this sort I was assisting him through the Ettrick, and we had both got upon the same tottering stone in the middle of the stream, when some story about a *kelpie* occurring to him, he must needs stop and tell it with all his usual vivacity—and then laughing heartily at his own joke, he slipped his foot, or the stone shuffled beneath him, and down he went headlong into the pool, pulling me after him. We escaped, however, with no worse than a thorough drenching and the loss of his stick, which floated down the river, and he was as ready as ever for a similar exploit before his clothes were half dried upon his back."

About this time Mr. and Mrs. Scott made a short excursion to the Lakes of Cumberland and Westmoreland, and visited some of their finest scenery, in company with Mr. Wordsworth. I have found no written narrative of this little tour, but I have often heard Scott speak with enthusiastic delight of the reception he met with in the humble cottage which his brother poet then inhabited on the banks of Grasmere; and at least one of the days they spent together was destined to furnish a theme for the verse of each, namely, that which they gave to the ascent of Helvellyn, where, in the course of the preceding spring, a young gentleman having lost his way and perished by falling over a precipice, his remains were discovered, three months afterwards, still watched by " a faithful terrier-bitch, his constant attendant during frequent rambles among the wilds." [1] This day they were accompanied by an illustrious philosopher, who was also a true poet—and might have been one of the greatest of poets had he chosen; and I have heard Mr. Wordsworth say, that it would be difficult to express the feelings with which he, who so often had climbed Helvellyn alone, found himself standing on its summit with two such men as Scott and Davy.

After leaving Mr. Wordsworth, Scott carried his wife to spend a few days at Gilsland, among the scenes where they had first met; and his reception by the company at the wells was such as to make him look back with something of regret, as well as of satisfaction, to the change that had occurred in his circumstances since 1797. They were, however, enjoying themselves much there, when he received intelligence which induced him to believe that a French force was about to land in Scotland :—the alarm indeed had spread far and wide; and a mighty gathering of volunteers, horse and foot, from the Lothians and the Border country, took place in consequence at Dalkeith. He was not slow to obey the summons. He had luckily chosen to accompany on horseback the carriage in which Mrs. Scott travelled. His good steed carried him to the spot of rendezvous, full a hundred miles from Gilsland, within twenty-four hours; and on reaching it, though no doubt to his disappointment the alarm had already blown over, he was delighted with the general enthusiasm that had thus been put to the test—and, above all, by the rapidity with which the yeomen of Ettrick Forest had poured down from their glens, under the guidance of his good friend and neighbour, Mr. Pringle of Torwoodlee. These fine fellows were quartered along with the Edinburgh troop when he reached Dalkeith and Musselburgh; and after some sham battling, and a few evenings of high

[1] See *Poetical Works,* edit. 1841, p. 629; and compare Wordsworth—8vo edit., vol. iii. p. 96.

jollity had crowned the needless muster of the beacon-
fires, he immediately turned his horse again towards the
south, and rejoined Mrs. Scott at Carlisle.[1]

By the way, it was during his fiery ride from Gilsland to
Dalkeith, on the occasion above mentioned, that he composed his Bard's Incantation :—

> " The forest of Glenmore is drear,
>   It is all of black pine and the dark oak-tree," &c.—

and the verses bear the full stamp of the feelings of the
moment.

Meantime, the affair of the Clerkship, opened nine or
ten months before, had not been neglected by the friends
on whose counsel and assistance Scott had relied.
Whether Mr. Pitt's hint to Mr. William Dundas, that he
would willingly find an opportunity to promote the interests of the author of the Lay, or some conversation
between the Duke of Buccleuch and Lord Melville, first
encouraged him to this direction of his views, I am not
able to state distinctly; but I believe that the desire to
see his fortunes placed on some more substantial basis,
was at this time partaken pretty equally by the three
persons who had the principal influence in the distribution
of the Crown patronage in Scotland; and as his object was
rather to secure a future than an immediate increase of
official income, it was comparatively easy to make such
an arrangement as would satisfy his ambition.   George
Home of Wedderburn, an old friend of his family, had
now held a Clerkship for upwards of thirty years.   In
those days there was no system of retiring pensions for
the worn-out functionary of this class, and the usual
method was, either that he should resign in favour of a
successor who advanced a sum of money according to the
circumstances of his age and health, or for a coadjutor to
be associated with him in his patent, who undertook the
duty on condition of a division of salary.   Scott offered
to relieve Mr. Home of all the labours of his office, and
to allow him, nevertheless, to retain its emoluments entire;
and the aged clerk of course joined his exertions to procure a conjoint-patent on these very advantageous terms.
About the close of 1805, a new patent was drawn out
accordingly; but, by a clerical inadvertency, it was drawn
out solely in Scott's favour, no mention of Mr. Home

[1] See Note, " Alarm of Invasion," Antiquary, vol. ii. p. 338.

being inserted in the instrument. Although, therefore, the sign-manual had been affixed, and there remained nothing but to pay the fees and take out the commission, Scott, on discovering this error, could not proceed in the business; since, in the event of his dying before Mr. Home, that gentleman would have lost the vested interest which he had stipulated to retain. A pending charge of pecuniary corruption had compelled Lord Melville to retire from office some time before Mr. Pitt's death (January 23, 1806); and the cloud of popular obloquy under which he now laboured, rendered it impossible that Scott should expect assistance from the quarter to which, under any other circumstances, he would naturally have turned for extrication from this difficulty. He therefore, as soon as the Fox and Grenville cabinet had been nominated, proceeded to London, to make in his own person such representations as might be necessary to secure the issuing of the patent in the right shape.

It seems wonderful that he should ever have doubted for a single moment of the result; since, had the new cabinet been purely Whig, and had he been the most violent and obnoxious of Tory partisans, neither of which was the case, the arrangement had been not only virtually, but, with the exception of an evident official blunder, formally completed; and no Secretary of State, as I must think, could have refused to rectify the paltry mistake in question, without a dereliction of every principle of honour. At this period, however, Scott had by no means measured either the character, the feelings, or the arrangements of great public functionaries, by the standard with which observation and experience subsequently furnished him. He had breathed hitherto, as far as political questions of all sorts were concerned, the hot atmosphere of a very narrow scene—and seems (from his letters) to have pictured to himself Whitehall and Downing Street as only a wider stage for the exhibition of the bitter and fanatical prejudices that tormented the petty circles of the Parliament House at Edinburgh; the true bearing and scope of which no man in after days more thoroughly understood, or more sincerely pitied. The seals of the Home Office had been placed in the hands of a nobleman of the highest character—moreover, an ardent lover of literature;—while the chief of the new Ministry was one of the most generous as well as tasteful of mankind; and there occurred no hesitation whatever on their parts. In communicating his success to the Earl of Dalkeith, whose warm personal kindness, without doubt, had first animated in his favour both the Duke of Buccleuch and Lord Melville, he says (London, February 11):—" Lord Spencer, upon the nature of the transaction being explained in an audience with which he favoured me, was pleased to direct the commission to be issued, as an act of justice, regretting, he said, it had not been from the beginning his own deed. This was doing the thing handsomely, and like an English nobleman. I have been very much fêted and caressed here, almost indeed to suffocation, but have been made amends by meeting some old friends. . . . . After all, a little literary reputation is of some use here. I suppose Solomon, when he compared a good name to a pot of ointment, meant that it oiled the hinges of the hall-doors into which the possessors of that inestimable treasure wished to penetrate. What a *good* name was in Jerusalem, a *known* name seems to be in London. If you are celebrated for writing verses or for slicing cucumbers, for being two feet taller or two feet less than any other biped, for acting plays when you should be whipped at school, or for attending schools and institutions when you should be preparing for your grave,—your notoriety becomes a talisman—an ' Open Sesame ' before which every thing gives way—till you are voted a bore, and discarded for a new plaything. As this is a consummation of notoriety which I am by no means ambitious of experiencing, I hope I shall be very soon able to shape my course northward, to enjoy my good fortune at my leisure and snap my fingers at the Bar and all its works. . . . . I dine to-day at Holland-house; I refused to go before, lest it should be thought I was soliciting interest in that quarter, as I abhor even the shadow of changing or turning with the tide." He says elsewhere,—" I never saw Mr. Fox on this or any other occasion, and never made any application to him, conceiving, that in doing so, I might have been supposed to express political opinions different from those which I had always professed. In his private capacity, there is no man to whom I would have been more proud to owe an obligation—had I been so distinguished." [1]

Among other eminent men with whom he on this occa-

[1] Introduction to Marmion, 1830.

sion first made acquaintance, were Ellis's bosom friends, Frere and Canning; with the latter of whom his intercourse became afterwards close and confidential. It was now also that he first saw Joanna Baillie, of whose Plays on the Passions he had been, from their first appearance, an enthusiastic admirer. The late Mr. Sotheby, the translator of Oberon, etc., etc., was the friend who introduced him to the poetess of Hampstead. Being asked in 1836 what impression he made upon her at this interview—" I was at first," she answered, " a little disappointed, for I was fresh from the Lay, and had pictured to myself an ideal elegance and refinement of feature; but I said to myself, If I had been in a crowd, and at a loss what to do, I should have fixed upon that face among a thousand, as the sure index of the benevolence and the shrewdness that would and could help me in my strait. We had not talked long, however, before I saw in the expressive play of his countenance far more even of elegance and refinement than I had missed in its mere lines." The acquaintance thus begun, soon ripened into a most affectionate intimacy; and thenceforth Mrs. Joanna and her distinguished brother, Dr. Matthew Baillie, were among the friends to whose society Scott looked forward with the greatest pleasure when about to visit the metropolis. I ought to have mentioned before that he had known Mr. Sotheby at a very early period of life,—that amiable and excellent man having been stationed for some time at Edinburgh while serving his Majesty as a captain of dragoons. Scott ever retained for him a sincere regard; he was always, when in London, a frequent guest at his hospitable board, and owed to him the personal acquaintance of not a few of their most eminent contemporaries.

Caroline, Princess of Wales, was in those days considered among the Tories, whose politics her husband had uniformly opposed, as the victim of unmerited misfortune, cast aside, from the mere wantonness of caprice, by a gay and dissolute voluptuary; while the Prince's Whig associates had espoused his quarrel, and were already, as the event shewed, prepared to act, publicly as well as privately, as if they believed her to be among the most abandoned of her sex. I know not by whom Scott was first introduced to her little Court at Blackheath; but I think it was probably through Mrs. Hayman, a lady of her bedchamber, several of whose notes and letters occur about this time in the collection of his correspondence. The careless levity of the Princess's manner was observed by him, I have heard him say, with much regret, as likely to bring the purity of heart and mind, for which he gave her credit, into suspicion. For example, when, in the course of the evening, she conducted him by himself to admire some flowers in a conservatory, and, the place being rather dark, his lameness occasioned him to hesitate for a moment in following her down some steps which she had taken at a skip, she turned round, and said, with mock indignation, "Ah! false and faint-hearted troubadour! you will not trust yourself with me for fear of your neck!"

I find from one of Mrs. Hayman's letters, that on being asked, at Montague House, to recite some verses of his own, he replied that he had none unpublished which he thought worthy of her Royal Highness's attention, but introduced a short account of the Ettrick Shepherd, and repeated one of the ballads of the *Mountain Bard*, for which he was then endeavouring to procure subscribers. The Princess appears to have been interested by the story, and she affected, at all events, to be pleased with the lines; she desired that her name might be placed on the Shepherd's list, and thus he had at least one gleam of royal patronage.

I shall not dwell at present upon Scott's method of conduct in the circumstances of an eminently popular author beleaguered by the importunities of fashionable admirers; his bearing when first exposed to such influences was exactly what it was to the end, and I shall have occasion in the sequel to produce the evidence of more than one deliberate observer.

His nomination as Clerk of Session appeared in the Gazette (March 8, 1806), which announced the instalment of the Hon. Henry Erskine and John Clerk of Eldin as Lord Advocate and Solicitor-General for Scotland. The promotion at such a moment, of a distinguished Tory, might well excite the wonder of the Parliament House, and even when the circumstances were explained, the inferior local adherents of the triumphant cause were far from considering the conduct of their superiors in this matter with feelings of satisfaction. The indication of such humours was deeply resented by his haughty spirit; and he in his turn shewed his irritation in a manner well calculated to extend to higher quarters the spleen with which his advancement had been regarded by persons unworthy of his attention. In short, it was almost immediately after a Whig Ministry had gazetted his appointment to an office which had for twelve months formed a principal object of his ambition, that, rebelling against the implied suspicion of his having accepted something like a personal obligation at the hands of adverse politicians, he for the first time put himself forward as a decided Tory partisan.

The impeachment of Lord Melville was among the first measures of the new Government; and personal affection and gratitude graced as well as heightened the zeal with which Scott watched the issue of this, in his eyes, vindictive proceeding; but, though the ex-minister's ultimate acquittal was, as to all the charges involving his personal honour, complete, it must now be allowed that the investigation brought out many circumstances by no means creditable to his discretion; and the rejoicings of his friends ought not, therefore, to have been scornfully jubilant. Such they were, however—at least in Edinburgh; and Scott took his share in them by inditing a song, which was sung by James Ballantyne, and received with clamorous applauses, at a public dinner given in honour of the event on the 27th of June 1806. [1]

[1] The reader may turn to this song in the later editions of Scott's Poetical Works. Mr. W. Savage Landor, a man of great learning and great abilities, has in a recent collective edition of his writings reproduced many uncharitable judgments on distinguished contemporaries, which the reflection of advanced life might have been expected to cancel. Sir Walter Scott has his full share in these, but he suffers in good company. I must, however, notice the distinct assertion (vol. i. p. 339) that Scott "composed and sung a triumphal song on the death of a minister who, in his lifetime, he had flattered, and who was just in his coffin when the minstrel sang *The fox is run to earth.* Constable of Edinburgh heard him, and related the fact to Curran, who expressed his incredulity with great vehemence, and his abhorrence was greater than his incredulity." The only possible foundation on which this story can have been built is the occurrence in one stanza of the song mentioned in my text of the words, *Tally-ho to the fox.* That song was written and sung in June 1806. Mr. Fox was then minister, and died in September 1806. The lines which Mr. Landor speaks of as "flattering Fox during his lifetime," are very celebrated lines: they appeared in the epistle prefixed to the first canto of Marmion, which was published in February 1808, and their subject is the juxtaposition of the tombs of Pitt and Fox in Westminster Abbey. Everybody who knew Scott knows that he never sang a song in his life; and if that had not been

But enough of this. Scott's Tory feelings certainly appear to have been kept in a very excited state during the whole of that short reign of the Whigs. He then, for the first time, mingled keenly in the details of county politics,—canvassed electors—harangued meetings; and, in a word, made himself conspicuous as a leading instrument of his party—more especially as an indefatigable local manager, wherever the parliamentary interest of the Buccleuch family was in peril. But he was, in truth, earnest and serious in his belief that the new rulers of the country were disposed to abolish many of its most valuable institutions; and he regarded with special jealousy certain schemes of innovation with respect to the courts of law and the administration of justice, which were set on foot by the Crown officers for Scotland. At a debate of the Faculty of Advocates on some of these propositions, he made a speech much longer than any he had ever before delivered in that assembly; and several who heard it have assured me, that it had a flow and energy of eloquence for which those who knew him best had been quite prepared. When the meeting broke up, he walked across *the Mound*, on his way to Castle Street, between Mr. Jeffrey and another of his reforming friends, who complimented him on the rhetorical powers he had been displaying, and would willingly have treated the subject-matter of the discussion playfully. But his feelings had been moved to an extent far beyond their apprehension : he exclaimed, "No, no—'tis no laughing matter; little by little, whatever your wishes may be, you will destroy and undermine, until nothing of what makes Scotland Scotland shall remain." And so saying, he turned round to conceal his agitation—but not before Mr. Jeffrey saw tears gushing down his cheek—resting his head until he recovered himself on the wall of the Mound. Seldom, if ever, in his more advanced age, did any feelings obtain such mastery.

Before any of these scenes occurred he had entered upon his duties as Clerk of Session ; and as he continued to dis-

notorious, who but Mr. Landor could have heard without " incredulity " that he sang a triumphal song on the death of Fox, in the presence of the publisher of Marmion and proprietor of the Edinburgh Review? I may add, though it is needless, that Constable's son-in-law and partner, Mr. Cadell, " never heard of such a song as that described by Mr. Landor."

charge them with exemplary regularity, and to the entire satisfaction both of the Judges and the Bar, during the long period of twenty-five years, I think it proper to tell precisely in what they consisted.

The Court of Session sat, in his time, from the 12th of May to the 12th of July, and again from the 12th of November, with a short interval at Christmas, to the 12th of March. The Judges of the Inner Court took their places on the Bench, every morning not later than ten o'clock, and remained according to the amount of business ready for despatch, but seldom for less than four or more than six hours daily; during which space the Principal Clerks continued seated at a table below the Bench, to watch the progress of the suits, and record the decisions—the cases of all classes being equally apportioned among their number. The Court of Session, however, does not sit on Monday, that day being reserved for the criminal business of the High Court of Justiciary, and there is also another blank day every other week,—the Teind Wednesday, as it is called, when the Judges are assembled for the hearing of tithe questions, which belong to a separate jurisdiction, of comparatively modern creation, and having its own separate establishment of officers. On the whole, then, Scott's attendance in Court may be taken to have amounted, on the average, to from four to six hours daily during rather less than six months out of the twelve.

Not a little of the Clerk's business in Court is merely formal, and indeed mechanical; but there are few days in which he is not called upon for the exertion of his higher faculties, in reducing the decisions of the Bench, orally pronounced, to technical shape; which, in a new, complex, or difficult case, cannot be satisfactorily done without close attention to all the previous proceedings and written documents, an accurate understanding of the principles or precedents on which it has been determined, and a thorough command of the whole vocabulary of legal forms. Dull or indolent men, promoted through the mere wantonness of political patronage, might, no doubt, contrive to devolve the harder part of their duty upon humbler assistants: but in general, the office had been held by gentlemen of high character and attainments; and more than one among Scott's own colleagues enjoyed the reputation of legal science that would have done honour to the Bench.   Such men, of course, prided themselves on doing well whatever it was their proper function to do; and it was by their example, not that of the drones who condescended to lean upon unseen and irresponsible inferiors, that Scott uniformly modelled his own conduct as a Clerk of Session.   To do this, required, of necessity, constant study of law-papers and authorities at home.   There was also a great deal of really base drudgery, such as the authenticating of registered deeds by signature, which he had to go through out of Court; he had, too, a Shrievalty, though not a heavy one, all the while upon his hands;—and, on the whole, it forms one of the most remarkable features in his history, that, throughout the most active period of his literary career, he must have devoted a large proportion of his hours, during half at least of every year, to the conscientious discharge of professional duties.

Henceforth, then, when in Edinburgh, his literary work was performed chiefly before breakfast; with the assistance of such evening hours as he could contrive to rescue from the consideration of Court papers, and from those social engagements in which, year after year, as his celebrity advanced, he was of necessity more and more largely involved; and of those entire days during which the Court of Session did not sit—days which, by most of those holding the same official station, were given to relaxation and amusement.   So long as he continued quarter-master of the Volunteer Cavalry, of course he had, even while in Edinburgh, some occasional horse exercise; but, in general, his town life henceforth was in that respect as inactive as his country life ever was the reverse.   He scorned for a long while to attach any consequence to this complete alternation of habits; but we shall find him confessing in the sequel that it proved highly injurious to his bodily health.

I may here observe, that the duties of his clerkship brought him into close daily connection with a set of gentlemen, most of whom were soon regarded by him with the most cordial affection and confidence.   One of his new colleagues was David Hume (the nephew of the historian), whose lectures on the Law of Scotland are characterised with just eulogy in the Ashestiel Memoir, and who subsequently became a Baron of the Exchequer; a man as virtuous and amiable, as conspicuous for masculine vigour

of intellect and variety of knowledge. Another was Hector
Macdonald Buchanan of Drummakiln, a frank-hearted and
generous gentleman, not the less acceptable to Scott for
the Highland prejudices which he inherited with the high
blood of Clanranald; at whose beautiful seat of Ross
Priory, on the shores of Lochlomond, he was henceforth
almost annually a visitor—a circumstance which has left
many traces in the Waverley Novels. A third (though I
believe of later appointment), with whom his intimacy was
not less strict, was the late excellent Sir Robert Dundas
of Beechwood, Bart. ; and the fourth, was the friend of his
boyhood, one of the dearest he ever had, Colin Mackenzie
of Portmore. With these gentlemen's families, he and his
lived in such constant familiarity of kindness, that the
children all called their fathers' colleagues *uncles*, and the
mothers of their little friends, *aunts*; and in truth, the
establishment was a brotherhood.

CHAPTER V

Marmion—Edition of Dryden, &c.—Morritt—Domestic Life—
  Quarrel with Constable and Co.—John Ballantyne started as a
  Publisher—The Quarterly Review begun. 1806-1809.

DURING the whole of 1806 and 1807 Dryden continued to
occupy the greater share of Scott's literary hours; but in
the course of the former year he found time and (notwithstanding a few political bickerings) inclination to draw up
three papers for the Edinburgh Review; one being that
exquisite piece of humour, the article on the Miseries of
Human Life, to which Mr. Jeffrey added some, if not all,
of the *Reviewers' Groans.* He also edited, with Preface
and Notes, " Original Memoirs written during the Great
Civil Wars; being the Life of Sir Henry Slingsby, and
Memoirs of Captain Hodgson," &c. This volume was put
forth in October, 1806, by Constable; and in November he
began *Marmion,*—the first of his own Poems in which that
enterprising firm had a primary part.

He was at this time in communication with several
booksellers, each of whom would willingly have engrossed
his labour; but from the moment that his undertakings
began to be serious, he seems to have acted on the maxim,
that no author should ever let any one house fancy that

they had obtained a right of monopoly over his works—
or, as he expressed it, in the language of the Scottish
feudalists, " that they had completely thirled him to their
mill." Of the conduct of Messrs. Longman, he has attested that it was liberal beyond his expectation; but,
nevertheless, a negotiation which they now opened proved
fruitless. Constable offered a thousand guineas for the
poem very shortly after it was begun, and without having
seen one line of it. It is hinted in the Introduction of
1830, that private circumstances rendered it desirable for
Scott to obtain the immediate command of such a sum;
the price was actually paid long before the book was published; and it suits very well with Constable's character
to suppose that his readiness to advance the money may
have outstripped the calculations of more established
dealers, and thus cast the balance in his favour. He was
not, however, so unwise as to keep the whole adventure to
himself. His bargain being concluded, he tendered one-
fourth of the copyright to Miller of Albemarle Street, and
another to John Murray, then of Fleet Street; and the
latter at once replied, " We both view it as honourable,
profitable, and glorious to be concerned in the publication
of a new poem by Walter Scott." The news that a thousand guineas had been paid for an unseen and unfinished
MS. seemed in those days portentous; and it must be
allowed that the man who received such a sum for a performance in embryo, had made a great step in the hazards
as well as in the honours of authorship. The private circumstances which he alludes to as having precipitated his
re-appearance as a poet were connected with his brother
Thomas's final withdrawal from his practice as a Writer to
the Signet; but it is extremely improbable that, in the
absence of any such occurrence, a young, energetic, and
ambitious man would have long resisted the stimulus of
such success as had attended the Last Minstrel.

" I had formed," he says, " the prudent resolution to
bestow a little more labour than I had yet done, and to be
in no hurry again to announce myself as a candidate for
literary fame. Accordingly, particular passages of a poem
which was finally called *Marmion* were laboured with a
good deal of care by one by whom much care was seldom
bestowed. Whether the work was worth the labour or
not, I am no competent judge; but I may be permitted to
say, that the period of its composition was a very happy

one in my life; so much so, that I remember with pleasure
at this moment (1830) some of the spots in which particular passages were composed." The first four of the
Introductory Epistles are dated Ashestiel, and they point
out very distinctly some of these spots. There is a knoll
with some tall old ashes on the adjoining farm of the Peel,
where he was very fond of sitting by himself, and it still
bears the name of the *Sheriff's Knowe*. Another favourite
seat was beneath a huge oak hard by the river, at the
extremity of the *haugh* of Ashestiel. It was here that
while meditating his verses he used

> " To waste the solitary day
> In plucking from yon fen the reed,
> And watch it floating down the Tweed."

He frequently wandered far from home, however, attended
only by his dog, and would return late in the evening,
having let hour after hour slip away among the soft and
melancholy wildernesses where Yarrow creeps from her
fountains. The lines,

> " Oft in my mind such thoughts awake,
> By lone Saint Mary's silent lake," etc.

paint a scene not less impressive than what Byron found
amidst the gigantic pines of the forest of Ravenna; and
how completely does he set himself before us in the moment
of his gentler and more solemn inspiration, by the closing
couplet,—

> " Your horse's hoof-tread sounds too rude,
> So stilly is the solitude."

But when the theme was of a more stirring order, he enjoyed pursuing it over brake and fell at the full speed of
his *Lieutenant*. I well remember his saying, as I rode
with him across the hills from Ashestiel to Newark one
day in his declining years—" Oh, man, I had many a grand
gallop among these braes when I was thinking of Marmion, but a trotting canny pony must serve me now."

Mr. Skene, however, informs me that many of the more
energetic descriptions, and particularly that of the battle of
Flodden, were struck out while he was in quarters again
with his cavalry, in the autumn of 1807. " In the intervals of drilling," he says, " Scott used to delight in
walking his powerful black steed up and down by himself
upon the Portobello sands, within the beating of the surge;
and now and then you would see him plunge in his spurs,

and go off as if at the charge, with the spray dashing about him. As we rode back to Musselburgh, he often came and placed himself beside me, to repeat the verses that he had been composing during these pauses of our exercise."

He seems to have communicated fragments of the poem very freely during the whole of its progress. As early as the 22nd February 1807, I find Mrs. Hayman acknowledging, in the name of the Princess of Wales, the receipt of a copy of the Introduction to Canto III., in which occurs the tribute to her heroic father, mortally wounded the year before at Jena—a tribute so grateful to her feelings, that she sent the poet an elegant silver vase as a memorial of her thankfulness. And about the same time, the Marchioness of Abercorn expresses the delight with which both she and her lord had read the generous verses on Pitt and Fox. But his connection with this family was no new one; for his father, and afterwards his brother, had been the auditors of their Scotch rental.

In March, his researches concerning Dryden carried him again to the south. For several weeks he gave his day pretty regularly to the pamphlets and MSS. of the British Museum, and the evening to the brilliant societies that now courted him whenever he came within their sphere. " As I had," he writes to his brother-in-law in India, " contrary to many who avowed the same opinions in sunshine, held fast my integrity during the Foxites' interval of power, I found myself of course very well with the new administration." But he uniformly reserved his Saturday and Sunday either for Mr. Ellis at Sunninghill, or Lord and Lady Abercorn at Stanmore; and the press copy of Cantos I. and II. of Marmion attests that most of it reached Ballantyne in sheets franked by the Marquis, or his son-in-law Lord Aberdeen. Before he turned homeward, he made a short visit to his friend William Rose in Hampshire, and enjoyed in his company various long rides in the New Forest, a day in the dockyard of Portsmouth, and two or three more in the Isle of Wight. Several sheets of Canto III. are also under covers franked from Gundimore. In the first week of May we find him at Lichfield, having diverged from the great road to Scotland for the purpose of visiting Miss Seward. Her account of her correspondent, whom till now she had never seen, was addressed to Mr. Cary, the translator of Dante. " This proudest boast of the Caledonian muse is tall," she says, "and rather robust than slender, but lame in the same manner as Mr. Hayley, and in a greater measure. Neither the contour of his face nor yet his features are elegant; his complexion healthy, and somewhat fair, without bloom. We find the singularity of brown hair and eyelashes, with flaxen eyebrows; and a countenance open, ingenuous, and benevolent. When seriously conversing or earnestly attentive, though his eyes are rather of a lightish grey, deep thought is on their lids; he contracts his brow, and the rays of genius gleam aslant from the orbs beneath them. An upper lip too long prevents his mouth from being decidedly handsome; but the sweetest emanations of temper and heart play about it when he talks cheerfully or smiles —and in company he is much oftener gay than contemplative—his conversation an overflowing fountain of brilliant wit, apposite allusion, and playful archness—while on serious themes it is nervous and eloquent; the accent decidedly Scotch, yet by no means broad. Not less astonishing than was Johnson's memory is that of Mr. Scott; like Johnson, also, his recitation is too monotonous and violent to do justice either to his own writings or those of others." Miss Seward adds, that she showed him the passage in Cary's Dante where Michael Scott occurs, and that though he admired the spirit and skill of the version, he confessed his inability to find pleasure in the Divina Commedia. "The plan," he said, "appeared to him unhappy; the personal malignity and strange mode of revenge presumptuous and uninteresting." By the 12th of May he was at Edinburgh for the commencement of the summer session, and the printing of his Poem seems thenceforth to have gone on at times with great rapidity, at others slowly and irregularly; the latter Cantos having no doubt been merely blocked out when the first went to press, and his professional avocations, but above all his Dryden, occasioning frequent interruptions.

Mr. Guthrie Wright, who was among the familiar associates of the Troop, has furnished me with some details which throw light on the construction of Marmion. This gentleman had, through Scott's good offices, succeeded his brother Thomas in the charge of the Abercorn business. —"In the summer of 1807," he says, "I had the pleasure of making a trip with Sir Walter to Dumfries, for the purpose of meeting Lord Abercorn on his way to Ireland. His Lordship did not arrive for two or three days, and we

employed the interval in visiting Sweetheart Abbey, Caer-
laverock Castle, and some other ancient buildings in the
neighbourhood.   He recited poetry and old legends from
morn till night; and it is impossible that anything could
be more delightful than his society; but what I particularly allude to is the circumstance, that at that time he was
writing *Marmion*, the three or four first cantos of which he
had with him, and which he was so good as read to me.
It is unnecessary to say how much I was enchanted with
them; but as he good-naturedly asked me to state any
observations that occurred to me, I said in joke that it
appeared to me he had brought his hero by a very strange
route into Scotland. ' Why,' says I, ' did ever mortal
coming from England to Edinburgh go by Gifford, Crichton Castle, Borthwick Castle, and over the top of Blackford Hill?   Not only is it a circuitous *détour*, but there
never was a road that way since the world was created ! '
' That is a most irrelevant objection,' said Sir Walter;
' it was my good pleasure to bring Marmion by that
route, for the purpose of describing the places you have
mentioned, and the view from Blackford Hill—it was his
business to find his road and pick his steps the best way
he could.   But, pray, how would you have me bring him?
Not by the post-road, surely, as if he had been travelling
in a mail-coach?'—'No,' I replied; ' there were neither
post-roads nor mail-coaches in those days; but I think you
might have brought him with a less chance of getting into
a swamp, by allowing him to travel the natural route by
Dunbar and the sea-coast; and then he might have tarried
for a space with the famous Earl of Angus, surnamed
Bell-the-Cat, at his favourite residence of Tantallon Castle,
by which means you would have had not only that fortress
with all his feudal followers, but the Castle of Dunbar,
the Bass, and all the beautiful scenery of the Forth to
describe.'   This observation seemed to strike him much,
and after a pause he exclaimed—' By Jove, you are right !
I ought to have brought him that way;' and he added,
' but before he and I part, depend upon it he shall visit
Tantallon.'   He then asked if I had ever been there, and
upon saying I had frequently, he desired me to describe it,
which I did; and I verily believe it is from what I then said
that the accurate description contained in the fifth canto
was given—at least I never heard him say he had afterwards gone to visit the castle; and when the poem was

published, I remember he laughed, and asked me how I liked Tantallon."

Just a year had elapsed from his beginning the poem, when he penned the Epistle for Canto IV. at Ashestiel; and who, that considers how busily his various pursuits and labours had been crowding the interval, can wonder to be told that

> " Even now, it scarcely seems a day
> Since first I tuned this idle lay—
> A task so often laid aside
> When leisure graver cares denied—
> That now November's dreary gale,
> Whose voice inspired my opening tale,
> That same November gale once more
> Whirls the dry leaves on Yarrow shore."

The fifth Introduction was written in Edinburgh in the month following; that to the last Canto, during the Christmas festivities of Mertoun-house, where, from the first days of his ballad-rhyming to the close of his life, he, like his bearded ancestor, usually spent that season with the immediate head of the race. The bulky appendix of notes, including a mass of curious antiquarian quotations, must have moved somewhat slowly through the printers' hands; but Marmion was at length ready for publication by the middle of February 1808.

Among the " graver cares " which he alludes to as having interrupted his progress, were those of preparing himself for an office to which he was formally appointed soon afterwards, namely, that of Secretary to a Parliamentary Commission for the improvement of Scottish Jurisprudence. This Commission, at the head of which was Sir Islay Campbell, Lord President of the Court of Session, continued in operation for two or three years. Scott's salary, as secretary, was a mere trifle; but he had been led to expect that his exertions in this capacity would lead to better things. In giving a general view of his affairs to his brother-in-law in India, he says—" I am principally pleased with my new appointment as being conferred on me by our chief law lords and King's counsel, and consequently an honourable professional distinction. The employment will be but temporary, but may have consequences important to my future lot in life, if I give due satisfaction in the discharge of it." He appears accordingly to have submitted to a great deal of drudgery, in mastering the technical controversies which had called for legislatorial interference; and he discharged his functions, as usual, with the warm approbation of his superiors; but no result followed.

Not only did he write sundry articles for the Edinburgh Review while Marmion was on hand, but having now frequent correspondence with Mr. Southey, whose literature had not as yet been very lucrative to him, he made an effort to enlist that friend also in the same critical corps. Thalaba and Madoc had been handled by them in no very flattering style; the early works of Wordsworth still more irreverently; but Southey declined these offers of intermediation on the score mainly of politics—expressing, at the same time, some regret that Wordsworth, in his magnificent sonnet on Killiecrankie, should have introduced that type of ultra-toryism, the Viscount of Dundee, without apparent censure of his character. In reply (15th December 1807), Scott admits his own " extreme dislike " of the tone of the Review as to the war with Bonaparte. He says :—" Who ever thought he did a service to a person engaged in an arduous conflict, by proving to him, or attempting to prove, that he must necessarily be beaten? and what effect can such language have but to accelerate the accomplishment of the prophecy which it contains? And as for Catholic Emancipation—I am not, God knows, a bigot in religious matters, nor a friend to persecution; but if a particular sect of religionists are *ipso facto* connected with foreign politics—and placed under the spiritual direction of a class of priests, whose unrivalled dexterity and activity are increased by the rules which detach them from the rest of the world—I humbly think that we may be excused from intrusting to them those places in the State where the influence of such a clergy, who act under the direction of a passive tool of our worst foe, is likely to be attended with the most fatal consequences. If a gentleman chooses to walk about with a couple of pounds of gunpowder in his pocket, if I give him the shelter of my roof, I may at least be permitted to exclude him from the seat next to the fire. So thinking, I have felt your scruples in doing anything for the Review of late. As for my good friend Dundee, I cannot admit his culpability in the extent you allege; and it is scandalous of the Sunday bard to join in your condemnation, ' and yet come of a noble Græme ! ' [1] I admit he was *tant soit peu sauvage*—

---

[1] James Grahame, author of *The Sabbath*, &c.

but he was a noble savage; and the beastly Covenanters against whom he acted, hardly had any claim to be called men, unless what was founded on their walking upon their hind feet. You can hardly conceive the perfidy, cruelty, and stupidity of these people, according to the accounts they have themselves preserved. But I admit I had many cavalier prejudices instilled into me, as my ancestor was a Killiecrankie man."

Mr. Southey happened to be in London when Marmion came out, and he wrote thus to the author on his return to Keswick—" Half the poem I had read at Heber's before my own copy arrived. I went punctually to breakfast with him, and he was long enough dressing to let me devour so much of it. The story is made of better materials than the Lay, yet they are not so well fitted together. As a whole, it has not pleased me so much—in parts, it has pleased me more. There is nothing so finely conceived in your former poem as the death of Marmion : there is nothing finer in its conception anywhere. The introductory epistles I did not wish away, because, as poems, they gave me great pleasure; but I wished them at the end of the volume, or at the beginning—anywhere except where they were. My taste is perhaps peculiar in disliking all interruptions in narrative poetry. When the poet lets his story sleep, and talks in his own person, it has to me the same sort of unpleasant effect that is produced at the end of an act. You are alive to know what follows, and lo—down comes the curtain, and the fiddlers begin with their abominations."

I pass over a multitude of the congratulatory effusions of inferior names, but must not withhold part of a letter on a folio sheet, written not in the first hurry of excitement, but two months after Marmion had reached Ellis. He then says :—" All the world are agreed that you are like the elephant mentioned in the Spectator, who was the greatest elephant in the world except himself, and consequently, that the only question at issue is, whether the Lay or Marmion shall be reputed the most pleasing poem in our language—save and except one or two of Dryden's fables. But, with respect to the two rivals, I think the Lay is, on the whole, the greater favourite. It is admitted that the fable of Marmion is greatly superior—that it contains a greater diversity of character—that it inspires more interest—and that it is by no means inferior in point of poetical expression; but it is contended that the incident of Deloraine's journey to Melrose surpasses anything in Marmion, and that the personal appearance of the Minstrel, who, though the last, is by far the most charming of all minstrels, is by no means compensated by the idea of an author shorn of his picturesque beard, deprived of his harp, and writing letters to his intimate friends. These introductory epistles, indeed, though excellent in themselves, are in fact only interruptions to the fable; and accordingly, nine out of ten have perused them separately, either after or before the poem—and it is obvious that they cannot have produced, in either case, the effect which was proposed—viz., of relieving the reader's attention, and giving variety to the whole. Perhaps, continue these critics, it would be fair to say that Marmion delights us in spite of its introductory epistles—while the Lay owes its principal charm to the venerable old minstrel—the two poems may be considered as equally respectable to the talents of the author; but the first, being a more perfect whole, will be more constantly preferred. Now, all this may be very true—but it is no less true that everybody has already read Marmion *more than once*—that it is the subject of general conversation—that it delights all ages and all tastes, and that it is universally allowed to improve upon a second reading. My own opinion is, that both the productions are equally good in their different ways : yet, upon the whole, I had rather be the author of Marmion than of the Lay, because I think its species of excellence of much more difficult attainment. What degree of bulk may be essentially necessary to the corporeal part of an epic poem, I know not; but sure I am that the story of Marmion might have furnished twelve books as easily as six—that the masterly character of Constance would not have been less bewitching had it been much more minutely painted—and that De Wilton might have been dilated with great ease, and even to considerable advantage;—in short, that had it been your intention merely to exhibit a spirited romantic story, instead of making that story subservient to the delineation of the manners which prevailed at a certain period of our history, the number and variety of your characters would have suited any scale of painting. Marmion is to Deloraine what Tom Jones is to Joseph Andrews;—the varnish of high breeding nowhere diminishes the prominence of the features—and the minion of a king is as light and sinewy a cavalier as the Borderer,—rather less ferocious, more wicked, less fit for the hero of a ballad, and far more for the hero of a regular poem. On the whole, I can sincerely assure you, ' *sans phrase*,' that had I seen Marmion without knowing the author, I should have ranked it with Theodore and Honoria,—that is to say, on the very top shelf of English poetry.'' This elegant letter may no doubt be considered as an epitome of the very highest and most refined of London table-talk on Marmion, during the first freshness of its popularity, and before the only critical journal of which any one in those days thought very seriously, had pronounced its verdict.

When we consider some parts of that judgment, together with the author's personal intimacy with the editor, and the aid which he had of late been affording to the Review itself, it must be allowed that Mr. Jeffrey acquitted himself on this occasion in a manner highly creditable to his courageous sense of duty. The number for April 1808 was accompanied by this note:—'' Queen Street, Tuesday.—Dear Scott,—If I did not give you credit for more magnanimity than other of your irritable tribe, I should scarcely venture to put this into your hands. As it is, I do it with no little solicitude, and earnestly hope that it will make no difference in the friendship which has hitherto subsisted between us. I have spoken of your poem exactly as I think, and though I cannot reasonably suppose that you will be pleased with everything I have said, it would mortify me very severely to believe I had given you pain. If you have any amity left for me, you will not delay very long to tell me so. In the meantime, I am very sincerely yours,—F. Jeffrey.''

The reader will, I hope, pause here and read the article as it stands; endeavouring to put himself into the situation of Scott when it was laid upon his desk, together with this ominous billet from the editor, who, as it happened, had been for some time engaged to dine that same Tuesday in Castle Street. The detailed criticism of the paper is, I am sure, done in a style on which the writer cannot now reflect with perfect equanimity, any more than on the lofty and decisive tone of the sweeping paragraphs by which it was introduced. All this, however, I can suppose Scott to have gone through with great composure; but he must, I think, have wondered, to say the least, when he

found himself accused of having " throughout neglected
Scottish feelings and Scottish characters " !—he who had
just poured out all the patriotic enthusiasm of his soul in
so many passages of Marmion, which every Scotchman to
the end of time will have by heart; painted the capital, the
court, the camp, the heroic old chieftains of Scotland, in
colours instinct with a fervour that can never die; and
dignified the most fatal of her national misfortunes by a
celebration as loftily pathetic as ever blended pride with
sorrow,—a battle-piece which even his critic had pronounced to be the noblest save in Homer ! But not even
this injustice was likely to wound him very deeply. Coming from one of the recent witnesses of his passionate
agitation on *the Mound*, perhaps he would only smile at it.
At all events, he could make allowance for the petulancies
into which men the least disposed to injure the feelings of
others will sometimes be betrayed, when the critical rod is
in their hands. He assured Mr. Jeffrey that the article
had not disturbed his digestion, though he hoped neither
his booksellers nor the public would agree with the
opinions it expressed; and begged he would come to
dinner at the hour previously appointed. Mr. Jeffrey
appeared accordingly, and was received by his host with
the frankest cordiality; but had the mortification to observe that the mistress of the house, though perfectly
polite, was not quite so easy with him as usual. She, too,
behaved herself with exemplary civility during the dinner;
but could not help saying, in her broken English, when
her guest was departing, " Well, good-night, Mr. Jeffrey
—dey tell me dat you have abused Scott in de Review,
and I hope Mr. Constable has paid *you* very well for writing it." This anecdote was not perhaps worth giving;
but it has been printed already in an exaggerated shape,
so I thought it as well to present the edition which I have
derived from the lips of all the three persons concerned.
No one, I am sure, will think the worse of any of them for
it,—least of all of Mrs. Scott. She might well be pardoned, if she took to herself more than her own share in
the misadventures as well as the successes of the most
affectionate of protectors. It was, I believe, about this
time when, as Scott has confessed, " the popularity of
Marmion gave him such a *heeze*, he had for a moment
almost lost his footing," that a shrewd and sly observer,

Mrs. Grant of Laggan, said, wittily enough, upon leaving a brilliant assembly where the poet had been surrounded by all the buzz and glare of fashionable ecstasy—" Mr. Scott always seems to me like a glass, through which the rays of admiration pass without sensibly affecting it; but the bit of paper that lies beside it will presently be in a blaze—and no wonder."

I shall not, after so much about criticism, say anything more of Marmion in this place, than that I have always considered it as on the whole the greatest of Scott's poems. There is a certain light, easy, virgin charm about the Lay, which we look for in vain through the subsequent volumes of his verse; but the superior strength, and breadth, and boldness both of conception and execution in the Marmion appear to me indisputable. The great blot, the combination of *mean felony* with so many noble qualities in the character of the hero, was, as the poet says, severely commented on at the time by the most ardent of his early friends, Leyden; but though he admitted the justice of that criticism, he chose " to let the tree lie as it had fallen." He was also sensible that many of the subordinate and connecting parts of the narrative are flat, harsh, and obscure—but would never make any serious attempt to do away with these imperfections; and perhaps they, after all, heighten by contrast the effect of the passages of high-wrought enthusiasm which alone he considered, in after days, with satisfaction. As for the " epistolary dissertations " (as Jeffrey called them), it must, I take it, be allowed that they interfered with the flow of the story, when readers were turning the leaves in the first glow of curiosity; and they were not, in fact, originally intended to be interwoven in any fashion with the romance of Marmion. Though the author himself does not allude to, and had perhaps forgotten, the circumstance, when writing the Introductory Essay of 1830— they were announced by an advertisement early in 1807 as " Six Epistles from Ettrick Forest," to be published in a separate volume; and perhaps it might have been better that this first plan had been adhered to. But however that may be, are there any pages, among all he ever wrote, that one would be more sorry he should not have written? They are among the most delicious portraitures that genius ever painted of itself,—buoyant, virtuous, happy genius—exulting in its own energies, yet possessed and mastered by a clear, calm, modest mind, and happy only in diffusing happiness around it.

The feelings of political partisanship find no place in this poem; but though Mr. Jeffrey chose to complain of its " manifest neglect of *Scottish* feelings," I take leave to suspect that the boldness and energy of *British* patriotism which breathes in so many passages, may have had more share than that alleged omission in pointing the pen that criticised Marmion. Scott had sternly and indignantly rebuked and denounced the then too prevalent spirit of anti-national despondence; he had put the trumpet to his lips, and done his part at least to sustain the hope and resolution of his countrymen in that struggle from which it was the doctrine of the Edinburgh Review that no sane observer of the times could anticipate anything but ruin and degradation. He must ever be considered as the " mighty minstrel " of the Antigallican war; and it was Marmion that first announced him in that character.

Be all this as it may, his connection with the Review was now broken off; and indeed it was never renewed, except in one instance, many years after, when the strong wish to serve poor Maturin shook him for a moment from his purpose. The loftiest and purest of human beings seldom act but under a mixture of motives, and I shall not attempt to guess in what proportions he was swayed by aversion to the political doctrines which the journal had lately been avowing with increased openness—by dissatisfaction with its judgments of his own works—or, lastly, by the feeling that, whether those judgments were or were not just, it was but an idle business for him to assist by his own pen the popularity of the vehicle that diffused them. That he was influenced more or less by all of these considerations, appears highly probable; and I fancy I can trace some indications of each of them in a letter with which I am favoured by a warm lover of literature, and a sincere admirer both of Scott and Jeffrey, and though numbered among the Tories in the House of Commons, yet one of the most liberal section of his party[1]— who happened to visit Scotland shortly after the article on Marmion appeared, and has set down his recollections of the course of table-talk at a dinner where he for the first time met the poet in company with his censor :—" There were," he says, " only a few people besides the two lions

[1] The late Mr. Morritt of Rokeby.—1848.

—and assuredly I have seldom passed a more agreeable day. A thousand subjects of literature, antiquities, and manners, were started; and much was I struck, as you may well suppose, by the extent, correctness, discrimination, and accuracy of Jeffrey's information; equally so with his taste, acuteness, and wit, in dissecting every book, author, and story that came in our way. Nothing could surpass the variety of his knowledge, but the easy rapidity of his manner of producing it. He was then in his meridian. Scott, delighted to draw him out, delighted also to talk himself, and displayed, I think, even a larger range of anecdote and illustration; remembering every thing, whether true or false, that was characteristic or impressive; every thing that was good, or lovely, or lively. It struck me that there was this great difference—Jeffrey for the most part entertained us, when books were under discussion, with the detection of faults, blunders, absurdities, or plagiarisms : Scott took up the matter where he left it, recalled some compensating beauty or excellence for which no credit had been allowed, and by the recitation, perhaps, of one fine stanza, set the poor victim on his legs again. I believe it was just about this time that Scott had abandoned his place in Mr. Jeffrey's corps. The journal had been started among the clever young society with which Edinburgh abounded when they were both entering life as barristers; and Jeffrey's principal coadjutors for some time were Sydney Smith, Brougham, Horner, Scott himself—and on scientific subjects, Playfair; but clever contributors were sought for in all quarters. But it was not long before Brougham dipped the concern deep in witty Whiggery; and it was thought at the time that some very foolish neglects on the part of Pitt had a principal share in making several of these brilliant young men decide on carrying over their weapons to the enemy's camp. Scott was a strong Tory, nay, by family recollections and poetical feelings of association, a Jacobite. Jeffrey, however, was an early friend—and thus there was a confliction of feelings on both sides. Scott, as I was told, remonstrated against the deepening Whiggery—Jeffrey alleged that he could not resist the wit. Scott offered to try his hand at a witty bit of Toryism—but the editor pleaded off, upon the danger of inconsistency. These differences first cooled—and soon dissolved their federation.—To return to our gay dinner. As the claret was taking its rounds, Jeffrey introduced some good-natured eulogy of his old supporters—Sydney Smith, Brougham, and Horner. ' Come,' says Scott, ' you can't say too much about Sydney or Brougham, but I will not admire your Horner : he always put me in mind of Obadiah's bull, who, although, as Father Shandy observed, he never produced a calf, went through his business with such a grave demeanour, that he always maintained his credit in the parish ! ' The fun of the illustration tempted him to this sally, I believe; but Horner's talents did not lie in humour, and his economical labours were totally uncongenial to the mind of Scott."

Before quitting Marmion and its critics, I ought to say that, like the Lay, this and the subsequent great poems were all first published in a splendid quarto form. The 2,000 of the original Marmion, price a guinea and a half, were disposed of in less than a month; and twelve octavo editions, between 1808 and 1825, had carried the sale to upwards of 30,000 copies, before the author included it in the collection of his poetry with biographical prefaces in 1830; since which period there have been frequent reprints; making an aggregate legitimate circulation between 1808 and 1848 of about 60,000.

Ere the poem was published, a heavy task, begun earlier, and continued throughout its progress, had been nearly completed; and there appeared in the last week of April, 1808, The Works of John Dryden, now first collected; with notes historical, critical, and explanatory, and a Life of the Author.—Eighteen volumes 8vo. This was the bold speculation of William Miller of Albemarle Street; and the editor's fee, at forty guineas the volume, was £756. The bulk of the collection, the neglect into which a majority of the pieces had fallen, the obsoleteness of the party politics which had so largely exercised the author's pen, and the indecorum, not seldom running into flagrant indecency, by which transcendent genius had ministered to the appetites of a licentious age, all combined to make the warmest of Scott's admirers doubt whether even his skill and reputation would be found sufficient to ensure the success of this undertaking. It was, however, better received than anyone, except perhaps the courageous bookseller himself, had anticipated. The entire work was reprinted in 1821. Since then the Life of Dryden has had its place in various editions of Scott's prose miscellanies; nor perhaps does that class of his writings include any piece which keeps a higher estimation.

This Dryden was criticised in the Edinburgh Review for October 1808, with great ability, and, on the whole, with admirable candour. The industry and perspicacity with which Scott had carried through his editorial researches and annotations were acknowledged in terms which, had he known the name of his reviewer, must have been doubly gratifying; and it was confessed that, in the Life of his author, he had corrected with patient honesty, and filled up with lucid and expansive detail, the sometimes careless and often naked outline of Johnson's masterly Essay. It would be superfluous to quote in this place a specimen of critical skill which has already enjoyed wide circulation, and which will hereafter, no doubt, be included in the miscellaneous prose works of HALLAM. The points of political faith on which that great writer dissents from the Editor of Dryden, would, even if I had the inclination to pursue such a discussion, lead me far astray from the immediate object of these pages; they embrace questions on which the best and wisest of our countrymen will probably continue to take opposite sides, as long as our past history excites a living interest, and our literature is that of an active nation. On the poetical character of Dryden, I think the editor and his critic will be found to have expressed substantially much the same judgment; when they appear to differ, the battle strikes me as being about words rather than things, as is likely to be the case when men of such abilities and attainments approach a subject remote from their personal passions. As might have been expected, the terse and dexterous reviewer has often the better in this logomachy; but when the balance is struck, we discover here, as elsewhere, that Scott's broad and masculine understanding had, by whatever happy hardihood, grasped the very result to which others win their way by the more cautious processes of logical investigation. While nothing has been found easier than to attack his details, his general views on critical questions have seldom, if ever, been successfully impugned.

I wish I could believe that Scott's labours had been sufficient to recall Dryden to his rightful station, not in the opinion of those who make literature the business or chief solace of their lives—for with them he had never forfeited it—but in the general favour of the intelligent public. That such has been the case, however, the not rapid sale of two editions, aided as they were by the greatest of living names, can be no proof; nor have I observed among the numberless recent speculations of the English booksellers, a single reprint of even those tales, satires, and critical essays, not to be familiar with which would, in the last age, have been considered as disgraceful in any one making the least pretension to letters.

Scott's Biography of Dryden—the only Life of a great poet which he has left us, and also his only detailed work on the personal fortunes of one to whom literature was a profession—was penned just when he had begun to apprehend his own destiny. On this point of view, forbidden to contemporary delicacy, we may now pause with blameless curiosity. Seriously as he must have in those days been revolving the hazards of literary enterprise, he could not, it is probable, have handled any subject of this class without letting out here and there thoughts and feelings proper to his own biographer's province; but, widely as he and his predecessor may appear to stand apart as regards some of the most important both of intellectual and moral characteristics, they have nevertheless many features of resemblance, both as men and as authors; and I doubt if the entire range of our annals could have furnished a theme more calculated to keep Scott's scrutinising interest awake, than that which opened on him as he contemplated step by step the career of Dryden. There are grave lessons which that story was not needed to enforce upon his mind; he required no such beacon to make him revolt from paltering with the dignity of woman, or the passions of youth, or insulting by splenetic levities the religious convictions of any portion of his countrymen. But Dryden's prostitution of his genius to the petty bitternesses of political warfare, and the consequences both as to the party he served, and the antagonists he provoked, might well supply matter for serious consideration to the author of the Melville song. "Where," says Scott, "is the expert swordsman that does not delight in the flourish of his weapon? and a brave man will least of all withdraw himself from his ancient standard when the tide of battle beats against it." But he says also,—and I know enough of his own then recent experiences, in his intercourse with some who had been among his earliest and dearest associates, not to apply the language to the circumstances that suggested it—" He who keenly engages in political controversy must not only encounter the vulgar abuse which he may justly contemn, but the altered eye of friends whose regard is chilled." Nor, when he adds that " the protecting zeal of his party did not compensate Dryden for the loss of those whom he alienated in their service," can I help connecting this reflection too with his own subsequent abstinence from party personalities, in which had the expert swordsman's delight in the flourish of his weapon prevailed he might have rivalled the success of either Dryden or Swift, to be repaid like them by the settled rancour of Whigs and the jealous ingratitude of Tories.

It is curious enough to compare the hesitating style of his apology for that tinge of evanescent superstition which seems to have clouded occasionally Dryden's bright and solid mind, with the open avowal that he has " pride in recording his author's decided admiration of old ballads and popular tales " ; and perhaps his personal feelings were hardly less his prompter where he dismisses with brief scorn the sins of negligence and haste which had been so often urged against Dryden. " Nothing," he says, " is so easily attained as the power of presenting the extrinsic qualities of fine painting, fine music, or fine poetry ; the beauty of colour and outline, the combination of notes, the melody of versification, may be imitated by artists of mediocrity ; and many will view, hear, or peruse their performances, without being able positively to discover why they should not, since composed according to all the rules, afford pleasure equal to those of Raphael, Handel, or Dryden. The deficiency lies in the vivifying spirit, which, like *alcohol*, may be reduced to the same principle in all the fine arts. The French are said to possess the best possible rules for building ships of war, although not equally remarkable for their power of fighting them. When criticism becomes a pursuit separate from poetry, those who follow it are apt to forget that the legitimate ends of the art for which they lay down rules, are instruction and delight ; and that these points being attained, by what road soever, entitles a poet to claim the prize of successful merit. Neither did the learned authors of these disquisitions sufficiently attend to the general disposition of mankind, which cannot be contented even with the happiest imitations of former excellence, but demands novelty as a necessary ingredient for amusement. To insist that every epic poem shall have the plan of the Iliad, and every tragedy be modelled by the rules of Aristotle, resembles the principle of the architect who should build all his houses with the same number of windows and of storeys. It happened, too, inevitably, that the critics, in the pleni-potential authority which they exercised, often assumed as indispensable requisites of the drama, or epopeia, cir-cumstances which, in the great authorities they quoted, were altogether accidental or indifferent. These they erected into laws, and handed down as essential; although the forms prescribed have often as little to do with the merit and success of the original from which they are taken as the shape of the drinking-glass with the flavour of the wine which it contains." These sentences appear, from the dates, to have been penned immediately after the bio-grapher of Dryden had perused the Edinburgh Review on *Marmion.*

I conclude with a passage, in writing which he seems to have anticipated the only serious critical charge that was ever brought against his edition of Dryden as a whole—namely, the loose and irregular way in which his own æsthetical notions are indicated, rather than expounded. " While Dryden," says Scott, " examined, discussed, ad-mitted, or rejected the rules proposed by others, he for-bore, from *prudence, indolence,* or *a regard for the free-dom of Parnassus,* to erect himself into a legislator. His doctrines are scattered without system or pretence to it : it is impossible to read far without finding some maxim for doing, or forbearing, which every student of poetry will do well to engrave upon the tablets of his memory; but the author's mode of instruction is neither harsh nor dictatorial."

On the whole, it is impossible to doubt that the success of Dryden in rapidly reaching, and till the end of a long life holding undisputed, the summit of public favour and reputation, in spite of his " brave neglect " of minute finishing, narrow laws, and prejudiced authorities, must have had a powerful effect in nerving Scott's hope and resolution for the wide ocean of literary enterprise into which he had now fairly launched his bark. Like Dryden, he felt himself to be " amply stored with acquired know-ledge, much of it the fruits of early reading and applica-tion "; anticipated that though, " while engaged in the hurry of composition, or overcome by the lassitude of continued literary labour," he should sometimes " draw with too much liberality on a tenacious memory," no " occasional imperfections would deprive him of his praise "; in short, made up his mind that " pointed and nicely-turned lines, sedulous study, and long and repeated correction and revision " would all be dispensed with—provided their place were supplied as in Dryden by " rapidity of conception, a readiness of expressing every idea without losing anything by the way—perpetual animation and elasticity of thought—and language never laboured, never loitering, never (in Dryden's own phrase) *cursedly confined.*"

I believe that Scott had, in 1807, agreed with London booksellers as to the superintendence of two other large collections, the Somers' Tracts and the Sadler State Papers; but it seems that Constable first heard of these engagements when he accompanied the second cargo of Marmion to the great southern market; and, alarmed at the prospect of losing his hold on Scott's industry, he at once invited him to follow up his Dryden by an Edition of Swift on the same scale—offering, moreover, to double the rate of payment; that is to say, to give him £1,500 for the new undertaking. This munificent tender was accepted; and as early as May, 1808, I find Scott writing in all directions for books, pamphlets, and MSS., likely to be serviceable in illustrating the Life and Works of the Dean of St. Patrick's. While these were accumulating about him, which they soon did in greater abundance than he had anticipated, he concluded his labours on Sadler, and kept pace, at the same time with Ballantyne, as the Somers' Tracts continued to move through the press. The Sadler was published in 1809, in three large volumes, quarto; but the last of the thirteen equally ponderous tomes to which Somers extended, was not dismissed from his desk until towards the conclusion of 1812.

He also edited this year, for Murray, Strutt's unfinished romance of Queenhoo-hall, with a conclusion in the fashion of the original; for Constable, Carleton's Memoirs of the War of the Spanish Succession, to which he gave a lively preface and various notes; and the Memoirs of Robert Cary, Earl of Monmouth. The republication of Carleton,[1]

[1] It seems to be now pretty generally believed that *Carleton's Memoirs* were among the numberless fabrications of De Foe; but in this case (if the fact indeed be so), as in that of his *Cavalier,* he no doubt had before him the rude journal of some officer who had fought and bled in the campaigns described with such an air of truth.

Johnson's eulogy of which fills a pleasant page in Boswell, had probably been suggested by the interest which Scott took in the first outburst of Spanish patriotism consequent on Napoleon's transactions at Bayonne. There is one passage in the preface which I must transcribe. Speaking of the absurd recall of Peterborough from the command in which he had exhibited such a wonderful combination of patience and prudence with military daring, he says :— " One ostensible reason was, that Peterborough's parts were of too lively and mercurial a quality, and that his letters shewed more wit than became a General;—a commonplace objection, raised by the dull malignity of commonplace minds, against those whom they see discharging with ease and indifference the tasks which they themselves execute (if at all) with the sweat of their brow and in the heaviness of their hearts. There is a certain hypocrisy in business, whether civil or military, as well as in religion, which they will do well to observe who, not satisfied with discharging their duty, desire also the good repute of men." It was not long before some of the dull malignants of the Parliament House began to insinuate what at length found a dull and dignified mouthpiece in the House of Commons—that if a Clerk of Session had any real business to do, it could not be done well by a man who found time for more literary enterprises than any other author of the age undertook—" wrote more books," Lord Archibald Hamilton serenely added, " than any body could find leisure to read "—and, moreover, mingled in general society as much as many that had no pursuit but pleasure.

The eager struggling of the different booksellers to engage Scott at this time, is a very amusing feature in the voluminous correspondence before me. Had he possessed treble the energy for which it was possible to give any man credit, he could never have encountered a tithe of the projects that the post brought day after day to him, announced with extravagant enthusiasm, and urged with all the arts of conciliation. I shall mention only one out of at least a dozen gigantic schemes which were thus proposed before he had well settled himself to his Swift; and I do so, because something of the kind was a few years later carried into execution. This was a General Edition of British Novelists,—beginning with De Foe and reaching to the end of the last century—to be set forth with prefaces and notes by Scott, and printed of course by Ballantyne.

The projector was Murray, who was now eager to start on all points in the race with Constable; but this was not, as we shall see presently, the only business that prompted my enterprising friend's first visit to Ashesfiel.

Conversing with Scott, towards the end of his toils, about the tumult of engagements in which he was thus involved, he said, "Aye—it was enough to tear me to pieces—but there was a wonderful exhilaration about it all : my blood was kept at fever-pitch—I felt as if I could have grappled with anything and everything; then there was hardly one of all my schemes that did not afford me the means of serving some poor devil of a brother author. There were always huge piles of materials to be arranged, sifted, and indexed—volumes of extracts to be transcribed —journeys to be made hither and thither, for ascertaining little facts and dates,—in short, I could commonly keep half-a-dozen of the ragged regiment of Parnassus in tolerable case." I said he must have felt something like what a locomotive engine on a railway might be supposed to do, when a score of coal waggons are seen linking themselves to it the moment it gets the steam up, and it rushes on its course regardless of the burden. "Yes," said he, laughing, and making a crashing cut with his axe (for we were felling larches); "but there was a cursed lot of dung carts too." He was seldom, in fact, without some of these appendages; and I admired nothing more in him than the patient courtesy, the unwearied gentle kindness with which he always treated them, in spite of their delays and blunders, to say nothing of the almost incredible vanity and presumption which more than one of them often exhibited in the midst of their fawning; and, I believe, with all their faults, the worst and weakest of them repaid him by a canine fidelity of affection. This part of Scott's character recalls by far the most pleasing trait in that of his last predecessor in the plenitude of literary authority—Dr. Johnson. There was perhaps nothing (except the one great blunder) that had a worse effect on the course of his pecuniary fortunes, than the readiness with which he exerted his interest with the booksellers on behalf of inferior writers. Even from the commencement of his connection with Constable in particular, I can trace a continual series of such applications. They stimulated the already too sanguine publisher to numberless risks; and when these failed, the result was, in one shape or another, some corresponding deduction from the fair profits of his own literary labour. "I like well," Constable was often heard to say in the sequel, " I like well Scott's *ain bairns*—but heaven preserve me from those of his fathering ! "

Every now and then, however, he had the rich compensation of finding that his interference had really promoted the interests of some meritorious obscure. None more meritorious could be named than John Struthers, a shoemaker of Glasgow, whose very striking poem *The Poor Man's Sabbath*, being seen in MS. by Miss Joanna Baillie when on a visit to her native district, was by her recommended to Scott, and by him to Constable, who published it in 1808. Mr. Struthers made a pilgrimage of gratitude to Ashestiel, where he was received with hearty kindness ; and it is pleasing to add, that he ended his life in a very respectable position—as keeper of Stirling's Library, an old endowment in Glasgow.

James Hogg was by this time beginning to be appreciated ; and the popularity of his *Mountain Bard* encouraged Scott to more strenuous intercession in his behalf. I have before me a long array of letters on this subject, which passed between Scott and the Earl of Dalkeith and his brother Lord Montagu, in 1808. Hogg's prime ambition at this period was to procure an ensigncy in a militia regiment, and he seems to have set little by Scott's representations that the pay of such a situation was very small, and that, if he obtained it, he would probably find his relations with his brother officers far from agreeable. There was, however, another objection which Scott could not hint to the aspirant himself, but which seems to have been duly considered by those who were anxious to promote his views. Militia officers of that day were by no means unlikely to see their nerves put to the test ; and the Shepherd's—though he wrote some capital war-songs, especially *Donald Macdonald*—were not heroically strung. This was in truth no secret among his early intimates, though he had not measured himself at all exactly on that score, and was even tempted, when he found there was no chance of the militia epaulette, to threaten that he would " list for a soldier " in a marching regiment. Notwithstanding at least one melancholy precedent, the Excise, which would have suited him almost as badly as " hugging Brown Bess," was next thought of ; and the

Shepherd himself seems to have entered into that plan with considerable alacrity : but I know not whether he changed his mind, or what other cause prevented such an appointment from taking place. After various shiftings, he at last obtained from the Duke of Buccleuch's kindness, the gratuitous life-rent of a small farm in the vale of Yarrow; and had he contented himself with the careful management of its fields, the rest of his days might have been easy. But he could not withstand the attractions of Edinburgh, which carried him away from Altrive for months every year; and when at home, a warm and hospitable disposition, so often stirred by vanity less pardonable than his, made him convert his cottage into an unpaid hostelrie for the reception of endless troops of thoughtless admirers; and thus, in spite of much help and much forbearance, he was never out of one set of pecuniary difficulties before he had begun to weave the meshes of some fresh entanglement. In *pace requiescat.* There will never be such an Ettrick Shepherd again.

In May 1808, Joanna Baillie spent a week or two under Scott's roof in Edinburgh. Their acquaintance was thus knit into a deep and respectful affection on both sides; and henceforth they maintained a close epistolary correspondence, which will always be read with special interest. But within a few weeks after her departure, he was to commence another intimacy not less sincere and cordial; and one productive of a still more important series of his letters. He had now reached a period of life after which real friendships are but seldom formed; and it is fortunate that another with an Englishman of the highest class of accomplishments had been thoroughly compacted before death cut the ties between him and George Ellis—because his dearest intimates within Scotland had of course but a slender part in his written correspondence. Mr. Morritt of Rokeby and his wife had long been intimate with Lady Louisa Stuart and Mr. William Rose; and the meeting, therefore, had been well prepared for. It took place at Edinburgh in June. Scott shewed them the lions of the town and its vicinity, exactly as if he had nothing else to attend to but their gratification; and Mr. Morritt recollected with particular pleasure one long day spent in rambling along the Esk by Roslin and Hawthornden,

Where Jonson sat in Drummond's social shade,

down to the old haunts of Lasswade. "When we approached that village," he writes,—"Scott, who had laid hold of my arm, turned along the road in a direction not leading to the place where the carriage was to meet us. After walking some minutes towards Edinburgh, I suggested that we were losing the scenery of the Esk, and, besides, had Dalkeith Palace yet to see. 'Yes,' said he, 'and I have been bringing you where there is little enough to be seen—only that Scotch cottage—(one by the road side, with a small garth)—but, though not worth looking at, I could not pass it. It was our first country-house when newly married, and many a contrivance we had to make it comfortable. I made a dining-table for it with my own hands. Look at these two miserable willow-trees on either side the gate into the enclosure; they are tied together at the top to be an arch, and a cross made of two sticks over them is not yet decayed. To be sure, it is not much of a lion to shew a stranger; but I wanted to see it again myself, for I assure you that after I had constructed it, *mamma* (Mrs. Scott) and I both of us thought it so fine, we turned out to see it by moonlight, and walked backwards from it to the cottage door, in admiration of our own magnificence and its picturesque effect. I did want to see if it was still there—so now we will look after the barouche, and make the best of our way to Dalkeith.' Such were the natural feelings that endeared the Author of Marmion and the Lay to those who saw him in 'the happier hour of social pleasure.' His person at that time may be exactly known from Raeburn's first picture, which had just been executed for his bookseller Constable, and which was a most faithful likeness of him and his dog Camp. The literal fidelity of the portraiture, however, is its principal merit. The expression is serious and contemplative, very unlike the hilarity and vivacity then habitual to his speaking face, but quite true to what it was in the absence of such excitement. His features struck me at first as commonplace and heavy,—but they were almost always lighted up by the flashes of the mind within. This required a hand more masterly than Raeburn's; and indeed, in my own opinion, Chantrey alone has in his bust attained that, in his case, most difficult task of portraying the features faithfully, and yet giving the real and transient expression of the countenance when animated.

" We passed a week in Edinburgh, chiefly in his society and that of his friends the Mackenzies. We were so far on our way to Brahan Castle, in Ross-shire. Scott unlocked all his antiquarian lore, and supplied us with numberless *data*, such as no guide-book could have furnished, and such as his own Monkbarns might have delighted to give. It would be idle to tell how much pleasure and instruction his advice added to a tour in itself so productive of both, as well as of private friendships and intimacies, now too generally terminated by death, but never severed by caprice or disappointment. His was added to the number by our reception now in Edinburgh, and, on our return from the Highlands, at Ashestiel—where he had made us promise to visit him, saying that the farm-house had pigeon-holes enough for such of his friends as could live, like him, on Tweed salmon and Forest mutton. There he was the cherished friend and kind neighbour of every middling Selkirkshire yeoman, just as easily as in Edinburgh he was the companion of clever youth and narrative old age in refined society. He carried us one day to Melrose Abbey or Newark—another, to course with mountain greyhounds by Yarrow braes or St. Mary's Loch, repeating every ballad or legendary tale connected with the scenery—and on a third, we must all go to a farmer's *kirn*, or harvest-home, to dance with Border lasses on a barn floor, drink whisky punch, and enter with him into all the gossip and good-fellowship of his neighbours, on a complete footing of unrestrained conviviality, equality, and mutual respect. His wife and happy young family were clustered round him, and the cordiality of his reception would have unbent a misanthrope.

" At this period his conversation was more equal and animated than any man's that I ever knew. It was most characterised by the extreme felicity and fun of his illustrations, drawn from the whole encyclopædia of life and nature, in a style sometimes too exuberant for written narrative, but which to him was natural and spontaneous. A hundred stories, always apposite, and often interesting the mind by strong pathos, or eminently ludicrous, were daily told, which, with many more, have since been transplanted, almost in the same language, into the Waverley novels and his other writings. These, and his recitations of poetry, which can never be forgotten by those

who knew him, made up the charm that his boundless
memory enabled him to exert to the wonder of the gaping
lovers of wonders. But equally impressive and powerful
was the language of his warm heart, and equally wonderful were the conclusions of his vigorous understanding,
to those who could return or appreciate either. Among
a number of such recollections, I have seen many of the
thoughts which then passed through his mind embodied
in the delightful prefaces annexed late in life to his poetry
and novels. Those on literary quarrels and literary irritability are exactly what he then expressed. Keenly
enjoying literature as he did, and indulging his own love
of it in perpetual composition, he always maintained the
same estimate of it as subordinate and auxiliary to the
purposes of life, and rather talked of men and events than
of books and criticism. Literary fame, he always said,
was a bright feather in the cap, but not the substantial
cover of a well-protected head. This sound and manly
feeling was what I have seen described by some of his
biographers as *pride*; and it will always be thought so by
those whose own *vanity* can only be gratified by the
admiration of others, and who mistake shows for realities.
None valued the love and applause of others more than
Scott; but it was to the love and applause of those he
valued in return that he restricted the feeling—without
restricting the kindness. Men who did not, or would not,
understand this, perpetually mistook him—and, after
loading him with undesired eulogy, perhaps in his own
house neglected common attention or civility to other
parts of his family. It was on such an occasion that I
heard him murmur in my ear, ' Author as I am, I wish
these good people would recollect that I began with being
a gentleman, and don't mean to give up the character.'
Such was all along his feeling, and this, with a slight
prejudice common to Scotchmen in favour of ancient and
respectable family descent, constituted what in Grub
Street is called his *pride*. It was, at least, what Johnson would have justly called *defensive* pride. From all
other, and still more from mere vanity, I never knew any
man so remarkably free."

The farmer at whose annual *kirn* Scott and all his
household were, in those days, regular guests, was Mr.
Laidlaw, the Duke of Buccleuch's tenant on the lands of
Peel, which are only separated from the eastern terrace

of Ashestiel by the ravine and its brook. Mr. Laidlaw
was himself possessed of some landed property in the same
neighbourhood, and being considered as wealthy, and
fond of his wealth, he was usually called among the
country people *Laird Nippy*; an expressive designation
which it would be difficult to translate. Though a very
dry, demure, and taciturn old Presbyterian, he could not
resist the Sheriff's jokes; nay, he even gradually subdued
his scruples so far as to become a pretty constant attendant at his "*English printed prayers*" on the Sundays;
which, indeed, the parish-kirk being eight miles distant,
attracted by degrees more neighbours than quite suited
the capacity of the parlour-chapel. Mr. Laidlaw's wife
was a woman of superior mind and manners—a great
reader, and one of the few to whom Scott liked lending
his books; for most strict and delicate was he always in
the care of them, and indeed, hardly any trivial occurrence
ever seemed to touch his temper at all, except anything
like irreverent treatment of a book. The intercourse
between the family at Ashestiel and this worthy woman
and her children, was a constant interchange of respect
and kindness; but I remember to have heard Scott say
that the greatest compliment he had ever received in his
life was from the rigid old farmer himself, for, years after
he had left Ashestiel, he discovered casually that special
care had been taken to keep the turf seat on *the Shirra's
knowe* in good repair; and this was much from Nippy.

And here I must set down a story, which, most readers
will smile to be told, was often repeated by Scott, and
always with an air that seemed to me, in spite of his
endeavours to the contrary, as grave as the usual aspect
of Laird Nippy of the Peel. This neighbour was a distant
kinsman of his dear friend William Laidlaw;—so distant,
that elsewhere in that condition they would scarcely have
remembered any community of blood;—but they both
traced their descent, in the ninth degree, to an ancestress
who, in the days of John Knox, fell into trouble from a
suspicion of witchcraft. In her time the Laidlaws were
rich and prosperous, and held rank among the best gentry
of Tweeddale; but in some evil hour, her husband, the
head of his blood, reproached her with her addiction to
the black art, and she, in her anger, cursed the name and
lineage of Laidlaw. Her youngest son, who stood by,
implored her to revoke the malediction; but in vain. Next

day, however, on the renewal of his entreaties, she carried him with her into the woods, made him slay a heifer, sacrificed it to the power of evil in his presence, and then, collecting the ashes in her apron, invited the youth to see her commit them to the river. " Follow them," said she, " from stream to pool, as long as they float visible, and as many streams as you shall then have passed, for so many generations shall your descendants prosper. After that, they shall, like the rest of the name, be poor, and take their part in my curse." The streams he counted were nine; "and now," Scott would say, "look round you in this country, and sure enough the Laidlaws are one and all landless men, with the single exception of Auld Nippy!" Many times had I heard both him and William Laidlaw tell this story, before any suspicion got abroad that Nippy's wealth rested on insecure foundations. Year after year, we never escorted a stranger by the Peel, but I heard the tale;—and at last it came with a new conclusion;—" and now, think whatever we choose of it, my good friend is landless." He had sold his own land and quitted the Peel.

Mr. Morritt's mention of the " happy young family clustered round him " at Mr. Laidlaw's *kirn,* reminds me that I ought to say a few words on Scott's method of treating his children in their early days. He had now two boys and two girls;[1]—and he never had more. He was not one of those who take much delight in a mere infant; but no father ever devoted more time and tender care to his offspring than he did to each of his, as they reached the age when they could listen to him, and understand his talk. Like their playmates, Camp and the greyhounds, they had at all times free access to his study; he never considered their prattle as any disturbance; they went and came as pleased their fancy; he was always ready to answer their questions; and when they, unconscious how he was engaged, entreated him to lay down his pen and tell them a story, he would take them on his knee, repeat a ballad or a legend, kiss them, and set them down again to their marbles or ninepins, and resume his labour, as if refreshed by the interruption. From a very early age he made them dine at table, and " to sit up to supper " was the great reward when they had been " very good bairns."

[1] Charlotte Sophia, born in October, 1799; Walter, October, 1801; Anne, February, 1803; Charles, December, 1805.

In short, he considered it as the highest duty as well as the sweetest pleasure of a parent to be the companion of his children; he partook all their little joys and sorrows, and made his kind informal instructions to blend so easily and playfully with the current of their own sayings and doings, that so far from regarding him with any distant awe, it was never thought that any sport or diversion could go on in the right way, unless *papa* were of the party, or that the rainest day could be dull, so he were at home.

Of the irregularity of his own education he speaks with regret, in the autobiographical fragment written this year at Ashestiel; yet his practice does not look as if that feeling had been strongly rooted in his mind;--for he never did show much concern about regulating systematically what is usually called *education* in the case of his children.   It seemed, on the contrary, as if he attached little importance to anything else, so he could perceive that the young curiosity was excited—the intellect, by whatever springs of interest, set in motion.   He detested and despised the whole generation of modern children's books, in which the attempt is made to convey accurate notions of scientific minutiæ: delighting cordially, on the other hand, in those of the preceding age, which, addressing themselves chiefly to the imagination, obtain through it, as he believed, the best chance of stirring our graver faculties also.   He exercised the memory by selecting for tasks of recitation passages of popular verse the most likely to catch the fancy of children; and gradually familiarised them with the ancient history of their own country, by arresting attention, in the course of his own oral narrations, on incidents and characters of a similar description.   Nor did he neglect to use the same means of quickening curiosity as to the events of sacred history.   On Sunday he never rode —at least not until his growing infirmity made his pony almost necessary to him—for it was his principle that all domestic animals have a full right to their Sabbath of rest; but after he had read the prayers and lessons of the day, he usually walked with his whole family, dogs included, to some favourite spot at a considerable distance from the house—most frequently the ruined tower of Elibank—and there dined with them in the open air on a basket of cold provisions, mixing his wine with the water of the brook beside which they all were grouped around him on the turf; and here, or at home, if the weather kept them from

their ramble, his Sunday talk was just such a series of
biblical lessons as that which we have preserved for the
permanent use of rising generations, in his Tales of a
Grandfather on the early history of Scotland. I wish he had
committed that other series to writing too;—how different
that would have been from our thousand compilations of
dead epitome and imbecile cant! He had his Bible, the
Old Testament especially, by heart; and on these days in-
wove the simple pathos or sublime enthusiasm of Scripture,
in whatever story he was telling, with the same picturesque
richness as in his week-day tales the quaint Scotch of Pit-
scottie, or some rude romantic old rhyme from Barbour's
Bruce or Blind Harry's Wallace.

By many external accomplishments, either in girl or boy,
he set little store. He delighted to hear his daughters
sing an old ditty, or one of his own framing; but, so the
singer appeared to feel the spirit of her ballad, he was not
at all critical of the technical execution. There was one
thing, however, on which he fixed his heart hardly less
than the ancient Persians of the Cyropædia : like them,
next to love of truth, he held love of horsemanship for the
prime point of education. As soon as his eldest girl could
sit a pony, she was made the regular attendant of his
mountain rides; and they all, as they attained sufficient
strength, had the like advancement. He taught them to
think nothing of tumbles, and habituated them to his own
reckless delight in perilous fords and flooded streams; and
they all imbibed in great perfection his passion for horses
—as well, I may venture to add, as his deep reverence
for the more important article of that Persian training.
" Without courage," he said, " there cannot be truth;
and without truth there can be no other virtue."

He had a horror of boarding-schools; never allowed his
girls to learn anything out of his own house; and chose
their governess—Miss Miller—who about this time was
domesticated with them, and never left them while they
needed one,—with far greater regard to her kind, good
temper and excellent moral and religious principles, than
to the measure of her attainments in what are called
fashionable accomplishments. The admirable system of
education for boys in Scotland combines all the advantages
of public and private instruction ; his carried their satchels
to the High-School, when the family was in Edinburgh,
just as he had done before them, and shared of course the

evening society of their happy home. But he rarely,
if ever, left them in town, when he could himself be
in the country; and at Ashestiel he was, for better or
for worse, his eldest boy's daily tutor, after he began
Latin.

His letters of this autumn to such friends as Rose, Morritt, and Miss Baillie, give additional details of the pleasant
domestic life of Ashestiel. In one (Sept.) he says to Miss
Joanna :—" If you ask what I am doing, I am very like
a certain ancient king, distinguished in the Edda, who,
when Lok paid him a visit,—

> Was twisting of collars his dogs to hold,
> And combing the mane of his courser bold.

If this idle man's employment required any apology, we
must seek it in the difficulty of seeking food to make
savoury messes for our English guests ; for we are eight
miles from market, and must call in all the country sports
to aid the larder." Scott, however, had business enough
at this time, besides combing the mane of Brown Adam,
and twisting couples for Douglas and Percy. He was deep
in Swift; and the Ballantyne press was groaning under a
multitude of works, with almost all of which his hand as
well as his head had something, more or less, to do. But
a serious change was about to take place in his relations
with the spirited publishing house which had hitherto been
the most efficient supporters of that press ; and his letters
begin to be much occupied with disputes which cost him
many anxious hours in the apparently idle autumn of 1808.
Mr. Constable had then for his partner Mr. Hunter, afterwards Laird of Blackness, to whose intemperate language
much more than to any part of Constable's own conduct,
Scott ascribed this unfortunate alienation ; which, however, as well as most of my friend's subsequent misadventures, I am inclined to trace in no small degree to the influence which a third person, hitherto unnamed, was about
this time beginning to exercise over the concerns of James
Ballantyne.

John Ballantyne, a younger brother of Scott's schoolfellow, was originally destined for the paternal trade of a
merchant—(that is to say, a dealer in everything from fine
broadcloth to children's tops)—at Kelso. The father seems
to have sent him when very young to London, where, whatever else he may have done in the way of professional

training, he spent some time in the banking-house of
Messrs. Currie. On returning to Kelso, however, the
" *department* " which more peculiarly devolved upon him
was the tailoring one.[1] His personal habits had not been
improved by his brief sojourn in the Great City, and the
business, in consequence (by his own statement) of the irregularity of his life, gradually melted to nothing in his
hands. Early in 1805, his goods were sold off, and barely
sufficed to pay his debts. The worthy old couple found
refuge with their ever affectionate eldest son, who provided his father with some little occupation (real or
nominal) about the printing office; and thus John himself
again quitted his native place, under circumstances which,
as I shall shew in the sequel, had left a deep and painful
trace even upon that volatile mind. He had, however,
some taste, and he at least fancied himself to have some
talent for literature;[2] and the rise of his brother, who also
had met with no success in his original profession, was
before him. He had acquired in London great apparent
dexterity in book-keeping and accounts. He was married by this time; and it might naturally be hoped that
with the severe lessons of the past, he would now apply
sedulously to any duty that might be entrusted to him.
The concern in the Canongate was a growing one, and
James Ballantyne's somewhat indolent habits were already
severely tried by its management. The Company offered
John a salary of £200 a year as clerk, and the destitute
ex-*merchant* was too happy to accept the proposal.

He was a quick, active, intrepid little fellow; and in
society so very lively and amusing, so full of fun and merriment—such a thoroughly light-hearted droll, all-over
quaintness and humorous mimicry; and, moreover, such
a keen and skilful devotee to all manner of field-sports,
from fox-hunting to badger-baiting inclusive, that it was
no wonder he should have made a favourable impression
on Scott, when he appeared in Edinburgh in this destitute
plight, and offered to assist James in book-keeping, which
the latter never understood, or could bring himself to attend to with regularity. The contrast between the two

[1] The first time that William Laidlaw saw John Ballantyne, he
had come to Selkirk to measure the troopers of the Yeomanry
Cavalry, of whom Laidlaw was one, for new breeches.

[2] John Ballantyne, upon the marvellous success of Waverley,
wrote and published a wretched novel, called " The Widow's Lodgings."

brothers was not the least of the amusement; indeed that
continued to amuse him to the last. The elder of these is
painted to the life in an early letter of Leyden's, which, on
the Doctor's death, he, though not (I fancy) without
wincing, permitted Scott to print:—" Methinks I see you
with your confounded black beard, bull-neck, and upper
lip turned up to your nose, while one of your eyebrows is
cocked perpendicularly, and the other forms pretty well
the base of a right-angled triangle, opening your great
gloating eyes, and crying—*But Leyden!!!*" James was
a short, stout, well-made man, and would have been
considered a handsome one, but for these grotesque
frowns, starts, and twistings of his features, set off by a
certain mock-majesty of walk and gesture, which he had
perhaps contracted from his usual companions, the emperors and tyrants of the stage. His voice in talk was
grave and sonorous, and he sung well (theatrically well),
in a fine rich bass. John's tone in singing was a sharp
treble—in conversation something between a croak and a
squeak. Of *his* style of story-telling it is sufficient to say
that the late Charles Mathews's " old Scotch lady " was
but an imperfect copy of the original, which the great
comedian first heard in my presence from his lips.[1] He
was shorter than James, but lean as a scarecrow, and he
rather hopped than walked; his features, too, were naturally good, and he twisted them about quite as much, but
in a very different fashion. The elder brother was a gour-
mand—the younger liked his bottle and his bowl, as well
as, like Johnny Armstrong, " a hawk, a hound, and a fair
woman." Scott used to call the one Aldiborontiphoscophornio—the other Rigdumfunnidos. They both entertained him; they both loved and revered him; and I believe
would have shed their heart's blood in his service; but
James had serious deficiencies as a man of business, and
John was not likely to supply them. A more reckless,
thoughtless, improvident adventurer never rushed into the
serious responsibilities of commerce; but his cleverness,
his vivacity, his unaffected zeal, his gay fancy always
seeing the light side of everything, his imperturbable
good-humour, and buoyant elasticity of spirits, made and
kept him such a favourite, that I believe Scott would as
soon have ordered his dog to be hanged, as harboured, in

[1] The reader will find an amusing anecdote of Johnny in the
Memoirs of Mathews, by his widow, vol. ii. p. 382.

his darkest hour of perplexity, the least thought of dis-
carding " jocund Johnny."

The great bookseller of Edinburgh was a man of calibre
infinitely beyond the Ballantynes. Though with a strong
dash of the sanguine (without which, indeed, there can be
no great projector in any walk of life), Archibald Constable
was one of the most sagacious persons that ever followed
his profession. Mr. Thomas Campbell writes to Scott,
a year or two before this time,—" Our butteracious friend
at the Cross turns out a deep draw-well; " and another
eminent literator, still more closely connected with Constable, had already, I believe, christened him " The
Crafty." Indeed, his fair and very handsome physiognomy carried a bland astuteness of expression, not to be
mistaken by one who could read the plainest of nature's
handwriting. He made no pretensions to literature—
though he was in fact a tolerable judge of it generally, and
particularly well skilled in the department of Scotch antiquities. He distrusted himself, however, in such matters,
being conscious that his early education had been very
imperfect; and, moreover, he wisely considered the business of a critic as quite as much out of his " proper line "
as authorship itself. But of that "proper line," and his own
qualifications for it, his estimation was ample; and—often
as I may have smiled at the lofty serenity of his self-
complacence—I confess I now doubt whether he rated
himself too highly as a master in the true science of the
bookseller. He had, indeed, in his mercantile character
one deep and fatal flaw—for he hated accounts, and systematically refused, during the most vigorous years of his
life, to examine or sign a balance-sheet; but for casting a
keen eye over the remotest indications of popular taste—
for anticipating the chances of success and failure in any
given variety of adventure—for the planning and invention of his calling—he was not, in his own day at least,
surpassed; and among all his myriad of undertakings, I
question if any one that really originated with himself, and
continued to be superintended by his own care, ever did
fail. He was as bold as far-sighted—and his disposition
was as liberal as his views were wide. Had he and Scott
from the beginning trusted as thoroughly as they understood each other; had there been no third parties to step
in, flattering an overweening vanity on the one hand into
presumption, and on the other side spurring the enterprise

that wanted nothing but a bridle, I have no doubt their joint career might have been one of unbroken prosperity. But the Ballantynes were jealous of the superior mind, bearing, and authority of Constable; and though he too had a liking for them both personally—esteemed James's literary tact, and was far too much of a humorist not to be very fond of the younger brother's company—he could never away with the feeling that they intervened unnecessarily, and left him but the shadow, where he ought to have had the substantial lion's share, of confidence. On his part, again, he was too proud a man to give entire confidence where that was withheld from himself.

But in tracing the progress of the coldness which this year advanced to a complete rupture, it must be especially kept in mind that the Edinburgh Review had been the great primary source of the wealth and influence of the house of Constable. The then comparatively little-known bookseller of London, who was destined to be ultimately its most formidable rival in more than one department, has told me, that when he read the article on Marmion, and another on general politics in the same Number, he said to himself—" Walter Scott has feelings both as a gentleman and a Tory, which these people must now have wounded ;—the alliance between him and the whole clique of the Review, its proprietor included, is shaken; " and, as far at least as the political part of the affair was concerned, John Murray's sagacity was not at fault. We have seen with what thankful alacrity he accepted a small share in the adventure of Marmion—and with what brilliant success that was crowned; nor is it wonderful that a young bookseller, conscious of ample energies, should now have watched with eagerness the circumstances which seemed not unlikely to place within his own reach a more intimate connection with the first great living author in whose works he had ever had any direct interest. He forthwith took measures for improving and extending his relations with James Ballantyne, through whom, as he guessed, Scott could best be approached. His tenders of employment for the Canongate press were such that the apparent head of the firm proposed a conference at Ferry-bridge in Yorkshire; and there Murray, after detailing some of his own literary plans—particularly that already alluded to, of a Novelist's Library—in his turn sounded Ballantyne so far as to resolve on pursuing his journey

into Scotland. Ballantyne had said enough to satisfy him
that the project of setting up a new publishing house in
Edinburgh, in opposition to Constable, was already all
but matured; and he, on the instant, proposed himself for
its active co-operator in the metropolis. The printer proceeded to open his budget farther, mentioning, among other
things, that the author of Marmion had " both another
Scotch poem and a *Scotch novel* on the stocks " ; and had
moreover chalked out the design of an Edinburgh Annual
Register to be conducted in opposition to the politics and
criticism of Constable's Review. These tidings might
have been enough to make Murray proceed farther northwards; but there was a scheme of his own which had for
some time deeply occupied his mind, and the last article of
this communication determined him to embrace the opportunity of opening it in person at Ashestiel. He arrived
there about the middle of October. The 26th Number of
the Edinburgh Review, containing Mr. Brougham's article
entitled " Don Cevallos on the Usurpation of Spain," had
just been published; and one of the first things Scott
mentioned in conversation was, that he had so highly
resented the tone of that essay, as to give orders that his
name might be discontinued on the list of subscribers.[1]
Mr. Murray could not have wished better auspices for the
matter he had come to open; it was no other than the
project of a London Review on the scale of the Edinburgh;
and, for weeks ensuing, Scott's letters to Ellis, Morritt,
and other literary Tories, attest with what eager zeal he
had embraced the new scheme.

It is impossible to include more than a fragment of this
copious and curious correspondence in the present narrative; but the first letter to Ellis (Nov. 2) seems to contain,
in a few sentences, a sufficiently intelligible summary of
his main views. He says :—" The present Ministry are
not all that I could wish them—for (Canning excepted) I
doubt there is among them too much *self-seeking,* as it
was called in Cromwell's time; and what is their misfortune, if not their fault, there is not among them one in the

---

[1] When the 26th Number appeared, Mr. Scott wrote to Constable
in these terms :—" The Edinburgh Review *had* become such as to
render it impossible for me to continue a contributor to it.—*Now,*
it is such as I can no longer continue to receive or read it." The
list of the then subscribers exhibits, in an indignant dash of Constable's pen opposite Mr. Scott's name, the word " STOPT ! ! ! ".
—*R. Cadell.*

decided situation of paramount authority, both with respect to the others and to the Crown, which is, I think, necessary, at least in difficult times, to produce promptitude, regularity, and efficiency in measures of importance. But their political principles are sound English principles, and, compared to the greedy and inefficient horde which preceded them, they are angels of light and of purity. It is obvious, however, that they want defenders both in and out doors. Pitt's

> ——' Love and fear glued many friends to him;
> And now he's fallen, those tough commixtures melt.'[1]

Were this only to affect a change of hands, I should expect it with more indifference; but I fear a change of principles is designed. The Edinburgh Review tells you coolly, ' We foresee a speedy revolution in this country, as well as Mr. Cobbett; ' and, to say the truth, by degrading the person of the Sovereign—exalting the power of the French armies, and the wisdom of their counsels—holding forth that peace (which they allow can only be purchased by the humiliating prostration of our honour) is indispensable to the very existence of this country—I think, that for these two years past, they have done their utmost to hasten the accomplishment of their own prophecy. Of this work 9,000 copies are printed quarterly, and no genteel family *can* pretend to be without it, because, independent of its politics, it gives the only valuable literary criticism which can be met with. Consider, of the numbers who read this work, how many are likely to separate the literature from the politics—how many youths are there upon whose minds the flashy and bold character of the work is likely to make an indelible impression. Now, I think there is balm in Gilead for all this; and that the cure lies in instituting such a Review in London as should be conducted totally independent of bookselling influence, on a plan as liberal as that of the Edinburgh, its literature as well supported, and its principles English and constitutional. Accordingly, I have been given to understand that Mr. William Gifford is willing to become the conductor of such a work, and I have written to him a very voluminous letter on the subject. Now, should this plan succeed, you must hang your birding-piece on its hooks, take down your old Antijacobin armour, and ' remember your swashing blow.'

[1] See 3d *K. Henry IV.* Act II. Scene 6.

In point of learning, you Englishmen have ten times our scholarship; and as for talent and genius, ' Are not Abana and Pharpar, rivers of Damascus, better than any of the rivers in Israel? ' Have we not yourself and your cousin, the Roses, Malthus, Matthias, Gifford, Heber, and his brother? Can I not procure you a score of blue-caps, who would rather write for us than for the Edinburgh Review if they got as much pay by it? ' A good plot, good friends, and full of expectation—an excellent plot, very good friends ! ' "[1]

The excellent plot had too many good friends to be long a secret; nor could the rumours of Scott's share in it and other new schemes tend to soothe the irritation between him and the house of Constable. Something occurred before the end of 1808 which induced Scott to suspect that among other sources of uneasiness had been a repentant grudge as to their bargain about Swift; and on the 2nd of January 1809 I find him requesting, that if, on reflection, they thought they had hastily committed themselves, the deed might be cancelled. To this the firm did not assent : their letter expresses regret that Scott should have attached importance to " an unguarded expression " of the junior partner, " our Mr. Hunter," and the hope that " the old footing may be restored hereafter, when the misrepresentations of interested persons may cease to be remembered." Scott replies coldly, requesting that a portrait for which he had sat to Raeburn may be considered as done for himself, charged to his account, and sent to him. Mr. Constable declined, in very handsome terms, to give up the picture. But for the present the breach was complete. Among other negotiations which Scott had patronised twelve months before, was one concerning the publication of Miss Seward's Poems. On the 19th of March, he writes as follows to that lady :—" Constable, like many other folks who learn to undervalue the means by which they have risen, has behaved, or rather suffered his partner to behave, very uncivilly towards me. But they may both live to know that they should not have kicked down the ladder till they were sure of their footing. The very last time I spoke to him on business was about your poems. I understood him to decline your terms; but I had neither influence to change his opinion, nor inclination to interfere with his resolution. He is a very enterprising, and, I believe, a

[1] Hotspur—1st K. Henry IV. Act II. Scene 3.

thoroughly honest man, but his vanity in some cases over-powers his discretion."

"Our Mr. Hunter" was, I am told by friends of mine who knew him well, a man of considerable intelligence and accomplishments, to whose personal connections the house of Constable owed a great accession of business and influ-ence. He was, however, a very keen politician—in Scott's phrase, "a sort of Whig gone mad";—regarded Scott's Toryism with a fixed bitterness; and, moreover, could never conceal his impression that Scott ought to have em-barked in no other literary undertakings whatever until he had completed his edition of Swift. It is not wonderful that, not having been bred regularly to the bookselling business, he should have somewhat misapprehended the obligation which Scott had incurred when the bargain for that work was made; and his feeling of his own station and consequence was no doubt such as to give his style of conversation, on doubtful questions of business, a tone for which Scott had not been prepared by his previous inter-course with Mr. Constable. The defection of the poet was, however, at once regretted and resented by both these partners; and Constable, I am told, often vented his wrath in figures as lofty as Scott's own. "Ay," he would say, stamping on the ground with a savage smile, "Ay, there is such a thing as rearing the oak until it can support itself."

The project of the Quarterly Review was not the only declaration of hostilities. The scheme of starting a new bookselling house in Edinburgh, begun in the short-sighted heat of pique, had now been matured;—I cannot add, either with composed observation or rational forecast—for it was ultimately settled that the ostensible and chief managing partner should be a person without capital, and neither by training nor by temper in the smallest degree qualified for such a situation; more especially where the field was to be taken against long experience, consummate skill, and resources which, if not so large as all the world supposed them, were still in comparison vast, and admir-ably organised. The rash resolution was, however, carried into effect, and a deed, deposited for secrecy's sake in the hands of Scott, laid the foundation of the firm of "John Ballantyne and Co., booksellers, Edinburgh. Scott appears to have supplied all the capital, at any rate his own *one-half* share, and *one-fourth,* the portion of James, who, not having any funds to spare, must have become indebted to some one for it. It does not appear from what source John acquired his, the remaining *fourth*; but *Rigdum-funnidos* was thus installed in Hanover Street as the avowed rival of " The Crafty."

This was arranged in January. Under the same month I must mention an event often alluded to in its correspondence :—the death of Camp, the first of several dogs whose names will be " freshly remembered " as long as their master's works are popular. This favourite preserved his affection and sagacity to the last. At Ashestiel, as the servant was laying the cloth for dinner, he would say, " Camp, my good fellow, the Sheriff's coming home by the ford—or by the hill; " and the sick animal would immediately bestir himself to welcome his master, going out at the back door or the front door according to the direction given, and advancing as far as he was able, either towards the Tweed, or the Glenkinnon burn. He was buried on a fine moonlight night, in the little garden behind the house in Castle Street, immediately opposite to the window at which Scott usually sat writing. My wife told me that she remembered the whole family standing in tears about the grave, as her father himself smoothed down the turf above Camp with the saddest expression of face she had ever seen in him. He had been engaged to dine abroad that day, but apologised on account of " the death of a dear old friend "; and Mr. Macdonald Buchanan was not at all surprised that he should have done so, when it came out next morning that Camp was no more.

CHAPTER VI

London—Theatrical Anecdotes—Byron's Satire—The Lady of the Lake—Excursion to the Hebrides—Vision of Don Roderick—Byron—Davy—Crabbe—Purchase of Abbotsford. 1809–1812.

In February Mr. John Ballantyne proceeded to London, for the purpose of introducing himself to the chief publishers there in his new capacity, and especially of taking Mr. Murray's instructions respecting the Scotch management of the Quarterly Review. As soon as the spring vacation began, Mr. and Mrs. Scott followed him by sea. They stayed two months, and this being the first visit to

town since his fame had been crowned by Marmion, he
was more than ever the object of curiosity and attention.
Mr. Morritt saw much of him, and I transcribe a few
sentences from his *Memoranda* of the period.

" Scott," his friend says, " more correctly than any
other man I ever knew, appreciated the value of that
apparently enthusiastic *engouement* which the world of
London shews to the fashionable wonder of the year. The
homage paid him neither altered his opinions, nor produced the affectation of despising it; on the contrary, he
received it, cultivated it, and repaid it in its own coin.
' All this is very flattering,' he would say, ' and very civil;
and if people are amused with hearing me tell a parcel of
old stories, or recite a pack of ballads to lovely young
girls and gaping matrons, they are easily pleased, and a
man would be very ill-natured who would not give pleasure
so cheaply conferred.' If he dined with us and found any
new faces, ' Well, do you want me to play lion to-day?'
was his usual question—' I will roar if you like it to your
heart's content.' He would, indeed, in such cases put
forth all his inimitable powers of entertainment—and day
after day surprise me by their unexpected extent and
variety. Then, as the party dwindled, and we were left
alone, he laughed at himself, quoted—' Yet know that I
one Snug the joiner am—no lion fierce,' etc.—and was at
once himself again.

" He often lamented the injurious effects for literature
and genius resulting from the excitement of ambition for
this ephemeral *réputation du salon*. ' It may be a pleas-
sant gale to sail with,' he said, ' but it never yet led to a
port that I should like to anchor in;' nor did he willingly
endure, either in London or in Edinburgh, the little exclusive circles of literary society, much less their occasional fastidiousness and petty partialities. One story
which I heard of him from Dr. Howley, now Archbishop
of Canterbury (for I was not present), was very characteristic. The Doctor was one of a grand congregation of
lions, where Scott and Coleridge, *cum multis aliis*, attended at Sotheby's. Poets and poetry were the topics of
the table, and there was plentiful recitation of effusions as
yet unpublished, which of course obtained abundant applause. Coleridge repeated more than one, which, as Dr.
H. thought, were eulogised by some of the company with
something like affectation, and a desire to humble Scott

by raising a poet of inferior reputation on his shoulders. Scott, however, joined in the compliments as cordially as anybody, until, in his turn, he was invited to display some of his occasional poetry. Scott said he had nothing of his own worth their hearing, but he would repeat a little copy of verses which he had shortly before seen in a provincial newspaper, and which seemed to him almost as good as anything they had been listening to. He repeated ' Fire, Famine, and Slaughter.' The applauses that ensued were faint—then came slight criticisms, from which Scott defended the unknown author. At last a more bitter antagonist opened, and fastening upon one line, cried, ' This at least is absolute nonsense.' Scott denied the charge— the Zoilus persisted—until Coleridge, out of all patience, exclaimed, ' For God's sake let Mr. Scott alone—I wrote the poem.'

" He often complained of the dulness of parties where each guest arrived under the implied obligation of exhibiting some extraordinary powers of talk or wit. ' If,' he said, ' I encounter men of the world, men of business, odd or striking characters of professional excellence in any department, I am in my element, for they cannot lionise me without my returning the compliment and learning something from them.' He was much with George Ellis, Canning, and Croker, and delighted in them —as indeed who did not?—but he loved to study eminence of every class and sort, and his rising fame gave him easy access to gratify all his curiosity."

The meetings with Canning, Croker, and Ellis, to which Morritt alludes, were, as may be supposed, chiefly occupied with the affairs of the Quarterly Review. The first number appeared while Scott was in London: and contained three articles from his pen.

On his way back to Scotland, he spent some days more with Morritt, at Rokeby Park, on the northern boundary of Yorkshire; and he was so delighted by the scenery of the rivers Tees and Greta, which have their confluence within the demesne, and so interested with his host's traditional anecdotes of the Cavaliers of the Rokeby lineage, that he resolved on connecting a poem with these fair landscapes. But he had already, I presume, begun the Lady of the Lake; for, on his arrival at Edinburgh, he undertook that it should be finished by the end of the year. In July he revisited all the localities so dear to him

in the days of his juvenile rambling, which he had chosen
for the scene of his fable. He gave a week to Cambusmore, and ascertained, in his own person, that a good
horseman might gallop from Loch Vennachar to Stirling
within the space allotted to Fitz-James. He then, under
the guidance of Mr. Macdonald Buchanan, explored Loch
Lomond, Arrochar, Loch Sloy, and all the scenery of a
hundred conflicts between the Macfarlanes, the Col-
quhouns, and the Clan Alpine. At Buchanan House,
which is very near Ross Priory, Lady Douglas and Lady
Louisa Stuart were visiting the Duke of Montrose; he
joined them there, and read to them the Stag Chase,
which he had just completed under the full influence of
the *genius loci.*

It was at Buchanan that he first saw Lord Byron's
" English Bards and Scotch Reviewers." I need not reprint here what he says, in an essay in 1830, on his " share
in the flagellation of their famous satire," viz.—

> Next view in state, proud prancing on his roan,
> The golden-crested haughty Marmion—

down to

> For this we spurn Apollo's venal son,
> And bid a long *good-night to Marmion.*

But it is amusing enough to contrast with that graceful
" Introduction " the plain words of a letter to Southey,
written in August 1809. He there says :—" If I were
once in possession of my reversionary income, I would do
nothing but what I pleased, which might be another
phrase for doing very little. I was always an admirer of
the modest wish of a retainer in one of Beaumont and
Fletcher's plays—

> ' I would not be a serving man, to carry the cloak-bag still,
> Nor would I be a falconer, the greedy hawks to fill ;
> But I would be in a good house, and have a good master too,
> For I would eat and drink of the best, and *no* work would I do.' [1]

In the meantime, it is funny enough to see a whelp of a
young Lord Byron abusing me, of whose circumstances he
knows nothing, for endeavouring to scratch out a living
with my pen. God help the bear, if, having little else to
eat, he must not even suck his own paws. I can assure
the noble imp of fame it is not my fault that I was not
born to a park and £5,000 a year, as it is not his lordship's merit, although it may be his great good fortune,

[1] *The Knight of the Burning Pestle.*

that he was not born to live by his literary talents or success."

About this time several travesties of Scott's poetry, I do not recollect by whom, were favourably noticed in some of the minor reviews, and appear to have annoyed Mr. Morritt. Scott's only remark on *The Lay of the Scotch Fiddle*, etc., etc., is in a very miscellaneous letter to that friend :—" As to those terrible parodies which have come forth, I can only say with Benedict, *A college of such wit-mongers cannot flout me out of my humour.* Had I been conscious of one place about my temper, were it even, metaphorically speaking, the tip of my heel, vulnerable to this sort of aggression, I have that respect for mine own ease, that I would have shunned being a candidate for public applause, as I would avoid snatching a honey-comb from among a hive of live bees." When, three years later, all the world laughed over James Smith's really admirable *Death of Clutterbuck*, in the " Rejected Addresses," no one laughed more heartily than the author of Marmion.

To this period belong two stories, which it would be unfair to suppress. It is a rare case when a large family does not include a frail member. Walter Scott's youngest brother Daniel was such.[1] After many luckless adventures, he obtained, through the poet's connection with George Ellis, a post of responsibility on a West Indian estate; but in a moment of danger, his nerves shewed the effects of continued dissipation. He was dismissed, and died soon afterwards at Edinburgh, under his mother's roof—but his brother would never see him, nor would he attend his funeral, or wear mourning for him. Thus sternly, when in the height and pride of his blood, could Scott, whose heart was never hardened against the distress of an enemy, recoil from the disgrace of a brother. It is a more pleasing part of my duty to add, that he spoke to me, twenty years afterwards, in terms of great and painful contrition for the austerity with which he had conducted himself on this occasion. I must add, moreover, that he took a warm interest in a natural child whom Daniel had bequeathed to his mother's care; and after the old lady's death, religiously supplied her place as the boy's protector.

The other story is connected with his ever dear brother

[1] See Chap. I., ante, p. 12.

Thomas, in whose hands, as has been mentioned above, the business that he inherited did not prosper. Walter, as Clerk of Session, had the patronage of several offices in the Register House at Edinburgh, and he appointed Thomas to one of these, by no means so lucrative as others at his disposal, but welcome under the circumstances. Thomas soon after found it convenient to withdraw for a time to the Isle of Man; and while he was there the Government introduced a Bill, by which his *extractorship*, and many other little places of the sort, were to be abolished, the holders receiving some compensation by way of annuity. Some keen Edinburgh partisans suggested to the Earl of Lauderdale (then at the head of the Whig interest in Scotland) that Walter Scott had foreseen the abolition of the post when he bestowed it on Thomas—that Thomas was discharging its small duties by deputy—and that in his case *compensation* would be only the successful crowning of a job. Scott, in his letters to friends, both Whig and Tory, denies indignantly that either he or Thomas had anticipated the abolition of the office, and intimates his conviction that the parliamentary opposition to the compensation sprang entirely from the wish to hurt his own feelings. Lord Lauderdale's amendment was lost in the House of Peers. Indeed no other Peer spoke in favour of it except Lord Holland; and Scott resented that speech warmly, because his Lordship seemed to have " gone out of his way " in meddling about a small Scotch matter. It happened unluckily that Lord Holland visited Edinburgh within a few weeks afterwards, and he was then introduced by Scott's friend, Mr. Thomas Thomson, at a dinner of *the Friday Club*.[1] The poet, in a letter to his brother, says : " We met accidentally at a public party. He made up to me, but I remembered his part in your affair, and *cut* him with as little remorse as an old pen." Two gentlemen who were present inform me that they distinctly remember a very painful scene for which, knowing Scott's habitual good-nature and urbanity, they had been wholly unprepared. One of them (Lord Jeffrey) adds, that this was the only example of rudeness he ever witnessed in him in the course of a lifelong

[1] *The Friday Club* was instituted in June 1803—on the model, I believe, of Johnson's at the Turk's Head. Scott, Thomson, and most of their intimates at the Bar were original members. The great majority were Whigs. They dined at Fortune's tavern.

familiarity. It is consolatory to add, that he enjoyed much agreeable intercourse in after days with Lord Holland.

I willingly turn from these dregs of politics to some other matters, which about this time occupied a large share of his thoughts. He had from his boyish days a great love for theatrical representation; and so soon as circumstances enabled him to practise extended hospitality, the chief actors of his time, whenever they happened to be in Scotland, were among the most acceptable of his guests. Mr. Charles Young was, I believe, the first of them of whom he saw much : as early as 1803 I find him writing of that gentleman to the Marchioness of Abercorn as a valuable addition to the society of Edinburgh; and down to the end of Scott's life, Mr. Young was never in the north without visiting him. Another graceful performer, of whom he saw a great deal in his private circle, was Miss Smith, afterwards Mrs. Bartley. But at the period of which I am now treating, his principal theatrical intimacy was with John Philip Kemble, and his sister Mrs. Siddons, both of whom he appears to have often met at Lord Abercorn's villa near Stanmore. Of John Kemble's character and manners, he has recorded his impressions in a pleasing reviewal of Mr. Boaden's Memoir. The great tragedian's love of black-letter learning afforded a strong bond of fellowship; and I have heard Scott say that the only man who ever seduced him into very deep potations in his middle life was Kemble. He was frequently at Ashestiel, and a grave butler, by name *John Macbeth*, made sore complaints of the bad hours kept on such occasions in one of the most regular of households; but the watchings of the night were not more grievous to " Cousin Macbeth," as Kemble called the honest *beauffetier*, than were the hazards and fatigues of the morning to the representative of " the Scotch usurper." Kemble's miseries during a rough gallop were quite as grotesque as those of his namesake, and it must be owned that species of distress was one from the contemplation of which his host could never derive anything but amusement.

I have heard Scott chuckle with particular glee over the recollection of an excursion to the vale of the Ettrick, near which river the party were pursued by a bull. " Come, King John," said he, " we must even take the water ; " and accordingly he and his daughter Sophia plunged into the stream. But King John, halting on the bank, and surveying the river, which happened to be full and turbid, exclaimed, in his usual solemn manner,

> ——" The flood is angry, Sheriff;
> Methinks I'll get me up into a tree."[1]

It was well that the dogs had succeeded in diverting the bull, because there was no tree at hand which could have sustained King John, nor, had that been otherwise, could so stately a personage have dismounted and ascended with such alacrity as circumstances would have required. He at length followed his friends through the river with the rueful dignity of Don Quixote.

It was this intercourse which led Scott to exert himself strenuously about 1809, to prevail on Mr. Henry Siddons, the nephew of Kemble, to undertake the lease and management of the Edinburgh Theatre. On this occasion he purchased a share, and became one of the acting trustees; and thenceforth, during a long series of years, he continued to take a very lively concern in the proceedings of the Edinburgh company. In this he was plentifully encouraged by his domestic *camarilla*; for his wife had all a Frenchwoman's passion for the *spectacle*; and the elder Ballantyne was a regular newspaper critic of theatrical affairs, and in that capacity had already attained a measure of authority supremely gratifying to himself.

The first new play produced by Henry Siddons was the Family Legend of Joanna Baillie. This was, I believe, the first of her dramas that ever underwent the test of representation in her native kingdom; and Scott exerted himself most indefatigably in its behalf. He was consulted about all the *minutiæ* of costume, attended every rehearsal and supplied the prologue. The play was better received than any other which the gifted authoress has since subjected to the same experiment; and how ardently Scott enjoyed its success may be seen in many letters which he addressed to his friend on the occasion.

It was at a rehearsal of this piece that Scott was first

---

[1] John Kemble's most familiar table-talk often flowed into blank verse; and so indeed did his sister's. Scott (who was a capital mimic) often repeated her tragic exclamation to a footboy during a dinner at Ashestiel—

> " You've brought me water, boy—I ask'd for beer."

Another time, dining with a Provost of Edinburgh, she ejaculated, in answer to her host's apology for his *pièce de resistance*—

> " Beef cannot be too salt for me, my lord!"

introduced to another theatrical performer—who ere long acquired a large share of his regard and confidence—Mr. Daniel Terry. He had received a good education, and been regularly trained as an architect; but abandoned that profession at an early period of life, and was now beginning to attract attention as a valuable actor in Henry Siddons's company. Already he and the Ballantynes were constant companions, and through his familiarity with them, Scott had abundant opportunities of appreciating his many excellent and agreeable qualities. He had the manners and feelings of a gentleman. Like John Kemble, he was deeply skilled in the old literature of the drama, and he rivalled Scott's own enthusiasm for the antiquities of *vertu*. Their epistolary correspondence in after days was frequent, and none so well illustrates many of the poet's minor tastes and habits. As their letters lie before me, they appear as if they had all been penned by the same hand. Terry's idolatry of his new friend induced him to imitate his writing so zealously, that Scott used to say, if he were called on to swear to any document, the utmost he could venture to attest would be, that it was either in his own hand or in Terry's. The actor, perhaps unconsciously, mimicked him in other matters with hardly inferior pertinacity. His small lively features had acquired, before I knew him, a truly ludicrous cast of Scott's graver expression; he had taught his tiny eyebrow the very trick of the poet's meditative frown; and to crown all, he so habitually affected his tone and accent, that, though a native of Bath, a stranger could hardly have doubted he must be a Scotchman. These things afforded all their acquaintance much diversion; but perhaps no Stoic could have helped being secretly gratified by seeing a clever and sensible man convert himself into a living type and symbol of admiration.

Charles Mathews and Terry were once thrown out of a gig together, and the former received an injury which made him halt ever afterwards, while the latter escaped unhurt. "Dooms, *Dauniel*," said Mathews when they next met, "what a pity that it wasna your luck to get the game leg, mon! Your *Shirra* would hae been the very thing, ye ken, an' ye wad hae been croose till ye war coffined!" Terry, though he did not always relish bantering on this subject, replied readily and good-humouredly by a quotation from Peter Pindar's *Bozzy and Piozzi* :—

" When Foote his leg by some misfortune broke,
    Says I to Johnson, all by way of joke,
    Sam, sir, in Paragraph will soon be clever,
    He'll take off Peter better now than ever."

Mathews's mirthful caricature of Terry's sober mimicry of Scott was one of the richest extravaganzas of his social hours; but indeed I have often seen this Proteus dramatise the whole Ballantyne group with equal success—while Rigdumfunnidos screamed with delight, and Aldiborontiphoscophornio faintly chuckled, and the Sheriff, gently smiling, pushed round his decanters.[1]

Scott had by the end of 1809 all but completed his third great poem; yet this year also was crowded with miscellaneous literary labours. In it he made great progress with Swift, and in it he finished and saw published his edition of the Sadler Papers; the notes copious, curious, lively and entertaining, and the Life of Sir Ralph a very pleasing specimen of his style. Several volumes of the huge Somers' Collection, illustrated throughout with similar care, were also issued in 1809; and I suppose he received his fee for each volume as it appeared—the whole sum amounting, when the last came out in 1812, to 1,300 guineas. His labours on these collections were gradually storing his mind with that minute knowledge of the leading persons and events both of Scotch and English history, which made his conversation on such subjects that of one who had rather lived with than read about the departed. He delighted in them, and never complained that they interrupted disadvantageously the works of his higher genius. But he submitted to many less agreeable tasks—among others, at this same period, to a good deal of trouble entailed on him by the will of Miss Seward. Dying in March 1809, she bequeathed her poetry to Scott, with an injunction to publish it speedily, and prefix a sketch of her life; while she made her letters (of which she had kept copies) the property of Constable. Scott superintended, accordingly, the edition of the lady's verses which was published in three volumes by John Ballantyne; and Constable lost no time in announcing her corre-

[1] Perhaps the very richest article in Mathews's social budget was the scene alleged to have occurred when he himself communicated to the two Ballantynes the new titles which the Sheriff had conferred on them. Rigdum's satisfaction with his own cap and bells, and the other's indignant incredulity, passing by degrees into tragical horror, made, I am told, a delicious contrast.

spondence—an announcement which the poet observed with trepidation; for few had suffered more than himself from her epistolary restlessness. He says to an authoress of a different breed (Miss Baillie)—" The despair which I used to feel on receiving poor Miss Seward's letters, whom I really liked, gave me a most unsentimental horror for sentimental letters. I am now doing penance for my ill-breeding, by submitting to edit her posthumous poetry, most of which is absolutely execrable. This, however, is the least of my evils, for when she proposed this bequest to me, which I could not in decency refuse, she combined it with a request that I would publish her whole literary correspondence. This I declined on principle, having a particular aversion at perpetuating that sort of gossip; but what availed it? Lo! to ensure the publication, she left it to an Edinburgh bookseller; and I anticipate the horror of seeing myself advertised for a live poet like a wild beast on a painted streamer; for I understand all her friends are depicted therein in body, mind, and manners."

Mr. Constable, however, took this opportunity of re-opening his intercourse with Scott, and gave him essential relief by allowing him to draw his pen through Miss Seward's extravagant eulogies on himself and his poetry. This attention so gratified him, that he authorised John Ballantyne to ask, in his name, that experienced bookseller's advice respecting the poem now nearly completed, the amount of the first impression, and other professional details. Mr. Constable readily gave the assistance thus requested, and would willingly have taken any share they pleased in the adventure. They had completed their copyright arrangements before these communications occurred, and the triumphant success of the *coup d'essai* of the new firm was sufficient to close Scott's ears for a season against any propositions of the like kind from the house at the Cross; but from this time there was no return of anything like personal ill-will between the parties.

Early in May the Lady of the Lake came out—as her two elder sisters had done—in all the majesty of quarto, with every accompanying grace of typography, and with moreover an engraved frontispiece of Saxon's portrait of Scott; the price of the book two guineas. For the copyright the poet had nominally received 2,000 guineas, but as John Ballantyne and Co. retained three-fourths of the

# Life of Sir Walter Scott 211

property to themselves (Miller of London purchasing the other fourth), the author's profits were, or should have been, more than this.

Mr. Cadell, the publisher of this Memoir, then a young man in training for his profession, retains a strong impression of the interest which the quarto excited before it was on the counter. "James Ballantyne," he says, "read the cantos from time to time to select coteries, as they advanced at press. Common fame was loud in their favour; a great poem was on all hands anticipated. I do not recollect that any of all the author's works was ever looked for with more intense anxiety, or that any one of them excited a more extraordinary sensation when it did appear. The whole country rang with the praises of the poet—crowds set off to view the scenery of Loch Katrine, till then comparatively unknown; and as the book came out just before the season for excursions, every house and inn in that neighbourhood was crammed with a constant succession of visitors. It is a well-ascertained fact, that from the date of the publication of the Lady of the Lake, the post-horse duty in Scotland rose in an extraordinary degree, and indeed it continued to do so regularly for a number of years, the author's succeeding works keeping up the enthusiasm for our scenery which he had thus originally created."—Mr. Cadell adds, that four 8vo editions followed the quarto within the space of twelve months; that these carried the early sale to 20,000 copies; and that by July 1836 the legitimate sale in Great Britain had been not less than 50,000 copies; since which date I understand that, in spite of legal and illegal piracies, the fair demand has been well kept up.

In their reception of this work, the critics were for once in full harmony with each other, and with the popular voice. The article in the Quarterly was written by George Ellis; but its eulogies, though less discriminative, are not a whit more emphatic than those of Mr. Jeffrey in the rival Review. Indeed, I have always considered this last paper as the best specimen of contemporary criticism on Scott's poetry. The Lay, if I may venture to state the creed now established, is, I should say, generally considered as the most natural and original, Marmion as the most powerful and splendid, the Lady of the Lake as the most interesting, romantic, picturesque, and graceful of his great poems.

Of its success he speaks as follows in 1830:—" It was certainly so extraordinary as to induce me for the moment to conclude that I had at last fixed a nail in the proverbially inconstant wheel of Fortune. But, as the celebrated John Wilkes is said to have explained to King George the Third, that he himself was never a Wilkite, so I can with honest truth exculpate myself from having been at any time a partisan of my own poetry, even when it was in the highest fashion with the million."

James Ballantyne has preserved in his *Memorandum* an anecdote strikingly confirmative of the most remarkable statement in this page of Scott's confessions. " I remember," he says, " going into his library shortly after the publication of the Lady of the Lake, and finding Miss Scott (who was then a very young girl) there by herself. I asked her—' Well, Miss Sophia, how do you like the Lady of the Lake?' Her answer was given with perfect simplicity—' Oh, I have not read it: papa says there's nothing so bad for young people as reading bad poetry.'"

In fact, his children in those days had no idea of the source of his distinction—or rather, indeed, that his position was in any respect different from that of other Advocates, Sheriffs, and Clerks of Session. The eldest boy came home one afternoon about this time from the High School, with tears and blood hardened together upon his cheeks.—" Well, Wat," said his father, " what have you been fighting about to-day?" With that the boy blushed and hung his head, and at last stammered out—that he had been called a *lassie*. " Indeed!" said Mrs. Scott, " this was a terrible mischief, to be sure." "You may say what you please, mamma," Wat answered roughly, " but I dinna think there's a *waufer* (shabbier) thing in the world than to be a lassie, to sit boring at a clout." Upon further inquiry it turned out that one or two of his companions had dubbed him *The Lady of the Lake*, and the phrase was to him incomprehensible, save as conveying some imputation on his prowess, which he accordingly vindicated in the usual style of the Yards. Of the poem he had never before heard. Shortly after, this story having got wind, one of Scott's colleagues of the Clerks' Table said to the boy—(who was in the home circle called *Gilnockie*, from his admiration of Johnny Armstrong)— ' Gilnockie, my man, you cannot surely help seeing that great people make more work about your papa than they do about me or any other of your *uncles*—what is it do you suppose that occasions this?" The little fellow pondered for a minute or two, and then answered very gravely— "It's commonly *him* that sees the hare sitting." And yet this was the man that had his children all along so very much with him. In truth, however, young Walter had guessed pretty shrewdly in the matter, for his father had all the tact of the Sutherland Highlander, whose detection of an Irish rebel up to the neck in a bog, he has commemorated in a note upon Rokeby. Like him, he was quick to catch the *sparkle* of the victim's eye; and often said jestingly of himself, that whatever might be thought of him as a *maker* (poet), he was an excellent *trouveur*.

Ballantyne adds:—"One day about this same time, when his fame was supposed to have reached its acmé, I said to him—'Will you excuse me, Mr. Scott, but I should like to ask you what you think of your own genius as a poet, in comparison with that of Burns?' He replied— 'There is no comparison whatever—we ought not to be named in the same day.' 'Indeed!' I answered; 'would you compare Campbell to Burns?' 'No, James, not at all—If you wish to speak of a real poet, Joanna Baillie is now the highest genius of our country.'—But, in fact," (continues Ballantyne)—"he had often said to me that neither his own nor any modern popular style of composition was that from which he derived most pleasure. I asked him what it was. He answered—Johnson's; and that he had more pleasure in reading *London*, and *The Vanity of Human Wishes,* than any other poetical composition he could mention; and I think I never saw his countenance more indicative of high admiration than while reciting aloud from those productions."

In his sketch of Johnson's Life, Scott says—"The deep and pathetic morality of *The Vanity of Human Wishes* has often extracted tears from those whose eyes wander dry over pages professedly sentimental." The last line of MS. that he sent to the press was a quotation from the same piece. Yet it is the cant of our day—above all, of its poetasters—that Johnson was no poet. To be sure, they say the same of Pope—and hint it occasionally even of Dryden.

Walter Scott was at this epoch in the highest spirits, and having strong reasons of various kinds for his resolution to avail himself of the gale of favour, only hesitated in which quarter to explore the materials of some new romance. His first and most earnest desire was " to take a peep at Lord Wellington and his merrymen in the Peninsula,—where," he says, " I daresay I should have picked up some good materials for battle scenery "; and he afterwards writes with envy of the way in which a young barrister of his acquaintance (the late excellent John Miller of Lincoln's Inn, K.C.) spent the long vacation of that year—having the good luck to arrive at Oporto when our army was in retreat for the frontier, and after travelling through a country totally deserted, to hear suddenly, in a low glen, the distant sound of a bagpipe—be welcomed by the officers of a Highland Regiment—and next day witness (rifle in hand) the Battle of Busaco. But Scott dropped his Peninsular plan on perceiving that it gave his wife " more distress than could be compensated by any gratification of his own curiosity." He then thought of revisiting Rokeby—for, as was mentioned already, he had from the first day that he spent there designed to connect its localities with his verse. But the burst of enthusiasm which followed the appearance of the Lady of the Lake finally swayed him to undertake a journey, deeper than he had as yet gone, into the *Highlands*, and a warm invitation from the Laird of Staffa easily induced him to add a voyage to the *Hebrides*. He was accompanied by his wife, his daughter Sophia, Miss Hannah Mackenzie, daughter of " The Man of Feeling," and a dear friend and distant relation, Mrs. Apreece (now Lady Davy), who had been, as he says in one of his letters, " a lioness of the first magnitude in Edinburgh " during the preceding winter. He travelled slowly with his own horses, through Argyleshire, as far as Oban; but even where post-horses might have been had, this was the mode he always preferred in these family excursions, for he delighted in the liberty it afforded him of alighting and lingering as often and as long as he chose; and, in truth, he often performed the far greater part of the day's journey on foot—examining the map in the morning so as to make himself master of the bearings—and following his own fancy over some old disused riding track, or along the margin of a stream, while the carriage, with its female occupants, adhered to the proper road. Of the insular part of the expedition we have many details in the appendages to the Lord of

the Isles—and others not less interesting in the Notes
which he contributed to Croker's Edition of Boswell. The
private letters of 1810 dwell with delight on a scene which
it was, indeed, special good fortune for him to witness :—
the arrival among the Mackinnons of their young chief
(since well known as M.P. for Lymington), whose ancestors had sold or forfeited their insular territory, but could
not alienate the affectionate veneration of their clan. He
also expatiates with hearty satisfaction on the patriarchal
style of the hospitality of Mulva, where the Laird of Staffa
(a brother of his colleague Mr. Macdonald Buchanan)
lived among " a people distractedly fond of him," cheered
by their adherence to the native soil from which so
many of the neighbouring tribes were yearly emigrating,
proudly and hopefully encouraging their growth in numbers, and doing whatever he could to keep up the old
manners and the old spirit of his region—" his people
doubled and his income trebled." But this is a picture to
which we cannot now revert without pain and regret; for
changes in public polity within a few years destroyed
utterly the ease and prosperity which the poet witnessed.
Like so many others of his class, that gay and high-
spirited gentleman was destined to see his fond people
pine around him in destitution, until the majority of them
also took refuge beyond the Atlantic,—and there was left
to himself only the name and shadow of that fair possession, of which, on his death, the last fragment—the rocky
Staffa itself—had to be parted with by his children.

On returning from this pleasant expedition, and establishing himself at Ashestiel, Scott, in searching an old
desk for fishing-flies one morning, found the forgotten
MS. of the first two or three chapters of *Waverley*.
From a letter of James Ballantyne's on now reading these
chapters, it is plain that he was not their unfavourable
critic of 1805; but though he augured " success " if the
novel were completed, he added that he could not say
" how much," and honestly confessed that the impression
made on his mind was far from resembling that he had
received from the first specimen of the *Lady of the Lake* :
and once more the fated MS. was restored to its hiding-
place. But this was not the only unwelcome communication from that quarter. Already their publishing adventure began to wear a bad aspect. Between 1805 and the
Christmas of 1809, Scott invested in the Ballantyne firms

not less than £9,000; by this time probably there had been a farther demand on his purse; and now the printer's triumph in the fast multiplying editions of the Lady of the Lake was darkened with ominous reports about their miscellaneous speculations—such as the Beaumont and Fletcher of Weber—the "Tixall Poetry"—and the History of the Culdees by Dr. Jamieson. But a still more serious business was the Edinburgh Annual Register. Its two first volumes were issued about this time, and expectation had been highly excited by the announcement that the historical department was in the hands of Southey, while Scott and other eminent persons were to contribute to its miscellaneous literature and science. Mr. Southey was fortunate in beginning his narrative with the great era of the Spanish Revolt against Napoleon, and it exhibited his usual research, reflection, elegance, and spirit. The second volume contained some of his most admired minor poems; and Scott enriched it both with verse and prose. Nevertheless, the public were alarmed by the extent of the history, and the prospect of two volumes annually. This was, in short, a new periodical publication on a large scale; all such adventures are hazardous; none of them can succeed, unless there be a skilful bookseller, and a zealous editor, who give a large share of their industry and intelligence, day after day, to its arrangements. Such a bookseller John Ballantyne was not; such an editor, with Scott's multifarious engagements, he could not be. The volumes succeeded each other at irregular intervals; there was soon felt the want of one ever active presiding spirit; and though the work was continued during a long series of years, it never profited the projectors.

The first *livraison* included an essay of some length by Scott on the proposed changes in the Scotch law and judicature, which had occupied Sir Ilay Campbell's Commission : and the sagacity of this piece appears as creditable to him as the clear felicity of its language. I fancy few English lawyers will now deny that their criminal system at least had more need to borrow from Scotland, than hers from theirs. However, his essay strongly deprecated the commencement of a general innovation; and though the condition of the Ballantyne affairs was already uneasy, and his correspondence shews that he fretted occasionally under the unrecompensed drudgery of his clerkship, still I cannot but suspect that his repugnance to these legal novelties had a share in producing the state of mind indicated by a letter of November 1810, to his brother Thomas. He there says : " I have no objection to tell you in confidence, that, were Dundas to go out Governor-General to India, and were he willing to take me with him in a good situation, I would not hesitate to pitch the Court of Session and the booksellers to the Devil, and try my fortune in another climate." He adds, " but this is strictly *entre nous* "—nor indeed was I aware, until I found this letter, that he had ever entertained such a design as that which it communicates. Mr. Dundas (now Lord Melville) being highly acceptable to the Court of Directors in the office of President of the Board of Control, which he long filled, was spoken of at various times as likely to be appointed Governor-General. He had no doubt hinted to Scott, that in case he should ever assume that station, it would be agreeable for him to be accompanied by his early friend : and there could be little question of Scott's capacity to have filled with distinction the part either of an Indian secretary or of an Indian judge. But enough of what was but a passing dream. The buoyancy of his temperament had sustained no lasting depression—and his circumstances before the lapse of another year underwent a change which for ever fixed his destiny to the soil of his best affections and happiest inspirations.

Meantime, unflagging was the interest with which, among whatever labours and anxieties, he watched the progress of the great contest in the Peninsula. It was so earnest, that he never on any journey, not even in his very frequent passages between Edinburgh and Ashestiel, omitted to take with him the largest and best map he had been able to procure of the seat of war ; upon this he was perpetually poring, tracing the marches and countermarches of the French and English by means of black and white pins ; and not seldom did Mrs. Scott complain of this constant occupation of his attention and her carriage. In the beginning of 1811 a committee was formed in London to collect subscriptions for the relief of the Portuguese, who had seen their lands wasted and their houses burnt in the course of Massena's last campaign ; and Scott, on reading the advertisement, addressed the chairman, begging to contribute the profits, to whatever they might amount, of the first edition of a poem connected with the localities of the patriotic struggle.   His offer was accepted.   The *Vision of Don Roderick* was published, in 4to, in July; and the money forwarded to the board. Lord Dalkeith writes thus :—" Those with ample fortunes and thicker heads may easily give 100 guineas to a subscription, but the man is really to be envied who can draw that sum from his own brains, and apply the produce to so exalted a purpose."

The *Vision* had features of novelty, both as to the subject and the manner of the composition, which gave rise to some sharp controversy.   The main fable was indeed from the most picturesque region of old romance; but it was made throughout the vehicle of feelings directly adverse to those with which the Whig critics had all along regarded the interference of Britain in behalf of the nations of the Peninsula; and the silence which, while celebrating our other generals on that scene of action, had been preserved with respect to Scott's own gallant countryman, Sir John Moore, was considered or represented by them as an odious example of genius hoodwinked by the influence of party.   Nor were there wanting persons who affected to discover that the charm of Scott's poetry had to a great extent evaporated under the severe test to which he had exposed it, by adopting, in place of those comparatively light and easy measures in which he had hitherto dealt, the most elaborate one that our literature exhibits.   The piece, notwithstanding the complexity of the Spenserian stanza, had been very rapidly executed; and it shows, accordingly, many traces of negligence.   But the patriotic inspiration of it found an echo in the vast majority of British hearts; many of the Whig oracles themselves acknowledged that the difficulties of the metre had been on the whole successfully overcome; and even the hardest critics were compelled to express unqualified admiration of various detached pictures and passages, which, in truth, as no one now disputes, neither he nor any other poet ever excelled.   The whole setting or framework—whatever relates to the Last of the Goths himself—was, I think, even then unanimously pronounced admirable; and no party feeling could blind any man to the heroic splendour of such stanzas as those in which the three equally gallant elements of a British army are contrasted.   I incline to

believe that the choice of the measure had been in no small
degree the result of hints from more than one friendly
critic on the subject of his favourite octosyllabics.

Of the letters addressed to him soon after the *Vision*
appeared, he has preserved several which had no doubt
interested and gratified him at the time. But I am very
sure no one was so welcome as that which reached him,
some months after his poem had ceased to be new in
England, from a dear friend who, after various chances
and changes, was then serving as a captain in the 58th
regiment. "Last spring," says he (Lisbon, Aug. 31), " I
was so fortunate as to get a reading of the Lady of the
Lake, when in the lines of Torres Vedras, and thought
I had no inconsiderable right to enter into and judge of
its beauties, having made one of the party on your first
visit to the Trossachs. While the book was in my
possession, I had nightly invitations to *evening parties!*
and I must say that (though not conscious of much merit
in the way of recitation) my attempts to do justice to the
grand opening of the stag-hunt were always followed
with bursts of applause—for this canto was the favourite
among the rough sons of the fighting Third Division.
At that time supplies of various kinds were scanty;—
and, in gratitude, I am bound to declare that to the good
offices of the Lady I owed many a nice slice of ham and
rummer of hot punch." The gallant and gastronomical
Captain (now Sir Adam) Fergusson (who did not by the
by escape suspicions of having been a little glanced at
in *Dalgetty*) was no less heartily regaled on the arrival
of The Vision " *ex dono auctoris.*" He again writes
(6th October), " I relished much the wild and fanciful
opening of the introductory part; yet what particularly
delighted me were the stanzas announcing the approach
of the British fleets and armies; and I can assure you the
Pats are, to a man, enchanted with the picture drawn
of their countrymen, and the mention of the great man
himself. Your swearing, in the true character of a minstrel, ' shiver my harp, and burn its every chord,' amused
me not a little.—Should it be my fate to survive, I am
resolved to try my hand on a snug little farm either up
or down the Tweed, somewhere in your neighbourhood;
and on this dream many a delightful castle do I build."
At least one of the knight's *chateaux en Espagne* was, as
we shall see, realised in the sequel. I must not omit a

circumstance which Scott learned from another source, and which he always took special pride in relating. In the course of the day when the Lady of the Lake first reached Fergusson, he was posted with his company on a point of ground exposed to the enemy's artillery. The men were ordered to lie prostrate on the ground; while they kept that attitude, the Captain, kneeling at their head, read aloud the battle of Canto VI., and the listening soldiers only interrupted him by a joyous huzza whenever the shot struck the bank close above them.

I have alluded to some hints of Ellis, Canning, and others, in disparagement of octosyllabics. Having essayed, probably to please these friends, the most difficult of all English measures in Don Roderick, Scott this year tried also the heroic couplet, and produced *The Poacher*—on seeing which, Crabbe, as his biographer tells us, exclaimed, " This man, whoever he is, can do all that I can, and *something more*." This piece, an imitation of Moore, and another of *Scott*, were published in the Register, with a preface, entitled The Inferno of Altesidora, in which he shadows out the chief reviewers of the day, especially Jeffrey and Gifford, with admirable breadth and yet lightness of pleasantry; but he kept his secret as to this Inferno and all its appendages, even from Miss Baillie—to whom he says, on their appearance, that —" the imitation of Crabbe had struck him as good; that of Moore as bad; and that of himself as beginning well, but falling off grievously to the close." It is curious to trace the beginnings of the systematic mystification which he afterwards put in practice. The quarto edition of Don Roderick having rapidly gone off, instead of reprinting the poem as usual in a separate octavo, he inserted it entire in the Register; a proof how much that undertaking was felt to require extraordinary efforts.

Throughout 1811 his serious labour continued to be bestowed on the Swift; but this and all other literary tasks were frequently interrupted in consequence of a step which he took early in the year. He had now at last the near prospect of emolument from his Edinburgh post. For, connected with the other reforms in the Scotch judicature, was a plan for allowing the retirement of functionaries, who had served to an advanced period of life, upon pensions—while the effective Clerks of Session were to be paid not by fees, but by fixed salaries of

£1,300; and contemplating a speedy accession of income so considerable as this, he resolved to place himself in the situation to which he had probably from his earliest days looked forward as the highest object of ambition, that of a Tweedside Laird.—*Sit mihi sedes utinam senectæ!*

And the place on which he had fixed his views, though not to the common eye very attractive, had long been one of peculiar interest for him. I have often heard him tell, that when travelling in boyhood with his father from Selkirk to Melrose, the old man desired the carriage to halt at the foot of an eminence, and said, "We must get out here, Walter, and see a thing quite in your line." His father then conducted him to a rude stone on the edge of an acclivity about half a mile above the Tweed, which marks the spot—

> Where gallant Cessford's life-blood dear
> Reeked on dark Elliot's border spear.

This was the conclusion of the battle of Melrose, fought in 1526, between the Earls of Angus and Home and the two chiefs of the race of Kerr on the one side, and Buccleuch on the other, in sight of the young King James V., the possession of whose person was the object of the contest. This battle is often mentioned in the Border Minstrelsy, and the reader will find a long note on it, under the lines which I have just quoted from the Lay of the Last Minstrel. In the names of *Skirmish-field, Charge-Law,* and so forth, various incidents of the fight have found a lasting record; the spot where the retainer of Buccleuch terminated the pursuit by the mortal wound of Kerr of Cessford (ancestor of the Dukes of Rox-burghe), has always been called *Turn-again.* In his own future domain the young minstrel had before him the scene of the last great Clan-battle of the Borders.

On the 12th of May 1811, he writes thus to James Ballantyne,—"My lease of Ashestiel is out. I have, therefore, resolved to purchase a piece of ground sufficient for a cottage and a few fields. There are two pieces, either of which would suit me, but both would make a very desirable property indeed. They stretch along the Tweed, on the opposite side from Lord Somerville, and could be had for between £7,000 and £8,000—or either separate for about half the sum. I have serious thoughts of one or both, and must have recourse to my pen to make the matter easy. The worst is the difficulty which John might find in advancing so large a sum as the copyright of a new poem; supposing it to be made payable within a year at farthest from the work going to press,—which would be essential to my purpose. Yet the Lady of the Lake came soon home. I have a letter this morning giving me good hope of my Treasury business being carried through : if this takes place, I will buy both the little farms, which will give me a mile of the beautiful turn of Tweed above Gala-foot—if not, I will confine myself to one. It is proper John and you should be as soon as possible apprised of these my intentions, which I believe you will think reasonable in my situation, and at my age, while I may yet hope to sit under the shade of a tree of my own planting. I hope this Register will give a start to its predecessors ; I assure you I shall spare no pains. John must lend his earnest attention to clear his hands of the quire stock, and to taking in as little as he can unless in the way of exchange ; in short, reefing our sails, which are at present too much spread for our ballast."

It would no doubt have been wise not to buy land at all until he had seen the Treasury arrangement as to his clerkship completed—until he had completed also the poem on which he relied mainly for the purchase-money ; above all, until " John reefed his sails " ; but he contented himself with one of the farms, that comprising the scene of Cessford's slaughter; the cost being £4,000 —one-half of which was borrowed of his brother, Major John Scott, the other, raised by the Ballantynes, on the security of the long-meditated *Rokeby*. The seller, the Rev. Dr. Douglas, holding the living of Galashiels, in the same neighbourhood, had never resided on the property, and his efforts to embellish it had been limited to one stripe of firs, so long and so narrow that Scott likened it to a black hair-comb. It ran from the precincts of the homestead to near *Turn-again*, and has bequeathed the name of *the Doctor's redding-kame* to the mass of nobler trees amidst which its dark straight line can now hardly be traced. The farm consisted of a meadow or *haugh* along the banks of the river, and a tract of undulated ground behind, all in a neglected state, undrained, wretchedly enclosed, much of it covered with the native heath. The house was small and poor, with a common

kail-yard on one flank, and a staring barn on the other;
while in front appeared a filthy pond covered with ducks
and duckweed, from which the whole tenement had
derived the unharmonious designation of *Clarty Hole.*
But the Tweed was everything to him—a beautiful river,
flowing broad and bright over a bed of milkwhite pebbles,
unless here and there where it darkened into a deep pool,
overhung as yet only by the birches and alders which
had survived the statelier growth of the primitive Forest;
and the first hour that he took possession he claimed for
his farm the name of the adjoining *ford*, situated just
above the influx of the classical tributary Gala. As might
be guessed from the name of *Abbotsford*, these lands
had all belonged of old to the great Abbey of Melrose;
and indeed the Duke of Buccleuch, as the territorial
representative of that religious brotherhood, still retains
some seignorial rights over them and almost all the surrounding district. Another feature of no small interest in
Scott's eyes was an ancient Roman road leading from the
Eildon hills to this ford, the remains of which, however,
are now mostly sheltered from view amidst his numerous
plantations. The most graceful and picturesque of all
the monastic ruins in Scotland, the Abbey of Melrose
itself, is visible from any points in the immediate neighbourhood of the house; and last, not least, on the rising
ground full in view across the river, the traveller may
still observe the chief traces of that celebrated British
barrier, the *Catrail.* Such was the territory on which his
prophetic eye already beheld rich pastures, embosomed
among flourishing groves, where his children's children
should thank the founder. To his brother-in-law Mr.
Carpenter he writes, " I have bought a property extending along the banks of the river Tweed for about half-a-
mile. This is the greatest incident which has lately taken
place in our domestic concerns, and I assure you we are
not a little proud of being greeted as *laird* and *lady* of
Abbotsford. We will give a grand gala when we take
possession of it, and as we are very *clannish* in this
corner, all the Scots in the country, from the Duke to
the peasant, shall dance on the green to the bagpipes,
and drink whisky punch."

About the same time he tells Miss Baillie:—" My
dreams about my cottage go on. My present intention
is to have only two spare bed-rooms, with dressing-

rooms, each of which will on a pinch have a couch bed; but I cannot relinquish my Border principle of accommo- dating all the cousins and *duniwastles*, who will rather sleep on chairs, and on the floor, and in the hay-loft, than be absent when folks are gathered together; and truly I used to think Ashestiel was very much like the tent of Periebanou, in the Arabian Nights, that suited alike all numbers of company equally; ten people fill it at any time, and I remember its lodging thirty-two with- out any complaint. As for the *go-about* folks, they generally pay their score one way or other; and to con- fess the truth, I do a little envy my old friend Abouhassan his walks on the bridge of Bagdad, and evening conver- sations and suppers with the guests whom he was never to see again in his life; he never fell into a scrape till he met with the Caliph—and, thank God, no Caliphs frequent the brigg of Melrose, which will be my nearest Rialto at Abbotsford."

In answering this letter, Miss Baillie says, very prettily :—" Yourself and Mrs. Scott, and the children, will feel sorry at leaving Ashestiel, which will long have a consequence, and be the object of kind feelings with many, from having once been the place of your residence. If I should ever be happy enough to be at Abbotsford, you must take me to see Ashestiel too. I have a kind of tenderness for it, as one has for a man's first wife, when you hear he has married a second." The same natural sentiment is expressed in a manner character- istically different, in a letter from the Ettrick Shepherd : —" Are you not sorry at leaving *auld Ashestiel* for *gude an' a*, after being at so much trouble and expense in making it a complete thing? Upon my word I was, on seeing it in the papers."

In January 1812, Scott entered upon the enjoyment of his proper salary as a Clerk of Session, which, with his sheriffdom, gave him from this time till very near the close of his life a professional income of £1,600 a year.

The next of his letters to Joanna Baillie is curious, as giving his first impressions on reading Childe Harold. " It is, I think, a very clever poem, but gives no good symptom of the writer's heart or morals. Although there is a caution against it in the preface, you cannot for your soul avoid concluding that the author, as he gives an account of his own travels, is also doing so in his own character. Now really this is too bad : vice ought to be a little more modest, and it must require impudence at least equal to the noble Lord's other powers, to claim sympathy gravely for the ennui arising from his being tired of his wassailers and his paramours. Yet with all this conceit and assurance, there is much poetical merit in the book, and I wish you would read it." A month later, he writes in a similar strain to Morritt (May 12), but concludes thus :—" This is upon the whole a piece of most extraordinary power, and may rank its author with our first poets."

Lord Byron was, I need not say, the prime object of interest this season in the fashionable world of London ; nor did the Prince Regent owe the subsequent hostilities of the noble Poet to any nelgect on his part. Mr. Murray, the publisher of the Romaunt, on hearing, on the 29th of June, Lord Byron's account of his introduction to his Royal Highness, conceived that, by communicating it to Scott, he might afford the opportunity of such a personal explanation between his two poetical friends, as should obliterate whatever painful feelings had survived the allusions to Marmion in the English Bards and Scotch Reviewers; and this good-natured step had the desired consequences. Whether or not Scott supposed that Byron had been privy to Murray's movement, I cannot say; but the senior and the offended party considered that it became him to take the initiative. In his first letter to Byron, after some warm praise of Childe Harold, he passes to the old Marmion story and says :—" The poem, my Lord, was *not* written upon contract for a sum of money—though it is too true that it was sold and published in a very unfinished state (which I have since regretted), to enable me to extricate myself from some engagements which fell suddenly upon me, by the unex-pected misfortunes of a very near relation. So that, to quote statute and precedent, I really come under the case cited by Juvenal, though not quite in the extremity of the classic author—

> Esurit, intactam Paridi nisi vendit Agaven.

As for my attachment to literature, I sacrificed for the pleasure of pursuing it very fair chances of opulence and professional honours, at a time of life when I fully knew their value; and I am not ashamed to say that in deriving

advantages in compensation from the partial favour of
the public, I have added some comforts and elegancies
to a bare independence. I am sure your Lordship's good
sense will easily put this unimportant egotism to the
right account, for—though I do not know the motive
would make me enter into controversy with a fair or an
unfair literary critic—I may be well excused for a wish
to clear my personal character from any tinge of mer-
cenary or sordid feeling in the eyes of a contemporary
of genius. Your Lordship will likewise permit me to add,
that you would have escaped the trouble of this explanation, had I not understood that the satire alluded to had
been suppressed, not to be reprinted. For in removing a
prejudice on your Lordship's own mind, I had no intention of making any appeal by or through you to the
public, since my own habits of life have rendered my
defence as to avarice or rapacity rather too easy." Lord
Byron in answer says:—" I feel sorry that you should
have thought it worth while to notice the evil works of
my nonage, as the thing is suppressed *voluntarily*, and
your explanation is too kind not to give me pain. The
Satire was written when I was very young and very
angry, and fully bent on displaying my wrath and my wit,
and now I am haunted by the ghosts of my wholesale
assertions. I cannot sufficiently thank you for your
praise; and now, waiving myself, let me talk to you of
the Prince Regent. He ordered me to be presented to
him at a ball : and after some sayings, peculiarly pleasing
from royal lips, as to my own attempts, he talked to me
of you and your immortalities; he preferred you to
every bard past and present, and asked which of your
works pleased me most. It was a difficult question. I
answered, I thought the Lay. He said his own opinion
was nearly similar. In speaking of the others, I told him
that I thought you more particularly the poet of *Princes*,
as *they* never appeared more fascinating than in Marmion
and the Lady of the Lake. He was pleased to coincide,
and to dwell on the description of your Jameses as no
less royal than poetical. He spoke alternately of Homer
and yourself, and seemed well acquainted with both. I
defy Murray to have exaggerated his Royal Highness's
opinion of your powers; but it may give you pleasure to
hear that it was conveyed in language which would only
suffer by my attempting to transcribe it; and with a tone

and taste which gave me a very high idea of his abilities
and accomplishments, which I had hitherto considered as
confined to *manners*, certainly superior to those of any
living *gentleman*."—Scott immediately (July 16) rejoined
in terms of frank kindness, inviting Byron to visit him
at Abbotsford, where he had now established himself.—
"Although," he says, "I am living in a gardener's hut,
and although the adjacent ruins of Melrose have little to
tempt one who has seen those of Athens, yet, should you
take a tour which is so fashionable at this season, I
should be very happy to have an opportunity of introducing you to anything remarkable in my fatherland.
The fair, or shall I say the sage, Apreece that was, Lady
Davy that is, is soon to show us how much science she
leads captive in Sir Humphry; so your Lordship sees,
as the citizen's wife says in the farce, ' Threadneedle
Street has some charms,' since they procure us such celebrated visitants. As for me, I would rather cross-question
your Lordship about the outside of Parnassus, than learn
the nature of the contents of all the other mountains in
the world. Pray, when under ' its cloudy canopy ' did
you hear anything of the celebrated Pegasus? Some say
he has been brought off with other curiosities to Britain,
and now covers at Tattersall's. I would fain have a cross
from him out of my little moss-trooper's Galloway, and
I think your Lordship can tell me how to set about it,
as I recognise his true paces in the high-mettled description of Ali Pacha's military court."

The correspondence thus begun erelong assumed a
tone of unaffected friendliness equally honourable to both
these great competitors, without rivalry, for the favour of
the literary world.

The date of the letter last quoted immediately preceded
that of Scott's second meeting with another of the most
illustrious of his contemporaries. He had met Davy at
Mr. Wordsworth's when in the first flush of his celebrity
in 1804, and been, as one of his letters states, much
delighted with "the simple and unaffected style of his
bearing—the most agreeable characteristic of high
genius." Sir Humphry, now at the summit of his fame,
had come, by his marriage with Scott's accomplished
relation, into possession of an ample fortune; and he and
his bride were among the first of the poet's visitants in
the original cabin at Abbotsford.

It was also this year that the first correspondence took place between Scott and Crabbe. The contrast of their epistolary styles is highly amusing; for Mr. Crabbe was as yet quite the simple country clergyman; but there is something better than amusement to be derived from observing the cordial confidence which a very little intercourse was sufficient to establish between men so different from each other in most of the habits of life. It will always be considered as one of the most pleasing peculiarities in Scott's history, that he was the friend of every great contemporary poet; yet I could hardly name one of them who, manly principles and the cultivation of literature apart, had many points of resemblance to him; and surely not one who had fewer than Crabbe.

He had finally left Ashestiel at Whitsuntide; and the day when this occurred was a sad one for many a poor neighbour—for they lost, both in him and his wife, very generous protectors.   In such a place, among the few evils which counterbalance so many good things in the condition of the peasantry, the most afflicting is the want of access to medical advice.   As far as their means and skill would go, they had both done their utmost to supply this want; and Mrs. Scott, in particular, had made it her business to visit the sick in their scattered cottages, and bestowed on them the contents of her medicine-chest as well as of the larder and cellar, with the same unwearied kindness that I observed in her afterwards as lady of Abbotsford.   Their children remembered the parting scene as one of unmixed affliction—but it had had its lighter features.   Among the English friends whom Scott owed to his frequent visits at Rokeby, none had a higher place in his regard than Lady Alvanley, the widow of the celebrated Chief-Justice of the Common Pleas.   To her, on the 25th, he says,—"The neighbours have been much delighted with the procession of my furniture, in which old swords, bows, targets, and lances made a very conspicuous show.   A family of turkeys was accommodated within the helmet of some *preux* chevalier of ancient Border fame; and the very cows, for aught I know, were bearing banners and muskets.   I assure your ladyship that this caravan, attended by a dozen of ragged rosy peasant children, carrying fishing-rods and spears, and leading ponies, greyhounds, and spaniels, would, as it crossed the Tweed, have furnished no bad subject for the pencil, and really reminded me of one of the gypsey groups of Callot upon their march."

The necessary alterations on the old farm-house immediately commenced; and besides raising its roof and projecting some of the lower windows, a rustic porch, a supplemental cottage at one end, and a fountain to the south, soon made their appearance.

CHAPTER VII

Publication of Rokeby and the Bridal of Triermain—Commercial Difficulties—Reconciliation with Constable—Death of Weber—Voyage to the Shetland, Orkney, and Hebridean Islands—Publication of the Life and Works of Swift—and of Waverley. 1812–1814.

THIS was one of the busiest summers of his busy life. Till the 12th of July he was at his post in the Court of Session five days every week; but every Saturday evening found him at Abbotsford, to observe the progress his labourers had made within doors and without in his absence; and on Monday night he returned to Edinburgh. Even before the Summer Session commenced, he appears to have made some advance in his Rokeby, for he writes to Mr. Morritt, from Abbotsford, on the 4th of May—" As for the house and the poem, there are twelve masons hammering at the one, and one poor noddle at the other —so they are both in progress "; and his literary tasks throughout the long vacation were continued under the same sort of disadvantage. That autumn he had, in fact, no room at all for himself. The only parlour which had been hammered into habitable condition served at once for dining-room, drawing-room, school-room, and study. A window looking to the river was kept sacred to his desk; an old bed-curtain was nailed up across the room close behind his chair, and there, whenever the spade, the dibble, or the chisel (for he took his full share in all the work on hand) was laid aside, he plied his pen, apparently undisturbed and unannoyed by the surrounding confusion of masons and carpenters, to say nothing of the lady's small talk, the children's babble among themselves, or their repetition of their lessons. The truth no doubt was, that when at his desk he did little more, as far as regarded *poetry*, than write down the lines which he had fashioned in his mind while pursuing his vocation as a planter. By and by, he says to Terry:—" The acorns are coming up fast, and Tom Purdie is the happiest and most consequential person in the world. My present work is building up the well with some *débris* from the Abbey. The worst of all is, that while my trees grow and my fountain fills, my purse, in an inverse ratio, sinks to zero." He then adds that he has at least been relieved of one of his daily labours, that of hearing his boy Walter's lesson, by " a gallant son of the church, who with one leg of wood, and another of oak, walks to and fro from Melrose every day for that purpose." This was Mr. George Thomson, son of the minister of Melrose, who, when the house afforded better accommodation, was and continued for many years to be domesticated at Abbotsford. Scott had always a particular tenderness towards persons afflicted with any bodily misfortune; and Thomson, whose leg had been amputated in consequence of a rough casualty of his boyhood, had a special share in his favour from the high spirit with which he refused at the time to betray the name of the companion that had occasioned his mishap, and continued ever afterwards to struggle against its disadvantages. Tall, vigorous, athletic, a dauntless horseman, and expert at the singlestick, George formed a valuable as well as picturesque addition to the *tail* of the new laird, who often said, " In the Dominie, like myself, accident has spoiled a capital lifeguardsman." His many oddities and eccentricities in no degree interfered with the respect due to his amiable feelings, upright principles, and sound learning; nor did *Dominie Thamson* at all quarrel in after times with the universal credence of the neighbourhood that he had furnished many features for the inimitable personage whose designation so nearly resembled his own; and if he never " wagged his head " in a " pulpit o' his ain," he well knew it was not for want of earnest and long-continued intercession on the part of the author of Guy Mannering.

For many years Scott had accustomed himself to proceed in the composition of poetry along with that of prose essays of various descriptions; but it is a remarkable fact that he chose this period of perpetual noise and bustle, when he had not even a summer-house to himself, for the new experiment of carrying on two poems at the

same time—and this too without suspending the heavy
labour of his Swift, to say nothing of lesser matters in
which the Ballantynes were, from day to day, calling for
the assistance of his judgment and his pen. In the same
letter in which Erskine acknowledges the receipt of the
first four pages of Rokeby, he adverts also to the Bridal
of Triermain as in rapid progress. Certain fragments of
verse which were mentioned as being inserted in the
Register of 1811 under the guise of *Imitations of Walter
Scott*, had attracted considerable notice; the secret of
their authorship was well kept; and by some means,
even in the shrewdest circles of Edinburgh, the belief had
become prevalent that they came from Erskine. Scott
had no sooner completed his bargain as to Rokeby, than
he resolved to pause from time to time in its composition,
and weave those fragments into a lighter romance, to be
published anonymously, in a small volume, as nearly as
possible on the same day with the avowed quarto. He
expected great amusement from the comparisons which
the critics would no doubt indulge themselves in drawing
between himself and this humble candidate; and Erskine
good-humouredly entered into the scheme, undertaking to
do nothing which should effectually suppress the notion
of his having set himself up as a modest rival to his
friend. Nay, he suggested a further refinement, which
in the sequel had no small share in the success of this
little plot upon the sagacity of the reviewers. " To prevent," he writes, " any discovery from your prose, what
think you of putting down your ideas of what the preface
ought to contain, and allowing me to write it over? And
perhaps a quizzing review might be concocted." This
hint was welcome; and among other parts of the preface
to *The Bridal of Triermain* which " threw out the knowing ones," certain Greek quotations are now accounted
for. Scott, on his part, appears to have studiously interwoven into the piece allusions to personal feelings and
experiences more akin to his friend's history and character than to his own; and he did so still more largely,
when repeating this experiment, in Harold the Dauntless.

The same post which conveyed Erskine's letter above
quoted, brought him an equally wise and kind one in
answer to a fresh application for details about the Valley
of the Tees. Scott had promised to spend part of this
autumn with Morritt; but now, busied with his planting,

and continually urged by Ballantyne to have the Quarto ready by Christmas, he would willingly have trusted his friend's knowledge in place of his own research. Morritt urgently represented, in reply, the expediency of a leisurely personal inspection; adding, " I shall always feel your friendship as an honour : we all wish our honours to be permanent : and yours promises mine at least a fair chance of immortality. I hope, however, you will not be obliged to write in a hurry. If you want a few hundreds independent of these booksellers, your credit is so very good, now that you have got rid of your Old Man of the Sea, that it is no great merit to trust you, and I happen at this moment to have five or six for which I have no sort of demand :—so rather than be obliged to spur Pegasus beyond the power of pulling him up when he is going too fast, do consult your own judgment, and set the midwives of the trade at defiance." This appeal was not to be resisted. Scott accepted Morritt's friendly offer so far as to ask his assistance in having some of his printer's bills discounted : and he proceeded the week after to Rokeby, travelling on horseback, his eldest boy and girl on their ponies, while Mrs. Scott followed in the carriage. Halting at Flodden to expound the field to his young folks, he found that Marmion had benefited the public house there very largely; and the village Boniface, overflowing with gratitude, expressed his anxiety to have a *Scott's Head* for his sign-post. The poet demurred to this proposal, and assured mine host that nothing could be more appropriate than the portraiture of a foaming tankard, which already surmounted his doorway. "Why, the painter-man has not made an ill job," said the landlord, " but I would fain have something more connected with the book that has brought me so much custom." He produced a well-thumbed copy, and handing it to the author, begged he would at least suggest a motto from the tale of Flodden Field. Scott opened the book at the death scene of the hero, and his eye was immediately caught by the " Inscription " in black letter—

> " Drink, weary pilgrim, drink, and pray
> For the kind soul of Sibyl Grey."

" Well, my friend," said he, " what more would you have? You need but strike out one letter in the first of these lines, and make your painter-man, the next time he

comes this way, print between the jolly tankard and your
own name

'Drink, weary pilgrim, drink, and PAY.'"

Scott was delighted to find, on his return, that this
suggestion had been adopted, and for aught I know, the
romantic legend may still be visible.

At Rokeby he remained about a week; and how he
spent it is well told in Mr. Morritt's *Memorandum*:—
" The morning after he arrived he said—' You have often
given me materials for romance—now I want a good
robber's cave, and an old church of the right sort.' We
rode out, and he found what he wanted in the ancient
slate quarries of Brignal and the ruined Abbey of Egglestone. I observed him noting down even the peculiar
little wild-flowers and herbs on the side of a bold crag
near his intended cave of Guy Denzil; and could not
help saying, that as he was not to be upon oath in his
work, daisies, violets, and primroses would be as poetical
as any of the humble plants he was examining. I
laughed, in short, at his scrupulousness; but I understood him when he replied, ' that in nature herself no
two scenes were exactly alike, and that whoever copied
truly what was before his eyes, would possess the same
variety in his descriptions, and exhibit apparently an
imagination as boundless as the range of nature in the
scenes he recorded; whereas—whoever trusted to imagination, would soon find his own mind circumscribed
and contracted to a few favourite images, and the repetition of these would sooner or later produce that very
monotony and barrenness which had always haunted
descriptive poetry in the hands of any but the patient
worshippers of truth. Besides which,' he said, ' local
names and peculiarities make a fictitious story look so
much better in the face.' In fact, from his boyish habits,
he was but half satisfied with the most beautiful scenery
when he could not connect with it some local legend; and
when I was forced sometimes to confess with the Knife-
grinder, 'Story! God bless you! I have none to tell,
sir '—he would laugh and say, ' Then let us make one—
nothing so easy as to make a tradition.'" Mr. Morritt
adds, that he had brought with him about half the Bridal
of Triermain—and promised himself particular satisfaction in *laying a trap for Jeffrey.*

Crowded as this year was with multifarious cares and tasks—the romance of Rokeby was finished before the close of 1812. Though it had been long in hand, the MS. bears abundant evidence of its being the *prima cura*: three cantos at least reached the printer through the Melrose post—written on paper of various sorts and sizes—full of blots and interlineations—the closing couplets of a despatch now and then encircling the page, and mutilated by the breaking of the seal.

According to the recollection of Mr. Cadell, though James Ballantyne read the poem, as the sheets were advancing, to his usual circle of *dilettanti*, their whispers were far from exciting in Edinburgh such an intensity of expectation as had been witnessed in the case of The Lady of the Lake. He adds, however, that it was looked for with undiminished anxiety in the south. I well remember, being in those days a young student at Oxford, how the booksellers' shops there were beleaguered for the earliest copies, and how he that had been so fortunate as to secure one was followed to his chambers by a tribe of friends, all as eager to hear it read as ever horse-jockeys were to see the conclusion of a match at Newmarket; and indeed not a few of those enthusiastic academics had bets depending on the issue of the struggle, which they considered the elder favourite as making to keep his own ground against the fiery rivalry of Childe Harold.

On the day of publication (January 12, 1813), Scott writes gaily enough to Morritt, from his seat at the Clerks' table:—" The book has gone off here very bobbishly; for the impression of 3,000 and upwards is within two or three score of being exhausted, and the demand for these continuing faster than they can be boarded. I am heartily glad of this, for now I have nothing to fear but a bankruptcy in the Gazette of Parnassus; but the loss of five or six thousand pounds to my good friends and school companions would have afflicted me very much. I wish we could whistle you here to-day. Ballantyne always gives a christening dinner, at which the Duke of Buccleuch[1] and a great many of my friends are formally feasted. He has always the best singing that can be heard in Edinburgh, and we have usually a very pleasant

[1] Charles Earl of Dalkeith became Duke of Buccleuch in January 1812, on the death of Duke Henry his father.

party, at which your health as patron and proprietor of
Rokeby will be faithfully and honourably remembered."

It will surprise no one to hear that Mr. Morritt assured
his friend he considered Rokeby as the best of all his
poems. The admirable, perhaps the unique fidelity of the
local descriptions, might alone have swayed, for I will not
say it perverted, the judgment of the lord of that beautiful
and thenceforth classical domain; and, indeed, I must
admit that I never understood or appreciated half the charm
of this poem until I had become familiar with its scenery.
But Scott himself had not designed to rest his strength on
these descriptions. He said to his printer while the work
was in progress (September), " I hope the thing will do,
chiefly because the world will not expect from *me* a
poem of which the interest turns upon *character* "; and in
another letter (October), " I think you will see the same
sort of difference taken in all my former poems,—of which
I would say, if it is fair for me to say anything, that the
force in the Lay is thrown on style—in Marmion on description—and in the Lady of the Lake, on incident." Possibly
some of these distinctions may have been matters of after-
thought; but as to Rokeby there can be no mistake. Of
its principal characters no one who compares the poem
with his novels will doubt that, had he undertaken their
portraiture in prose, they would have come forth with effect
hardly inferior to any of all the groups he ever created.
As it is, I question whether even in his prose there is anything more exquisitely wrought out, as well as fancied, than
the whole contrast of the two rivals for the love of the
heroine; and that heroine herself has a very particular interest attached to her. Writing to Miss Edgeworth five
years after this time (1818), he says, " I have not read
one of my poems since they were printed, excepting last
year the Lady of the Lake, which I liked better than I
expected, but not well enough to induce me to go through
the rest—so I may truly say with Macbeth—

> I am afraid to think of what I've done—
> Look on't again I dare not.

This much of *Matilda* I recollect—(for that is not so easily
forgotten)—that she was attempted for the existing person
of a lady who is now no more, so that I am particularly
flattered with your distinguishing it from the others, which
are in general mere shadows." I can have no doubt that
the lady he here alludes to was the object of his own un-

fortunate first love; and as little, that in the romantic
generosity both of the youthful poet who fails to win her
higher favour, and of his chivalrous competitor, we have
before us something more than a mere shadow.

In spite of these graceful characters, the inimitable
scenery on which they are presented, and the splendid vivacity and thrilling interest of several chapters in the story—
such as the opening interview of Bertram and Wycliff—the
flight up the cliff on the Greta—the first entrance of the
cave at Brignal—the firing of Rokeby Castle—and the
catastrophe in Egglestone Abbey;—in spite certainly of
exquisitely happy lines profusely scattered throughout the
whole composition, and of some detached images—that of
the setting of the tropical sun in Canto VI., for example—
which were never surpassed by any poet;—in spite of all
these merits, the immediate success of Rokeby was greatly
inferior to that of the Lady of the Lake; nor has it ever
since been so much a favourite with the public at large as
any other of his poetical romances.   He ascribes this
failure, in his Introduction of 1830, partly to the radically
unpoetical character of the Roundheads; but surely their
character has its poetical side also, had his prejudices allowed him to enter upon its study with impartial sympathy.
Partly he blames the satiety of the public ear, which had
had so much of his rhythm, not only from himself, but
from dozens of mocking-birds, male and female, all more
or less applauded in their day, and now all equally forgotten.   This circumstance, too, had probably no slender
effect; the more that, in defiance of all the hints of his
friends, he now repeated (with more negligence) the uniform octosyllabic couplets of the Lady of the Lake, instead
of recurring to the more varied cadence of the Lay or
Marmion.   It is fair to add that, among the London circles
at least, some sarcastic flings in Mr. Moore's " Twopenny
Post Bag " may have had an unfavourable influence on this
occasion.[1]   But the cause of failure which the poet himself
places last, was unquestionably the main one.   The deeper
and darker passion of Childe Harold, the audacity of its
morbid voluptuousness, and the melancholy majesty of the
numbers in which it defied the world, had taken the general
imagination by storm; and Rokeby, with many beauties
and some sublimities, was pitched, as a whole, on a key
which seemed tame in the comparison.

[1] See the Epistle of Lady Corke—and that of Messrs. Lackington.

I have already adverted to the fact that Scott felt it a relief, not a fatigue, to compose the Bridal of Triermain *pari passu* with Rokeby. In answer, for example, to one of his printer's letters, he says, " I fully share in your anxiety to get forward the grand work; but, I assure you, I feel the more confidence from coquetting with the guerilla." The quarto was followed, within two months, by the small volume which had been designed for a twin-birth;—the MS. had been transcribed by one of the Ballantynes themselves, in order to guard against any indiscretion of the press-people; and the mystification, aided and abetted by Erskine, in no small degree heightened the interest of its reception. Except Morritt, Scott had no English confidant. Whether any of his companions in the Parliament House were in the secret, I have never heard; but I can scarcely believe that any of those who had known him and Erskine from their youth upwards, could have believed the latter capable either of the invention or the execution of this airy and fascinating romance in little. Mr. Jeffrey, as it happened, made a voyage that year to America, and thus lost the opportunity of immediately expressing his opinion either of Rokeby or of Triermain. The Quarterly critic seems to have been completely deceived. " The diction (he says) undoubtedly reminds us of a rhythm and cadence we have heard before; but the sentiments, descriptions, and characters, have qualities that are native and unborrowed." If this writer was (as I suppose) Ellis, he no doubt considered it as impossible that Scott should have engaged in such a scheme without giving him a hint of it; but to have admitted into the secret any one who was likely to criticise the piece seriously, would have been to sacrifice the very object of the device. Erskine's own suggestion, that " perhaps a quizzical review might be got up," led, I believe, to nothing more important than a paragraph in one of the Edinburgh newspapers. He may be pardoned for having been not a little flattered to find it generally considered as not impossible that he should have written such a poem; and I have heard James Ballantyne say, that nothing could be more amusing than the style of his coquetting on the subject while it was yet fresh; but when this first excitement was over, his natural feeling of what was due to himself, as well as to his friend, dictated many a remonstrance; and, though he ultimately acquiesced in permitting another minor romance to be put forth in the same manner, he did so reluctantly, and was far from acting his part so well.

Scott says, in the Introduction to the Lord of the Isles —" As Mr. Erskine was more than suspected of a taste for poetry, and as I took care, in several places, to mix something that might resemble (as far as was in my power) my friend's feeling and manner, the train easily caught, and two large editions were sold." Among the passages to which he here alludes, are no doubt those in which the character of the minstrel Arthur is shaded with the colourings of an almost effeminate gentleness. Yet, in the midst of them, the "mighty minstrel" himself, from time to time, escapes; as, for instance, where the lover bids Lucy, in that exquisite picture of crossing a mountain stream, trust to his " stalwart arm "—

> " Which could yon oak's prone trunk uprear."

Nor can I pass the compliment to Scott's own fair patroness, where Lucy's admirer is made to confess, with some momentary lapse of gallantry, that he

> " Ne'er won—best meed to minstrel true—
> One favouring smile from fair Buccleuch."

But, above all, the choice of the scenery reveals the treasured predilections of the poet. For who that remembers the circumstances of his first visit to the vale of St. John, but must recognise the impress of his own real romance?

As a whole, the Bridal of Triermain appears to me as characteristic of Scott as any of his larger poems. His genius pervades and animates it beneath a thin and playful veil, which perhaps adds as much of grace as it takes away of splendour. As Wordsworth says of the eclipse on the lake of Lugano—

> " 'Tis sunlight sheathed and gently charmed ; "

and I think there is at once a lightness and a polish of versification beyond what he has elsewhere attained. If it be a miniature, it is such a one as a Cooper might have hung fearlessly beside the masterpieces of Vandyke.

The Introductions contain some of the most exquisite passages he ever produced; but their general effect has always struck me as unfortunate. No art can reconcile us to contemptuous satire of the merest frivolities of modern life—some of them already grown obsolete—interlaid between such bright visions of the old world of romance.

The fall is grievous from the hoary minstrel of Newark and his feverish tears on Killiecrankie, to a pathetic swain who can stoop to denounce as objects of his jealousy

> "The landaulet and four blood bays—
> The Hessian boot and pantaloon."

Before Triermain came out, Scott had taken wing for Abbotsford; and indeed he seems to have so contrived it in his earlier period, that he should not be in Edinburgh when any unavowed work was published; whereas, from the first, in the case of books that bore his name on the title-page, he walked as usual to the Parliament House, and bore all the buzz and tattle of friends and acquaintance with an air of good-humoured equanimity, or rather of total indifference.

The limits of this narrative do not admit of minute details concerning the commercial adventures in which Scott was entangled; and those of the period we have now reached are so painful that I am very willing to spare them. By the spring of 1813 the crisis in the war affected credit universally; and while the oldest firms in every department of the trade of literature had difficulties to contend with, the pressure brought many of humbler resources to extremity. It was so with the house of *John Ballantyne and Co.*; which had started with no solid capital except what Scott supplied; and had been entrusted to one who never looked beyond the passing day—availed himself with a blind recklessness of the system of discounting and renewing bills—and, though attached to Scott by the strongest ties of grateful veneration, yet allowed himself to neglect month after month the most important of his duties—that of keeping the only moneyed partner accurately informed as to the actual obligations and resources of the establishment.

Mr. John's loose methods of transacting business had soon cooled the alliance between his firm and the great Tory publisher of London. Murray's Scotch agency was taken away—he retained hardly any connection with Scott himself, except as a contributor to his Review, and from time to time a friendly visitor in Albemarle Street; and under these altered circumstances, I do not see how the whole concern of John Ballantyne and Co. could have escaped the necessity of an abrupt and disastrous exposure within but a few weeks after the appearance of the *Triermain,* had not the personal differences with Constable been by that time healed. Mr. Hunter had now retired from that house; and Constable, released from his influence, had been watching with hope the unconcealable complication in the affairs of this fragile rival. Constable had never faltered in his conviction that Scott must continue to be the ruling spirit in the literature of their age : and there were few sacrifices which that sanguine man would not have made to regain his hold on the unmatched author. The Ballantynes saw the opening for help, and their advances were well met; but some quite unexpected calls on Scott compelled him to interfere directly, and he began in his own person a negotiation which, though at the time he likened it to that of the treaty of Amiens, was far from being capriciously protracted, or from leading only to a brief and barren truce. Constable, flattered *in limine* by the offer, on fair terms, of a fourth part of the remaining copyright of Rokeby, agreed to relieve the labouring firm of a mass of its stock : the partners to exert themselves in getting rid of the residue, and then wind up their publishing concern with all convenient speed. This was a great relief : on the 18th of May 1813, Scott writes to Mr. John—" For the first time these many weeks, I shall lay my head on a quiet pillow : " but there was still much to be achieved. The warehouse must still groan under unsaleable quires—the desk, too late explored, shewed a dismal vista of approaching demand. Scott was too just not to take something of the blame upon himself; the accumulated stock bore witness against too many of his own plans and suggestions : nor could he acquit himself of carelessness in not having forced the manager to greater exactness in the detailing of accounts. But still he felt that he had serious reason for complaint; and the letter of which a sentence has just been quoted ends in these words, which ought to have produced the deeper impression because of their gentleness :—" Adieu, my dear John. If I have ever expressed myself with irritation in speaking of this business, you must impute it to *the sudden, extensive, and unexpected embarrassments in which I found myself involved all at once*. If to your real goodness of heart and integrity, and to the quickness and acuteness of your talents, you added habits of more universal circumspection, and, above all, the courage to tell disagreeable truths to those whom you hold in regard, I pronounce that the world never held such a man of business. These it must be your study to add to your other good qualities. Meantime, as some one says to Swift, I love you with all your failings. Pray make an effort and love me with all mine.—Yours truly, W.S.

" P.S.—James has behaved very well during this whole transaction, and has been most steadily attentive to business. I am convinced that the more he works the better his health will be. *One or other of you will need to be constantly in the printing-office henceforward*—it is the sheet-anchor."

The allusion in this *postscript* to the printer's health reminds me that Scott's letters to himself are full of hints on that subject, even from a very early period of their connection; and these hints are all to the same effect. One letter (Ashestiel, 1810) will be a sufficient specimen : —" I am very sorry for the state of your health, and should be still more so, were I not certain that I can prescribe for you as well as any physician in Edinburgh. You have naturally an athletic constitution and a hearty stomach, and these agree very ill with a sedentary life and the habits of indolence which it brings on. You must positively put yourself on a regimen as to eating, not for a month or two, but for a year at least, and take regular exercise—and my life for yours."—Among the early pets at Abbotsford there was a huge raven, whose powers of speech were remarkable, and who died in consequence of an equally remarkable voracity. Thenceforth, Scott often repeated to his old friend, and occasionally scribbled by way of postscript to his notes on business—

> " When you are craving,
> Remember the Raven."

Sometimes the formula is varied to—

> " When you've dined half,
> Think on poor Ralph ! "

His preachments of regularity in book-keeping to John, and of abstinence from good cheers to James, were equally vain; but, on the other hand, it must be allowed that the " hard skirmishes," as he calls them, of May 1813, do not seem to have left on himself all the impression that might have been anticipated. He was in the most vigorous of his prime : his temperament was buoyant and hopeful : nothing had occurred to check his confidence in the resources of his own genius and industry. So it was,

that ere many weeks had passed, he was preparing fresh
embarrassments for himself by bidding for another parcel
of land.   As early as the 20th of June he writes to Constable as being already aware of this matter, and alleges
his anxiety " to close at once with a very capricious
person," as the only reason that could have induced him
to offer for £5,000 the whole copyright of an as yet
unwritten poem, to be called " The Nameless Glen."   A
long correspondence ensued, in the course of which Scott
mentions " the Lord of the Isles " as a title which had
suggested itself to him in place of " The Nameless Glen ";
but as the negotiation did not succeed, I may pass its
details.   The new property which he was so eager to acquire was that hilly tract stretching from the old Roman
road near Turn-again towards the Cauldshiels Loch : a
then desolate and naked mountain-mere, which he likens,
in a letter of this summer, to the Lake of the Genie and
the Fisherman in the Arabian Tale.   To obtain this lake
at one extremity of his estate, as a contrast to the Tweed
at the other, was a prospect for which hardly any sacrifice
would have appeared too much; and he contrived to
gratify his wishes in the course of July.   Nor was he, I
must add, more able to control some of his minor tastes.
I find him writing to Terry on the same 20th of June,
about " that splendid lot of ancient armour, advertised by
Winstanley," a celebrated auctioneer in London, of which
he had the strongest fancy to make spoil, though he was
at a loss to know where it should be placed when it
reached Abbotsford; and on the 2nd of July this acquisition also having been settled, he says to the same correspondent—" I have written to Mr. Winstanley.   My bargain with Constable was otherwise arranged, but little
John is to find the needful article, and I shall take care of
Mr. Winstanley's interest, who has behaved too handsomely in this matter to be trusted to the mercy of our
little friend the Picaroon, who is, notwithstanding his
many excellent qualities, a little on the score of old Gobbo
—doth somewhat smack—somewhat grow to."

On the 12th of July, as usual, he removed to Tweedside; but he had not long enjoyed himself in sketching out
woods and walks for the borders of his Fairy Lake before
he received sharp admonishment.   Two lines of a letter to
the " little Picaroon," dated July 24th, speak already to a
series of annoyances :—" Dear John,—I sent you the

order and have only to hope it arrived safe and in good time. I waked the boy at three o'clock myself, having slept little, less on account of the money than of the time. Surely you should have written, three or four days before, the probable amount of the deficit, and, as on former occasions, I would have furnished you with means of meeting it. These expresses, besides every other inconvenience, excite surprise in my family and in the neighbourhood. I know no justifiable occasion for them but the unexpected return of a bill. I do not consider you as answerable for the success of plans, but I do and must hold you responsible for giving me, in distinct and plain terms, your opinion as to any difficulties which may occur, and that in such time that I may make arrangements to obviate them if possible."

The affair of the 24th itself was aggravated by the circumstance that Scott had been prepared to start on the 25th for a visit in a different county : so that the worst consequences that had so late alarmed his *manager*, must have been after all unavoidable if he had deferred his messenger but a few hours more.

Scott proceeded, accordingly, to join a gay and festive circle, whom the Duke of Buccleuch had assembled about him on first taking possession of the magnificent Castle of Drumlanrig, in Nithsdale, the principal messuage of the dukedom of Queensberry, which had recently lapsed into his family. But *post equitem sedet atra cura*—a second and a third of these unwelcome missives, rendered necessary by neglect of precisely the same kind, reached him in the midst of this scene of rejoicing.

He had been engaged also to meet the Marquis of Abercorn at Carlisle, in the first week of August, on business connected with his brother Thomas's late administration of that nobleman's affairs ; and he had designed to pass from Drumlanrig to Carlisle for his purpose, without going back to Abbotsford. In consequence of these repeated harassments, however, he so far altered his plans as to cut short his stay at Drumlanrig, and turn homewards for two or three days, where James Ballantyne met him with such a statement as in some measure relieved his mind.

He then proceeded to fulfil his engagement with Lord Abercorn, whom he encountered travelling in a rather peculiar style between Carlisle and Longtown. The ladies of the family and the household occupied four or five carriages, all drawn by the Marquis's own horses, while the noble Lord himself brought up the rear, mounted on horseback, and decorated with the ribbon of the Garter. On meeting the cavalcade, Scott turned with them, and he was not a little amused when they reached the village of Longtown, which he had ridden through an hour before, with the preparations which he found there made for the dinner of the party. The Marquis's major-domo and cook had arrived there early in the morning, and everything was now arranged for his reception in the little public house, as nearly as possible in the style of his own mansions. The ducks and geese that had been dabbling three or four hours ago in the village pond, were now ready to make their appearance under numberless disguises ; a regular bill-of-fare flanked the Marquis's allotted cover ; every huckaback towel in the place had been pressed to do service as a napkin ; and the landlady's poor remnants of crockery had been furbished up, and mustered in solemn order on a crazy beauffet, which was to represent a sideboard worthy of Lucullus. I think it worth while to preserve this anecdote, which Scott delighted in telling, as perhaps the last relic of a style of manners now passed away, and never likely to be revived among us.

Having despatched this dinner and his business, Scott again turned southwards, intending to spend a few days at Rokeby; but on reaching Penrith, the landlord placed a letter in his hands : *ecce iterum*—it was once more a cry of distress from John Ballantyne. Having once more despatched a cheque and a gentle remonstrance to Edinburgh, he rode on to Brough; but there he received such a painful account of Mrs. Morritt's health, that he abandoned his intention of proceeding to Rokeby; and indeed it was much better that he should be at Abbotsford again, for by this time the whole of these affairs had reached a second *crisis*. Again Constable was consulted; and now a detailed statement was submitted to him. On examining it, he so expressed himself, that all the partners concurred in the necessity of submitting forthwith to steps not less decisive than painful. Constable again relieved them of some of their crushing stock; but he frankly owned that he could not do in that way enough to serve them effectually; and Scott was constrained to have recourse to the Duke of Buccleuch, who with the kindest promptitude gave him a guarantee to the extent of £4,000, immediately available in the money market—the poet insuring his life for that sum, and depositing the insurance as security with the Duke; while John Ballantyne agreed, in place of a leisurely winding up of the publishing affair, to terminate it with the utmost possible speed, and endeavour to establish himself as an auctioneer of books, antiquities, and objects of *vertu*. How bitterly must Scott have felt his situation when he wrote thus to John on the 16th August: —" With regard to the printing, it is my intention to retire from that also so soon as I can possibly do so with safety to myself, and with the regard I shall always entertain for James's interest. Whatever loss I may sustain will be preferable to the life I have lately led, when I seem surrounded by a sort of magic circle, which neither permits me to remain at home in peace, nor to stir abroad with pleasure. Your first exertion as an auctioneer may probably be on ' that distinguished, select, and inimitable collection of books, made by an amateur of this city retiring from business.' I do not feel either health or confidence in my own powers sufficient to authorise me to take a long price for a new poem, until these affairs shall have been in some measure digested." There still remained a difficult digestion. His correspondence on to Christmas is deeply chequered; but the nature of the details may be guessed by such as have had experience in the merchandise of literature; and few others, I suppose, will regret their curtailment.

It was in the midst of these distressing occurrences that Scott received two letters—one from Dr. Stanier Clarke, private librarian to the Regent, and another, more formal, from the Marquis of Hertford, Lord Chamberlain, announcing His Royal Highness's desire to nominate him to the office of Poet Laureate, which had just fallen vacant by the death of Mr. Pye. Its emoluments were understood by him to be " £400, or at least £300 a year "; at that time such an accession of income must have been welcome; and at any rate, what the Sovereign designed as a favour and a distinction could not be lightly waived by Walter Scott. He felt, however, that holding already two lucrative offices in the gift of the Crown, he could not gracefully accept a third, entirely unconnected with his own legal profession, while so many eminent men remained wholly dependent on their literary exertions; and the friends whom he consulted, especially the Duke of Buccleuch, all concurring in the propriety of these scruples, he declined the royal offer. It is evident that from the first he had had Mr. Southey's case in his contemplation. The moment he made up his mind as to himself, he wrote to Mr. Croker and others in the Prince Regent's confidence, suggesting that name : and he had soon to congratulate his friend of Keswick on assuming the official laurel, which " had been worn of old by Dryden and more lately by Warton." Mr. Southey, in an essay long subsequent to his death, says— " Sir Walter's conduct was, as it always was, character- istically friendly and generous."

This happened in September. October brought another succession of John Ballantyne's missives, to one of which Scott answers :—" For Heaven's sake, treat me as a man, not as a milch-cow ; "—and a third crisis, at the approach of the Martinmas term, was again weathered with the narrowest difficulty—chiefly, as before, through the inter- vention of Constable. All these annoyances produced no change whatever in his habits of industry. During these anxious months of September, October, and November he kept feeding the press from day to day both with the annotated text of the closing volumes of Swift's works, and with the MS. of his Life of the Dean. He had also pro- ceeded to mature in his mind the plan of the Lord of the Isles, and executed such a portion of the First Canto as gave him confidence to renew his negotiation with Con- stable for the sale of the whole, or part of its copyright. It was, moreover, at this period, that his eye chanced to light once more on the Ashestiel fragment of *Waverley*. He read over those introductory chapters—thought they had been undervalued—and determined to finish the story.

It is proper to mention, that, in the very agony of these perplexities, the unfortunate Maturin received from him a timely succour of £50, rendered doubly acceptable by the kind and judicious letter of advice in which it was en- closed ; and I have before me ample evidence that his benevolence had been extended to other struggling brothers of the trade, even when he must often have had actual difficulty to meet the immediate expenditure of his own family.

The great successes of the Allied Powers in the cam- paigns of 1813 gave a salutary stimulus to commercial enterprise : and the return of general confidence facilitated many arrangements in which Scott's interests were involved. He, however, needed no such considerations to heighten his patriotic enthusiasm, which overflowed in two songs—one of them never since, I believe, omitted at any celebration of the anniversary of Mr. Pitt's death—

> " O dread was the time and more dreadful the omen,
>   When the brave on Marengo lay slaughter'd in vain."

He also wrote an address to the Sovereign for the Magistracy of Edinburgh, which was privately acknowledged to the penman, by His Royal Highness's command, as " the most elegant congratulation a sovereign ever received or a subject offered." The Magistrates accordingly found particular graciousness at Carlton House; and on their return (Christmas, 1813) presented Scott with the freedom of his native city and a very handsome piece of plate.

I must, however, open the year 1814 with a melancholy story. Mention has been made in connection with an unlucky edition of Beaumont and Fletcher, of Henry Weber, a German scholar, who, escaping to this country in 1804, from misfortunes in his own, excited Scott's compassion, and was thenceforth furnished, through his means, with literary employment of various sorts. Weber was a man of considerable learning; but Scott, as was his custom, appears to have formed an exaggerated notion of his capacity, and certainly countenanced him, to his own severe cost, in several most unhappy undertakings. When not engaged on things of a more ambitious character, he had acted for ten years as his protector's amanuensis, and when the family were in Edinburgh he very often dined with them. There was something very interesting in his appearance and manners : he had a fair, open countenance, in which the honesty and the enthusiasm of his nation were alike visible; his demeanour was gentle and modest; and he had not only a stock of curious antiquarian knowledge, but the reminiscences, which he detailed with amusing simplicity, of an early life chequered with many strange-enough adventures. He was, in short, much a favourite with Scott and all the household; and was invited to dine with them so frequently, chiefly because his friend was aware that he had an unhappy propensity to drinking, and was anxious to keep him away from places where he might have been more likely to indulge it. This vice had been growing on him; and of late Scott had found it necessary to make some rather severe remonstrances about habits which were at once injuring his health and interrupting his literary industry. They had, however, parted kindly when Scott left Edinburgh at Christmas; and the day after his return, Weber attended him as usual in his library— being employed in transcribing extracts during several hours, while his friend, seated over against him, continued working at the Life of Swift. The light beginning to fail, Scott threw himself back in his chair, and was about to ring for candles, when he observed the German's eyes fixed upon him with an unusual solemnity of expression. "Weber," said he, "what's the matter with you?" "Mr. Scott," said Weber, rising, "you have long insulted me, and I can bear it no longer. I have brought a pair of pistols with me, and must insist on your taking one of them instantly;" and with that he produced the weapons, which had been deposited under his chair, and laid one of them on Scott's manuscript. "You are mistaken, I think," said Scott, "in your way of setting about this affair—but no matter. It can, however, be no part of your object to annoy Mrs. Scott and the children; therefore, if you please, we will put the pistols into the drawer till after dinner, and then arrange to go out together like gentlemen." Weber answered with equal coolness, "I believe that will be better," and laid the second pistol also on the table. Scott locked them both in his desk, and said, "I am glad you have felt the propriety of what I suggested—let me only request farther, that nothing may occur while we are at dinner to give my wife any suspicion of what has been passing." Weber again assented, and Scott withdrew to his dressing-room, from which he despatched a message to one of Weber's companions,—and then dinner was served, and Weber joined the circle as usual. He conducted himself with composure, and everything seemed to go on in the ordinary way, until whisky and hot water being produced, Scott, instead of inviting his guest to help himself, mixed two moderate tumblers of toddy, and handed one of them to Weber, who, upon that, started up with a furious countenance, but instantly sat down again, and when Mrs. Scott expressed her fear that he was ill, answered placidly that he was liable to spasms, but that the pain was gone. He then took the glass, eagerly gulped down its contents, and pushed it back to Scott. At this moment the friend who had been sent for made his appearance; and Weber, on seeing him enter the room, rushed past him and out of the house, without stopping to put on his hat. The friend, who pursued instantly, came up with him at the end of the street, and did all he could to soothe his agitation, but in vain. The same evening he was obliged to be put into a strait-waistcoat; and though in a few days he exhibited such symptoms of recovery that he was allowed to go by himself to pay a visit in the North of England, he there soon relapsed, and continued ever afterwards a hopeless lunatic, being supported to the end of his life, in June 1818, at Scott's expense, in an asylum at York.

On the first of July 1814, the Swift, nineteen volumes 8vo, at length issued from the press. This adventure, undertaken by Constable in 1808, had been proceeded in during all the variety of their personal relations, and now came forth when author and publisher felt more warmly towards each other than perhaps they had ever before done. The impression was of 1,250 copies; and a reprint of similar extent was called for in 1824. Scott added to his edition many admirable pieces, both in prose and verse, which had never before been printed, and still more, which had escaped notice amidst old bundles of pamphlets and broadsides. To the illustration of these and of all the better known writings of the Dean, he brought the same qualifications which had, by general consent, distinguished his Dryden: "uniting," as the Edinburgh Review expresses it, "to the minute knowledge and patient research of the Malones and Chalmerses, a vigour of judgment and a vivacity of style to which they had no pretensions." His biographical narrative, introductory essays, and notes show, indeed, an intimacy of acquaintance with the obscurest details of the political, social, and literary history of the period of Queen Anne, which it is impossible to consider without feeling a lively regret that he never accomplished a long-cherished purpose of editing Pope. It has been specially unfortunate for that "true deacon of the craft," as Scott often called him, that first Goldsmith, and then Scott, should have taken up, only to abandon it, the project of writing his life and annotating his works.

The Edinburgh Reviewer thus characterises the Memoir of the Dean of St. Patrick's :—

" It is not much like the production of a mere man of letters, or a fastidious speculator in sentiment and morality; but exhibits throughout, and in a very pleasing form, the good sense and large toleration of a man of the world, with much of that generous allowance for the

'Fears of the brave and follies of the wise,'

which genius too often requires, and should therefore always be most forward to show. It is impossible, however, to avoid noticing that Mr. Scott is by far too favourable to the personal character of his author, whom we think it would really be injurious to the cause of morality to allow to pass either as a very dignified or a very amiable person. The truth is, we think, that he was extremely ambitious, arrogant, and selfish; of a morose, vindictive, and haughty temper; and though capable of a sort of patronising generosity towards his dependents, and of some attachment towards those who had long known and flattered him, his general demeanour, both in public and private life, appears to have been far from exemplary; destitute of temper and magnanimity, and we will add, of principle, in the former; and in the latter, of tenderness, fidelity, or compassion."—Vol. xvii. p. 9.

I have no desire to break a lance in this place in defence of Swift. It does not appear to me that he stands at all distinguished among politicians (least of all, among the politicians of his time) for laxity of principle; nor can I consent to charge his private demeanour with the absence either of tenderness, or fidelity, or compassion. But who ever dreamed—most assuredly not Scott—of holding up the Dean of St. Patrick's as on the whole an " exemplary character " ?   The biographer felt, whatever his critic may have thought on the subject, that a vein of morbid humour ran through Swift's whole existence, both mental and physical, from the beginning. " He early adopted," says Scott, " the custom of observing his birthday as a term not of joy but of sorrow, and of reading, when it recurred, the striking passage of Scripture in which Job laments and execrates the day upon which it was said in his father's house *that a man-child was born*; " and I should have expected that any man who had considered the black close of the career thus early clouded, and read the entry of Swift's diary on the funeral of Stella, his epitaph on himself, and the testament by which he disposed of his fortune, would have been willing, like Scott, to dwell on the splendour of his immortal genius, and the many traits of manly generosity " which he unquestionably exhibited," rather than on the faults and foibles of

nameless and inscrutable disease, which tormented and
embittered the far greater part of his earthly being.
What the critic says of the practical and business-like
style of Scott's biography, appears very just—and I think
the circumstance eminently characteristic; nor, on the
whole, could his edition, as an edition, have been better
dealt with than in the Essay which I have quoted.   It
was, by the way, written by Mr. Jeffrey at Constable's
particular request.   " It was, I think, the first time I ever
asked such a thing of him," the bookseller said to me;
" and I assure you the result was no encouragement to
repeat such petitions."   Mr. Jeffrey attacked Swift's
whole character at great length, and with consummate
dexerity; and, in Constable's opinion, his article threw
such a cloud on the Dean as materially checked for a
time the popularity of his writings.   Admirable as the
paper is in point of ability, I think Mr. Constable may
have considerably exaggerated its effects; but in those
days it must have been difficult for him to form an impartial opinion upon such a question; for, as Johnson said
of Cave that " he could not spit over his window without
thinking of The Gentleman's Magazine," I believe Constable allowed nothing to interrupt his paternal pride in
the concerns of his Review, until Waverley opened
another periodical publication still more important to his
fortunes.

And this consummation was not long delayed.   Before
Christmas, Erskine had perused the greater part of the
first volume, and expressed his decided opinion that
Waverley would prove the most popular of all his friend's
writings.   The MS. was forthwith copied by John Ballantyne, and sent to press.   As soon as a volume was
printed, Ballantyne conveyed it to Constable, who did not
for a moment doubt from what pen it proceeded, but took
a few days to consider of the matter, and then offered
£700 for the copyright.   When we recollect what the
state of novel literature in those days was, and that the
only exceptions to its mediocrity, the Irish Tales of Miss
Edgeworth, however appreciated in refined circles, had a
circulation so limited that she had never realised a tithe
of £700 by the best of them—it must be allowed that
Constable's offer was a liberal one.   Scott's answer, however, was, that £700 was too much in case the novel
should not be successful, and too little if it should.   He

added, " If our fat friend had said £1,000, I should have been staggered." John did not forget to convey this last hint to Constable, but the latter did not choose to act upon it; and ultimately agreed to an equal division of profits between himself and the author.

There was a considerable pause between the finishing of the first volume and the beginning of the second. Constable, eager about an extensive *Supplement* to his Encyclopædia Britannica, earnestly requested Scott to undertake a few articles; and, anxious to gratify the generous bookseller, he laid aside his tale until he had finished two essays—those on Chivalry and the Drama. They were written in the course of April and May, and he received for each of them £100.

A letter of the 9th July to Mr. Morritt gives in more exact detail than the author's own recollection could supply in 1830, the history of the completion of Waverley: which had then been two days published. " I must now " (he says) " account for my own laziness, by referring you to a small anonymous sort of a novel, which you will receive by the mail of this day. It was a very old attempt of mine to embody some traits of those characters and manners peculiar to Scotland, the last remnants of which vanished during my own youth. I had written great part of the first volume, and sketched other passages, when I mislaid the MS., and only found it by the merest accident as I was rummaging the drawers of an old cabinet; and I took the fancy of finishing it. It has made a very strong impression here, and the good people of Edinburgh are busied in tracing the author, and in finding out originals for the portraits it contains. Jeffrey has offered to make oath that it is mine, and another great critic has tendered his affidavit *ex contrario*; so that these authorities have divided the Gude Town. Let me know your opinion about it. The truth is that this sort of muddling work amuses me, and I am something in the condition of Joseph Surface, who was embarrassed by getting himself too good a reputation; for many things may please people well enough anonymously, which, if they have me in the title-page, would just give me that sort of ill name which precedes hanging—and that would be in many respects inconvenient, if I thought of again trying a *grande opus.*"

Morritt, as yet the only English confidant, conveyed on

volume by volume as he read them his honest criticism : at last vehemently protesting against the maintenance of the incognito. Scott in his reply (July 24th) says :—" I shall *not* own Waverley; my chief reason is, that it would prevent me the pleasure of writing again. David Hume, nephew of the historian, says the author must be of a Jacobite family and predilections, a yeoman-cavalry man, and a Scottish lawyer, and desires me to guess in whom these happy attributes are united. I shall not plead guilty, however; and as such seems to be the fashion of the day, I hope charitable people will believe my *affidavit* in contradiction to all other evidence. The Edinburgh faith now is, that Waverley is written by Jeffrey, having been composed to lighten the tedium of his late Transatlantic voyage. So you see the unknown infant is like to come to preferment. In truth, I am not sure it would be considered quite decorous for me, as a Clerk of Session to write novels. Judges being monks, Clerks are a sort of lay brethren, from whom some solemnity of walk and conduct may be expected. So whatever I may do of this kind, ' I shall whistle it down the wind, and let it prey at fortune.' [1] The second edition is, I believe, nearly through the press. It will hardly be printed faster than it was written; for though the first volume was begun long ago, and actually lost for a time, yet the other two were begun and finished between the 4th June and the first July, during all which I attended my duty in Court, and proceeded without loss of time or hindrance of business."

This statement as to the time occupied by the second and third volumes of Waverley, recalls to my memory a trifling anecdote, which, as connected with a dear friend of my youth, whom I have not seen for many years, and may very probably never see again in this world, I shall here set down, in the hope of affording him a momentary, though not an unmixed pleasure, when he may chance to read this compilation on a distant shore—and also in the hope that my humble record may impart to some active mind in the rising generation a shadow of the influence which the reality certainly exerted upon his. Happening to pass through Edinburgh in June, 1814, I dined one day with the gentleman in question (now the Honourable William Menzies, one of the Supreme Judges at the Cape

[1] *Othello,* Act III. Scene 3.

of Good Hope), whose residence was then in George Street, situated very near to, and at right angles with, North Castle Street. It was a party of very young persons, most of them, like Menzies and myself, destined for the Bar of Scotland, all gay and thoughtless, enjoying the first flush of manhood, with little remembrance of the yesterday, or care of the morrow. When my companion's worthy father and uncle, after seeing two or three bottles go round, left the juveniles to themselves, the weather being hot, we adjourned to a library which had one large window looking northwards. After carousing here for an hour or more, I observed that a shade had come over the aspect of my friend, who happened to be placed immediately opposite to myself, and said something that intimated a fear of his being unwell. " No," said he, " I shall be well enough presently, if you will only let me sit where you are, and take my chair; for there is a confounded hand in sight of me here, which has often bothered me before, and now it won't let me fill my glass with a good will." I rose to change places with him accordingly, and he pointed out to me this hand which, like the writing on Belshazzar's wall, disturbed his hour of hilarity. " Since we sat down," he said, " I have been watching it—it fascinates my eye— it never stops—page after page is finished and thrown on that heap of MS., and still it goes on unwearied—and so it will be till candles are brought in, and God knows how long after that. It is the same every night—I can't stand a sight of it when I am not at my books."—" Some stupid, dogged, engrossing clerk, probably," exclaimed myself, or some other giddy youth in our society. " No, boys," said our host, " I well know what hand it is—'tis Walter Scott's." This was the hand that, in the evenings of three summer weeks, wrote the two last volumes of Waverley.

The gallant composure with which Scott, when he had dismissed a work from his desk, awaited the decision of the public—and the healthy elasticity of spirit with which he could meanwhile turn his whole zeal upon new or different objects—are among the features in his character which will always, I believe, strike the student of literary history as most remarkable. It would be difficult to exaggerate the importance to his fortunes of this his first novel. Yet before he had heard of its reception in the south, except the whisper of one partial friend, he started on a voyage which was likely to occupy two months, and during which he could hardly expect to receive any letters.

He had been invited to accompany the Commissioners of the Northern Light Houses in their annual expedition; and as its programme included the Hebrides, and he had already made some progress in the Lord of the Isles, the opportunity for refreshing and enlarging his acquaintance with that region would alone have been a strong temptation. But there were many others. The trip was also to embrace the isles of Shetland and Orkney, and a vast extent of the mainland coasts, no part of which he had ever seen—or but for such an offer might ever have much chance of seeing. The Commissioners were all familiar friends of his—William Erskine, then Sheriff of the Orkneys, Robert Hamilton, Sheriff of Lanarkshire, Adam Duff, Sheriff of Forfarshire; but the real chief was the Surveyor-General, the celebrated engineer, Mr. Stephenson, and Scott anticipated special pleasure in his society. " I delight," he told Morritt, " in these professional men of talent. They always give you some new lights by the peculiarity of their habits and studies—so different from the people who are rounded and smoothed and ground down for conversation, and who can say all that every other person says—and no more."

To this voyage we owe many of the most striking passages in the Lord of the Isles, and the noble romance of the Pirate wholly. The leisure of the yacht allowed him to keep a very minute diary, from which he gave sundry extracts in his notes to both these works, and which may now be read entire in the larger memoirs of his life and correspondence. It abounds in interest—in sketches of scenery which could have come from his hand alone—in most curious details of insular manners; but its chief value is in its artless portraiture of the penman. I question if any man ever drew his own character more fully or more pleasingly. We have before us, according to the scene and occasion, the poet, the antiquary, the magistrate, the planter, and the agriculturist; but everywhere the warm yet sagacious philanthropist—everywhere the courtesy, based on the unselfishness, of the thoroughbred gentleman. It concludes with these words :—" But I must not omit to say, that among five or six persons, some of whom were doubtless different in tastes and pursuits,

there did not occur, during the close communication of more than six weeks aboard a small vessel, the slightest difference of opinion. Each seemed anxious to submit his own wishes to those of his friends. The consequence was, that by judicious arrangement all were gratified in their turn, and frequently he who made some sacrifices to the views of his companions was rewarded by some unexpected gratification calculated particularly for his own amusement. We had constant exertion, a succession of wild and uncommon scenery, good humour on board, and objects of animation and interest when we went ashore :—
Sed fugit interea—fugit irrevocabile tempus."

I have been told by one of the companions of this voyage, that heartily as he entered throughout into their social enjoyments, they all perceived him, when inspecting for the first time scenes of remarkable grandeur, to be in such an abstracted and excited mood, that they felt it would be the kindest and discreetest plan to leave him to himself. " I often," said Lord Kinnedder, " on coming up from the cabin at night, found him pacing the deck rapidly, muttering to himself—and went to the forecastle, lest my presence should disturb him. I remember, that at Loch Corriskin, in particular, he seemed quite overwhelmed with his feelings; and we all saw it, and retiring unnoticed, left him to roam and gaze about by himself, until it was time to muster the party and be gone." Scott used to mention the surprise with which he himself witnessed Erskine's emotion on first entering the Cave of Staffa. " Would you believe it? " he said—" my poor Willie sat down and wept like a woman ! " Yet his own sensibilities, though betrayed in a more masculine and sterner guise, were perhaps as keen as well as deeper than his amiable friend's.

A few days before his voyage ended he heard casually of the death of Harriet Duchess of Buccleuch, who ever since the days of Lasswade had been his most kind friend. The sad intelligence was confirmed on his arrival in the Clyde, by a most touching and manly letter from the Duke. Its closing paragraph has these sentences :— " Endeavouring to the last to conceal her suffering, she evinced a fortitude, a resignation, a Christian courage, beyond all power of description. Her last injunction was to attend to her poor people. I have learned that the most truly heroic spirit may be lodged in the tenderest and the gentlest breast. If ever there was a proof of the efficacy of our religion in moments of the deepest affliction, and in the hour of death, it was exemplified in her conduct. I will endeavour to do in all things what I know she would wish. I have therefore determined to lay myself open to all the comforts my friends can afford me. I shall be most happy to cultivate their society as heretofore. I shall love them more and more because I know they loved her. Whenever it suits your convenience I shall be happy to see you here. I feel that it is particularly my duty not to make my house the house of mourning to my children; for I know it was *her* decided opinion that it is most mischievous to give an early impression of gloom to the mind."

The Duke survived for some years, and he continued in the line of conduct which he had from the first resolved upon; but he never recovered the blow: and this no one perceived more clearly than Scott.

In his letter to Morritt on reaching Edinburgh, he says (September 14th),—" We sailed from Leith, and skirted the Scottish coast, visiting the Buller of Buchan and other remarkable objects—went to Shetland—thence to Orkney—from thence round Cape Wrath to the Hebrides, making descents everywhere, where there was anything to be seen—thence to Lewis and the Long Island—to Skye—to Iona—and so forth, lingering among the Hebrides as long as we could. Then we stood over to the coast of Ireland, and visited the Giant's Causeway and Port Rush, where Dr. Richardson, the inventor (discoverer, I would say) of the celebrated fiorin grass, resides. By the way, he is a chattering charlatan, and his fiorin a mere humbug. But if he were Cicero, and his invention were potatoes, or anything equally useful, I should detest the recollection of the place and the man, for it was there I learned the death of my friend. Adieu, my dear Morritt; like poor Tom, ' I cannot daub it farther.' "

As he passed through Edinburgh, the negotiation as to the Lord of the Isles, which had been protracted through several months, was completed : Constable agreeing to give fifteen hundred guineas for one-half of the copyright, while the other moiety was retained by the author. The same sum had been offered at an early stage of the affair, but it was not until now accepted, in consequence of the earnest wish of Messrs. Ballantyne to saddle the publisher of the new poem with another pyramid of their old " quire stock,"—which, however, Constable ultimately persisted in refusing. It may easily be believed that John's management during a six weeks' absence had been such as to render it doubly convenient for the poet to have this matter settled; and it may also be supposed that the progress of Waverley during that interval had tended to put the chief parties in good humour with each other. For nothing can be more unfounded than the statement repeated in various memoirs of Scott's life, that the sale of the first edition of this immortal Tale was slow. It appeared on the 7th of July, and the whole impression (1,000 copies) had disappeared within five weeks; an occurrence then unprecedented in the case of an anonymous novel, put forth at what is called among publishers *the dead season.* A second edition of 2,000 copies was at least projected by the 24th of the same month :—that appeared before the end of August, and it too had gone off so rapidly that Scott now, in September, found Constable eager to treat, on the same terms as before, for a third of 1,000 copies. This third edition was published in October; and when a fourth of the like extent was called for in November, I find Scott writing to John Ballantyne :—" I suppose Constable won't quarrel with a work on which he has netted £612 in four months, with a certainty of making it £1,000 before the year is out." It would be idle to enumerate subsequent reprints. Well might Constable regret that he had not ventured to offer £1,000 for the whole copyright of Waverley !

The only private friends originally intrusted with his secret appear to have been Erskine and Morritt. But there was one with whom it would, of course, have been more than vain to affect any concealment. On the publication of the third edition, I find him writing thus to his brother, then in Canada :—" Dear Tom, a novel here, called Waverley, has had enormous success. I sent you a copy, and will send you another with the Lord of the Isles which will be out at Christmas. The success which it has had, with some other circumstances, has induced people

    ' To lay the bantling at a certain door,
      Where lying store of faults, they'd fain heap more.' [1]

---

[1] Garrick's Epilogue to *Polly Honeycombe,* 1760.

You will guess for yourself how far such a report has credibility; but by no means give the weight of your opinion to the Transatlantic public; for you must know there is also a counter-report, that *you* have written the said Waverley. Send me a novel intermixing your exuberant and natural humour, with any incidents and descriptions of scenery you may see—particularly with characters and traits of manners. I will give it all the cobbling that is necessary, and if you do but exert yourself, I have not the least doubt it will be worth £500; and, to encourage you, you may, when you send the MS., draw on me for £100, at fifty days' sight—so that your labours will at any rate not be quite thrown away. You have more fun and descriptive talent than most people; and all that you want—*i.e.* the mere practice of composition—I can supply, or the devil's in it. Keep this matter a dead secret, and look knowing when Waverley is spoken of. If you are not Sir John Falstaff, you are as good a man as he, and may therefore face Colville of the Dale. You may believe I don't want to make you the author of a book you have never seen; but if people will, upon their own judgment, suppose so, and also on their own judgment give you £500 to try your hand on a novel, I don't see that you are a pin's-point the worse. Mind that your MS. attends the draft. I am perfectly serious and confident, that in two or three months you might clear the cobs. I beg my compliments to the hero who is afraid of Jeffrey's scalping-knife.''

In truth, no one of Scott's intimate friends ever had, or could have had, the slightest doubt as to the parentage of Waverley; nor, although he abstained from communicating the fact formally to most of them, did he ever affect any real concealment in the case of such persons; nor, when any circumstance arose which rendered the withholding of direct confidence on the subject incompatible with perfect freedom of feeling on both sides, did he hesitate to make the avowal. Nor do I believe that the mystification ever answered much purpose among literary men of eminence beyond the circle of his personal acquaintance. But it would be difficult to suppose that he had ever wished that to be otherwise; it was sufficient for him to set the mob of readers at gaze, and above all, to escape the annoyance of having productions, actually known to be his, made the daily and hourly topics of discussion in his presence—especially (perhaps) productions in a new walk, to which it might be naturally supposed that Lord Byron's poetical successes had diverted him.

Mr. Jeffrey had known Scott from his youth—and in reviewing Waverley he was at no pains to conceal his conviction of its authorship. He quarrelled as usual with carelessness of style and some inartificialities of plot, but rendered justice to the substantial merits of the work. The Quarterly was far less favourable. Indeed the articles on Waverley and Guy Mannering in that journal will bear the test of ultimate opinion as badly as any critical pieces which our time has produced. They are written in a captious, cavilling strain of quibble, which shews as complete blindness to the essential interest of the narrative, as the critic betrays on the subject of the Scottish dialogue, which forms its liveliest ornament, when he pronounces that to be " a dark dialect of Anglified Erse." With this remarkable exception, the censors of any note were not slow to confess their belief that, under a hackneyed name and trivial form, there had appeared a work of original creative genius, worthy of being placed by the side of the very few real masterpieces of prose fiction. Loftier romance was never blended with easier, quainter humour, by Cervantes. In his familiar delineations he had combined the strength of Smollett with the native elegance and unaffected pathos of Goldsmith; in his darker scenes he had revived that real tragedy which appeared to have left our theatre with the age of Shakespeare; and elements of interest so diverse had been blended and interwoven with that nameless grace, which, more surely perhaps than even the highest perfection in the command of any one strain of sentiment, marks the master-mind cast in Nature's most felicitous mould.

CHAPTER VIII

Publication of the Lord of the Isles and Guy Mannering—Meeting with Byron—Carlton House Dinner—Excursion to Paris—Publication of the Field of Waterloo—Paul's Letters—The Antiquary—Harold the Dauntless—and the first Tales of my Landlord. 1815-1816.

THE voyage and these good news sent him back in high vigour to his desk at Abbotsford. For lighter work he had on hand *The Memorie of the Somervilles*, a very curious specimen of family history, which he had undertaken to edit at the request of his neighbour Lord Somerville. This was published in October. His serious labour was on the Lord of the Isles : of which only three cantos had been written when he concluded his bargain with Constable. He had carried with him in the yacht some proof-sheets of a little book that Ballantyne was printing, entitled *Poems illustrative of Traditions in Galloway and Ayrshire, by Joseph Train, Supervisor of Excise at Castle-Stewart :* and, being struck with the notes, wrote, on his arrival at home, to the author, whom he had never seen, requesting information concerning the ruins of Turnberry, on the Ayrshire coast, of which he wished to say something in connection with one of Bruce's adventures in the forthcoming poem. Mr. Train did much more than Scott had meant to ask ;—for he had never himself been at Turnberry—but instantly rode over the hills to the spot, and transmitted ample details of the castle and all its legends :—not omitting a local superstition, that on the anniversary of the night when Bruce landed there from Arran, the meteoric gleam which had attended his voyage re-appeared unfailingly in the same quarter of the heavens. What use Scott made of this and other parts of Mr. Train's paper, we see from the fifth canto of the Lord of the Isles and its notes : and the date of the communication (November 2) is therefore important as to the history of the composition ; but this was the beginning of a correspondence which had many other happy consequences. From this time the worthy supervisor, who had had many literary plans and schemes, dropt all notion of authorship in his own person, and devoted his leisure with most generous assiduity to the collection of whatever stories he fancied likely to be of use to his new acquaintance, who, after one or two meetings, had impressed him with unbounded enthusiasm of attachment. To no one individual did Scott owe so much of the materials of his novels : and one of the very earliest packets from Castle-Stewart (November 7) contained a ballad called *The Durham Garland,* which, reviving Scott's recollection of a story told in his youth by a servant of his father's, suggested the groundwork of the second of the series. James Ballantyne, in writing by desire of " The Author of Waverley " to Miss Edgeworth, with a copy of the fourth edition of that novel (November 11), mentioned that another might soon be expected; but, as he added, that it would treat of manners more ancient than those of 1745, it is clear that no outline resembling that of *Guy Mannering* was then in the printer's view: most probably Scott had signified to him that he designed to handle the period of the Covenanters.   There can, I think, be as little doubt that he began Guy Mannering as soon as Train's paper of the 7th November reached him.

He writes on the 25th December, to Constable, that he " had corrected the last proofs of the Lord of the Isles, and was setting out for Abbotsford to refresh the machine."   And in what did his refreshment of the machine consist?   The poem was published on the 15th January; and he says, *on that day*, to Morritt, " I want to shake myself free of Waverley, and accordingly have made a considerable exertion to finish an odd little tale within such time as will mystify the public, I trust—unless they suppose me to be Briareus.   Two volumes are already printed, and the only persons in my confidence, W. Erskine and Ballantyne, are of opinion that it is much more interesting than Waverley.   It is a tale of private life, and only varied by the perilous exploits of smugglers and excisemen."   Guy Mannering was published on the 24th of February—that is, exactly two months after the Lord of the Isles was dismissed from the author's desk; and—making but a narrow allowance for the operations of the transcriber, printer, bookseller, etc., I think the dates I have gathered together confirm the accuracy of what I have often heard Scott say, that his second novel " was the work of six weeks at a Christmas."   Such was his recipe " for refreshing the machine."

I am sorry to have to add, that this severity of labour, like the repetition of it which had deplorable effects at a later period, was the result of difficulties about the discount of John Ballantyne's bills.

Finding that Constable would not meet his views as to some of these matters, Mr. John suggested to Scott that some other house might prove more accommodating if he were permitted to offer them not only the new novel, but the next edition of the established favourite Waverley : but upon this ingenious proposition Scott at once set his *veto.*   " Dear John," he writes, " your expedients are all wretched, as far as regards me.   I never will give Constable, or any one, room to say I have broken my word with him in the slightest degree.   If I lose everything else, I will at least keep my honour unblemished; and I do hold myself bound in honour to offer him a Waverley, while he shall continue to comply with the conditions annexed." The result was, that Messrs. Longman undertook the Guy Mannering, relieving John of some of his encumbering stock; but Longman, in compliance with Scott's wish, admitted Constable to a share in the adventure; and with one or two exceptions, originating in circumstances nearly similar, the house of Constable published all the subsequent novels.

I must not, however, forget that *The Lord of the Isles* was published a month before *Guy Mannering*.   The poem was received with an interest much heightened by the recent and growing success of the mysterious Waverley. Its appearance, so rapidly following that novel, and accompanied with the announcement of another prose tale, just about to be published, by the same hand, puzzled and confounded the mob of dulness.   The more sagacious few said to themselves—Scott is making one serious effort more in his old line, and by this it will be determined whether he does or does not altogether renounce that for his new one.

The most important remarks of the principal Reviewers on the details of the plot and execution are annexed to the last edition of the poem; and show such an exact coincidence of judgment in two masters of their calling, as had not hitherto been exemplified in the professional criticism of his metrical romances.   The defects which both point out, are, I presume, but too completely explained by the preceding statement of the rapidity with which this, the last of those great performances, had been thrown off; nor do I see that either Reviewer has failed to do sufficient justice to the beauties which redeem the imperfections of the Lord of the Isles—except as regards the whole character of Bruce, its real hero, and the picture of the Battle of Bannockburn, which, now that one can compare these works from something like the same point of view, does not appear to me in the slightest particular inferior to the Flodden of Marmion.

This poem is now, I believe, about as popular as Rokeby; but it has never reached the same station in general favour with the Lay, Marmion, or the Lady of the Lake.   The instant consumption of 1,800 quartos, followed by 8vo reprints to the number of 12,000, would, in the case of

almost any other author, have been splendid success; but
as compared with what he had previously experienced,
even in his Rokeby, and still more so as compared with
the enormous circulation at once attained by Lord Byron's
early tales, which were then following each other in almost
breathless succession, the falling off was decided. One
evening, some days after the poem had been published,
Scott requested James Ballantyne to call on him, and the
printer found him alone in his library, working at the third
volume of Guy Mannering.—" Well, James," he said, " I
have given you a week—what are people saying about the
Lord of the Isles?"—" I hesitated a little," says the
printer, " after the fashion of Gil Blas, but he speedily
brought the matter to a point—' Come,' he said, ' speak
out, my good fellow; what has put it into your head to be
on so much ceremony *with me* all of a sudden? But, I
see how it is, the result is given in one word—*Disappointment.*' My silence admitted his inference to the fullest extent. His countenance certainly did look rather blank for
a few seconds; in truth, he had been wholly unprepared
for the event; for it is a singular fact, that before the
public, or rather the booksellers, had given their decision,
he no more knew whether he had written well or ill, than
whether a die thrown out of a box was to turn up a size or
an ace. However, he instantly resumed his spirit, and expressed his wonder rather that his poetical popularity
should have lasted so long, than that it should have now
at last given way. At length he said, with perfect cheerfulness, ' Well, well, James, so be it—but you know we must
not droop, for we can't afford to give over. Since one line
has failed, we must just stick to something else : '—and so
he dismissed me, and resumed this novel....He spoke thus,
probably, unaware of the undiscovered wonders then
slumbering in his mind. Yet still he could not but have
felt that the production of a few poems was nothing in
comparison of what must be in reserve for him, for he was
at this time scarcely more than forty. An evening or two
after I called again on him, and found on the table a copy
of the Giaour, which he seemed to have been reading.
Having an enthusiastic young lady in my house, I asked
him if I might carry the book home with me, but chancing
to glance on the autograph blazon, ' *To the Monarch of
Parnassus from one of his subjects,*' instantly retracted my
request, and said I had not observed Lord Byron's inscrip-

tion before. ' What inscription? ' said he; ' O yes, I had forgot, but, inscription or no inscription, you are equally welcome.'   I again took it up, and he continued—' James, Byron hits the mark where I don't even pretend to fledge my arrow.'   At this time he had never seen Byron, but I knew he meant soon to be in London, when, no doubt, the mighty consummation of the meeting of the two bards would be accomplished—and I ventured to say that he must be looking forward to it with some interest.   His counten-ance became fixed, and he answered impressively, ' O, of course.'   In a minute or two afterwards he rose from his chair, paced the room at a very rapid rate, which was his practice in certain moods of mind, then made a dead halt, and bursting into an extravaganza of laughter, ' James, cried he, ' I'll tell you what Byron should say to me when we are about to accost each other—

Art thou the man whom men famed Grizzle call?

And then how germane would be my answer—

Art thou the still more famed Tom Thumb the small? '

This,'' concludes Mr. B., '' kept him full of mirth for the rest of the evening.''

The whole scene is delightfully characteristic : and not more of Scott than of his printer : for Ballantyne, with all his profound worship of his benefactor, was an undoubting acquiescer in '' the decision of the public, or rather of the booksellers ''; and among the many absurdities into which his reverence for the popedom of Paternoster Row led him, I never could but consider with special astonishment, the facility with which he seemed to have adopted the notion that the Byron of 1814 was really entitled to supplant Scott as a popular poet.   Appreciating, as no man of his talents could fail to do, the original glow and depth of Childe Harold, he always appeared quite blind to the fact that in the Giaour, the Bride of Abydos, Parisina, and in-deed in all his early narratives, Byron owed at least half his success to imitation of Scott, and no trivial share of the rest to the lavish use of materials which Scott never em-ployed, only because his genius was under the guidance of high feelings of moral rectitude.   All this Lord Byron himself seems to have felt most completely : witness his letters and diaries; and I think I see many symptoms that both the decision of the million, and its index, '' the de-cision of the booksellers,'' tend the same way at present.

If January brought " disappointment," there was abundant consolation in store for February 1815. Guy Mannering was received with eager curiosity, and pronounced by acclamation fully worthy to share the honours of Waverley. The easy transparent flow of its style; the beautiful simplicity, and here and there the wild solemn magnificence of its sketches of scenery; the rapid, ever heightening interest of the narrative; the unaffected kindliness of feeling, the manly purity of thought, everywhere mingled with a gentle humour and a homely sagacity; but, above all, the rich variety and skilful contrast of characters and manners at once fresh in fiction, and stamped with the unforgeable seal of truth and nature— these were charms that spoke to every heart and mind; and the few murmurs of pedantic criticism were lost in the voice of general delight, which never fails to welcome the invention that introduces to the sympathy of imagination a new group of immortal realities.

The first edition was, like that of Waverley, in three little volumes, with a humility of paper and printing which the meanest novelist would now disdain to imitate; the price a guinea. The 2,000 copies of which it consisted were sold the day after the publication; and within three months came a second and a third impression, making together 5,000 copies more. Of the subsequent vogue it is needless to speak.

On the rising of the Court of Session in March, Scott went by sea to London with his wife and their eldest girl. Six years had elapsed since he last appeared in the metropolis; and brilliant as his reception had then been, it was still more so on the present occasion. Scotland had been visited in the interim, chiefly from the interest excited by his writings, by crowds of the English nobility, most of whom had found introduction to his personal acquaintance—not a few had partaken of his hospitality at Ashestiel or Abbotsford. The generation among whom, I presume, a genius of this order feels his own influence with the proudest and sweetest confidence—on whose fresh minds and ears he has himself made the first indelible impressions—the generation with whose earliest romance of the heart and fancy his idea had been blended, was now grown to the full stature; the success of these recent novels, seen on every table, the subject of every conversation, had, with those who did not doubt their parentage, far more than counter-weighed his declination, dubious after all, in the poetical balance; while the mystery that hung over them quickened the curiosity of the hesitating and conjecturing many—and the name on which ever and anon some new circumstance accumulated stronger suspicion, loomed larger through the haze in which he had thought fit to envelope it. Moreover, this was a period of high national pride and excitement. At such a time, Prince and people were well prepared to hail him who, more perhaps than any other master of the pen, had contributed to sustain the spirit of England through-out the struggle, which was as yet supposed to have been terminated on the field of Toulouse. " Thank Heaven, you are coming at last "—Joanna Baillie had written a month or two before—" Make up your mind to be stared at only a little less than the Czar of Muscovy or old Blücher."

And now took place James Ballantyne's " mighty con-summation of the meeting of the two bards." " Report," says Scott to Moore, " had prepared me to meet a man of peculiar habits and a quick temper, and I had some doubts whether we were likely to suit each other in society. I was most agreeably disappointed in this respect. I found Lord Byron in the highest degree courteous, and even kind. We met for an hour or two almost daily, in Mr. Murray's drawing-room, and found a great deal to say to each other. We also met frequently in parties and even-ing society, so that for about two months I had the advan-tage of a considerable intimacy with this distinguished individual. Our sentiments agreed a good deal, except upon the subjects of religion and politics, upon neither of which I was inclined to believe that Lord Byron enter-tained very fixed opinions. I remember saying to him, that I really thought that if he lived a few years he would alter his sentiments. He answered, rather sharply—' I suppose you are one of those who prophesy I shall turn Methodist.' I replied—' No; I don't expect your conver-sion to be of such an ordinary kind. I would rather look to see you retreat upon the Catholic faith, and distinguish yourself by the austerity of your penances.' He smiled gravely, and seemed to allow I might be right. On poli-tics, he used sometimes to express a high strain of what is now called Liberalism; but it appeared to me that the pleasure it afforded him, as a vehicle for displaying his

wit and satire against individuals in office, was at the
bottom of this habit of thinking, rather than any real conviction of the political principles on which he talked.   He
was certainly proud of his rank and ancient family, and
in that respect, as much an aristocrat as was consistent
with good sense and good breeding.   Some disgusts, how
adopted I know not, seemed to me to have given this
peculiar and (as it appeared to me) contradictory cast of
mind; but, at heart, I would have termed Byron a
patrician on principle. . . . Lord Byron's reading did
not seem to me to have been very extensive, either in
poetry or history.   Having the advantage of him in that
respect, and possessing a good competent share of such
reading as is little read, I was sometimes able to put
under his eye objects which had for him the interest of
novelty.   I remember particularly repeating to him the
fine poem of Hardyknute, an imitation of the old Scottish ballad, with which he was so much affected, that
some one who was in the same apartment asked me what
I could possibly have been telling Byron by which he
was so much agitated. . . . Like the old heroes in
Homer, we exchanged gifts.   I gave Byron a beautiful
dagger mounted with gold, which had been the property
of the redoubted Elfi Bey.   But I was to play the part of
Diomed in the Iliad, for Byron sent me, some time after,
a large sepulchral vase of silver.   It was full of dead
men's bones, and had inscriptions on two sides of the
base.   One ran thus :—' The bones contained in this urn
were found in certain ancient sepulchres within the long
walls of Athens, in the month of February 1811.'   The
other face bears the lines of Juvenal—' Expende—quot
libras in duce summo invenies?—Mors sola fatetur quan-
tula sint hominum corpuscula.'   To these I have added
a third inscription, in these words—' The gift of Lord
Byron to Walter Scott.'   There was a letter with this
vase, more valuable to me than the gift itself, from the
kindness with which the donor expressed himself towards
me.   I left it naturally in the urn with the bones; but it
is now missing.   As the theft was not of a nature to be
practised by a mere domestic, I am compelled to suspect
the inhospitality of some individual of higher station,
most gratuitously exercised certainly, since, after what I
have here said, no one will probably choose to boast of
possessing this literary curiosity.   We had a good deal of

laughing, I remember, on what the public might be supposed to think, or say, concerning the gloomy and ominous nature of our mutual gifts. He was often melancholy—almost gloomy. When I observed him in this humour, I used either to wait till it went off of its own accord, or till some natural and easy mode occurred of leading him into conversation, when the shadows almost always left his countenance, like the mist rising from a landscape. In conversation, he was very animated. . . . I think I also remarked in his temper starts of suspicion, when he seemed to pause and consider whether there had not been a secret, and perhaps offensive, meaning in something casually said to him. In this case I also judged it best to let his mind, like a troubled spring, work itself clear, which it did in a minute or two. I was considerably older, you will recollect, than my noble friend, and had no reason to fear his misconstruing my sentiments towards him, nor had I ever the slightest reason to doubt that they were kindly returned on his part. If I had occasion to be mortified by the display of genius which threw into the shade such pretensions as I was then supposed to possess, I might console myself that, in my own case, the materials of mental happiness had been mingled in a greater proportion. . . . . I have always continued to think that a crisis of life was arrived, in which a new career of fame was opened to him, and that had he been permitted to start upon it, he would have obliterated the memory of such parts of his life as friends would wish to forget.''

It was also in the spring of 1815 that Scott had, for the first time, the honour of being presented to the Prince Regent. His Royal Highness, on reading his Edinburgh Address, had said to William Dundas, that '' Walter Scott's charming behaviour about the laureateship made him doubly desirous of seeing him at Carlton House '': and there had been other messages from the Prince's librarian. On hearing from Mr. Croker (then Secretary to the Admiralty) that Scott was to be in town by the middle of March, the Prince said—'' Let me know when he comes, and I'll get up a snug little dinner that will suit him;'' and, after he had been presented and graciously received at the *levée,* he was invited to dinner accordingly, through his excellent friend Mr. Adam (afterwards Lord Chief Commissioner of the Jury Court in

Scotland),[1] who at that time held a confidential office in the royal household. The Regent had consulted with Mr. Adam also as to the composition of the party. " Let us have," said he, " just a few friends of his own—and the more Scotch the better ; " and both the Chief Commissioner and Mr. Croker assure me that the party was the most interesting and agreeable one in their recollection. It comprised, I believe, the Duke of York—the late Duke of Gordon (then Marquess of Huntly)—the late Marquess of Hertford (then Lord Yarmouth)—the Earl of Fife— and Scott's early friend Lord Melville. " The Prince and Scott," says Mr. Croker, " were the two most brilliant story-tellers in their several ways, that I have ever happened to meet ; they were both aware of their *forte*, and both exerted themselves that evening with delightful effect. On going home, I really could not decide which of them had shone the most. The Regent was enchanted with Scott, as Scott with him ; and on all his subsequent visits to London, he was a frequent guest at the royal table." The Lord Chief Commissioner remembers that the Prince was particularly delighted with the poet's anecdotes of the old Scotch judges and lawyers, which his Royal Highness sometimes *capped* by ludicrous traits of certain ermined sages of his own acquaintance. Scott told, among others, a story which he was fond of telling ; and the commentary of, his Royal Highness on hearing it amused Scott, who often mentioned it afterwards. The anecdote is this :—A certain Judge, whenever he went on a particular circuit, was in the habit of visiting a gentleman of good fortune in the neighbourhood of one of the assize towns, and staying at least one night, which, being both of them ardent chess-players, they usually concluded with their favourite game. One Spring circuit the battle was not decided at daybreak, so the Judge said—" Weel, Donald, I must e'en come back this gate in the harvest, and let the game lie ower for the present ; " and back he came in October, but not to his old friend's hospitable house ; for that gentleman had in the interim been appre-

---

[1] This most amiable and venerable gentleman, my dear and kind friend, died at Edinburgh on the 17th February 1839, in the 89th year of his age. He retained his strong mental faculties in their perfect vigour to the last days of this long life, and with them the warmth of social feelings which had endeared him to all who were so happy as to have any opportunity of knowing him—to none more than Scott.

hended on a capital charge (of forgery), and his name
stood on the *Porteous Roll*, or list of those who were
about to be tried under his former guest's auspices. The
laird was indicted and tried accordingly, and the jury returned a verdict of *guilty*. The Judge forthwith put on
his cocked hat (which answers to the black cap in England) and pronounced the sentence of the law in the usual
terms :—" To be hanged by the neck until you be dead;
and may the Lord have mercy upon your unhappy soul ! "
Having concluded this awful formula in his most sonorous
cadence, the Judge, dismounting his formidable beaver,
gave a familiar nod to his unfortunate acquaintance, and
said to him in a sort of chuckling whisper—" And now,
Donald, my man, I think I've checkmated you for ance."
The Regent laughed heartily at this specimen of judicial
humour : and " I'faith, Walter," said he, " this old big-
wig seems to have taken things as coolly as my tyrannical
self. Don't you remember Tom Moore's description of
me at breakfast—

'The table spread with tea and toast,
    Death-warrants and the Morning Post '? "

Towards midnight, the Prince called for " a bumper,
with all the honours, to the Author of Waverley," and
looked significantly, as he was charging his own glass, to
Scott. Scott seemed somewhat puzzled for a moment,
but instantly recovering himself, and filling his glass to
the brim, said, " Your Royal Highness looks as if you
thought I had some claim to the honours of this toast.
I have no such pretensions, but shall take good care that
the real Simon Pure hears of the high compliment that
has now been paid him." He then drank off his claret,
and joined in the cheering, which the Prince himself
timed. But before the company could resume their seats,
his Royal Highness exclaimed—" Another of the same,
if you please, to the Author of Marmion—and now,
Walter, my man, I've checkmated you for *ance*." The
second bumper was followed by cheers still more prolonged; and Scott then rose and returned thanks in a
short address, which struck the Lord Chief Commissioner
as " alike grave and graceful." This story has been circulated in a very perverted shape. I now give it on the
authority of my venerated friend.—He adds, that having
occasion, the day after, to call on the Duke of York, his
Royal Highness said to him : " Upon my word, Adam,

my brother went rather too near the wind about Waverley
—but nobody could have turned the thing more prettily
than Walter Scott did—and upon the whole I never had
better fun." [1]

The Regent, as was his custom with those he most delighted to honour, uniformly addressed the poet, even at
their first dinner, by his Christian name, " Walter."

Before he left town, he again dined at Carlton House,
when the party was a still smaller one than before, and
the merriment, if possible, still more free. That nothing
might be wanting, the Prince sung several capital songs
in the course of that evening—as witness the lines in
Sultan Serendib—

> " I love a Prince will bid the bottle pass,
> Exchanging with his subjects glance and glass ;
> In fitting time can, gayest of the gay,
> Keep up the jest and mingle in the lay.
> Such Monarchs best our freeborn humour suit,
> But despots must be stately, stern, and mute."

Before he returned to Edinburgh, on the 22nd of May,
the Regent sent him a gold snuff-box, set in brilliants,
with a medallion of his Royal Highness's head on the lid,
" as a testimony " (writes Mr. Adam, in transmitting it)
" of the high opinion his Royal Highness entertains of
your genius and merit."

I transcribe what follows from James Ballantyne's
Memoranda :—" After Mr. Scott's first interview with
his Sovereign, one or two intimate friends took the liberty
of inquiring, what judgment he had formed of the
Regent's talents? He declined giving any definite answer
—but repeated, that ' he was the first gentleman he had
seen—certainly the first *English* gentleman of his day ;
—there was something about him which, independently
of the *prestige*, the ' divinity, which hedges a King,'
marked him as standing entirely by himself : but as to his
abilities, spoken of as distinct from his charming manners, how could any one form a fair judgment of that
man who introduced whatever subject he chose, discussed

[1] Since this narrative was first published, I have been told by
two gentlemen who were at this dinner, that, according to their
recollection, the Prince *did not* on that occasion run " so near the
wind " as my text represents : and I am inclined to believe that a
subsequent scene may have been unconsciously blended with a
gentler rehearsal. The Chief Commissioner had promised to revise
my sheets for the second edition ; but alas ! he never did so—and I
must now leave the matter as it stands.

it just as long as he chose, and dismissed it when he chose?'" Ballantyne adds—"What I have now to say is more important, not only in itself, but as it will enable you to give a final contradiction to an injurious report which has been in circulation; viz. that the Regent asked him as to the authorship of Waverley, and received a distinct and solemn denial. I took the bold freedom of requesting to know *from him* whether his Royal Highness had questioned him on that subject, and what had been his answer. He glanced at me with a look of wild surprise, and said—'What answer I might have made to such a question, put to me by my Sovereign, perhaps I do not, or rather perhaps I do know; but I was never put to the test. He is far too well-bred a man ever to put so ill-bred a question.'"

During his brief residence in London, Scott lost his dear friend George Ellis—which threw a heavy cloud over a bright sky. But the public events of the time must alone have been sufficient to keep him in a state of fervid excitement. Before his return to the north, Napoleon had been fully reinstated, and the allied forces were fast assembling in the Netherlands. His official duties compelled him to defer once more his old anxiety for "a peep at Wellington and his merry men," until the fate of Europe had been decided at Waterloo. But his friends were well aware of his resolution to visit the Continent as soon as the session was over; and he very kindly accepted the proposal of three young neighbours of Tweedside who were eager to make the excursion in his society.

With these gentlemen, Alexander Pringle of Whytbank (since M.P. for Selkirkshire), Robert Bruce (now Sheriff of Argyle), and his kinsman, the late accomplished John Scott of Gala, he left Edinburgh accordingly on the 27th of July. They travelled by the stage-coach, and took the route of Cambridge; for *Gala* and *Whytbank*, both members of that university, were desirous of showing its architecture to their friend. After this wish had been gratified, they proceeded to Harwich. "The weather was beautiful," says *Gala*, "so we all went outside the coach. At starting, there was a general complaint of thirst, the consequence of some experiments over-night on the celebrated *bishop* of my *Alma Mater*; our friend, however, was in great glee, and never was a merrier *basket* than he made it all the morning. He had cautioned us, on leaving Edinburgh, never to *name names* in such situations, and our adherence to this rule was rewarded by some amusing incidents. For example, as we entered the town where we were to dine, a heavy-looking man, who was to stop there, took occasion to thank Scott for the pleasure his anecdotes afforded him : ' You have a good memory, sir,' said he : ' mayhap, now, you sometimes write down what you hear or be a-reading about? ' He answered, very gravely, that he did occasionally put down a *few* notes, if anything struck him particularly. In the afternoon, it happened that he sat on the box, while the rest of us were behind him. Here, by degrees, he became absorbed in his own reflections. He frequently repeated to himself, or *composed* perhaps, for a good while, and often smiled or raised his hand, seeming completely occupied and amused. His neighbour, a vastly scientific and rather grave professor, in a smooth drab Benjamin and broad-brimmed beaver, cast many a curious sidelong glance at him, evidently suspecting that all was not right with the upper story, but preserved perfect politeness. The poet was, however, discovered by the captain of the vessel in which we crossed to Helvoestsleys; and a perilous passage it was, chiefly in consequence of the unceasing tumblers in which this worthy kept drinking his health.''

Before Scott reached Harwich, he received Constable's acceptance of an offer to compose, during the journey, a series of sketches, which he undertook to have ready for publication '' by the second week of September ''; and thenceforth he threw his daily letters to his wife into the form of communications meant for an imaginary group, consisting of a spinster sister, a statistical laird, a rural clergyman of the Presbyterian Kirk, and a brother, a veteran officer on half-pay. The rank of this last personage corresponded, however, exactly with that of his own elder brother, John Scott, who also, like the Major of the book, had served in the Duke of York's unfortunate campaign of 1797; the sister is only a slender disguise for his aunt Christian Rutherfurd, already often mentioned; Lord Somerville, long President of the Board of Agriculture, was Paul's laird; and the shrewd and unbigoted Dr. Douglas of Galashiels was his '' minister of the gospel.'' These epistles, after having been devoured by the little circle at Abbotsford, were transmitted to Major John Scott, his mother, and Miss Rutherfurd, in Edinburgh; from their hands they passed to those of James Ballantyne and Mr. Erskine, both of whom assured me that the copy ultimately sent to the press consisted, in great part, of the identical sheets that had successively reached Melrose through the post. The rest had of course been, as Ballantyne expresses it, " somewhat cobbled "; but, on the whole, *Paul's Letters to his Kinsfolk* are to be considered as a true and faithful journal of this expedition. The kindest of husbands and fathers never portrayed himself with more unaffected truth than in this vain effort, if such he really fancied he was making, to sustain the character of " a cross old bachelor." The whole man, just as he was, breathes in every line, with all his compassionate and benevolent sympathy of heart, all his sharpness of observation, and sober shrewdness of reflection; all his enthusiasm for nature, for country life, for simple manners and simple pleasures, mixed up with an equally glowing enthusiasm, at which many may smile, for the tiniest relics of feudal antiquity—and last, not least, a pulse of physical rapture for the " circumstance of war," which bears witness to the blood of *Boltfoot* and *Fire-the-Braes*. I shall not trespass on the reader of that delightful record, except by a few particulars which I owe to the juniors of the party.

Paul modestly acknowledges in his last letter, the personal attentions which he received, while in Paris, from Lords Cathcart, Aberdeen, and Castlereagh; and hints that, through their intervention, he had witnessed several of the splendid *fêtes* given by the Duke of Wellington, where he saw half the crowned heads of Europe grouped among the gallant soldiers who had cut a way for them to the guilty capital of France. Scott's reception, however, had been distinguished to a degree of which Paul's language gives no notion. The Noble Lords above named welcomed him with cordial satisfaction; and the Duke of Wellington, to whom he was first presented by Sir John Malcolm, treated him then, and ever afterwards, with a kindness and confidence, which, I have often heard him say, he considered as " the highest distinction of his life." He used to tell, with great effect, the circumstances of his introduction to the Emperor Alexander, at a dinner given by the Earl of Cathcart. Scott appeared, on that occasion, in the blue and red dress of the Selkirkshire Lieutenancy; and the Czar's first question, glancing at his lameness, was, " In what affair were you wounded? " Scott signified that he suffered from a natural infirmity; upon which the Emperor said, " I thought Lord Cathcart mentioned that you had served." Scott observed that the Earl looked a little embarrassed at this, and promptly answered, " O yes; in a certain sense I have served—that is, in the yeomanry cavalry; a home force resembling the Landwehr, or Landsturm."—" Under what commander? "—" Sous M. le Chevalier Rae."—" Were you ever engaged? "—" In some slight actions—such as the battle of the Cross Causeway and the affair of Moredun-Mill." —" This," says Mr. Pringle of Whytbank, " was, as he saw in Lord Cathcart's face, quite sufficient, so he managed to turn the conversation to some other subject." It was at the same dinner that he first met Platoff,[1] who seemed to take a great fancy to him, though, adds my friend, " I really don't think they had any common language to converse in." Next day, however, when Pringle and Scott were walking together in the Rue de la Paix, the Hetman happened to come up, cantering with some of his Cossacks; as soon as he saw Scott, he jumped off his horse, leaving it to the Pulk, and, running up to him, kissed him on each side of the cheek with extra-ordinary demonstrations of affection—and then made him understand, through an aide-de-camp, that he wished him to join his staff at the next great review, when he would take care to mount him on the gentlest of his Ukraine horses.

It will seem less surprising that Scott should have been honoured with much attention by the leading soldiers and statesmen of Germany then in Paris. The fame of his poetry had already been established for some years in that country. Yet it may be doubted whether Blücher had heard of Marmion any more than Platoff; and old

[1] Scott acknowledges, in a note to St. Ronan's Well (vol. i. p. 252), that he took from Platoff this portrait of Mr. Touchwood :— " His face, which at the distance of a yard or two seemed hale and smooth, appeared, when closely examined, to be seamed with a million of wrinkles, crossing each other in every direction possible, but as fine as if drawn by the point of a very fine needle." Thus did every little peculiarity remain treasured in his memory, to be used in due time for giving the air of minute reality to some imaginary personage.

Blücher struck Scott's fellow-travellers as taking more interest in him than any foreign general, except only the Hetman.

A striking passage in Paul's tenth letter indicates the high notion which Scott had formed of the personal qualities of the Prince of Orange. After depicting, with almost prophetic accuracy, the dangers to which the then recent union of Holland and Belgium must be exposed, he concludes with expressing his hope that the firmness and sagacity of the King of the Netherlands, and the admiration which his heir's character and bearing had already excited among all, even Belgian observers, might ultimately prove effective in redeeming this difficult experiment from the usual failure of " *arrondissements*, indemnities, and all the other terms of modern date, under sanction of which cities and districts, and even kingdoms, have been passed from one government to another, as the property of lands or stock is transferred by a bargain between private parties."

It is not less curious to compare, with the subsequent course of affairs in France, the following brief hint in Paul's 16th letter:—" The general rallying point of the *Liberalistes* is an avowed dislike to the present monarch and his immediate connections. They will sacrifice, they pretend, so much to the general inclinations of Europe, as to select a king from the Bourbon race; but he must be one of their own choosing, and the Duke of Orleans is most familiar in their mouths." Thus, in its very bud, had his eye detected the *conjuration de quinze ans!*

As yet, the literary reputation of Scott had made but little way among the French nation; but some few of their eminent men vied even with the enthusiastic Germans in their courteous and unwearied attentions to him. The venerable *Chevalier*, in particular, seemed anxious to embrace every opportunity of acting as his cicerone; and many mornings were spent in exploring, under his guidance, the most remarkable scenes and objects of historical and antiquarian interest both in Paris and its neighbourhood. He several times also entertained Scott and his young companions at dinner; but the last of those dinners was thoroughly poisoned by a preliminary circumstance. The poet, on entering the saloon, was presented to a stranger, whose physiognomy struck him as the most hideous he had ever seen; nor was his disgust lessened, when he found, a few minutes afterwards, that he had undergone the *accollade* of David " of the blood-stained brush."

From Paris, Mr. Bruce and Mr. Pringle went on to Switzerland, leaving the Poet and Gala to return home together, which they did by way of Dieppe, Brighton, and London. It was here, on the 14th of September, that Scott had his last meeting with Byron. He carried his young friend in the morning to call on Lord Byron, who agreed to dine with them at their hotel, where he met also Charles Mathews and Daniel Terry. Gala has recorded it in his note-book as the most interesting day he ever spent. " How I did stare," he says, " at Byron's beautiful pale face, like a spirit's—good or evil. But he was *bitter*—what a contrast to Scott! Among other anecdotes of British prowess and spirit, Scott mentioned that a young gentleman —— —— —— had been awfully shot in the head while conveying an order from the Duke, and yet staggered on, and delivered his message when at the point of death. ' Ha ! ' said Byron, ' I daresay he could do as well as most people without his head—it was never of much use to him.' Waterloo did not delight him, probably—and Scott could talk or think of scarcely anything else."

Mathews accompanied them as far as Warwick and Kenilworth, both of which castles the poet had seen before, but now re-examined with particular curiosity. They spent a night at Sheffield; and early next morning Scott sallied forth to provide himself with a planter's knife of the most complex contrivance and finished workmanship. Having secured one to his mind, and which for many years after was his constant pocket-companion, he wrote his name on a card, " Walter Scott, Abbotsford," and directed it to be engraved on the handle. On his mentioning this acquisition at breakfast, young Gala expressed his desire to equip himself in like fashion, and was directed to the shop accordingly. When he had purchased a similar knife, and produced his name in turn for the engraver, the master cutler eyed the signature for a moment, and exclaimed—" John Scott of Gala ! Well, I hope your ticket may serve me in as good stead as another Mr. Scott's has just done. Upon my word, one of my best men, an honest fellow from the North, went out of his senses when he saw it—he offered me a week's work if I would let him keep it to himself—and I took *Saunders* at his word." Scott used to talk of this as one of the most gratifying compliments he ever received in his literary capacity.

In a letter to Morritt, he says :—" We visited Corby Castle on our return to Scotland, which remains, in point of situation, as beautiful as when its walks were celebrated by David Hume, in the only rhymes he was ever known to be guilty of. Here they are, from a pane of glass in an inn at Carlisle :—

> ' Here chicks in eggs for breakfast sprawl,
> Here godless boys God's glories squall,
> Here Scotchmen's heads do guard the wall,
> But Corby's walks atone for all.'

Would it not be a good quiz to advertise *The Poetical Works of David Hume,* with notes, critical, historical, and so forth—with an historical inquiry into the use of eggs for breakfast; a physical discussion on the causes of their being addled; a history of the English Church music, and of the choir of Carlisle in particular; a full account of the affair of 1745, with the trials, last speeches, and so forth of the poor *plaids* who were strapped up at Carlisle; and lastly, a full and particular description of Corby, with the genealogy of every family who ever possessed it? I think, even without more than the usual waste of margin, the Poems of David would make a decent twelve shilling touch. I shall think about it when I have exhausted mine own *century of inventions.*"

Reaching Abbotsford, Scott found with his family his old friend Mr. Skene of Rubislaw, who had expected him to come home sooner, and James Ballantyne, who had arrived with a copious budget of bills, calendars, book-sellers' letters, and proof-sheets. From each of these visitors' *memoranda* I now extract an anecdote. Mr. Skene's is of a small enough matter, but still it places the man so completely before myself, that I am glad he thought it worth setting down. " During Scott's absence," says his friend, " his wife had had the tiny drawing-room of the cottage fitted up with new chintz furniture—everything had been set out in the best style—and she and her girls had been looking forward to the pleasure which they supposed the little surprise of the arrangements would give him. He was received in the spruce fresh room, set himself comfortably down in the chair prepared for him, and remained in the full enjoyment of his own fireside, and a return to his family circle, without the least consciousness that any change had taken place—until, at length, Mrs. Scott's patience could hold out no longer, and his attention was expressly called to it. The vexation he showed at having caused such a disappointment, struck me as amiably characteristic—and in the course of the evening he every now and then threw out some word of admiration to reconsole *mamma.*"

Ballantyne's note of their next morning's conference is in these terms :—" He had just been reviewing a pageant of emperors and kings, which seemed, like another Field of the Cloth of Gold, to have been got up to realise before his eyes some of his own splendid descriptions. I begged him to tell me what was the general impression left on his mind. He answered, that he might now say he had seen and conversed with all classes of society, from the palace to the cottage, and including every conceivable shade of science and ignorance—but that he had never felt awed or abashed except in the presence of one man—the Duke of Wellington. I expressed some surprise. He said I ought not, for that the Duke of Wellington possessed every one mighty quality of the mind in a higher degree than any other man did, or had ever done. He said he beheld in him a great soldier and a great statesman—the greatest of each. When it was suggested that the Duke, on his part, saw before him a great poet and novelist, he smiled, and said, ' What would the Duke of Wellington think of a few *bits of novels*, which perhaps he had never read, and for which the strong probability is that he would not care a sixpence if he had? ' You are not," (adds Ballantyne) " to suppose that he looked sheepish or embarrassed in the presence of the Duke—indeed you well know that he did not, and could not do so; but the feeling, qualified and modified as I have described it, unquestionably did exist to a certain extent. Its origin forms a curious moral problem ; and may probably be traced to a secret consciousness, which he might not himself advert to, that the Duke, however great as a soldier and statesman, was so defective in imagination as to be incapable of appreciating that which had formed the charm of his own life, as well as of his works."[1]

[1] It is proper to add to Mr. Ballantyne's solution of his " curious moral problem," that he was in his latter days a strenuous opponent

Two years after this time, when Mr. Washington Irving visited Scott, he walked with him to a quarry, where his people were at work. " The face of the humblest dependent," he says, "brightened at his approach—all paused from their labour to have a pleasant ' crack wi' the laird.' Among the rest was a tall straight old fellow, with a healthful complexion and silver hairs, and a small round-crowned white hat. He had been about to shoulder a hod, but paused, and stood looking at Scott with a slight sparkling of his blue eye as if waiting his turn; for the old fellow knew he was a favourite. Scott accosted him in an affable tone, and asked for a pinch of snuff. The old man drew forth a horn snuff-box. ' Hoot, man,' said Scott, ' not that old mull. Where's the bonnie French one that I brought you from Paris?' ' Troth, your honour,' replied the old fellow, 'sic a mull as that is nae for week-days.' On leaving the quarry, Scott informed me, that, when absent at Paris, he had purchased several trifling articles as presents for his dependents, and, among others, the gay snuff-box in question, which was so carefully reserved for Sundays by the veteran. ' It was not so much the value of the gifts,' said he, ' that pleased them, as the idea that the laird should think of them when so far away.' "

One more incident of this return—it was told to me by himself, some years afterwards, with gravity, and even sadness. "The last of my chargers," he said, "was a high-spirited and very handsome one, by name Daisy, all over white, without a speck, and with such a mane as Rubens delighted to paint. He had, among other good qualities, one always particularly valuable in

of the Duke of Wellington's politics; to which circumstance he ascribes, in these same *memoranda*, the only coolness that ever occurred between him and Scott. I think it very probable that Scott had his own first interview with the Duke in his mind when he described the introduction of Roland Græme to the Regent Murray in the Abbot:—" Such was the personage before whom Roland Graham now presented himself with a feeling of breathless awe, very different from the usual boldness and vivacity of his temper. In fact he was, from education and nature, much more easily controlled by the moral superiority arising from the elevated talents and renown of those with whom he conversed, than by pretensions founded only on rank or external show. He might have braved with indifference the presence of an Earl merely distinguished by his belt and coronet; but he felt overawed in that of the eminent soldier and statesman, the wielder of a nation's power, and the leader of her armies."

my case, that of standing like a rock to be mounted. When he was brought to the door, after I came home from the Continent, instead of signifying, by the usual tokens, that he was pleased to see his master, he looked askant at me like a devil; and when I put my foot in the stirrup, he reared bolt upright, and I fell to the ground rather awkwardly. The experiment was repeated twice or thrice, always with the same result. It occurred to me that he might have taken some capricious dislike to my dress; and Tom Purdie, who always falls heir to the white hat and green jacket, and so forth, when Mrs. Scott has made me discard a set of garments, was sent for, to try whether these habiliments would produce him a similar reception from his old friend Daisy:—but Daisy allowed Tom to back him with all manner of gentleness. The thing was inexplicable—but he had certainly taken some part of my conduct in high dudgeon and disgust; and after trying him again, at the interval of a week, I was obliged to part with Daisy—and wars and rumours of wars being over, I resolved thenceforth to have done with such dainty blood. I now stick to a good sober cob." Somebody suggested, that Daisy might have considered himself as ill-used, by being left at home when *the Laird* went on his journey. " Ay," said he, " these creatures have many thoughts of their own, no doubt, that we can never penetrate." Then laughing, " Troth," said he, " maybe some bird had whispered Daisy that I had been to see the grand reviews at Paris on a little scrag of a Cossack, while my own gallant trooper was left behind bearing Peter and the post-bag to Melrose."

Scott had written verse as well as prose during his travels. " The Field of Waterloo " was published before the end of October; the profits of the first edition being his contribution to the fund raised for the relief of the widows and children of the soldiers slain in the battle. This piece appears to have disappointed those most disposed to sympathise with the author's views and feelings. The descent is indeed heavy from his Bannockburn to his Waterloo : the presence, or all but visible reality of what his dreams cherished, seems to have overawed his imagination, and tamed it into a weak pomposity of movement. The burst of pure native enthusiasm upon the *Scottish* heroes that fell around the Duke of Welling-

ton's person, bears, however, the broadest marks of the
" Mighty Minstrel ".

> ——" Saw gallant Miller's fading eye
> Still bent where Albyn's standards fly,
> And Cameron, in the shock of steel,
> Die like the offspring of Lochiel," &c. :—

and this is far from being the only redeeming passage.
The poem was the first upon a subject likely to be sufficiently hackneyed ; and, having the advantage of coming
out in a small cheap form—(prudently imitated from
Murray's innovation with the tales of Byron, which was
the deathblow to the system of verse in quarto)—it attained rapidly a measure of circulation above what had
been reached either by Rokeby or the Lord of the Isles.

Meanwhile the revision of Paul's Letters was proceeding ; and Scott had almost immediately on his return concluded his bargain for the first edition of a third novel—
The Antiquary; nor was it much later that he completed
rather a tedious negotiation with another bonnet-laird,
and added the lands of *Kaeside* to Abbotsford—witness
the last words of a letter to Miss Baillie, dated Nov. 12 :

—" My eldest boy is already a bold horseman and a fine
shot, though only about fourteen years old.   I assure you
I was prouder of the first black-cock he killed, than I
have been of anything whatever since I first killed one
myself, and that is twenty years ago.   This is all stupid
gossip ; but, as Master Corporal Nym says, ' things must
be as they may ' : you cannot expect grapes from thorns,
or much amusement from a brain bewildered with thorn
hedges at Kaeside, for such is the sonorous title of my new
possession, in virtue of which I subscribe myself,
                    " ABBOTSFORD & KAESIDE."

His pride in the young heir of *Abbotsford and Kaeside*
was much gratified about this time, on occasion of a
solemn football match *more majorum,* held under the
auspices of the Duke of Buccleuch on the famous field
of Carterhaugh, the scene of Montrose's last battle.
The combatants on one side were picked men of the town
of Selkirk, duly marshalled and led by their Provost ; on
the other, yeomen and shepherds of the vale of Yarrow,
at whose head marched the Duke's gay and good-
humoured brother-in-law, Lord Home, well pleased with
this festive mockery of old feuds, which would have been

forgotten ages before but for the ballad so dear to the
burghers,—

> *'Tis up wi' the Sutors o' Selkirk,*
> *And 'tis down wi' the Earl of Home.*

His Lordship's lieutenant was James Hogg, now ranked
among the tenantry of Yarrow; and the muster being
complete—to quote the Edinburgh newspaper of 15th
December—" The ancient banner of the Buccleuch family,
a curious and venerable relique, emblazoned with
armorial bearings, and with the word *Bellendaine,* the
ancient warcry of the clan of Scott, was displayed, as on
former occasions when the chief took the field in person,
whether for the purpose of war or sport. The
banner was delivered by Lady Ann Scott to Master
Walter Scott, younger of Abbotsford, who attended
suitably mounted and armed, and, riding over the
field, displayed it to the sound of the warpipes,
and amid the acclamations of the assembled spectators, who could not be fewer than 2,000 in number.
That this singular renewal of an ancient military custom
might not want poetical celebrity, verses were distributed
among the spectators, composed for the occasion by Mr.
Walter Scott and the Ettrick Shepherd. . . . . The
parties parted with equal honours, but, before they left
the ground, *the Sheriff* threw up his hat, and in Lord
Dalkeith's name and his own, challenged the Yarrow men,
on the part of the Sutors, to a match to be played upon
the first convenient opportunity." The newspaper then
gives Scott's " Lifting of the Banner " :—

> " Then up with the Banner! let forest winds fan her!
> She has blazed over Ettrick eight ages and more;
> In sport we'll attend her, in battle defend her,
> With heart and with hand, like our Fathers before; "

—and that excellent ditty by Hogg, entitled " The Ettrick
Garland to the Ancient Banner of the House of Buccleuch " :—

> " All hail! memorial of the brave
> The liegemen's pride, the Border's awe!
> May thy grey pennon never wave
> On sterner field than Carterhaugh."

I have no doubt the Sheriff of the Forest was a prouder
man, when he saw his boy ride about Carterhaugh with
the pennon of Bellenden, than when Platoff mounted himself for the imperial review of the *Champ de Mars.*

Mr. Hogg in his Autobiography informs us that when

the more distinguished part of the company assembled on
the conclusion of the sport to dine at Bowhill, he was proceeding to place himself at a particular table—but the
Sheriff seized his arm, told him *that* was reserved for the
nobility, and seated him at an inferior board—" between
himself and the Laird of Harden." " The fact is," says
Hogg, " I am convinced he was sore afraid of my getting
to be too great a favourite among the young ladies of
Buccleuch ! " Who can read this, and not be reminded of
Sancho Panza and the Duchess? And, after all, he quite
mistook what Scott had said to him; there was no *high
table for the nobility*—but there was a *side-table for the
children*, at which when the Shepherd was about to seat
himself, his friend probably whispered that it was reserved
for the " *little* lords and ladies, and their playmates."—
Hogg was incurable; if it had been otherwise, he must
have been cured, for a little time at least, by some incidents of the preceding winter. He then, being as usual
in pecuniary straits, projected a work, to be called " The
Poetic Mirror," in which should appear some piece by
each popular poet of the time, the whole to be edited by
himself, and published for his benefit; and he addressed,
accordingly, to his brother bards a circular petition for
their best assistance. Scott—like Byron and most others
—declined the proposition. His letter has not been preserved, but nobody can suspect that it was uncourteous.
The Shepherd, however, took some phrase in high
dudgeon, and penned an answer virulently insolent in
spirit and in language, accusing him of base jealousy of
his own genius. I am not sure whether it was on this
or another occasion of the like sort, that James varied the
usual formulas of epistolary composition, by beginning
with " Damned Sir," and ending, " Believe me, Sir,
yours with disgust, &c."; but the performance was such
that no intercourse took place for some weeks, or perhaps
months afterwards. The letter in which Hogg at length
solicits a renewal of kindliness, says nothing, it may be
observed, of the circumstance which, according to his
Autobiography, had caused him to repent of his suspicions.
The fact was, that hearing, shortly after the receipt of the
offensive epistle, that the Shepherd was confined to his
lodgings, in an obscure alley of Edinburgh, by a dangerous
illness, Scott called on a kind friend and protector of his,
Mr. John Grieve (a hatter on the North Bridge), to make

inquiries about him, and to offer to take on himself the
expenses of the best medical attendance. He had, however, cautioned the worthy hatter that no hint of this offer
must reach Hogg; and in consequence, it might perhaps
be the Shepherd's feeling at the time that he should not,
in addressing his life-long benefactor, betray any acquaintance with this recent interference on his behalf.
There can be no doubt, however, that he obeyed the
genuine dictates of his better nature when he penned this
apologetic effusion :—

"*Gabriel's Road, February* 28, 1815.

"Mr. Scott,—I think it is great nonsense for two men
who are friends at heart, and who ever must be so—
indeed it is not in the nature of things that they can be
otherwise—should be professed enemies.

"Mr. Grieve and Mr. Laidlaw, who were very severe
on me, and to whom I was obliged to show your letter,
have long ago convinced me that I mistook part of it, and
that it was not me you held in such contempt, but the
opinion of the public. The idea that you might mean
that (though I still think the reading will bear either construction) has given me much pain; for I know I answered
yours intemperately, and in a mortal rage. I meant to
have enclosed yours, and begged of you to return mine,
but I cannot find it, and am sure that some one to whom
I have been induced to show it, has taken it away. However, as my troubles on that subject were never like to
wear to an end, I could not longer resist telling you that
I am extremely vexed about it. I desire not a renewal of
our former intimacy, for haply, after what I have written,
your family would not suffer it; but I wish it to be understood that, when we meet *by chance*, we might shake
hands, and speak to one another as old acquaintances, and
likewise that we may exchange a letter occasionally, for
I find there are many things which I yearn to communicate
to you, and the tears rush to my eyes when I consider
that I may not. If you allow this, pray let me know, and
if you do not, let me know. Indeed, I am anxious to hear
from you, for ' as the day of trouble is with me, so shall my
strength be.' To be friends *from the teeth forwards* is
common enough; but it strikes me that there is something
still more ludicrous in the reverse of the picture, and so to
be enemies—and why should I be, *from the teeth forwards*,
yours sincerely,   James Hogg? "

Scott's reply was, as Hogg says, " a brief note, telling him to think no more of the business, and come to breakfast next morning."

The year 1815 may be considered as, for Scott's peaceful tenor of life, an eventful one. That which followed has left almost its only traces in the successive appearance of nine volumes, which attest the prodigal genius and hardly less astonishing industry of the man. Early in January were published Paul's Letters to his Kinsfolk, of which I need not now say more than that they were received with lively curiosity, and general, though not vociferous applause. The first edition was an octavo of 6,000 copies; and it was followed in the course of the next two or three years by a second and a third, amounting together to 3,000 more. The popularity of the novelist was at its height; and this admitted, if not avowed, specimen of Scott's prose, must have been perceived by all who had any share of discrimination, to flow from the same pen.

Mr. Terry produced, in the spring of 1816, a dramatic piece entitled " Guy Mannering," which met with great success on the London boards, and still continues to be a favourite with the theatrical public. What share the novelist himself had in this first specimen of what he used to call the " art of *Terryfying*," I cannot exactly say; but his correspondence shews that the pretty song of the *Lullaby* was not his only contribution to it; and I infer that he had taken the trouble to modify the plot, and rearrange, for stage purposes, a considerable part of the original dialogue.

Early in May appeared the novel of " The Antiquary," which seems to have been begun a little before the close of 1815. It came out at a moment of domestic distress. His brother, Major John Scott, whose health had long been feeble, died on the 8th of May. The Major, from all I have heard, was a sober, sedate bachelor, of dull mind and frugal tastes, who, after his retirement from the army, divided his time between his mother's primitive fireside, and the society of a few whist-playing brother officers, that met for an evening rubber at Fortune's tavern. He left some £6,000 to be divided between his two surviving brothers; and Walter thus writes on the occasion to his friend at Rokeby : " Though we were always on fraternal terms of mutual kindness and good-will, yet our habits of life, our tastes for society and circles of friends, were so totally different, that there was less frequent intercourse between us than our connection and real liking to each other might have occasioned. Yet it is a heavy consideration to have lost the last but one who was interested in our early domestic life, our habits of boyhood, and our first friends and connections. It makes one look about and see how the scene has changed around him, and how he himself has been changed with it. My only remaining brother is in Canada, and seems to have an intention of remaining there; so that my mother, now upwards of eighty, has now only one child left to her out of thirteen whom she has borne. She is a most excellent woman, possessed, even at her advanced age, of all the force of mind and sense of duty which have carried her through so many domestic griefs, as the successive deaths of eleven children, some of them come to men and women's estate, naturally infer. She is the principal subject of my attention at present, and is, I am glad to say, perfectly well in body and composed in mind. . . . I sent you, some time since, The Antiquary. It is not so interesting as its predecessors—the period did not admit of so much romantic situation. But it has been more fortunate than any of them in the sale, for 6,ooo went off in the first six days, and it is now at press again; which is very flattering to the unknown author." In a letter of the same date to Terry, Scott says—" It wants the romance of Waverley and the adventure of Guy Mannering; and yet there is some salvation about it, for if a man will paint from nature, he will be likely to amuse those who are daily looking at it."

After a little pause of hesitation, it attained popularity not inferior to Guy Mannering; and though the author appears for a moment to have shared the doubts which he read in the countenance of James Ballantyne, it certainly was, in the sequel, his chief favourite among all his novels. Nor is it difficult to account for this preference, without laying any stress on the fact that, during a few short weeks, it was pretty commonly talked of as a falling off from its immediate predecessors—and that some minor critics re-echoed this in print. In that view, there were many of its successors that had stronger claims on the parental instinct of protection. But the

truth is, that although Scott's Introduction of 1830 represents him as pleased with fancying that, in the principal
personage, he had embalmed a worthy friend of his
boyish days, his own antiquarian propensities, originating
perhaps in the kind attentions of George Constable of
Wallace-Craigie, and fostered not a little, at about as
ductile a period, by those of old Clerk of Eldin, and John
Ramsay of Ochtertyre, had by degrees so developed themselves, that he could hardly, even when the Antiquary
was published, have scrupled about recognising a quaint
caricature of the founder of Abbotsford Museum, in the
inimitable portraiture of the Laird of Monkbarns. The
Descriptive Catalogue of that collection which he began
towards the close of his life, but, alas! never finished, is
entitled " *Reliquiæ Trottcosianæ—or the Gabions of the
late Jonathan Oldbuck, Esq.*" But laying this, which
might have been little more than a good-humoured pleasantry, out of the question, there is assuredly no one of
all his works on which more of his own early associations have left their image. Of those early associations,
as his full-grown tastes were all the progeny, so his
genius, in all its happiest efforts, was the " Recording
Angel "; and when George Constable first expounded his
" Gabions " to the child that was to immortalise his
name, they were either wandering hand-in-hand over the
field where the grass still grew rank upon the grave of
Balmawhapple, or sauntering on the beach where the
Mucklebackets of Prestonpans dried their nets, singing

" Weel may the boatie row, and better may she speed,
   O weel may the boatie row that wins the bairns' bread "—

or telling wild stories about cliff-escapes and the funerals
of shipwrecked fishermen.

   Considered by itself, this novel seems to me to possess,
almost throughout, in common with its two predecessors,
a kind of simple unsought charm, which the subsequent
works of the series hardly reached, save in occasional
snatches :—like them it is, in all its humbler and softer
scenes, the transcript of actual Scottish life, as observed
by the man himself. And I think it must also be allowed
that he has nowhere displayed his highest art, that of
skilful contrast, in greater perfection. Even the tragic
romance of Waverley does not set off its MacWheebles
and Callum Begs better than the oddities of Jonathan

Oldbuck and his circle are relieved, on the one hand by
the stately gloom of the Glenallans, on the other by the
stern affliction of the poor fisherman, who, when discovered repairing the " auld black bitch o' a boat " in
which his boy had been lost, and congratulated by his
visitor on being capable of the exertion, makes answer—
" And what would you have me to do, unless I wanted
to see four children starve, because one is drowned?
*It's weel wi' you gentles, that can sit in the house wi'
handkerchers at your een, when ye lose a friend; but the
like o' us maun to our wark again, if our hearts were
beating as hard as my hammer.*"

It may be worth noting, that it was in correcting the
proof-sheets of this novel that Scott first took to equip-
ping his chapters with mottoes of his own fabrication.
On one occasion he happened to ask John Ballantyne,
who was sitting by him, to hunt for a particular passage
in Beaumont and Fletcher. John did as he was bid, but
did not succeed in discovering the lines.   " Hang it,
Johnnie," cried Scott, " I believe I can make a motto
sooner than you will find one."   He did so accordingly;
and from that hour, whenever memory failed to suggest
an appropriate epigraph, he had recourse to the inexhaustible mines of " *old play* " or " *old ballad*," to which
we owe some of the most exquisite verses that ever
flowed from his pen.

Unlike, I believe, most men, whenever Scott neared the
end of one composition, his spirit seems to have caught
a new spring of buoyancy, and before the last sheet was
sent from his desk he had crowded his brain with the
imagination of another fiction.   The Antiquary was published, as we have seen, in May, but by the beginning of
April he had already opened to the Ballantynes the plan
of the first *Tales of my Landlord*; and—to say nothing
of *Harold the Dauntless*, which he began shortly after
the Bridal of Triermain was finished, and which he seems
to have kept before him for two years as a congenial
plaything, to be taken up whenever the coach brought
no proof-sheets to jog him as to serious matters—he had
also, before this time, undertaken to write the historical
department of the Register for 1814.   He had not yet
collected the materials requisite for his historical sketch
of a year distinguished for the importance and complexity

of its events; but these, he doubted not, would soon
reach him, and he felt no hesitation about pledging himself to complete, not only that sketch, but four new
volumes of prose romances—and his Harold the Dauntless also, if Ballantyne could make any suitable arrangement on that score—between the April and the Christmas of 1816.

The Antiquary had been published by Constable, but I
presume that, in addition to the usual stipulations, he had
been again, on that occasion, solicited to relieve John
Ballantyne's stock to an extent which he did not find quite
convenient; and at all events he had of late shewn a
considerable reluctance to employ James Ballantyne and
Co. as printers. One or other of these impediments is
alluded to in this queer note of Scott's :—" Dear John,—
I have seen the great swab, who is supple as a glove,
and will do ALL, which some interpret NOTHING. However, we shall do well enough.—W. S." "The great
swab" had been admitted, almost from the beginning,
into the *secret* of the Novels—and for that, among other
reasons, it would have been desirable for the Novelist to
have him continue the publisher without interruption; but
Scott was led to suspect, that if he were called upon to
conclude a bargain for a fourth novel before the third
had made its appearance, his scruples as to the matter of
printing might at least protract the treaty; and why Scott
should have been urgently desirous of seeing the transaction settled at once is sufficiently explained by the fact,
that though so much of Mr. John's old unfortunate stock
still remained on hand—and with it some occasional recurrence of difficulty as to *floating-bills* must be expected
—while Mr. James Ballantyne's management of pecuniary
affairs had not been very careful [1]—nevertheless, the sanguine author had gone on purchasing one patch of land
after another, until his estate had already grown from
150 to nearly 1,000 acres. The property all about his
original farm had been in the hands of small holders
(Scotticè, *cock-lairds*); these were sharp enough to understand that their neighbour could with difficulty resist any
temptation that might present itself in the shape of acres;

[1] In February 1816, when James Ballantyne married, it appears from letters in his handwriting that he owed to Scott more
than £3,000 of personal debt.

and thus he proceeded buying up lot after lot of unim-
proved ground, at extravagant prices,—his " appetite increasing by what it fed on " ; while the ejected yeomen
set themselves down elsewhere, to fatten at their leisure
upon the profits—most commonly the anticipated profits
—of " The Scotch Novels."

He was ever and anon pulled up with a momentary
misgiving,—and resolved that the latest acquisition
should be the last, until he could get rid entirely of " John
Ballantyne and Co." But, after the first and more
serious embarrassments had been overcome, John was far
from continuing to hold by his patron's anxiety for the
total abolition of their unhappy copartnership. He,
unless when some sudden emergency arose, flattered
Scott's own gay imagination, by representing everything
in the most smiling colours ; and though Scott, in his
replies, seldom failed to introduce some hint of caution—
such as " *Nullum numen abest si sit prudentia* "—he
more and more took home to himself the agreeable cast
of his *Rigdum's* anticipations, and wrote to him in a vein
as merry as his own—*e.g.*—" As for our stock,

" 'Twill be wearing awa,' John,
    Like snaw-wreaths when it's thaw, John," &c., &c., &c.

John could never have forgotten that it was to Constable alone that his firm had more than once owed its
escape from dishonour ; and he must have known that,
after the triumphant career of the Waverley series had
once commenced, nothing could have been more easy than
to bring all the affairs of " back-stock, &c." to a close,
by entering into a distinct and candid treaty on that subject, in connection with the future works of the great
Novelist, either with Constable or with any other first-
rate house in the trade : but he also knew that, were that
unhappy firm wholly extinguished, he must himself sub-
side into a clerk of the printing company. Therefore, in
a word, he appears to have systematically disguised from
Scott the extent to which the whole Ballantyne concern
had been sustained by Constable—especially during his
Hebridean tour of 1814, and his Continental one of 1815
—and prompted and enforced the idea of trying other
booksellers from time to time, instead of adhering to Constable, merely for the selfish purposes,—first, of facilitating the immediate discount of bills ;—secondly, of
further perplexing Scott's affairs, the entire disentangle-

ment of which would have been, as he fancied, prejudicial to his own personal importance.

It was resolved, accordingly, to offer the risk and half profits of the first edition of another new novel—or rather collection of novels—to Mr. Murray of Albemarle Street, and Mr. Blackwood, who was then Murray's agent in Scotland; but it was at the same time resolved, partly because Scott wished to try another experiment on the public sagacity, but partly also, no question, from the wish to spare Constable's feelings, that the title-page of the "Tales of my Landlord" should not bear the magical words "by the Author of Waverley." The facility with which both Murray and Blackwood embraced such a proposal, as no untried novelist, being sane, could have dreamt of hazarding, shews that neither of them had any doubt as to the identity of the author. They both considered the withholding of the avowal on the forthcoming title-page as likely to check very much the first success of the book; but they were both eager to prevent Constable's acquiring a sort of prescriptive right to publish for the unrivalled novelist, and agreed to all the terms, including a considerable burden of the endless "back-stock."

Scott's intention originally was to give in the four volumes as many tales, each having its scene laid in a different province of Scotland; but this scheme was soon abandoned: and the series included only the two stories of the Black Dwarf and Old Mortality. When the former had been printed off, Murray shewed it to Gifford, who expressed some disapprobation: and Blackwood, on hearing what the Quarterly critic thought, ventured to write to James Ballantyne, intimating his own apprehension likewise, that the Dwarf would be considered as hardly worthy of the author: he said that the groundwork was excellent, but that the execution had been too rapid —that the conclusion seemed to him very disappointing: and that if the author would recast the latter chapters, he (Mr. Blackwood) would gladly take on himself the expense of cancelling the sheets. Scott, on receiving this communication, wrote to Ballantyne in terms of violent indignation, of which Blackwood had the sternest share apparently, but which I doubt not was chiefly stirred against the "coadjutor" referred to in the new publisher's epistle. "Tell him and his coadjutor," said he, "that I belong to the Black Hussars of Literature, who neither give nor receive quarter. I'll be cursed but this is the most impudent proposal that ever was made." Ballantyne translated this into courtly phrase for the eye of the parties—but Scott heard no more of preliminary criticism.

On the first of December the Tales appeared, and notwithstanding the silence of the title-page, the change of publishers, and the attempt which had certainly been made to vary the style both of delineation and of language, all doubts whether they were or were not from the same hand with Waverley had worn themselves out before the lapse of a week. On the 14th the London publisher was unable to suppress his exultation, and addressed to Scott himself a letter concluding in these words:—" Heber says there are only two men in the world—Walter Scott and Lord Byron. Between you, you have given existence to a THIRD —ever your faithful servant, *John Murray.*" To this cordial effusion, Scott returned a dexterous answer. It was necessary, since he had resolved against compromising his incognito, that he should be prepared not only to repel the impertinent curiosity of strangers, but to evade the proffered congratulations of overflowing kindness. He contrived, however, to do so, on this and all similar occasions, in a style of equivoque which could never be seriously misunderstood. He says to Murray:—" I give you heartily joy of the success of the Tales, although I do not claim that paternal interest in them which my friends do me the credit to assign me. I assure you I have never read a volume of them until they were printed, and can only join with the rest of the world in applauding the true and striking portraits which they present of old Scottish manners. I do not expect implicit reliance to be placed on my disavowal, because I know very well that he who is disposed not to own a work must necessarily deny it, and that otherwise his secret would be at the mercy of all who choose to ask the question, since silence in such a case must always pass for consent, or rather assent. But I have a mode of convincing you that I am perfectly serious in my denial—pretty similar to that by which Solomon distinguished the fictitious from the real mother—and that is, by reviewing the work, which I take to be an operation equal to that of quartering the child. But this is only on condition I can have Mr. Erskine's assistance, who admires the work greatly more than I

Life of Sir Walter Scott   295

do, though I think the painting of the second Tale both
true and powerful.   The first tale is not very original in
its concoction, and lame and impotent in its conclusion.''

Murray, gladly embracing this offer of an article for his
journal on the Tales of my Landlord, begged Scott to
take a wider scope, and dropping all respect for the idea
of a divided parentage, to place together any materials he
might have for the illustration of the Scotch Novels in
general.   What Scott's original conception had been I
know not; but the able biographer of John Knox, Dr.
M'Crie, had, in the meantime, considered the representation of the Covenanters, in the story of Old Mortality,
as so unfair as to demand at his hands a very serious
rebuke.   The Doctor forthwith published, in a religious
magazine, a set of papers, in which the historical foundations of that tale were attacked with indignant warmth;
and Scott found the impression they were producing so
strong, that he finally devoted a very large part of his
article for the Quarterly to an elaborate defence of his
own picture of the Covenanters.[1]

[1] Since I have mentioned this reviewal, I may express here my
conviction, that Erskine, not Scott, was the author of the critical
estimate of the Waverley novels which it embraces—although for
the purpose of mystification Scott had taken the trouble to transcribe the paragraphs in which that estimate is contained.   At the
same time I cannot but add that, had Scott really been the sole
author of the article, he need not have incurred the severe censure
which has been applied to his supposed conduct in the matter.   After
all, his judgment of his own works must have been allowed to be
not above, but very far under the mark : and the whole affair would
I think, have been considered by every candid person exactly as the
letter about Solomon and the rival mothers was by Murray, Gifford,
and " the four o'clock visitors " of Albemarle Street—as a good joke.
A better joke, certainly, than the allusion to the report of Thomas
Scott being the author of Waverley, at the close of the paper, was
never penned ; and I think it includes a confession over which a
misanthrope might have chuckled :—" We intended here to conclude
this long article, when a strong report reached us of certain Transatlantic confessions, which, if genuine (though of this we know
nothing), assign a different author to these volumes than the party
suspected by our Scottish correspondents.   Yet a critic may be excused seizing upon the nearest suspicious persons, on the principle
happily expressed by Claverhouse, in a letter to the Earl of Linlith-
gow.   He had been, it seems, in search of a gifted weaver, who
used to hold forth at conventicles : ' I sent for the webster (weaver),
they brought in his *brother* for him ; though he, may be, cannot
preach like his brother, I doubt not but he is as well-principled as
he, wherefore I thought it would be no great fault to give him the
trouble to go to jail with the rest ! ' "—*Miscell. Prose*, xix. p. 85.

The answer to Dr. M'Crie, and the Introduction of
1830, have exhausted the historical materials on which he
constructed his Old Mortality; and the origin of the Black
Dwarf—as to the conclusion of which story he appears on
reflection to have adopted the opinion of honest Blackwood—has already been mentioned in an anecdote of his
early wanderings. The latter Tale, however imperfect,
and unworthy as a work of art to be placed high in the
catalogue of his productions, derives a singular interest
from its delineation of the dark feelings so often connected with physical deformity; feelings which appear to
have diffused their shadow over the whole genius of Byron
—and which, but for this single picture, we should hardly
have conceived ever to have passed through Scott's happier mind. All the bitter blasphemy of spirit which, from
infancy to the tomb, swelled up in Byron against the unkindness of nature; which sometimes perverted even his
filial love into a sentiment of diabolical malignity; all
this black and desolate train of reflections must have been
encountered and deliberately subdued by the manly parent
of the Black Dwarf. Old Mortality, on the other hand,
is remarkable as the *novelist's* first attempt to re-people
the past by the power of imagination working on materials
furnished by books. In Waverley he revived the fervid
dreams of his boyhood, and drew, not from printed
records, but from the artless oral narratives of his
Invernahyles. In Guy Mannering and the Antiquary he
embodied characters and manners familiar to his own
wandering youth. But whenever his letters mention Old
Mortality in its progress, they represent him as strong in
the confidence that the industry with which he had pored
over a library of forgotten tracts would enable him to
identify himself with the time in which they had birth,
as completely as if he had listened with his own ears
to the dismal sermons of Peden, ridden with Claverhouse
and Dalzell in the rout of Bothwell, and been an advocate
at the bar of the Privy Council when Lauderdale cate-
chised and tortured the assassins of Archbishop Sharpe.
To reproduce a departed age with such minute and life-
like accuracy as this tale exhibits, demanded a far more
energetic sympathy of imagination than had been called
for in any effort of his serious verse. It is indeed most
curiously instructive for any student of art to compare
the Roundheads of Rokeby with the Bluebonnets of Old

Mortality. For the rest—the story is framed with a deeper skill than any of the preceding novels; the canvass is a broader one; the characters are contrasted and projected with a power and felicity which neither he nor any other master ever surpassed; and notwithstanding all that has been urged against him as a disparager of the Covenanters, it is to me very doubtful whether the inspiration of romantic chivalry ever prompted him to nobler emotions than he has lavished on the re-animation of their stern and solemn enthusiasm. This work has always appeared to me the Marmion of his novels.

I have disclaimed the power of farther illustrating its historical groundworks, but I am enabled by Mr. Train's kindness to give some interesting additions to Scott's own account of this novel as a composition. The generous Supervisor visited him in Edinburgh in May 1816, a few days after the publication of the Antiquary, carrying with him a purse that had belonged to Rob Roy, and also a fresh heap of traditionary gleanings—among others some story by a Mr. Broadfoot, " schoolmaster at the clachan of Penningham." Broadfoot had facetiously signed his communication *Clashbottom*,—" a professional appellation derived," says Mr. Train, " from the use of the birch, and by which he was usually addressed among his companions, —who assembled, not at the Wallace Inn of Gandercleuch, but at the sign of the Shoulder of Mutton in Newton-Stewart." Scott (who already possessed Rob Roy's gun) received these gifts with benignity, and invited the friendly donor to breakfast next morning. He found him at work in his library, and surveyed with enthusiastic curiosity the furniture of the room, especially its only picture, a portrait of Graham of Claverhouse. Train expressed the surprise with which every one who had known Dundee only in the pages of the Presbyterian Annalists, must see for the first time that beautiful and melancholy visage, worthy of the most pathetic dreams of romance. Scott replied, " that no character had been so foully traduced as the Viscount of Dundee—that, thanks to Wodrow, Cruickshanks, and such chroniclers, he, who was every inch a soldier and a gentleman, still passed among the Scottish vulgar for a ruffian desperado, who rode a goblin horse, was proof against shot, and in league with the Devil." " Might he not," said Mr. Train, " be made, in good hands, the hero of a national romance as interesting as any about either Wallace or Prince Charlie?" "He might," said Scott, "but your western zealots would require to be faithfully portrayed in order to bring him out with the right effect." "And what," resumed Train, "if the story were to be delivered as if from the mouth of *Old Mortality?* Would *he* not do as well as *the Minstrel* did in the Lay?" I think it certain that to this interview with Train we owe the framework of the Gandercleuch Series, as well as the adoption of Claverhouse's period for one of its first fictions. It seems also probable that we owe a further obligation to the Supervisor's presentation of Rob Roy's *spleuchan.*

Within less than a month, the Black Dwarf and Old Mortality were followed by "Harold the Dauntless, by the author of the Bridal of Triermain." This poem had been, it appears, begun several years back; nay, part of it had been actually printed before the appearance of Childe Harold, though that circumstance had escaped the author's remembrance when he penned, in 1830, his Introduction to the Lord of the Isles; for he there says, "I am still astonished at my having committed the gross error of selecting the very name which Lord Byron had made so famous." The volume was published by Messrs. Constable, and had, in those booksellers' phrase, "considerable success." It has never, however, been placed on a level with Triermain; and though it contains many vigorous pictures, and splendid verses, and here and there some happy humour, the confusion and harsh transitions of the fable, and the dim rudeness of character and manners, seem sufficient to account for this inferiority in public favour. It is not surprising that the author should have redoubled his aversion to the notion of any more serious performances in verse. He had seized on an instrument of wider compass, and which, handled with whatever rapidity, seemed to reveal at every touch treasures that had hitherto slept unconsciously within him. He had thrown off his fetters, and might well go forth rejoicing in the native elasticity of his strength.

It is at least a curious coincidence in literary history, that as Cervantes, driven from the stage of Madrid by the success of Lope de Vega, threw himself into prose romance, and produced, at the moment when the world considered him as silenced for ever, the Don Quixote which has outlived Lope's two thousand triumphant

dramas—so Scott, abandoning verse to Byron, should
have rebounded from his fall by the only prose romances,
which seem to be classed with the masterpiece of Spanish
genius, by the general judgment of Europe.

CHAPTER IX

Serious Illness—Laidlaw settled at Kaeside and the Fergussons at
   Huntley-Burn—New House begun—Washington Irving—Publication of Rob Roy—and the Heart of Mid-Lothian—Scott in Edinburgh. 1817–1818.

Not to disturb the narrative of his literary proceedings,
I have deferred until now the mention of an attempt which
Scott made during the winter of 1816-1817, to exchange
his seat at the Clerk's table for one on the Bench of the
Scotch Court of Exchequer. It had often occurred to me,
in the most prosperous years of his life, that such a situation would have suited him better in every respect than
that which he held, and that his never attaining a promotion, which the Scottish public would have considered so
naturally due to his character and services, reflected little
honour on his political allies. But at the period when I
was entitled to hint this to him, he appeared to have made
up his mind that the rank of Clerk of Session was more
compatible than that of a Supreme Judge with the habits
of a literary man, who was perpetually publishing, and
whose writings were generally of the imaginative order.
I had also witnessed the zeal with which he seconded the
views of more than one of his own friends, when their
ambition was directed to the Exchequer Bench. I remained, in short, ignorant that he ever had seriously
thought of it for himself, until the ruin of his worldly
fortunes in 1826; nor had I any information that his wish
to obtain it had ever been distinctly stated, until his letters
to the late Duke of Buccleuch were placed in my hands
after his death. The Duke's answers show the warmest
anxiety to serve Scott, but refer to private matters, which
rendered it inconsistent with his Grace's feelings to interfere at the time with the distribution of Crown patronage.
I incline to think, on the whole, that the death of this
nobleman, which soon after left the influence of his house
in abeyance, must have, far more than any other circumstance, determined Scott to renounce all notions of altering his professional position.

Early in 1817, he was visited, for the first time since his childish years, with a painful illness, which proved the harbinger of a series of attacks, all nearly of the same kind, continued at short intervals during more than two years. The reader has been told already how widely his habits of life when in Edinburgh differed from those of Abbotsford. They at all times did so to a great extent; but he had pushed his liberties with a most robust constitution to a perilous extreme while the affairs of the Ballantynes were labouring. "I had," he writes to Morritt (12th March), "been plagued all through this winter with cramps in my stomach, which I endured as a man of mould might, and endeavoured to combat them by drinking scalding water, and so forth. As they grew rather unpleasantly frequent, I had reluctant recourse to Baillie. But before his answer arrived, on the 5th, I had a most violent attack, which broke up a small party at my house, and sent me to bed roaring like a bull-calf. All sorts of remedies were applied, as in the case of Gil Blas' pretended colic, but such was the pain of the real disorder that it out-devilled the Doctor hollow. Even heated salt, which was applied in such a state that it burned my shirt to rags, I hardly felt when clapped to my stomach. At length the symptoms became inflammatory, and dangerously so, the seat being the diaphragm. They only gave way to very profuse bleeding and blistering, which, under higher assistance, saved my life. My recovery was slow and tedious from the state of exhaustion. I could neither stir for weakness and giddiness, nor read for dazzling in my eyes, nor listen for a whizzing sound in my ears, nor even think for lack of the power of arranging my ideas. So I had a comfortless time of it for about a week. Even yet I by no means feel, as the copy-book hath it,

'The lion bold, which the lamb doth hold—'

on the contrary, I am as weak as water. They tell me (of course) I must renounce every creature comfort, as my friend Jedediah calls it. As for dinner and so forth, I care little about it—but toast and water, and three glasses of wine, sound like hard laws to me. However, to parody the lamentation of Hassan, the camel-driver,

'The lily health outvies the grape's bright ray,
And life is dearer than the usquebæ.' "

The scene of the 5th was more than once repeated. His

friends in Edinburgh continued all that spring in great
anxiety on his account. Scarcely, however, had the first
symptoms yielded to severe medical treatment, than he is
found to have beguiled the intervals of his suffering by
planning a drama on a story supplied to him by one of
Train's communications, which he desired to present to
Terry, on behalf of the actor's first-born son, who had
been christened by the name of Walter Scott Terry.[1]
Such was the origin of " The Fortunes of Devorgoil "—a
piece which, though completed soon afterwards, and submitted by Terry to many manipulations with a view to the
stage, was never received by any manager, and was first
published, towards the close of the author's life, under
the title, slightly altered for an obvious reason, of " The
Doom of Devorgoil."

On the 29th of March John Philip Kemble, after going
through the round of his chief parts, to the delight of the
Edinburgh audience, took his final leave of them as
Macbeth, and in the costume of that character delivered
a farewell address, penned for him by Scott. No one who
witnessed that scene, and heard the lines as then recited,
can ever expect to be again interested to the same extent
by anything occurring within the walls of a theatre; nor
was I ever present at any public dinner in all its circumstances more impressive than that which occurred a few
days afterwards, when Kemble's Scotch friends and
admirers assembled around him—Francis Jeffrey being
chairman, Walter Scott and John Wilson the croupiers.

His letters to Terry about this time prove sufficiently
that, whatever pain he endured, he had no serious apprehensions as to his health; for a principal theme is the plan
of founding a new house at Abbotsford; and by and by
the details of that project wholly engross the correspondence. The foundation was in part laid early in the ensuing
summer : an unfortunate feature in Scott's history; for he
was by degrees tempted to extend his design, and the
ultimate expense very greatly exceeded all his and his
friends' calculations.

Shortly before this time, Mr. William Laidlaw had met
with misfortunes, which rendered it necessary for him
to give up his farm. He was now anxiously looking
about him for some new establishment, and Scott invited

[1] Mr. W. S. Terry lived to distinguish himself as an officer in
the East India army; and fell in action against the Affghans.

him to occupy a house on his property, and endeavour, under his guidance, to make such literary exertions as might improve his income. The prospect of obtaining such a neighbour was, no doubt, the more welcome to "Abbotsford and Kaeside," from its opening at this period of fluctuating health; and Laidlaw, who had for twenty years loved and revered him, considered the proposal with far greater delight than the most lucrative appointment on any noble domain in the island could have afforded him. Though possessed of a lively and searching sagacity as to things in general, he had always been as to his own worldly interests simple as a child. His tastes and habits were all modest; and when he looked forward to spending the remainder of what had not hitherto been a successful life, under the shadow of the genius that he had worshipped almost from boyhood, his gentle heart was all happiness. He surveyed with glistening eyes the humble cottage in which his friend proposed to lodge him, his wife, and his little ones, and said to himself that he should write no more sad songs on *Forest Flittings*.[1]

He soon procured a little employment from Mr. Blackwood, who was then starting his Magazine; and Scott being at the moment too unwell to write himself, dictated to and *for* him the anecdotes of gypsies which appeared in Blackwood's opening Number, and have since been placed among the appendages of Guy Mannering. By and by, when the Laird had made other additions to his territory, and especially to his woodlands, Laidlaw's active watchfulness over the habits and comforts of the cottars employed well entitled him to a regular salary as *factor*. Meantime occasional literary jobs both amused and helped him; and any deficiency of funds was no doubt supplied in the way that may be guessed from Scott's delicate and thoughtful notes and letters to his most amiable friend: for example, this of November 1817:—" Dear Willie,—I hope you will not quarrel with my last. Believe me that, to a sound judging and philosophical mind, this same account of Dr. and Cr. which fills up so much time in the world, is comparatively of very small value. When

---

[1] Laidlaw's song of "Lucy's Flitting"—a simple and pathetic picture of a poor Ettrick maiden's feelings in leaving a service where she had been happy—must ever be a favourite with all who understand the delicacies of the Scottish dialect, and the manners of the district in which the scene is laid.

you get rich, unless I thrive in the same proportion, I will request your assistance for less, for little, or for nothing, as the case may require; but while I wear my seven-leagued boots to stride in triumph over moss and muir, it would be very silly in either of us to let a cheque twice a-year of £25 make a difference between us. But all this we will talk over when we meet. I meditate one day a *coup-de-maître,* which will make my friend's advice and exertion essential—indeed worthy of much better remuneration."

Neither the recurring fits of cramp, nor anything else, could, as yet, interrupt Scott's literary industry. Before Whitsuntide he had made his bargain for another novel. This was at once tendered to Constable, who was delighted to interrupt in his turn the connection with Murray and Blackwood, and readily agreed to meet John Ballantyne at Abbotsford, where all was speedily settled.

As to *Rob Roy,* the title was suggested by Constable, and he told me years afterwards the difficulty he had to get it adopted by the author. " What ! " said he, " Mr. Accoucheur, must you be setting up for Mr. Sponsor too? —but let's hear it." Constable said the name of the real hero would be the best possible name for the book. "Nay," answered Scott, "never let me have to write up to a name. You well know I have generally adopted a title that told nothing."—The bookseller, however, persevered ; and after the trio had dined, these scruples gave way.

On rising from table, according to Constable they sallied out to the green before the door of the cottage, and all in the highest spirits enjoyed the fine May evening. John Ballantyne, hopping up and down in his glee, exclaimed, " Is Rob's gun here, Mr. Scott; would you object to my trying the auld barrel with a *few de joy?* " —" Nay, Mr. Puff," said Scott, "it would burst, and blow you to the devil before your time."—" Johnny, my man," said Constable, "what the mischief puts drawing at sight into *your* head? " Scott laughed heartily at this innuendo ; and then observing that the little man felt somewhat sore, called attention to the notes of a bird in the adjoining shrubbery. " And by the bye," said he, as they continued listening, " 'tis a long time, Johnny, since we have had the Cobbler of Kelso." Mr. Puff forthwith jumped up on a mass of stone, and seating himself in the proper attitude of one working with his awl, began a favourite interlude, mimicking a certain son of Crispin, at whose stall Scott and he had often lingered when they were schoolboys, and a blackbird, the only companion of his cell, that used to sing to him, while he talked and whistled to it all day long. With this performance Scott was always delighted : nothing could be richer than the contrast of the bird's wild sweet notes, some of which he imitated with wonderful skill, and the accompaniment of the Cobbler's hoarse cracked voice, uttering all manner of endearing epithets, which Johnny multiplied and varied in a style worthy of the Old Women in Rabelais at the birth of Pantagruel. I often wondered that Mathews, who borrowed so many good things from John Ballantyne, allowed this Cobbler, which was certainly the masterpiece, to escape him.

Scott himself had probably exceeded that evening the three glasses of wine sanctioned by his Sangrados. " I never," said Constable, " had found him so disposed to be communicative about what he meant to do. Though he had had a return of his illness but the day before, he continued for an hour or more to walk backwards and forwards on the green, talking and laughing—he told us he was sure he would make a hit in a Glasgow weaver, whom he would *ravel up with Rob*; and fairly outshone the Cobbler, in an extempore dialogue between the bailie and the cateran—something not unlike what the book gives us as passing in the Glasgow tolbooth."

Mr. Puff might well exult in the " full and entire success " of his trip to Abbotsford. His friend had made it a *sine qua non* with Constable that he should have a third share in the bookseller's moiety of the bargain—and though Johnny had no more trouble about the publishing or selling of Rob Roy than his own Cobbler of Kelso, this stipulation had secured him a *bonus* of £1,200 before two years passed. Moreover, one must admire his adroitness in persuading Constable, during their journey back to Edinburgh, to relieve him of that fraction of his own old stock, with which his unhazardous share in the new transaction was burdened. Scott's kindness continued as long as John Ballantyne lived, to provide for him a constant succession of similar advantages at the same easy rate; and Constable, from deference to Scott's wishes, and from views of bookselling policy, appears to have submitted to this heavy tax on his most important ventures.

During the summer term, Scott seems to have laboured chiefly on his History of 1815 for the Register, which was published in August; but he also found time to draw up a valuable introductory Essay for the richly embellished quarto, entitled " Border Antiquities," which came out a month later. Upon the rising of the Court, he made an excursion to the Lennox, chiefly that he might visit a cave at the head of Loch Lomond, said to have been a favourite retreat of his hero, Rob Roy, and thence to Glasgow, where, under the auspices of a kind and intelligent acquaintance, Mr. John Smith, bookseller, he refreshed his recollection of the noble cathedral, and other localities of the birthplace of Bailie Jarvie.

By this time, the foundations of that part of the existing house of Abbotsford, which extends from the hall westwards to the original court-yard, had been laid; and Scott, on reaching home, found a new source of constant occupation in watching the proceedings of his masons. He had, moreover, no lack of employment further a-field,—for he was now negotiating with another neighbouring landowner for the purchase of an addition of more consequence than any he had hitherto made to his estate. In the course of the autumn he concluded this matter, and became, for the price of £10,000, proprietor of the lands of *Toftfield*, on which there had recently been erected a substantial mansion-house. This circumstance offered a temptation which much quickened Scott's zeal for completing his arrangement. The venerable Professor Fergusson had died a year before; his son Adam had been placed on half-pay; and Scott now saw the means of securing for himself, henceforth, the immediate neighbourhood of the companion of his youth, and his amiable sisters. Fergusson, who had written from the lines of Torres Vedras his hopes of finding, when the war should be over, some sheltering cottage upon the Tweed, within a walk of Abbotsford, was delighted to see his dreams realised; and the family took up their residence next spring at the new house of Toftfield, on which Scott then bestowed, at the ladies' request, the name of Huntley Burn :—this more harmonious designation being taken from the mountain brook which passes through its garden, —the same famous in tradition as the scene of Thomas the Rhymer's interviews with the Queen of Fairy. The upper part of the *Rhymer's Glen*, through which this

brook finds its way from the Cauldsheilds Loch to Toftfield, had been included in a previous purchase. He was
now master of all these haunts of "True Thomas," and
of the whole ground of the battle of Melrose, from
Skirmish-field to *Turn-again*. His enjoyment of the new
territory was, however, interrupted by various returns of
his cramp, and the depression of spirit which always attended, in his case, the use of opium, the only medicine
that seemed to have power over the disease.

A pleasant incident belongs to August 1817. Scott
had read "the History of New York by Knickerbocker,"
shortly after its appearance in 1812; and the admirable
humour of this early work had led him to anticipate the
brilliant career which its author has since run. Campbell,
being no stranger to Scott's estimation of Washington
Irving's genius, gave him a letter of introduction, which,
halting his chaise on the high-road above Abbotsford, he
modestly sent down to the house "with a card on which
he had written, that he was on his way to the ruins of
Melrose, and wished to know whether it would be agreeable to Mr. Scott to receive a visit from him in the course
of the morning."

"The noise of my chaise," says Irving, "had disturbed the quiet
of the establishment. Out sallied the warder of the castle, a black
greyhound, and leaping on one of the blocks of stone, began a
furious barking. This alarm brought out the whole garrison of
dogs, all open-mouthed and vociferous. In a little while the lord of
the castle himself made his appearance. I knew him at once, by
the likenesses that had been published of him. He came limping up
the gravel walk, aiding himself by a stout walking-staff, but moving
rapidly and with vigour. By his side jogged along a large iron-grey
staghound, of most grave demeanour, who took no part in the
clamour of the canine rabble, but seemed to consider himself bound,
for the dignity of the house, to give me a courteous reception.—
Before Scott reached the gate, he called out in a hearty tone, welcoming me to Abbotsford, and asking news of Campbell. Arrived
at the door of the chaise, he grasped me warmly by the hand :
'Come, drive down, drive down to the house,' said he, 'ye're just
in time for breakfast, and afterwards ye shall see all the wonders of
the Abbey.' I would have excused myself on the plea of having
already made my breakfast. 'Hut, man,' cried he, 'a ride in the
morning in the keen air of the Scotch hills is warrant enough for a
second breakfast.' I was accordingly whirled to the portal of the
cottage, and in a few moments found myself seated at the breakfast
table. There was no one present but the family, which consisted
of Mrs. Scott; her eldest daughter, Sophia, then a fine girl about
seventeen ; Miss Anne Scott, two or three years younger ; Walter, a
well-grown stripling ; and Charles, a lively boy, eleven or twelve

years of age.—I soon felt myself quite at home, and my heart in a glow, with the cordial welcome I experienced. I had thought to make a mere morning visit, but found I was not to be let off so lightly. ' You must not think our neighbourhood is to be read in a morning like a newspaper,' said Scott; ' it takes several days of study for an observant traveller, that has a relish for auld-world trumpery. After breakfast you shall make your visit to Melrose Abbey; I shall not be able to accompany you, as I have some household affairs to attend to; but I will put you in charge of my son Charles, who is very learned in all things touching the old ruin and the neighbourhood it stands in; and he and my friend Johnnie Bower, will tell you the whole truth about it, with a great deal more that you are not called upon to believe, unless you be a true and nothing-doubting antiquary. When you come back, I'll take you out on a ramble about the neighbourhood. To-morrow we will take a look at the Yarrow, and the next day we will drive over to Dryburgh Abbey, which is a fine old ruin, well worth your seeing.'—In a word, before Scott had got through with his plan, I found myself committed for a visit of several days, and it seemed as if a little realm of romance was suddenly open before me."

After breakfast, while Scott, no doubt, wrote a chapter of Rob Roy, Mr. Irving, under young Charles's guidance, saw Melrose Abbey, and had much talk with old Bower, the showman of the ruins, who was eager to enlighten in all things the Sheriff's friends. " He'll come here sometimes," said Johnny, " with great folks in his company, and the first I'll know of it is his voice calling out Johnny! —Johnny Bower!—and when I go out I'm sure to be greeted with a joke or a pleasant word. He'll stand an' crack an' laugh wi' me just like an auld wife—and *to think that of a man that has such an awfu' knowledge o' history!* "

On his return from the Abbey, Irving found Scott ready for a ramble.

" As we sallied forth," he writes, " every dog in the establishment turned out to attend us. There was the old staghound, Maida, that I have already mentioned, a noble animal, and Hamlet, the black greyhound, a wild thoughtless youngster, not yet arrived at the years of discretion; and Finette, a beautiful setter, with soft, silken hair, long pendant ears, and a mild eye, the parlour favourite. When in front of the house, we were joined by a superannuated greyhound, who came from the kitchen wagging his tail; and was cheered by Scott as an old friend and comrade. In our walks, he would frequently pause in conversation, to notice his dogs, and speak to them as if rational companions; and, indeed, there appears to be a vast deal of rationality in these faithful attendants on man, derived from their close intimacy with him. Maida deported himself with a gravity becoming his age and size, and seemed to consider himself called upon to preserve a great degree of dignity and decorum in our society. As he jogged along a little distance ahead of us, the young dogs would gambol about him, leap on his neck, worry at his ears, and endeavour to tease him into a gambol. The old dog would keep on for a long time with imperturbable solemnity, now and then seeming to rebuke the wantonness of his young companions. At length he would make a sudden turn, seize one of them, and tumble him in the dust, then giving a glance at us, as much as to say, ' You see, gentlemen, I can't help giving way to this nonsense,' would resume his gravity, and jog on as before. Scott amused himself with these peculiarities. 'I make no doubt,' said he, ' when Maida is alone with these young dogs, he throws gravity aside, and plays the boy as much as any of them; but he is ashamed to do so in our company, and seems to say—Ha' done with your nonsense, youngsters; what will the laird and that other gentleman think of me if I give way to such foolery?' Scott amused himself with the peculiarities of another of his dogs, a little shamefaced terrier, with large glassy eyes, one of the most sensitive little bodies to insult and indignity in the world. ' If ever he whipped him,' he said, ' the little fellow would sneak off and hide himself from the light of day in a lumber garret, from whence there was no drawing him forth but by the sound of the chopping-knife, as if chopping up his victuals, when he would steal forth with humiliated and downcast look, but would skulk away again if any one regarded him.'—His domestic animals were his friends. Everything about him seemed to rejoice in the light of his countenance. Our ramble took us on the hills commanding an extensive prospect. ' Now,' said Scott, ' I have brought you, like the pilgrim in the Pilgrim's Progress, to the top of the Delectable Mountains, that I may shew you all the goodly regions hereabouts.' . . . I gazed about me for a time with mute surprise, I may almost say with disappointment. I beheld a mere succession of grey waving hills, line beyond line, as far as my eye could reach, monotonous in their aspect, and so destitute of trees, that one could almost see a stout fly walking along their profile; and the far-famed Tweed appeared a naked stream, flowing between bare hills, without a tree or thicket on its banks; and yet such had been the magic web of poetry and romance thrown over the whole, that it had a greater charm for me than the richest scenery I had beheld in England. I could not help giving utterance to my thoughts. Scott hummed for a moment to himself, and looked grave; he had no idea of having his muse complimented at the expense of his native hills. ' It may be pertinacity,' said he at length; ' but to my eye, these grey hills, and all this wild border country, have beauties peculiar to themselves. I like the very nakedness of the land; it has something bold, and stern, and solitary about it. When I have been for some time in the rich scenery about Edinburgh, which is like ornamented garden land, I begin to wish myself back again among my own honest grey hills; and if I did not see the heather, at least once a-year, *I think I should die!*' The last words were said with an honest warmth, accompanied by a thump on the ground with his staff, by way of emphasis, that shewed his heart was in his speech. He vindicated the Tweed, too, as a beautiful stream in itself, and observed, that he did not dislike it for being bare of trees, probably from having been much of an angler in his time; and an angler does not like to have a stream overhung by trees, which embarrass him in the exercise of his rod and line. I took occasion

Life of Sir Walter Scott

to plead, in like manner, the associations of early life for my disappointment in respect to the surrounding scenery. I had been so
accustomed to see hills crowned with forests, and streams breaking
their way through a wilderness of trees, that all my ideas of romantic
landscape were apt to be well wooded. ' Ay, and that's the great
charm of your country,' cried Scott. ' You love the forest as I do
the heather; but I would not have you think I do not love the glory
of a great woodland prospect. There is nothing I should like more
than to be in the midst of one of your grand wild original forests,
with the idea of hundreds of miles of untrodden forest around me.
I once saw at Leith an immense stick of timber just landed from
America. It must have been an enormous tree when it stood in its
native soil, at its full height, and with all its branches. I gazed at it
with admiration; it seemed like one of the gigantic obelisks which are
now and then brought from Egypt to shame the pigmy monuments of
Europe; and, in fact, these vast aboriginal trees, that have sheltered
the Indians before the intrusion of the white men, are the monuments
and antiquities of your country.'

" The conversation here turned upon Campbell's poem of Gertrude
of Wyoming, as illustrative of the poetic materials furnished by
American scenery. Scott cited several passages of it with great
delight. ' What a pity it is,' said he, ' that Campbell does not
write more and oftener, and give full sweep to his genius! He has
wings that would bear him to the skies; and he does, now and then,
spread them grandly, but folds them up again, and resumes his
perch, as if he was afraid to launch away. What a grand idea is
that,' said he, ' about prophetic boding, or, in common parlance,
second sight—

> "Coming events cast their shadows before!"—

The fact is,' added he, ' Campbell is, in a manner, a bugbear to
himself. The brightness of his early success is a detriment to all
his further efforts. *He is afraid of the shadow that his own fame
casts before him.*'

" We had not walked much farther, before we saw the two Miss
Scotts advancing along the hillside to meet us. The morning's
studies being over, they had set off to take a ramble on the hills,
and gather heather blossoms with which to decorate their hair for
dinner. As they came bounding lightly like young fawns, and their
dresses fluttering in the pure summer's breeze, I was reminded
of Scott's own description of his children, in his introduction to one
of the cantos of Marmion:—

> ' My imps, though hardy, bold, and wild,
>   As best befits the mountain child,' &c.

As they approached, the dogs all sprung forward, and gambolled
around them. They joined us with countenances full of health and
glee. Sophia, the eldest, was the most lively and joyous, having
much of her father's varied spirit in conversation, and seeming to
catch excitement from his words and looks; Anne was of a quieter
mood, rather silent, owing, in some measure, no doubt, to her being
some years younger."

Having often, many years afterwards, heard Irving
speak warmly of William Laidlaw, I must not omit the
following passage :—

"One of my pleasantest rambles with Scott about the neighbourhood of Abbotsford, was taken in company with Mr. William Laidlaw, the steward of his estate. This was a gentleman for whom Scott entertained a particular value. He had been born to a competency, had been well educated, his mind was richly stored with varied information, and he was a man of sterling moral worth. Having been reduced by misfortune, Scott had got him to take charge of his estate. He lived at a small farm, on the hillside above Abbotsford, and was treated by Scott as a cherished and confidential friend, rather than a dependant. That day at dinner we had Mr. Laidlaw and his wife, and a female friend who accompanied them. The latter was a very intelligent respectable person, about the middle age, and was treated with particular attention and courtesy by Scott. Our dinner was a most agreeable one, for the guests were evidently cherished visitors to the house, and felt that they were appreciated. When they were gone, Scott spoke of them in the most cordial manner. ' I wish to show you,' said he, ' some of our really excellent, plain Scotch people; not fine gentlemen and ladies, for such you can meet everywhere, and they are everywhere the same. The character of a nation is not to be learnt from its fine folks.' He then went on with a particular eulogium on the lady who had accompanied the Laidlaws. She was the daughter, he said, of a poor country clergyman, who had died in debt, and left her an orphan and destitute. Having had a good plain education, she immediately set up a child's school, and had soon a numerous flock under her care, by which she earned a decent maintenance. That, however, was not her main object. Her first care was to pay off her father's debts, that no ill word or ill will might rest upon his memory. This, by dint of Scotch economy, backed by filial reverence and pride, she accomplished, though in the effort she subjected herself to every privation. Not content with this, she in certain instances refused to take pay for the tuition of the children of some of her neighbours, who had befriended her father in his need, and had since fallen into poverty. ' In a word,' added Scott, ' she's a fine old Scotch girl, and I delight in her more than in many a fine lady I have known, and I have known many of the finest.'

"The evening having passed away delightfully in a quaint-looking apartment, half study, half drawing-room, Scott read several passages from the old Romance of Arthur, with a fine deep sonorous voice, and a gravity of tone that seemed to suit the antiquated black-letter volume. It was a rich treat to hear such a work read by such a person, and in such a place; and his appearance, as he sat reading, in a large arm-chair, with his favourite hound Maida at his feet, and surrounded by books and reliques and Border trophies, would have formed an admirable and most characteristic picture. When I retired for the night, I found it almost impossible to sleep : the idea of being under the roof of Scott; of being on the Borders on the Tweed; in the very centre of that region which had, for some time past, been the favourite scene of romantic fiction; and, above all the recollections of the ramble I had taken, the company in which I had taken it, and the conversation which had passed, all fermented in my mind, and nearly drove sleep from my pillow.

"On the following morning the sun darted his beams from over the hills through the low lattice of my window. I rose at an early hour, and looked out between the branches of eglantine which over-hung the casement. To my surprise, Scott was already up, and forth, seated on a fragment of stone, and chatting with the work-men employed in the new building. I had supposed, after the time he had wasted upon me yesterday, he would be closely occupied this morning; but he appeared like a man of leisure, who had nothing to do but bask in the sunshine and amuse himself. I soon dressed myself and joined him. He talked about his proposed plans of Abbotsford: happy would it have been for him could he have con-tented himself with his delightful little vine-covered cottage, and the simple, yet hearty and hospitable, style in which he lived at the time of my visit."

These lines to the elder Ballantyne are without date. They accompanied, no doubt, the last proof-sheet of Rob Roy, and were therefore in all probability written about ten days before the 31st of December 1817—on which day the novel was published.

" With great joy
  I send you Roy.
  'Twas a tough job,
But we're done with Rob."

The novel had indeed been " a tough job "—for lightly and airily as it reads, the author had struggled almost throughout with the pains of cramp or the lassitude of opium. Calling on him one day to dun him for copy, James found him with a clean pen and a blank sheet before him, and uttered some rather solemn exclamation of sur-prise. " Ay, ay, Jemmy," said he, " 'tis easy for you to bid me get on, but how the deuce can I make Rob Roy's wife speak, with such a *curmurring* in my guts? "

Rob and his wife, Bailie Jarvie and his housekeeper, Die Vernon and Rashleigh Osbaldistone—these boldly drawn and happily contrasted personages—were welcomed as warmly as the most fortunate of their predecessors. Constable's resolution to begin with an edition of 10,000 proved to have been as sagacious as brave; for within a fortnight a second 3,000 was called for.

Scott, however, had not waited for this new burst of applause. As soon as he came within view of the com-pletion of Rob Roy, he desired John Ballantyne to propose to Constable a second series of the Tales of my Landlord, to be comprised, like the first, in four volumes, and ready for publication by " the King's birth-day "; that is, the 4th of June 1818. " I have hungered and thirsted," he wrote, " to see the end of those shabby borrowings among

friends; they have all been wiped out except the good
Duke's £4,000—and I will not suffer either new offers of
land or anything else to come in the way of that clearance.
I expect that you will be able to arrange this resurrection
of Jedediah, so that £5,000 shall be at my order."

Mr. Rigdum used to glory in recounting that he
acquitted himself on this occasion with a species of dexterity not contemplated in his commission.   He well knew
how sorely Constable had been wounded by seeing the
first Tales of Jedediah published by Murray and Blackwood—and that the utmost success of Rob Roy would
only double his anxiety to keep them out of the field, when
the hint should be dropped that a second MS. from Gandercleuch might shortly be looked for.   John therefore took
a convenient opportunity to mention the new scheme as
if casually—so as to give Constable the impression that
the author's purpose was to divide the second series also
between his old rival in Albemarle Street, of whom his
jealousy was always sensitive, and his neighbour Blackwood, whom, if there had been no other grudge, the recent
conduct and rapidly increasing sale of his Magazine would
have been sufficient to make Constable hate with a perfect
hatred.   To see not only his old "Scots Magazine"
eclipsed, but the authority of the Edinburgh Review itself
bearded on its own soil by this juvenile upstart, was to
him gall and wormwood; and, moreover, he himself had
come in for his share in some of those grotesque *jeux
d'esprit* by which Blackwood's young Tory wags delighted
to assail their elders and betters of the Whig persuasion.
To prevent the proprietor of this new journal from acquiring anything like a hold on the author of Waverley, and
thus competing with himself not only in periodical literature, but in the highest of the time, was an object for
which, as John Ballantyne shrewdly guessed, Constable
would have made at that moment almost any sacrifice.
When, therefore, the haughty but trembling bookseller—
"The Lord High Constable" (as he had been dubbed by
these jesters)—signified his earnest hope that the second
Tales of my Landlord were destined to come out under
the same auspices with Rob Roy, the plenipotentiary
answered with an air of deep regret, that he feared it
would be impossible for the author to dispose of the
work—unless to publishers who should agree to take with
it *the whole* of the remaining stock of "John Ballantyne

& Co."; and Constable, pertinaciously as he had stood out against many more modest propositions of this nature, was so worked upon by his jealous feelings, that his resolution at once gave way. He agreed on the instant to do all that John seemed to shrink from asking—and at one sweep cleared the Augean stable in Hanover Street of unsaleable rubbish to the amount of £5,270! I am assured by his surviving partner, that when he had finally redisposed of the stock, he found himself a loser by fully two-thirds of this sum. Burthened with this heavy condition, the agreement for the sale of 10,000 copies of the embryo series was signed before the end of November 1817; and on the 7th January 1818, Scott wrote to his noble friend of Buccleuch,—" I have the great pleasure of enclosing the discharged bond which your Grace stood engaged in on my account."

The time now approached when a Commission to examine the Crown-room in the Castle of Edinburgh, which had sprung from one of Scott's conversations with the Prince Regent in 1815, was at length to be acted upon; and the result was the discovery of the long lost regalia of Scotland. Of the official proceedings of the 4th Feb. 1818, the reader has a full and particular account in an Essay which Scott penned shortly afterwards; but I may add a little incident of the 5th. He and several of his brother Commissioners then revisited the Castle, accompanied by some of the ladies of their families. His daughter Sophia told me that her father's conversation had worked her feelings up to such a pitch, that when the lid was again removed, she nearly fainted, and drew back from the circle. As she was retiring, she was startled by his voice exclaiming, in a tone of the deepest emotion, " something between anger and despair," as she expressed it, " By G—, no ! " One of the Commissioners, not quite entering into the solemnity with which Scott regarded this business, had it seems made a sort of motion as if he meant to put the crown on the head of one of the young ladies near him, but the voice and aspect of the Poet were more than sufficient to make the worthy gentleman understand his error; and respecting the enthusiasm with which he had not been taught to sympathise, he laid down the ancient diadem with an air of painful embarrassment. Scott whispered, " Pray forgive me "; and turning round at the moment, observed his daughter deadly pale, and leaning by the door. He immediately drew her out of the room, and when the air had somewhat recovered her, walked with her across the Mound to Castle Street. "He never spoke all the way home," she said, "but every now and then I felt his arm tremble; and from that time I fancied he began to treat me more like a woman than a child. I thought he liked me better, too, than he had ever done before."

At this moment, his position, take it for all in all, was, I am inclined to believe, what no other man had ever won for himself by the pen alone. His works were the daily food, not only of his countrymen, but of all educated Europe. His society was courted by whatever England could shew of eminence. Station, power, wealth, beauty, and genius, strove with each other in every demonstration of respect and worship, and—a few political fanatics and envious poetasters apart—wherever he appeared in town or country, whoever had Scotch blood in him, "gentle or simple," felt it move more rapidly through his veins when he was in the presence of Scott. To descend to what many looked on as higher things, he considered himself, and was considered by all about him, as rapidly consolidating a large fortune:—the annual profits of his novels alone had, for several years, been not less than £10,000; his domains were daily increased —his castle was rising—and perhaps few doubted that ere long he might receive from the just favour of his Prince some distinction in the way of external rank, such as had seldom before been dreamt of as the possible consequences of a mere literary celebrity. It was about this time that the compiler of these pages first had the opportunity of observing the plain easy modesty which had survived the many temptations of such a career; and the kindness of heart pervading, in all circumstances, his gentle deportment, which made him the rare, perhaps the solitary, example of a man signally elevated from humble beginnings, and loved more and more by his earliest friends and connections, in proportion as he had fixed on himself the homage of the great and the wonder of the world.

It was during the sitting of the General Assembly of the Kirk in May 1818, that I first had the honour of meeting him in private society : the party was not a large one,

at the house of a much-valued common friend—Mr. Home
Drummond, the grandson of Lord Kames. Mr. Scott,
ever apt to consider too favourably the literary efforts of
others, and more especially of very young persons, received me, when I was presented to him, with a cordiality
which I had not been prepared to expect from one filling
a station so exalted. This, however, is the same story
that every individual, who ever met him under similar
circumstances, has had to tell. When the ladies retired
from the dinner-table, I happened to sit next him; and he,
having heard that I had lately returned from a tour in
Germany, made that country and its recent literature the
subject of some conversation. In the course of it, I told
him that when, on reaching the inn at Weimar, I asked
the waiter whether Goethe was then in the town, the man
stared as if he had not heard the name before; and that
on my repeating the question, adding *Goethe der grosse
Dichter* (the great poet), he shook his head as doubtfully
as before—until the landlady solved our difficulties, by
suggesting that perhaps the traveller might mean " the
Herr Geheimer-Rath (Privy Councillor) *Von Goethe.*"—
Scott seemed amused with this, and said, " I hope you
will come one of these days and see me at Abbotsford;
and when you reach Selkirk or Melrose, be sure you ask
even the landlady for nobody but *the Sheriff.*" He appeared particularly interested when I described Goethe as
I first saw him, alighting from a carriage crammed with
wild plants and herbs which he had picked up in the
course of his morning's botanising among the hills above
Jena. " I am glad," said he, " that my old master has
pursuits somewhat akin to my own. I am no botanist,
properly speaking; and though a dweller on the banks of
the Tweed, shall never be knowing about Flora's beauties;[1]
but how I should like to have a talk with him about
trees ! " I mentioned how much any one must be struck
with the majestic beauty of Goethe's countenance—the
noblest certainly by far that I have ever yet seen—
" Well," said he, " the grandest demigod I ever saw was
Dr. Carlyle, minister of Musselburgh, commonly called
Jupiter Carlyle, from having sat more than once for the
king of gods and men to Gavin Hamilton—and a shrewd,

[1] " What beauties does Flora disclose,
How sweet are her smiles upon Tweed," &c.
CRAWFORD.

clever old carle was he, no doubt, but no more a poet than his precentor. As for poets, I have seen, I believe, all the best of our own time and country—and though Burns had the most glorious eyes imaginable, I never thought any of them would come up to an artist's notion of the character, except Byron.'' Principal Nicol of St. Andrew's expressed his regret that he had never seen Lord Byron. '' And the prints,'' resumed Scott, '' give one no impression of him—the lustre is there, Doctor, but it is not lighted up. Byron's countenance is *a thing to dream of*. A certain fair lady, whose name has been too often mentioned in connection with his, told a friend of mine, that when she first saw Byron, it was in a crowded room, and she did not know who it was, but her eyes were instantly nailed, and she said to herself, *that pale face is my fate*. And, poor soul, if a godlike face and godlike powers could have made any excuse for devilry, to be sure she had one.'' In the course of this talk, Sir P. Murray of Ochtertyre, an old friend and schoolfellow of Scott's, asked him, across the table, if he had any faith in the antique busts of Homer. '' No, truly,'' he answered, smiling, '' for if there had been either limners or stuccoyers worth their salt in those days, the owner of such a headpiece would never have had to trail the poke. They would have alimented the honest man decently among them for a lay-figure.''

A few days after this, I received a communication from the Messrs. Ballantyne, to the effect that Mr. Scott's various avocations had prevented him from fulfilling his agreement with them as to the historical department of the Edinburgh Annual Register for 1816, and that it would be acceptable to him as well as them, if I could undertake to supply it in the course of the autumn. This proposal was agreed to, and I had consequently occasion to meet him pretty often during that summer session. He told me, that if the war had gone on, he should have liked to do the historical summary as before; but that the prospect of having no events to record but radical riots, and the passing or rejecting of corn bills and poor bills, sickened him; that his health was no longer what it had been; and that though he did not mean to give over writing altogether—(here he smiled significantly, and glanced his eye towards a pile of MS. on the desk by him)—he thought himself now entitled to write nothing but what

would rather be an amusement than a fatigue to him—
" *Juniores ad labores.*"

He at this time occupied as his *den* a small square
room, behind the dining parlour in Castle Street. It had
but a single Venetian window, opening on a patch of turf
not much larger than itself, and the aspect of the place
was on the whole sombrous. The walls were entirely
clothed with books; most of them folios and quartos, and
all in that complete state of repair which at a glance reveals a tinge of bibliomania. A dozen volumes or so,
needful for immediate purposes of reference, were placed
close by him on a small movable frame—something like
a dumb-waiter. All the rest were in their proper niches,
and wherever a volume had been lent, its room was occupied by a wooden block of the same size, having a card
with the name of the borrower and date of the loan,
tacked on its front. The old bindings had obviously been
retouched and regilt in the most approved manner; the
new, when the books were of any mark, were rich, but
never gaudy—a large proportion of blue morocco—all
stamped with his *device* of the portcullis, and its motto,
clausus tutus ero—being an anagram of his name in
Latin. Every case and shelf was accurately lettered, and
the works arranged systematically; history and biography on one side—poetry and the drama on another—
law books and dictionaries behind his own chair. The
only table was a massive piece of furniture which he had
had constructed on the model of one at Rokeby; with a
desk and all its appurtenances on either side, that an
amanuensis might work opposite to him when he chose;
and with small tiers of drawers, reaching all round to the
floor. The top displayed a goodly array of session
papers, and on the desk below were, besides the MS.
at which he was working, sundry parcels of letters, proof-
sheets, and so forth, all neatly done up with red tape.
His own writing apparatus was a very handsome old
box, richly carved, lined with crimson velvet, and containing ink-bottles, taper-stand, &c., in silver—the whole in
such order that it might have come from the silversmith's
window half an hour before. Besides his own huge
elbow-chair, there were but two others in the room, and
one of these seemed, from its position, to be reserved
exclusively for the amanuensis. I observed, during the
first evening I spent with him in this *sanctum*, that while

he talked, his hands were hardly ever idle; sometimes he folded letter-covers—sometimes he twisted paper into matches, performing both tasks with great mechanical expertness and nicety; and when there was no loose paper fit to be so dealt with, he snapped his fingers, and the noble Maida aroused himself from his lair on the hearth-rug, and laid his head across his master's knees, to be caressed and fondled. The room had no space for pictures except one, a portrait of Claverhouse, which hung over the chimneypiece, with a Highland target on either side, and broadswords and dirks (each having its own story) disposed star-fashion round them. A few green tin-boxes, such as solicitors keep title-deeds in, were piled over each other on one side of the window; and on the top of these lay a fox's tail, mounted on an antique silver handle, wherewith, as often as he had occasion to take down a book, he gently brushed the dust off the upper leaves before opening it. I think I have mentioned all the furniture of the room except a sort of ladder, low, broad, well carpeted, and strongly guarded with oaken rails, by which he helped himself to books from his higher shelves. On the top step of this convenience, Hinse of Hinsteldt (so called from one of the German *Kinder-Märchen*), a venerable tom-cat, fat and sleek, and no longer very locomotive, usually lay watching the proceedings of his master and Maida with an air of dignified equanimity; but when Maida chose to leave the party, he signified his inclinations by thumping the door with his huge paw, as violently as ever a fashionable footman handled a knocker in Grosvenor Square; the Sheriff rose and opened it for him with courteous alacrity,—and then Hinse came down purring from his perch, and mounted guard by the footstool, *vice* Maida absent upon furlough. Whatever discourse might be passing, was broken every now and then by some affectionate apostrophe to these four-footed friends. He said they understood everything he said to them—and I believe they did understand a great deal of it. But at all events, dogs and cats, like children, have some infallible tact for discovering at once who is, and who is not, really fond of their company; and I venture to say, Scott was never five minutes in any room before the little pets of the family, whether dumb or lisping, had found out his kindness for all their generation.

I never thought it lawful to keep a journal of what

passes in private society, so that no one need expect from the sequel of this narrative any detailed record of Scott's familiar talk. What fragments of it have happened to adhere to a tolerably retentive memory, and may be put into black and white without wounding any feelings which my friend, were he alive, would have wished to spare, I shall introduce as the occasion suggests or serves. But I disclaim on the threshold anything more than this; and I also wish to enter a protest once for all against the general fidelity of several literary gentlemen who have kindly forwarded to me private lucubrations of theirs, designed to *Boswellise* Scott, and which they may probably publish hereafter. To report conversations fairly, it is a necessary pre-requisite that we should be completely familiar with all the interlocutors, and understand thoroughly all their minutest relations, and points of common knowledge and common feeling, with each other. He who does not, must be perpetually in danger of misinterpreting sportive allusions into serious statement; and the man who was only recalling, by some jocular phrase or half-phrase, to an old companion, some trivial reminiscence of their boyhood or youth, may be represented as expressing, upon some person or incident casually tabled, an opinion which he had never framed, or if he had, would never have given words to in any mixed assemblage—not even among what the world calls *friends* at his own board. In proportion as a man is witty and humorous, there will always be about him and his a widening maze and wilderness of cues and catchwords, which the uninitiated will, if they are bold enough to try interpretation, construe, ever and anon, egregiously amiss—not seldom into arrant falsity. For this one reason, to say nothing of many others, I consider no man justified in journalising what he sees and hears in a domestic circle where he is not thoroughly at home; and I think there are still higher and better reasons why he should not do so where he is.

Before I ever met Scott in private, I had, of course, heard many people describe and discuss his style of conversation. Everybody seemed to agree that it overflowed with hearty good-humour, as well as plain unaffected good sense and sagacity; but I had heard not a few persons of undoubted ability and accomplishment maintain, that the genius of the great poet and novelist rarely, if

ever, revealed itself in his talk. It is needless to say,
that the persons I allude to were all his own countrymen,
and themselves imbued, more or less, with the conversa-
tional habits derived from a system of education in which
the study of metaphysics occupies a very large share of
attention. The best table-talk of Edinburgh was, and
probably still is, in a very great measure made up of
brilliant disquisition—such as might be transferred without alteration to a professor's note-book, or the pages of
a critical Review—and of sharp word-catchings, ingenious
thrusting and parrying of dialectics, and all the quips and
quibblets of bar pleading. It was the talk of a society to
which lawyers and lecturers had, for at least a hundred
years, given the tone. From the date of the Union, Edinburgh ceased to be the headquarters of the Scotch nobility
—and long before the time of which I speak, they had all
but entirely abandoned it as a place of residence. I
think I never knew above two or three of the Peerage to
have houses there at the same time—and these were
usually among the poorest and most insignificant of their
order. The wealthier gentry had followed their example.
Very few of that class ever spent any considerable part
of the year in Edinburgh, except for the purposes of educating their children, or superintending the progress of a
lawsuit; and these were not more likely than a score or
two of comatose and lethargic old Indians, to make head
against the established influences of academical and forensic celebrity. Now Scott's tastes and resources had
not much in common with those who had inherited and
preserved the chief authority in this provincial hierarchy
of rhetoric. He was highly amused with watching their
dexterous logomachies—but his delight in such displays
arose mainly, I cannot doubt, from the fact of their being,
both as to subject-matter and style and method, remote *a Scævolæ studiis*. He sat by, as he would have
done at a stage-play or a fencing-match, enjoying and
applauding the skill exhibited, but without feeling much
ambition to parade himself as a rival either of the foil or
the buskin. I can easily believe, therefore, that in the
earlier part of his life—before the blaze of universal fame
had overawed local prejudice, and a new generation, accustomed to hear of that fame from their infancy, had
grown up—it may have been the commonly adopted creed
in Edinburgh, that Scott, however distinguished other-

wise, was not to be named as a table-companion in the
same day with this or that master of luminous dissertation
or quick rejoinder, who now sleeps as forgotten as his
grandmother. It was natural enough that persons
brought up in the same circle with him, who remembered
all his beginnings, and had but slowly learned to acquiesce
in the justice of his claim to unrivalled honour in literature, should have clung all the closer for that late acquiescence to their original estimate of him as inferior to
themselves in other titles to admiration. It was also
natural that their prejudice on that score should be
readily taken up by the young aspirants who breathed,
as it were, the atmosphere of their professional renown.
Perhaps, too, Scott's steady Toryism, and the effect of his
genius and example in modifying the intellectual sway of
the long dominant Whigs in the north, may have some
share in this matter. However all that may have been,
the substance of what I had been accustomed to hear certainly was, that Scott had a marvellous stock of queer
stories, which he often told with happy effect, but that,
bating these drafts on a portentous memory, set off with
a simple old-fashioned *naïveté* of humour and pleasantry,
his strain of talk was remarkable neither for depth of
remark nor felicity of illustration; that his views and
opinions on the most important topics of practical interest were hopelessly perverted by his blind enthusiasm
for the dreams of by-gone ages; and that, but for the
grotesque phenomenon presented by a great writer of the
nineteenth century gravely uttering sentiments worthy of
his own Dundees and Invernahyles, the main texture of
his discourse would be pronounced by any enlightened
member of modern society, rather bald and poor than
otherwise. I think the epithet most in vogue was *commonplace.*

It will be easily believed, that, in companies such as I
have been alluding to, made up of, or habitually domi-
neered over, by voluble Whigs and political economists,
Scott was often tempted to put forth his Tory doctrines
and antiquarian prejudices in an exaggerated shape, in
colours, to say the truth, altogether different from what
they assumed under other circumstances, or which had
any real influence upon his mind and conduct on occasions
of practical moment. But I fancy it will seem equally
credible, that the most sharp-sighted of these social critics

may not always have been capable of tracing, and doing
justice to, the powers which Scott brought to bear upon
the topics which they, not he, had chosen for discussion.
In passing from a gas-lit hall into a room with wax
candles, the guests sometimes complain that they have
left splendour for gloom; but let them try by what sort of
light it is most satisfactory to read, write, or embroider,
or consider at leisure under which of the two either men
or women look their best.

The strongest, purest, and least observed of all lights,
is, however, daylight; and his talk was commonplace,
just as sunshine is, which gilds the most indifferent objects, and adds brilliancy to the brightest. As for the
old-world anecdotes which these clever persons were condescending enough to laugh at as pleasant extravagances,
serving merely to relieve and set off the main stream of
debate, they were often enough, it may be guessed, connected with the theme in hand by links not the less apt
that they might be too subtle to catch their bedazzled and
self-satisfied optics. There might be keener knowledge
of human nature than was " dreamt of in their philosophy "—which passed with them for *commonplace*, only
because it was clothed in plain familiar household words,
not dressed up in some pedantic masquerade of antithesis.
" There are people," says Landor, " who think they write
and speak finely, merely because they have forgotten the
language in which their fathers and mothers used to talk
to them "; and surely there are a thousand homely old
proverbs, which many a dainty modern would think it
beneath his dignity to quote either in speech or writing,
any one of which condenses more wit (take that word in
any of its senses) than could be extracted from all that
was ever said or written by the *doctrinaires* of the Edinburgh school. Many of those gentlemen held Scott's conversation to be commonplace exactly for the same reason
that a child thinks a perfectly limpid stream, though perhaps deep enough to drown it three times over, must
needs be shallow. But it will be easily believed that the
best and highest of their own idols had better means and
skill of measurement: I can never forget the pregnant
expression of one of the ablest of that school and party—
Lord Cockburn—who, when some glib youth chanced to
echo in his hearing the consolatory tenet of local mediocrity, answered quietly—" I have the misfortune to think

differently from you—in my humble opinion, Walter
Scott's *sense* is a still more wonderful thing than his
genius."

Indeed I have no sort of doubt that, long before 1818,
full justice was done to Scott, even in these minor things,
by all those of his Edinburgh acquaintance, whether
Whig or Tory, on whose personal opinion he could have
been supposed to set much value. With few exceptions,
the really able lawyers of his own or nearly similar standing, had ere that time obtained stations of judicial dignity,
or were in the springtide of practice; and in either case
they were likely to consider general society much in his
own fashion, as the joyous relaxation of life, rather than
the theatre of exertion and display. Their tables were
elegantly, some of them sumptuously spread; and they
lived in a pretty constant interchange of entertainments,
in every circumstance of which, conversation included, it
was their ambition to imitate those voluptuous metropoli-
tan circles, wherein most of them had from time to time
mingled, and several of them with distinguished success.
Among such prosperous gentlemen, like himself past the
mezzo cammin, Scott's picturesque anecdotes, rich easy
humour, and gay involuntary glances of mother-wit, were,
it is not difficult to suppose, appreciated above contributions of a more ambitious stamp; and no doubt his
London *reputation de salon* (which had by degrees risen
to a high pitch, although he cared nothing for it) was
not without its effect in Edinburgh. But still the old
prejudice lingered on in the general opinion of the place,
especially among the smart praters of *the Outer-House.*

In truth, it was impossible to listen to Scott's oral
narrations, whether gay or serious, or to the felicitous
fun with which he parried absurdities of all sorts, without
discovering better qualities in his talk than *wit*—and of a
higher order; I mean especially a power of *vivid painting*
—the true and primary sense of what is called *Imagination.*
He was like Jacques—though not a "Melancholy
Jacques"; and "moralised" a common topic "into a
thousand similitudes." Shakespeare and the banished
Duke would have found him "full of matter." He disliked mere disquisitions in Edinburgh, and prepared *im-
promptus* in London; and puzzled the promoters of such
things sometimes by placid silence, sometimes by broad
merriment. To such men he seemed *commonplace*—not

so to the most dexterous masters in what was to some of them almost a science; not so to Rose, Hallam, Moore, or Rogers,—to Ellis, Mackintosh, Croker, or Canning.

Scott managed to give and receive such great dinners as I have been alluding to, at least as often as any other private gentleman in Edinburgh; but he very rarely accompanied his wife and daughters to the evening assemblies, which commonly ensued under other roofs—for *early to rise*, unless in the case of spare-fed anchorites, takes for granted *early to bed*. When he had no dinner engagement, he frequently gave a few hours to the theatre; but still more frequently, when the weather was fine, and still more, I believe, to his own satisfaction, he drove out with some of his family, or a single friend, in an open carriage; the favourite rides being either to the Blackford Hills, or to Ravelston, and so home by Corstorphine; or to the beach of Portobello, where Peter was always instructed to keep his horses as near as possible to the sea. More than once, even in the first summer of my acquaintance with him, I had the pleasure of accompanying him on these evening excursions; and never did he seem to enjoy himself more fully than when placidly surveying, at such sunset or moonlight hours, either the massive outlines of his " own romantic town," or the tranquil expanse of its noble estuary. He delighted, too, in passing when he could, through some of the quaint windings of the ancient city itself, now deserted, except at mid-day, by the upper world. How often have I seen him go a long way round about, rather than miss the opportunity of halting for a few minutes on the vacant esplanade of Holyrood, or under the darkest shadows of the Castle rock, where it overhangs the Grassmarket, and the huge slab that still marks where the gibbet of Porteous and the Covenanters had its station. His coachman knew him too well to move at a Jehu's pace amidst such scenes as these. No funeral hearse crept more leisurely than did his landau up the Canongate or the Cowgate; and not a queer tottering gable but recalled to him some long-buried memory of splendour or bloodshed, which, by a few words, he set before the hearer in the reality of life. His image is so associated in my mind with the antiquities of his native place, that I cannot now revisit them without feeling as if I were treading on his gravestone.

Whatever might happen on the other evenings of the week, he always dined at home on Sunday, and usually some few friends were then with him, but never any person with whom he stood on ceremony. These were, it may be readily supposed, the most agreeable of his entertainments. He came into the room rubbing his hands, his face bright and gleesome, like a boy arriving at home for the holidays, his Peppers and Mustards gambolling about his heels, and even the stately Maida grinning and wagging his tail in sympathy. Among the most regular guests on these happy evenings were, in my time, as had long before been the case, Mrs. Maclean Clephane of Torloisk (with whom he agreed cordially on all subjects except the authenticity of Ossian), and her daughters, whose guardian he had become at their choice. The eldest of them had been for some years married to the Earl of Compton (now Marquis of Northampton), and was of course seldom in the north; but the others had much of the same tastes and accomplishments which so highly distinguished the late Lady Northampton; and Scott delighted especially in their proficiency in the poetry and music of their native isles. Mr. and Mrs. Skene of Rubislaw were frequent attendants—and so were the Macdonald-Buchanans of Drumakiln, whose eldest daughter, Isabella, was his chief favourite among all his *nieces* of the Clerk's table—as was, among the *nephews*, my own dear friend and companion, Joseph Hume, a singularly graceful young man, rich in the promise of hereditary genius, but, alas! cut off in the early bloom of his days. The well-beloved Erskine was seldom absent; and very often Terry or James Ballantyne came with him—sometimes, though less frequently, Constable. Among other persons who now and then appeared at these "dinners without the silver dishes," as Scott called them, I may mention—to say nothing of such old cronies as Mr. Clerk, Mr. Thomson, and Mr. Kirkpatrick Sharpe—Sir Alexander Boswell of Auchinleck, who had all his father *Bozzy's* cleverness, good-humour, and joviality, without one touch of his meaner qualities—wrote *Jenny dang the Weaver*, and some other popular songs, which he sang capitally— and was moreover a thorough bibliomaniac; the late Sir Alexander Don of Newton, in all courteous and elegant accomplishments the model of a cavalier; and last, not least, William Allan, R.A., who had shortly before this time returned to Scotland from several years of travel in Russia and Turkey. At one of these plain hearty dinners, however, the company rarely exceeded three or four, besides the as yet undivided family.

Scott had a story of a topping goldsmith on the Bridge, who prided himself on being the mirror of Amphitryons, and accounted for his success by stating that it was his invariable custom to set his own stomach at ease, by a beef-steak and a pint of port in his back-shop, half-an-hour before the arrival of his guests. But the host of Castle Street had no occasion to imitate this prudent arrangement, for his appetite at dinner was neither keen nor nice. Breakfast was his chief meal. Before that came, he had gone through the severest part of his day's work, and then he set to with the zeal of Crabbe's Squire Tovell—

     " And laid at once a pound upon his plate."

No foxhunter ever prepared himself for the field by more substantial appliances. His table was always provided, in addition to the usually plentiful delicacies of a Scotch breakfast, with some solid article, on which he did most lusty execution—a round of beef—a pasty, such as made Gil Blas's eyes water—or, most welcome of all, a cold sheep's head, the charms of which primitive dainty he has so gallantly defended against the disparaging sneers of Dr. Johnson and his bear-leader.[1] A huge brown loaf flanked his elbow, and it was placed upon a broad wooden trencher, that he might cut and come again with the bolder knife. Often did the *Clerks' coach*, commonly called among themselves *the Lively*—which trundled round every morning to pick up the brotherhood, and then deposited them at the proper minute in the Parliament Close—often did this lumbering hackney arrive at his door before he had fully appeased what Homer calls " the sacred rage of hunger " ; and vociferous was the merriment of the learned *uncles*, when the surprised poet swung forth to join them, with an extemporised sandwich, that looked like a ploughman's luncheon, in his hand. But this robust supply would have served him in fact for the day. He never tasted anything more before dinner, and at dinner he ate almost as sparingly as Squire Tovell's niece from the boarding-school—

    ——" Who cut the sanguine flesh in frustums fine,
And marvelled much to see the creatures dine."

---

     [1] See *Croker's Boswell* (edit. 1831), vol iii. p. 38.

The only dishes he was at all fond of were the old-fashioned ones to which he had been accustomed in the days of Saunders Fairford; and which really are excellent dishes,—such, in truth, as Scotland borrowed from France before Catherine de Medicis brought in her Italian *virtuosi* to revolutionise the kitchen like the court. Of most of these, I believe, he has in the course of his novels found some opportunity to record his esteem. But above all, who can forget that his King Jamie, amidst the splendours of Whitehall, thinks himself an ill-used monarch unless his first course includes *cockyleekie?*

It is a fact, which some philosophers may think worth setting down, that Scott's organisation, as to more than one of the senses, was the reverse of exquisite. He had very little of what musicians call an ear; his smell was hardly more delicate. I have seen him stare about, quite unconscious of the cause, when his whole company betrayed their uneasiness at the approach of an over-kept haunch of venison; and neither by the nose or the palate could he distinguish corked wine from sound. He could never tell Madeira from Sherry; nay, an Oriental friend having sent him a butt of *sheeraz,* when he remembered the circumstance some time afterwards, and called for a bottle to have Sir John Malcolm's opinion of its quality, it turned out that his butler, mistaking the label, had already served up half the binn as *sherry.* Port he considered as physic: he never willingly swallowed more than one glass of it, and was sure to anathematise a second, if offered, by repeating John Home's epigram :—

> " Bold and erect the Caledonian stood,
> Old was his mutton, and his claret good;
> Let him drink port, the English statesman cried—
> He drank the poison, and his spirit died."

In truth, he liked no wines except sparkling champagne and claret; but even as to this last he was no connoisseur; and sincerely preferred a tumbler of whisky-toddy to the most precious " liquid ruby " that ever flowed in the cup of a prince. He rarely took any other potation when quite alone with his family; but at the Sunday board he circulated the champagne briskly during dinner, and considered a pint of claret each man's fair share afterwards. I should not omit, however, that his Bordeaux was uniformly preceded by a small libation of the genuine *mountain dew,* which he poured with his own hand, *more majorum*, for each guest—making use for the purpose of such a multifarious collection of ancient Highland *quaighs* (little cups of curiously dovetailed wood, inlaid with silver) as no Lowland sideboard but his was ever equipped with —but commonly reserving for himself one that was peculiarly precious in his eyes, as having travelled from Edinburgh to Derby in the canteen of Prince Charlie. This relic had been presented to "the wandering Ascanius" by some very careful follower, for its bottom is of glass, that he who quaffed might keep his eye the while upon the dirk hand of his companion.

The sound of music—(even, I suspect, of any sacred music but psalm-singing)—would be considered indecorous in the streets of Edinburgh on a Sunday night; so, upon the occasions I am speaking of, the harp was silent, and *Otterburne* and *The Bonnie House of Airlie* must needs be dispensed with. To make amends, after tea in the drawing-room, Scott usually read some favourite author for the amusement of his little circle; or Erskine, Ballantyne, or Terry, did so, at his request. He himself read aloud high poetry with far greater simplicity, depth, and effect, than any other man I ever heard; and in Macbeth or Julius Cæsar, or the like, I doubt if Kemble could have been more impressive. Yet the changes of intonation were so gently managed, that he contrived to set the different interlocutors clearly before us, without the least approach to theatrical artifice. Not so the others I have mentioned; they all read cleverly and agreeably, but with the decided trickery of stage recitation. To them he usually gave the book when it was a comedy, or, indeed, any other drama than Shakspeare's or Joanna Baillie's. Dryden's Fables, Johnson's two Satires, and certain detached scenes of Beaumont and Fletcher, especially that in the *Lover's Progress*, where the ghost of the musical innkeeper makes his appearance, were frequently selected. Of the poets, his contemporaries, however, there was not one that did not come in for his part. In Wordsworth, his pet pieces were, I think, the *Song for Brougham Castle*, the *Laodamia*, and some of the early sonnets :—in Southey, *Queen Orraca, Fernando Ramirez*, the *Lines on the Holly Tree*—and, of his larger poems, the *Thalaba*. Crabbe was perhaps, next to Shakspeare, the standing resource; but in those days Byron was pouring out his spirit fresh and full; and, if a new piece from his hand had appeared, it was sure to be read by Scott the Sunday evening after-wards, and that with such delighted emphasis as shewed how completely the elder bard had kept all his enthusiasm for poetry at the pitch of youth, all his admiration of genius, free, pure, and unstained by the least drop of literary jealousy. Rare and beautiful example of a happily constituted and virtuously disciplined mind and character !

Let me turn, meanwhile, to a table very different from his own, at which, from this time forward, I often met Scott.

James Ballantyne then lived in St. John Street, a row of good, old-fashioned, and spacious houses, adjoining the Canongate and Holyrood, and at no great distance from his printing establishment. He had married a few years before the daughter of a wealthy farmer in Berwickshire— a quiet, amiable woman, of simple manners, and perfectly domestic habits : a group of fine young children were growing up about him; and he usually, if not constantly, had under his roof his aged mother, his and his wife's tender care of whom it was most pleasing to witness. As far as a stranger might judge, there could not be a more exemplary household, or a happier one; and I have occa-sionally met the poet in St. John Street when there were no other guests but Erskine, Terry, George Hogarth,[1] and another intimate friend or two, and when James Ballan-tyne was content to appear in his own true and best colours, the kind head of his family, the respectful but honest schoolfellow of Scott, the easy landlord of a plain, comfortable table. But when any great event was about to take place in the business, especially on the eve of a new novel, there were doings of a higher strain in St. John Street; and to be present at one of those scenes was truly a rich treat, even—if not especially—for persons who, like myself, had no more *knowledge* than the rest of the world as to the authorship of Waverley. Then where con-gregated about the printer all his own literary allies, of whom a considerable number were by no means personally familiar with " THE GREAT UNKNOWN " :—who, by the way, owed to him that widely adopted title;—and He appeared among the rest with his usual open aspect of

[1] George Hogarth, Esq., W.S., brother of Mrs. James Ballantyne. This gentleman is now well known in the literary world ; especially by a History of Music, of which all who understand that science speak highly.

buoyant good-humour—although it was not difficult to
trace, in the occasional play of his features, the diversion
it afforded him to watch all the procedure of his swelling
confidant, and the curious neophytes that surrounded the
well-spread board.

The feast was, to use one of James's own favourite
epithets, *gorgeous;* an aldermanic display of turtle and
venison, with the suitable accompaniments of iced punch,
potent ale, and generous Madeira.   When the cloth was
drawn, the burly preses arose, with all he could muster
of the port of John Kemble, and spouted with a sonorous
voice the formula of Macbeth—

> " Fill full !
> I drink to the general joy of the whole table ! "

This was followed by " The King, God bless him ! " and
second came—" Gentlemen, there is another toast which
never has been nor shall be omitted in this house of mine
—I give you the health of Mr. Walter Scott with three
times three ! "—All honour having been done to this
health, and Scott having briefly thanked the company
with some expressions of warm affection to their host,
Mrs. Ballantyne retired;—the bottles passed round twice
or thrice in the usual way;—and then James rose once
more, every vein on his brow distended, his eyes solemnly
fixed upon vacancy, to propose, not as before in his stentorian key, but with " 'bated breath," in the sort of
whisper by which a stage conspirator thrills the gallery—
" *Gentlemen, a bumper to the immortal Author of
Waverley !* "—The uproar of cheering, in which Scott
made a fashion of joining, was succeeded by deep silence,
and then Ballantyne proceeded—

> " In his Lord-Burleigh look, serene and serious,
> A something of imposing and mysterious "—

to lament the obscurity in which his illustrious but too
modest correspondent still chose to conceal himself from
the plaudits of the world—to thank the company for the
manner in which the *nominis umbra* had been received—
and to assure them that the Author of Waverley would,
when informed of the circumstance, feel highly delighted
—" the proudest hour of his life," &c., &c.   The cool
demure fun of Scott's features during all this mummery
was perfect; and Erskine's attempt at a gay *nonchalance*
was still more ludicrously meritorious.   Aldiborontiphoscophornio, however, bursting as he was, knew too well to

allow the new novel to be made the subject of discussion. Its name was announced, and success to it crowned another cup; but after that, no more of Jedediah.   To cut the thread, he rolled out unbidden some one of his many theatrical songs, in a style that would have done no dishonour to almost any orchestra—*The Maid of Lodi*—or perhaps, *The Bay of Biscay, oh!*—or *The sweet little cherub that sits up aloft*.   Other toasts followed, interspersed with ditties from other performers;—old George Thomson, the friend of Burns, was ready, for one, with *The Moorland Wedding*, or *Willie brew'd a peck o' maut*; —and so it went on, until Scott and Erskine, with any clerical or very staid personage that had chanced to be admitted, saw fit to withdraw.   Then the scene was changed.   The claret and olives made way for broiled bones and a mighty bowl of punch; and when a few glasses of the hot beverage had restored his powers, James opened *ore rotundo* on the merits of the forthcoming romance.   "One chapter—one chapter only"—was the cry.   After " *Nay, by'r Lady, nay!* " and a few more coy shifts, the proof-sheets were at length produced, and James, with many a prefatory hem, read aloud what he considered as the most striking dialogue they contained.

The first I heard so read was the interview between Jeanie Deans, the Duke of Argyle, and Queen Caroline, in Richmond Park; and notwithstanding some spice of the pompous tricks to which he was addicted, I must say he did the inimitable scene great justice.   At all events, the effect it produced was deep and memorable, and no wonder that the exulting typographer's *one bumper more to Jedediah Cleishbotham* preceded his parting stave, which was uniformly *The Last Words of Marmion*, executed certainly with no contemptible rivalry of Braham.

What a different affair was a dinner, although probably including many of the same guests, at the junior partner's!   He in those days retained, I think, no private apartments attached to his auction-rooms in Hanover Street, over the door of which he still kept emblazoned " John Ballantyne and Company, Booksellers."   At any rate, such of his entertainments as I ever saw Scott partake of, were given at his villa near to the Firth of Forth, by Trinity;—a retreat which the little man had invested with an air of dainty voluptuous finery, contrasting strikingly enough with the substantial citizen-like snugness of his elder brother's domestic appointments. His house was surrounded by gardens so contrived as to seem of considerable extent, having many a shady tuft, trellised alley, and mysterious alcove, interspersed among their bright parterres. His professional excursions to Paris and Brussels in quest of objects of *vertu*, had supplied both the temptation and the means to set forth the interior in a fashion that might have satisfied the most fastidious *petite maîtresse* of Norwood or St. Denis. John, too, was a married man: he had, however, erected for himself a private wing, the accesses to which, whether from the main building or the bosquet, were so narrow that it was physically impossible for the handsome and portly lady who bore his name to force her person through any one of them. His dinners were in all respects Parisian, for his wasted palate disdained such John Bull luxuries as were all in all with James. The piquant pasty of Strasburg or Perigord was never to seek; and even the *pièce de résistance* was probably a boar's head from Coblentz, or a turkey ready stuffed with truffles from the Palais Royal. The pictures scattered among John's innumerable mirrors were chiefly of theatrical subjects—many of them portraits of beautiful actresses—the same Peg Woffingtons, Bellamys, Kitty Clives, and so forth, that found their way in the sequel to Charles Mathews's gallery at Highgate. Here that exquisite comedian's own mimicries and parodies were the life and soul of many a festival, and here, too, he gathered from his facetious host not a few of the richest materials for his *at homes* and *monopolylogues*. But, indeed, whatever actor or singer of eminence visited Edinburgh, of the evenings when he did not perform several were sure to be reserved for Trinity. Here Braham quavered, and here Liston drolled his best—here Johnstone, and Murray, and Yates, mixed jest and stave—here Kean revelled and rioted—and here the Roman Kemble often played the Greek from sunset to dawn. Nor did the popular *danseuse* of the time disdain to freshen her roses, after a laborious week, amidst these Paphian arbours.

Johnny had other tastes that were equally expensive. He had a well-furnished stable, and followed the fox-hounds whenever the covert was within an easy distance. His horses were all called after heroes in Scott's poems or novels; and at this time he usually rode up to his auction on a tall milk-white hunter, yclept *Old Mortality*, attended by a leash or two of greyhounds,—Die Vernon, Jenny Dennison, and so forth, by name. The featherweight himself appeared uniformly, hammer-in-hand, in the half-dress of some sporting-club—a light grey frock, with emblems of the chase on its silver buttons, white cord breeches, and jockey-boots in Meltonian order. Yet he affected in the pulpit rather a grave address; and was really one of the most plausible and imposing of the Puff tribe. Probably Scott's presence overawed his ludicrous propensities; for the poet was, when sales were going on, almost a daily attendant in Hanover Street, and himself not the least energetic of the numerous competitors for Johnny's uncut *fifteeners*, Venetian lamps, Milanese cuirasses, and old Dutch cabinets. Maida, by the way, was so well aware of his master's habits, that about the time when the Court of Session was likely to break up for the day, he might usually be seen couched in expectation among Johnny's own *tail* of greyhounds at the threshold of the mart.

It was at one of those Trinity dinners this summer that I first saw Constable. Being struck with his appearance, I asked Scott who he was, and he told me—expressing some surprise that anybody should have lived a winter or two in Edinburgh without knowing, by sight at least, a citizen whose name was so familiar to the world. I happened to say that I had not been prepared to find the great bookseller a man of such gentlemanlike and even distinguished bearing. Scott smiled, and answered— "Ay, Constable is indeed a grand-looking chield. He puts me in mind of Fielding's apology for Lady Booby— to wit, that Joseph Andrews had an air which, to those who had not seen many noblemen, would give an idea of nobility." I had not in those days been much initiated in the private jokes of what is called, by way of excellence, *the trade*, and was puzzled when Scott, in the course of the dinner, said to Constable, "Will your Czarish Majesty do me the honour to take a glass of champagne?" I asked the master of the feast for an explanation. "Oh!" said he, "are you so green as not to know that Constable long since dubbed himself *The Czar of Muscovy*, John Murray *The Emperor of the West*, and Longman and his string of partners *The Divan*?"—"And what title," I asked, "has Mr. John Ballantyne himself

found in this new *almanach impérial*? ''—" Let that flee
stick to the wa'," quoth Johnny : " When I set up for a
bookseller, The Crafty christened me *The Dey of Alljeers*
—but he now considers me as next thing to dethroned."
He added—" His Majesty the autocrat is too fond of
these nicknames. One day a partner of the house of
Longman was dining with him in the country, to settle
an important piece of business, about which there
occurred a good deal of difficulty. ' What fine swans you
have in your pond there ! ' said the Londoner, by way of
parenthesis.—' Swans ! ' cried Constable; ' they are only
geese, man. There are just five of them, if you please to
observe, and their names are Longman, Hurst, Rees,
Orme, and Brown.' This skit cost The Crafty a good
bargain."

It always appeared to me that James Ballantyne felt
his genius rebuked in the presence of Constable; his
manner was constrained, his smile servile, his hilarity
elaborate. Not so with Johnny : the little fellow never
seemed more airily frolicsome than when he capered for
the amusement of the Czar.

When I visited Constable, as I often did at a period
somewhat later than that of which I now speak, and for
the most part in company with Scott, I found the bookseller established in a respectable country gentleman's
seat, some six or seven miles out of Edinburgh, and doing
the honours of it with all the ease that might have been
looked for had he been the long-descended owner of the
place;—there was no foppery, no show, no idle luxury,
but to all appearance the plain abundance and simple
enjoyment of hereditary wealth. His conversation was
manly and vigorous, abounding in Scotch anecdotes of
the old time, which he told with a degree of spirit and
humour only second to his great author's. No man could
more effectually control, when he had a mind, either the
extravagant vanity, which, on too many occasions, made
him ridiculous, or the despotic temper which habitually
held in fear and trembling all such as were in any sort
dependent on his Czarish Majesty's pleasure. In him I
never saw (at this period) anything but the unobtrusive
sense and the calm courtesy of a well-bred gentleman.
His very equipage kept up the series of contrasts between
him and the two Ballantynes. Constable went back and
forward between the town and Polton in a deep hung

Life of Sir Walter Scott 335

and capacious green barouche, without any pretence at
heraldic blazonry, drawn by a pair of sleek, black, long-
tailed horses, and conducted by a grave old coachman in
plain blue livery. The Printer of the Canongate drove
himself and his wife about the streets and suburbs in a
snug machine, which did not overburthen one powerful
and steady cob;—while the gay Auctioneer, whenever he
left the saddle for the box, mounted a bright blue dog-
cart, and rattled down the Newhaven road with two high-
mettled steeds prancing *tandem* before him.

The Sheriff told with peculiar unction the following
anecdote of this spark :—The first time he went over to
pick up curiosities at Paris, it happened that he met, in
the course of his traffickings, a certain brother bookseller
of Edinburgh, as unlike him as one man could well be to
another—a grave, dry Presbyterian, rigid in all his notions
as the buckle of his wig. This precise worthy having
ascertained John's address, went to call on him a day or
two afterwards, with the news of some richly illuminated
missal, which he might possibly be glad to make prize
of. On asking for his friend, a smiling *laquais de place* informed him that *Monsieur* had gone out, but that *Madame*
was at home. Not doubting that Mrs. Ballantyne had
accompanied her husband on his trip, he desired to pay
his respects to *Madame*, and was ushered in accordingly.
" But oh, Mr. Scott! " said, or rather groaned the
austere elder on his return from this modern Babylon—
" oh, Mr. Scott, there was nae Mrs. John yonder, but a
painted Jezabel sittin' up in her bed, wi' a wheen impudent French limmers like hersel', and twa or three
whiskered blackguards, takin' their collation o' nicknacks
and champagne wine. I ran out o' the house as if I had
been shot. What judgment will this wicked warld come
to ! The Lord pity us ! " Scott was a severe enough
censor in the general of such levities, but somehow, in the
case of Rigdumfunnidos, he seemed to regard them with
much the same toleration as the naughty tricks of a
monkey in the " Jardin des Plantes."

Why did Scott persist in mixing up all his most important concerns with these Ballantynes? The reader of
these pages will have all my materials for an answer; but
in the meantime let it suffice to say, that he was the most
patient, long-suffering, affectionate, and charitable of
mankind; that in the case of both the brothers he could

count, after all, on a sincerely, nay, a passionately devoted attachment to his person; that, with the greatest
of human beings, use is in all but unconquerable power;
and that he who so loftily tossed aside the seemingly
most dangerous assaults of flattery, the blandishment of
dames, the condescension of princes, the enthusiasm of
crowds—had still his weak point, upon which two or three
humble besiegers, and one unwearied, though most
frivolous underminer, well knew how to direct their ap-
proaches. It was a favourite saw of his own, that the
wisest of our race often reserve the average stock of folly
to be all expended upon some one flagrant absurdity.

I alluded to James Ballantyne's reading of the famous
scene in Richmond Park. According to Scott's original
intention, the second series of *Jedediah* was to have included two tales; but his Jeanie Deans soon grew so on
his fancy as to make this impossible; and the Heart of
Mid-Lothian alone occupied the four volumes which appeared in June 1818, and were at once placed by acclamation in the foremost rank of his writings. Lady
Louisa Stuart's picture of the southern rapture may be
found elsewhere; but I must not omit here her own
remarks on the principal character :—" People were beginning to say the author would wear himself out; it was
going on too long in the same key, and no striking notes
could possibly be produced. On the contrary, I think the
interest is stronger here than in any of the former ones—
(always excepting my first-love Waverley)—and one may
congratulate you upon having effected what many have
tried to do, and nobody yet succeeded in, making the perfectly good character the most interesting. Of late days,
especially since it has been the fashion to write moral and
even religious novels, one might almost say of some of the
wise good heroines, what a lively girl once said of her
well-meaning aunt—' Upon my word she is enough to
make anybody wicked.' And though beauty and talents
are heaped on the right side, the writer, in spite of himself, is sure to put agreeableness on the wrong; the person
from whose errors he means you should take warning,
runs away with your secret partiality in the meantime.
Had this very story been conducted by a common hand,
Effie would have attracted our concern and sympathy—
Jeanie only cold approbation. Whereas Jeanie, without
youth, beauty, genius, warm passions, or any other novel-

perfection, is here our object from beginning to end. This is ' enlisting the affections in the cause of virtue ' ten times more than ever Richardson did; for whose male and female pedants, all-excelling as they are, I never could care half so much as I found myself inclined to do for Jeanie before I finished the first volume.''

From the choice of localities, and the splendid blazoning of tragical circumstances that had left the strongest impression on the memory and imagination of every inhabitant, the reception of this tale in Edinburgh was a scene of all-engrossing enthusiasm, such as I never witnessed there on the appearance of any other literary novelty. But the admiration and delight were the same all over Scotland. Never before had he seized such really noble features of the national character as were canonised in the person of his homely heroine : no art had ever devised a happier running contrast than that of her and her sister, or interwoven a portraiture of lowly manners and simple virtues, with more graceful delineations of polished life, or with bolder shadows of terror, guilt, crime, remorse, madness, and all the agony of the passions.

CHAPTER X

Sketches of Abbotsford—Illness and Domestic Afflictions—The Bride of Lammermoor—The Legend of Montrose—Ivanhoe. 1818–1819.

THE 12th of July [1818] restored Scott as usual to the supervision of his trees and carpenters; but he had already told the Ballantynes, that the story which he had found it impossible to include in the recent series should be forthwith taken up as the opening one of a third; and instructed John to embrace the first favourable opportunity of offering Constable the publication of this, on the footing of 10,000 copies again forming the first edition; but now at length without any more stipulations connected with the " old stock.''

One of his visitors of September was Mr. R. Cadell, who was now in all the secrets of his father-in-law and partner Constable; and observing how his host was harassed with lion-hunters, and what a number of hours he spent daily in the company of his work-people, he expressed, during one of their walks, his wonder that Scott should ever be able to write books at all while in the country. " I know," he said, "that you contrive to get a few hours in your own room, and that may do for the mere penwork; but when is it that you think?"—"Oh," said Scott, "I lie *simmering* over things for an hour or so before I get up —and there's the time I am dressing to overhaul my half-sleeping, half-waking *projet de chapitre*—and when I get the paper before me, it commonly runs off pretty easily. Besides, I often take a dose in the plantations, and while Tom marks out a dyke or a drain as I have directed, one's fancy may be running its ain riggs in some other world."

It was in the month following that I first saw Abbotsford. He invited my friend John Wilson (now Professor of Moral Philosophy at Edinburgh) and myself to visit him for a day or two on our return from an excursion to Mr. Wilson's beautiful villa on Windermere, but named the particular day (October 8th) on which it would be most convenient for him to receive us; and we discovered on our arrival, that he had fixed it from a good-natured motive. We found him walking at no great distance from the house, with five or six young people, and his friends Lord Melville and Adam Fergusson. Having presented us to the First Lord of the Admiralty, he fell back a little and said, "I am glad you came to-day, for I thought it might be of use to you both, some time or other, to be known to my old schoolfellow here, who is, and I hope will long continue to be, the great giver of good things in the Parliament-House. I trust you have had enough of certain pranks with your friend Ebony, and if so, Lord Melville will have too much sense to remember them." [1] We then walked round a plantation called *the Thicket*, and came back to the house by a formidable work which he was constructing for the defence of his *haugh* against the wintry violences of the Tweed; and he discoursed for some time with keen interest upon the comparative merits of different methods of embankment, but stopped now and then to give us the advantage of any point of view in which his new building on the eminence above pleased his eye. It had a fantastic appearance—being but a fragment of the existing edifice—and not at all harmonis-

---

[1] *Ebony* was Mr. Blackwood's own usual designation in the *jeux d'esprit* of his young Magazine, in many of which the persons thus addressed by Scott were conjoint culprits. They both were then, as may be inferred, sweeping the board of the Parliament-House as "briefless barristers."

ing in its outline with the original tenement to the eastward. Scott, however, expatiated *con amore* on the rapidity with which, being chiefly of darkish granite, it was assuming a "time-honoured" aspect. Fergusson, with a grave and respectful look, observed, "Yes, it really has much the air of some old fastness hard by the river Jordan." This allusion to a so-called *Chaldee MS.*, in the manufacture of which Fergusson fancied Wilson and myself to have had a share, gave rise to a burst of laughter among Scott's merry young folks, while he himself drew in his nether lip and rebuked the Captain with "Toots, Adam! Toots, Adam!" He then returned to his embankment, and described how a former one had been entirely swept away in one night's flood. But the Captain was ready with another verse of the *Oriental MS.*, and groaned out by way of echo—"Verily my fine gold hath perished!"[1] Whereupon the "Great Magician" elevated his huge oaken staff as if to lay it on the waggish soldier's back—but flourished it gaily over his own head, and laughed louder than the youngest of the company. As we walked and talked, the Pepper and Mustard terriers kept snuffing about among the bushes and heather near us, and started every five minutes a hare, which scudded away before them and the ponderous staghound Maida—the Sheriff and all his tail holloaing and cheering in perfect confidence that the dogs could do no more harm to poor puss than the venerable tom-cat, Hinse of Hinsfeldt, who pursued the vain chase with the rest.

At length we drew near *Peterhouse*, and found sober Peter himself, and his brother-in-law the facetious factotum Tom Purdie, superintending, pipe in mouth, three or four sturdy labourers busy in laying down the turf for a bowling-green. " I have planted hollies all round it, you see," said Scott, "and laid out an arbour on the right-hand side for the laird; and here I mean to have a game at bowls after dinner every day in fine weather—for I take that to have been among the indispensables of our old *vie de château*." But I must not forget the reason he gave me some time afterwards for having fixed on that spot for his bowling-green. " In truth," he then said, " I wished to have a smooth walk and a canny seat for myself within ear-shot of Peter's evening psalm." The coachman was a devout Presbyterian, and many a time

[1] See Blackwood for October 1817.

have I in after years accompanied Scott on his evening
stroll, when the principal object was to enjoy, from the
bowling-green, the unfailing melody of this good man's
family worship—and heard him repeat, as Peter's manly
voice led the humble choir within, that beautiful stanza of
Burns's Saturday Night :—

> " They chant their artless notes in simple guise;
>   They tune their hearts, by far the noblest aim," &c.

It was near the dinner-hour before we reached the house,
and presently I saw assembled a larger company than I
should have fancied to be at all compatible with the existing accommodations of the place; but it turned out that
Adam Fergusson, and the friends whom I have not as yet
mentioned, were to find quarters elsewhere for the night.
His younger brother, Captain John Fergusson of the
Royal Navy (a favourite lieutenant of Lord Nelson's), had
come over from Huntley Burn; there were present also,
Mr. Scott of Gala, whose residence is within an easy
distance; Sir Henry Hay Macdougal of Mackerston, an
old baronet, with gay, lively, and highly polished manners, related in the same degree to both Gala and the
Sheriff; Sir Alexander Don, the member for Roxburghshire, whose elegant social qualities had been alluded to
in a preceding chapter; and Dr. Scott of Darnlee, a
modest and intelligent gentleman, who, having realised a
fortune in the East India Company's medical service, had
settled within two or three miles of Abbotsford, and,
though no longer practising his profession, had kindly
employed all the resources of his skill in the endeavour to
counteract his neighbour's recent liability to attacks of
cramp.   Our host and one or two others appeared, as was
in those days a common fashion with country gentlemen,
in the lieutenancy uniform of their county.   How fourteen
or fifteen people contrived to be seated in the then dining-
room of Abbotsford I know not—for it seemed quite full
enough when it contained only eight or ten; but so it was
—nor, as Sir Harry Macdougal's fat valet, warned by
former experience, did not join the train of attendants,
was there any perceptible difficulty in the detail of the
arrangements.   Everything about the dinner was, as the
phrase runs, in excellent style; and in particular the *potage
à la Meg Merrilees*, announced as an attempt to imitate a
device of the Duke of Buccleuch's celebrated cook—by

name Monsieur Florence—seemed, to those at least who were better acquainted with the Kaim of Derncleugh than with the *cuisine* of Bowhill,[1] a very laudable specimen of the art. The champagne circulated nimbly—and I never was present at a gayer dinner. It had advanced a little beyond the soup when it received an accompaniment which would not, perhaps, have improved the satisfaction of southern guests, had any such been present. A tall and stalwart bagpiper, in complete Highland costume, appeared pacing to and fro on the green before the house, and the window being open, it seemed as if he might as well have been straining his lungs within the parlour. At a pause of his strenuous performance, Scott took occasion to explain, that *John of Skye* was a recent acquisition to the rising hamlet of Abbotstown; that the man was a capital hedger and ditcher, and only figured with the pipe and philabeg on high occasions in the after part of the day; "but indeed," he added, laughing, "I fear John will soon be discovering that the hook and mattock are unfavourable to his chanter hand." When the cloth was drawn, and the never-failing salver of *quaighs* introduced, John Bruce, upon some well-known signal, entered the room, but *en militaire*, without removing his bonnet, and taking his station behind the landlord, received from his hand the largest of the Celtic bickers brimful of Glenlivet. The man saluted the company in his own dialect, tipped off the contents (probably a quarter of an English pint of raw aquavitæ) at a gulp, wheeled about as solemnly as if the whole ceremony had been a movement on parade, and forthwith recommenced his pibrochs and gatherings, which continued until long after the ladies had left the table, and the autumnal moon was streaming in upon us so brightly as to dim the candles.

I had never before seen Scott in such buoyant spirits as he shewed this evening—and I never saw him in higher afterwards; and no wonder, for this was the first time that he, Lord Melville, and Adam Fergusson, daily companions at the High School of Edinburgh, and partners in many joyous scenes of the early volunteer period, had met since the commencement of what I may call the serious part of any of their lives. The great poet and novelist was

---

[1] I understand that this now celebrated soup was *extemporised* by M. Florence on Scott's first visit to Bowhill after the publication of *Guy Mannering*.

receiving them under his own roof, when his fame was at its *acmé*, and his fortune seemed culminating to about a corresponding height—and the generous exuberance of his hilarity might have overflowed without moving the spleen of a Cynic. Old stories of *the Yards* and *the Crosscauseway* were relieved by sketches of real warfare, such as none but Fergusson (or Charles Mathews, had he been a soldier) could ever have given; and they toasted the memory of *Greenbreeks* and the health of *the Beau* with equal devotion.

When we rose from table, Scott proposed that we should all ascend his western turret, to enjoy a moonlight view of the valley. The younger part of his company were too happy to do so; some of the seniors, who had tried the thing before, found pretexts for hanging back. The stairs were dark, narrow, and steep; but the Sheriff piloted the way, and at length there were as many on the top as it could well afford footing for. Nothing could be more lovely than the panorama; all the harsher and more naked features being lost in the delicious moonlight; the Tweed and the Gala winding and sparkling beneath our feet; and the distant ruins of Melrose appearing, as if carved of alabaster, under the black mass of the Eildons. The poet, leaning on his battlement, seemed to hang over the beautiful vision as if he had never seen it before. " If I live," he exclaimed, " I will build me a higher tower, with a more spacious platform, and a staircase better fitted for an old fellow's scrambling." The piper was heard returning his instrument below, and he called to him for *Lochaber no more*. John of Skye obeyed, and as the music rose, softened by the distance, Scott repeated in a low key the melancholy words of the song of exile.

On descending from the tower, the whole company were assembled in the new dining-room, which was still under the hands of the carpenters, but had been brilliantly illuminated for the occasion. Mr. Bruce took his station, and old and young danced reels to his melodious accompaniment until they were weary, while Scott and the Dominie looked on with gladsome faces, and beat time now and then, the one with his staff, the other with his wooden leg. A tray with mulled wine and whisky punch was then introduced, and Lord Melville proposed a bumper, with all the honours, to the *Roof-tree*. Captain Fergusson having sung *Johnnie Cope*, called on the young ladies for *Ken-*

mure's on and awa'; and our host then insisted that the
whole party should join, standing in a circle hand-in-hand
more majorum, in the hearty chorus of

" Weel may we a' be,
Ill may we never see,
God bless the king and the gude companie ! "

—which being duly performed, all dispersed. Such was
the handsel—(for Scott protested against its being considered as *the househeating*)—of the new Abbotsford.

Awakening between six and seven next morning, I heard
the Sheriff's voice close to me, and looking out of the
little latticed window of the then detached cottage called
the Chapel, saw him and Tom Purdie pacing together on
the green before the door, in earnest deliberation over what
seemed to be a rude daub of a drawing ; and every time
they approached my end of their parade, I was sure to
catch the words *Blue Bank.* It turned out in the course
of the day, that a field of clay near Toftfield went by this
name, and that the draining of it was one of the chief
operations then in hand. My friend Wilson, meanwhile,
who lodged also in the chapel, tapped also at the door,
and asked me to rise and take a walk with him by the
river, for he had some angling project in his head. He
went out and joined in the consultation about the Blue
Bank, while I was dressing ; presently Scott hailed me at
the casement, and said he had observed a volume of a new
edition of Goethe on my table—would I lend it him for a
little? He carried off the volume accordingly, and re-
treated with it to his den. It contained the Faust, and I
believe in a more complete shape than he had before seen
that masterpiece of his old favourite. When we met at
breakfast, a couple of hours after, he was full of the poem
—dwelt with enthusiasm on the airy beauty of its lyrics,
the terrible pathos of the scene before the *Mater Dolorosa,*
and the deep skill shewn in the various subtle shadings of
character between Mephistopheles and poor Margaret. He
remarked, however, of the Introduction (which I suspect
was new to him), that blood would out—that, consummate
artist as he was, Goethe was a German, and that nobody
but a German would ever have provoked a comparison with
the book of Job, " the grandest poem that ever was written." He added, that he suspected the end of the story
had been left *in obscuro,* from despair to match the closing
scene of our own Marlowe's *Doctor Faustus.* Mr. Wilson

mentioned a report that Coleridge was engaged on a translation of the Faust. " I hope it is so," said Scott:
" Coleridge made Schiller's Wallenstein far finer than he
found it, and so he will do by this. No man has all
the resources of poetry in such profusion, but he cannot
manage them so as to bring out anything of his own on
a large scale at all worthy of his genius. He is like a
lump of coal rich with gas, which lies expending itself in
puffs and gleams, unless some shrewd body will clap it into
a cast-iron box, and compel the compressed element to do
itself justice. His fancy and diction would have long ago
placed him above all his contemporaries, had they been
under the direction of a sound judgment and a steady
will. I don't now expect a great original poem from
Coleridge, but he might easily make a sort of fame for
himself as a poetical translator, that would be a thing
completely unique and *sui generis.*"

While this criticism proceeded, Scott was cutting away
at his brown loaf and a plate of kippered salmon, in a
style which strongly reminded me of Dandie Dinmont's
luncheon at Mump's Hall; nor was his German topic at
all the predominant one. On the contrary, the sentences
which have dwelt on my memory dropped from him now
and then, in the pauses, as it were, of his main talk;—for
though he could not help recurring, ever and anon, to the
subject, it would have been quite out of his way to make
any literary matter the chief theme of his conversation,
when there was a single person present who was not likely
to feel much interested in its discussion.—How often have
I heard him quote on such occasions, Mr. Vellum's advice
to the butler in Addison's excellent play of *The Drummer*
—" Your conjuror, John, is indeed a twofold personage—
but he *eats and drinks like other people !* "

Before breakfast was over the post-bag arrived, and its
contents were so numerous, that Lord Melville asked Scott
what election was on hand—not doubting that there must
be some very particular reason for such a shoal of letters.
He answered that it was much the same most days, and
added, " though no one has kinder friends in the franking
line, and though Freeling and Croker especially [1] are always ready to stretch the point of privilege in my favour,
I am nevertheless a fair contributor to the revenue, for I

[1] Scott's excellent friend Sir Thomas Freeling was Secretary of the
Post-Office for a long series of years : Mr. Croker was Secretary of
the Admiralty from 1809 to 1827.

think my bill for letters seldom comes under £150 a year; and as to coach-parcels, they are a perfect ruination." He then told with high merriment a disaster that had lately befallen him. " One morning last spring," he said, " I opened a huge lump of a despatch, without looking how it was addressed, never doubting that it had travelled under some omnipotent frank like the First Lord of the Admiralty's, when, lo and behold, the contents proved to be a MS. play, by a young lady of New York, who kindly requested me to read and correct it, equip it with prologue and epilogue, procure for it a favourable reception from the manager of Drury Lane, and make Murray or Constable bleed handsomely for the copyright; and on inspecting the cover, I found that I had been charged five pounds odd for the postage. This was bad enough, but there was no help, so I groaned and submitted. A fortnight or so after, another packet, of not less formidable bulk, arrived, and I was absent enough to break its seal too without examination. Conceive my horror when out jumped the same identical tragedy of *The Cherokee Lovers*, with a second epistle from the authoress, stating that, as the winds had been boisterous, she feared the vessel intrusted with her former communication might have foundered, and therefore judged it prudent to forward a duplicate."

Scott said he must retire to answer his letters, but that the sociable and the ponies would be at the door by one o'clock, when he proposed to shew Melrose and Dryburgh to Lady Melville and any of the rest of the party that chose to accompany them; adding that his son Walter would lead anybody who preferred a gun to the likeliest place for a black-cock, and that Charlie Purdie (Tom's brother) would attend on Mr. Wilson, and whoever else chose to try a cast of the salmon-rod. He withdrew when all this was arranged, and appeared at the time appointed, with perhaps a dozen letters sealed for the post, and a coach parcel addressed to James Ballantyne, which he dropped at the turnpike-gate as we drove to Melrose. Seeing it picked up by a dirty urchin, and carried into a hedge pot-house, where half-a-dozen nondescript wayfarers were smoking and tippling, I could not but wonder that it had not been the fate of some one of those innumerable packets to fall into unscrupulous hands, and betray the grand secret. That very morning we had seen two post-chaises drawn up at his gate, and the enthusiastic travellers, seemingly decent tradesmen and their families, who must have been packed in a manner worthy of Mrs. Gilpin, lounging about to catch a glimpse of him at his going forth. But it was impossible in those days to pass between Melrose and Abbotsford without encountering some odd figure, armed with a sketch-book, evidently bent on a peep at the Great Unknown; and it must be allowed that many of these pedestrians looked as if they might have thought it very excusable to make prize, by hook or by crook, of a MS. chapter of the Tales of my Landlord.

Scott shewed us the ruins of Melrose in detail; and as we proceeded to Dryburgh, descanted learnedly and sagaciously on the good effects which must have attended the erection of so many great monastic establishments in a district so peculiarly exposed to the inroads of the English in the days of the Border wars. " They were now and then violated," he said, " as their aspect to this hour bears witness; but for once that they suffered, any lay property similarly situated must have been *harried* a dozen times. The bold Dacres, Liddells, and Howards, that could get easy absolution at York or Durham for any ordinary breach of a truce with the Scots, would have had *to dree a heavy dole* had they confessed plundering from the fat brothers, of the same order perhaps, whose lines had fallen to them on the wrong side of the Cheviot." He enlarged too on the heavy penalty which the Crown of Scotland had paid for its rash acquiescence in the wholesale robbery of the Church at the Reformation. " The proportion of the soil in the hands of the clergy had," he said, " been very great—too great to be continued. If we may judge by their share in the public burdens, they must have had nearly a third of the land in their possession. But this vast wealth was now distributed among a turbulent nobility, too powerful before; and the Stuarts soon found, that in the bishops and lord abbots they had lost the only means of balancing their factions, so as to turn the scale in favour of law and order; and by and by the haughty barons themselves, who had scrambled for the worldly spoil of the Church, found that the spiritual influence had been concentrated in hands as haughty as their own, and connected with no feelings likely to buttress their order any more than the

Crown—a new and sterner monkery, under a different name, and essentially plebeian. Presently the Scotch were on the verge of republicanism, in state as well as kirk, and I have sometimes thought it was only the accession of King Jamie to the throne of England that could have given monarchy a chance of prolonging its existence here." One of his friends asked what he supposed might have been the annual revenue of the abbey of Melrose in its best day. He answered, that he suspected, if all the sources of their income were now in clever hands, the produce could hardly be under £100,000 a-year; and added—"Making every allowance for modern improvements, there can be no question that the sixty brothers of Melrose divided a princely rental. The superiors were often men of very high birth, and the great majority of the rest were younger brothers of gentlemen's families. I fancy they may have been, on the whole, pretty near akin to your Fellows of All Souls—who, according to their statute, must be *bene nati, bene vestiti, et mediocriter docti.* They had a good house in Edinburgh, where, no doubt, my lord abbot and his chaplains maintained a hospitable table during the sittings of Parliament." Some one regretted that we had no lively picture of the enormous revolution in manners that must have followed the downfall of the ancient Church of Scotland. He observed that there were, he fancied, materials enough for constructing such a one, but that they were mostly scattered in records—"of which," said he, "who knows anything to the purpose except Tom Thomson and John Riddell? It is common to laugh at such researches, but they pay the good brains that meddle with them;—and had Thomson been as diligent in setting down his discoveries as he has been in making them, he might, long before this time of day, have placed himself on a level with Ducange or Camden. The change in the country-side," he continued, "must indeed have been terrific; but it does not seem to have been felt very severely by a certain Boniface of St. Andrews, for when somebody asked him, on the subsidence of the storm, what he thought of all that had occurred,—'Why,' answered mine host, 'it comes to this, that the mode*rautor* sits in my meikle chair, where the dean sat before, and in place of calling for the third stoup of Bordeaux, bids Jenny bring ben anither bowl of toddy.'"

At Dryburgh Scott pointed out to us the sepulchral aisle of his Haliburton ancestors, and said he hoped, in God's appointed time, to lay his bones among their dust. The spot was, even then, a sufficiently interesting and impressive one; but I shall not say more of it at present.

On returning to Abbotsford, we found Mrs. Scott and her daughters doing penance under the merciless curiosity of a couple of tourists who had arrived from Selkirk soon after we set out for Melrose. They were rich specimens— tall, lanky young men, both of them rigged out in new jackets and trousers of the Macgregor tartan; the one, as they had revealed, being a lawyer, the other a Unitarian preacher, from New England. These gentlemen, when told on their arrival that Mr. Scott was not at home, had shewn such signs of impatience, that the servant took it for granted they must have serious business, and asked if they would wish to speak a word with his lady. They grasped at this, and so conducted themselves in the interview, that Mrs. Scott never doubted they had brought letters of introduction to her husband, and invited them accordingly to partake of her luncheon. They had been walking about the house and grounds with her and her daughters ever since that time, and appeared at the porch, when the Sheriff and his party returned to dinner, as if they had been already fairly enrolled on his visiting list. For the moment, he too was taken in—he fancied that his wife must have received and opened their credentials— and shook hands with them with courteous cordiality. But Mrs. Scott, with all her overflowing good-nature, was a sharp observer; and she, before a minute had elapsed, interrupted the ecstatic compliments of the strangers, by reminding them that her husband would be glad to have the letters of the friends who had been so good as to write by them. It then turned out that there were no letters to be produced—and Scott, signifying that his hour for dinner approached, added, that as he supposed they meant to walk to Melrose, he could not trespass further on their time. The two lion-hunters seemed quite unprepared for this abrupt escape. But there was about Scott, in perfection, when he chose to exert it, the power of civil repulsion; he bowed the overwhelmed originals to his door, and on re-entering the parlour, found Mrs. Scott complaining very indignantly that they had gone so far as to pull out their note-book, and beg an exact account, not

only of his age—but of her own. Scott, already half
relenting, laughed heartily at this misery. He observed,
however, that " if he were to take in all the world, he had
better put up a sign-post at once,—

> ' Porter, ale, and British spirits,
> Painted bright between twa trees '; [1]

and that no traveller of respectability could ever be at a
loss for such an introduction as would ensure his best hospitality." Still he was not quite pleased with what had
happened—and as we were about to pass, half an hour
afterwards, from the drawing-room to the dining-room, he
said to his wife, " Hang the Yahoos, Charlotte—but we
should have bid them stay dinner." " Devil a bit," quoth
Captain John Fergusson, who had again come over from
Huntley Burn, and had been latterly assisting the lady to
amuse her Americans—" Devil a bit, my dear,—they were
quite in a mistake, I could see. The one asked Madame
whether she deigned to call her new house Tullyveolan or
Tillietudlem; and the other, when Maida happened to lay
his nose against the window, exclaimed *Pro-di-gi-ous!*" In
short, they evidently meant all the humbug not for you,
but for the culprit of Waverley, and the rest of that there
rubbish." " Well, well, Skipper," was the reply,—" for
a' that, the loons would hae been nane the waur o' their
kail."

From this banter it may be inferred that the younger
Fergusson had not as yet been told the Waverley secret—
which to any of that house could never have been any
mystery. Probably this, or some similar occasion soon
afterwards, led to his formal initiation; for during the
many subsequent years that the veil was kept on, I used
to admire the tact with which, when in their topmost high-
jinks humour, both " Captain John " and " The Auld
Captain " eschewed any the most distant allusion to the
affair.

And this reminds me, that at the period of which I am
writing, none of Scott's own family, except of course his
wife, had the advantage in that matter of the Skipper.
Some of them, too, were apt, like him, so long as no
regular confidence had been reposed in them, to avail
themselves of the author's reserve for their own sport
among friends. Thus, one morning, just as Scott was

---

[1] Macneill's *Will and Jean.*

opening the door of the parlour, the rest of the party being already seated at the breakfast-table, the Dominie was
in the act of helping himself to an egg, marked with a
peculiar hieroglyphic by Mrs. Thomas Purdie, upon which
Anne Scott, then a lively rattling girl of sixteen, lisped
out, "That's a mysterious-looking egg, Mr. Thomson—
what if it should have been meant for *the Great
Unknown?*" Ere the Dominie could reply, her father
advanced to the foot of the table, and having seated himself and deposited his stick on the carpet beside him, with
a sort of whispered whistle, "What's that Lady Anne's [1]
saying?" quoth he; "I thought that it had been well
known that the *keelavined* egg must be a soft one for
the Sherra!" And so he took his egg, and while all
smiled in silence, poor Anne said gaily, in the midst of
her blushes, "Upon my word, papa, I thought Mr. John
Ballantyne might have been expected." This allusion to
Johnny's glory in being considered as the accredited representative of Jedediah Cleishbotham, produced a laugh
—at which the Sheriff frowned—and then laughed too.

I remember nothing particular about our second day's
dinner, except that it was then I first met my dear and
honoured friend William Laidlaw. The evening passed
rather more quietly than the preceding one. Instead of
the dance in the new dining-room, we had a succession of
old ballads sung to the harp and guitar by the young
ladies of the house; and Scott, when they seemed to have
done enough, found some reason for taking down a
volume of Crabbe, and read us one of his favourite tales—

"Grave Jonas Kindred, Sybil Kindred's sire,
  Was six feet high, and looked six inches higher," &c.

But jollity revived in full vigour when the supper-tray was
introduced, and to cap all merriment, Adam Fergusson
dismissed us with the *Laird of Cockpen.* Lord and Lady
Melville were to return to Melville Castle next morning,
and Mr. Wilson and I happened to mention that we were
engaged to dine and sleep at the seat of my friend and
relation Mr. Pringle of Torwoodlee, on our way to Edinburgh. Scott immediately said that he would send word
in the morning to the Laird, that he and Fergusson meant

[1] When playing in childhood with the young ladies of the Buccleuch
family, she had been overheard saying to her namesake Lady Anne
Scott, "Well, I do wish I were Lady Anne too—it is so much pret-
tier than Miss"; thenceforth she was commonly addressed in the
family by the coveted title.

to accompany us—such being the unceremonious style in which country neighbours in Scotland visit each other. Next day, accordingly, we all rode over together to the "*distant Torwoodlee*" of the Lay of the Last Minstrel, distant not above five or six miles from Abbotsford—coursing hares as we proceeded, but inspecting the antiquities of the *Catrail* to the interruption of our sport. We had another joyous evening at Torwoodlee. Scott and Fergusson returned home at night, and the morning after, as Wilson and I mounted for Edinburgh, our kind old host, his sides still sore with laughter, remarked that "the Sheriff and the Captain together were too much for any company."

Towards the end of this year Scott received from Lord Sidmouth the formal announcement of the Prince Regent's desire (which had been privately communicated some months earlier through the Lord Chief-Commissioner Adam) to confer on him the rank of Baronet. When he first heard of the Regent's intention, he signified considerable hesitation; for it had not escaped his observation that such airy sounds, however modestly people may be disposed to estimate them, are apt to entail in the upshot additional cost upon their way of living, and to affect accordingly the plastic fancies, feelings, and habits of their children. But Lord Sidmouth's letter happened to reach him a few months after he had heard of the sudden death of Charles Carpenter, who had bequeathed the reversion of his fortune to his sister's family; and this circumstance disposed Scott to waive his scruples, chiefly with a view to the professional advantage of his eldest son, who had by this time fixed on the life of a soldier. As is usually the case, the estimate of Mr. Carpenter's property transmitted on his death to England proved to have been an exaggerated one; and at any rate no one of Scott's children lived to receive any benefit from the bequest. But it was thus he wrote at the time to Morritt: —" It would be easy saying a parcel of fine things about my contempt of rank, and so forth; but although I would not have gone a step out of my way to have asked, or bought, or begged, or borrowed a distinction, which to me personally will rather be inconvenient than otherwise, yet, coming as it does directly from the source of feudal honours, and as an honour, I am really gratified with it;—especially as it is intimated, that it is his Royal

Highness's pleasure to heat the oven for me expressly, without waiting till he has some new *batch* of Baronets ready in dough. My poor friend Carpenter's bequest to my family has taken away a certain degree of *impecuniosity*, a necessity of saving cheese-parings and candle-ends, which always looks inconsistent with any little pretension to rank. But as things now stand, Advance banners in the name of God and St. Andrew! Remember, I anticipate the jest, ' I like not such grinning honours as Sir Walter hath.' [1] After all, if one must speak for themselves, I have my quarters and emblazonments, free of all stain but Border theft, and High Treason, which I hope are gentlemanlike crimes; and I hope Sir Walter Scott will not sound worse than Sir Humphry Davy, though my merits are as much under his, in point of utility, as can well be imagined. But a name is something, and mine is the better of the two.''

His health prevented him from going up to the fountain of honour for more than a year. Meantime his building and other operations continued to tax his resources more than he had calculated upon; and he now completed an important negotiation with Constable, who agreed to give him bonds for £12,000 in consideration of all his existing copyrights; namely, whatever shares had been reserved to him in the earlier poems, and the whole property in his novels down to the third series of Tales of my Landlord inclusive. The deed included a clause by which Constable was to forfeit £2,000 if he ever " divulged the name of the Author of Waverley during the life of the said Walter Scott, Esq.'' It is perhaps hardly worth mentioning, that about this date a London bookseller announced certain volumes of Grub-Street manufacture, as " A New Series of the Tales of my Landlord ''; and when John Ballantyne, as the " agent for the author of Waverley,'' published a declaration that the volumes thus advertised were not from that writer's pen, met John's declaration by an audacious rejoinder—impeaching his authority, and asserting that nothing but the personal appearance in the field of the gentleman for whom Ballantyne pretended to act, could shake his belief that he was himself in the confidence of the true Simon Pure. Hereupon the dropping of Scott's mask seems to have been pronounced advisable by both Ballantyne and Constable. But he calmly replied,

[1] Sir Walter Blunt—1st *King Henry IV.*, Act V., Scene 3.

"The Author who lends himself to such a trick must be a blockhead—let them publish, and that will serve our purpose better than anything we ourselves could do." I have forgotten the names of the "tales," which, being published accordingly, fell still-born from the press.

During the winter he appears to have made little progress with the third series included in this negotiation;—his painful seizures of cramp were again recurring frequently, and he probably thought it better to allow the novels to lie over until his health should be re-established, In the meantime he drew up a set of topographical and historical essays, which originally appeared in the successive numbers of the splendidly illustrated work, entitled Provincial Antiquities of Scotland.[1] But he did this merely to gratify his own love of the subject, and because, well or ill, he must be doing something. He declined all pecuniary recompense; but afterwards, when the success of the publication was secure, accepted from the proprietors some of the beautiful drawings by Turner, Thomson, and other artists, which had been prepared to accompany his text. He also wrote that winter his article on the Drama for the Encyclopædia Supplement, and the review of the fourth canto of Childe Harold for the Quarterly.

On the 15th of February 1819, he witnessed the first representation, on the Edinburgh boards, of the most meritorious and successful of all the Terryfications, though Terry himself was not the manufacturer. The drama of Rob Roy will never again be got up so well in all its parts, as it then was by William Murray's Company; the manager's own Captain Thornton was excellent—and so was the Dugald Creature of a Mr. Duff—there was also a good Mattie—(about whose equipment, by the bye, Scott felt such interest that he left his box between the acts to remind Mr. Murray that she "must have a mantle with her lanthorn")—but the great and unrivalled attraction was the personification of Bailie Jarvie, by Charles Mackay, who, being himself a native of Glasgow, entered into the minutest peculiarities of the character with high gusto, and gave the west-country dialect in its most racy perfection. It was extremely diverting to watch the play of Scott's features during this admirable realisation of his

[1] These charming essays are now included in his Miscellaneous Prose Works.

conception; and I must add, that the behaviour of the
Edinburgh audience on all such occasions, while the secret
of the novels was preserved, reflected great honour on
their good taste and delicacy of feeling. He seldom, in
those days, entered his box without receiving some mark
of general respect and admiration; but I never heard of
any pretext being laid hold of to connect these demonstrations with the piece he had come to witness, or, in
short, to do or say anything likely to interrupt his quiet
enjoyment of the evening in the midst of his family and
friends.

This *Rob Roy* had a continued run of forty-one nights;
and when the Bailie's benefit-night arrived, he received
an epistle of kind congratulation signed *Jedediah Cleishbotham*, and enclosing a five-pound note: but all the
while, Scott was in a miserable state, and when he left
Edinburgh, in March, the alarm about him in the Parliament-House was very serious. He had invited me to
visit him in the country during the recess; but I should
not have ventured to keep my promise, had not the Ballantynes reported amendment towards the close of April.
John then told me that his "illustrious friend" (for so
both the brothers usually spoke of him) was so much
recovered as to have resumed his usual literary tasks,
though with this difference, that he now, for the first time
in his life, found it necessary to employ the hand of
another.

He had now begun in earnest his Bride of Lammermoor,
and his amanuenses were William Laidlaw and John Ballantyne;—of whom he preferred the latter, when he could
be at Abbotsford, on account of the superior rapidity of
his pen; and also because John kept his pen to the paper
without interruption, and, though with many an arch
twinkle in his eyes, and now and then an audible smack of
his lips, had resolution to work on like a well-trained
clerk; whereas good Laidlaw entered with such keen zest
into the interest of the story as it flowed from the author's
lips, that he could not suppress exclamations of surprise
and delight—" Gude keep us a'!—the like o' that!—eh
sirs! eh sirs!"—and so forth—which did not promote
despatch. I have often, however, in the sequel, heard
both these secretaries describe the astonishment with
which they were equally affected when Scott began this
experiment. The affectionate Laidlaw beseeching him to

stop dictating, when his audible suffering filled every pause, "Nay, Willie," he answered, "only see that the doors are fast. I would fain keep all the cry as well as all the wool to ourselves; but as to giving over work, that can only be when I am in woollen." John Ballantyne told me, that after the first day, he always took care to have a dozen of pens made before he seated himself opposite to the sofa on which Scott lay, and that though he often turned himself on his pillow with a groan of torment, he usually continued the sentence in the same breath. But when dialogue of peculiar animation was in progress, spirit seemed to triumph altogether over matter —he arose from his couch and walked up and down the room, raising and lowering his voice, and as it were acting the parts. It was in this fashion that Scott produced the far greater portion of The Bride of Lammermoor—the whole of the Legend of Montrose—and almost the whole of Ivanhoe. Yet when his health was fairly re-established, he disdained to avail himself of the power of dictation, which he had thus put to the sharpest test, but resumed, and for many years resolutely adhered to, the old plan of writing everything with his own hand. When I once, some time afterwards, expressed my surprise that he did not consult his ease, and spare his eye-sight at all events, by occasionally dictating, he answered—"I should as soon think of getting into a sedan-chair while I can use my legs."

But to return:—I rode out to Abbotsford with John Ballantyne towards the end of the spring vacation, and though he had warned me of a sad change in Scott's appearance, it was far beyond what I had been led to anticipate. He had lost a great deal of flesh—his clothes hung loose about him—his countenance was meagre, haggard, and of the deadliest yellow of the jaundice—and his hair, which a few weeks before had been but slightly sprinkled with grey, was now almost literally snow-white. His eye, however, retained its fire unquenched; indeed it seemed to have gained in brilliancy from the new languor of the other features; and he received us with all the usual cordiality, and even with little perceptible diminishment in the sprightliness of his manner. He sat at the table while we dined, but partook only of some rice pudding; and after the cloth was drawn, while sipping his toast and water, pushed round the bottle in his old style, and talked with easy cheerfulness of the stout battle he had fought, and which he now seemed to consider as won.

" One day there was," he said, " when I certainly began to have great doubts whether the mischief was not getting at my mind—and I'll tell you how I tried to reassure myself on that score. I was quite unfit for anything like original composition; but I thought if I could turn an old German ballad I had been reading into decent rhymes, I might dismiss my worst apprehensions—and you shall see what became of the experiment." He then desired his daughter Sophia to fetch the MS. of *The Noble Moringer,* as it had been taken down from his dictation, partly by her and partly by Mr. Laidlaw, during one long and painful day while he lay in bed. He read it to us as it stood, and seeing that both Ballantyne and I were much pleased with the verses, he said he should c\ ɔy them over,—make them a little " tighter about the joints,"—and give them to the Register for 1816.

The reading of this long ballad, however,—(it consists of forty-three stanzas)[1]—seemed to have exhausted him : he retired to his bedroom; and an hour or two after, when we were about to follow his example, his family were distressed by the well-known symptoms of another sharp recurrence of his affliction. A large dose of opium and the hot bath were immediately put in requisition. His good neighbour, Dr. Scott of Darnlee, was sent for, and soon attended; and in the course of three or four hours we learned that he was once more at ease. But I can never forget the groans which, during that space, his agony extorted from him. Well knowing the iron strength of his resolution, to find him confessing its extremity, by cries audible not only all over the house, but even to a considerable distance from it—it may be supposed that this was sufficiently alarming, even to my companion ; how much more to me, who had never before listened to that voice, except in the gentle accents of kindness and merriment.

I told Ballantyne that I saw this was no time for my visit, and that I should start for Edinburgh again at an early hour—and begged he would make my apologies—in the propriety of which he acquiesced. But as I was dressing, about seven next morning, Scott himself tapped at my door, and entered, looking better I thought than at

[1] See *Scott's Poetical Works,* royal 8vo, p. 618.

my arrival the day before. "Don't think of going," said he; "I feel hearty this morning, and if my devil does come back again, it won't be for three days at any rate. For the present, I want nothing to set me up except a good trot in the open air, to drive away the accursed vapours of the laudanum I was obliged to swallow last night. You have never seen Yarrow, and when I have finished a little job I have with Jocund Johnny, we shall all take horse and make a day of it." When I said something about a ride of twenty miles being rather a bold experiment after such a night, he answered, that he had ridden more than forty, a week before, under similar circumstances, and felt nothing the worse. He added, that there was an election on foot, in consequence of the death of Sir John Riddell of Riddell, Member of Parliament for the Selkirk district of Burghs, and that the bad health and absence of the Duke of Buccleuch rendered it quite necessary that he should make exertions on this occasion. "In short," said he, laughing, "I have an errand which I shall perform—and as I must pass Newark, you had better not miss the opportunity of seeing it under so excellent a cicerone as the old minstrel,

> ‘ Whose withered cheek and tresses grey
> Shall yet see many a better day.’ ”

About eleven o'clock, accordingly, he was mounted, by the help of Tom Purdie, upon a staunch active cob, yclept *Sybil Grey*,—exactly such a creature as is described in Mr. Dinmont's *Dumple*—while Ballantyne sprung into the saddle of noble *Old Mortality*, and we proceeded to the town of Selkirk, where Scott halted to do business at the Sheriff-Clerk's, and begged us to move onward at a gentle pace until he should overtake us. He came up by and by at a canter, and seemed in high glee with the tidings he had heard about the canvass. And so we rode by Philiphaugh, Carterhaugh, Bowhill, and Newark, he pouring out all the way his picturesque anecdotes of former times —more especially of the fatal field where Montrose was finally overthrown by Leslie. He described the battle as vividly as if he had witnessed it; the passing of the Ettrick at daybreak by the Covenanting General's heavy cuirassiers, many of them old soldiers of Gustavus Adolphus, and the wild confusion of the Highland host when exposed to their charge on an extensive *haugh* as flat as a bowling-green. He drew us aside at *Slain-men's-lee*, to observe the green mound that marks the resting-place of the slaughtered royalists; and pointing to the apparently precipitous mountain, Minchmoor, over which Montrose and his few cavaliers escaped, mentioned that, rough as it seemed, his mother remembered passing it in her early days in a coach and six, on her way to a ball at Peebles—several footmen marching on either side of the carriage to prop it up, or drag it through bogs, as the case might require. He also gave us, with all the dramatic effect of one of his best chapters, the history of a worthy family who, inhabiting at the time of the battle a cottage on his own estate, had treated with particular kindness a young officer of Leslie's army quartered on them for a night or two before. When parting from them to join the troops, he took out a purse of gold, and told the goodwoman that he had a presentiment he should not see another sun set, and in that case would wish his money to remain in her kind hands; but, if he should survive, he had no doubt she would restore it honestly. The young man returned mortally wounded, but lingered a while under her roof, and finally bequeathed to her and hers his purse and his blessing. " Such," he said, " was the origin of the respectable lairds of ——, now my good neighbours."

The prime object of this expedition was to talk over the politics of Selkirk with one of the Duke of Buccleuch's great store farmers, who, as the Sheriff had learned, possessed private influence with a doubtful bailie or deacon among the Souters. I forget the result, if ever I heard it. But next morning, having, as he assured us, enjoyed a good night in consequence of this ride, he invited us to accompany him on a similar errand across Bowden Moor, and up the Valley of the Ayle; and when we reached a particular bleak and dreary point of that journey, he informed us that he perceived in the waste below a wreath of smoke, which was the appointed signal that a *wavering* Souter of some consequence had agreed to give him a personal interview where no Whiggish eyes were likely to observe them;—and so, leaving us on the road, he proceeded to thread his way westwards, across moor and bog, until we lost view of him. I think a couple of hours might have passed before he joined us again, which was, as had been arranged, not far from the village of Lilliesleaf. In

that place, too, he had some negotiation of the same sort
to look after; and when he had finished it, he rode with us
all round the ancient woods of Riddell, but would not go
near the house; I suppose lest any of the afflicted family
might still be there. Many were his lamentations over the
catastrophe which had just befallen them. "They are,"
he said, "one of the most venerable races in the south of
Scotland—they were here long before these glens had ever
heard the name of Soulis or Douglas—to say nothing of
Buccleuch: they can shew a Pope's bull of the tenth century, authorising the then Riddell to marry a relation
within the forbidden degrees. Here they have been for a
thousand years at least; and now all the inheritance is to
pass away, merely because one good worthy gentleman
would not be contented to enjoy his horses, his hounds,
and his bottle of claret, like thirty or forty predecessors,
but must needs turn scientific agriculturist, take almost all
his fair estate into his own hand, superintend for himself
perhaps a hundred ploughs, and try every new nostrum
that has been tabled by the quackish *improvers* of the
time. And what makes the thing ten times more wonderful is, that he kept day-book and ledger, and all the rest
of it, as accurately as if he had been a cheesemonger in
the Grassmarket." Some of the most remarkable circumstances in Scott's own subsequent life have made me often
recall this conversation—with more wonder than he expressed about the ruin of the Riddells.

I remember he told us a world of stories, some tragical,
some comical, about the old lairds of this time-honoured
lineage; and among others, that of the seven Bibles and
the seven bottles of ale, which he afterwards inserted in a
note to a novel then in progress.[1] He was also full of
anecdotes about a friend of his father's, a minister of
Lilliesleaf, who reigned for two generations the most
popular preacher in Teviotdale; but I forget the orator's
name. When the original of Saunders Fairford congratulated him in his latter days on the undiminished
authority he still maintained—every kirk in the neighbourhood being left empty when it was known he was to mount
the *tent* at any country sacrament—the shrewd divine
answered, "Indeed, Mr. Walter, I sometimes think it's
vera surprising. There's aye a talk of this or that wonderfully gifted young man frae the college; but whenever

[1] See *The Bride of Lammermoor*, Note to chap. xiv.

I'm to be at the same *occasion* with ony o' them, I e'en mount the white horse in the Revelations, and he dings them a'."

Thus Scott amused himself and us as we jogged homewards : and it was the same the following day, when (no election matters pressing) he rode with us to the western peak of the Eildon hills, that he might shew me the whole panorama of his Teviotdale, and expound the direction of the various passes by which the ancient forayers made their way into England, and tell the names and the histories of many a monastic chapel and baronial peel, now mouldering in glens and dingles that escape the eye of the traveller on the highways. Among other objects on which he descanted with particular interest, were the ruins of the earliest residence of the Kerrs of Cessford, so often opposed in arms to his own chieftains of Branksome, and a desolate little kirk on the adjoining moor, where the Dukes of Roxburghe are still buried in the same vault with the hero who fell at Turn-again. Turning to the northward, he shewed us the crags and tower of Smailholme, and behind it the shattered fragment of Ercildoune—and repeated some pretty stanzas ascribed to the last of the real wandering minstrels of this district, by name *Burn* :—

> " Sing Ercildoune, and Cowdenknowes,
>   Where Holmes had ance commanding," &c.

That night he had again an attack of his cramp, but not so serious as the former. Next morning he was again at work with Ballantyne at an early hour; and when I parted from him after breakfast, he spoke cheerfully of being soon in Edinburgh for the usual business of his Court. I left him, however, with dark prognostications; and the circumstances of this little visit to Abbotsford have no doubt dwelt on my mind the more distinctly, from my having observed and listened to him throughout under the painful feeling that it might very probably be my last.

Within a few days he heard tidings perhaps as heavy as ever reached him. His ever steadfast friend, to whom he looked up, moreover, with the feelings of the true old border clansman, Charles Duke of Buccleuch, died on the 20th of April at Lisbon. Captain Adam Fergusson had accompanied the Duke, whose health had for years been breaking, to the scene of his own old campaigns : he now attended his Grace's remains to England; and on landing received a letter in which Scott said :—" I have had another eight days' visit of my disorder, which has confined me chiefly to my bed. It will perhaps shade off into a mild chronic complaint—if it returns frequently with the same violence, I shall break up by degrees, and follow my dear chief. I thank God I can look at this possibility without much anxiety, and without a shadow of fear."

On the 11th of May he returned to Edinburgh, and was present at the opening of the Court; when all who saw him were as much struck as I had been at Abbotsford with the change in his appearance. He was unable to persist in attendance at the Clerks' table—for several weeks afterwards I think he seldom if ever attempted it; and I well remember that, when the Bride of Lammermoor and Legend of Montrose at length came out (which was on the 10th of June), he was known to be confined to bed, and the book was received amidst the deep general impression that we should see no more of that parentage.

" The *Bride of Lammermoor* " (says James Ballantyne) " was not only written, but published before Mr. Scott was able to rise from his bed; and he assured me that when it was first put into his hands in a complete shape, he did not recollect one single incident, character, or conversation it contained. He did not desire me to understand, nor did I understand that his illness had erased from his memory the original incidents of the story, with which he had been acquainted from his boyhood. These remained rooted where they had ever been; or, to speak more explicitly, he remembered the general facts of the existence of the father and mother, of the son and daughter, of the rival lovers, of the compulsory marriage, and the attack made by the bride upon the hapless bridegroom, with the general catastrophe of the whole. All these things he recollected just as he did before he took to his bed : but he literally recollected nothing else—not a single character woven by the romancer, not one of the many scenes and points of humour, nor anything with which he was connected as the writer of the work. 'For a long time,' he said, ' I felt myself very uneasy in the course of my reading, lest I should be startled by meeting something altogether glaring and fantastic. However, I recollected that you had been the printer, and I felt sure that you would not have permitted anything of this sort to pass.' ' Well,' I said, ' upon the whole, how did you like it?'—' Why,' he said, ' as a whole, I felt it monstrous gross and grotesque; but still the worst of it made me laugh, and I trusted the good-natured public would not be less indulgent.' I do not think I ever ventured to lead to the discussion of this singular phenomenon again; but you may depend upon it, that what I have now said is as distinctly reported as if it had been taken down in short-hand at the moment; I believe you will agree with me in thinking that the history of the human mind contains nothing more wonderful.''

One day, soon after he reappeared in the Parliament-House, he asked me to walk home with him. He moved languidly, and said, if he were to stay in town many days, he must send for Sybil Grey; but his conversation was heart-whole; and, in particular, he laughed till, despite his weakness, the stick was flourishing in his hand, over the following almost incredible specimen of the eleventh Earl of Buchan.

Hearing one morning shortly before this time, that Scott was actually *in extremis*, the Earl proceeded to Castle Street, and found the knocker tied up. He then descended to the door in the area, and was there received by honest Peter Mathieson, whose face seemed to confirm the woful tidings, for in truth his master was ill enough. Peter told his Lordship that he had the strictest orders to admit no visitor; but the Earl would take no denial, pushed the bashful coachman aside, and elbowed his way up stairs to the door of Scott's bed-chamber. He had his fingers upon the handle before Peter could give warning to Miss Scott; and when she appeared to remonstrate against such an intrusion, he patted her on the head like a child, and persisted in his purpose of entering the sick-room so strenuously, that the young lady found it necessary to bid Peter see the Earl down stairs again, at whatever damage to his dignity. Peter accordingly, after trying all his eloquence in vain, gave the tottering, bustling, old, meddlesome coxcomb a single shove,—as respectful, doubt not, as a shove can ever be,—and he accepted that hint, and made a rapid exit. Scott, meanwhile, had heard the confusion, and at length it was explained to him; when fearing that Peter's gripe might have injured Lord Buchan's feeble person, he desired James Ballantyne, who had been sitting by his bed, to follow the old man home—make him comprehend, if he could, that the family were in such bewilderment of alarm that the ordinary rules of civility were out of the question—and, in fine, inquire what had been the object of his Lordship's intended visit. James proceeded forthwith to the Earl's house in George Street, and found him strutting about his library in a towering indignation. Ballantyne's elaborate demonstrations of respect, however, by degrees softened him, and he condescended to explain himself. "I wished," said he, "to embrace Walter Scott before he died, and inform him that I had long considered it as a satisfactory circumstance that he and I were destined to rest together in the same place of sepulchre. The principal thing, however, was to relieve his mind as to the arrangements of his funeral—to shew him a plan which I had prepared for the procession— and, in a word, to assure him that I took upon myself the whole conduct of the ceremonial at Dryburgh." He then exhibited to Ballantyne a formal programme, in which, as may be supposed, the predominant feature was not Walter Scott, but David Earl of Buchan. It had been settled, *inter alia*, that the said Earl was to pronounce an eulogium over the grave, after the fashion of French Academicians in the *Père la Chaise.*

And this was the elder brother of Thomas and Henry Erskine! But the story is well known of his boasting one day to the late Duchess of Gordon of the extraordinary talents of his family—when her unscrupulous Grace asked him, very coolly, whether the wit had not come by the mother, and been all settled on the younger branches?

I must not forget to set down what Sophia Scott afterwards told me of her father's conduct upon one night in June, when he really did despair of himself. He then called his children about his bed, and took leave of them with solemn tenderness. After giving them, one by one, such advice as suited their years and characters, he added, —"For myself, my dears, I am unconscious of ever having done any man an injury, or omitted any fair opportunity of doing any man a benefit. I well know that no human life can appear otherwise than weak and filthy in the eyes of God : but I rely on the merits and intercession of our Redeemer." He then laid his hand on their heads, and said—"God bless you! Live so that you may all hope to meet each other in a better place hereafter. And now leave me, that I may turn my face to the wall." They obeyed him; but he presently fell into a deep sleep;

and when he awoke from it after many hours, the crisis of
extreme danger was felt by himself, and pronounced by
his physician, to have been overcome.

The Tales of the Third Series would have been read
with indulgence, had they needed it; for the painful circumstances under which they must have been produced
were in part known wherever an English newspaper made
its way; but I believe that, except in typical errors, from
the author's inability to correct proof-sheets, no one ever
affected to perceive in either work the slightest symptom
of his malady. Dugald Dalgetty was placed by acclamation in the same rank with Bailie Jarvie—a conception
equally new, just, and humorous, and worked out in all the
details, as if it had formed the luxurious entertainment of
a chair as easy as was ever shaken by Rabelais; and
though the character of Montrose himself seemed hardly
to have been treated so fully as the subject merited, the
accustomed rapidity of the novelist's execution would have
been enough to account for any such defect. Caleb
Balderstone—(the hero of one of the many ludicrous
delineations which he owed to the late Lord Haddington)—
was pronounced at the time, by more than one critic, a
mere caricature; and, though he himself would never, in
after days, admit this censure to be just, he allowed that
" he might have sprinkled rather too much parsley over
his chicken." But even that blemish, for I grant that I
think it a serious one, could not disturb the profound
interest and pathos of the Bride of Lammermoor—to my
fancy the most pure and powerful of all the tragedies that
Scott ever penned.

These volumes, as was mentioned, came out before the
middle of June; and though at that moment he was unable
to quit his room, he did not hesitate to make all arrangements as to another romance. Nay, though his condition
still required an amanuensis, he had advanced considerably
in the new work before the Session closed in July. That
he felt much more security as to his health by that time,
must be inferred from his then allowing his son Walter to
proceed to Ireland to join the 18th regiment of Hussars.
The Cornet was only in the eighteenth year of his age;
and the fashion of education in Scotland is such, that he
had scarcely ever slept a night under a different roof from
his parents, until this separation occurred. He had been
treated from his cradle with all the indulgence that a man

of sense can ever permit himself to shew to any of his children; and for several years he had now been his father's daily companion in all his out-of-doors occupations and amusements. The parting was a painful one: but Scott's ambition centred in the heir of his name, and instead of fruitless pinings and lamentings, he henceforth made it his constant business to keep up such a frank correspondence with the young man as might enable himself to exert over him, when at a distance, the gentle influence of kindness, experience, and wisdom. The series of his letters to his son is, in my opinion, by far the most interesting and valuable, as respects the personal character and temper of the writer. His manly kindness to his boy, whether he is expressing approbation or censure of his conduct, is a model for the parent; and his practical wisdom was of that liberal order, based on such comprehensive views of man and the world, that I am persuaded it will often be found available to the circumstances of their own various cases, by young men of whatever station or profession.

Abbotsford had, in the ensuing autumn, the honour of a visit from Prince Leopold, now King of Belgium, who had been often in Scott's company in Paris in 1815; and his Royal Highness was followed by many other distinguished guests; none of whom, from what they saw, would have doubted that the masons and foresters fully occupied their host's time. He was all the while, however, making steady progress with his Ivanhoe—and that although he was so far from entire recovery, that Mr. Laidlaw continued to produce most of the MS. from his dictation.

The approach of winter brought a very alarming aspect of things in our manufacturing districts; and there was throughout Scotland a general revival of the old volunteer spirit. Scott did not now dream of rejoining the Light Horse of Edinburgh, which he took much pleasure in seeing re-organised; but in conjunction with his neighbour the laird of Gala, he planned the raising of a body of Border Sharpshooters, and was highly gratified by the readiness with which a hundred young men from his own immediate neighbourhood sent in their names, making no condition but that the Sheriff himself should be the commandant. He was very willing to accept that stipulation; and Laidlaw was instantly directed to look out for a

stalwart charger, a fit successor for the Brown Adams of
former days. But the progress of disaffection was
arrested before this scheme could be carried into execution. It was in the midst of that alarm that he put
forth the brief, but beautiful series of papers entitled *The
Visionary*.

In December he had an extraordinary accumulation of
distress in his family circle. Within ten days he lost his
uncle Dr. Rutherford; his dear aunt Christian Rutherford;
and his excellent mother. On her death he says to Lady
Louisa Stuart (who had seen and been much pleased with
the old lady):—" If I have been able to do anything in the
way of painting the past times, it is very much from the
studies with which she presented me. She connected a
long period of time with the present generation, for she
remembered, and often spoken with, a person who
perfectly recollected the battle of Dunbar, and Oliver
Cromwell's subsequent entry into Edinburgh. She preserved her faculties to the very day before her final illness; for our friends Mr. and Mrs. Scott of Harden
visited her on the Sunday, and, coming to our house
after, were expressing their surprise at the alertness of
her mind, and the pleasure which she had in talking over
both ancient and modern events. She had told them with
great accuracy the real story of the Bride of Lammermoor, and pointed out wherein it differed from the novel.
She had all the names of the parties, and detailed (for she
was a great genealogist) their connection with existing
families. On the subsequent Monday she was struck with
a paralytic affection, suffered little, and that with the
umost patience; and what was God's reward, and a great
one to her innocent and benevolent life, she never knew
that her brother and sister, the last thirty years younger
than herself, had trodden the dark path before her. She
was a strict economist, which she said enabled her to be
liberal; out of her little income of about £300 a-year, she
bestowed at least a third in well-chosen charities, and with
the rest lived like a gentlewoman, and even with hospitality more general than seemed to suit her age; yet I
could never prevail on her to accept of any assistance.
You cannot conceive how affecting it was to me to see the
little preparation of presents which she had assorted for
the New Year—for she was a great observer of the old
fashions of her period—and to think that the kind heart

was cold which delighted in all these acts of kindly affection.''

There is in the library at Abbotsford a fine copy of Baskerville's folio Bible, two volumes, printed at Cambridge in 1763; and there appears on the blank leaf, in the trembling handwriting of Scott's mother, this inscription —"*To my dear son, Walter Scott, from his affectionate Mother, Anne Rutherford—January 1st, 1819.*" Under these words her son has written as follows :—" This Bible was the gift of my grandfather Dr. John Rutherford, to my mother, and presented by her to me; being alas ! the last gift which I was to receive from that excellent parent, and, as I verily believe, the thing which she most loved in the world,—not only in humble veneration of the sacred contents, but as the dearest pledge of her father's affection to her. As such she gave it to me; and as such I bequeath it to those who may represent me—charging them carefully to preserve the same, in memory of those to whom it has belonged. 1820.''

On the 18th of December, while his house was thus saddened, appeared his *Ivanhoe*. It was received throughout England with a more clamorous delight than any of the *Scotch novels* had been. The volumes (three in number) were now, for the first time, of the post 8vo form, with a finer paper than hitherto, the press-work much more elegant, and the price accordingly raised from eight shillings the volume to ten; yet the copies sold in this original shape were twelve thousand.

I ought to have mentioned sooner, that the original intention was to bring out Ivanhoe as the production of a new hand, and that to assist this impression, the work was printed in a size and manner unlike the preceding ones; but Constable, when the day of publication approached, remonstrated against this experiment, and it was accordingly abandoned.

The reader has already been told that Scott dictated the greater part of this romance. The portion of the MS. which is his own, appears, however, not only as well and firmly executed as that of any of the Tales of my Landlord, but distinguished by having still fewer erasures and interlineations, and also by being in a smaller hand. The fragment is beautiful to look at—many pages together without one alteration. It is, I suppose, superfluous to add, that in no instance did Scott re-write his prose before sending it to the press. Whatever may have been the case with his poetry, the world uniformly received the *prima cura* of the novelist.

As a work of art, Ivanhoe is perhaps the first of all Scott's efforts, whether in prose or in verse; nor have the strength and splendour of his imagination been displayed to higher advantage than in some of the scenes of this romance. But I believe that no reader who is capable of thoroughly comprehending the author's Scotch character and Scotch dialogue will ever place even Ivanhoe, as a work of genius, on the same level with Waverley, Guy Mannering, or the Heart of Mid-Lothian.

The introduction of the charming Jewess and her father originated, I find, in a conversation that Scott held with his friend Skene during the severest season of his bodily sufferings in the early part of this year. " Mr. Skene," says that gentleman's wife, " sitting by his bedside, and trying to amuse him as well as he could in the intervals of pain, happened to get on the subject of the Jews, as he had observed them when he spent some time in Germany in his youth. Their situation had naturally made a strong impression; for in those days they retained their own dress and manners entire, and were treated with considerable austerity by their Christian neighbours, being still locked up at night in their own quarter by great gates; and Mr. Skene, partly in seriousness, but partly from the mere wish to turn his mind at the moment upon something that might occupy and divert it, suggested that a group of Jews would be an interesting feature if he could contrive to bring them into his next novel." Upon the appearance of Ivanhoe, he reminded Mr. Skene of this conversation, and said, " You will find this book owes not a little to your German reminiscences."

By the way, before Ivanhoe made its appearance, I had myself been formally admitted to the author's secret; but had he favoured me with no such confidence, it would have been impossible for me to doubt that I had been present some months before at the conversation which suggested, and indeed supplied all the materials of, one of its most amusing chapters. I allude to that in which our Saxon terms for animals in the field, and our Norman equivalents for them as they appear on the table, and so on, are explained and commented on. All this Scott owed to the after-dinner talk one day in Castle Street of his old friend Mr. William Clerk,—who, among other elegant pursuits, has cultivated the science of philology very deeply.

I cannot conclude without observing that the publication of Ivanhoe marks the most brilliant epoch in Scott's history as the literary favourite of his contemporaries. With the novel which he next put forth, the immediate sale of these works began gradually to decline; and though, even when that had reached its lowest declension, it was still far above the most ambitious dreams of any other novelist, yet the publishers were afraid the announcement of anything like a falling-off might cast a damp over the spirits of the author. He was allowed to remain for several years under the impression that whatever novel he threw off commanded at once the old triumphant sale of ten or twelve thousand, and was afterwards, when included in the collective edition, to be circulated in that shape also as widely as Waverley or Ivanhoe. In my opinion, it would have been very unwise in the booksellers to give Scott any unfavourable tidings upon such subjects after the commencement of the malady which proved fatal to him,—for that from the first shook his mind; but I think they took a false measure of the man when they hesitated to tell him exactly how the matter stood, throughout 1820 and the three or four following years, when his intellect was as vigorous as it ever had been, and his heart as courageous; and I regret their scruples (among other reasons), because the years now mentioned were the most costly ones in his life; and for every twelve months in which any man allows himself, or is encouraged by others, to proceed in a course of unwise expenditure, it becomes proportionably more difficult for him to pull up when the mistake is at length detected or recognised.

In the correspondence of this winter (1819-1820), there occurs frequent mention of the Prince Gustavus Vasa, who spent some months in Edinburgh, and his Royal Highness's accomplished attendant, the Baron Polier. I met them often in Castle Street, and remember as especially interesting the first evening that they dined there. The only portrait in Scott's Edinburgh dining-room was one of Charles XII. of Sweden, and he was struck, as indeed everyone must have been, with the remarkable resemblance which the exiled Prince's air and features

presented to the hero of his race. Young Gustavus, on
his part, hung with keen and melancholy enthusiasm on
his host's anecdotes of the expedition of Charles Edward.
The Prince, accompanied by Scott and myself, witnessed
the ceremonial of the proclamation of King George IV. on
the 2nd of February, at the Cross, from a window over
Mr. Constable's shop in the High Street; and on that
occasion also the air of sadness that mixed in his features
with eager curiosity was very affecting. Scott explained
all the details to him, not without many lamentations over
the barbarity of the Auld Reekie bailies, who had removed
the beautiful Gothic Cross itself, for the sake of widening
the thoroughfare. The weather was fine, the sun shone
bright; and the antique tabards of the heralds, the trumpet
notes of *God save the King*, and the hearty cheerings of
the immense uncovered multitude that filled the noble old
street, produced altogether a scene of great splendour and
solemnity. The Royal Exile surveyed it with a flushed
cheek and a watery eye, and Scott, observing his emotion,
withdrew with me to another window, whispering " Poor
lad ! poor lad ! God help him." Later in the season the
Prince spent a few days at Abbotsford, where he was
received with at least as much reverence as any eldest son
of a reigning sovereign could have been. He gave Scott,
at parting, a seal, which he almost constantly used ever
after.

About the middle of February—it having been ere that
time arranged that I should marry his eldest daughter in
the course of the spring,—I accompanied him and part of
his family on one of those flying visits to Abbotsford, with
which he often indulged himself on a Saturday during
term. Upon such occasions Scott appeared at the usual
hour in Court, but wearing, instead of the official suit of
black, his country morning dress—green jacket and so
forth—under the clerk's gown; a licence of which many
gentlemen of the long robe had been accustomed to avail
themselves in the days of his youth—it being then considered as the authentic badge that they were lairds as well
as lawyers—but which, to use the dialect of the place, had
fallen into *desuetud*e before I knew the Parliament-House.
He was, I think, one of the two or three, or at most the
half-dozen, who still adhered to this privilege of their
order; and it has now, in all likelihood, become quite
obsolete, like the ancient custom, a part of the same

system, for all Scotch barristers to appear without gowns or wigs, and in coloured clothes, when upon circuit. At noon, when the Court broke up, Peter Mathieson was sure to be in attendance in the Parliament Close, and five minutes after, the gown had been tossed off, and Scott, rubbing his hands for glee, was under weigh for Tweed-side. On this occasion, he was, of course, in mourning; but I have thought it worth while to preserve the circumstance of his usual Saturday's costume. As we proceeded, he talked without reserve of the novel of the Monastery, of which he had the first volume with him: and mentioned, what he had probably forgotten when he wrote the Introduction of 1830, that a good deal of that volume had been composed before he concluded Ivanhoe. "It was a relief," he said, "to interlay the scenery most familiar to me, with the strange world for which I had to draw so much on imagination."

Next morning there appeared at breakfast John Ballantyne, who had at this time a hunting-box a few miles off, in the vale of the Leader—and with him Mr. Constable, his guest; and it being a fine clear day, as soon as Scott had read the Church service and one of Jeremy Taylor's sermons, we all sallied out, before noon, on a perambulation of his upland territories; Maida and the rest of the favourites accompanying our march. At starting we were joined by the constant henchman, Tom Purdie—and I may save myself the trouble of any attempt to describe his appearance, for his master has given us an inimitably true one in introducing a certain personage of his Redgauntlet: —"He was, perhaps, sixty years old; yet his brow was not much furrowed, and his jet black hair was only grizzled, not whitened, by the advance of age. All his motions spoke strength unabated; and though rather undersized, he had very broad shoulders, was square made, thin-flanked, and apparently combined in his frame muscular strength and activity; the last somewhat impaired, perhaps, by years, but the first remaining in full vigour. A hard and harsh countenance; eyes far sunk under projecting eyebrows, which were grizzled like his hair; a wide mouth, furnished from ear to ear with a range of unimpaired teeth of uncommon whiteness, and a size and breadth which might have become the jaws of an ogre, completed this delightful portrait." Equip this figure in Scott's cast-off green jacket, white hat and drab trousers; and imagine that years of kind treatment, comfort, and the honest consequence of a confidential *grieve*, had softened away much of the hardness and harshness originally impressed on the visage by anxious penury and the sinister habits of a *blackfisher*;—and the Tom Purdie of 1820 stands before us.[1]

We were all delighted to see how completely Scott had recovered his bodily vigour, and none more so than Constable, who, as he puffed and panted after him up one ravine and down another, often stopped to wipe his forehead, and remarked that "it was not every author who should lead him such a dance." But Purdie's face shone with rapture as he observed how severely the swag-bellied bookseller's activity was taxed. Scott exclaiming exultingly, though perhaps for the tenth time, "This will be a glorious spring for our trees, Tom!"—"You may say that, Shirra," quoth Tom,—and then lingering a moment for Constable,—"'My certy,' he added, scratching his head, "and I think it will be a grand season for *our buiks* too." But indeed Tom always talked of *our buiks* as if they had been as regular products of the soil as *our aits* and *our birks*. Having threaded, first the Hexilcleugh, and then the Rhymer's Glen, we arrived at Huntley Burn, where the hospitality of the kind *Weird-Sisters*, as Scott called the Miss Fergussons, re-animated our exhausted Bibliopoles, and gave them courage to extend their walk a little further down the same famous brook. Here there was a small cottage in a very sequestered situation, by making some little additions to which Scott thought it might be converted into a suitable summer residence for his daughter and future son-in-law. The details of that plan were soon settled—it was agreed on all hands that a sweeter scene of seclusion could not be fancied. He repeated some verses of Rogers' "Wish," which paint the spot :—

> "Mine be a cot beside the hill—
> A bee-hive's hum shall soothe my ear;
> A willowy brook that turns a mill,
> With many a fall shall linger near:" &c.

But when he came to the stanza—

> "And Lucy at her wheel shall sing,
> In russet-gown and apron blue,"

he departed from the text, adding—

[1] There is in the dining-room at Abbotsford a clever little sketch in oil of Tom Purdie by Edwin Landseer, R.A.—who often enjoyed Tom's company in sports both of flood and field.

" But if Bluestockings here you bring,
  The Great Unknown won't dine with you."

Johnny Ballantyne, a projector to the core, was particularly zealous about this embryo establishment. Foreseeing that he should have had walking enough ere he reached Huntley Burn, his dapper little Newmarket groom had been ordered to fetch Old Mortality thither, and now, mounted on his fine hunter, he capered about us, looking pallid and emaciated as a ghost, but as gay and cheerful as ever, and would fain have been permitted to ride over hedge and ditch to mark out the proper line of the future avenue. Scott admonished him that the country-people, if they saw him at such work, would take the whole party for heathens; and clapping spurs to his horse, he left us. "The deil's in the body," quoth Tom Purdie; "he'll be ower every *yett* atween this and Turn-again, though it be the Lord's day. I wadna wonder if he were to be *ceeted* before the Session."—"Be sure, Tam," cries Constable, "that you egg on the Dominie to blaw up his father—I wouldna grudge a hundred miles o' gait to see the ne'er-do-weel on the stool, and neither, I'll be sworn, would the Sheriff."—"Na, na," quoth the Sheriff, "we'll let sleeping dogs be, Tam."

As we walked homeward, Scott, being a little fatigued, laid his left hand on Tom's shoulder, and leaned heavily for support, chatting to his "Sunday pony," as he called the affectionate fellow, just as freely as with the rest of the party, and Tom put in his word shrewdly and manfully, and grinned and grunted whenever the joke chanced to be within his apprehension. It was easy to see that his heart swelled within him from the moment that the Sheriff got his collar in his gripe.

There arose a little dispute between them about what tree or trees ought to be cut down in a hedge-row that we passed; and Scott seemed somewhat ruffled with finding that some previous hints of his on that head had not been attended to. When we got into motion again, his hand was on Constable's shoulder—and Tom dropped a pace or two to the rear, until we approached a gate, when he jumped forward and opened it. "Give us a pinch of your snuff, Tom," quoth the Sheriff. Tom's mull was produced, and the hand resumed its position. I was much diverted with Tom's behaviour when we at length reached Abbotsford. There were some garden chairs on the green

in front of the cottage porch. Scott sat down on one of
them to enjoy the view of his new tower as it gleamed in
the sunset, and Constable and I did the like. Mr. Purdie
remained lounging near us for a few minutes, and then
asked the Sheriff " to speak a word." They withdrew
together into the garden—and Scott presently rejoined us
with a particularly comical expression of face. As soon as
Tom was out of sight, he said—" Will ye guess what he
has been saying, now?—Well, this is a great satisfaction !
Tom assures me that he has thought the matter over, and
will take my advice about the thinning of that clump behind Captain Fergusson's." [1]

I must not forget, that whoever might be at Abbotsford,
Tom always appeared at his master's elbow on Sunday,
when dinner was over, and drank long life to the Laird and
the Lady and all the good company, in a quaigh of whisky,
or a tumbler of wine, according to his fancy. I believe
Scott has somewhere expressed in print his satisfaction
that, among all the changes of our manners, the ancient
freedom of personal intercourse may still be indulged between a master and an *out-of-doors'* servant; but in truth
he kept by the old fashion even with domestic servants,
to an extent which I have hardly seen practised by any
other gentleman. He conversed with his coachman if he
sat by him, as he often did on the box—with his footman,
if he happened to be in the rumble; and when there was
any very young lad in the household, he held it a point of

[1] I was obliged to the Sheriff's companion of 1815, John Scott of
Gala, for reminding me of the following trait of Tom Purdie. The
first time John Richardson of Fludyer Street (one of Sir Walter's
dearest friends) came to Abbotsford, Tom (who took him for a
Southron) was sent to attend upon him while he tried for a *fish* (*i.e.*
a salmon) in the neighbourhood of Melrose Bridge. As they walked
thither, Tom boasted grandly of the size of the fish he had himself
caught there, evidently giving the stranger no credit for much skill
in the Waltonian craft. By and by, however, Richardson, who is an
admirable angler, hooked a vigorous fellow, and after a beautiful
exhibition of the art, landed him in safety. " A fine *fish,* Tom."—
" Oo, aye, Sir," quoth Tom—" it's a bonny grilse." " A *grilse,*
Tom ! " says Mr. R.—" it's as heavy a *salmon* as the heaviest you
were telling me about." Tom shewed his teeth in a smile of bitter
incredulity ; but while they were still debating, Lord Sommerville's
fisherman came up with scales in his basket, and Richardson insisted
on having his victim weighed. The result was triumphant for the
captor. " Weel," says Tom, letting the salmon drop on the turf—
" weel, ye *are* a meikle fish, mon—and a meikle *fule* too " (he added
in a lower key) " to let yoursell be kilt by an Englander."

duty to see that his employments were so arranged as to leave time for advancing his education, made him bring his copy-book once a week to the library, and examined him as to all that he was doing. Indeed he did not confine this humanity to his own people. Any steady servant of a friend of his was soon considered as a sort of friend too, and was sure to have a kind little colloquy to himself at coming and going. With all this, Scott was a very rigid enforcer of discipline—contrived to make it thoroughly understood by all about him, that they must do their part by him as he did his by them; and the result was happy. I never knew any man so well served as he was—so carefully, so respectfully, and so silently; and I cannot help doubting if in any department of human operations real kindness ever compromised real dignity.

CHAPTER XI

Scott's Baronetcy—Portrait by Lawrence and Bust by Chantrey—Presidency of the Royal Society of Edinburgh—Hospitalities and Sports at Abbotsford—Publication of the Monastery—The Abbot—and Kenilworth. 1820.

THE novel of The Monastery was published in the beginning of March 1820. It appeared not in the post 8vo form of Ivanhoe, but in 3 vols. 12mo, like the earlier works of the series. In fact, a few sheets of The Monastery had been printed before Scott agreed to let Ivanhoe have " By the Author of Waverley " on its title-page; and the different shapes of the two books belonged to the abortive scheme of passing off " Mr. Laurence Templeton " as a hitherto unheard-of candidate for literary success.

At the rising of his Court on the 12th, he proceeded to London, for the purpose of receiving his baronetcy, which he had been prevented from doing in the spring of the preceding year by illness, and again at Christmas by family afflictions. The Prince Regent was now King.

One of his first visitors was Sir Thomas Lawrence, who informed him that his Majesty had resolved to adorn the great gallery, then in progress at Windsor Castle, with portraits by his hand of his most distinguished contemporaries; all the reigning monarchs of Europe, and their chief ministers and generals, had already sat for this purpose; on the same walls the King desired to see exhibited those of his own subjects who had attained the highest honours of literature and science—and it was his pleasure that this series should commence with Walter Scott. The portrait was begun immediately, and the head was finished before Scott left town. Sir Thomas has caught and fixed with admirable skill one of the loftiest expressions of his countenance at the proudest period of his life : to the perfect truth of the representation, every one who ever surprised him in the act of composition at his desk will bear witness. The expression, however, was one with which many who had seen the man often, were not familiar; and it was extremely unfortunate that Sir Thomas filled in the figure from a separate sketch after he had quitted London. When I first saw the head, I thought nothing could be better; but there was an evident change for the worse when the picture appeared in its finished state—for the rest of the person had been done on a different scale, and this neglect of proportion takes considerably from the majestic effect which the head itself, and especially the mighty pile of forehead, had in nature. I hope one day to see a good engraving of the head alone, as I first saw it floating on a dark sea of canvass.

Lawrence told me several years afterwards that, in his opinion, the two greatest men he had painted were the Duke of Wellington and Sir Walter Scott; " and it was odd," said he, " that they both chose usually the same hour for sitting—seven in the morning. They were both as patient sitters as I ever had. Scott, however, was, in my case at least, a very difficult subject. I had selected what struck me as his noblest look; but when he was in the chair before me, he talked away on all sorts of subjects in his usual style, so that it cost me great pains to bring him back to solemnity, when I had to attend to anything beyond the outline of a subordinate feature. I soon found that the surest recipe was to say something that would lead him to recite a bit of poetry. I used to introduce by hook or by crook a few lines of Campbell or Byron; he was sure to take up the passage where I left it, or *cap* it by something better—and then—when he was, as Dryden says of one of his heroes,

' Made up of three parts fire—so full of heaven
It sparkled at his eyes'—

then was my time—and I made the best use I could of it.

The hardest day's work I had with him was once when ****** [1] accompanied him to my painting room. ****** was in particularly gay spirits, and nothing would serve him but keeping both artist and sitter in a perpetual state of merriment by anecdote upon anecdote about poor Sheridan. The anecdotes were mostly in themselves black enough— but the style of the *conteur* was irresistibly quaint and comical. When Scott came next, he said he was ashamed of himself for laughing so much as he listened to them; ' for truly,' quoth he, ' if the tithe was fact, ****** might have said to Sherry—as Lord Braxfield once said to an eloquent culprit at the bar—' Ye're a verra clever chiel', man, but ye wad be nane the waur o' a hanging.' ''

It was also during this visit to London that Scott sat to Chantrey for that bust which alone preserves for posterity the cast of expression most fondly remembered by all who ever mingled in his domestic circle. Chantrey's request that Scott would sit to him was communicated through Allan Cunningham, clerk of the works in the great sculptor's establishment. "Honest Allan," in his early days, when gaining his bread as a stone-mason in Nithsdale, made a pilgrimage on foot into Edinburgh, for the sole purpose of seeing the author of Marmion as he passed along the street. He was now in possession of a celebrity of his own, and had mentioned to his patron his purpose of calling on Scott to thank him for some kind message he had received, through a common friend, on the subject of those "Remains of Nithsdale and Galloway Song," which first made his poetical talents known to the public. Chantrey embraced this opportunity of conveying to Scott his own long-cherished ambition of modelling his head; and Scott at once assented to the flattering proposal. " It was about nine in the morning," says Mr. Cunningham, " that I sent in my card to him at Miss Dumergue's in Piccadilly. It had not been gone a minute, when I heard a quick heavy step coming, and in he came, holding out both hands, as was his custom, and saying, as he pressed mine —' Allan Cunningham, I am glad to see you.' I said something," continues Mr. C., " about the pleasure I felt in touching the hand that had charmed me so much. He moved his hand, and with one of his comic smiles said, ' Ay—and a big brown hand it is.' I was a little abashed at first : Scott saw it, and soon put me at my ease; he had

---

[1] A distinguished Whig friend.

the power—I had almost called it the art, but art it was not —of winning one's heart, and restoring one's confidence beyond any man I ever met.''

Chantrey's purpose had been the same as Lawrence's— to seize a poetical phasis of the countenance; and when the poet first sat, he proceeded to model the head as looking upwards, gravely and solemnly. The talk that passed, meantime, had amused and gratified both, and fortunately at parting, Chantrey requested that Scott would come and breakfast with him next morning before they recommenced operations in the studio. He accepted the invitation, and when he arrived again in Ecclestone Street, found two or three acquaintances assembled to meet him,—among others, his old friend Richard Heber. The breakfast was, as any party in Sir Francis Chantrey's house was sure to be, a gay one, and not having seen Heber in particular for several years, Scott's spirits were unusually excited. '' In the midst of the mirth,'' says Cunningham, '' John (commonly called *Jack*) Fuller, the member for Surrey, and standing jester of the House of Commons, came in. Heber, who was well acquainted with the free and joyous character of that worthy, began to lead him out by relating some festive anecdotes : Fuller growled approbation, and indulged us with some of his odd sallies; things which he assured us ' were damned good, and true too, which was better.' Mr. Scott, who was standing when Fuller came in, eyed him at first with a look grave and considerate; but as the stream of conversation flowed, his keen eye twinkled brighter and brighter; his stature increased, for he drew himself up, and seemed to take the measure of the hoary joker, body and soul. An hour or two of social chat had meanwhile induced Chantrey to alter his views as to the bust, and when Scott left us, he said to me privately, ' This will never do—I shall never be able to please myself with a perfectly serene expression. I must try his conver- sational look, take him when about to break out into some sly funny old story.' As Chantrey said this, he took a string, cut off the head of the bust, put it into its present position, touched the eyes and mouth slightly, and wrought such a transformation, that when Scott came to his third sitting, he smiled and said—' Ay, ye're mair like yoursel now !—Why, Mr. Chantrey, no witch of old ever performed such cantrips with clay as this.''

The baronetcy was conferred on him, not in consequence

of any Ministerial suggestion, but by the King personally, and of his own unsolicited motion; and when the poet kissed his hand, he said to him—" I shall always reflect with pleasure on Sir Walter Scott's having been the first creation of my reign."

The Gazette announcing this was dated March 30, 1820; and the Baronet, as soon afterwards as he could get away from Lawrence, set out on his return to the North; for he had such respect for the ancient prejudice (a classical as well as a Scottish one) against marrying in May, that he was anxious to have the ceremony in which his daughter was concerned over before that unlucky month should commence. He reached Edinburgh late in April, and on the 29th of that month he gave me the hand of his daughter Sophia. The wedding, *more Scotico*, took place in the evening; and, adhering on all such occasions to ancient modes of observance with the same punctiliousness which he mentions as distinguishing his worthy father, he gave a jolly supper afterwards to all the friends and connections of the young couple.

In May 1820, he received from both the English Universities the highest compliment which it was in their power to offer him. The Vice-Chancellors of Oxford and Cambridge communicated to him, in the same week, their request that he would attend at the approaching Commemorations, and accept the honorary degree of Doctor in Civil Law. It was impossible for him to leave Scotland again in time; and on various subsequent renewals of the same flattering proposition from either body, he was prevented by similar circumstances from availing himself of their distinguished kindness.

About the middle of August, my wife and I went to Abbotsford; and we remained there for several weeks, during which I became familiarised to Sir Walter Scott's mode of existence in the country. The humblest person who stayed merely for a short visit, must have departed with the impression that what he witnessed was an occasional variety; that Scott's courtesy prompted him to break in upon his habits when he had a stranger to amuse; but that it was physically impossible that the man who was writing the Waverley romances at the rate of nearly twelve volumes in the year, could continue, week after week, and month after month, to devote all but a hardly perceptible fraction of his mornings to out-of-doors' occupations, and the whole of his evenings to the entertainment of a constantly varying circle of guests. The hospitality of his afternoons must alone have been enough to exhaust the energies of almost any man; for his visitors did not mean, like those of country-houses in general, to enjoy the landlord's good cheer and amuse each other; but the far greater proportion arrived from a distance, for the sole sake of the Poet and Novelist himself, whose person they had never before seen, and whose voice they might never again have an opportunity of hearing. No other villa in Europe was ever resorted to from the same motives, and to anything like the same extent, except Ferney; and Voltaire never dreamt of being visible to his *hunters*; except for a brief space of the day;—few of them ever dined with him, and none of them seem to have slept under his roof. Scott's establishment, on the contrary, resembled in every particular that of the affluent idler, who, because he has inherited, or would fain transmit political influence in some province, keeps open house—receives as many as he has room for, and sees their apartments occupied, as soon as they vacate them, by another troop of the same description. Even on gentlemen guiltless of inkshed, the exercise of hospitality upon this sort of scale is found to impose a heavy tax; few of them, now-a-days, think of maintaining it for any large portion of the year : very few indeed below the highest rank of the nobility—in whose case there is usually a staff of led-captains, led-chaplains, servile dandies, and semi-professional talkers and jokers from London, to take the chief part of the burden. Now, Scott had often in his mouth the pithy verses—

> " Conversation is but carving :—
> Give no more to every guest,
> Than he's able to digest :
> Give him always of the prime,
> And but little at a time ;
> Carve to all but just enough,
> Let them neither starve nor stuff ;
> *And that you may have your due,*
> *Let your neighbours carve for you* " :—

and he, in his own familiar circle always, and in other circles where it was possible, furnished a happy exemplification of these rules and regulations of the Dean of St. Patrick's. But the same sense and benevolence which dictated adhesion to them among his old friends and acquaintance, rendered it necessary to break them when he was

receiving strangers of the class I have described above at
Abbotsford : he felt that their coming was the best homage
they could pay to his celebrity, and that it would have
been as uncourteous in him not to give them their fill of
his talk, as it would be in your every-day lord of manors
to make his casual guests welcome indeed to his venison,
but keep his grouse-shooting for his immediate allies and
dependants.

Every now and then he received some stranger who was
not indisposed to take his part in the *carving*; and how
good-humouredly he surrendered the lion's share to any
one that seemed to covet it—with what perfect placidity he
submitted to be bored even by bores of the first water
must have excited the admiration of many besides the daily
observers of his proceedings. I have heard a spruce
Senior Wrangler lecture him for half an evening on the
niceties of the Greek epigram; I have heard the poorest
of all parliamentary blunderers try to detail to him the
pros and *cons* of what he called the *Truck system*; and in
either case the same bland eye watched the lips of the tor-
mentor. But, with such ludicrous exceptions, Scott was
the one object of the Abbotsford pilgrims; and evening followed evening only to shew him exerting, for their amusement, more of animal spirits, to say nothing of intellectual
vigour, than would have been considered by any other man
in the company as sufficient for the whole expenditure of a
week's existence. Yet this was not the chief marvel : he
talked of things that interested himself, because he knew
that by doing so he should give most pleasure to his guests.
But how vast was the range of subjects on which he could
talk with unaffected zeal; and with what admirable delicacy of instinctive politeness did he select his topic according to the peculiar history, study, pursuits, or social habits
of the stranger ! And all this was done without approach
to the unmanly trickery of what is called *catching the tone*
of the person one converses with. Scott took the subject
on which he thought such a man or woman would like best
to hear him speak—but not to handle it in their way, or
in any way but what was completely, and most simply his
own;—not to flatter them by embellishing, with the illustration of his genius, the views and opinions which they
were supposed to entertain,—but to let his genius play out
its own variations, for his own delight and theirs, as freely
and easily, and with as endless a multiplicity of delicious

novelties, as ever the magic of Beethoven or Mozart could fling over the few primitive notes of a village air.

It is the custom in some, perhaps in many country-houses, to keep a register of the guests, and I have often regretted that nothing of the sort was ever attempted at Abbotsford. It would have been a curious record—especially if so contrived—(as I have seen done)—that the names of each day should, by their arrangement on the page, indicate the exact order in which the company sat at dinner. It would hardly, I believe, be too much to affirm, that Sir Walter Scott entertained, under his roof, in the course of the seven or eight brilliant seasons when his prosperity was at its height, as many persons of distinction in rank, in politics, in art, in literature, and in science, as the most princely nobleman of his age ever did in the like space of time.—I turned over, since I wrote the preceding sentence, Mr. Lodge's compendium of the British Peerage, and on summing up the titles which suggested *to myself* some reminiscence of this kind, I found them nearly as one out of six.—I fancy it is not beyond the mark to add, that of the eminent foreigners who visited our island within this period, a moiety crossed the Channel mainly in consequence of the interest with which his writings had invested Scotland—and that the hope of beholding the man under his own roof was the crowning motive with half that moiety. As for countrymen of his own, like him ennobled, in the higher sense of that word, by the display of their intellectual energies, if any one such contemporary can be pointed out as having crossed the Tweed, and yet not spent a day at Abbotsford, I shall be surprised.

It is needless to add, that Sir Walter was familiarly known, long before the days I am speaking of, to almost all the nobility and higher gentry of Scotland; and consequently, that there seldom wanted a fair proportion of them to assist him in doing the honours of his country. It is still more superfluous to say so respecting the heads of his own profession at Edinburgh: *Sibi et amicis*— Abbotsford was their villa whenever they pleased to resort to it, and few of them were ever absent from it long. He lived meanwhile in a constant interchange of easy visits with the gentlemen's families of Teviotdale and the Forest; so that mixed up with his superfine admirers of the May-fair breed, his staring worshippers from foreign parts, and his quick-witted coevals of the Parliament-House—there was found generally some hearty home-spun laird, with his dame, and the young laird—a bashful bumpkin, perhaps, whose ideas did not soar beyond his gun and pointer —or perhaps a little pseudo-dandy, for whom the Kelso race-course and the Jedburgh ball were Life and the World. To complete the *olla podrida*, we must remember that no old acquaintance, or family connections, however remote their actual station or style of manners from his own, were forgotten or lost sight of. He had some, even near relations, who, except when they visited him, rarely if ever found admittance to what the haughty dialect of the upper world is pleased to designate exclusively as *society*. These were welcome guests, let who might be under that roof; and it was the same with many a worthy citizen of Edinburgh, habitually moving in an obscure circle, who had been in the same class with Scott at the High School, or his fellow-apprentice when he was proud of earning threepence a page by the use of his pen. To dwell on nothing else, it was surely a beautiful perfection of real universal humanity and politeness, that could enable this great and good man to blend guests so multifarious in one group, and contrive to make them all equally happy with him, with themselves, and with each other.

I remember saying to William Allan one morning as the whole party mustered before the porch after breakfast— " A faithful sketch of what you at this moment see, would be more interesting a hundred years hence, than the grandest so-called historical picture that you will ever exhibit at Somerset House "; and my friend agreed with me so cordially, that I often wondered afterwards he had not attempted to realise the suggestion. The subject ought, however, to have been treated conjointly by him (or Wilkie) and Edwin Landseer. It was a clear, bright September morning, with a sharpness in the air that doubled the animating influence of the sunshine, and all was in readiness for a grand coursing match on Newark Hill. The only guest who had chalked out other sport for himself was the staunchest of anglers, Mr. Rose; but he, too, was there on his *shelty*, armed with his salmon-rod and landing-net, and attended by his humorous squire Hinves, and Charlie Purdie, a brother of Tom, in those days the most celebrated fisherman of the district. This little group of Waltonians, bound for Lord Somerville's preserve, remained lounging about to witness the start of the main

cavalcade. Sir Walter, mounted on Sybil, was mar-
shalling the order of procession with a huge hunting-
whip; and, among a dozen frolicsome youths and maidens,
who seemed disposed to laugh at all discipline, appeared,
each on horseback, each as eager as the youngest sportsman in the troop, Sir Humphrey Davy, Dr. Wollaston,
and the patriarch of Scottish belles-lettres, Henry
Mackenzie. The Man of Feeling, however, was persuaded with some difficulty to resign his steed for the
present to his faithful negro follower, and to join Lady
Scott in the sociable, until we should reach the ground of
our *battue*. Laidlaw, on a long-tailed wiry Highlander,
yclept *Hoddin Grey*, which carried him nimbly and
stoutly, although his feet almost touched the ground as he
sat, was the adjutant. But the most picturesque figure
was the illustrious inventor of the safety-lamp. He had
come for his favourite sport of angling, and had been
practising it successfully with Rose, his travelling companion, for two or three days preceding this, but he had
not prepared for coursing fields, or had left Charlie
Purdie's troop for Sir Walter's on a sudden thought; and
his fisherman's costume—a brown hat with flexible brims,
surrounded with line upon line, and innumerable fly-hooks
—jack-boots worthy of a Dutch smuggler, and a fustian
surtout dabbled with the blood of salmon, made a fine
contrast with the smart jackets, white cord-breeches, and
well-polished jockey-boots of the less distinguished cavaliers about him. Dr. Wollaston was in black, and with
his noble serene dignity of countenance might have passed
for a sporting archbishop. Mr. Mackenzie, at this time
in the 76th year of his age, with a white hat turned up
with green, green spectacles, green jacket, and long
brown leathern gaiters buttoned upon his nether anatomy,
wore a dog-whistle round his neck, and had all over the
air of as resolute a devotee as the gay captain of Huntley
Burn. Tom Purdie and his subalterns had preceded us by
a few hours with all the greyhounds that could be collected
at Abbotsford, Darnick, and Melrose; but the giant Maida
had remained as his master's orderly, and now gambolled
about Sybil Grey, barking for mere joy like a spaniel
puppy.

The order of march had been all settled, and the sociable
was just getting under weigh, when *the Lady Anne* broke
from the line, screaming with laughter, and exclaimed—

" Papa, papa, I knew you could never think of going
without your pet."—Scott looked round, and I rather
think there was a blush as well as a smile upon his face,
when he perceived a little black pig frisking about his
pony, and evidently a self-elected addition to the party of
the day. He tried to look stern, and cracked his whip at
the creature, but was in a moment obliged to join in the
general cheers. Poor piggy soon found a strap round its
neck, and was dragged into the background :—Scott,
watching the retreat, repeated with mock pathos the first
verse of an old pastoral song—

> " What will I do gin my hoggie [1] die?
> My joy, my pride, my hoggie!
> My only beast, I had nae mae,
> And wow! but I was vogie!"

—the cheers were redoubled—and the squadron moved
on.

This pig had taken—nobody could tell how—a most
sentimental attachment to Scott, and was constantly
urging its pretensions to be admitted a regular member
of his *tail* along with the greyhounds and terriers; but
indeed I remember him suffering another summer under
the same sort of pertinacity on the part of an affectionate
hen. I leave the explanation for philosophers—but such
were the facts. I have too much respect for the vulgarly
calumniated donkey to name him in the same category of
pets with the pig and the hen; but a year or two after this
time, my wife used to drive a couple of these animals in
a little garden chair, and whenever her father appeared
at the door of our cottage, we were sure to see Hannah
More and Lady Morgan (as Anne Scott had wickedly
christened them) trotting from their pasture to lay their
noses over the paling, and, as Washington Irving says of
the old white-haired hedger with the Parisian snuff-box,
" to have a pleasant crack with the laird."

But to return to the *chasse*. On reaching Newark
Castle, we found Lady Scott, her eldest daughter, and the
venerable Mackenzie, all busily engaged in unpacking a
basket that had been placed in their carriage, and arranging the luncheon it contained upon the mossy rocks
overhanging the bed of the Yarrow. When such of the

---

[1] *Hog* signifies in the Scotch dialect a young sheep that has never
been shorn. Hence, no doubt, the name of the Poet of Ettrick—
derived from a long line of shepherds.

company as chose had partaken of this refection, the
Man of Feeling resumed his pony, and all ascended the
mountain, duly marshalled at proper distances, so as to
beat in a broad line over the heather, Sir Walter directing the movement from the right wing—towards Black-
andro. Davy, next to whom I chanced to be riding,
laid his whip about the fern like an experienced hand,
but cracked many a joke, too, upon his own jackboots,
and surveying the long eager battalion of bushrangers,
exclaimed—"Good heavens! is it thus that I visit the
scenery of the Lay of the Last Minstrel?" He then kept
muttering to himself, as his glowing eye—(the finest and
brightest that I ever saw)—ran over the landscape, some of
those beautiful lines from the *Conclusion* of the Lay—

> ————" But still,
> When summer smiled on sweet Bowhill,
> And July's eve, with balmy breath,
> Waved the blue bells on Newark heath,
> When throstles sung on Hareheadshaw,
> And corn was green in Carterhaugh,
> And flourished, broad, Blakandro's oak,
> The aged harper's soul awoke," &c.

Mackenzie, spectacled though he was, saw the first
sitting hare, gave the word to slip the dogs, and spurred
after them like a boy. All the seniors, indeed, did well
as long as the course was upwards, but when puss took
down the declivity, they halted and breathed themselves
upon the knoll—cheering gaily, however, the young
people, who dashed at full speed past and below them.
Coursing on such a mountain is not like the same sport
over a set of fine English pastures. There were gulfs
to be avoided and bogs enough to be threaded—many a
stiff nag stuck fast—many a bold rider measured his
length among the peat-hags—and another stranger to the
ground besides Davy plunged neck-deep into a treacherous
well-head, which, till they were floundering in it, had
borne all the appearance of a piece of delicate green
turf. When Sir Humphrey emerged from his involuntary bath, his habiliments garnished with mud, slime, and
mangled watercresses, Sir Walter received him with a
triumphant *encore!* But the philosopher had his revenge, for joining soon afterwards in a brisk gallop,
Scott put Sibyl Grey to a leap beyond her prowess, and
lay humbled in the ditch, while Davy, who was better

mounted, cleared it and him at a bound.   Happily there
was little damage done—but no one was sorry that the
sociable had been detained at the foot of the hill.

I have seen Sir Humphry in many places, and in company of many different descriptions; but never to such
advantage as at Abbotsford.   His host and he delighted
in each other, and the modesty of their mutual admiration was a memorable spectacle.   Davy was by nature a
poet—and Scott, though anything but a philosopher in
the modern sense of that term, might, I think it very
likely, have pursued the study of physical science with
zeal and success, had he chanced to fall in with such an
instructor as Sir Humphry would have been to him, in
his early life.   Each strove to make the other talk—and
they did so in turn more charmingly than I ever heard
either on any other occasion whatsoever.   Scott in his
romantic narratives touched a deeper chord of feeling
than usual, when he had such a listener as Davy; and
Davy, when induced to open his views upon any question of scientific interest in Scott's presence, did so with
a degree of clear energetic eloquence, and with a flow of
imagery and illustration, of which neither his habitual
tone of table-talk (least of all in London), nor any of his
prose writings (except, indeed, the posthumous Conso-
lations of Travel) could suggest an adequate notion.   I
say his prose writings—for who that has read his sublime quatrains on the doctrine of Spinoza can doubt that
he might have united, if he had pleased, in some great
didactic poem, the vigorous ratiocination of Dryden and
the moral majesty of Wordsworth?   I remember William
Laidlaw whispering to me, one night, when their " rapt
talk " had kept the circle round the fire until long after
the usual bedtime of Abbotsford—" Gude preserve us !
this is a very superior occasion !   Eh, sirs ! " he added,
cocking his eye like a bird, " I wonder if Shakspeare and
Bacon ever met to screw ilk other up? "

Since I have touched on the subject of Sir Walter's
autumnal diversions in these his latter years, I may as
well notice here two annual festivals, when sport was
made his pretext for assembling his rural neighbours
about him—days eagerly anticipated, and fondly remembered by many.   One was a solemn bout of salmon fishing for the neighbouring gentry and their families, instituted originally, I believe, by Lord Somerville, but

now, in his absence, conducted and presided over by the Sheriff. Charles Purdie, Tom's brother, had charge (partly as lessee) of the salmon fisheries for three or four miles of the Tweed, including all the water attached to the lands of Abbotsford, Gala, and Allwyn; and this festival had been established with a view, besides other considerations, of recompensing him for the attention he always bestowed on any of the lairds or their visitors that chose to fish, either from the banks or the boat, within his jurisdiction. His selection of the day, and other precautions, generally secured an abundance of sport for the great anniversary; and then the whole party assembled to regale on the newly-caught prey, boiled, grilled, and roasted in every variety of preparation, beneath a grand old ash, adjoining Charlie's cottage at Boldside, on the northern margin of the Tweed, about a mile above Abbotsford. This banquet took place earlier in the day or later, according to circumstances; but it often lasted till the harvest moon shone on the lovely scene and its revellers. These formed groups that would have done no discredit to Watteau—and a still better hand has painted the background in the Introduction to the Monastery:—" On the opposite bank of the Tweed might be seen the remains of ancient enclosures, surrounded by sycamores and ash-trees of considerable size. These had once formed the crofts or arable ground of a village, now reduced to a single hut, the abode of a fisherman, who also manages a ferry. The cottages, even the church which once existed there, have sunk into vestiges hardly to be traced without visiting the spot, the inhabitants having gradually withdrawn to the more prosperous town of Galashiels, which has risen into consideration within two miles of their neighbourhood. Superstitious eld, however, has tenanted the deserted grove with aërial beings to supply the want of the mortal tenants who have deserted it. The ruined and abandoned churchyard of Boldside has been long believed to be haunted by the Fairies, and the deep broad current of the Tweed, wheeling in moonlight round the foot of the steep bank, with the number of trees originally planted for shelter round the fields of the cottagers, but now presenting the effect of scattered and detached groves, fill up the idea which one would form in imagination for a scene that Oberon and Queen Mab might love to revel

in. There are evenings when the spectator might believe,
with Father Chaucer, that the

> ——' Queen of Faëry,
> With harp, and pipe, and symphony,
> Were dwelling in the place.' "——

Sometimes the evening closed with a " burning of the
water "; and then the Sheriff, though now not so agile
as when he practised that rough sport in the early times
of Ashestiel, was sure to be one of the party in the boat,—
held a torch, or perhaps took the helm,—and seemed to
enjoy the whole thing as heartily as the youngest of his
company—

> " 'Tis blythe along the midnight tide,
> With stalwart arm the boat to guide—
> On high the dazzling blaze to rear,
> And heedful plunge the barbed spear ;
> Rock, wood, and scaur, emerging bright,
> Fling on the stream their ruddy light,
> And from the bank our band appears
> Like Genii armed with fiery spears." [1]

The other " superior occasion " came later in the
season ; the 28th of October, the birthday of Sir Walter's
eldest son, was, I think, that usually selected for *the
Abbotsford Hunt*. This was a coursing-field on a large
scale, including, with as many of the young gentry as
pleased to attend, all Scott's personal favourites among
the yeomen and farmers of the surrounding country.
The Sheriff always took the field, but latterly devolved the
command upon his good friend Mr. John Usher, the ex-
laird of Toftfield ; and he could not have had a more
skilful or better-humoured lieutenant. The hunt took
place either on the moors above the Cauldshields' Loch,
or over some of the hills on the estate of Gala, and we had
commonly, ere we returned, hares enough to supply the
wife of every farmer that attended with soup for a week
following. The whole then dined at Abbotsford, the
Sheriff in the chair, Adam Fergusson croupier, and Dominie Thompson, of course, chaplain. George, by the
way, was himself an eager partaker in the preliminary
sport ; and now he would favour us with a grace, in
Burns's phrase " as long as my arm," beginning with
thanks to the Almighty, who had given man dominion
over the fowls of the air, and the beasts of the field, and
expatiating on this text with so luculent a commentary,

[1] See *Poetical Works*, royal 8vo, p. 694.

that Scott, who had been fumbling with his spoon long
before he reached Amen, could not help exclaiming as
he sat down, " Well done, Mr. George ! I think we've
had everything but the view holla ! " The company,
whose onset had been thus deferred, were seldom, I
think, under thirty in number, and sometimes they exceeded forty. The feast was such as suited the occasion
—a baron of beef at the foot of the table, a salted
round at the head, while tureens of hare-soup and hotch-
potch extended down the centre, and such light articles
as geese, turkeys, a sucking-pig, a singed sheep's head,
and the unfailing haggis, were set forth by way of side-
dishes. Blackcock and moorfowl, bushels of snipe, *black
puddings, white puddings*, and pyramids of pancakes,
formed the second course. Ale was the favourite beverage during dinner, but there was plenty of port and
sherry for those whose stomachs they suited. The quaighs
of Glenlivet were tossed off as if they held water. The
wine decanters made a few rounds of the table, but the
hints for hot punch soon became clamorous. Two or
three bowls were introduced, and placed under the supervision of experienced manufacturers—one of these being
usually the Ettrick Shepherd—and then the business of
the evening commenced in good earnest. The faces
shone and glowed like those at Camacho's wedding : the
chairman told his richest stories of old rural life, Lowland or Highland ; Fergusson and humbler heroes fought
their Peninsular battles o'er again ; the stalwart Dandie
Dinmonts lugged out their last winter's snow-storm, the
parish scandal, perhaps, or the dexterous bargain of the
Northumberland *tryste*; and every man was knocked
down for the song that he sung best, or took most pleasure in singing. Sheriff-substitute Shortreed—(a cheerful, hearty, little man, with a sparkling eye and a most in-
fectious laugh)—gave us *Dick o' the Cow*, or *Now Liddesdale has ridden a raid*; his son Thomas (Sir Walter's
assiduous disciple and assistant in Border Heraldry and
Genealogy) shone without a rival in *The Douglas Tragedy*
and *The Twa Corbies*; a weather-beaten, stiff-bearded
veteran, *Captain* Ormistoun, as he was called (though I
doubt if his rank was recognised at the Horse Guards),
had the primitive pastoral of *Cowdenknowes* in sweet perfection ; Hogg produced *The Women folk*, or *The Kye
comes hame*; and, in spite of many grinding notes, con-

trived to make everybody delighted whether with the fun
or the pathos of his ballad; the Melrose doctor sang in
spirited style some of Moore's masterpieces; a couple of
retired sailors joined in *Bould Admiral Duncan upon the
high sea*;—and the gallant croupier crowned the last
bowl with *Ale, good ale, thou art my darling!* Imagine
some smart Parisian *savant*—some dreamy pedant of
Halle or Heidelberg—a brace of stray young lords from
Oxford or Cambridge, or perhaps their prim college
tutors, planted here and there amidst these rustic wassailers—this being their first vision of the author of Marmion and Ivanhoe, and he appearing as heartily at home
in the scene as if he had been a veritable *Dandie* himself
—his face radiant, his laugh gay as childhood, his chorus
always ready. And so it proceeded until some worthy,
who had fifteen or twenty miles to ride home, began to
insinuate that his wife and bairns would be getting sorely
anxious about the fords, and the Dumples and Hoddins
were at last heard neighing at the gate, and it was voted
that the hour had come for *doch an dorrach*—the stirrup-
cup—to wit, a bumper all round of the unmitigated
mountain dew. How they all contrived to get home in
safety, Heaven only knows—but I never heard of any
serious accident except upon one occasion, when James
Hogg made a bet at starting that he would leap over his
wall-eyed pony as she stood, and broke his nose in this
experiment of " o'ervaulting ambition." One comely
goodwife, far off among the hills, amused Sir Walter by
telling him, the next time he passed her homestead after
one of these jolly doings, what her husband's first words
were when he alighted at his own door—" Ailie, my
woman, I'm ready for my bed—and oh lass (he gallantly
added), I wish I could sleep for a towmont, for there's
only ae thing in this warld worth living for, and that's
the Abbotsford hunt ! "

It may well be supposed that the President of the Boldside Festival and the Abbotsford Hunt did not omit the
good old custom of *the Kirn*. Every November, before
quitting the country for Edinburgh, he gave a *harvest
home*, on the most approved model of former days, to all
the peasantry on his estate, their friends and kindred, and
as many poor neighbours besides as his barn could hold.
Here old and young danced from sunset to sunrise,—John
of Skye's bagpipe being relieved at intervals by the violin

of some Wandering Willie;—and the laird and all his family were present during the early part of the evening— he and his wife to distribute the contents of the first tub of whisky-punch, and his young people to take their due share in the endless reels and hornpipes of the earthen floor. As Mr. Morritt has said of him as he appeared at Laird Nippy's kirn of earlier days, " to witness the cordiality of his reception might have unbent a misanthrope." He had his private joke for every old wife or " gausie carle," his arch compliment for the ear of every bonny lass, and his hand and his blessing for the head of every little *Eppie Daidle* from Abbotstown or Broomielees.

The whole of the ancient ceremonial of the *daft days*, as they are called in Scotland, obtained respect at Abbotsford. He said it was *uncanny*, and would certainly have felt it very uncomfortable, not to welcome the new year in the midst of his family, and a few old friends, with the immemorial libation of a *het pint*; but of all the consecrated ceremonies of the time none gave him such delight as the visit which he received as *Laird* from all the children on his estate, on the last morning of every December— when, in the words of an obscure poet often quoted by him,

"The cottage bairns sing blythe and gay,
  At the ha' door for *hogmanay*."

The following is from a new-year's day letter to Joanna Baillie:—" The Scottish labourer is in his natural state perhaps one of the best, most intelligent, and kind-hearted of human beings; and in truth I have limited my other habits of expense very much since I fell into the habit of employing mine honest people. I wish you could have seen about a hundred children, being almost entirely supported by their fathers' or brothers' labour, come down yesterday to dance to the pipes, and get a piece of cake and bannock, and pence a-piece (no very deadly largess) in honour of *hogmanay*. I declare to you, my dear friend, that when I thought the poor fellows who kept these children so neat, and well taught, and well behaved, were slaving the whole day for eighteen-pence or twenty-pence at the most, I was ashamed of their gratitude, and of their becks and bows. But after all, one does what one can, and it is better twenty families should be comfortable according to their wishes and habits, than half that num-

ber should be raised above their situation. Besides, like
Fortunio in the fairy tale, I have my gifted men—the best
wrestler and cudgel-player—the best runner and leaper—
the best shot in the little district; and, as I am partial to
all manly and athletic exercises, these are great favourites,
being otherwise decent persons, and bearing their faculties
meekly. All this smells of sad egotism, but what can I
write to you about save what is uppermost in my own
thoughts? And here am I, thinning old plantations and
planting new ones; now undoing what has been done, and
now doing what I suppose no one would do but myself,
and accomplishing all my magical transformations by the
arms and legs of the aforesaid genii, conjured up to my
aid at eighteen-pence a day."

"The notable paradox," he says in one of the most
charming of his essays, "that the residence of a proprietor
upon his estate is of as little consequence as the bodily
presence of a stockholder upon Exchange has, we believe,
been renounced. At least, as in the case of the Duchess
of Suffolk's relationship to her own child, the vulgar continue to be of opinion that there is some difference in
favour of the next hamlet and village, and even of the
vicinage in general, when the squire spends his rents at
the manor-house, instead of cutting a figure in France or
Italy. A celebrated politician used to say he would
willingly bring in one Bill to make poaching felony,
another to encourage the breed of foxes, and a third to
revive the decayed amusements of cock-fighting and bull-
baiting—that he would make, in short, any sacrifice to
the humours and prejudices of the country gentlemen, in
their most extravagant form, provided only he could prevail upon them to 'dwell in their own houses, be the
patrons of their own tenantry, and the fathers of their
own children.'"[1]

In September 1820 appeared *The Abbot*—the con-
tinuation, to a certain extent, of The Monastery, of which
I barely mentioned the publication under the preceding
March. I have nothing of any consequence to add to the
information which the Introduction of 1830 affords us
respecting the composition and fate of the former of these
novels. It was considered as a failure—the first of the
series on which any such sentence was pronounced;—nor

[1] *Miscellaneous Prose Works*, i. p. viii.

have I much to allege in favour of the White Lady of
Avenel, generally criticised as the primary blot—or of
Sir Percy Shafton, who was loudly, though not quite
so generally, condemned. In either case, considered
separately, he seems to have erred from dwelling (in the
German taste) on materials that might have done very well
for a rapid sketch. The phantom, with whom we have
leisure to become familiar, is sure to fail—even the witch
of Endor is contented with a momentary appearance and
five syllables of the shade she evokes. And we may say
the same of any grotesque absurdity in human manners.
Scott might have considered with advantage how lightly
and briefly Shakspeare introduces *his* Euphuism—though
actually the prevalent humour of the hour when he was
writing. But perhaps these errors might have attracted
little notice had the novelist been successful in finding
some reconciling medium capable of giving consistence
and harmony to his naturally incongruous materials.
"These," said one of his ablest critics, "are joined—but
they refuse to blend: Nothing can be more poetical in
conception, and sometimes in language, than the fiction of
the White Maid of Avenel; but when this ethereal personage, who rides on the cloud which ' for Araby is
bound '—who is

> ' Something between heaven and hell,
> Something that neither stood nor fell,'—

whose existence is linked by an awful and mysterious
destiny to the fortunes of a decaying family; when such a
being as this descends to clownish pranks, and promotes a
frivolous jest about a tailor's bodkin, the course of our
sympathies is rudely arrested, and we feel as if the author
had put upon us the old-fashioned pleasantry of selling a
bargain."[1]

The beautiful natural scenery, and the sterling Scotch
characters and manners introduced in The Monastery, are,
however, sufficient to redeem even these mistakes; and,
indeed, I am inclined to believe it will ultimately occupy a
securer place than some romances enjoying hitherto a far
higher reputation, in which he makes no use of *Scottish*
materials.

Sir Walter himself thought well of *The Abbot* when he
had finished it. When he sent me a complete copy, I

[1] Adolphus's *Letters to Heber*, p. 13.

found on a slip of paper at the beginning of volume first
these two lines from *Tom Cribb's Memorial to Congress*—

" Up he rose in a funk, lapped a toothful of brandy,
And *to it* again !—any odds upon Sandy !"—

and whatever ground he had been supposed to lose in The
Monastery, part at least of it was regained by this tale,
and especially by its most graceful and pathetic portraiture
of Mary Stuart. "The Castle of Lochleven," says the
Chief-Commissioner Adam, "is seen at every turn from
the northern side of Blair-Adam. This castle, renowned
and attractive above all the others in my neighbourhood,
became an object of much increased attention, and a theme
of constant conversation, after the author of Waverley
had, by his inimitable power of delineating character—
by his creative poetic fancy in representing scenes of
varied interest—and by the splendour of his romantic
descriptions, infused a more diversified and a deeper tone
of feeling into the history of Queen Mary's captivity and
escape."

I have introduced this quotation from a little book
privately printed for the amiable Judge's own family and
familiar friends, because Sir Walter owned to myself at
the time, that the idea of *The Abbot* had arisen in his mind
during a visit to Blair-Adam. In the pages of the tale
itself, indeed, the beautiful localities of that estate are
distinctly mentioned, with an allusion to the virtues and
manners that adorned its mansion, such as must have been
intended to satisfy the possessor (if he could have had any
doubts on the subject) as to the authorship of those novels.

About Midsummer 1816, the Judge received a visit from
his near relation William Clerk, Adam Fergusson, his
hereditary friend and especial favourite, and their lifelong
intimate, Scott. They remained with him for two or three
days, in the course of which they were all so much
delighted with their host, and he with them, that it was
resolved to reassemble the party, with a few additions, at
the same season of every following year. This was the
origin of the Blair-Adam Club, the regular members of
which were in number nine. They usually contrived to
meet on a Friday; spent the Saturday in a ride to some
scene of historical interest within an easy distance;
enjoyed a quiet Sunday at home—"duly attending divine
worship at the Kirk of Cleish (not Cleishbotham)"—gave
Monday morning to another antiquarian excursion, and

returned to Edinburgh in time for the Courts of Tuesday. From 1816 to 1831 inclusive, Sir Walter was a constant attendant at these meetings. He visited in this way Castle-Campbell, Magus Moor, Falkland, Dunfermline, St. Andrews, and many other scenes of ancient celebrity: to one of those trips we must ascribe his dramatic sketch of *Macduff's Cross*—and to that of the dog-days of 1819 we owe the weightier obligation of *The Abbot*.

To return—for reasons connected with the affairs of the Ballantynes, Messrs. Longman published the first edition of The Monastery; and similar circumstances induced Sir Walter to associate this house with that of Constable in the succeeding novel. Constable disliked its title, and would fain have had *The Nunnery* instead; but Scott stuck to his *Abbot*. The bookseller grumbled a little, but was soothed by the author's reception of his request that Queen Elizabeth might be brought into the field in his next romance, as a companion to the Mary Stuart of The Abbot. Scott would not indeed indulge him with the choice of the particular period of Elizabeth's reign, indicated in the proposed title of *The Armada*; but expressed his willingness to take up his own old favourite legend of Meikle's ballad. He wished to call the novel, like the ballad, *Cumnor Hall*, but in further deference to Constable's wishes, substituted "Kenilworth." John Ballantyne objected to this title, and told Constable the result would be "something worthy of the kennel"; but Constable had all reason to be satisfied with the child of his christening. His partner, Mr. Cadell, says—"His vanity boiled over so much at this time, on having his suggestion gone into, that, when in his high moods, he used to stalk up and down his room, and exclaim, 'By G—, I am all but the author of the Waverley Novels!'" Constable's bibliographical knowledge, however, it is but fair to say, was really of most essential service to Scott upon many of these occasions; and his letter proposing the subject of *The Armada*, furnished such a catalogue of materials for the illustration of the period as may, probably enough, have called forth some very energetic expression of thankfulness.

Scott's kindness secured for John Ballantyne the usual interest in the profits of Kenilworth,—the last of his great works in which his friend was to have any concern. I have already mentioned the obvious drooping of his health

and strength; yet his manners continued as airy as ever;
—nay, it was now, after his maladies had taken a very
serious shape, and it was hardly possible to look on him
without anticipating a speedy termination of his career,
that the gay hopeful spirit of the shattered and trembling
invalid led him to plunge into a new stream of costly
indulgence. It was an amiable point in his character, that
he had always retained a tender fondness for his native
place. He had now taken up the ambition of rivalling his
illustrious friend, in some sort, by providing himself with
a summer retirement amidst the scenery of his boyhood;
and it need not be doubted, at the same time, that in
erecting a villa at Kelso, he calculated on substantial advantages from its vicinity to Abbotsford.

One fine day of this autumn I accompanied Sir Walter
to inspect the progress of this edifice, which was to have
the title of *Walton Hall*. John had purchased two or
three old houses with notched gables and thatched roofs,
near the end of the long original street of Kelso, with
their small gardens and paddocks running down to the
Tweed. He had already fitted up convenient bachelor's
lodgings in one of the primitive tenements, and converted
the others into a goodly range of stabling, and was now
watching the completion of his new *corps de logis* behind,
which included a handsome entrance-hall, or saloon,
destined to have old Piscator's bust on a stand in the
centre, and to be embellished all round with emblems of
his sport. Behind this were spacious rooms overlooking
the little *pleasance*, which was to be laid out somewhat in
the Italian style, with ornamental steps, a fountain and
jet d'eau, and a broad terrace hanging over the river. In
these new dominions John received us with pride and
hilarity; we dined gaily, *al fresco*, by the side of his
fountain; and after not a few bumpers to the prosperity of
Walton Hall, he mounted Old Mortality, and escorted us
for several miles on our ride homewards. It was this day
that, overflowing with kindly zeal, Scott revived one of
the long-forgotten projects of their early connection in
business, and offered his gratuitous services as editor of a
Novelist's Library, to be printed and published for the sole
benefit of his host. The offer was eagerly embraced, and
when, two or three mornings afterwards, John returned
Sir Walter's visit, he had put into his hands the MS. of
that admirable Life of Fielding, which was followed at

brief intervals, as the arrangements of the projected work required, by fourteen others of the same class and excellence. The publication of the first volume of " Ballantyne's Novelist's Library " did not take place, however, until February 1821 ; and notwithstanding its Prefaces, in which Scott combines all the graces of his easy narrative with a perpetual stream of deep and gentle wisdom in commenting on the tempers and fortunes of his best predecessors in novel literature, and also with expositions of his own critical views, which prove how profoundly he had investigated the principles and practice of those masters before he struck out a new path for himself—in spite of these delightful and valuable essays, the Collection was not a prosperous speculation.

Sir James Hall of Dunglass resigned, in November 1820, the Presidency of the Royal Society of Edinburgh ; and the Fellows, though they had on all former occasions selected a man of science to fill that post, paid Sir Walter the compliment of unanimously requesting him to be Sir James's successor in it. He felt and expressed a natural hesitation about accepting this honour—which at first sight seemed like invading the proper department of another order of scholars. But when it was urged upon him that the Society is really a double one—embracing a section for literature as well as one of science—and that it was only due to the former to let it occasionally supply the chief of the whole body,—Scott acquiesced in the flattering proposal ; and his gentle skill was found effective, so long as he held the Chair, in maintaining and strengthening the tone of good feeling and good manners which can alone render the meetings of such a society either agreeable or useful. The new President himself soon began to take a lively interest in many of their discussions—those at least which pointed to any discovery of practical use ;—and he by and by added some eminent men of science, with whom his acquaintance had hitherto been slight, to the list of his most valued friends :—in particular Sir David Brewster.

I may mention his introduction about the same time to an institution of a far different description,—that called " The Celtic Society of Edinburgh " ; a club established mainly for the patronage of ancient Highland manners and customs, especially the use of " the Garb of Old Gaul "—though part of their funds have always heed

applied to the really important object of extending education in the wilder districts of the north. At their annual
meetings Scott was henceforth a regular attendant. He
appeared, as in duty bound, in the costume of the
Fraternity, and was usually followed by " John of Skye,"
in all his plumage.

His son Charles left home for the first time towards the
close of 1820—a boy of exceedingly quick and lively parts,
with the gentlest and most affectionate and modest of dispositions. This threw a cloud over the domestic circle;
but, as on the former occasion, Sir Walter sought and
found comfort in a constant correspondence with the
absent favourite. Charles had gone to Lampeter, in
Wales, to be under the care of the celebrated scholar John
Williams, Archdeacon of Cardigan; whose pains were well
rewarded in the progress of his pupil.

About Christmas appeared Kenilworth, in 3 vols. post
8vo, like Ivanhoe, which form was adhered to with all
the subsequent novels of the series. Kenilworth was one
of the most successful of them all at the time of publication; and it continues, and, I doubt not, will ever continue
to be placed in the very highest rank of prose fiction.
The rich variety of character, and scenery, and incident in
this novel, has never indeed been surpassed; nor, with the
one exception of the Bride of Lammermoor, has Scott bequeathed us a deeper and more affecting tragedy than
that of Amy Robsart.

CHAPTER XII

Death of John Ballantyne—and William Erskine—George IV. at
Edinburgh—Visits of Mr. Crabbe and Miss Edgeworth—Reminis-
cences by Mr. Adolphus—Publication of Lives of the Novelists—
Halidon Hill—The Pirate—The Fortunes of Nigel—Peveril of the
Peak—Quentin Durward—and St. Ronan's Well. 1821-1823.

BEFORE the end of January 1821, he went to London at
the request of the other Clerks of Session, that he might
watch over the progress of an Act of Parliament designed
to relieve them from a considerable part of their drudgery
in attesting recorded deeds by signature;—and his stay
was prolonged until near the beginning of the summer term
of his Court. On his return he found two matters of

domestic interest awaiting him. On the 23rd April he
writes to the Cornet :—" The noble Captain Fergusson
was married on Monday last. I was present at the bridal,
and I assure you the like hath not been seen since the
days of Lesmahago. Like his prototype, the Captain advanced in a jaunty military step, with a kind of leer on
his face that seemed to quiz the whole affair. You should
write to your brother sportsman and soldier, and wish the
veteran joy of his entrance into the band of Benedicts.
Odd enough that I should christen a grandchild and
attend the wedding of a contemporary within two days of
each other. I have sent John of Skye, with Tom, and all
the rabblement which they can collect, to play the pipes,
shout, and fire guns below the Captain's windows this
morning ; and I am just going over to hover about on my
pony, and witness their reception. The happy pair returned to Huntley Burn on Saturday ; but yesterday being
Sunday, we permitted them to enjoy their pillows in quiet.
This morning they must not expect to get off so well."

The Captain and his Lady soon pitched a tent for themselves—but it was in the same parish, and *Gattonside* was
but an additional Huntley Burn. I may as well introduce
here, however, Scott's description to Lord Montagu of
the Glen and its yet undivided community :—" The Captain is a very singular fellow ; for, with all his humour and
knowledge of the world, he by nature is a remarkably shy
and modest man, and more afraid of the possibility of intrusion than would occur to any one who only sees him in
the full stream of society. His sister Margaret is extremely like him in the turn of thought and of humour,
and he has two others who are as great curiosities in their
way. The eldest is a complete old maid, with all the
gravity and shyness of the character, but not a grain of
its bad humour or spleen ; on the contrary, she is one of
the kindest and most motherly creatures in the world.
The second, Mary, was in her day a very pretty girl ;
but her person became deformed, and she has the sharpness of features with which that circumstance is sometimes attended. She rises very early in the morning, and
roams over all my wild land in the neighbourhood, wearing the most complicated pile of handkerchiefs of different
colours on her head, and a stick double her own height
in her hand, attended by two dogs, whose powers of yelping are truly terrific. With such garb and accompani-

ments, she has very nearly established the character in the neighbourhood of being *something no canny*—and the urchins of Melrose and Darnick are frightened from gathering hazel-nuts and cutting wands in my cleuch, by the fear of meeting *the daft lady*. With all this quizzicality, I do not believe there ever existed a family with so much mutual affection, and such an overflow of benevolence to all around them, from men and women down to hedge-sparrows and lame ass-colts, more than one of which they have taken under their direct and special protection."

On the 16th of June 1821, died at Edinburgh John Ballantyne. Until within a week or two before, Sir Walter had not entertained any thought that his end was near. I was present at one of their last interviews, and John's deathbed was a thing not to be forgotten. We sat by him for perhaps an hour, and I think half that space was occupied with his predictions of a speedy end, and details of his last will, which he had just been executing, and which lay on his coverlid; the other half being given, five minutes or so at a time, to questions and remarks, which intimated that the hope of life was still flickering before him—nay, that his interest in all its concerns remained eager. The proof-sheets of a volume of his Novelist's Library lay also by his pillow; and he passed from them to his will, and then back to them, as by jerks and starts the unwonted veil of gloom closed upon his imagination, or was withdrawn again. He had, he said, left his great friend and patron £2,000 towards the completion of the new library at Abbotsford—and the spirit of the auctioneer virtuoso flashed up as he began to describe what would, he thought, be the best style and arrangement of the bookshelves. He was interrupted by an agony of asthma, which left him with hardly any signs of life; and ultimately he did expire in a fit of the same kind. Scott was visibly and profoundly shaken by this scene and sequel. As we stood together a few days afterwards, while they were smoothing the turf over John's remains in the Canongate churchyard, the heavens, which had been dark and slaty, cleared up suddenly, and the midsummer sun shone forth in his strength. Scott, ever awake to the "skiey influences," cast his eye along the overhanging line of the Calton Hill, with its gleaming walls and towers, and then turning to the grave again, " I feel,"

he whispered in my ear,—" I feel as if there would be
less sunshine for me from this day forth."

As we walked homewards, he told me, among other
favourable *traits* of his friend, one little story which I must
not omit. He remarked one day to a poor student of
divinity attending his auction, that he looked as if he
were in bad health. The young man assented with a
sigh. "Come," said Ballantyne, "I think I ken the
secret of a sort of draft that would relieve you—particularly," he added, handing him a cheque for £5 or £10—
" particularly, my dear, if taken upon an empty stomach."

I am sorry to take leave of John Ballantyne with the
remark, that his last will was a document of the same class
with too many of his *states* and *calendars*. So far from
having £2,000 to bequeath to Sir Walter, he died as he
had lived, ignorant of the situation of his affairs, and deep
in debt.

The coronation of George IV. had been deferred in
consequence of the unhappy affair of the Queen's Trial.
The 19th of July 1821 was now announced for this solemnity, and Sir Walter resolved to be among the spectators.
It occurred to him that if the Ettrick Shepherd were to
accompany him, and produce some memorial of the scene
likely to catch the popular ear in Scotland, good service
might thus be done to the cause of loyalty. But this was
not his only consideration. Hogg had married a handsome and most estimable young woman, a good deal
above his own original rank in life, the year before; and
expecting with her a dowry of £1,000, he had forthwith
revived the grand ambition of an earlier day, and taken
an extensive farm on the Buccleuch estate, at a short
distance from Altrive Lake. Misfortune pursued the
Shepherd—the bankruptcy of his wife's father interrupted
the stocking of the sheep-walk; and the arable part was
sadly mismanaged. Scott hoped that a visit to London,
and a coronation poem, or pamphlet, might end in some
pension or post that would relieve these difficulties, and
when writing to Lord Sidmouth, to ask a place for himself in the Hall and Abbey of Westminster, begged suitable accommodation for Hogg also. Lord Sidmouth
answered that Sir Walter's wishes should be gratified,
provided they would both dine with him the day after
the coronation, in Richmond Park, "where," says the
letter of the Under-Secretary, "his Lordship will invite

the Duke of York and a few other Jacobites to meet you."
All this being made known to the tenant of Mount-Benger,
he wrote to Scott, as he says, "with the tear in his
eye," to signify, that if he went to London he must miss
attending the great annual Border fair, held on St. Boswell's Green, on the 18th of every July; and that his
absence from that meeting so soon after entering upon
business as a store-farmer would be considered by his
new compeers as highly imprudent and discreditable. "In
short," James concludes, " the thing is impossible. But
as there is no man in his Majesty's dominions admires
his great talents for government, and the energy and
dignity of his administration, so much as I do, I will
write something at home, and endeavour to give it you
before you start." The Shepherd probably expected that
these pretty compliments would reach the royal ear; but
however that may have been, his own Muse turned a deaf
ear to him—at least I never heard of anything that he
wrote on this occasion. Scott embarked without him, on
board a new steam-ship called *the City of Edinburgh*,
which, as he suggested to the master, ought rather to
have been christened the *New Reekie*.

On the day after the coronation, Sir Walter addressed
a letter descriptive of the whole ceremonial to Ballantyne,
who published it in his newspaper. It has been since reprinted frequently : and will probably possess considerable interest for the student of English history and manners in future times; for the two next coronations were
conducted on a vastly inferior scale of splendour and
expense—and the precedent of curtailment in any such
matters is now seldom neglected.

At the close of that brilliant scene, he received a mark
of homage to his genius which delighted him not less than
Laird Nippy's reverence for the *Sheriff's Knoll*, and the
Sheffield cutler's dear acquisition of his signature on a
visiting ticket. Missing his carriage, he had to return
home on foot from Westminster, after the banquet—that
is to say, between two and three o'clock in the morning ;—
when he and a young gentleman his companion found
themselves locked in the crowd, somewhere near Whitehall, and the bustle and tumult were such that his friend
was afraid some accident might happen to the lame limb.
A space for the dignitaries was kept clear at that point
by the Scots Greys. Sir Walter addressed a sergeant of

this celebrated regiment, begging to be allowed to pass by him into the open ground in the middle of the street. The man answered shortly, that his orders were strict—that the thing was impossible. While he was endeavouring to persuade the sergeant to relent, some new wave of turbulence approached from behind, and his young companion exclaimed in a loud voice, " Take care, Sir Walter Scott, take care ! " The stalwart dragoon, on hearing the name, said, " What ! Sir Walter Scott? He shall get through anyhow ! " He then addressed the soldiers near him—" Make room, men, for Sir Walter Scott, our illustrious countryman ! " The men answered, " Sir Walter Scott !—God bless him ! "—and he was in a moment within the guarded line of safety.

" I saw Sir Walter again," says Allan Cunningham, " when he attended the coronation. In the meantime his bust had been wrought in marble, and the sculptor desired to take the advantage of his visit to communicate such touches of expression or lineament as the new material rendered necessary. This was done with a happiness of eye and hand almost magical : for five hours did the poet sit, or stand, or walk, while Chantrey's chisel was passed again and again over the marble, adding something at every touch. ' Well, Allan,' he said, ' were you at the coronation? it was a splendid sight.'—' No, Sir Walter,' I answered,—' places were dear and ill to get : I am told it was magnificent : but having seen the procession of King Crispin at Dumfries, I was satisfied.' Scott laughed heartily.—' That's not a bit better than Hogg ' he said. ' He stood balancing the matter whether to go to the coronation or the fair of Saint Boswell—and the fair carried it.' During this conversation, Mr. Bolton the engineer came in. Something like a cold acknowledgment passed between the poet and him. On his passing into an inner room Scott said, ' I am afraid Mr. Bolton has not forgot a little passage that once took place between us. We met in a public company, and in reply to the remark of some one, he said, " That's like the old saying, —in every quarter of the world you will find a Scot, a rat, and a Newcastle grindstone." This touched my Scotch spirit, and I said, " Mr. Bolton, you should have added— and a Brummagem button." There was a laugh at this, and Mr. Bolton replied, " We make something better in Birmingham than buttons—we make steam-engines, sir."

—' I like Bolton,' continued Sir Walter; ' he is a brave man,—and who can dislike the brave? He shewed this on a remarkable occasion. He had engaged to coin for some foreign prince a large quantity of gold. This was found out by some desperadoes, who resolved to rob the premises, and as a preliminary step tried to bribe the porter. The porter was an honest fellow,—he told Bolton that he was offered a hundred pounds to be blind and deaf next night. " Take the money," was the answer, " and I shall protect the place." Midnight came—the doors, secured with patent locks, opened as of their own accord—and three men with dark lanterns entered and went straight to the gold. Bolton had prepared some flax steeped in turpentine—he dropped fire upon it,—a sudden light filled all the place, and with his assistants he rushed forward on the robbers; the leader saw in a moment he was betrayed, turned on the porter, and shooting him dead, burst through all obstruction, and with an ingot of gold in his hand, scaled the wall and escaped.' ' That is quite a romance in robbing,' I said; and I had nearly said more, for the cavern scene and death of Meg Merrilees rose in my mind—perhaps the mind of Sir Walter was taking the direction of the Solway, too, for he said, ' How long have you been from Nithsdale? ' "

Sir F. Chantrey presented the bust, of which Mr. Cunningham speaks, to Sir Walter himself; by whose remotest descendants it will undoubtedly be held in additional honour on that account. The poet had the further gratification of learning that three copies were executed in marble before the original quitted the studio : One for Windsor Castle—a second for Apsley House—and a third for the friendly sculptor's own private collection. The casts of this bust have since been multiplied beyond all numeration. Some years later Scott gave Chantrey some more sittings : and a second bust, rather graver in the expression, was then produced for Sir Robert Peel's gallery at Drayton.

When Sir Walter returned from London, he brought with him the detailed plans of Mr. Atkinson for the completion of his house at Abbotsford;—which, however, did not extend to the gateway or the beautiful screen between the court and the garden—for these graceful parts of the general design were conceptions of his own, reduced to shape by the skill of the Messrs. Smith of Darnick. It would not, indeed, be easy for me to apportion rightly the constituent members of the whole edifice;—throughout there were numberless consultations with Mr. Blore, Mr. Terry, and Mr. Skene, as well as with Mr. Atkinson—and the actual builders placed considerable inventive talents, as well as admirable workmanship, at the service of their friendly employer. Every preparation was now made by them, and the foundations might have been set about without farther delay; but he was very reluctant to authorise the demolition of the rustic porch of the old cottage, with its luxuriant overgrowth of roses and jessamines; and, in short, could not make up his mind to sign the death-warrant of his favourite bower until winter had robbed it of its beauties. He then made an excursion from Edinburgh, on purpose to be present at its downfall—saved as many of the creepers as seemed likely to survive removal, and planted them with his own hands about a somewhat similar porch, erected expressly for their reception, at his daughter Sophia's little cottage of Chiefswood.

There my wife and I spent this summer and autumn of 1821—the first of several seasons which will ever dwell on my memory as the happiest of my life. We were near enough Abbotsford to partake as often as we liked of its brilliant society; yet could do so without being exposed to the worry and exhaustion of spirit which the daily reception of new-comers entailed upon all the family except Sir Walter himself. But, in truth, even he was not always proof against the annoyances connected with such a style of open-house-keeping. Even his temper sunk sometimes under the solemn applauses of learned dulness, the vapid raptures of painted and periwigged dowagers, the horse-leech avidity with which underbred foreigners urged their questions, and the pompous simpers of condescending magnates. When sore beset at home in this way, he would every now and then discover that he had some very particular business to attend to on an outlying part of his estate, and, craving the indulgences of his guests overnight, appear at the cabin in the glen before its inhabitants were astir in the morning. The clatter of Sybil Grey's hoofs, the yelping of Mustard and Spice, and his own joyous shout of *réveille* under our windows, were the signal that he had burst his toils, and meant for that day to "take his ease in his inn." On descending, he was to be found seated with all his dogs and ours about him, under a spreading ash that overshadowed half the bank between the cottage and the brook, pointing the edge of his woodman's axe for himself, and listening to Tom Purdie's lecture touching the plantation that most needed thinning. After breakfast, he would take possession of a dressing-room up stairs, and write a chapter of *The Pirate*; and then, having made up and despatched his packet for the printer, away to join Purdie wherever the foresters were at work—and sometimes to labour among them strenuously himself—until it was time either to rejoin his own party at Abbotsford, or the quiet circle of the cottage.—When his guests were few and friendly, he often made them come over and meet him at Chiefswood in a body towards evening; and surely he never appeared to more amiable advantage than when helping his young people with their little arrangements upon such occasions. He was ready with all sorts of devices to supply the wants of a narrow establishment; he used to delight particularly in sinking the wine in a well under the *brae* ere he went out, and hauling up the basket just before dinner was announced—this primitive process being, he said, what he had always practised when a young housekeeper—and, in his opinion, far superior in its results to any application of ice; and, in the same spirit, whenever the weather was sufficiently genial, he voted for dining out-of-doors altogether, which at once got rid of the inconvenience of very small rooms, and made it natural and easy for the gentlemen to help the ladies, so that the paucity of servants went for nothing. Mr. Rose used to amuse himself with likening the scene and the party to the closing act of one of those little French dramas, where " Monsieur le Comte " and " Madame la Comtesse " appear feasting at a village bridal under the trees; but, in truth, our " M. le Comte " was only trying to live over again for a few simple hours his own old life of Lasswade.

When circumstances permitted, he usually spent one evening at least in the week at our little cottage; and almost as frequently he did the like with the Fergussons, to whose table he could bring chance visitors, when he pleased, with equal freedom as to his daughter's. Indeed it seemed to be much a matter of chance, any fine day when there had been no alarming invasion of the Southron, whether the three families (which, in fact, made but one) should dine at Abbotsford, at Huntley Burn, or at Chiefswood; and at none of them was the party considered quite complete, unless it included also Mr. Laidlaw. Death has laid a heavy hand upon that circle—as happy a circle, I believe, as ever met. Bright eyes now closed in dust, gay voices for ever silenced, seem to haunt me as I write.

During several weeks of that summer Scott had under his roof Mr. William Erskine and two of his daughters; this being, I believe, their first visit to Tweedside since the death of Mrs. Erskine in September 1819. He had probably made a point of having his friend with him at this particular time, because he was desirous of having the benefit of his advice and corrections from day to day as he advanced in the composition of The Pirate—with the localities of which romance the Sheriff of Orkney and Zetland was of course thoroughly familiar. At all events, the constant and eager delight with which Erskine watched the progress of the tale has left a deep impression on my memory; and indeed I heard so many of the chapters first read from the MS. by him, that I can never open the book now without thinking I hear his voice. Sir Walter used to give him at breakfast the pages he had written that morning; and very commonly, while he was again at work in his study, Erskine would walk over to Chiefswood, that he might have the pleasure of reading them aloud to my wife and me under our favourite tree, before the packet had to be sealed up for Edinburgh. I cannot paint the pleasure and the pride with which he acquitted himself on such occasions. The little artifice of his manner was merely superficial, and was wholly forgotten as tender affection and admiration, fresh as the impulses of childhood, glistened in his eye, and trembled in his voice.

Erskine was, I think, the only man in whose society Scott took great pleasure, during the more vigorous part of his life, that had neither constitution nor inclination for any of the rough bodily exercises in which he himself delighted. The Counsellor (as the survivors of The Mountain always called him) was a little man of feeble make, who seemed unhappy when his pony got beyond a foot-pace, and had never, I should suppose, addicted himself to any out-of-doors sport whatever. He would, I fancy, have as soon thought of slaying his own mutton as of handling a fowling-piece; he used to shudder when he saw a party equipped for coursing, as if murder were in the wind; but the cool meditative angler was in his eyes the abomination of abominations. His small elegant features, hectic cheek, and soft hazel eyes, were the index of the quick sensitive gentle spirit within. He had the warm heart of a woman, her generous enthusiasm, and some of her weaknesses. A beautiful landscape, or a fine strain of music, would send the tears rolling down his cheek; and though capable, I have no doubt, of exhibiting, had his duty called him to do so, the highest spirit of a hero or a martyr, he had very little command over his nerves amidst circumstances such as men of ordinary mould (to say nothing of iron fabrics like Scott's) regard with indifference. He would dismount to lead his horse down what his friend hardly perceived to be a descent at all; grew pale at a precipice; and, unlike the White Lady of Avenel, would go a long way round for a bridge.

Erskine had as yet been rather unfortunate in his professional career, and thought a sheriffship by no means the kind of advancement due to his merits, and which his connections might naturally have secured for him. These circumstances had at the time when I first observed him tinged his demeanour; he had come to intermingle a certain wayward snappishness now and then with his forensic exhibitions, and in private seemed inclined (though altogether incapable of abandoning the Tory party) to say bitter things of people in high places; but, with these exceptions, never was benevolence towards all the human race more lively and overflowing than his evidently was, even when he considered himself as one who had reason to complain of his luck in the world. Now, however, these little asperities had disappeared; one great real grief had cast its shadow over him, and submissive to the chastisement of Heaven, he had no longer any thoughts for the petty misusage of mankind. Meanwhile he shrunk from the collisions of general society, and lived almost exclusively in his own little circle of intimates. His conversation, though somewhat precise and finical on the first impression, was rich in knowledge. His literary ambition, active and aspiring at the outset, had long before this time merged in his profound veneration for Scott; but he still read a great deal, and did so as much, I believe, with a view to assisting Scott by hints and

suggestions, as for his own amusement. He had much of
his friend's tact in extracting the picturesque from old,
and, generally speaking, dull books; and in bringing out
his stores he often shewed a great deal of quaint humour
and sly wit.   Scott, on his side, respected, trusted, and
loved him, much as an affectionate husband does the wife
who gave him her heart in youth, and thinks his thoughts
rather than her own in the evening of life; he soothed,
cheered, and sustained Erskine habitually.   I do not believe a more entire and perfect confidence ever subsisted
than theirs was and always had been in each other; and
to one who had duly observed the creeping jealousies of
human nature, it might perhaps seem doubtful on which
side the balance of real nobility of heart and character, as
displayed in their connection at the time of which I am
speaking, ought to be cast.

In the course of a few months more, Sir Walter had
the great satisfaction of seeing Erskine at length promoted
to a seat on the Bench of the Court of Session, by the
title of Lord Kinnedder; and his pleasure was enhanced
doubtless by the reflection that his friend owed his elevation very much, if not mainly, to his own unwearied
exertions on his behalf.   He writes thus on the occasion
to Joanna Baillie:—"There is a degree of melancholy
attending the later stages of a barrister's profession,
which, though no one cares for sentimentalities attendant
on a man of fifty or thereabout, in a rusty black bombazine
gown, are not the less cruelly felt : their business sooner
or later fails, for younger men will work cheaper, and
longer, and harder—besides that the cases are few, comparatively, in which senior counsel are engaged, and it is
not etiquette to ask any one in that advanced age to take
the whole burden of a cause.   Insensibly, without decay
of talent, and without losing the public esteem, there is a
gradual decay of employment, which almost no man ever
practised thirty years without experiencing; and thus the
honours and dignities of the Bench, so hardly earned, and
themselves leading but to toils of another kind, are
peculiarly desirable.   Erskine would have sat there ten
years ago, but for wretched intrigues."

In August appeared the volume of the Novelist's
Library containing Scott's Life of Smollett; and it being
now ascertained that John Ballantyne had died a debtor,
the editor offered to proceed with this series of prefaces,

on the footing that the whole profits of the work should
go to his widow. Mr. Constable, whose own health was
now beginning to break, had gone southwards in quest of
more genial air, and was residing near London when he
heard of this proposition. He immediately wrote to me,
entreating me to represent to Sir Walter that the undertaking, having been coldly received at first, was unlikely
to grow in favour if continued on the same plan—that in
his opinion the bulk of the volumes, and the small type of
their text, had been unwisely chosen, for a work of mere
entertainment, and could only be suitable for one of reference; that Ballantyne's Novelist's Library, therefore,
ought to be stopped at once, and another in a lighter
shape, to range with the late collected edition of the first
series of the Waverley Romances, announced with his
own name as publisher and Scott's as editor. He proposed at the same time to commence the issue of a Select
Library of English Poetry, with prefaces and a few notes
by the same hand; and calculating that each of these
collections should extend to twenty-five volumes, and that
the publication of both might be concluded within two
years—"The writing of the prefaces, &c., forming perhaps an occasional relief from more important labours"!
—the bookseller offered to pay their editor £6,000; a
small portion of which sum, as he hinted, would undoubtedly be more than Mrs. John Ballantyne could ever
hope to derive from the prosecution of her husband's last
publishing adventure. Various causes combined to prevent the realisation of these magnificent projects. Scott
now, as at the beginning of his career, had views about
what a collection of English Poetry should be, in which
even Constable could not be made to concur; and one of
his letters to Lady Louisa Stuart sufficiently explains the
coldness with which he regarded further attempts upon
our Elder Novelists. The Ballantyne Library crept on to
the tenth volume, and was then dropped abruptly; and the
double negotiation with Constable was never renewed.

Lady Louisa had not, I fancy, read Scott's Lives of the
Novelists until, some years after this time, they were collected into two little piratical duodecimos by a Parisian
bookseller; and on her then expressing her admiration of
them, together with her astonishment that the speculation
of which they formed a part should have attracted little
notice of any sort, he answered as follows :—" I am

delighted they afford any entertainment, for they are
rather flimsily written, being done merely to oblige a
friend : they were yoked to a great ill-conditioned,
lubberly, double-columned book, which they were as useful
to tug along as a set of fleas would be to draw a mail-
coach. It is very difficult to answer your Ladyship's
curious question concerning change of taste; but whether
in young or old, it takes place insensibly without the
parties being aware of it. A grand-aunt of my own, Mrs.
Keith of Ravelstone, who was a person of some condition, being a daughter of Sir John Swinton of Swinton,
lived with unabated vigour of intellect to a very advanced age. She was very fond of reading, and enjoyed it
to the last of her long life. One day she asked me, when
we happened to be alone together, whether I had ever
seen Mrs. Behn's novels?—I confessed the charge.—
Whether I could get her a sight of them?—I said, with
some hesitation, I believed I could; but that I did not
think she would like either the manners, or the language,
which approached too near that of Charles II.'s time to
be quite proper reading. 'Nevertheless,' said the good
old lady, 'I remember them being so much admired, and
being so much interested in them myself, that I wish to
look at them again.' To hear was to obey. So I sent
Mrs. Aphra Behn, curiously sealed up, with 'private and
confidential' on the packet, to my gay old grand-aunt.
The next time I saw her afterwards, she gave me back
Aphra, properly wrapped up, with nearly these words :—
'Take back your bonny Mrs. Behn; and, if you will
take my advice, put her in the fire, for I found it impossible to get through the very first novel. But is it
not,' she said, 'a very odd thing that I, an old woman of
eighty and upwards, sitting alone, feel myself ashamed
to read a book which, sixty years ago, I have heard read
aloud for the amusement of large circles, consisting of the
first and most creditable society in London?' This, of
course, was owing to the gradual improvement of the
national taste and delicacy. The change that brings into
and throws out of fashion particular styles of composition. is something of the same kind. It does not signify
what the greater or less merit of the book is :—the reader,
as Tony Lumpkin says, must be in a concatenation
accordingly—the fashion, or the general taste, must have
prepared him to be pleased, or put him on his guard

against it. It is much like *dress*. If Clarissa should appear before a modern party in her lace ruffles and head-dress, or Lovelace in his wig, however genteelly powdered, I am afraid they would make no conquests; the fashion which makes conquests of us in other respects, is very powerful in literary composition, and adds to the effect of some works, while in others it forms their sole merit."

Among other miscellaneous work of this autumn, Scott amused some leisure hours with writing a series of "Private Letters," supposed to have been discovered in the repositories of a Noble English Family, and giving a picture of manners in town and country during the early part of the reign of James I. These letters were printed as fast as he penned them, in a handsome quarto form, and he furnished the margin with a running commentary of notes, drawn up in the character of a disappointed chaplain, a keen Whig, or rather Radical, overflowing on all occasions with spleen against Monarchy and Aristo-cracy. When the printing had reached the 72nd page, however, he was told candidly by Erskine, by James Ballantyne, and also by myself, that, however clever his imitation of the epistolary style of the period in question, he was throwing away in these letters the materials of as good a romance as he had ever penned; and a few days afterwards he said to me—patting Sybil's neck till she danced under him—" You were all quite right; if the letters had passed for genuine they would have found favour only with a few musty antiquaries; and if the joke were detected, there was not story enough to carry it off. I shall burn the sheets, and give you Bonny King Jamie and all his tail in the old shape, as soon as I can get Captain Goffe within view of the gallows."

I think it must have been about the middle of October that he dropped the scheme of this fictitious corres-pondence. I well remember the morning that he began *The Fortunes of Nigel*. The day being destined for Newark Hill, I went over to Abbotsford before breakfast, and found Mr. Terry walking about with his friend's master-mason. While Terry and I were chatting, Scott came out, bareheaded, with a bunch of MS. in his hand, and said, " Well, lads, I've laid the keel of a new lugger this morning—here it is—be off to the waterside, and let me hear how you like it." Terry took the papers, and walking up and down by the river, read to me the first

chapter of Nigel. He expressed great delight with the
animated opening, and especially with the contrast
between its thorough stir of London life and a chapter
about Norna of the Fitfulhead, in the third volume of
The Pirate, which had been given to him in a similar
manner the morning before. I could see that (according
to the Sheriff's phrase) *he smelt roast meat*; here there
was every prospect of a fine field for the art of *Terryfication*. The actor, when our host met us returning from
the haugh, did not fail to express his opinion that the new
novel would be of this quality. Sir Walter, as he took the
MS. from his hand, eyed him with a gay smile, in which
genuine benevolence mingled with mock exultation, and
then throwing himself into an attitude of comical dignity,
he rolled out, in the tones of John Kemble, one of the
loftiest bursts of Ben Johnson's Mammon—

> "Come on, sir. Now you set your foot on shore
> In *Novo orbe*—Pertinax, my Surly,[1]
> Again I say to thee aloud, Be rich,
> This day thou shalt have ingots."

This was another period of "refreshing the machine."
Early in November, I find Sir Walter writing thus to
Constable's partner, Mr. Cadell:—" I want two books,
Malcolm's London Redivivus, or some such name, and
Derham's Artificial Clockmaker." [The reader of Nigel
will understand these requests.] "All good luck to you,
commercially and otherwise. I am grown a shabby letter-
writer, for my eyes are not so young as they were, and
I grudge everything that does not go to press."

Sir Walter concluded, before he went to town in
November, another negotiation of importance with this
house. They agreed to give for the remaining copyright
of the four novels published between December 1819 and
January 1821—to wit, Ivanhoe, The Monastery, The
Abbot, and Kenilworth—the sum of five thousand guineas.
The stipulation about not revealing the author's name,
under a penalty of £2,000, was repeated. By these four
novels, the fruits of scarcely more than twelve months'
labour, he had already cleared at least £10,000 before

---

1 The fun of this application of "my Surly" will not escape any
one who remembers the kind and good-humoured Terry's power of
assuming a peculiarly saturnine aspect. This queer grimness of look
was invaluable to the comedian ; and in private he often called it up
when his heart was most cheerful.

this bargain was completed. I cannot pretend to guess
what the actual state of his pecuniary affairs was at the
time when John Ballantyne's death relieved them from
one great source of complication and difficulty. But I
have said enough to satisfy every reader, that when he
began the second, and far the larger division of his
building at Abbotsford, he must have contemplated the
utmost sum it could cost him as a mere trifle in relation
to the resources at his command. He must have reckoned
on clearing £30,000 at least in the course of a couple of
years by the novels written within such a period. The
publisher of his Tales, who best knew how they were
produced, and what they brought of gross profit, and
who must have had the strongest interest in keeping the
author's name untarnished by any risk or reputation of
failure, would willingly, as we have seen, have given him
£6,000 more within a space of two years for works of a
less serious sort, likely to be despatched at leisure hours,
without at all interfering with the main manufacture.
But alas! even this was not all. Messrs. Constable had
such faith in the prospective fertility of his imagination,
that they were by this time quite ready to sign bargains
and grant bills for novels and romances to be produced
hereafter, but of which the subjects and the names were
alike unknown to them and to the man from whose pen
they were to proceed.[1] A forgotten satirist well says :—

> " The active principle within
>   Works on some brains the effect of gin " ;

but in Sir Walter's case, every external influence combined to stir the flame, and swell the intoxication of restless exuberant energy. His allies knew indeed, what he
did not, that the sale of his novels was rather less than it
had been in the days of Ivanhoe; and hints had sometimes
been dropped to him that it might be well to try the effect
of a pause. But he always thought—and James Ballantyne had decidedly the same opinion—that his best things
were those which he threw off the most easily and swiftly;
and it was no wonder that his booksellers, seeing how
immeasurably even his worst excelled in popularity, as
in merit, any other person's best, should have shrunk

---

[1] Mr. Cadell says :—" This device for raising the wind was the only
real legacy left by John Ballantyne to his generous friend; it was
invented to make up for the bad book stock of the Hanover Street
concern, which supplied so much good money for the passing hour."

from the experiment of a decisive damper. On the contrary, they might be excused for from time to time flattering themselves, that if the books sold at less rate, this might be counterpoised by still greater rapidity of production. They could not make up their minds to cast the peerless vessel adrift, and, in short, after every little whisper of prudential misgiving, echoed the unfailing burden of Ballantyne's song—to push on, hoisting more and more sail as the wind lulled.

He was as eager to do as they could be to suggest—and this I well knew at the time. I had, however, no notion, until all his correspondence lay before me, of the extent to which he had permitted himself thus early to build on the chances of life, health, and continued popularity. Before The Fortunes of Nigel issued from the press, Scott had exchanged instruments, and received his booksellers' bills, for no less than four " works of fiction "—not one of them otherwise described in the deeds of agreement— to be produced in unbroken succession, each of them to fill at least three volumes, but with proper saving clauses as to increase of copy-money in case any of them should run to four. And within two years all this anticipation had been wiped off by Peveril of the Peak, Quentin Durward, St. Ronan's Well, and Redgauntlet; and the new castle was by that time complete. But by that time the end also was approaching.

The splendid romance of The Pirate was published in the beginning of December 1821 ; and the wild freshness of its atmosphere, the beautiful contrast of Minna and Brenda, and the exquisitely drawn character of Captain Cleveland, found the reception which they deserved. The work was analysed with remarkable care in the Quarterly Review—by a critic second to few, either in the manly heartiness of his sympathy with the felicities of genius, or in the honest acuteness of his censure in cases of negligence and confusion. This was the second of a series of articles in that Journal, conceived and executed in a tone widely different from those given to Waverley, Guy Mannering, and The Antiquary. I fancy Mr. Gifford had become convinced that he had made a grievous mistake in this matter, before he acquiesced in Scott's proposal about " quartering the child " in January 1816; and if he was fortunate in finding a contributor able and willing to treat the rest of Father Jedediah's progeny

with excellent skill, and in a spirit more accordant with
the just and general sentiments of the public, we must also
recognise a pleasing and honourable trait of character in
the frankness with which the recluse and often despotic
editor now delegated the pen to Mr. Senior.

On the 13th December, Sir Walter received a copy of
CAIN, as yet unpublished, from Lord Byron's bookseller,
who had been instructed to ask whether he had any
objection to having the " Mystery " dedicated to him.
He says, in answer to Mr. Murray,—" I accept with feelings of great obligation the flattering proposal of Lord
Byron to prefix my name to the very grand and tremendous
drama of Cain.   Some part of the language is bold, and
may shock one class of readers, whose tone will be
adopted by others out of affectation or envy.   But then
they must condemn the Paradise Lost, if they have a mind
to be consistent.   The fiend-like reasoning and bold
blasphemy of the fiend and of his pupil lead exactly to
the point which was to be expected—the commission of
the first murder, and the ruin and despair of the per-
petrator."   Such was Scott's opinion of the drama which,
when pirated, Lord Eldon refused to protect.   It may be
doubted if the great Chancellor had ever read *Paradise
Lost.*

Whoever reads Scott's letters to Terry might naturally
suppose that during this winter his thoughts were almost
exclusively occupied with the rising edifice on Tweedside.
The pains he takes about every trifle of arrangement,
exterior and interior, is truly most remarkable : it is not
probable that many idle lords or lairds ever look half so
much about such matters.   But his literary industry was
all the while unresting.   His Nigel was completed by April
1822.   He had edited Lord Fountainhall's Chronological
Notes, and several other antiquarian publications.   Nor
had he neglected a promise of the summer before to supply
Miss Baillie with a contribution for a volume of miscellaneous verse, which she had undertaken to compile for
the benefit of a friend in distress.   With that view he
now produced—and that, as I well remember, in the
course of two rainy mornings at Abbotsford—the dramatic
sketch of Halidon Hill; but on concluding it, he found
that he had given it an extent quite incompatible with
his friend's arrangements for her charitable picnic.   He
therefore cast about for another subject likely to be em-

braced in smaller compass; and the Blair-Adam meeting of the next June supplied him with one in Macduff's Cross. Meantime, on hearing a whisper about Halidon Hill, Constable's junior partner, without seeing the MS., forthwith tendered £1,000 for the copyright—the same sum that had appeared almost irrationally munificent, when offered in 1807 for the embryo Marmion. It was accepted, and a letter about to be quoted will shew how well the head of the firm was pleased with this wild bargain.

The Nigel was published on the 30th of May 1822; and was, I need not say, hailed as ranking in the first class of Scott's romances. Indeed, as a historical portraiture, his of James I. stands forth pre-eminent, and almost alone; nor, perhaps, in reperusing these novels deliberately as a series, does any one of them leave so complete an impression as the picture of an age. It is, in fact, the best commentary on the old English drama—hardly a single picturesque point of manners touched by Ben Jonson and his contemporaries but has been dovetailed into this story, and all so easily and naturally, as to form the most striking contrast to the historical romances of authors who *cram*, as the schoolboys phrase it, and then set to work oppressed and bewildered with their crude and undigested burden.

On the day after the publication, Constable, then near London, wrote thus to the author:—" I was in town yesterday, and so keenly were the people devouring my friend *Jingling Geordie*, that I actually saw them reading it in the streets as they passed along. I assure you there is no exaggeration in this. A new novel from the Author of Waverley puts aside—in other words, puts down for the time—every other literary performance. The smack Ocean, by which the new work was shipped, arrived at the wharf on Sunday; the bales were got out by *one* on Monday morning, and before half-past ten o'clock 7,000 copies had been dispersed! I was truly happy to hear of Halidon Hill, and of the satisfactory arrangements made for its publication. I wish I had the power of prevailing with you to give us a similar production every three months; and that our ancient enemies on this side the Border might not have too much their own way, perhaps your next dramatic sketch might be Bannockburn. It would be presumptuous in me to point out subjects—[had he quite forgotten the *Lord of the Isles*?]—but you know

my craving to be great, and I cannot resist mentioning
here that I should like to see a battle of Hastings—a
Cressy—a Bosworth field—and many more."—The Nigel
was just launched—Constable knew that *Peveril of the
Peak* was already on the stocks: yet see how quietly he
suggests that a little pinnace of the Halidon class might
easily be rigged out once a quarter by way of diversion,
and thus add another £4,000 per annum to the £10,000
or £15,000, on which all parties counted as the sure yearly
profit of the three-deckers *in fore*! But Constable, during
that residence in England, was in the habit of writing
every week or two to Sir Walter, and his letters are all
of the same complexion. The ardent bookseller's brain
seems to have been well-nigh unsettled; and I have often
thought that the foxglove which he then swallowed (his
complaint being a threatening of water in the chest) might
have had a share in the extravagant excitement of his
mind. Occasionally, however, he enters on details, as to
which, or at least as to Sir Walter's share in them, there
could not have been any mistake; and these were, it must
be owned, of a nature well calculated to nourish and sustain in the author's fancy a degree of almost mad exhilaration, near akin to his publisher's own predominant mood.
In a letter of the ensuing month, for example, after
returning to the progress of Peveril of the Peak, under
10,000 copies of which (or nearly that number) Ballantyne's presses were now groaning, and glancing gaily to
the prospect of their being kept regularly employed to the
same extent until three other novels, as yet unchristened,
had followed Peveril, he adds a summary of what was
then, had just been, or was about to be, the amount of
occupation furnished to the same office by reprints of
older works of the same pen:—" a summary," he exclaims, " to which I venture to say there will be no rival
in our day!" And well might Constable say so; for the
result is, that James Ballantyne and Co. had just executed, or were on the eve of executing, by his order—

" A new edition of Sir W. Scott's Poetical Works,

      in 10 vols. (miniature)   ...   ...   5,000 copies.
" Novels and Tales, 12 vols. ditto   ...   5,000   —
" Historical Romances, 6 vols. ditto   ...   5,000   —
" Poetry from Waverley, &c., 1 vol. 12 mo.   5,000   —
" Paper required, ...   7,772 reams.
" Volumes produced from Ballantyne's press, 145,000!

To which we may safely add from 30,000 to 40,000 volumes more as the immediate produce of the author's daily industry within the space of twelve months. The scale of these operations was, without question, enough to turn any bookseller's wits;—Constable's, in his soberest hours, was as inflammable a head-piece as ever sat on the shoulders of a poet; and his ambition, in truth, had been moving *pari passu*, during several of these last stirring and turmoiling years, with that of *his* poet. He, too, as I ought to have mentioned ere now, had, like a true Scotchman, concentrated his dreams on the hope of bequeathing to his heir the name and dignity of a lord of acres; he, too, had considerably before this time purchased a landed estate in his native county of Fife; he, too, I doubt not, had, while Abbotsford was rising, his own rural castle *in petto*; and alas ! for " Archibald Constable of Balniel " also, and his overweening intoxication of worldly success, Fortune had already begun to prepare a stern rebuke.

I must pass on to a different excitement—that of the King's visit to his northern dominions in the autumn of 1822. Before this time no Prince of the House of Hanover was known to have touched the soil of Scotland, except one, whose name had ever been held there in universal detestation—the cruel conqueror of Culloden,—" the butcher Cumberland." Now that the very last dream of Jacobitism had expired with the Cardinal of York, there could be little doubt that all the northern Tories, of whatever shade of sentiment, would concur to give their lawful Sovereign a greeting of warm and devoted respect; but the feelings of the Liberals towards George IV. personally had been unfavourably tinctured, in consequence of several incidents in his history—above all—(speaking of the mass of population addicted to that political creed) —the unhappy dissensions and scandals which had terminated, as it were but yesterday, in the trial of his Queen. On the whole it was, in the opinion of cool observers, a very doubtful experiment, which the new, but not young king, had resolved on trying. That he had been moved to do so in a very great measure, both directly and indirectly, by Scott, there can be no question; and I believe it will be granted by all who recall the particulars as they occurred, that his Majesty mainly owed to Scott's personal influence, authority and zeal, the more than full realisation of the highest hopes he could have indulged on the occasion of this progress.

Whether all the arrangements which Sir Walter dictated or enforced were conceived in the most accurate taste is a different question. It appeared to be very generally thought, when the first programmes were issued, that kilts and bagpipes were to occupy a great deal too much space. With all respect for the generous qualities which the Highland clans have often exhibited, it was difficult to forget that they had always constituted a small, and almost always an unimportant part of the Scottish population; and when one reflected how miserably their numbers had of late years been reduced in consequence of the selfish and hard-hearted policy of their landlords, it almost seemed as if there was a cruel mockery in giving so much prominence to their pretensions. But there could be no question that they were picturesque—and their enthusiasm was too sincere not to be catching; so that by and by even the coolest-headed Sassenach felt his heart, like John of Argyle's, "warm to the tartan"; and high and low were in the humour, not only to applaud, but each, according to his station, to take a share in what might really be described as a sort of grand *Terryfication* of the Holyrood chapters in Waverley;—George IV., *anno ætatis* 60, being well contented to enact Prince Charlie, with the Great Unknown himself for his Baron Bradwardine, " *ad exuendas vel detrahendas caligas domini regis post battalliam.*"

But Sir Walter had as many parts to play as ever tasked the Protean genius of his friend Mathews; and he played them all with as much cordial energy as animated the exertions of any Henchman or Piper in the company. His severest duties, however, were those of stage-manager, and under these I sincerely believe any other human being's temper would very soon have given way. The magistrates, bewildered with the rush of novelty, threw themselves on him for advice about the merest trifles; and he had to arrange everything, from the order of a procession to the embroidering of a cross. Ere the green-room in Castle Street had dismissed provosts and bailies, it was sure to be besieged by swelling chieftains, who could not agree on the relative positions their clans had occupied at Bannockburn, which they considered as constituting the authentic precedent for determining their

own places, each at the head of his little theatrical *tail*,
in the line of the King's escort between the Pier of Leith
and the Canongate. It required all Scott's unwearied
good humour, and imperturbable power of face, to hear in
becoming gravity the sputtering controversies of such
fiery rivals, each regarding himself as a true potentate,
the representative of princes as ancient as Bourbon; and
no man could have coaxed them into decent co-operation,
except him whom all the Highlanders, from the haughtiest
MacIvor to the slyest Callum Beg, agreed in looking up to
as the great restorer and blazoner of their traditionary
glories. He had, however, in all this most delicate part of
his administration, an admirable assistant in one who had
also, by the direction of his literary talents, acquired no
mean share of authority among the Celts—General David
Stewart of Garth, the historian of the Highland Regiments. On Garth (seamed all over with the scars of
Egypt and Spain) devolved the Toy-Captainship of the
Celtic Club, already alluded to as an association of young
civilians enthusiastic for the promotion of the philabeg;—
and he drilled and conducted that motley array in such
style, that they formed, perhaps, the most splendid feature
in the whole of this plaided panorama. But he, too, had
a potential voice in the conclave of rival chieftains,—and
with the able backing of this honoured veteran, Scott
succeeded finally in assuaging all their heats, and reducing
their conflicting pretensions to terms of truce, at least,
and compromise. A ballad (now included in his works),
wherein these magnates were most adroitly flattered, was
understood to have had a considerable share of the merit
in this peace-making; but the constant hospitality of his
table was a not less efficient organ of influence.

About noon of the 14th of August, the royal yacht and
the attendant vessels of war cast anchor in the Roads of
Leith; but although Scott's ballad-prologue had entreated
the clergy to "warstle for a sunny day," the weather was
so unpropitious that it was found necessary to defer the
landing until the 15th. In the midst of the rain, however, Sir Walter rowed off to the Royal George; and, says
the newspaper of the day,—"When his arrival alongside
the yacht was announced to the King.—'What!' exclaimed his Majesty, 'Sir Walter Scott! The man in
Scotland I most wish to see! Let him come up.'"
When he stepped on the quarter-deck, his Majesty called

for a bottle of Highland whisky, and having drunk his health, desired a glass to be filled for him. Sir Walter, after draining his bumper, made a request that the King would condescend to bestow on him the glass out of which his Majesty had just drunk his health; and this being granted, the precious vessel was immediately wrapped up and carefully deposited in what he conceived to be the safest part of his dress. So he returned with it to Castle Street; but—to say nothing at this moment of graver distractions—on reaching his house he found a guest established there of a sort rather different from the usual visitors of the time. The poet Crabbe, after repeatedly promising an excursion to the north, had at last arrived in the midst of these tumultuous preparations for the royal advent. Notwithstanding all such impediments, he found his quarters ready for him, and Scott entering, wet and hurried, embraced the venerable man with brotherly affection. The royal gift was forgotten—the ample skirt of the coat within which it had been packed, and which he had hitherto held cautiously in front of his person, slipped back to its more usual position—he sat down beside Crabbe, and the glass was crushed to atoms. His scream and gesture made his wife conclude that he had sat down on a pair of scissors or the like: but very little harm had been done except the breaking of the glass, of which alone he had been thinking. This was a damage not to be repaired: as for the scratch that accompanied it, its scar was of no great consequence, as even when mounting the "*cat-dath*, or battle garment" of the Celtic Club, he adhered, like his hero Waverley, to *the trews*.

By six o'clock next morning, Sir Walter, arrayed in the garb of old Gaul (which he had of the Campbell tartan, in memory of one of his great-grandmothers), was attending a muster of these gallant Celts in the Queen-Street Gardens, where he had the honour of presenting them with a set of colours, and delivered a suitable exhortation, crowned with their rapturous applause. Some members of the Club, all of course in their full costume, were invited to breakfast with him. He had previously retired for a little to his library, and when he entered the parlour, Mr. Crabbe, dressed in the highest style of professional neatness and decorum, with buckles in his shoes, and whatever was then considered as befitting an English clergyman of his years and station, was standing in the midst of half-a-dozen stalwart Highlanders, exchanging elaborate civilities with them in what was at least meant to be French. He had come into the room shortly before, without having been warned about such company, and hearing the party conversing together in an unknown tongue, the polite old man had adopted, in his first salutation, what he considered as the universal language. Some of the Celts, on their part, took him for some foreign abbé or bishop, and were doing their best to explain to him that they were not the wild savages for which, from the startled glance he had thrown on their hirsute proportions, there seemed but too much reason to suspect he had taken them; others, more perspicacious, gave in to the thing for the joke's sake; and there was high fun when Scott dissolved the charm of their stammering, by grasping Crabbe with one hand and the nearest of these figures with the other, and greeted the whole group with the same hearty *good-morning*.

Perhaps no Englishman of these recent days ever arrived in Scotland with a scantier stock of information about the country and the people than (judging from all that he said, and more expressively looked) this illustrious poet had brought with him in August 1822. It seemed as if he had never for one moment conceived that the same island in which his peaceful parsonage stood contained actually a race of men, and gentlemen too, owing no affinity with Englishmen either in blood or in speech, and still proud in wearing, whenever opportunity served, a national dress of their own, bearing considerably more resemblance to an American Indian's than to that of an old-fashioned divine from the Vale of Belvoir. But the aspect of the city on the 15th was as new to the inhabitants as it could have been even to the Rector of Muston :—every height and precipice occupied by military of the regular army, or by detachments of these more picturesque irregulars from beyond the Grampians—lines of tents, flags, and artillery, circling Arthur's Seat, Salisbury Crags, and the Calton Hill—and the old black Castle and its rock, wreathed in the smoke of repeated salvoes, while a huge banner royal, such as had not waved there since 1745, floated and flapped over all :—every street, square, garden, or open space below, paved with solid masses of silent expectants, except only where glittering lines of helmets marked the avenue guarded for the approaching procession. All captiousness of criticism sunk into nothing before the grandeur of this vision : and it was the same, or nearly so, on every subsequent day when the King chose to take part in the devised ceremonial. I forget where Sir Walter's place was on the 15th; but on one or other of these occasions I remember him seated in an open carriage, in the Highland dress, armed and accoutred as heroically as Garth himself (who accompanied him), and evidently in a most bardish state of excitement, while honest Peter Mathieson managed as best he might four steeds of a fierier sort than he had usually in his keeping— though, perhaps, after all, he might be less puzzled with them than with the cocked-hat and regular London Jehu's flaxen wig, which he, for the first and last time, displayed during " the royal fortnight."

It is, I believe, of the dinner of this 15th August in Castle Street that Crabbe penned the following brief record in his Journal :—" Whilst it is fresh in my memory, I should describe the day which I have just passed, but I do not believe an accurate description to be possible. What avails it to say, for instance, that there met at the sumptuous dinner, in all the costume of the Highlanders, the great chief himself, and officers of his company. This expresses not the singularity of appearance and manners— the peculiarities of men all gentlemen, but remote from our society—leaders of clans—joyous company. Then we had Sir Walter Scott's national songs and ballads, exhibiting all the feelings of clanship. I thought it an honour that Glengarry even took notice of me, for there were those, and gentlemen too, who considered themselves honoured by following in his train. There were also Lord Errol, and the Macleod, and the Fraser, and the Gordon, and the Fergusson ; and I conversed at dinner with Lady Glengarry, and did almost believe myself a harper, or bard, rather—for harp I cannot strike ; and Sir Walter was the life and soul of the whole. It was a splendid festivity, and I felt I know not how much younger. "

In the glittering and tumultuous assemblages of that season, the elder bard was (to use one of his friend's favourite similitudes) very like *a cow in a fremd loaning* ; and though Scott could never have been seen in colours more likely to excite admiration, Crabbe had hardly any opportunity of observing him in the everyday lovableness of his converse. Sir Walter's enthusiastic excitement about the kilts and the processions seemed at first utterly incomprehensible to him; but by degrees he perceived and appreciated the dexterous management of prejudices and pretensions. He exclaims, in his Journal,—" What a keen discriminating man is my friend!" But I shall ever regret that Crabbe did not see him at Abbotsford among his books, his trees, and his own good simple peasants. They had, I believe, but one quiet walk together, and it was to the ruins of St. Anthony's Chapel and Muschat's Cairn, which the deep impression made on Crabbe by the Heart of Mid-Lothian had given him an earnest wish to see. I accompanied them; and the hour so spent, in the course of which the fine old man gave us some most touching anecdotes of his early struggles, was a truly delightful contrast to the bustle and worry of miscellaneous society which consumed so many of his few hours in Scotland.

The King took up his residence at Dalkeith Palace; and here his dinner party almost daily included Sir Walter, who, however, appeared to have derived more deep-felt gratification from his Majesty's kind and paternal attention to his juvenile host (the Duke of Buccleuch was at that time only in his sixteenth year), than from all the flattering condescension lavished on himself. From Dalkeith the King repaired to Holyroodhouse two or three times, for the purposes of a levee or drawing-room. One Sunday he attended divine service in the Cathedral of St. Giles', when the decorum and silence preserved by the multitudes in the streets struck him as a most remarkable contrast to the rapturous excitement of his reception on week-days; and the scene was not less noticeable in the eyes of Crabbe, who says in his Journal,—" The silence of Edinburgh on the Sunday is in itself devout."

There is in the armoury at Abbotsford a sword presented by Charles I. to the great Marquis of Montrose—with Prince Henry's arms and cypher on one side of the blade, and his own on the other. One day the late Duke of Montrose happened to sit next to Sir Walter, and complimented him on the vigorous muster of Border Yeomanry which Portobello Sands had exhibited that morning. " Indeed," said Scott, " there's scarcely a man left to guard our homesteads."—" I've a great mind," quoth the Duke, " to send a detachment of my tail to Abbotsford to make prize of my ancestor's sword."—" Your Grace," says Sir Walter, drily, " is very welcome to try—but we're near Philiphaugh yonder."

Another very splendid day was that of a procession from Holyrood to the Castle, whereof the whole ceremonial had obviously been arranged under Scott's auspices, for the purpose of calling up, as exactly as might be, the time-hallowed observance of "the Riding of the Parliament." Mr. Peel (the Secretary of State for the Home Department) was desirous of witnessing this procession privately, instead of taking a place in it, and he walked up the High Street accordingly in company with Scott, some time before the royal cavalcade was to get into motion. The Poet was as little desirous of attracting notice as the Secretary, but he was soon recognised—and his companion, when revisiting Scotland, after the lapse of fourteen years, expressed his lively remembrance of the enthusiastic veneration with which Scott's person was then greeted by all classes of his countrymen. In proposing Sir Walter's memory at a public dinner given to him in Glasgow, in December 1836, Sir Robert Peel said, —" I had the honour of accompanying his late Majesty as his Secretary of State, when he paid a visit to Edinburgh. I suppose there are many of you here who were present on that occasion, at that memorable scene, when the days of ancient chivalry were recalled—when every man's friendship seemed to be confirmed—when men met for the first time, who had always looked to each other with distrust, and resolved in the presence of their Sovereign to forget their hereditary feuds and animosities. In the beautiful language of Dryden—

> ' Men met each other with erected look—
> The steps were higher that they took ;
> Friends to congratulate their friends would haste
> And long inveterate foes saluted as they pass'd.'

Sir Walter Scott took an active lead in these ceremonies. On the day on which his Majesty was to pass from Holyroodhouse, he proposed to me to accompany him up the High Street, to see whether the arrangements were completed. I said to him—' You are trying a dangerous experiment—you will never get through in privacy.' He said, ' They are entirely absorbed in loyalty.' But I was the better prophet : he was recognised from the one extremity of the street to the other, and never did I see such an instance of national devotion expressed."

The King at his first levee diverted many, and delighted
Scott, by appearing in the full Highland garb,—the same
brilliant *Stuart Tartans*, so called, in which certainly no
Stuart, except Prince Charles, had ever presented himself in the saloons of Holyrood. His Majesty's Celtic
toilette had been carefully watched and assisted by the
gallant Laird of Garth, who was not a little proud of the
result of his dexterous manipulations of the royal plaid,
and pronounced the King " a verra pretty man." And he
did look a most stately and imposing person in that
beautiful dress—but his satisfaction therein was cruelly
disturbed, when he discovered, towering and blazing
among and above the genuine Glengarries and Macleods
and MacGregors, a figure even more portly than his own,
equipped, from a sudden impulse of loyal ardour, in an
equally complete set of the self-same conspicuous Stuart
tartans :—

> " He caught Sir William Curtis in a kilt—
> While throng'd the chiefs of every Highland clan
> To hail their brother, Vich Ian Alderman." [1]

In truth, this portentous apparition cast an air of
ridicule and caricature over the whole of Sir Walter's
Celtified pageantry. A sharp little bailie from Aberdeen,
who had previously made acquaintance with the worthy
Guildhall Baronet, and tasted the turtle-soup of his voluptuous yacht, tortured him, as he sailed down the long
gallery of Holyrood, by suggesting that, after all, his
costume was not quite perfect. Sir William, who had
been rigged out, as the auctioneer's advertisements say,
" regardless of expense," exclaimed that he must be mistaken—begged he would explain his criticism—and as
he spoke, threw a glance of admiration on a *skene dhu*
(black knife), which, like a true " warrior and hunter of
deer," he wore stuck into one of his garters. " Oo ay—
oo ay," quoth the Aberdonian ; " the knife's a' right,
mon ; but faar's your speen ? " (where's your spoon?) Such
was Scott's story—but whether he " gave it a cocked-hat
and walking-cane," in the hope of restoring the King's
good-humour, so grievously shaken by this heroical *doppel-
ganger*, it is not very necessary to inquire.

As in Hamlet, there was to be a play within the play ;
and, by his Majesty's desire, William Murray's company
performed in his presence the drama of *Rob Roy*. The

[1] Byron's *Age of Bronze.*

audience were enchanted with the King's hearty laughter at Bailie Jarvie's jokes;—but I particularly remember his Majesty's shout at *Mattie's* "nane o' your Lunnan tricks."

On the 24th the Magistrates entertained their Sovereign with a banquet in the Parliament House; and Sir Walter Scott was invited to preside over one of the tables. But the most striking homage (though apparently an unconscious one) that his genius received during this festive period was when the King, after proposing the health of the Magistrates, rose and said there was one toast more, and but one, in which he must request the assembly to join him,—"I shall simply give you," said he, "*The Chieftains and Clans of Scotland*—and prosperity to the Land of Cakes." So completely had this hallucination taken possession, that nobody seems to have been startled at the time by language which thus distinctly conveyed his Majesty's impression that the marking and crowning glory of Scotland consisted in the Highland clans and their chieftains.

Scott's early associations, and the prime labours and honours of his life, had been so deeply connected with the Highlands, that it was no wonder he should have taught himself to look on their clans and chiefs with almost as much affection and respect as if he had had more than a scantling of their blood in his veins. But it was necessary to be an eye-witness of this royal visit, in order to comprehend the extent to which he had allowed his imagination to get the mastery over him as to all these matters; and perhaps it was necessary to understand him thoroughly on such points, in his personal relations, feelings, and demeanour, before one could follow his genius to advantage in some of his most favoured and delightful walks of exertion. The strongest impression, however, which the whole affair left on my mind was, that I had never till then formed any just notion of his capacity for practical dealing and rule among men. I do not think he had much in common with the statesmen and diplomatists of his own age and country; but I am mistaken if Scott could not have played in other days either the Cecil or the Gondomar; and I believe no man, after long and intimate knowledge of any other great poet, has ever ventured to say that he could have conceived the possibility of any such parts being adequately filled on the active stage of the world, by a person in whom the powers of fancy and imagination had such predominant sway as to make him in fact live three or four lives habitually in place of one. I have known other literary men of energy perhaps as restless as his; but all such have been entitled to the designation of *busybodies*—busy almost exclusively about trifles, and, above all, supremely and constantly conscious of their own remarkable activity, and rejoicing and glorying in it. Whereas Scott, neither in literary labour nor in continual contact with the affairs of the world, ever did seem aware that he was making any very extraordinary exertion. The machine, thus gigantic in its impetus, moved so easily that the master had no perception of the .obstructions it overcame—in fact, no measure for its power. Compared to him, all the rest of the *poet* species that I have chanced to observe nearly— with but one glorious exception—have seemed to me to do little more than sleep through their lives—and at best to fill the sum with dreams; and I am persuaded that, taking all ages and countries together, the rare examples of indefatigable energy, in union with serene self-possession of mind and character, such as Scott's, must be sought for in the roll of great sovereigns or great captains, rather than in that of literary genius.

In the case of such renowned practical masters, it has been usual to account for their apparent calmness amidst the stirring troubles of the world, by imputing to them callousness of the affections. Perhaps injustice has been done by the supposition; but, at all events, hardly could anv one extend it to the case of the placid man of the imaginative order;—a great depictor of man and nature, especially, would seem to be, *ex vi termini*, a profound sympathiser with the passions of his brethren, with the weaknesses as well as with the strength of humanity. Such assuredly was Scott. His heart was as " ramm'd with life " (to use a phrase of Ben Jonson's) as his brain; and I never saw him tried in a tenderer point than he was during the full whirl of splendour and gaiety that seemed to make every brain but his dizzy in the Edinburgh of August 1822.

Few things had ever given him so much pleasure as William Erskine's promotion to the Bench. It seemed to have restored his dearest friend to content and cheerfulness, and thus to have doubled his own sources of enjoyment. But Erskine's constitution had been shaken before he attained this dignity; and the anxious delicacy of his conscience rendered its duties oppressive and overwhelming. In a feeble state of body, and with a sensitive mind stretched and strained, a silly calumny, set afoot by some envious gossip, was sufficient literally to chase him out of life. On his return to Edinburgh about the 20th of July, Scott found him in visible danger; he did whatever friendship could do to comfort and stimulate him; but all was in vain. Lord Kinnedder survived his elevation hardly half-a-year—and who that observed Scott's public doings during the three or four weeks I have been describing could have suspected that he was daily and nightly the watcher of a deathbed, or the consoler of orphans; striving all the while against

> " True earnest sorrows, rooted miseries,
>   Anguish in grain, vexations ripe and blown? "

I am not aware that I ever saw him in such a state of dejection as he was when I accompanied him and his friend Mr. Thomas Thomson from Edinburgh to Queensferry, in attendance upon Lord Kinnedder's funeral. Yet that was one of the noisiest days of the royal festival, and he had to plunge into some scene of high gaiety the moment after he returned. As we halted in Castle Street, Mr. Crabbe's mild, thoughtful face appeared at the window, and Scott said, on leaving me,—" Now for what our old friend there puts down as the crowning curse of his poor player in the Borough—

> ' To hide in rant the heart-ache of the night.' "

The very few letters that he adressed to friends at a distance during the King's stay are chiefly occupied with Erskine. In one of them he says :—" It would be rather difficult for any one who has never lived much among my good country-people to comprehend that an idle story of a love intrigue, a story alike base and baseless, should be the death of an innocent man of high character, high station, and well advanced in years. It struck into poor Erskine's heart and soul, however, quite as cruelly as any similar calumny ever affected a modest woman—he withered and sunk. There is no need that I should say peace be with him ! If ever a pure spirit quitted this vale of tears, it was William Erskine's. I must turn to and see what can be done about getting some pension for his daughters."

The King's stay in Scotland was protracted until the 29th of August. He then embarked from the Earl of Hopetoun's magnificent seat on the Firth of Forth, and Sir Walter had the gratification of seeing his Majesty, in the moment of departure, confer the honour of knighthood on two of his friends—both of whom, I believe, owed some obligation in this matter to his good offices—namely, Captain Adam Fergusson, deputy-keeper of the Regalia, and Henry Raeburn, R.A., properly selected as the representative of the fine arts in Scotland. This amiable man and excellent artist, however, did not long survive the receipt of his title. Sir Henry died on the 8th of July 1823—the last work of his pencil having been a portrait of Scott for Lord Montagu.

On the eve of the King's departure he received a letter from Mr. Peel, saying:—"The king has commanded me to acquaint you that he cannot bid adieu to Scotland without conveying to you individually his warm personal acknowledgments. His Majesty well knows how many difficulties have been smoothed, and how much has been effected by your unremitting activity, by your knowledge of your countrymen, and by the just estimation in which they hold you. The King wishes to make you the channel of conveying to the Highland chiefs and their followers, who have given to the varied scene which we have witnessed so peculiar and romantic a character, his particular thanks for their attendance, and his warm approbation of their uniform deportment."

Though Mr. Crabbe found it necessary to leave Scotland without seeing Abbotsford, this was not the case with many less celebrated friends from the south, who had flocked to the Royal Festival. Sir Walter's house was, in his own phrase, "like a cried fair," during several weeks after the King's departure; and as his masons were then in the highest activity, the tumult within doors and without was really perplexing. He says in his letters, that the excitement of the Edinburgh scenes had thrown him into a fever, and, I believe, it was very lucky that an eruption took place, which compelled him to keep his chamber for some days.

Nor was an unusual influx of English pilgrims the only legacy of "the glorious days" of August. A considerable number of persons who had borne a part in the ceremonies fancied that their exertions had entitled them to some substantial mark of approbation; and post after post brought despatches from these enthusiasts, to him who was supposed to enjoy, as to matters of this description, the readiest access to the fountain of honour. To how many of these applications he accorded more than a civil answer I cannot tell; but the Duke of York was too good a *Jacobite* not to grant favourable consideration to his request that one or two half-pay officers who had distinguished themselves in the van of *the Celts* might be replaced in Highland regiments, and so re-invested with the untheatrical " Garb of old Gaul." Sir Walter had also a petition of his own. This related to a certain gigantic piece of ordnance, celebrated in the history of the Scottish Jameses under the title of *Mons Meg*, which had been removed from Edinburgh Castle to the Tower in 1746. When Scott next saw the King, after he had displayed his person on the chief bastion of the old fortress, he lamented the absence of Mons Meg on that occasion in language which his Majesty could not resist. There ensued a correspondence with the official guardians of Meg—among others, with the Duke of Wellington, then Master-General of the Ordnance, and though circumstances deferred her restoration, it was never lost sight of, and took place when the Duke was Prime Minister, in 1828.

A more serious petition was a written one in which Sir Walter expressed feelings in which I believe every class of his countrymen were disposed to concur with him cordially —and certainly none more so than George IV. himself. The object was the restoration of the peerages forfeited in consequence of the insurrections of 1715 and 1745; and the honourable families, in whose favour this liberal measure was soon afterwards adopted, appear to have vied with each other in the expression of their gratefulness for his exertions on their behalf.

Early in October, he had another attack of illness. He says to Terry, in a letter full of details about silk hangings, ebony-cabinets, and so forth :—" I have not been very well—a whoreson thickness of blood, and a depression of spirits, arising from the loss of friends, have annoyed me much; and Peveril will, I fear, smell of the apoplexy. I propose a good rally, however, and hope it will be a powerful effect. My idea is, *entre nous*, a Scotch archer in the French king's guard, *tempore* Louis XI., the most picturesque of all times." This is the first allusion to *Quentin Durward* and also the species of malady that ultimately proved fatal to Sir Walter Scott. He never mentioned to his family the symptoms which he here speaks of; but long before any serious apoplectic seizure occurred it had been suspected by myself and by others of his friends, that he had sustained slight attacks of that nature, and concealed them. The depression of spirits could not, however, have hung over him long. Peveril was completed, and some progress had also been achieved with Quentin Durward, before the year reached its close. Nor had he ceased to contemplate future labour with firmness and hopefulness. He, in October, received Constable's bills for another unnamed " work of fiction "; and this was the last such work in which the great bookseller was destined to have any concern. The engagement was in fact that redeemed three years afterwards by *Woodstock*.

Peveril of the Peak appeared in January 1823. Its reception was somewhat colder than that of its three immediate predecessors. The rapidity of the Novelist's execution was put to a severe trial, from his adoption of so wide a canvas as was presented by a period of twenty busy years, filled by so large and multifarious an assemblage of persons, not a few of them, as it were, struggling for prominence. Finella was an unfortunate conception; what is good in it is not original, and the rest absurd and incredible. Even worse was that condescension to the practice of vulgar romancers, in his treatment of the trial scenes—scenes usually the very citadels of his strength— which outraged every feeling of probability with those who had studied the terrible tragedies of the Popish Plot, in the authentic records of, perhaps, the most disgraceful epoch in our history. The story is clumsy and perplexed; the catastrophe (another signal exception to his rules) foreseen from the beginning, and yet most inartificially brought about. All this is true; and yet might not criticisms of the same sort be applied to half the masterpieces of Shakspeare? And did any dramatist—to say nothing of any other novelist—ever produce, in spite of all the surrounding bewilderment of the fable, characters more powerfully conceived, or, on the whole, more happily portrayed, than those (I name but a few) of Christian, Bridgenorth, Buckingham, and Chiffinch?—sketches more vivid than those of young Derby, Colonel Blood, and the keeper of Newgate?

Among the lounging barristers of the *Outer*-House in those days, Sir Walter, in the intervals of his duty as Clerk, often came forth and mingled much in the style of his own coeval *Mountain*. Indeed the pleasure he seemed to take in the society of his professional juniors was one of the most remarkable, and certainly not the least agreeable features of his character at this period of his consummate honour and celebrity—but I should rather have said, perhaps, of young people generally, male or female, law or lay, gentle or simple. I used to think it was near of kin to another feature in him, his love of a bright light. It was always, I suspect, against the grain with him, when he did not even work at his desk with the sun full upon him. However, one morning soon after Peveril came out, one of our most famous wags (now famous for better things), namely, Patrick Robertson,[1] commonly called by the endearing Scottish *diminutive* " Peter," observed that tall conical white head advancing above the crowd towards the fireplace, where the usual roar of fun was going on among the briefless, and said, " Hush, boys, here comes old Peveril—I see *the Peak*." A laugh ensued, and the Great Unknown, as he withdrew from the circle after a few minutes' gossip, insisted that I should tell him what our joke upon his advent had been. When enlightened, being by that time half-way across the " babbling hall " towards his own *Division*, he looked round with a sly grin, and said, between his teeth, " Ay, ay, my man, as weel Peveril o' the Peak ony day, as Peter o' the Painch " (paunch)—which, being transmitted to the brethren of the *stove school*, of course delighted all of them, except their portly Coryphæus. But *Peter's* application stuck; to his dying day, Scott was in the Outer-House *Peveril of the Peak*, or *Old Peveril*—and, by and by, like a good Cavalier, he took to the designation kindly. He was well aware that his own family and younger friends constantly talked of him under this *sobriquet*. Many a little note have I had from him (and so probably has *Peter* also), reproving, or perhaps encouraging, Tory mischief, and signed, " Thine, PEVERIL."

[1] Mr. R. became Dean of the Faculty of Advocates in 1842, and a Judge by the style of Lord Robertson in 1843. His first (and successful) appearance as a Poet was in 1847.

It was, perhaps, some inward misgiving towards the completion of Peveril, that determined Scott to break new ground in his next novel, and, as he had before awakened a fresh interest by venturing on English scenery and history, try the still bolder experiment of a continental excursion. However this may have been, he was encouraged and strengthened by the return of his friend Skene about this time, from a tour in France; in the course of which he had kept an accurate and lively journal, and executed a vast variety of clever drawings, representing landscapes and ancient buildings, such as would have been most sure to interest Scott had he been the companion of his wanderings. Mr. Skene's MS. collections were placed at his disposal, and he took from one of their chapters the substance of the *original* Introduction to Quentin Durward. Yet still his difficulties in this new undertaking were frequent, and of a sort to which he had hitherto been a stranger. I remember observing him many times in the Advocates' Library poring over maps and gazetteers with care and anxiety.

He was much amused with a mark of French admiration which reached him (opportunely enough) in February— one of the few such that his works seem to have brought him prior to the publication of Quentin Durward. He says to Constable,—" A funny Frenchman wants me to accept some champagne for a set of my works. I have written in answer that as my works cost me nothing I could not think of putting a value on them, but that I should apply to you. Send him a set of my children and god-children (poems and novels), and—if he found, on seeing them, that they were worth a dozen flasks of champagne, he might address the case," &c.

A compliment not less flattering was paid within a few weeks after the appearance of Peveril. In the epistle introductory of that novel, Clutterbuck amuses Dryasdust with an account of a recent visit from their common parent " the Author of Waverley," whose outward man, as it was in those days, is humorously caricatured, with a suggestion that he had probably sat to Geoffrey Crayon for his " Stout Gentleman of No. II."; and who is made to apologise for the heartiness with which he pays his duty to the viands set before him, by alleging that he is in training for the anniversary of the Roxburghe Club :—
" He was preparing himself " (said the gracious and

portly *Eidolon*) " to hobnob with the lords of the literary treasures of Althorpe and Hodnet in Maderia negus, brewed by the classical Dibdin." This drollery in fact alluded, not to the Roxburghe, but to an institution of the same class which was just at this time springing into life in Edinburgh—the *Bannatyne Club*, of which Scott was the founder and first president. The heroes of the Roxburghe, however, were not to penetrate the mystification of Captain Clutterbuck's report, and from their jovial and erudite board, when they next congregated around its " generous flasks of Burgundy, each flanked by an uncut fifteener "—their Secretary, Dr. Dibdin, wrote to Scott saying :—" The death of Sir M. Sykes having occasioned a vacancy in our CLUB, I am desired to request that you will have the goodness to make that fact known to the AUTHOR OF WAVERLEY, who, from the *Proheme* to PEVERIL OF THE PEAK seems disposed to become one of the members thereof ; and I am further desired to express the wishes of the said CLUB that the said AUTHOR may succeed to the said Baronet." —Sir Walter answered, that he would find means to convey the message to the " Author of Waverley " ; adding— " As his personal appearance in the fraternity is not like to be a speedy event, the table of the Roxburghe, like that of King Arthur, will have a vacant chair. But if this author, who ' hath fernseed and walketh invisible,' should not appear to claim it before I come to London, with permission of the Club, I, who have something of adventure in me, although a knight like Sir Andrew Aguecheek, ' dubbed with unhacked rapier, and on carpet consideration,' would, rather than lose the chance of a dinner with the Roxburghe Club, take upon me the adventure of the *siege perilous*, and reap some amends for perils and scandals into which the invisible champion has drawn me, by being his *locum tenens* on so distinguished an occasion."—The Club gladly accepted this offer ; and Scott writes again to their Secretary :—" Mad Tom tells us, that ' the Prince of Darkness is a gentleman ' ;[1] and this mysterious personage will, I hope, partake as much of his honourable feelings as his invisibility, and, retaining his incognito, permit me to enjoy, in his stead, an honour which I value more than I do that which has been bestowed on me by the credit of having written any of

[1] *King Lear*, Act III. Scene 5.

his novels."—In his way of taking both the Frenchman's civilities and those of the Roxburghers, we see evident symptoms that the mask had begun to be worn rather carelessly.   Sir Walter, it may be worth mentioning, was also about this time elected a member of " THE CLUB "— that famous one established by Johnson, Burke, and Reynolds.   Moreover, he had been chosen, on the death of the antiquary Lysons, Professor of Ancient History to the Royal Academy—a chair originally founded at Dr. Johnson's suggestion, " in order that *Goldy* might have a right to be at their dinners."   I believe he was present at more than one of the festivals of each of these fraternities.   A particular dinner of the Royal Academy, at all events, is recorded with some picturesque details in his essay on the life of Kemble, who sat next to him upon that occasion.

The Bannatyne Club was a child of his own, and from first to last he took a most fatherly concern in all its proceedings.   His practical sense dictated a direction of their funds differènt from what had been adopted by the Roxburghe.   Their *Club Books* already constitute a very curious and valuable library of Scottish history and antiquities : their example was soon followed with not inferior success by the Maitland Club of Glasgow, of which too Sir Walter was a zealous associate; by the Spalding Club of Aberdeen—and since his death by a fourth, founded at Edinburgh in his honour, and styled *The Abbotsford Club*—which last has taken a still wider range —not confining their printing to works connected with Scotland, but admitting all materials that can throw light on the ancient history or literature of any country described or handled by the Author of Waverley.

At the meetings of the Bannatyne he presided from 1823 to 1831; and in the chair on their anniversary dinners, surrounded by some of his oldest and dearest friends—Thomas Thomson (the Vice-President), John Clerk (Lord Eldin), the Chief-Commissioner Adam, the Chief-Baron Shepherd, Lord Jeffrey, Mr. Constable—and let me not forget his kind, intelligent, and industrious ally, Mr. David Laing, bookseller, the Secretary of the Club— he from this time forward was the unfailing source and centre of all sorts of merriment, " within the limits of becoming mirth."   Of the origin and early progress of their institution the reader has a full account in his review of

Pitcairn's Criminal Trials; and the last edition of his
Poems includes that excellent song composed for their
first dinner—that of March 9, 1823—and then sung by
James Ballantyne, and heartily chorused by all the aforesaid dignitaries :—

> " Assist me, ye friends of old books and old wine,
> To sing in the praises of sage Bannatyne,
> Who left such a treasure of old Scottish lore,
> As enables each age to print one volume more.
>> One volume more, my friends—one volume more,
>> We'll ransack old Banny for one volume more,"—&c.

Various passages in Scott's correspondence have recalled to my recollection the wonder with which the
friends best acquainted with the extent of his usual
engagements observed, about this period, his readiness in
mixing himself up with the business of associations far
different from the Bannatyne Club. I cannot doubt that
his conduct as President of the Royal Society, and as
manager of the preparations for the King's visit, had a
main influence in this matter. In these capacities he had
been thrown into contact with many of the most eminent
of his fellow-citizens, who had previously been accustomed to flavour their notions of him with something of
the gall of local politics ; and they had soon appreciated
his influence, for they must all have had abundant opportunities of observing the ease with which ill humours are
engendered, to the disturbance of all really useful discussion, wherever social equals assemble in conclave,
without having some official preses, uniting the weight
of strong and quick intellect with the calmness and
moderation of a brave spirit, and the conciliating grace
of habitual courtesy. Presumption, dogmatism, and
arrogance shrunk from the over-awing contrast of his
modest greatness : the poison of every little passion was
shamed and neutralised beneath the charitable dignity of
his penetration : and jealousy, fretfulness, and spleen felt
themselves transmuted in the placid atmosphere of good
sense, good humour, and good manners. And whoever
might be apt to plead off on the score of personal duty of
any sort, Scott had always leisure as well as temper at
command, when invited to take part in any business connected with a rational hope of public advantage. These
things opened, like the discovery of some new element of
wealth, upon certain eager spirits who considered the
Royal Society as the great local parent and minister of

practical inventions and mechanical improvements; and they found it no hard matter to inspire their genial chief with a warm sympathy in not a few of their then predominant speculations. He was invited, for example, to place himself at the head of a new company for improving the manufacture of oil gas, and in the spring of this year began to officiate regularly in that capacity. Other associations of a like kind called for his countenance, and received it. The fame of his ready zeal and happy demeanour grew and spread; and from this time, until bodily infirmities disabled him, Sir Walter occupied, as the most usual, acceptable, and successful chairman of public meetings of almost every sort, apart from politics, a very prominent place among the active citizens of his native town. Any foreign student of statistics who should have happened to peruse the files of an Edinburgh newspaper for the period to which I allude would, I think, have concluded that there must be at least two Sir Walter Scotts in the place—one the miraculously fertile author whose works occupied two-thirds of its literary advertisements and critical columns—another some retired magistrate or senator of easy fortune and indefatigable philanthropy, who devoted the rather oppressive leisure of an honourable old age to the promotion of patriotic ameliorations, the watchful guardianship of charities, and the ardent patronage of educational institutions.

The reader of his correspondence will find hints about various little matters connected with Scott's own advancing edifice, in which he may trace the President of the Royal Society and the Chairman of the Gas Company. But I cannot say that the "century of inventions" at Abbotsford turned out very happily. His bells to move by compression of air in a piston proved a poor succedaneum for the simple wire; and his application of gas-light to the interior of a dwelling-house was in fact attended with so many inconveniences, that ere long all his family heartily wished it had never been thought of. Moreover, he had deceived himself as to the expense of such an apparatus when constructed and maintained for the use of a single domestic establishment. The effect of the apparatus was at first superb. In sitting down to table, in autumn, no one observed that in each of three chandeliers, there lurked a tiny bead of red light. Dinner passed off, and the sun went down, and suddenly

at the turning of a screw, the room was filled with a gush
of splendour worthy of the palace of Aladdin; but, as in
the case of Aladdin, the old lamp would have been better
in the upshot. Jewellery sparkled, but cheeks and lips
looked cold and wan in this fierce illumination; and the
eye was wearied, and the brow ached, if the sitting was
at all protracted. I confess, however, that my chief
enmity to the whole affair arises from my conviction that
Sir Walter's own health was damaged, in his latter years,
in consequence of his habitually working at night under
the intense and burning glare of a broad star of gas.

In June Quentin Durward was published; and sur-
passing as its popularity was eventually Constable, who
was in London at the time, wrote in cold terms of its
immediate reception.

Very shortly before the bookseller left Edinburgh for
that trip, he had concluded another bargain (his last of
the sort) for the purchase of Waverley copyrights—acquiring the author's property in the Pirate, Nigel, Peveril,
and also Quentin Durward, out and out, at the price of
five thousand guineas. He had thus paid for the copyright of novels (over and above the half profits of the
early separate editions) the sum of £22,500; and his
advances upon "works of fiction" still in embryo,
amounted at this moment to £10,000 more. He began,
in short, and the wonder is that he began so late, to
suspect that the process of creation was moving too
rapidly. The publication of different sets of the Tales in
a collective shape may probably have had a share in opening his eyes to the fact, that the voluminousness of an
author is anything but favourable to the rapid diffusion of
his works as library books—the great object with any publisher who aspires at founding a solid fortune. But he
merely intimated on this occasion that, considering the
usual chances of life and health, he must decline contract-
ing for any more novels until those already bargained for
were written. Scott himself appears to have admitted
for a moment the suspicion that he had been overdoing in
the field of romance; and opened the scheme of a work
on popular superstitions in the form of dialogue, for
which he had long possessed ample materials in his
curious library of *diablerie*. But before Constable had
leisure to consider this proposal in all its bearings,
Quentin Durward, from being, as Scott expressed it,

frost-bit, had emerged into most fervid and flourishing life. In fact, the sensation which this novel on its first appearance created in Paris was extremely similar to that which attended the original Waverley in Edinburgh, and Ivanhoe afterwards in London. For the first time Scott had ventured on foreign ground, and the French public, long wearied of the pompous tragedians and feeble romancers, who had alone striven to bring out the ancient history and manners of their country in popular forms, were seized with a fever of delight when Louis XI. and Charles the Bold started into life again at the beck of the Northern Magician. The result of Quentin Durward, as regards the contemporary literature of the Continent, would open a field for ample digression. As concerns the author himself, the rays of foreign enthusiasm speedily thawed the frost of Constable's unwonted misgivings; the Dialogues on Superstition, if he ever began them, were very soon dropped, and the Novelist resumed his pen. He had not sunk under the short-lived frown—for he wrote to Ballantyne, on first ascertaining that a damp was thrown on his usual manufacture,

> " The mouse who only trusts to one poor hole,
> Can never be a mouse of any soul ";

and, while his publisher yet remained irresolute as to the plan of Dialogues, threw off his excellent Essay on Romance for the Encyclopædia Britannica; and I cannot but consider it as another display of his high self-reliance, that, though he well knew to what influence Quentin owed its ultimate success in the British market, he, the instant he found himself encouraged to take up the trade of story-telling again, sprang back to Scotland —nay, voluntarily encountered new difficulties, by selecting the comparatively tame and unpicturesque realities of modern manners in his native province.

A conversation, which much interested me at the time, had, I fancy, some share at least in this determination. As he, Laidlaw, and myself, were lounging on our ponies, one fine calm afternoon, along the brow of the Eildon Hill where it overhangs Melrose, he mentioned to us gaily the *row*, as he called it, that was going on in Paris about Quentin Durward, and said, " I can't but think that I could make better play still with something German." Laidlaw grumbled at this, and said, like a true Scotchman, " Na, na, sir—take my word for it, you are always best, like Helen MacGregor, when your foot is on your native heath; and I have often thought that if you were to write a novel, and lay the scene *here* in the very year you were writing it, you would exceed yourself."— " Hame's hame," quoth Scott, smiling, " be it ever sae hamely. There's something in what you say, Willie. What suppose I were to take Captain Clutterbuck for a hero, and never let the story step a yard beyond the village below us yonder? "—" The very thing I want," says Laidlaw; " stick to Melrose in July 1823."—" Well, upon my word," he answered, " the field would be quite wide enough—and *what for no?*"—(This pet phrase of Meg Dods was a *Laidlawism.*)—Some fun followed about the different real persons in the village that might be introduced with comical effect; but as Laidlaw and I talked and laughed over our worthy neighbours, his air became graver and graver; and he at length said, " Ay, ay, if one could look into the heart of that little cluster of cottages, no fear but you would find materials enow for tragedy as well as comedy. I undertake to say there is some real romance at this moment going on down there, that, if it could have justice done to it, would be well worth all the fiction that was ever spun out of human brains." He then told us a tale of dark domestic guilt which had recently come under his notice as Sheriff, and of which the scene was not Melrose, but a smaller hamlet, on the other side of the Tweed, full in our view; but the details were not of a kind to be dwelt upon;—anything more dreadful was never conceived by Crabbe, and he told it so as to produce on us who listened all the effect of an- other *Hall of Justice.* It could never have entered into his head to elaborate such a tale; but both Laidlaw and I used to think that this talk suggested St. Ronan's Well— though my good friend was by no means disposed to accept that as payment in full of his demand, and from time to time afterwards would give the Sheriff a little poking about " Melrose in July."

Before Sir Walter settled to the new novel, he received Joanna Baillie's long-promised Collection of Poetical Mis- cellanies, in which appeared his dramatic sketch of Macduff's Cross. When Halidon Hill first came forth, there were not wanting reviewers who hailed it in a style of rapture, such as might have been expected had it been a Macbeth. But this folly soon sunk; and I only mention

it as an instance of the extent to which reputation be-
wilders and confounds even persons who have good brains
enough when they find it convenient to exercise them.
The second attempt of the class produced no sensation
whatever at the time; and both would have been long
since forgotten, but that they came from Scott's pen.
They both contain some fine passages—Halidon Hill has,
indeed, several grand ones. But, on the whole, they
always seemed to me unworthy of Sir Walter; and, now
that I have read his admirable letters on dramatic composition to Allan Cunningham, it appears doubly hard to
account for the rashness with which he committed himself
in even such slender attempts on a species of composition,
of which, in his cool hour, he so fully appreciated the
difficult demands. Nevertheless, I am very far from
agreeing with those critics who have gravely talked of
Halidon Hill and Macduff's Cross, and the still more
unfortunate Doom of Devorgoil, as proving that Sir
Walter could not have succeeded in the drama, either
serious or comic. It would be as fair to conclude, from
the abortive fragment of the Vampyre, that Lord Byron
could not have written a good novel or romance in prose.
Scott threw off these things *currente calamo*; he never
gave himself time to consider beforehand what could be
made of their materials, nor bestowed a moment on correcting them; and neither when they were new, nor even
after, did he seem to attach the slightest importance to
them.

The month of August 1823 was one of the happiest in
Scott's life. Never did I see a brighter day at Abbotsford
than that on which Miss Edgeworth first arrived there
—never can I forget her look and accent when she was
received by him at his archway, and exclaimed, " Everything about you is exactly what one ought to have had wit
enough to dream ! " The weather was beautiful, and the
edifice, and its appurtenances, were all but complete; and
day after day, so long as she could remain, her host had
always some new plan of gaiety. One day there was fishing on the Cauldshields' Loch, and a dinner on the heathy
bank. Another, the whole party feasted by Sir Thomas
the Rhymer's waterfall in the glen—and the stone on
which Maria that day sat was ever afterwards called
Edgeworth's Stone. A third day we had to go further
afield. He must needs shew her, not Newark only, but

all the upper scenery of the Yarrow, where "fair hangs the apple frae the rock,"—and the baskets were unpacked about sunset, beside the ruined Chapel overlooking St. Mary's Loch—and he had scrambled to gather blue-bells and heath-flowers, with which all the young ladies must twine their hair,—and they sang, and he recited, until it was time to go home beneath the softest of harvest moons. Thus a fortnight was passed—and the vision closed; for Miss Edgeworth never saw Abbotsford again during his life; and I am very sure she could never bear to look upon it now that the spirit is fled.

Another welcome guest of the same month was Mr. Adolphus—the author of the Letters to Heber; whose reminiscences of this and several subsequent visits are singularly vivid and interesting. He says :—" The circumstances under which I presented myself were peculiar, as the only cause of my being under his roof was one which could not without awkwardness be alluded to, while a strict reserve existed on the subject of the Waverley novels. This, however, did not create any embarrassment; and he entered into conversation as if anything that might have been said with reference to the origin of our acquaintance had been said an hour before. I never saw a man who, in his intercourse with all persons, was so perfect a master of courtesy. His manners were so plain and natural, and his kindness took such immediate possession of the feelings, that this excellence in him might for a while pass almost unobserved. I cannot pay a higher testimony to it than by owning that I first fully appreciated it from his behaviour to others. His air and aspect, at the moment of a first introduction, were placid, modest, and, for his time of life, venerable. Occasionally, where he stood a little on ceremony, he threw into his address a deferential tone, which had in it something of old-fashioned politeness, and became him extremely well.

" A point of hospitality in which Sir Walter Scott never failed, whatever might be the pretensions of the guest, was to do the honours of conversation. When a stranger arrived, he seemed to consider it as much a duty to offer him the resources of his mind as those of his table ; taking care, however, by his choice of subjects, to give the visitor an opportunity of making his own stores, if he had them, available. To me he addressed himself often as to a member of his own profession; and indeed he seemed always to have a real pleasure in citing from his own experience as an advocate and a law-officer.

"It would, I think, be extremely difficult to give a just idea of his general conversation to any one who had not known him. Considering his great personal and literary popularity, and the wide circle of society in which he had lived, it is perhaps remarkable that so few of his sayings, real or imputed, are in circulation. But he did not affect sayings; the points and sententious turns, which are so easily caught up and transmitted, were not natural to him: though he occasionally expressed a thought very pithily and neatly. For example, he once described the Duke of Wellington's style of debating as ' slicing the argument into two or three parts, and helping himself to the best.' But the great charm on his ' table-talk ' was in the sweetness and *abandon* with which it flowed,—always, however, guided by good sense and taste; the warm and unstudied eloquence with which he expressed rather sentiments than opinions; and the liveliness and force with which he narrated and described: and all that he spoke derived so much of its effect from indefinable felicities of manner, look, and tone—and sometimes from the choice of apparently insignificant words—that a moderately faithful transcript of his sentences would be but a faint image of his conversation:—" No one who has seen him can forget the surprising power of change which his countenance shewed when awakened from a state of composure. In 1823, his face, which was healthy and sanguine, and the hair about it, which had a strong reddish tinge, contrasted rather than harmonised with the sleek, silvery locks above; a contrast which might seem rather suited to a jovial and humorous, than to a pathetic expression. But his features were equally capable of both. The form and hue of his eyes (for the benefit of minute physiognomists it should be noted that the iris contained some small specks of brown) were wonderfully calculated for shewing great varieties of emotion. Their mournful aspect was extremely earnest and affecting; and when he told some dismal and mysterious story, they had a doubtful, melancholy, exploring look, which appealed irresistibly to the hearer's imagination. Occasionally, when he spoke of something very audacious or eccentric, they would dilate and light up with a tragi-comic, hare-brained expression, quite peculiar to himself; one might see in it a whole chap-

ter of *Cœur-de-lion* and the Clerk of Copmanhurst.
Never, perhaps, did a man go through all the gradations of
laughter with such complete enjoyment, and a countenance
so radiant. The first dawn of a humorous thought would
shew itself sometimes, as he sat silent, by an involuntary
lengthening of the upper lip, followed by a shy sidelong
glance at his neighbours, indescribably whimsical, and
seeming to ask from their looks whether the spark of
drollery should be suppressed or allowed to blaze out. In
the full tide of mirth he did indeed ' laugh the heart's
laugh,' like Walpole, but it was not boisterous and over-
powering, nor did it check the course of his words; he
could go on telling or descanting, while his lungs did
' crow like chanticleer,' his syllables, in the struggle,
growing more emphatic, his accent more strongly Scotch,
and his voice plaintive with excess of merriment.

" The habits of life at Abbotsford, when I first saw it,
ran in the same easy, rational, and pleasant course which I
believe they always afterwards took; though the family
was at this time rather straitened in its arrangements, as
some of the principal rooms were not finished. After
breakfast Sir Walter took his short interval of study in
the light and elegant little room afterwards called Miss
Scott's. That which he occupied when Abbotsford was
complete, though more convenient in some material
respects, seemed to me the least cheerful [1] and least private
in the house. It had, however, a recommendation which
perhaps he was very sensible of, that as he sat at his
writing-table, he could look out at his young trees. About
one o'clock he walked or rode, generally with some of his
visitors. At this period, he used to be a good deal on
horseback, and a pleasant sight it was to see the gallant
old gentleman, in his seal-skin cap and short green jacket,
lounging along a field-side on his mare, Sybil Grey, and
pausing now and then to talk, with a serio-comic look, to a
labouring man or woman, and rejoice them with some
quaint saying in broad Scotch. The dinner hour was
early; the sitting after dinner was hospitably but not im-
moderately prolonged; and the whole family party (for
such it always seemed, even if there were several visitors)
then met again for a short evening, which was passed in
conversation and music. I once heard Sir Walter say,

[1] It is, however, the only sitting-room in the house that looks
southward.

that he believed there was a ' pair ' of cards (such was his antiquated expression) somewhere in the house—but probably there is no tradition of their having ever been used. The drawing-room and library (unfurnished at the time of my first visit) opened into each other, and formed a beautiful evening apartment. By every one who has visited at Abbotsford they must be associated with some of the most delightful recollections of his life. Sir Walter listened to the music of his daughters, which was all congenial to his own taste, with a never-failing enthusiasm. He followed the fine old songs which Mrs. Lockhart sang to her harp with his mind, eyes, and lips, almost as if joining in an act of religion. To other musical performances he was a dutiful, and often a pleased listener; but I believe he cared little for mere music—the notes failed to charm him if they were not connected with good words, or immediately associated with some history or strong sentiment, upon which his imagination could fasten. A similar observation might, I should conceive, apply to his feeling of other arts. I do not remember any picture or print at Abbotsford which was remarkable merely as a work of colour or design. All, I think, either represented historical, romantic, or poetical subjects, or related to persons, places, or circumstances in which he took an interest. Even in architecture, his taste had the same bias; almost every stone of his house bore an allusion or suggested a sentiment.

" It seemed at first a little strange, in a scene where so many things brought to mind the Waverley novels, to hear no direct mention of them, or even allusion to their existence. But as forbearance on this head was a rule on which a complete tacit understanding subsisted, there was no embarrassment or appearance of mystery on the subject. Once or twice I have heard a casual reference made, in Sir Walter's presence, to some topic in the novels; no surprise or appearance of displeasure followed, but the conversation, so far as it tended that way, died a natural death. It has, I believe, happened that he himself has been caught unawares on the forbidden ground; I have heard it told by a very acute observer, not now living, that on his coming once to Abbotsford, after the publication of The Pirate, Sir Walter asked him, ' Well, and how is our friend Kemble? glorious John ! ' and then, recollecting, of course, that he was talking of Claud Halcro, he checked

himself, and could not for some moments recover from the
false step.   Had a man been ever so prone to indiscretion
on such subjects, it would have been unpardonable to betray it towards Sir Walter Scott, who (beside all his
other claims to respect and affection) was himself cautious,
even to nicety, of hazarding an inquiry or remark which
might appear to be an intrusion upon the affairs of those
with whom he conversed.   It may be observed, too, that
the publications of the day were by no means the staple of
conversation at Abbotsford, though they had their turn;
and with respect to his own works, Sir Walter did not
often talk even of those which were avowed.   If he ever
indulged in anything like egotism, he loved better to speak
of what he had done and seen than of what he had
written.

   "After all, there is perhaps hardly a secret in the
world which has not its safety-valve.   Though Sir Walter
abstained strictly from any mention of the Waverley
novels he did not scruple to talk, and that with great zest,
of the plays which had been founded upon some of them,
and the characters, as there represented.   Soon after our
first meeting, he described to me, with his usual dramatic
power, the deathbed scene of 'the original Dandie Dinmont'; of course referring, ostensibly at least, to the
opera of Guy Mannering.   He dwelt with extreme delight
upon Mackay's performances of the Bailie and Dominie
Sampson, and appeared to taste them with all the fresh
and disinterested enjoyment of a common spectator.   I do
not know a more interesting circumstance in the history of
the Waverley novels, than the pleasure which their illustrious author thus received, as it were at the rebound, from
those creations of his own mind which had so largely
increased the enjoyments of all the civilised world.

   "In one instance only did he, in my presence, say or do
anything which seemed to have an intentional reference to
the novels themselves, while they were yet unacknow-
ledged.   On the last day of my visit in 1823, I rode out
with Sir Walter and his friend Mr. Rose, who was then
his guest and frequent companion in these short rambles.
Sir Walter led us a little way down the left bank of the
Tweed, and then into the moors by a track called the
Girth Road, along which, he told us, the pilgrims from
that side of the river used to come to Melrose.   We traced
upward, at a distance, the course of the little stream called

the Elland. When we had ridden a little time on the moors, he said to me rather pointedly, ' I am going to shew you something that I think will interest you '; and presently, in a wild corner of the hills, he halted us at a place where stood three small ancient towers or castellated houses, in ruins, at short distances from each other. It was plain, upon the slightest consideration of the topography, that one (perhaps any one) of these was the tower of Glendearg, where so many romantic and marvellous adventures happen in The Monastery. While we looked at this forlorn group, I said to Sir Walter that they were what Burns called ' ghaist-alluring edifices.' ' Yes,' he answered carelessly, ' I dare say there are many stories about them.' "

Every friend of Sir Walter's must admire particularly Mr. Adolphus's exquisite description of his laugh; but indeed, every word of these memoranda is precious.

In September, the Highland Society, at the request of Sir Henry Stewart of Allanton, sent a deputation to his seat in Lanarkshire, to examine and report upon his famous improvements in the art of transplanting trees. Sir Walter was one of the committee, and he took a lively interest in it; witness his Essay on Landscape Gardening. He himself made several Allantonian experiments at Abbotsford; but found reason in the sequel to abate somewhat of the enthusiasm which his Essay expresses as to *the system.* The question, after all, comes to pounds, shillings, and pence—and, whether Sir Henry's accounts had or had not been accurately kept, the thing turned out greatly more expensive on Tweedside than he found it represented in Clydesdale.

I accompanied Sir Walter on this little expedition, in the course of which we paid several other visits, and explored not a few ancient castles in the upper regions of the Tweed and the Clyde. Even while the weather was most unpropitious, nothing could induce him to remain in the carriage when we approached any ruined or celebrated edifice. If he had never seen it before, his curiosity was like that of an eager stripling : if he had examined it fifty times, he must renew his familiarity, and gratify the tenderness of youthful reminiscences. While on the road, his conversation never flagged—story suggested story, and ballad came upon ballad in endless succession. But what struck me most was the apparently omnivorous grasp of his memory. That he should recollect every stanza of any ancient ditty of chivalry or romance that had once excited his imagination could no longer surprise me : but it seemed as if he remembered everything without exception, so it were in anything like the shape of verse, that he had ever read. For example, the morning after we left Allanton, we went across the country to breakfast with his friend Cranstoun (Lord Corehouse), who accompanied us in the same carriage; and his Lordship happening to repeat a phrase, remarkable only for its absurdity, from a Magazine poem of the very silliest feebleness, which they had laughed at when at College together, Scott immediately began at the beginning, and gave it us to the end, with apparently no more effort than if he himself had composed it the day before. I could after this easily believe a story often told by Hogg, to the effect that, lamenting in Scott's presence his having lost his only copy of a long ballad composed by him in his early days, and of which he then could recall merely the subject, and one or two fragments, Sir Walter forthwith said, with a smile, —" Take your pencil, Jamie, and I'll dictate your ballad to you, word for word ";—which was done accordingly.[1]

As this was among the first times that I ever travelled for a few days in company with Scott, I may as well add the surprise with which his literary diligence, when away from home and his books, could not fail to be observed. Wherever we slept, whether in the noble mansion or in the shabbiest of country inns, and whether the work was done after retiring at night or before an early start in the morning, he *very rarely* mounted the carriage again without having a packet of the well-known aspect, ready sealed

---

[1] " One morning at breakfast, in my father's house, shortly after one of Sir Walter's severe illnesses, he was asked to partake of some of ' the baked meats that coldly did furnish forth the *breakfast*-table.'—' No, no,' he answered ; ' I bear in mind at present, Bob, the advice of your old friend Dr. Weir—

> " From season'd meats avert your eyes,
> From hams, and tongues, and pigeon pies—
> A venison pasty set before ye,
> Each bit you eat—*Memento mori*." '

This was a verse of a clever rhyming prescription sent some thirty years before, and which my father then remembered to have repeated upon one of their Liddesdale raids. The verses had almost entirely escaped his memory, but Sir Walter was able to give us a long *screed of them.—Andrew Shortrede.*"

and corded, and addressed to his printer in Edinburgh. I used to suspect that he had adopted in his latter years the plan of writing everything on paper of the quarto form, in place of the folio which he at an earlier period used, chiefly because in this way, whatever he was writing, and wherever he wrote, he might seem to casual observers to be merely engaged upon a common letter ; and the rapidity of his execution, taken with the shape of his sheet, has probably deceived hundreds ; but when he had finished his two or three letters, St. Ronan's Well, or whatever was in hand, had made a chapter in advance.

The novel just mentioned was published in December, and in its English reception there was another falling off, which of course somewhat dispirited the bookseller for the moment. Scotch readers in general dissented stoutly from this judgment, alleging (as they might well do) that Meg Dods deserved a place by the side of Monkbarns, Bailie Jarvie, and Captain Dalgetty ;—that no one, who had lived in the author's own country, could hesitate to recognise vivid and happy portraitures in Touchwood, Mac-Turk, and the recluse minister of St. Ronan's ;—that the descriptions of natural scenery might rank with any he had given ;—and, finally, that the whole character of Clara Mowbray, but especially its development in the third volume, formed an original creation, destined to be classed by posterity with the highest efforts of tragic romance. Some Edinburgh critics, however—(both talkers and writers)—received with considerable grudgings certain sarcastic sketches of the would-be-fine life of the watering-place—sketches which their Southern brethren had kindly suggested *might* be drawn from *Northern* observation, but could never appear better than fantastic caricatures to any person who had visited even a third-rate English resort of the same nominal class. There is no doubt that the author dashed off these minor personages with, in the painter's phrase, *a rich brush* ; but I must confess my belief that they have far more truth about them than his countrymen seemed at the time willing to allow; and that while the Continent was shut, as it was in the days of Sir Walter's youthful wanderings, a trip to such a sequestrated place as Gilsland, or Moffat, or Innerleithen—(almost as inaccessible to London duns and bailiffs as the Isle of Man was then, or as Boulogne and Dieppe are now)—may have supplied the future novelist's note-book with authen-

Life of Sir Walter Scott 453

tic materials even for such worthies as Sir Bingo and
Lady Binks, Dr. Quackleben, and Mr. Winterblossom.
It should moreover be borne in mind, that during our insular blockade, northern watering-places were not alone
favoured by the resort of questionable characters from the
south. The comparative cheapness of living, and especially of education, procured for Sir Walter's " own romantic town " a constant succession of such visitants, so long
as they could have no access to the *tables d'hôte* and
dancing-masters of the Continent. When I first mingled
in the society of Edinburgh, it abounded with English,
broken in character and in fortune, who found a mere title
(even a baronet's one) of consequence enough to obtain
for them, from the proverbially cautious Scotch, a degree
of attention to which they had long been unaccustomed
nearer home; and I heard many name, when the novel was
new, a booby of some rank, in whom they recognised a
sufficiently accurate prototype for Sir Bingo.

Sir Walter had shewn a remarkable degree of good-
nature in the completion of this novel. When the end
came in view, James Ballantyne suddenly took vast alarm
about a particular feature in the history of the heroine.
In the original conception, and in the book as actually
written and printed, Miss Mowbray's mock marriage had
not halted at the profaned ceremony of the church; and
the delicate printer shrunk from the idea of obtruding on
the fastidious public the possibility of any personal con-
tamination having been incurred by a high-born damsel
of the nineteenth century. Scott was at first inclined to
dismiss his friend's scruples as briefly as he had done
those of Blackwood in the case of the Black Dwarf:—
" You would never have quarrelled with it," he said, " had
the thing happened to a girl in gingham :—the silk petti-
coat can make little difference." James reclaimed with
double energy, and called Constable to the rescue;—and
after some pause, the author very reluctantly consented
to cancel and re-write about twenty-four pages, which
was enough to obliterate to a certain extent the dreaded
scandal—and in a similar degree, as he always persisted,
to perplex and weaken the course of his narrative and the
dark effect of its catastrophe.

Whoever might take offence with different parts of the
book, it was rapturously hailed by the inhabitants of Innerleithen, who immediately identified the most striking of

its localities with those of their own pretty village and
picturesque neighbourhood, and foresaw in this celebration a chance of restoring the popularity of their long
neglected *Well*;—to which Scott had occasionally escorted
his mother and sister in the days of boyhood. The not-
ables of the little town voted by acclamation that the old
name of Innerleithen should be, as far as possible, dropped
thenceforth, and that of St. Ronan's adopted. Nor were
they mistaken in their auguries. An unheard-of influx of
water-bibbers forthwith crowned their hopes ; and spruce
hottles and huge staring lodging-houses soon arose to
disturb woefully every association that had induced Sir
Walter to make Innerleithen the scene of a romance.
Nor were they who profited by these invasions of the
genius loci at all sparing in their demonstrations of gratitude ;—the traveller reads on the corner of every new erection there, *Abbotsford Place, Waverley Row, The Marmion Hotel*, or some inscription of the like coinage.

Among other consequences of the revived fame of the
place, a yearly festival was instituted for the celebration
of *The St. Ronan's Border Games*. A club of *Bowmen
of the Border*, arrayed in doublets of Lincoln green, with
broad blue bonnets, and having the Ettrick Shepherd for
Captain, assumed the principal management of this exhibition ; and Scott was well pleased to be enrolled among
them, and during several years was a regular attendant,
both on the Meadow, where (besides archery) leaping,
racing, wrestling, stone-heaving, and hammer-throwing,
went on opposite to the noble old Castle of Traquair, and
at the susequent banquet, where Hogg in full costume
always presided as master of the ceremonies. A gayer
spectacle than that of *The St. Ronan's Games* in those
days could not well have been desired. The Shepherd,
even when on the verge of threescore, seldom failed to
carry off some of the prizes, to the astonishment of his
vanquished juniors ; and the *bon-vivants* of Edinburgh mustered strong among the gentry and yeomanry of Tweeddale to see him afterwards in his glory filling the president's chair with eminent success, and commonly supported on this—which was, in fact, the grandest evening
of his year—by Sir Walter Scott, Professor Wilson, Sir
Adam Fergusson, and *Peter* Robertson.

CHAPTER XIII

Publication of Redgauntlet—Abbotsford completed—Marriage of
Captain Scott—Constable's Miscellany projected—Life of Napoleon
begun—Tales of the Crusaders published—Tour in Ireland—Visit
to Windermere—Moore at Abbotsford—Rumours of evil among
the Booksellers. 1824-1825.

IMMEDIATELY on the conclusion of St. Ronan's Well,
Sir Walter began *Redgauntlet*;—but it had made considerable progress at press before Constable and Ballantyne could persuade him to substitute that title for *Herries*.
The book was published in June 1824, and was received
at the time somewhat coldly, though it has since, I believe,
found more justice. The reintroduction of the adventurous
hero of 1745, in the dulness and dimness of advancing
age and fortunes hopelessly blighted—and the presenting
him—with whose romantic portraiture at an earlier period
historical truth had been so admirably blended—as the
moving principle of events, not only entirely, but notori-
ously imaginary—this was a rash experiment, and could
not fail to suggest disadvantageous comparisons; yet, had
there been no Waverley, I am persuaded the fallen and
faded Ascanius of Redgauntlet would have been universally pronounced a masterpiece. About the secondary
personages there could be little ground for controversy.
What novel or drama has surpassed the grotesquely ludicrous, dashed with the profound pathos, of Peter Peebles
—the most tragic of farces?—or the still sadder merriment of that human shipwreck, Nantie Ewart?—or Wandering Willie—and his Tale—the wildest and most rueful
of dreams told by such a person, and in such a dialect?
With posterity, even apart from these grand features,
this novel will yield in interest to none of the series; for
it contains perhaps more of *Allan Fairford's* personal experiences than any other of them, or even than all the rest
put together.

This year—*mirabile dictu!*—produced but one novel;
and it is not impossible that the author had taken deeply
into his mind, though he would not *immediately* act upon
them, certain hints about the danger of " overcropping,"
which have been alluded to as dropping from his publishers in 1823. He had, however, a labour of some
weight to go through in a second edition of his Swift.

The additions to this reprint were numerous, and he corrected his notes, and the Life of the Dean throughout, with care. He also threw off several reviews and other petty miscellanies—among the rest his memorable tribute to the memory of Lord Byron, written immediately after the news of the catastrophe at Missolonghi reached him.

The arrangement of his library and museum was, however, the main care of the summer; and his woods were now in such a state that his most usual exercise out of doors was thinning them. He was an expert as well as powerful wielder of the axe, and competed with his ablest subalterns as to the paucity of blows by which a tree could be brought down. The wood rang ever and anon with laughter while he shared their labours; and if he had taken as he every now and then did, a whole day with them, they were sure to be invited home to Abbotsford, to sup gaily at Tom Purdie's. One of Sir Walter's transatlantic admirers, by the way, sent him a complete assortment of the tools employed in clearing the Backwoods, and both he and Tom made efforts to attain dexterity in using them; but neither succeeded. The American axe, having a longer shaft than ours, and a much smaller and narrower cutting-piece, was, in Tom's opinion, only fit for paring a *kebbuck* (*i.e.*, a cheese of skimmed milk). The old-fashioned weapon was soon resumed, and the belt that bore it had accommodation also for a chisel, a hammer, and a small saw. Among all the numberless portraits, why was there not one representing the " Belted Knight," accoutred with these appurtenances of his forest-craft, jogging over the heather on a breezy morning, with Thomas at his stirrup, and Maida stalking in advance?

Notwithstanding numberless letters to Terry about his upholstery, the far greater part of it was manufactured at home. The most of the articles from London were only models for the use of two or three neat-handed carpenters whom he had discovered in the villages near him; and he watched and directed their operations as carefully as a George Bullock could have done; and the results were such as even Bullock might have admired. The great table in the library, for example (a most complex and beautiful one), was done entirely in the room where it now stands, by Joseph Shillinglaw of Darnick—the Sheriff planning and studying every turn as zealously as ever an old lady pondered the development of an embroidered

cushion. The hangings and curtains, too, were chiefly
the work of a little hunch-backed tailor, by name *William*
Goodfellow—(save at Abbotsford, where he answered to
Robin)—who occupied a cottage on Scott's farm of the
Broomielees ; one of the race who creep from homestead
to homestead, welcomed wherever they appear by house-
wife and handmaiden, the great gossips and newsmen of
the parish,—in Scottish nomenclature *cardooers*. Proudly
and earnestly did all these vassals toil in his service ; and
I think it was one of them that, when some stranger asked
a question about his personal demeanour, answered in
these simple words—" Sir Walter speaks to every man as
if they were blood-relations." Not long after he had completed his work at Abbotsford, little Goodfellow fell sick,
and as his cabin was near Chiefswood, I had many opportunities of observing the Sheriff's kind attention to
him in his affliction. I can never forget the evening on
which the poor tailor died. When Scott entered the hovel
he found everything silent, and inferred from the looks of
the good women in attendance that their patient had fallen
asleep, and that they feared his sleep was the final one.
He murmured some syllables of kind regret ;—at the sound
of his voice the dying tailor unclosed his eyes, and eagerly
and wistfully sat up, clasping his hands with an expression
of rapturous gratefulness and devotion, that, in the midst
of deformity, disease, pain, and wretchedness, was at once
beautiful and sublime. He cried with a loud voice, " The
Lord bless and reward you ! " and expired with the effort.

  In the painting, too, Sir Walter personally directed
everything. He abominated the commonplace daubing
of walls, panels, doors, and window-boards, with coats of
white, blue, or grey, and thought that sparklings and
edgings of gilding only made their baldness and poverty
more noticeable. Except in the drawing-room, which he
abandoned to Lady Scott's taste, all the roofs were, in
appearance at least, of antique carved oak, relieved by
coats of arms duly blazoned at the intersections of beams,
and resting on cornices to the eye of the same material,
but composed of casts in plaster of Paris, after the
foliage, the flowers, the grotesque monsters and dwarfs,
and sometimes the beautiful heads of nuns and confessors,
on which he had doated from infancy among the cloisters
of Melrose and Roslin. In the painting of these things,
also, he had instruments who considered it as a labour of

love. The master-limner, in particular (Mr. D. R. Hay), had a devoted attachment to his person; and this was not wonderful, for he, in fact, owed a prosperous fortune to Scott's kind and sagacious counsel tendered at the very outset of his career. As a printer's apprentice, he had attracted notice by his attempts with the pencil, and Sir Walter was called upon, after often admiring his skill in representing dogs and horses and the like, to assist him with his advice, as ambition had been stirred, and the youth would fain give himself to the regular training of an artist. Scott took him into his room, and conversed with him at some length. He explained the difficulties and perils of this aspiring walk; and ended with saying, "It has often struck me that some clever fellow might make a good hit, if, in place of enrolling himself among the future Raphaels and Vandykes of the Royal Academy, he should resolutely set himself to introducing something of a more elegant style of house-painting."

Meantime, the progress of Abbotsford stimulated both friends and strangers to contribute articles of curiosity towards its adornment. Mr. Train's gift of this year was a handsome chair made from the oak of the house of Robroyston, the traditionary scene of the betrayal of Wallace by Menteith. This Sir Walter placed in his own *sanctum*: where there was no other chair but the one on which he sat at work. But the arrivals were endless: among the rest came, I think within the same week, a copy of Montfauçon's Antiquities, in fifteen volumes folio, richly bound in scarlet, the gift of King George IV., and a set of the Variorum Classics, in a hundred and forty volumes, together with a couple of really splendid carved chairs, the spoils of some Venetian palace, from Mr. Constable. These were his tokens of gratitude, by the way, for the MSS. of the Novels, which, on Lord Kinnedder's death, Scott drew from that friend's secret repositories, and transferred, with strict injunctions of watchfulness, to his delighted publisher.

Towards the close of this year, Sir Walter heard of the death of his dear brother Thomas, whose only son had been for some time domesticated at Abbotsford. In October, his own son Charles began his residence at Brazennose College, Oxford. The adoption of this plan implied finally dropping an appointment in the civil service of the East India Company, which had been placed at his disposal by Lord Bathurst in 1820; a step which, were there any doubt on that subject, would alone be sufficient to prove that the young gentleman's father at this time considered his own worldly fortunes as in a highly prosperous situation. A writership in India is early independence;—in the case of a son of Scott, so conducting himself as not to discredit the name he inherited, it could hardly have failed to be early wealth. And Sir Walter was the last man to deprive his boy of such safe and easy prospects of worldly advantage, turning him over to the precarious chances of a learned profession in Great Britain, unless in the confidence that his own resources were so great as to render ultimate failure in such a career a matter of no primary importance.

By Christmas the Tales of the Crusaders were begun, and Abbotsford was at last rid of carpenters and upholsterers. Young Walter arrived to see his father's house complete, and filled with a larger company than it could ever before accommodate. One of the guests was Captain Basil Hall, always an agreeable one : a traveller and a *savant*, full of stories and theories, inexhaustible in spirits, curiosity, and enthusiasm. Sir Walter was surprised and a little annoyed on observing that the Captain kept a note-book on his knee while at table, but made no remark. He kindly allowed me, in 1836, to read his Abbotsford Diaries, &c., and make what use of them I might then think proper. On the present occasion I must give but a specimen :—

"On coming to a broad path in the middle of the woods, we took notice of a finger-post, on which was written ' The *Rod* to Selkirk.' We made some remark about Tom's orthography, upon which he laughed, and said that that finger-post had gained him great popularity in the neighbourhood. ' I cannot say,' he remarked, ' that I had any such view when I ordered it to be put up. The public road, it is true, is not far off, and this leads through the very centre of my grounds, but I never could bring myself to make that a reason for excluding any person who finds it agreeable or advantageous to take over the hill if he likes. But although my practice in this respect had always been well known, the actual admission of it, the avowed establishment of it as a sort of right, by sticking up the finger-post, was received as a kind of boon, and I got a world of credit for a thing which had certainly not any popularity, for its object. Nevertheless,' he continued, ' I have no scruple in saying that what I did deserved the good people's acknowledgment; and I seriously disapprove of those proprietors who act on a different principle in these matters. Nothing on earth would induce me to put up boards threatening prosecution, or cautioning one's fellow-creatures to beware of man-traps and spring-guns. I hold that all such things are not only in the highest degree offensive and hurtful to the feelings of people whom it is every way important to conciliate, but that they are also quite inefficient—and I will venture to say, that not one of my young trees has ever been cut, nor a fence trodden down, or any kind of damage done in consequence of the free access which all the world has to my place. Round the house, of course, there is a set of walks set apart and kept private for the ladies—but over all the rest of my land any one may rove as he likes. I please myself with the reflection that many people of taste may be indulging their fancies in these grounds, and I often recollect how much of Burns's inspiration was probably due to his having near him the woods of Ballochmyle to ramble through at his will when he was a ragged callant.' Some one talked of the pains taken to provide the poor with receipts for making good dishes out of their ordinary messes. ' I dislike all such interference,' he said—' all your domiciliary, kind, impertinent visits;—they are all pretty much felt like insults, and do no manner of good : let people go on in their own way, in God's name. How would you like to have a nobleman coming to you to teach you how to dish up your beefsteak into a French kickshaw? Let the poor alone in their domestic habits : protect them, treat them kindly, trust them; but let them enjoy in quiet their dish of porridge, and their potatoes and herrings, or whatever it may be—for anysake don't torment them with your fashionable soups. And take care,' he added, ' not to give them anything gratis; except when they are under the gripe of immediate *misery*—what *they* think misery—consider it as a sin to do anything that can tend to make them lose the precious feeling of independence. For my part, I very very rarely give anything away. Now, for instance, this pile of branches which has been thinned out this morning is placed here for sale for the poor people's fires, and I am perfectly certain they are more grateful to me for selling it at the price I do (which, you may be sure, is no great matter), than if I were to give them ten times the quantity for nothing. Every shilling collected in this and other similar manners goes to a fund which pays the doctor for his attendance on them when they are sick; and this is my notion of charity.'—' I make not a rule to be on intimate terms,' he told us, ' with all my neighbours—that would be an idle thing to do. Some are good—some are not so good, and it would be foolish and ineffectual to treat all with the same cordiality; but to live in harmony with all is quite easy, and surely very pleasant. Some of them may be rough and *gruff* at first, but all men, if kindly used, come about at last, and by going on gently, and never being eager or noisy about what I want, and letting things glide on leisurely, I always find in the end that the object is gained on which I have set my heart, either by exchange or purchase, or by some sort of compromise by which both parties are obliged, and good-will begot if it did not exist before—strengthened if it did exist.'—I have never seen any person on more delightful terms with his family. The youngest of his nephews and nieces can joke with him, and seem at all times perfectly at ease in his presence—his coming into the room only increases the laugh, and never checks it—he either joins in what is going on or passes. No one notices him any more than if he were one of themselves. These are things which cannot be got up.''

Another entry says :—'' Last night there was a dance in honour of Sir Walter Scott's eldest son, who had recently come from Sandhurst College, after having passed through some military examinations with great credit. We had a great clan of Scotts. There were no less than nine Scotts of Harden, and ten of other families. There were others besides from the neighbourhood—at least half-a-dozen Fergussons, with the jolly Sir Adam at their head—Lady Fergusson, her niece Miss Jobson, the pretty heiress of Lochore,'' &c. But with all his acuteness, Hall does not seem to have caught any suspicion of the real purpose and meaning of this ball. That evening was one of the very proudest and happiest in Scott's brilliant existence. Its festivities were held in honour of the young lady, whom the Captain names cursorily as '' the pretty heiress of Lochore.'' It was known to not a few

of the party, and I should have supposed it might have
been surmised by the rest, that those halls were displayed
for the first time in all their splendour, on an occasion
not less interesting to the Poet than the conclusion of a
treaty of marriage between the heir of his name and fortunes, and the amiable niece of his friends Sir Adam and
Lady Fergusson.   It was the first regular ball given at
Abbotsford, and the last.   Nay, I believe nobody has ever
danced under that roof since then.   I myself never again
saw the whole range of apartments thrown open for the
reception of company except once—on the day of Sir
Walter Scott's funeral.

   The lady's fortune was a handsome one, and her guardians exerted the powers with which they were invested,
by requiring that the marriage-contract should settle Abbotsford (with reservation of Sir Walter's own life rent)
upon the affianced parties.   To this condition he gave a
ready assent, and the moment he had signed the deed, he
exclaimed—" I have now parted with my lands with more
pleasure than I ever derived from the acquisition or possession of them ; and if I be spared for ten years, I think
I may promise to settle as much more again upon these
young folks. "   It was well for himself and his children
that his auguries, which failed so miserably as to the
matter of worldly wealth, were destined to no disappointment as respected considerations of a higher description.

   The marriage took place at Edinburgh on the 3rd day
of February, and when the young couple left Abbotsford
two or three weeks afterwards, Sir Walter promised to
visit them at their regimental quarters in Ireland in the
course of the summer.   Before he fulfilled that purpose
he had the additional pleasure of seeing his son gazetted
as Captain in the King's Hussars—a step for which Sir
Walter advanced the large sum of £3,500.

   In May, Terry, and his able brother comedian, Frederick Yates, entered on a negotiation, which terminated in
their becoming joint lessees and managers of the Adelphi
Theatre.   Terry requested Scott and Ballantyne to assist
him on this occasion by some advance of money, or if
that should be inconvenient, by the use of their credit.
They were both very anxious to serve him ; but Sir Walter
had a poor opinion of speculations in theatrical property ;
and, moreover, entertained suspicions, too well justified by
the result, that Terry was not much qualified for conduct-

ing the pecuniary part of such a business. Ultimately Ballantyne, who shared these scruples, became Terry's security for a considerable sum (I think £500), and Sir Walter pledged his credit in like manner to the extent of £1,250. He had, in the sequel, to pay off both this sum and that for which the printer had engaged.

But at this time the chief subject of concern was a grand scheme of revolution in the whole art and traffic of publishing, which Constable first opened in detail one Saturday at Abbotsford—none being present except Sir Walter, Ballantyne, and myself. After dinner, there was a little pause of expectation, and the brave schemer suddenly started *in medias res,* saying:—" Literary genius may, or may not, have done its best; but the trade are in the cradle." Scott eyed the florid bookseller's beaming countenance, and the solemn stare with which the equally portly printer was listening, and pushing round the bottles with a hearty chuckle, bade me " Give our twa *soncie babbies* a drap mother's milk." Constable sucked in fresh inspiration, and proceeded to say that, wild as we might think him, certain new plans, of which we had all already heard some hints, had been suggested by, and were in fact mainly grounded upon, a sufficiently prosaic authority—namely, the annual schedule of assessed taxes, a copy of which interesting document he drew from his pocket, and substituted for his *D'Oyley*. It was copiously diversified, " text and margent," by figures and calculations in his own handwriting, which I for one might have regarded with less reverence, had I known at the time this " great arithmetician's " rooted aversion and contempt for all examination of his own balance-sheet. He had, however, taken vast pains to fill in the number of persons who might fairly be supposed to pay the taxes for each separate article of luxury, armorial bearings, hunters racers, four-wheeled carriages, &c., &c.; and having demonstrated that hundreds of thousands held, as neces sary to their comfort and station, articles upon articles of which their forefathers never dreamt, said, that our self-love never deceived us more grossly than when we fancied our notions as to the matter of books had advanced in at all a corresponding proportion. " On the contrary," cried Constable, " I am satisfied that the demand for Shakspeare's plays, contemptible as we hold it to have been, in the time of Elizabeth and James, was more creditable to the classes who really indulged in any sort of elegance then, than the sale of Childe Harold or Waverley is to this nineteenth century."

Scott helped him on by interposing, that at that moment he had a rich valley crowded with handsome houses under his view, and yet much doubted whether any laird within ten miles spent ten pounds per annum on the literature of the day. "No," said Constable, "there is no market among them that's worth one's thinking about. They are contented with a review or a magazine, or at best with a paltry subscription to some circulating library forty miles off. But if I live for half-a-dozen years, I'll make it as impossible that there should not be a good library in every decent house in Britain as that the shepherd's ingle-nook should want the *saut poke*. Ay, and what's that?" he continued, warming and puffing; "why should the ingle-nook itself want a shelf for *the novels*?"—"I see your drift, my man," says Sir Walter;—"you're for being like Billy Pitt in Gilray's print—you want to get into the salt-box yourself."—"Yes," he responded (using a favourite adjuration)—"I have hitherto been thinking only of the wax lights, but before I'm a twelvemonth older I shall have my hand upon the tallow."—"Troth," says Scott, "you are indeed likely to be 'The grand Napoleon of the realms of *print*.'"—"If you outlive me," says Constable, with a regal smile, "I bespeak that line for my tomb-stone, but, in the meantime, may I presume to ask you to be my right-hand man when I open my campaign of Marengo? I have now settled my outline of operations—a three-shilling or half-crown volume every month, which must and shall sell, not by thousands or tens of thousands, but by hundreds of thousands—ay, by millions! Twelve volumes in the year, a halfpenny of profit upon every copy of which will make me richer than the possession of all the copyrights of all the quartos that ever were, or will be, hot-pressed!—twelve volumes, so good that millions must wish to have them, and so cheap that every butcher's callant may have them, if he pleases to let me tax him sixpence a week!"

Many a previous consultation, and many a solitary meditation, too, prompted Scott's answer.—"Your plan," said he, "cannot fail, provided the books be really good; but you must not start until you have not only leading columns, but depth upon depth of reserve in thorough

order. I am willing to do my part in this grand enterprise. Often, of late, have I felt that the vein of fiction
was nearly worked out; often, as you all know, have I
been thinking seriously of turning my hand to history.
I am of opinion that historical writing has no more been
adapted to the demands of the increased circles among
which literature does already find its way, than you allege
as to the shape and price of books in general. What say
you to taking the field with a Life of the *other* Napoleon? "

The reader does not need to be told that the series of
cheap volumes, subsequently issued under the title of
" Constable's Miscellany," was the scheme on which this
great bookseller was brooding. Before he left Abbotsford, it was arranged that the first number of this collection should consist of one-half of Waverley; the second,
of the first section of a " Life of Napoleon Bonaparte by
the Author of Waverley "; that this Life should be comprised in four of these numbers; and that, until the whole
series of his novels had been issued, a volume every
second month, in this new and uncostly form, he should
keep the Ballantyne press going with a series of historical
works, to be issued on the alternate months.

Some circumstances in the progress of the Tales of the
Crusaders, now on the eve of publication, must have been
uppermost in Scott's mind when he met Constable's proposals with so much alacrity. The story of *The Betrothed*
—(to which he was mainly prompted by the lively conversation on Welsh antiquities of Archdeacon Williams)—
found no favour as it advanced with Ballantyne; and so
heavily did his critical remonstrances weigh on the author,
that he at length determined to cancel it for ever. The
tale, however, all but a chapter or two, had been printed
off, and both publisher and printer paused about committing such a mass to the flames. The sheets were hung up
meanwhile, and Scott began The Talisman—of which also
James criticised the earlier chapters in such a strain that
Scott was deeply vexed. " Is it wise," he wrote, " to
mend a dull overloaded fire by heaping on a shovelful of
wet coals? " and hinted some doubts whether he should
proceed. He did so, however; the critical printer by degrees warmed to the story, and he at last pronounced The
Talisman such a masterpiece, that The Betrothed might
venture abroad under its wing. Sir Walter was now
reluctant on that subject, and said he would rather write

two more new novels than the few pages necessary to
complete his unfortunate Betrothed. But while he hesitated, the German newspapers announced "*a new romance by the author of Waverley* " as about to issue from
the press of Leipsig. There was some ground for suspecting that a set of the suspended sheets might have been
purloined and sold to a pirate, and this consideration put
an end to his scruples. And when the German did publish the fabrication, entitled *Walladmor,* it could no longer
be doubtful that some reader of Scott's sheets had communicated at least the fact that he was breaking ground
in Wales.

Early in June, then, the Tales of the Crusaders were put
forth; and, as Mr. Ballantyne had predicted, the brightness of the Talisman dazzled the eyes of the million as to
the defects of the twin-story. Few of these publications
had a more enthusiastic greeting; and Scott's literary
plans were, as the reader will see reason to infer, considerably modified in consequence of the new burst of applause
which attended the brilliant procession of his Saladin and
Cœur de Lion.

To return for a moment to our merry conclave at
Abbotsford. Constable's vast chapter of embryo schemes
was discussed more leisurely on the following Monday
morning, when we drove to the crags of Smailholm and
the Abbey of Dryburgh, both poet and publisher talking
over the past and the future course of their lives, and agreeing, as far as I could penetrate, that the years to come
were likely to be more prosperous than any they had as
yet seen. In the evening, too, this being his friend's first
visit since the mansion had been completed, Scott (though
there were no ladies and few servants) had the hall and
library lighted up, that he might shew him everything to
the most sparkling advantage. With what serenity did he
walk about those apartments, handling books, expounding
armour and pictures, and rejoicing in the Babylon which
he had built!

He began, without delay, what was meant to be a very
short preliminary sketch of the French Revolution, prior
to the appearance of his hero upon the scene of action.
This, he thought, might be done almost *currente calamo*;
for his recollection of all the great events as they occurred
was vivid, and he had not failed to peruse every book of
any considerable importance on these subjects as it issued

from the press. He apprehended the necessity, on the
other hand, of more laborious study in the way of reading
than he had for many years had occasion for, before he
could enter with advantage upon Buonaparte's military
career; and Constable accordingly set about collecting a
new library of printed materials, which continued from
day to day pouring in upon him, till his little parlour in
Castle Street looked more like an auctioneer's premises
than an author's. The first waggon delivered itself of
about a hundred huge folios of the Moniteur; and London,
Paris, Amsterdam, and Brussels, were all laid under contribution to meet the bold demands of his purveyor.

In the meantime he advanced with his Introduction;
and, catching fire as the theme expanded before him, had
so soon several chapters in his desk, without having
travelled over half the ground assigned for them, that
Constable saw it would be in vain to hope for the completion of the work within four duodecimos. They resolved that it should be published, in the first instance, as
a separate book, in four volumes of the same size with the
Tales of the Crusaders, but with more pages and more
letterpress to each page. Scarcely had this been settled
before it became obvious, that four such volumes would
never suffice; and the number was week after week
extended—with corresponding alterations as to the rate of
the author's payment. Constable still considered the
appearance of the second edition of the Life of Napoleon
in his Miscellany as the great point on which the fortunes
of that undertaking were to turn; and its commencement
was in consequence adjourned; which, however, must have
been the case at any rate, as the stock of the Novels was
greater than he had calculated; and some interval must
elapse, before, with fairness to the retail trade, he could
throw that long series into any cheaper form.

Before the Court rose in July, Sir Walter had made
considerable progress in his Sketch of the French Revolution; but it was agreed that he should make his promised
excursion to Ireland before any MS. went to the printers.
He had seen no more of the sister island than Dunluce
and the Giant's Causeway; his curiosity about the scenery
and the people was lively; and besides the great object of
seeing his son and daughter-in-law under their own roof,
and the scarcely inferior pleasure of another meeting with
Miss Edgeworth, he looked forward to renewing his

acquaintance with several accomplished persons who had been serviceable to him in his labours upon Swift. But, illustriously as Ireland had contributed to the English Library, he had always been accustomed to hear that almost no books were now published there, and fewer sold than in any other country calling itself civilised; and he had naturally concluded that apathy and indifference prevailed as to literature itself, and of course as to literary men. He had not, therefore, formed the remotest anticipation of the kind of reception which awaited him. Miss Anne Scott and myself accompanied him. We left Edinburgh on the 8th of July in a light open carriage, and embarked at Glasgow for Belfast. The steam-boat, besides a crowd of passengers of all possible classes, was lumbered with a carge offensive enough to the eye and the nostrils, but still more disagreeable from the anticipations and reflections it could not fail to suggest. Hardly had our carriage been lashed on the deck before it disappeared from our view amidst mountainous packages of old clothes;—the cast-off raiment of the Scotch beggars was on its way to a land where beggary is the staple of life. A voyage down the Firth of Clyde, however, is enough to make anybody happy : nowhere can the home tourist, at all events, behold, in the course of one day, such a succession and variety of beautiful, romantic, and majestic scenery : on one hand, dark mountains and castellated shores—on the other, rich groves and pastures, interspersed with elegant villas and thriving towns—the bright estuary between, alive with shipping, and diversified with islands. It may be supposed how delightful such a voyage was in a fine day of July, with Scott, always as full of glee on any trip as a schoolboy; crammed with all the traditions and legends of every place we passed; and too happy to pour them out for the entertainment of his companions on deck. After dinner, too, he was the charm of the table. A worthy old Bailie of Glasgow sat by him, and shared fully in the general pleasure; though his particular source of interest and satisfaction was, that he had got into such close quarters with a live Sheriff and Clerk of Session,—and this gave him the opportunity of discussing sundry knotty points of police law, as to which our steerage passengers might perhaps have been more curious than most of those admitted to the symposium of the cabin. Sir Walter, however, was as ready for the rogueries of the Broomielaw, as for the mystic antiquities of Balclutha, or the discomfiture of the Norseman at Largs, or Bruce's adventures in Arran. The Bailie insisted for a second bowl of punch, and volunteered to be the manufacturer; "for," quoth he slily, "I am reckoned a fair hand, though not equal to *my father the deacon.*" Scott smiled in acquiescence.

We reached Belfast next morning. When we halted at Drogheda, a retired officer of dragoons, discovering that the party was Sir Walter's, sent in his card, with a polite offer to attend him over the field of the battle of the Boyne, about two miles off, which of course was accepted;—Sir Walter rejoicing the veteran's heart by his vigorous recitation of the famous ballad (*The crossing of the Water*), as we proceeded to the ground, and the eager and intelligent curiosity with which he received his explanations of it.

On Thursday the 14th we reached Dublin in time for dinner, and found young Walter and his bride established in one of those large and noble houses in St. Stephen's Green (the most extensive square in Europe), the founders of which little dreamt that they should ever be let at an easy rate as garrison lodgings. Never can I forget the fond joy and pride with which Sir Walter looked round him, as he sat for the first time at his son's table. I could not but recall Pindar's lines, in which, wishing to paint the gentlest rapture of felicity, he describes an old man with a foaming wine-cup in his hand at his child's wedding feast.

In the evening arrived a deputation from the Royal Society of Dublin, inviting Sir Walter to a public dinner; and next morning he found on his breakfast-table a letter from the Provost of Trinity College (Dr. Kyle, afterwards Bishop of Cork), announcing that the University desired to pay him the high compliment of a degree of Doctor of Laws by *diploma*. The Archbishop of Dublin (Dr. Magee) was among the earliest of his visitors; another was the Right Honourable Anthony Blake, who was the bearer of a message from the Marquis Wellesley, then Lord-Lieutenant, inviting him to dine next day at his Excellency's country residence, Malahide Castle. It would be endless to enumerate the distinguished persons who, morning after morning, crowded his *levee* in St. Stephen's Green. The courts of law were not then sitting, and most of the judges were out of town; but all the other great functionaries, and the leading noblemen and gentlemen of the city and its neighbourhood, of whatever sect or party, hastened to tender every conceivable homage and hospitality. But all this was less surprising to the companions of his journey (though, to say the truth, we had, no more than himself, counted on such eager enthusiasm among any class of Irish society), than the demonstrations of respect which, after the first day or two, awaited him, wherever he moved, at the hands of the less elevated orders of the Dublin population. If his carriage was recognised at the door of any public establishment, the street was sure to be crowded before he came out again, so as to make his departure as slow as a procession. When he entered a street, the watchword was passed down both sides like lightning, and the shopkeepers and their wives stood bowing and curtseying all the way down.

From Dublin, we made an excursion of some days into Wicklow, halting for a night at the villa of the Surgeon-General, Sir Philip Crampton, who kindly did the honours of Lough Breagh and the Dargle; and then for two or three at Old Connaught, near Bray, the seat of the Attorney-General, afterwards Lord Plunkett. Here there was a large and brilliant party assembled; and from hence, under the guidance of Mr. Attorney and his amiable family, we perambulated to all possible advantage the classical resorts of the Devil's Glyn, Rosanna, Kilruddery, and Glendalough, with its seven churches, and *St. Kevin's Bed*—the scene of the fate of Cathleen, celebrated in Moore's ballad—

> " By that lake whose gloomy shore
> Skylark never warbles over," &c.

It is a hole in the sheer surface of the rock, in which two or three people might sit. The difficulty of getting into this place has been exaggerated, as also the danger, for it would only be falling thirty or forty feet into very deep water. Yet I never was more pained than when Scott, in spite of all remonstrances, would make his way to it, crawling along the precipice. After he was gone, Plunkett told the female guide he was a poet. Cathleen treated this with indignation, as a quiz of Mr. Attorney's. —" *Poet!* " said she; " the devil a bit of him—but an honourable gentleman : he gave me half-a-crown."

On the 1st of August we proceeded from Dublin to Edgeworthstown, the party being now reinforced by

Captain and Mrs. Scott, and also by the delightful addition of the Surgeon-General. A happy meeting it was : we remained there for several days, making excursions to Loch Oel and other scenes of interest in Longford and the adjoining counties; the gentry everywhere exerting themselves with true Irish zeal to signalise their affectionate pride in their illustrious countrywoman, and their appreciation of her guest; while her brother, Mr. Lovell Edgeworth, had his classical mansion filled every evening with a succession of distinguished friends, the *élite* of Ireland. Here, above all, we had the opportunity of seeing in what universal respect and comfort a gentleman's family may live in that country, and in far from its most favoured district, provided only they live there habitually, and do their duty as the friends and guardians of those among whom Providence has appointed their proper place. Here we found neither mud hovels nor naked peasantry, but snug cottages and smiling faces all about. Here there was a very large school in the village, of which masters and pupils were in a nearly equal proportion Protestants and Roman Catholics—the Protestant squire himself making it a regular part of his daily business to visit the scene of their operations, and strengthen authority and enforce discipline by his personal superintendence. It is a curious enough coincidence that Oliver Goldsmith and Maria Edgeworth should both have derived their early love and knowledge of Irish character and manners from the same identical district. He received part of his education at this very school of Edgeworthstown; and Pallasmore (the *locus cui nomen est Pallas* of Johnson's epitaph), the little hamlet where the author of the Vicar of Wakefield first saw the light, is still, as it was in his time, the property of the Edgeworths. It may well be imagined with what lively interest Sir Walter surveyed the scenery with which so many of the proudest recollections of Ireland must ever be associated, and how curiously he studied the rural manners it presented to him, in the hope (not disappointed) of being able to trace some of his friend's bright creations to their first hints and germs. On the delight with which he contemplated her position in the midst of her own domestic circle, I need say still less. The reader is aware by this time how deeply he condemned and pitied the conduct and fate of those who, gifted with pre-eminent talents for the instruction and entertainment of their species at large, fancy themselves entitled to neglect those every-day duties and charities of life, from the mere shadowing of which in imaginary pictures the genius of poetry and romance has always reaped its highest and purest, perhaps its only true and immortal honours. In Maria he hailed a sister spirit—one who, at the summit of literary fame, took the same modest, just, and, let me add, *Christian* view of the relative importance of the feelings, the obligations, and the hopes in which we are all equally partakers, and those talents and accomplishments which may seem, to vain and short-sighted eyes, sufficient to constitute their possessors into an order and species apart from the rest of their kind. Such fantastic conceits found no shelter with either of these powerful minds. I was then a young man, and I cannot forget how much I was struck at the time by some words that fell from one of them, when, in the course of a walk in the park at Edgeworthstown, I happened to use some phrase which conveyed (though not perhaps meant to do so) the impression that I suspected Poets and Novelists of being a good deal accustomed to look at life and the world only as materials for art. A soft and pensive shade came over Scott's face as he said—"I fear you have some very young ideas in your head:—are you not too apt to measure things by some reference to literature—to disbelieve that anybody can be worth much care, who has no knowledge of that sort of thing, or taste for it? God help us! what a poor world this would be if that were the true doctrine! I have read books enough, and observed and conversed with enough of eminent and splendidly cultivated minds, too, in my time; but I assure you, I have heard higher sentiments from the lips of poor *uneducated* men and women, when exerting the spirit of severe yet gentle heroism under difficulties and afflictions, or speaking their simple thoughts as to circumstances in the lot of friends and neighbours, than I ever yet met with out of the pages of the Bible. We shall never learn to feel and respect our real calling and destiny, unless we have taught ourselves to consider everything as moonshine, compared with the education of the heart." Maria did not listen to this without some water in her eyes—(her tears are always ready when any generous string is touched:—for, as Pope says, " the finest minds, like the finest metals, dissolve the easiest ")—but she brushed them gaily aside, and said,

" You see how it is—Dean Swift said he had written his
books in order that people might learn to treat him like a
great lord—Sir Walter writes his in order that he may be
able to treat his people as a great lord ought to do."

Lest I should forget to mention it, I put down here a
rebuke which, later in his life, Sir Walter once gave in my
hearing to his daughter Anne. She happened to say of
something, I forget what, that she could not abide it—it
was *vulgar*. " My love," said her father, " you speak
like a very young lady; do you know, after all, the meaning of this word *vulgar*? 'Tis only *common*; nothing that
is common, except wickedness, can deserve to be spoken
of in a tone of contempt; and when you have lived to my
years, you will be disposed to agree with me in thanking
God that nothing really worth having or caring about in
this world is *uncommon*."

Miss Edgeworth, her sister Harriet, and her brother
William, were easily persuaded to join our party for the
rest of our Irish travels. We were anxious to make the
best of our way to the Lakes of Killarney; but posting
was not to be very rapidly accomplished in those regions
by so large a company as had now collected—and we were
more agreeably delayed by the hospitalities of Miss Edgeworth's old friends, and Sir Walter's new ones, at various
mansions on our line of route—of which I must note
especially Judge Moore's, at Lamberton, near Mary-
borough, because Sir Walter pronounced its beneficence
to be even beyond the usual Irish scale; for, on reaching
our next halting place, which was an indifferent country
inn, we discovered that we need be in no alarm as to our
dinner at all events, the Judge's people having privately
packed up in one of the carriages a pickled salmon, a
most lordly venison pasty, and half-a-dozen bottles of
champagne. But most of these houses seemed, like the
Judge's, to have been constructed on the principle of the
Peri Banou's tent. They seemed to have room not only
for the lion and lioness, and their respective tails, but for
all in the neighbourhood who could be held worthy to
inspect them at feeding-time.

It was a succession of festive gaiety wherever we halted;
and in the course of our movements we saw many castles,
churches, and ruins of all sorts—with more than enough
of mountain, wood, lake, and river, to have made a similar
progress in perhaps any other part of Europe truly

delightful. But those to whom the south of Ireland was new had almost continually before them spectacles of abject misery, which robbed these things of more than half their charm. Sir Walter, indeed, with the habitual hopefulness of his temper, persisted that what he saw even in Kerry was better than what books had taught him to expect; and insured, therefore, that improvement, however slow, was going on. But, ever and anon, as we moved deeper into the country, there was a melancholy in his countenance, and, despite himself, in the tone of his voice, which I for one could not mistake. The constant passings and repassings of bands of mounted policemen, armed to the teeth, and having quite the air of highly disciplined soldiers on sharp service;—the rueful squalid poverty that crawled by every way-side, and blocked up every village where we had to change horses, with exhibitions of human suffering and degradation, such as it had never entered into our heads to conceive;—and, above all, the contrast between these naked clamorous beggars, who seemed to spring out of the ground at every turn like swarms of vermin, and the boundless luxury and merriment surrounding the thinly scattered magnates who condescended to inhabit their ancestral seats, would have been sufficient to poison those landscapes, had nature dressed them out in the verdure of Arcadia, and art embellished them with all the temples and palaces of Old Rome and Athens. It is painful enough even to remember such things; but twenty years can have had but a trifling change in the appearance of a country which, so richly endowed by Providence with every element of wealth and happiness, could, at so advanced a period of European civilisation, sicken the heart of the stranger by such wide-spread manifestations of the wanton and reckless profligacy of human mis-management, the withering curse of feuds and factions, and the tyrannous selfishness of absenteeism; and I fear it is not likely that any contemporary critic will venture to call my melancholy picture overcharged. A few blessed exceptions—such an aspect of ease and decency, for example, as we met everywhere on the vast domain of the Duke of Devonshire—served only to make the sad reality of the rule more flagrant and appalling.

There were, however, abundance of ludicrous incidents to break this gloom; and no traveller ever tasted either the humours or the blunders of Paddy more heartily than

did Sir Walter.   I find recorded in one letter a very merry
morning at Limerick, where, amidst the ringing of all the
bells, in honour of the advent, there was ushered in a
brother-poet, who must needs pay his personal respects to
the author of Marmion.   He was a scarecrow figure—by
name O'Kelly; and he had produced on the spur of the
occasion this modest parody of Dryden's famous epigram :—

> " Three poets, of three different nations born,
>   The United Kingdom in this age adorn ;
>   Byron of England, Scott of Scotia's blood,
>   And Erin's pride—O'Kelly great and good."

Sir Walter's five shillings were at once forthcoming ; and
the bard, in order that Miss Edgeworth might display
equal generosity, pointed out, in a little volume of his
works (for which, moreover, we had all to subscribe), this
pregnant couplet—

> " Scott, Morgan, Edgeworth, Byron, prop of Greece,
>   Are characters whose fame not soon will cease."

We were still more amused (though there was real
misery in the case) with what befell on our approach to a
certain pretty seat, in a different county, where there was
a collection of pictures and curiosities not usually shewn
to travellers.   A gentleman, whom we had met in Dublin,
had been accompanying us part of the day's journey, and
volunteered, being acquainted with the owner, to procure
us easy admission.   At the entrance of the domain, to
which we proceeded under his wing, we were startled by
the dolorous apparition of two undertaker's men,   in
voluminous black scarfs, though there was little or nothing
of black about the rest of their habiliments, who sat upon
the highway before the gate, with a whisky-bottle on a
deal-table between them.   They informed us that the
master of the house had died the day before, and that they
were to keep watch and ward in this style until the
funeral, inviting all Christian passengers to drink a glass
to his repose.   Our cicerone left his card for the widow—
having previously, no doubt, written on it the names of
his two lions.   Shortly after we regained our post-house,
he received a polite answer from the lady.   To the best of
my memory it was in these terms :—" Mrs. —— presents
her kind compliments to Mr. ——, and much regrets that
she cannot shew the pictures to-day, as Major —— died

yesterday evening by apoplexy; which Mrs. —— the more regrets, as it will prevent her having the honour to see Sir Walter Scott and Miss Edgeworth.'' Sir Walter said it reminded him of a woman in Fife, who, summing up the misfortunes of a black year in her history, said—'' Let me see, sirs; first we lost our wee callant—and then Jenny—and then the gudeman himsel died—and then the *coo* died too, poor hizzey; but, to be sure, *her* hide brought me fifteen shillings.''

At one county gentleman's table where we dined, though two grand full-length daubs of William and Mary adorned the walls of the room, there was a mixed company—about as many Catholics as Protestants, all apparently on cordial terms, and pledging each other lustily in bumpers of capital claret. About an hour after dinner, however, punch was called for; tumblers and jugs of hot water appeared, and with them two magnums of whisky—the one bearing on its label King's, the other Queen's. We did not at first understand these inscriptions; but it was explained, *sotto voce*, that the King's had paid the duty, the Queen's was of contraband origin; and, in the choice of liquors, we detected a new shibboleth of party. The jolly Protestants to a man stuck to the King's bottle— the equally radiant Papists paid their duty to the Queen's.

Since I have alluded at all to the then grand dispute, I may mention, that, after our tour was concluded, we considered with some wonder that, having partaken liberally of Catholic hospitality, and encountered almost every other class of society, we had not sat at meat with one specimen of the Romish priesthood; whereas, even at Popish tables, we had met dignitaries of the Established Church. This circumstance we set down at the time as amounting pretty nearly to a proof that there were few gentlemen in that order; but we afterwards were willing to suspect that a prejudice of their own had been the source of it. The only incivility, which Sir Walter Scott ultimately discovered himself to have encountered—(for his friends did not allow him to hear of it at the time)—in the course of his Irish peregrination, was the refusal of a Roman Catholic gentleman, named O'Connell, who kept staghounds near Killarney, to allow of a hunt on the upper lake, the day he visited that beautiful scenery. This he did, as we were told, because he considered it as a notorious fact, that Sir Walter Scott was an enemy to the

Roman Catholic claims for admission to seats in Parliament. He was entirely mistaken, however; for, though no man disapproved of Romanism as a system of faith and practice more sincerely than Sir Walter always did, he had long before this period formed the opinion, that no good could come of farther resistance to the claim in question. He on all occasions expressed manfully his belief, that the best thing for Ireland would have been never to relax the strictly *political* enactments of the penal laws, however harsh these might appear. Had they been kept in vigour for another half century, it was his conviction that Popery would have been all but extinguished in Ireland. But he thought that, after admitting Romanists to the elective franchise, it was a vain notion that they could be permanently or advantageously debarred from using that franchise in favour of those of their own persuasion. The greater part of the charming society into which he fell while in Ireland entertained views and sentiments very likely to confirm these impressions; and it struck me that considerable pains were taken to enforce them. It was felt, probably, that the crisis of decision drew near; and there might be a natural anxiety to secure the suffrage of the great writer of the time.

Having crossed the hills from Killarney to Cork, where a repetition of the Dublin reception—corporation honours, deputations of the literary and scientific societies, and so forth—awaited him, he gave a couple of days to the hospitality of this flourishing town, and the beautiful scenery of the Lee; not forgetting an excursion to the groves of Blarney, among whose shades we had a right mirthful picnic. Sir Walter scrambled up to the top of the castle, and kissed, with due faith and devotion, the famous *Blarney stone*, one salute of which is said to emancipate the pilgrim from all future visitations of *mauvaise honte* :

> " The stone this is, whoever kisses,
>   He never misses to grow eloquent—
> 'Tis he may clamber to a lady's chamber,
>   Or be a member of Parliament."

From Cork we proceeded to Dublin by Fermoy, Lismore, Cashel, Kilkenny, and Holycross—at all of which places we were bountifully entertained, and assiduously ciceroned—to our old quarters in St. Stephen's Green; and after a morning or two spent in taking leave of many kind faces that he was never to see again, Sir Walter and his

original fellow-travellers started for Holyhead on the 18th
of August.   Our progress through North Wales produced
nothing worth recording, except perhaps the feeling of delight which everything in the aspect of the common people,
their dress, their houses, their gardens, and their husbandry, could not fail to call up in persons who had just been
seeing Ireland for the first time.   Scott had, while at
Edgeworthstown, been requested by Mr. Canning to meet
him at his friend Mr. Bolton's, on Windermere.   On
reaching that lake, we spent a pleasant day with Professor
Wilson at Elleray, and he then conducted us to Storrs.   A
large company had been assembled there in honour of the
Minister—among others was Mr. Wordsworth.   It has
not, I suppose, often happened, to a plain English merchant, wholly the architect of his own fortunes, to entertain at one time a party embracing so many illustrious
names.   He was proud of his guests; they respected him,
and honoured and loved each other; and it would have
been difficult to say which star in the constellation shone
with the brightest or the softest light.   There was " high
discourse," intermingled with as gay flashings of courtly
wit as ever Canning displayed; and a plentiful allowance,
on all sides, of those airy transient pleasantries, in which
the fancy of poets, however wise and grave, delights to
run riot when they are sure not to be misunderstood.
There were beautiful and accomplished women to adorn
and enjoy this circle.   The weather was as Elysian as the
scenery.   There were brilliant cavalcades through the
woods in the mornings, and delicious boatings on the
lake by moonlight; and the last day, " the Admiral of the
Lake " presided over one of the most splendid regattas
that ever enlivened Windermere.   Perhaps there were not
fewer than fifty barges following in the Professor's radiant
procession, when it paused at the point of Storrs to admit
into the place of honour the vessel that carried kind and
happy Mr. Bolton and his guests.   The bards of the Lakes
led the cheers that hailed Scott and Canning; and music
and sunshine, flags, streamers, and gay dresses, the
merry hum of voices, and the rapid splashing of innumerable oars, made up a dazzling mixture of sensations as the
flotilla wound its way among the richly-foliaged islands,
and along bays and promontories peopled with enthusiastic spectators.
     On at last quitting Storrs, we visited Mr. Wordsworth

at his charming retreat of Mount Rydal : and he thence accompanied us to Keswick, where we saw Mr. Southey in his unrivalled library. Mr. Wordsworth and his daughter then turned with us, and passing over Kirkstone to Ulls-water, conducted us first to his friend Mr. Marshall's elegant villa, near Lyulph's Tower, and on the next day to the noble castle of his lifelong friend and patron Lord Lonsdale. The Earl and Countess had their halls filled with another splendid circle of distinguished persons. Sir Walter remained a couple of days, and perambulated, under Wordsworth's guidance, the superb terraces and groves of the " fair domain " which that poet has connected with the noblest monument of his genius. He reached Abotsford again on the 1st of September, and said truly that " his tour had been one ovation."

Without an hour's delay he resumed his usual habits of life—the musing ramble among his own glens, the breezy ride over the moors, the merry spell at the woodman's axe, or the festive chase of Newark, Fernilee, Hanging-shaw, or Deloraine; the quiet old-fashioned contentment of the little domestic circle, alternating with the brilliant phantasmagoria of admiring, and sometimes admired, strangers—or the hoisting of the telegraph flag that called laird and bonnet-laird to the burning of the water, or the wassail of the hall. The hours of the closet alone had found a change. The preparation for the Life of Napoleon was a course of such hard reading as had not been called for while " the great magician," in the full sunshine of ease, amused himself, and delighted the world, by un-rolling, fold after fold, his endlessly varied panorama of romance. That miracle had to all appearance cost him no effort. Unmoved and serene among the multiplicities of worldly business, and the invasions of half Europe and America, he had gone on tranquilly enjoying, rather than exerting his genius, in the production of those master-pieces which have peopled all our firesides with inexpensive friends, and rendered the solitary supremacy of Shak-speare, as an all-comprehensive and genial painter of man, no longer a proverb.

He had, while this was the occupation of his few desk-hours, read only for his diversion. How much he read even then, his correspondence may have afforded some notion. Those who observed him the most constantly were never able to understand how he contrived to keep himself so thoroughly up with the stream of contemporary literature of almost all sorts, French and German, as well as English. That a rapid glance might tell him more than another man could gather by a week's poring may easily be guessed; but the grand secret was his perpetual practice of his own grand maxim, *never to be doing nothing.* He had no "unconsidered trifles" of time. Every moment was turned to account; and thus he had leisure for everything—except, indeed, the newspapers, which consume so many precious hours now-a-days with most men, and of which, during the period of my acquaintance with him, he certainly read less than any other man I ever knew that had any habit of reading at all. I should also except, speaking generally, the Reviews and Magazines of the time. Of these he saw few, and of the few he read little.

He had now to apply himself doggedly to the mastering of a huge accumulation of historical materials. He read, and noted, and indexed with the pertinacity of some pale compiler in the British Museum; but rose from such employment, not radiant and buoyant, as after he had been feasting himself among the teeming harvests of Fancy, but with an aching brow, and eyes on which the dimness of years had begun to plant some specks, before they were subjected again to that straining over small print and difficult manuscript which had, no doubt, been familiar to them in the early time, when in (Shortreed's phrase) "he was making himself." It was a pleasant sight when one happened to take a passing peep into his den, to see the white head erect, and the smile of conscious inspiration on his lips, while the pen, held boldly, and at a commanding distance, glanced steadily and gaily along a fast-blackening page of "The Talisman." It now often made me sorry to catch a glimpse of him, stooping and poring with his spectacles, amidst piles of authorities—a little note-book ready in the left hand, that had always used to be at liberty for patting Maida.

About this time, being again a traveller, I lost the opportunity of witnessing his reception of several eminent persons;—among others the late admirable Master of the Rolls, Lord Gifford, and his Lady; Dr. Philpotts, now Bishop of Exeter; and Mr. Thomas Moore. This last fortunately found Sir Walter in an interval of repose—no

one with him at Abbotsford but Lady and Miss Scott—
and no company at dinner except the Fergussons and
Laidlaw. The two poets had thus the opportunity of a
great deal of quiet conversation; and from the hour they
met, they seemed to have treated each other with a full
confidence, the record of which, however touchingly
honourable to both, could hardly be made public *in extenso*
while one of them survives. The first day they were alone
after dinner, and the talk turned chiefly on the recent death
of Byron—from which Scott passed unaffectedly to his
own literary history. Mr. Moore listened with great
interest to details, now no longer new, about the early
days of Mat Lewis, the Minstrelsy, and the Poems; and
" at last," says he, " to my no small surprise, as well as
pleasure, he mentioned the novels, without any reserve, as
his own. He gave me an account of the original progress
of those extraordinary works, the hints supplied for them,
the conjectures and mystification to which they had given
rise, &c., &c. ": he concluded with saying, " they have
been a mine of wealth to me—but I find I fail in them now
—I can no longer make them so good as at first." This
frankness was met as it should have been by the brother
poet; and when he entered Scott's room next morning, " he
laid his hand," says Mr. Moore, " with a sort of cordial
earnestness on my breast, and said—*Now, my dear Moore,
we are friends for life.*" They sallied out for a walk
through the plantations, and among other things, the com-
monness of the poetic talent in these days was alluded to.
" Hardly a Magazine is now published," said Moore,
" that does not contain verses which some thirty years
ago would have made a reputation."—Scott turned with
his look of shrewd humour, as if chuckling over his own
success, and said, " Ecod, we were in the luck of it to
come before these fellows "; but he added, playfully
flourishing his stick as he spoke, " we have, like Bobadil,
taught them to beat us with our own weapons."—" In
complete novelty," says Moore, " he seemed to think,
lay the only chance for a man ambitious of high literary
reputation in these days."

Moore says—" I parted from Scott with the feeling that
all the world might admire him in his works, but that
those only could learn to love him as he deserved who had
seen him at Abbotsford. I give you *carte blanche*, to say
what you please of my sense of his cordial kindness and

gentleness; perhaps not a very dignified phrase would express my feeling better than any fine one—it was that he was a *thorough good fellow.*" What Scott thought of his guest appears from this entry in a private note-book :—
" Tom Moore's is the most exquisite warbling I ever heard. . . . There is a manly frankness, with perfect ease and good-breeding, about him, which is delightful. Not the least touch of the poet or the pedant. A little—very little man—less, I think, than Lewis, and something like him in person; God knows, not in conversation, for Mat, though a clever fellow, was a bore of the first description. Moreover, he looked always like a schoolboy. Now Moore has none of this insignificance. His countenance is plain, but the expression so very animated, especially in speaking or singing, that it is far more interesting than the finest features could have rendered it. I was aware that Byron had often spoken of Moore and myself in the same breath, and with the same sort of regard; so I was curious to see what there could be in common betwixt us, Moore having lived so much in the gay world, I in the country, and with people of business, and sometimes with politicians; Moore a scholar, I none; he a musician and artist, I without knowledge of a note; he a democrat, I an aristocrat—with many other points of difference; besides his being an Irishman, I a Scotchman, and both tolerably national. Yet there is a point of resemblance, and a strong one. We are both good-humoured fellows, who rather seek to enjoy what is going forward than to maintain our dignity as Lions; and we have both seen the world too widely and too well not to contemn in our souls the imaginary consequence of literary people, who walk with their noses in the air, and remind me always of the fellow whom Johnson met in an alehouse, and who called himself ' *the great Twalmly—inventor of the flood-gate iron for smoothing linen.*' He also enjoys the *mot pour rire*, and so do I."

The author of Lalla Rookh's Kelso chaise was followed before many days by a more formidable equipage. The much-talked-of lady who began life as Miss Harriet Mellon, a comic actress in a provincial troupe, and died Duchess of St. Albans, was then making a tour in Scotland as Mrs. Coutts, the enormously wealthy widow of the first English banker of his time. No person of such consequence could, in those days, have thought a Scotch progress complete, unless it included a reception at Abbotsford; but Mrs. Coutts had been previously acquainted with Sir Walter, who indeed had some remote connection with her late husband's family, through the Stuarts of Allanbank. He had visited her occasionally in London during Mr. Coutts's life, and was very willing to do the honours of Teviotdale in return. But although she was considerate enough not to come on him with all her retinue (leaving four of the seven carriages with which she travelled at Edinburgh), the appearance of only three coaches, each drawn by four horses, was rather trying for poor Lady Scott. They contained Mrs. Coutts—her future lord the Duke of St. Albans—one of his Grace's sisters—a *dame de compagnie*—a brace of physicians—for it had been considered that one doctor might himself be disabled in the course of an expedition so adventurous—and, besides other menials of every grade, two bedchamber women for Mrs. Coutts's own person; she requiring to have this article also in duplicate, because, in her widowed condition, she was fearful of ghosts—and there must be one Abigail for the service of the toilette, a second to keep watch by night. With a little puzzling and cramming, all this train found accommodation;—but it so happened that there were already in the house several ladies, Scotch and English, of high birth and rank, who felt by no means disposed to assist their host and hostess in making Mrs. Coutts's visit agreeable to her. I need not observe how effectually women of fashion can contrive to mortify, without doing or saying anything that shall expose them to the charge of actual incivility.

Sir Walter, during dinner, did everything in his power to counteract this influence of *the evil eye*, and something to overawe it;—but the spirit of mischief had been fairly stirred, and it was easy to see that Mrs. Coutts followed these noble dames to the drawing-room in by no means that complacent mood which was customarily sustained, doubtless, by every blandishment of obsequious flattery, in this mistress of millions. He cut the gentlemen's sederunt short, and soon after joining the ladies, managed to withdraw the youngest, and gayest, and cleverest, who was also the highest in rank (the late Marchioness of Northampton), into his armorial-hall adjoining. " I said to her " (he told me), " I want to speak a word with you about Mrs. Coutts;—we have known each other a good while, and I

know you won't take anything I can say in ill part. It is,
I hear, not uncommon among the fine ladies in London to
be very well pleased to accept invitations, and even sometimes to hunt after them, to Mrs. Coutts's grand balls
and fêtes, and then, if they meet her in any private circle,
to practise on her the delicate *manœuvre* called *tipping the
cold shoulder*. This you agree with me is shabby; but it
is nothing new either to you or to me, that fine people will
do shabbiness for which beggars might blush, if they
once stoop so low as to poke for tickets. I am sure you
would not for the world do such a thing; but you must
permit me to take the great liberty of saying, that I think
the style you have all received my guest Mrs. Coutts in,
this evening, is, to a certain extent, a sin of the same
order. You were all told a couple of days ago that I had
accepted her visit, and that she would arrive to-day to
stay three nights. Now if any of you had not been disposed to be of my party at the same time with her, there
was plenty of time for you to have gone away before she
came; and as none of you moved, and it was impossible
to fancy that any of you would remain out of mere
curiosity, I thought I had a perfect right to calculate on
your having made up your minds to help me out with her.''
Lady Northampton (who had been his ward) answered—
'' I thank you, Sir Walter;—you have done me the great
honour to speak as if I had been your daughter, and depend upon it you shall be obeyed with heart and good
will.'' One by one, the other exclusives were seen
engaged in a little *tête-à-tête* with her ladyship. Sir
Walter was soon satisfied that things had been put into a
right train; the Marchioness was requested to sing a
particular song, *because* he thought it would please Mrs.
Coutts. '' Nothing could gratify her more than to please
Mrs. Coutts.'' Mrs. Coutts's brow smoothed, and in the
course of half an hour she was as happy and easy as ever
she was in her life, rattling away at comical anecdotes of
her early theatrical years, and joining in the chorus of Sir
Adam's *Laird of Cockpen*. She stayed out her three
days [1]—saw, accompanied by all the circle, Melrose, Dryburgh, and Yarrow—and left Abbotsford delighted with
her host, and, to all appearance, with his other guests.

[1] Sir Walter often quoted the maxim of an old lady in one of
Miss Ferrier's novels—that a visit should never exceed three days,
'' the *rest* day—the *drest* day—and the *prest* day.''

It may be said (for the most benevolent of men had in his lifetime, and still has, some maligners) that he was so anxious about Mrs. Coutts's comfort, because he worshipped wealth. I dare not deny that he set more of his affections, during great part of his life, upon worldly things, wealth among others, than might have become such an intellect. One may conceive a sober grandeur of mind, not incompatible with genius as rich as even his, but infinitely more admirable than any genius, incapable of brooding upon any of the pomps and vanities of this life—or caring about money at all, beyond what is necessary, for the easy sustenance of nature. But we must, in judging the most powerful of minds, take into account the influences to which they were exposed in the plastic period; and where imagination is visibly the predominant faculty, allowance must be made very largely indeed. Scott's autobiographical fragment, and the anecdotes annexed to it, have been printed in vain, if they have not conveyed the notion of such a training of the mind, fancy, and character, as could hardly fail to suggest dreams and aspirations very likely, were temptation presented, to take the shape of active external ambition—to prompt a keen pursuit of those resources, without which visions of worldly splendour cannot be realised. But I think the subsequent narrative and his own correspondence must also have satisfied every candid reader that his appetite for wealth was after all essentially a vivid yearning for the means of large beneficence. As to his being capable of the silliness—to say nothing of the meanness—of allowing any part of his feelings or demeanour towards others to be affected by their mere possession of wealth, I cannot consider such a suggestion as worthy of much remark. He had a kindness towards Mrs. Coutts, because he knew that, vain and pompous as her displays of equipage and attendance might be, she mainly valued wealth, like himself, as the instrument of doing good. Even of her apparently most fantastic indulgences he remembered, as Pope did when ridiculing the " lavish cost and little skill " of his Timon,

" Yet hence the poor are clothed, the hungry fed ";

but he interfered, to prevent her being made uncomfortable in his house, neither more nor less than he would have done, had she come there in her original character of a comic actress, and been treated with coldness as such by his Marchionesses and Countesses.

Since I have been led to touch on what many always considered as the weak part of his character—his over respect for worldly things in general,—I must say one word as to the matter of rank, which undoubtedly had far more effect on him than money. In the first place, he was all along courted by the great world—not it by him; and, secondly, pleased as he was with its attentions, he derived infinitely greater pleasure from the trusting and hearty affection of his old equals, and the inferiors whose welfare he so unweariedly promoted. But, thirdly, he made acute discriminations among the many different orders of claimants who jostle each other for pre-eminence in the curiously complicated system of modern British society. His imagination had been constantly exercised in recalling and embellishing whatever features of the past it was possible to connect with any pleasing ideas, and a historical name was a charm that literally stirred his blood. But not so a mere title. He reverenced the Duke of Buccleuch—but it was not as a Duke, but as the head of his clan, the representative of the old knights of Branxholm. In the Duke of Hamilton he saw not the premier peer of Scotland, but the lineal heir of the heroic old Douglasses; and he had profounder respect for the chief of a Highland Clan, without any title whatever, and with an ill-paid rental of two or three thousand a year, than for the haughtiest magnate in a blue ribbon, whose name did not call up any grand historical reminiscence. I remember once when he had some young Englishmen of high fashion in his house, there arrived a Scotch gentleman of no distinguished appearance, whom he received with a sort of eagernes and *empressement* of reverential courtesy that struck the strangers as quite out of common. His name was that of a Scotch Earl, however, and no doubt he was that nobleman's son. "Well," said one of the Southrons to me,—"I had never heard that the Earl of —— was one of your very greatest lords in this country; even a second son of his, booby though he be, seems to be of wonderful consideration." The young English lord heard with some surprise, that the visitor in question was a poor lieutenant on half-pay, heir to a tower, about as crazy as Don Quixote's, and noways related (at least according to English notions of relationship) to the Earl

of ——. " What, then," he cried, " what *can* Sir Walter
mean? " " Why," said I, " his meaning is very clear.
This gentleman is the male representative (which the Earl
of —— may possibly be in the female line) of a knight
who is celebrated by our old poet Blind Harry, as having
signalised himself by the side of Sir William Wallace, and
from whom every Scotchman that bears the name of ——
has at least the ambition of being supposed to descend."—
Sir Walter's own title came unsought; and that he accepted it, not in the foolish fancy that such a title, or any
title, could increase his own personal consequence, but
because he thought it fair to embrace the opportunity of
securing a certain external distinction to his heirs at
Abbotsford, was proved pretty clearly by his subsequently
declining the greatly higher, but intransmissible rank of
a Privy Councillor. At the same time, I dare say his ear
liked the knightly sound; and undoubtedly, he was much
pleased with the pleasure his wife took, and gaily
acknowledged she took, in being My Lady.

The circumstances of the King's visit in 1822, and
others already noted, leave no doubt that imagination
enlarged and glorified for him many objects to which it is
very difficult for ordinary men in our generation to attach
much importance; and perhaps he was more apt to attach
importance to such things, during the prosperous course
of his own fortunes, than even a liberal consideration of
circumstances can altogether excuse. To myself it seems to
have been so; yet I do not think the severe critics on this
part of his story have kept quite sufficiently in mind how
easy it is for us all to undervalue any species of temptation to which we have not happened to be exposed. I am
aware, too, that there are examples of men of genius,
situated to a certain extent like him, who have resisted
and repelled the fascinations against which he was not
entirely proof; but I have sometimes thought that they
did so at the expense of parts of their character nearer the
marrow of humanity than those which his weakness in
this way tended to endamage; that they mingled, in short,
in their virtuous self-denial, some grains of sacrifice at
the shrine of a cold, unsocial, even sulky species of self-
conceit. But this digression has already turned out
much longer than I intended. It is time to open occurrences which contrast sadly with the summer scenes of
1825.

Towards the end of September I returned to Scotland from a visit to London on some personal business. During that visit I had heard a great deal more than I understood about the commercial excitement of the time. There had been several years of extravagant speculation. Even persons who had extensive and flourishing businesses in their hands, partook the general rage of infatuation. He whose own shop, counting-house, or warehouse, had been sufficient to raise him to a decent and safely-increasing opulence, and was more than sufficient to occupy all his attention, drank in the vain delusion that he was wasting his time and energy on things unworthy of a masculine ambition, and embarked the resources necessary for the purposes of his lawful calling in schemes worthy of the land-surveyors of El Dorado. It was whispered that *the trade* (so called, *par excellence*) had been bitten with this fever; and persons of any foresight who knew the infinitely curious links by which booksellers, and printers, and paper-makers (and therefore authors) are bound together, for good and for evil, already began to prophesy that, whenever the general crash, which must come ere long, should arrive, its effects would be felt far and wide among all classes connected with the productions of the press. When it was rumoured that this great bookseller, or printer, had become a principal holder of South American mining shares—that another was the leading director of a gas company—while a third house had risked about £100,000 in a cast upon the most capricious of all agricultural products, *hops*—it was no wonder that bankers should begin to calculate balances, and pause upon discounts.

Among other hints were some concerning a bookselling establishment in London, with which I knew Constable to be closely connected. Little suspecting the extent to which any mischance of Messrs. Hurst and Robinson must involve Sir Walter's own responsibilities, I transmitted to him the rumours in question. Before I could have his answer, a legal friend told me that people were talking doubtfully about Constable's own stability. I thought it probable, that if Constable fell into any embarrassments, Scott might suffer the inconvenience of losing the copy-money of his last novel. Nothing more serious occurred to me. But I thought it my duty to tell him this whisper also; and heard from him, almost by return of post, that, shake who might in London, his friend in Edinburgh was " rooted, as well as branched, like the oak."

A few days, however, after my arrival at Chiefswood, I received a letter from the legal friend already alluded to —(Mr. William Wright, the eminent barrister of Lincoln's Inn,—who, by the way, was also on habits of great personal familiarity with Constable, and liked *the Czar* exceedingly)—which renewed my apprehensions, or rather, for the first time, gave me any suspicion that there really might be something " rotten in the state of *Muscovy*." Mr. Wright informed me that it was reported in London that Constable's London banker had thrown up his book. This letter reaching me about five o'clock, I rode over to Abbotsford, and found Sir Walter alone over his glass of whisky and water and cigar—at this time, whenever there was no company, " his custom always in the afternoon." I gave him Mr. Wright's letter to read. He did so, and returning it said, quite with his usual tranquil good-humour of look and voice, " I am much obliged to you for coming over; but you may rely upon it Wright has been hoaxed. I promise you, were the Crafty's book thrown up, there would be a pretty decent scramble among the bankers for the keeping of it. There may have been some little dispute or misunderstanding, which malice and envy have exaggerated in this absurd style; but I shan't allow such nonsense to disturb my *siesta*."

Seeing how coolly he treated my news, I went home relieved and gratified. Next morning, as I was rising, behold Peter Mathieson at my door, his horses evidently off a journey, and the Sheriff rubbing his eyes as if the halt had shaken him out of a sound sleep. I made what haste I could to descend, and found him by the side of the brook looking somewhat worn, but with a serene and satisfied countenance, busied already in helping his little grandson to feed a fleet of ducklings.—" You are surprised," he said, " to see me here. The truth is, I was more taken aback with Wright's epistle than I cared *to let on*; and so, as soon as you left me, I ordered the carriage to the door, and never stopped till I got to Polton, where I found Constable putting on his nightcap. I stayed an hour with him, and I have now the pleasure to tell you that *all is right*. There was not a word of truth in the story—he is fast as Ben Lomond; and as Mamma and Anne did not know what my errand was, I thought it as well to come and breakfast here, and set Sophia and you at your ease before I went home again."

We had a merry breakfast, and he chatted gaily afterwards as I escorted him through his woods, leaning on my shoulder all the way, which he seldom as yet did, except with Tom Purdie, unless when he was in a more than commonly happy and affectionate mood. But I confess the impression this incident left on my mind was not a pleasant one. It was then that I first began to harbour a suspicion, that if anything should befall Constable, Sir Walter would suffer a heavier loss than the non-payment of some one novel. The night journey revealed serious alarm. My wife suggested, as we talked things over, that his alarm had been, not on his own account, but Ballantyne's, who, in case evil came on the great employer of his types, might possibly lose a year's profit on them, which neither she nor I doubted must amount to a large sum—any more than that a misfortune of Ballantyne's would grieve her father as much as one personal to himself. His warm regard for his printer could be no secret; we well knew that James was his confidential critic—his trusted and trustworthy friend from boyhood. Nor was I ignorant that Scott had a share in the property of Ballantyne's Edinburgh Weekly Journal. That had been commonly reported before I was acquainted with them; and all doubt was removed at the time of the Queen's trial in 1820, when they had some warm debates in my presence as to the side to be taken on that unhappy question. But that Sir Walter was, and had all along been James's partner in the great printing concern, neither I, nor, I believe, any member of his family, had entertained the slightest suspicion prior to the coming calamities which were now "casting their shadows before."

It is proper to add here, that the story about the banker's throwing up Constable's book was groundless. Sir Walter's first guess as to its origin proved correct.

A few days afterwards, Mr. Murray sent me a transcript of Lord Byron's Ravenna Diary, with permission for my neighbour also to read it if he pleased. Sir Walter read those extraordinary pages with the liveliest interest, and filled several of the blank leaves and margins with illustrative annotations and anecdotes. In perusing what Byron had jotted down from day to day in the intervals of regular composition, it very naturally occurred to him that the noble poet had done well to avoid troubling himself by any adoption or affectation of plan or order—giving an opinion, a reflection, a reminiscence, serious or comic, or the incidents of the passing hour, just as the spirit moved him;—and seeing what a mass of curious things, such as " after times would not willingly let die," had been thus rescued from oblivion at a very slight cost of exertion,—he resolved to attempt keeping thenceforth a somewhat similar record. A thick quarto volume, bound in vellum, with a lock and key, was forthwith procured. The occupation of a few stray minutes in his dressing-room at getting up in the morning, or after he had retired for the night, was found a pleasant variety for him. He also kept the book by him when in his study, and often had recourse to it when anything puzzled him and called for a halt in the prosecution of what he considered (though posterity will hardly do so) a more important task. It was extremely fortunate that he took up this scheme exactly at the time when he settled seriously to the history of Buonaparte's personal career. The sort of preparation which every chapter of that book now called for has been already alluded to; and although, when he had fairly read himself up to any one great cycle of transactions, his old spirit roused itself in full energy, and he traced the record with as rapid and glowing a pencil as he had ever wielded —there were minutes enough, and hours,—possibly days of weariness, depression, and languor, when (unless this silent confidant had been at hand) even he perhaps might have made no use of his writing-desk.

Even the new resource of journalising, however, was not sufficient. He soon convinced himself that it would facilitate, not impede, his progress with Napoleon, to have a work of imagination in hand also. The success of the Tales of the Crusaders had been very high; and Constable, well aware that it had been his custom of old to carry on two romances at the same time, was now too happy to encourage him in beginning *Woodstock*, to be taken up whenever the historical MS. should be in advance of the press.

Thenceforth, as the Dairy shews, he continued to divide his usual desk-hours accordingly: but before he had filled many pages of the private quarto, it begins to record alarm—from day to day deepening—as to Constable, and the extent to which the great publisher's affairs had by degrees come to be connected and bound up with those of the printing firm.

Till John Ballantyne's death, as already intimated, the pecuniary management of that firm had been wholly in his hands. Of his conduct in such business I need add no more : the burden had since been on his surviving brother; and I am now obliged to say that, though his deficiencies were of a very different sort from John's, they were, as respected his commercial career and connections, great and unfortunate.

He had received the education, not of a printer, but of a solicitor; and he never, to his dying day, had the remotest knowledge or feeling of what the most important business of a master-printer consists in. He had a fine taste for the effect of types—no establishment turned out more beautiful specimens of the art than his; but he appears never to have understood that types need watching as well as setting. If the page looked handsome, he was satisfied. He had been instructed that on every £50 paid in his men's wages, the master-printer is entitled to an equal sum of gross profit; and beyond this *rule of thumb* calculation, no experience could bring him to penetrate his *mystery*. In a word, James never comprehended that in the greatest and most regularly employed manufactory of this kind (or indeed of any kind) the profits are likely to be entirely swallowed up, unless the acting master keeps up a most wakeful scrutiny, from week to week, and from day to day, as to the machinery and the materials. So far was he from doing this, that during several of the busiest and most important years of his connection with the establishment in the Canongate, he seldom crossed its doors. He sat in his own elbow-chair, in a comfortable library, situated in a different street—not certainly an idle man—quite the reverse, though naturally indolent—but the most negligent and inefficient of master-printers.

He was busy, indeed; and inestimably serviceable to Scott was his labour; but it consisted solely in the correction and revisal of proof-sheets. It is most true, that Sir Walter's hurried method of composition rendered it absolutely necessary that whatever he wrote should be subjected to far more than the usual amount of inspection required at the hands of a printer; and it is equally so, that it would have been extremely difficult to find another man willing and able to bestow such time and care on his proof-sheets as they uniformly received from James. But this was, in fact, not the proper occupation of the man who was at the head of the establishment—who had undertaken the pecuniary management. In every other great printing-house that I have known anything about, there are intelligent and well-educated men, called, technically, *readers*, who devote themselves to this species of labour, and who are, I fear, seldom paid in proportion to its importance. Dr. Goldsmith, in his early life, was such a *reader* in the printing-house of Richardson; but the author of Clarissa did not disdain to look after the presses and types himself, or he would never have accumulated the fortune that enabled him to be the liberal employer of *readers* like Goldsmith. In a letter addressed to John Ballantyne, when the bookselling house was breaking up, Scott says,— " One or other of you will need to be constantly in the printing-office *henceforth*; it is the sheet anchor." This was *ten* years after that establishment began. Thenceforth James, in compliance with this injunction, occupied, during many hours of every day, a cabinet within the premises in the Canongate; but whoever visited him there, found him at the same eternal business, that of a literator, not that of a printer. He was either editing his newspaper —or correcting sheets, or writing critical notes to the Author of Waverley. Shakspeare, Addison, Johnson, and Burke, were at his elbow; but not the ledger. We may thus understand poor John's complaint, in what I may call his dying memorandum, of the " large sums abstracted from the bookselling house for the use of the printing-office." Yet that bookselling house was from the first a hopeless one; whereas, under accurate superintendence, the other ought to have produced the partners a dividend of from £2,000 to £3,000 a year, at the very least.

On the other hand, the necessity of providing some remedy for this radical disorder must very soon have forced itself upon the conviction of all concerned, had not John introduced his fatal enlightenment on the subject of facilitating discounts, and raising cash by means of accommodation-bills. Hence the perplexed *states* and *calendars*—the wilderness and labyrinths of ciphers, through which no eye but that of a professed accountant could have betected any clue; hence the accumulation of bills and counter-bills drawn by both bookselling and printing-house, and gradually so mixed up with other obligations, that John died in utter ignorance of the condition of their affairs. The pecuniary detail then devolved upon James; and I fancy it will be only too apparent that he never made even one serious effort to master the formidable array of figures thus committed to his sole trust.

The reader has been enabled to trace from its beginnings the connection between Constable and the two Ballantyne firms. It has been seen how much they both owed to his interference on various occasions of pressure and alarm. But when he, in his overweening self-sufficiency, thought it involved no mighty hazard to indulge his better feelings, as well as his lordly vanity, in shielding these firms from commercial dishonour, he had estimated but loosely the demands of the career of speculation on which he was himself entering. And by and by, when advancing by one mighty plunge after another in that vast field, he felt in his own person the threatenings of more signal ruin than could have befallen them, this " Napoleon of the press "— still as of old buoyed up to the ultimate result of his grand operations by the most fulsome flatteries of imagination— appears to have tossed aside very summarily all scruples about the extent to which he might be entitled to tax their sustaining credit in requital. The Ballantynes, if they had comprehended all the bearings of the case, were not the men to consider grudingly demands of this nature, founded on service so important; and who can doubt that Scott viewed them from a chivalrous altitude? It is easy to see, that the moment the obligations became reciprocal, there arose extreme peril of their coming to be hopelessly complicated. It is equally clear, that Scott ought to have applied on these affairs, as their complication thickened, the acumen which he exerted, and rather prided himself in exerting, on smaller points of worldly business, to the utmost. That he did not, I must always regard as the enigma of his personal history; but various incidents in that history, which I have already narrated, prove incontestably that he had never done so; and I am unable to account for this having been the case, except on the supposition that his confidence in the resources of Constable and the prudence of James Ballantyne was so entire, that he willingly absolved himself from all duty of active and thoroughgoing superinspection.

It is the extent to which the confusion had gone that

constitutes the great puzzle. I have been told that John Ballantyne, in his hey-day, might be heard whistling for his clerk, John Stevenson (often alluded to in Scott's correspondence as *True* Jock), from the *sanctum* behind the shop with, "Jock, you lubber, fetch ben a sheaf o' stamps." Such things might well enough be believed of that hare-brained creature; but how sober solemn James could have made up his mind, as he must have done, to follow much the same wild course whenever any pinch occurred, is to me, I must own, incomprehensible. The books were kept at the printing-house; and of course Sir Walter (who alone in fact had capital at stake) might have there examined them as often as he liked : but it is to me very doubtful if he ever once attempted to do so : and it is certain that they were *never balanced* during the latter years of the connection. During several years it was almost daily my custom to walk home with Sir Walter from the Parliament-House, calling at James's on our way. For the most part I used to amuse myself with a newspaper or proof-sheet in the outer room, while they were closeted in the little cabinet at the corner; and merry were the tones that reached my ear while they remained in colloquy. If I were called in, it was because James, in his ecstasy, must have another to enjoy the dialogue that his friend was improvising—between Meg Dods and Captain MacTurk, for example, or Peter Peebles and his counsel.

The reader may perhaps remember a page in a former chapter where I described Scott as riding with Johnny Ballantyne and myself round the deserted halls of the ancient family of Riddell, and remarking how much it increased the wonder of their ruin that the late baronet had kept "day-book and ledger as regularly as any *cheesemonger in the Grassmarket*." It is nevertheless true, that Sir Walter kept from first to last as accurate an account of his own *personal* expenditure as Sir John Riddell could have done of his extravagant outlay on agricultural experiments. I could, I believe, place before my reader the sum-total of sixpences that it had cost him to ride through turnpike-gates during a period of thirty years. This was, of course, an early habit mechanically adhered to : but how strange that the man who could persist, however mechanically, in noting down every shilling that he actually drew from his purse, should have allowed others to pledge his credit, year after year, upon sheafs of accom-

modation paper, without keeping any efficient watch—
without knowing any one Christmas, for how many thousands he was responsible as *a printer in the Canongate!*

This is sufficiently astonishing—and had this been all,
the result must sooner or later have been sufficiently uncomfortable; but it must be admitted that Scott could
never have foreseen a step which Constable took in the
frenzied excitement of his day of pecuniary alarm. Owing
to the original habitual irregularities of John Ballantyne,
it had been adopted as the regular plan between that
person and Constable, that, whenever the latter signed a
bill for the purpose of the other's raising money among
the bankers, there should, in case of his neglecting to take
that bill up before it fell due, be deposited a counter-bill,
signed by Ballantyne, on which Constable might, if need
were, raise a sum equivalent to that for which he had
pledged his credit. I am told that this is an usual enough
course of procedure among speculative merchants; and
it may be so. But mark the issue. The plan went on
under James's management, just as John had begun it.
Under his management also—such was the incredible
looseness of it—the *counter-bills*, meant only for being
sent into the market in the event of the *primary bills* being
threatened with dishonour—these instruments of safe-
guard for Constable against contingent danger were allowed to lie uninquired about in Constable's desk, until
they had swelled to a truly monstrous "sheaf of stamps."
Constable's hour of distress darkened about him, and he
rushed with these to the money-changers. And thus it
came to pass, that, supposing Ballantyne and Co. to
have at the day of reckoning obligations against them,
in consequence of bill transactions with Constable, to
the extent of £25,000, they were legally responsible
for £50,000.

It is not my business to attempt any detailed history of
the house of Constable. The sanguine man had, almost
at the outset of his career, been "lifted off his feet," in
Burns's phrase, by the sudden and unparalleled success of
the Edinburgh Review. Scott's poetry and Scott's novels
followed: and had he confined himself to those three great
and triumphant undertakings, he must have died in
possession of a princely fortune. But his "appetite grew
with what it fed on," and a long series of less meritorious
publications, pushed on, one after the other, in the craziest

rapidity, swallowed up the gains which, however vast, he never counted, and therefore always exaggerated to himself. Finally, what he had been to the Ballantynes, certain other still more audacious " Sheafmen " had been to him. Hurst, Robinson, and Co. had long been his London correspondents; and he had carried on with them the same traffic in bills and counter-bills that the Canongate Company did with him—and upon a still larger scale. They had done what he did not—or at least did not to any very culpable extent : they had carried their adventures out of the line of their own business. It was they, for example, that must needs be embarking such vast sums in a speculation on hops ! When ruin threatened them, they availed themselves of Constable's credit without stint or limit—while he, feeling darkly that the net was around him, struggled and splashed for relief, no matter who might suffer, so he escaped ! And Sir Walter Scott, sorely as he suffered, was too plainly conscious of the " strong tricks " he had allowed his own imagination to play, not to make merciful allowance for all the apparently monstrous things that I have now been narrating of Constable.

For the rest, his friends, and above all posterity, are not left to consider his fate without consoling reflections. They who knew and loved him must ever remember that the real nobility of his character could not have exhibited itself to the world at large, had he not been exposed in his later years to the ordeal of adversity. And others as well as they may feel assured, that had not that adversity been preceded by the perpetual spur of pecuniary demands, he who began life with such quick appetites for all its ordinary enjoyments would never have devoted himself to the rearing of that gigantic monument of genius, labour, and power, which his works now constitute. The imagination which has bequeathed so much to delight and humanise mankind would have developed few of its miraculous resources, except in the embellishment of his own personal existence. The enchanted spring might have sunk into earth with the rod that bade it gush, and left us no living waters. We cannot understand, but we may nevertheless respect even the strangest caprices of the marvellous combination of faculties to which our debt is so weighty. We should try to picture to ourselves what the actual intellectual life must have been of the author of such a series of romances. We should ask ourselves whether, filling and discharging so soberly and gracefully as he did the common functions of social man, it was not, nevertheless, impossible but that he must have passed most of his life in other worlds than ours; and we ought hardly to think it a grievous circumstance that their bright visions should have left a dazzle sometimes on the eyes which he so gently reopened upon our prosaic realities. He had, on the whole, a command over the powers of his mind—I mean, that he could control and direct his thoughts and reflections with a readiness, firmness, and easy security of sway—beyond what I find it possible to trace in any other *artist's* recorded character and history; but he could not habitually fling them into the region of dreams throughout a long series of years, and yet be expected to find a corresponding satisfaction in bending them to the less agreeable considerations which the circumstances of any human being's practical lot in this world must present in abundance. The training to which he accustomed himself could not leave him as he was when he began. He must pay the penalty, as well as reap the glory of this lifelong abstraction of reverie, this self-abandonment of Fairyland.

This was for him the last year of many things; among others, of Sybil Grey and *the Abbotsford Hunt*. Towards the close of a hard run on his neighbour Gala's ground, he adventured to leap *the Catrail*—that venerable relic of the days of

" Reged wide and fair Strath-Clyde."

He was severely bruised and shattered; and never afterwards recovered the feeling of confidence, without which there can be no pleasure in horsemanship. He often talked of this accident with a somewhat superstitious mournfulness.

CHAPTER XIV

Ruin of the Houses of Constable and Ballantyne—Death of Lady Scott—Publication of Woodstock—Journey to London and Paris—Publication of the Life of Napoleon. 1825-1827.

JAMES BALLANTYNE says, in a paper dictated from his deathbed :—" I need not here enlarge upon the unfortunate facility which, at the period of universal confidence and indulgence, our and other houses received from the banks. Suffice it to say that all our appearances of prosperity, as well as those of Constable, and Hurst and Robinson, were merely shadows, and that from he moment the bankers exhibited symptoms of doubt, it might have been easy to discover what must be the ultimate result. During weeks, and even months, however, our house was kept in a state of very painful suspense. The other two, I have no doubt, saw the coming events more clearly. I must here say, that it was one of Sir Walter's weaknesses to shrink too much from looking evil in the face, and that he was apt to carry a great deal too far—' sufficient for the day is the evil thereof.' I do not think it was more than three weeks before the catastrophe that he became fully convinced it was impending—if indeed his feelings ever reached the length of conviction at all. Thus, at the last, his fortitude was very severely tried indeed."

Mr. Ballantyne had never seen Scott's Diary, and its entries from the 20th November 1825 (when it begins) until the middle of January 1826, are in perfect accordance with this statement. The first on the subject is in these terms :—" Here is matter for a May morning, but much fitter for a November one. The general distress in the city has affected H. and R., Constable's great agents. Should they *go*, it is not likely that Constable can stand ; and such an event would lead to great distress and perplexity on the part of J. B. and myself. Thank God, I have enough to pay more than 20s. in the pound, taking matters at the very worst. But much inconvenience must be the consequence. I had a lesson in 1814 which should have done good ; but success and abundance erased it from my mind. But this is no time for journalising or moralising either. Necessity is like a sourfaced cook-maid, and I a turn-spit she has flogged, ere now, till he mounted his wheel. If Woodstock can be out by 25th January it will do much,—and it is possible."

Thus he continued to labour on at his romance ; from time to time arrested amidst his visions by some fresh omen of the coming reality : but after suggesting or concurring in the commercial measure that seemed feasible, immediately commanding his mind into oblivion of whatever must prevent his pursuance of the task that depended solely on himself. That down to the 14th of December he

was far indeed from having brought home to himself anything like the extent of his danger, is clear enough from
the step recorded in that day's entry—namely, his consenting to avail himself of the power he had retained of borrowing £10,000 on the lands of Abbotsford, and advancing that sum to the struggling houses. Ballantyne hints
that in his opinion both Constable and his London agents
must have foreseen more clearly the issue of the struggle;
and it is certain that the only point in Constable's personal
conduct which Scott afterwards considered himself entitled to condemn and resent was connected with these
last advances.

My residence had been removed to London before Sir
Walter felt, or acknowledged, serious apprehensions : nor
can I on this occasion quote his Diary so largely as would
enable the reader to follow from day to day the fluctuations
of hope, anxiety, and fear. I must limit myself to a few
of what seem the most remarkable passages of that record.
On the 18th of December he writes thus :—'' If things go
badly in London, the magic wand of the Unknown will be
shivered in his grasp. He must then, faith, be termed the
Too-well-known. The feast of fancy will be over with the
feeling of independence. He shall no longer have he
delight of waking in the morning with bright ideas in his
mind, hasten to commit them to paper, and count them
monthly, as the means of planting such scaurs and purchasing such wastes; replacing dreams of fiction by other
prospective visions of walks by

    ' Fountain heads, and pathless groves;
      Places which pale passion loves.'

This cannot be; but I may work substantial husbandry,
i.e. write history, and such concerns. They will not be received with the same enthusiasm; at least, I much doubt
the general knowledge that an author must write for his
bread, at least for improving his pittance, degrades him
and his productions in the public eye. He falls into the
second-rate rank of estimation :

    ' While the harness sore galls, and the spurs his side goad,
      The high-mettled racer 's a hack on the road.'

It is a bitter thought; but if tears start at it, let them
flow. My heart clings to the place I have created—there is
scarce a tree on it that does not owe its being to me.—
What a life mine has been !—half-educated, almost wholly

neglected, or left to myself; stuffing my head with most nonsensical trash, and undervalued by most of my companions for a time; getting forward, and held a bold and a clever fellow, contrary to the opinion of all who thought me a mere dreamer; broken-hearted for two years; my heart handsomely pieced again—but the crack will remain till my dying day. Rich and poor four or five times; once on the verge of ruin, yet opened a new source of wealth almost overflowing. Now to be broken in my pitch of pride, and nearly winged (unless good news should come): because London chooses to be in an uproar, and in the tumult of bulls and bears, a poor inoffensive lion like myself is pushed to the wall. But what is to be the end of it? God knows; and so ends the catechism.—Nobody in the end can lose a penny by me—that is one comfort. Men will think pride has had a fall. Let them indulge their own pride in thinking that my fall will make them higher, or seem so at least. I have the satisfaction to recollect that my prosperity has been of advantage to many, and to hope that some at least will forgive my transient wealth on account of the innocence of my intentions, and my real wish to do good to the poor. Sad hearts, too, at Darnick, and in the cottages at Abbotsford. I have half resolved never to see the place again. How could I tread my hall with such a diminished crest?—how live a poor indebted man where I was once the wealthy, the honoured? I was to have gone there on Saturday in joy and prosperity to receive my friends. My dogs will wait for me in vain. It is foolish—but the thoughts of parting from these dumb creatures have moved me more than any of the painful reflections I have put down. Poor things! I must get them kind masters! There may be yet those who, loving me, may love my dog because it has been mine. I must end these gloomy forebodings, or I shall lose the tone of mind with which men should meet distress. I feel my dogs' feet on my knees—I hear them whining and seeking me everywhere. This is nonsense, but it is what they would do could they know how things may be.—An odd thought strikes me—When I die, will the journal of these days be taken out of the ebony cabinet at Abbotsford, and read with wonder, that the well-seeming Baronet should ever have experienced the risk of such a hitch?—or will it be found in some obscure lodging-house, where the decayed son of chivalry had hung up his scutcheon, and where one or two old friends will look grave, and whisper to each other, ' Poor gentleman '—' a well-meaning man '— ' nobody's enemy but his own '—' thought his parts would never wear out '—' family poorly left '—' pity he took that foolish title.' Who can answer this question?—Poor Will Laidlaw !—poor Tom Purdie !—such news will wring your hearts, and many a poor fellow's besides, to whom my prosperity was daily bread.

" Ballantyne behaves like himself, and sinks the prospect of his own ruin in contemplating mine. I tried to enrich him indeed, and now all—all is in the balance. He will have the Journal still, that is a comfort, for sure they cannot find a better editor. *They*—alas, who will *they* be—the *unbekannten obern* [1] who may have to dispose of my all as they will? Some hard-eyed banker—some of these men of millions !—I have endeavoured to give vent to thoughts naturally so painful, by writing these notes— partly to keep them at bay by busying myself with the history of the French Convention. I thank God I can do both with reasonable composure. I wonder how Anne will bear such an affliction. She is passionate, but stout-hearted and courageous in important matters, though irritable in trifles. I am glad Lockhart and his wife are gone. Why? I cannot tell—but I *am* pleased to be left to my own regrets, without being melted by condolences, though of the most sincere and affectionate kind.—*Half-past eight*. I closed this book under the impression of impending ruin. I open it an hour after (thanks be to God) with the strong hope that matters will be got over safely and honourably, in a mercantile sense. Cadell came at eight to communicate a letter from Hurst and Robinson, intimating they had stood the storm. I shall always think the better of Cadell for this—not merely because ' his feet are beautiful on the mountains who brings good tidings,' but because he shewed feeling—deep feeling, poor fellow. He, who I thought had no more than his numeration-table, and who, if he had had his whole counting-house full of sensibility, had yet his wife and children to bestow it upon—I will not forget this, if all keeps right. I love the virtues of rough-and-round men —the others are apt to escape in salt rheum, sal-volatile, and a white pocket handkerchief.

" *December* 19.—Ballantyne here before breakfast. He

¹ *Unbekannten obern*—unknown rulers.

looks on last night's news with confidence.   Constable
came in and sat an hour.   The old gentleman is firm as a
rock.   He talks of going to London next week.   But I
must go to work.

" *December* 21.—Dined with James Ballantyne, and
met R. Cadell, and my old friend Mathews the comedian.
The last time I saw him before, he dined with me in company with poor Sir Alexander Boswell, who was killed
within a week.   I never saw Sir A. more.   The time before was in 1815, when Gala and I were returning from
France, and passed through London, when we brought
Mathews down as far as Leamington.   Poor Byron made
an early dinner with us at Long's, and a most brilliant day
we had of it.   I never saw Byron so full of fun, frolic,
wit, and whim; he was as playful as a kitten.   Well, I
never saw *him* again.   So this man of mirth, with his
merry meetings, has brought me no luck.   I could not
help thinking, in the midst of the glee, what gloom had
lately been over the minds of three of the company.   What
a strange scene if the surge of conversation could suddenly ebb like the tide, and shew us the state of people's
real minds !

> ' No eyes the rocks discover
> Which lurk beneath the deep.'

Life could not be endured were it seen in reality.   Things
keep mending in London.

" *December* 22.—I wrote six of my close pages yesterday, which is about twenty-four pages in print.   What is
more, I think it comes off twangingly.   The air of *Bonnie
Dundee* running in my head to-day, I wrote a few verses
to it before dinner, taking the key-note from the story of
Clavers leaving the Scottish Convention of Estates in
1688-9.   I wonder if they are good.   Ah, poor Will Erskine ! thou couldst and wouldst have told me.   I must
consult J. B., who is as honest as was W. E.   But then,
though he has good taste too, there is a little of *Big bow-
wow* about it.   Can't say what made me take a frisk so
uncommon of late years as to write verses of free-will.   I
suppose the same impulse which makes birds sing when
the storm has blown over.

" *December* 24.—Constable has a new scheme of publishing the works of the Author of Waverley in a superior
style, at £1 1s. volume.   He says he will answer for

making £20,000 of this, and liberally offered me any share of the profits. I have no great claim to any, as I have only to contribute the notes, which are light work; yet a few thousands coming in will be a good thing—besides the Printing Office. Constable, though valetudinary, and cross with his partner, is certainly as good a pilot in these rough seas as ever man put faith in.

" *December* 25.—*Abbotsford.*—Arrived here last night at seven. Our halls are silent compared to last year, but let us be thankful—*Barbarus has segetes? Nullum numen abest, si sit prudentia.* There shall be no lack of wisdom. But come—*il faut cultiver notre jardin.* I will accept no invitation for dinner, save one to Newton-Don, and Mertoun to-morrow, instead of Christmas-Day. On this day of general devotion, I have a particular call for gratitude.

" *January* 14.—An odd mysterious letter from Constable, who has gone post to London. It strikes me to be that sort of letter which I have seen men write when they are desirous that their disagreeable intelligence should be rather apprehended than expressed. I thought he had been in London a fortnight ago, disposing of property to meet this exigence, and so I think he should. Well, I must have patience. But these terrors and frights are truly annoying. .... A letter from J. B., mentioning Constable's journey, but without expressing much apprehension. He knows C. well, and saw him before his departure, and makes no doubt of his being able easily to extricate whatever may be entangled. I will not therefore make myself uneasy. I can help doing so surely, if I will. At least, I have given up cigars since the year began, and have now no wish to return to the habit, as it is called. I see no reason why one should not, with God's assistance, shun noxious thoughts, which foretell evil, and cannot remedy it."

A few days after Sir Walter penned the last-quoted paragraph, Mr. Constable made his appearance in London. I saw him immediately. Having deferred his journey imprudently, he had performed it very rapidly; and this exertion, with mental excitement, had brought on a sharp access of gout, which confined him for a couple of days to his hotel in the Adelphi—*reluctantem draconem.* A more impatient spirit never boiled in a feverish frame. It was then that I received my first information of Sir W. Scott's implication as a partner in the firm of Ballantyne.

It was then also for the first time, that I saw full swing
given to the tyrannical temper of *the Czar*. He looked,
spoke, and gesticulated like some hoary despot, accustomed to nothing but the complete indulgence of every
wish and whim, against whose sovereign authority his
most trusted satraps and tributaries had suddenly revolted
—open rebellion in twenty provinces—confusion in the
capital—treason in the palace. I will not repeat his
haughty ravings of scorn and wrath. I listened to these with
wonder and commiseration; nor were such feelings miti-
gated when, having exhausted his violence of vituperation
against many persons of whom I had never before heard
him speak but as able and trusted friends, he cooled down
sufficiently to answer my question as to the practical business on which the note announcing his arrival in town had
signified his urgent desire to take my advice. Constable
told me that he had already seen one of the Hurst and
Robinson firm, and that the storm which had seemed to be
" blown over " had, he was satisfied, only been lulled for
a moment to burst out in redoubled fury. If they went,
however, he must follow. He had determined to support
them through the coming gale as he had done through the
last; and he had the means to do so effectually, provided
Sir Walter Scott would stand by him heartily and boldly.

The first and most obvious step was to make large sales
of copyrights; and it was not surprising that Constable
should have formed most extravagant notions of the mar-
ketable value of the property of this nature in his possession. Every bookseller is very apt to do so. A manuscript is submitted to him; he inspects it with coldness and
suspicion; with hesitation offers a sum for it; obtains it,
and sends it to be printed. He has hardly courage to look
at the sheets as they are thrown off; but the book is at
last laid on his counter, and he from that moment regards
it with an eye of parental fondness. It is *his*; he considers it in that light quite as much as does the author,
and is likely to be at least as sorely provoked by anything
in the shape of hostile criticism. If this be the usual
working of self-love or self-interest in such cases, what
wonder that the man who had at his disposal (to say
nothing of innumerable minor properties) the copyrights
of the Encyclopædia Britannica, a moiety of the Edinburgh Review, nearly all Scott's Poetry, the Waverley

Novels, and the advancing Life of Napoleon—who had made, besides, sundry contracts for novels by Scott, as yet unwritten—and who seriously viewed his plan of the new Miscellany as in itself the sure foundation of a gigantic fortune—what wonder that the sanguine Constable should have laid to his soul the flattering unction, that he had only to display such resources in some quarter totally above the momentary pressure of *the trade,* and command an advance of capital adequate to relieve him and all his allies from these unfortunate difficulties about a few paltry " sheafs " of stamped paper? To be brief, he requested me to accompany him, as soon as he could get into his carriage, to the Bank of England, and support him (as a confidential friend of the Author of Waverley) in his application for a loan of from £100,000 to £200,000 on the security of the copyrights in his possession. It is needless to say that, without distinct instructions from Sir Walter, I could not take upon me to interfere in such a business as this. Constable, when I refused, became livid with rage. After a long silence, he stamped on the ground, and swore that he could and would do alone. I left him in stern indignation.

There was another scene of the same kind a day or two afterwards, when his object was to get me to back his application to Sir Walter to borrow £20,000 in Edinburgh, and transmit it to him in London. I promised nothing but to acquaint Scott immediately with his request, and him with Scott's answer. Sir Walter, ere the message reached him, had been candidly told by Constable's own partner that any further advances would be mere folly.

Constable lingered on, fluctuating between wild hope and savage despair, until, I seriously believe, he at last hovered on the brink of insanity. When he returned to Edinburgh, it was to confront creditors whom he knew he could not pay.

Scott's Diary has—" *Edinburgh, January* 16.—Came through cold roads to as cold news. Hurst and Robinson have suffered a bill to come back upon Constable, which I suppose infers the ruin of both houses. We shall soon see. Dined with the Skenes."—Mr. Skene assures me that he appeared that evening quite in his usual spirits, conversing on whatever topic was started as easily and gaily as if there had been no impending calamity; but at part-

ing he whispered—" Skene, I have something to speak to
you about; be so good as to look in on me as you go to
the Parliament-House to-morrow." When Skene called
in Castle Street, about half-past nine o'clock next morning, he found Scott writing in his study. He rose, and
said—" My friend, give me a shake of your hand—mine is
that of a beggar." He then told him that Ballantyne had
just been with him, and that his ruin was certain and complete; explaining, briefly, the nature of his connection with
the three houses, whose downfall must that morning be
made public. He added—" Don't fancy I am going to
stay at home to brood idly on what can't be helped. I
was at work upon Woodstock when you came in, and I
shall take up the pen the moment I get back from Court.
I mean to dine with you again on Sunday, and hope then
to report progress to some purpose."—When Sunday came
he reported accordingly, that in spite of all the numberless
interruptions of meetings and conferences with his partner
and men of business—to say nothing of his anxieties on
account of his wife and daughter—he had written a chapter of his novel every intervening day. And the Diary
gives the precise detail. His exertions, he there says,
were suspended for the 17th and 18th; but in the course
of the 19th, 20th, and 21st, he wrote 38 pages of his novel
—such pages that 70 of them made " half a volume of the
usual size."

Diary.—" *January* 17.—James Ballantyne this morning,
good honest fellow, with a visage as black as the crook.
He hopes no salvation; has indeed taken measures to stop.
It is hard, after having fought such a battle. Have apologised for not attending the Royal Society Club, who have
a *gaudeamus* on this day, and seemed to count much on
my being the preses. My old acquaintance, Miss Elizabeth Clerk, sister of Willie, died suddenly, I cannot choose
but wish it had been Sir W. S.; and yet the feeling is
unmanly. I have Anne, my wife, and Charles, to look
after. I felt rather sneaking as I came home from the
Parliament-House—felt as if I were liable *monstrari digito*
in no very pleasant way. But this must be borne *cum
cæteris*; and, thank God, however uncomfortable, I do not
feel despondent."

The reader may be curious to see what account Ballantyne's memorandum gives of that dark announcement on
the morning of Tuesday the 17th. It is as follows :—

" On the evening of the 16th, I received from Mr. Cadell a distinct message putting me in possession of the truth. I called immediately in Castle Street, but found Sir Walter had gained an unconscious respite by being engaged out at dinner.   It was between eight and nine next morning that I made the final communication.   No doubt he was greatly stunned—but, upon the whole, he bore it with wonderful fortitude.   He then asked—' Well, what is the actual step we must first take?   I suppose we must do something?'   I reminded him that two or three thousand pounds were due that day, so that we had only to do what we must do—re-fuse payment—to bring the disclosure sufficiently before the world.   He took leave of me with these striking words —' Well, James, depend upon that, I will never forsake you.' "

In the course of that unhappy yet industrious week, Sir Walter's situation as Ballantyne's partner became uni-versally known.   Mr. Ballantyne, as an individual, had no choice but to resolve on the usual course of a commercial man unable to meet engagements ; but Scott from the first moment determined to avoid, if by his utmost efforts it could be avoided, the necessity of participating in such steps.   He immediately placed his whole affairs in the hands of three trustees (James Jollie, W.S., Alex. Mony-penny, W.S., and John Gibson, W.S.), all men of the highest honour and of great professional experience; and declined every offer of private assistance.   These were very numerous :—his eldest son and his daughter-in-law eagerly tendered the whole fortune at their disposal, and the principal banks of Edinburgh, especially the house of Sir William Forbes & Co., which was the one most deeply involved in Ballantyne's obligations, sent partners of the first consideration, who were his personal friends, to offer liberal additional accommodation.   What, I think, affected him most of all, was a letter from Mr. Poole, his daugh-ters' harp-master, offering £500,—" probably," says the Diary, " his all."   From London, also, he received various kind communications.   Among others, one tendering an instant advance of £30,000—a truly munificent message, conveyed through a distinguished channel, but the source of which was never revealed to him, nor to me until some years after his death, and even then under conditions of secrecy.   To all his answer was the same.   And within a few days he had reason to believe that the creditors would, as a body, assent to let things go in the course which he and his trustees suggested.

His Diary has this entry for the 24th January :—" I went to the Court for the first time to-day, and, like the man with the large nose, thought everybody was thinking of me and my mishaps. Many were, undoubtedly, and all rather regrettingly; some obviously affected. It is singular to see the difference of men's manner whilst they strive to be kind or civil in their way of addressing me. Some smiled as they wished me good-day, as if to say, ' Think nothing about it, my lad; it is quite out of our thoughts.' Others greeted me with the affected gravity which one sees and despises at a funeral. The best-bred—all I believe meaning equally well—just shook hands and went on. A foolish puff in the papers, calling on men and gods to assist a popular author, who having choused the public of many thousands, had not the sense to keep wealth when he had it. If I am hard pressed, and measures used against me, I must use all means of legal defence, and subscribe myself bankrupt in a petition for sequestration. It is the course one should, at any rate, have advised a client to take. But for this I would, in a Court of Honour, deserve to lose my spurs. No,—if they permit me, I will be their vassal for life, and dig in the mine of my imagination to find diamonds (or what may sell for such) to make good my engagements, not to enrich myself. And this from no reluctance to be called the Insolvent, which I probably am, but because I will not put out of the power of my creditors the resources, mental or literary, which yet remain to me."

Jan. 26.—" Gibson comes with a joyful face, announcing that almost all the creditors had agreed to a private trust. This is handsome and confidential, and must warm my best efforts to get them out of the scrape. I will not doubt—to doubt is to lose. Sir William Forbes took the chair, and behaved, as he has ever done, with the generosity of ancient faith and early friendship. That House is more deeply concerned than most. In what scenes have Sir William and I not borne share together ! desperate and almost bloody affrays, rivalries, deep drinking matches, and finally, with the kindliest feelings on both sides, somewhat separated by his retiring much within the bosom of his family, and I moving little beyond mine. It is fated our planets should cross, though, and that at the periods most interesting for me. Down — down — a hundred thoughts."

There soon, however, emerged new difficulties. It would indeed have been very wonderful if all the creditors of three companies, whose concerns were inextricably intertangled, had at once adopted the views of the meeting, composed entirely of eminent citizens of Edinburgh, over which Sir William Forbes presided on the 26th of January; nor, it is proper to add, was Scott himself aware, until some days later, of the extent to which the debts of the two houses of Constable and Hurst exceeded their assets; circumstances necessarily of the greatest importance to the holders of Ballantyne's paper. In point of fact, it turned out that the obligations of the three firms had, by what is termed cross-rankings, reached respectively sums far beyond the calculations of any of the parties. On the full revelation of this state of things, some of the printers' creditors felt great disinclination to close with Scott's proposals; and there ensued a train of harassment, the detail of which must be left in his Diary, but which was finally terminated according to his own original, and really most generous suggestion.

The day of calamity revealed the fact that James Ballantyne personally possessed no assets whatever. The claims against Sir Walter, as the sole really responsible partner in the printing firm, and also as an individual, settled into a sum of about £130,000. On much heavier debts Constable & Co. paid ultimately 2s. 9d. in the pound; Hurst & Robinson about 1s. 3d. The Ballantyne firm had as yet done nothing to prevent their following the same line of conduct. It might still have allowed itself (and not James Ballantyne merely as an individual) to be declared bankrupt, and obtained a speedy discharge, like these booksellers, from all its obligations. But for Scott's being a partner, the whole affair must have been settled in a very short time. If he could have at all made up his mind to let commercial matters take the usual commercial course, the creditors of the firm would have brought into the market whatever property, literary or otherwise, Scott at the hour of failure possessed; they would have had a right to his liferent of Abbotsford, among other things—and to his reversionary interest in the estate, in case either his eldest son or his daughter-in-law should die without leaving issue, and thus void the provisions of their marriage-contract. All this being disposed of, the result would have been a dividend very far superior to what the creditors of Constable and Hurst received; and in return, the partners in the printing firm would have been left at liberty to reap for themselves the profits of their future exertions. Things were, however, complicated in consequence of the transfer of Abbotsford in January 1825. Some creditors now had serious thoughts of contesting the validity of that transaction; but a little reflection and examination satisfied them that nothing could be gained by such an attempt. On the other hand, Sir Walter felt that he had done wrong in placing any part of his property beyond the reach of his creditors, by entering into that marriage-contract without a previous most deliberate examination into the state of his responsibilities. He must have felt in this manner, though I have no sort of doubt, that the result of such an examination in January 1825, if accompanied by an instant calling in of all *counter-bills*, would have been to leave him at perfect liberty to do all that he did upon that occasion. However that may have been, and whatever may have been his delicacy respecting this point, he persisted in regarding the embarrassment of his commercial firm with the feelings not of a merchant but of a gentleman. He thought that, by devoting the rest of his life to the service of his creditors, he could, in the upshot, pay the last farthing he owed them. They (with one or two exceptions) applauded his honourable intentions and resolutions, and partook, to a certain extent, in the self-reliance of their debtor. Nor had they miscalculated as to their interest. Nor had Sir Walter calculated wrongly. He paid the penalty of health and life, but he saved his honour and his self-respect :—

"The glory dies not, and the grief is past." [1]

As to the difficulty that occurred in February, a single extract from his Diary must here suffice. On the 16th he writes thus :—" 'Misfortune's growing bark' comes louder and louder. By assigning my whole property to trustees for behoof of creditors, with two works in progress and nigh publication, and with all my future literary labours, I conceived I was bringing into the field a large

---

[1] Sonnet on Scott's death, by Sir E. Brydges.

fund of payment, which could not exist without my exertions, and that thus far I was entitled to a corresponding degree of indulgence.   I therefore supposed, on selling this house, and various other property, and on receiving the price of Woodstock and Napoleon, that they would give me leisure to make other exertions, and be content with the rents of Abbotsford, without attempting a sale. But Gibson last night came in after dinner, and gave me to understand that the Bank of Scotland see this in a different point of view, and consider my contribution of the produce of past, present, and future labours, as compensated *in full* by their accepting of the trust-deed, instead of pursuing the mode of sequestration, and placing me in the Gazette.   They therefore expect the trustees to commence a lawsuit to reduce the marriage-settlement which settles the estate upon Walter; thus loading me with a most expensive suit, and I suppose selling library and whatever else they can lay hold on.   Now this seems unequal measure, and would besides of itself totally destroy any power of fancy—of genius, if it deserves the name, which may remain to me.   A man cannot write in the House of Correction; and this species of *peine forte et dure* which is threatened would render it impossible for one to help himself or others.   So I told Gibson I had my mind made up as far back as the 24th of January, not to suffer myself to be harder pressed than law would press me.   If they take the sword of the law, I must lay hold of the shield.   If they are determined to consider me as an irretrievable bankrupt, they have no title to object to my settling upon the usual terms which the statute requires. They probably are of opinion, that I will be ashamed to do this by applying publicly for a sequestration.   Now, my feelings are different.   I am ashamed to owe debts I cannot pay; but I am not ashamed of being classed with those to whose rank I belong.   The disgrace is in being an actual bankrupt, not in being made a legal one.   I had like to have been too hasty in this matter.   I must have a clear understanding that I am to be benefited or indulged in some way, if I bring in two such funds as those works in progress, worth certainly from £10,000 to £15,000.''

It was by and by settled that he should be left in the undisturbed possession of Abbotsford, on his pledging himself to dispose immediately of all his other property, of what kind soever, for the behoof of the creditors—to limit his personal expenses henceforth within his official salary—and, continuing his literary labour with his best diligence, to pay in all its profits until the debt should be wholly obliterated. Excepting from a single London Jew, a creditor originally of Hurst's, no practical interference with this arrangement was ever subsequently threatened. Scott, meanwhile, laboured on at his desk. In the very darkest period of his anxieties, he not only continued his novel and his Buonaparte, but threw off his graceful and humorous, as well as sagacious and instructive review of Pepys' Diary : and before that was published, he had also most effectually displayed his self-possession by a political demonstration under a new but thin disguise.

As soon as Parliament met, the recent convulsion in the commercial world became the subject of some very remarkable debates in the Lower House; and the Ministers, tracing it mainly to the rash facility of bankers in yielding credit to speculators, proposed to strike at the root of the evil by taking from private banks the privilege of circulating their own notes as money, and limiting even the Bank of England to the issue of notes of £5 value and upwards. The Government designed that this regulation should apply to Scotland as well as England; and the northern public received the announcement with almost universal reprobation. The Scotch banks apprehended a most serious curtailment of their profits; and the merchants and traders of every class were well disposed to back them in opposing the Ministerial innovation. Scott, ever sensitively jealous as to the interference of English statesmen with the internal affairs of his native kingdom, took the matter up with as much zeal as he could have displayed against the Union had he lived in the days of Queen Anne. His national feelings may have been somewhat stimulated, perhaps, by his deep sense of gratitude for the generous forbearance which several Edinburgh banking-houses had just been exhibiting toward himself; and I think it need not be doubted, moreover, that the *splendida bilis* which, as the Diary confesses, his own misfortunes had engendered, demanded some escape-valve. Hence the three *Letters of Malachi Malagrowther*, which appeared first in the Edinburgh Weekly Journal, and were afterwards collected into a pamphlet by the late Mr. Blackwood, who, on that occasion, for the first time, had justice done to his personal character by " the Black Hussar of Literature."

These diatribes produced in Scotland a sensation not, perhaps, inferior to that of the Drapier's letters in Ireland; a greater one, certainly, than any political tract had excited in the British public at large since the appearance of Burke's Reflections on the French Revolution. They were answered most elaborately and acutely in the London Courier (then the semi-official organ of Lord Liverpool's Government) by Sir Walter's friend, the secretary of the Admiralty, Mr. Croker : who perhaps hazarded, in the heat of his composition, a few personal allusions that might as well have been spared, and which might have tempted a less good-natured antagonist to a fiery rejoinder. Meeting, however, followed meeting, and petition on petition came up with thousands of signatures; and the Ministers ere long found that the opposition, of which Malachi had led the van, was, in spite of all their own speeches and Mr. Croker's essays, too strong and too rapidly strengthening, to be safely encountered. The Scotch part of the measure was dropped; and Scott, having carried his practical object, was not at all disposed to persist in a controversy which, if farther pursued, could scarcely, as he foresaw, fail to interrupt the kindly feelings that Croker and he had for many years entertained for each other, and also to aggravate and prolong, unnecessarily, the resentment with which several of his friends in the Cabinet had regarded his unlooked for appearance as a hostile agitator.

When the Court of Session was to rise for the spring vacation he had to take farewell of his house in Castle Street. Henceforth, his family were to stay always, as he designed, in the country—and a small hired lodging was to suffice for himself when his duty called him to be in Edinburgh. In one day's diary he says,—" Looked out a quantity of things, to go to Abbotsford; for we are flitting, if you please. It is with a sense of pain that I leave behind a parcel of trumpery prints and little ornaments, once the pride of Lady S——'s heart, but which she sees consigned with indifference to the chance of an auction. Things that have had their day of importance with me I cannot forget, though the merest trifles. But I am glad that she, with bad health, and enough to vex her, has not the same useless mode of associating recollections with this unpleasant business."—Again, on the 13th March—" I have hinted in these notes, that I am not entirely free from a sort of gloomy fits, with a fluttering of the heart and depression of spirits, just as if I knew not what was going to befall me. I can sometimes resist this successfully, but it is better to evade than to combat it. The hang-dog spirit may have originated in the confusion and chucking about of our old furniture, the stripping of walls of pictures, and rooms of ornaments; the leaving of a house we have so long called our home is altogether melancholy enough. Meanwhile, to make my recusant spirit do penance, I have set to work to clear away papers and pack them for my journey. What a strange medley of thoughts such a task produces ! There lie letters which made the heart throb when received, now lifeless and uninteresting—as are perhaps their writers—riddles which have been read—schemes which time has destroyed or brought to maturity—memorials of friendships and enmities which are now alike faded. Thus does the ring of Saturn consume itself. To-day annihilates yesterday, as the old tyrant swallowed his children, and the snake its tail. But I must say to my journal as poor Byron did to Moore—' D—n it, Tom, don't be poetical.'

" *March* 14.—J. B. called this morning to take leave, and receive directions about proofs, &c. Talks of the uproar about Malachi; but I am tired of Malachi—the humour is off, and I have said what I wanted to say, and put the people of Scotland on their guard, as well as Ministers, if they like to be warned. They are gradually destroying what remains of nationality, and making the country *tabula rasa* for doctrines of bold innovation. Their loosening and grinding down all those peculiarities which distinguished us as Scotsmen will throw the country into a state in which it will be universally turned to democracy, and instead of canny Saunders, they will have a very dangerous North-British neighbourhood. Some lawyer expressed to Lord Elibank an opinion, that at the Union the English law should have been extended all over Scotland. ' I cannot say how that might have answered our purpose,' said Lord Patrick, who was never non-suited for want of an answer, ' but it would scarce have suited *yours,* since by this time the *Aberdeen*

Advocates[1] would have possessed themselves of all the business in Westminster Hall.'

  "*March* 15.—This morning I leave No. 39 Castle Street, for the last time. ' The cabin was convenient,' and habit had made it agreeable to me. I never reckoned upon a change in this particular so long as I held an office in the Court of Session. In all my former changes of residence it was from good to better—this is retrograding. I leave this house for sale, and I cease to be an Edinburgh citizen, in the sense of being a proprietor, which my father and I have been for sixty years at least. So farewell, poor 39, and may you never harbour worse people than those who now leave you. Not to desert the Lares all at once, Lady S. and Anne remain till Sunday. As for me, I go, as aforesaid, this morning.

' Ha til mi tulidh ' !— ''[2]

  Sir Walter's Diary begins to be clouded with a darker species of distress than mere loss of wealth could bring to his spirit. His darling grandson is sinking at a distance from him under incurable disease. At home the misfortunes against which his manhood struggled with stern energy were encountered by his affectionate wife under the disadvantages of enfeebled health; and it seems but too evident that mental pain and mortification had a great share in hurrying her ailments to a fatal end. Nevertheless, all his afflictions do not seem to have interrupted for more than a day or two his usual course of labour. With rare exceptions, he appears, all through this trying period, to have finished his daily task—thirty printed pages of Woodstock—until that novel was completed; or, if he paused in it, he gave a similar space of time to some minor production; such as his paper on the Life of Kemble. He also corresponded much as usual (notwithstanding all he says about indolence on that score) with his absent friends; and I need scarcely add, that his duties as Sheriff claimed many hours every week. The picture of resolution and industry which this portion of his Journal presents is certainly as remarkable as the boldest imagination could have conceived.

  "*Abbotsford, March* 17.—A letter from Lockhart. My worst augury is verified;—the medical people think poor

[1] The *Solicitors* of Aberdeen enjoy somehow the title of *Advocates.*
[2] I return no more.

Johnnie is losing strength; he is gone with his mother to Brighton. The bitterness of this probably impending calamity is extreme. The child was almost too good for this world;—beautiful in features; and though spoiled by every one, having one of the sweetest tempers as well as the quickest intellect I ever saw; a sense of humour quite extraordinary in a child, and, owing to the general notice which was taken of him, a great deal more information than suited his years. The poor dear love had so often a slow fever, that when it pressed its little lips to mine, I always foreboded to my own heart what all I fear are now aware of.

"*March* 18.—Slept indifferently, and under the influence of Queen Mab, seldom auspicious to me. Dreamed of reading the tale of the Prince of the Black Marble Islands to Little Johnnie, extended on a paralytic chair, and yet telling all his pretty stories about Ha-Papa, as he calls me, and Chiefswood—and waked to think I should see the little darling no more, or see him as a thing that had better never have existed. Oh misery! misery! that the best I can wish for him is early death, with all the wretchedness to his parents that is likely to ensue!

"*March* 19.—Lady S., the faithful and true companion of my fortunes, good and bad, for so many years, has, but with difficulty, been prevailed on to see Dr. Abercrombie, and his opinion is far from favourable. Her asthmatic complaints are fast terminating in hydropsy, as I have long suspected; yet the announcement of the truth is overwhelming. They are to stay a little longer in town to try the effects of a new medicine. On Wednesday, they propose to return hither—a new affliction, where there was enough before; yet her constitution is so good, that if she will be guided by advice, things may be yet ameliorated. God grant it! for really these misfortunes come too close upon each other.

"*March* 28.—We have now been in solitude for some time—myself nearly totally so, excepting at meals. One is tempted to ask himself, knocking at the door of his own heart, Do you love this extreme loneliness?—I can answer conscientiously, *I do*. The love of solitude was with me a passion of early youth; when in my teens, I used to fly from company to indulge in visions and airy castles of my own, the disposal of ideal wealth, and the exercise of imaginary power.   This feeling prevailed even till I was eighteen, when love and ambition, awakening with other passions, threw me more into society, from which I have, however, at times withdrawn myself, and have been always even glad to do so.   I have risen from a feast satiated; and unless it be one or two persons of very strong intellect, or whose spirits and good humour amuse me, I wish neither to see the high, the low, nor the middling class of society.   This is a feeling without the least tinge of misanthropy, which I always consider as a kind of blasphemy of a shocking description.   If God bears with the very worst of us, we may surely endure each other.   If thrown into society, I always have, and always will endeavour to bring pleasure with me, at least to shew willingness to please.   But for all this, ' I had rather live alone,' and I wish my appointment, so convenient otherwise, did not require my going to Edinburgh. But this must be, and in my little lodging I shall be lonely enough.

  " *April* 1.—*Ex uno die disce omnes* —Rose at seven or sooner, studied and wrote till breakfast, with Anne, about a quarter before ten.   Lady Scott seldom able to rise till twelve or one.   Then I write or study again till one.   At that hour to-day I drove to Huntley Burn, and walked home by one of the hundred and one pleasing paths which I have made through the woods I have planted—now chatting with Tom Purdie, who carries my plaid and speaks when he pleases, telling long stories of hits and misses in shooting twenty years back—sometimes chewing the cud of sweet and bitter fancy—and sometimes attending to the humours of two curious little terriers of the Dandie Dinmont breed, together with a noble wolf-hound puppy which Glengarry has given me to replace Maida.   This brings me down to the very moment I do tell—the rest is prophetic.   I shall feel drowsy when this book is locked, and perhaps sleep until Dalgleish brings the dinner summons.   Then I shall have a chat with Lady S. and Anne; some broth or soup, a slice of plain meat—and man's chief business, in Dr. Johnson's estimation, is briefly despatched.   Half an hour with my family, and half an hour's coquetting with a cigar, a tumbler of weak whisky and water, and a novel perhaps, lead on to tea, which sometimes consumes another half hour of chat; then write and read in my own room till ten o'clock at night; a little bread, and then a glass of porter, and to bed; and this, very rarely varied by a visit from some one, is the tenor of my daily life—and a very pleasant one indeed, were it not for apprehensions about Lady S. and poor Johnnie. The former will, I think, do well; for the latter—I fear—I fear——

"*April* 3.—I have the extraordinary and gratifying news that *Woodstock* is sold for £8,228; all ready money—a matchless sale for less than three months' work." [The reader will understand that, the novel being sold for the behoof of J. B. and Co.'s creditors, this sum includes the cost of printing the first edition, as well as paper.] "If Napoleon does as well, or near it, it will put the trust affairs in high flourish. Four or five years of leisure and industry would, with such success, amply replace my losses. I have a curious fancy; I will go set two or three acorns, and judge by their success in growing whether I shall succeed in clearing my way or not. I have a little toothache keeps me from working much to-day—besides I sent off copy for Napoleon."

The price received for *Woodstock* shews what eager competition had been called forth among the booksellers, when, after the lapse of several years, Constable's monopoly of Sir Walter's novels was abolished by their common calamity. The interest excited, not only in Scotland and England, but all over civilised Europe, by the news of Scott's misfortunes, must also have had its influence in quickening this commercial rivalry. The reader need hardly be told, that the first meeting of James Ballantyne and Company's creditors witnessed the transformation, a month before darkly prophesied, of the "Great Unknown" into the "Too-well-known." Even for those who had long ceased to entertain any doubt as to the main source at least of the Waverley romances, there would have been something stirring in the first confession of the author; but it in fact included the avowal, that he had stood alone in the work of creation; and when the mighty claim came in the same breath with the announcement of personal ruin, the effect on the community of Edinburgh was electrical. It is, in my opinion, not the least striking feature in his Diary, that it contains no allusion (save the ominous one of 18th December) to this long withheld revelation. He notes his painful anticipation of returning to the Parliament-House—*monstrari digito*—as an insolvent. It does not seem even to have occurred to him, that when he appeared there the morning after his creditors had heard his confession, there could not be many men in the place but must gaze on his familiar features with a mixture of curiosity, admiration, and sympathy, of which a hero in the moment of victory might have been proud—which might have swelled the heart of a martyr as he was bound to the stake. The universal feeling was, I believe, much what the late amiable and accomplished Earl of Dudley expressed to Mr. Morritt when these news reached them at Brighton.—" Scott ruined !" said he, " the author of Waverley ruined ! Good God ! let every man to whom he has given months of delight give him a sixpence, and he will rise to-morrow morning richer than Rothschild !"

It is no wonder that the book, which it was known he had been writing during this crisis of distress, should have been expected with solicitude. Shall we find him, asked thousands, to have been master truly of his genius in the moment of this ordeal? Shall we trace anything of his own experiences in the construction of his imaginary personages and events?—I know not how others interpreted various passages in Woodstock, but there were not a few that carried deep meaning for such of Scott's own friends as were acquainted with, not his pecuniary misfortune alone, but the drooping health of his wife, and the consolation afforded him by the dutiful devotion of his daughter Anne, in whose character and demeanour a change had occurred exactly similar to that painted in poor Alice Lee : " A light joyous air, with something of a humorous expression, which seemed to be looking for amusement, had vanished before the touch of affliction, and a calm melancholy supplied its place, which seemed on the watch to administer comfort to others." In several *mottoes*, and other scraps of verse, the curious reader will find similar traces of the facts and feelings recorded in the author's Diary. As to the novel itself, though none can pretend to class it in the very highest rank of his works, since we feel throughout the effects of the great fundamental error, likened by a contemporary critic to that of the writer who should lay his scene at Rome immediately after the battle of Philippi, and introduce Brutus as the survivor in that conflict, and Cicero as his companion in victory ; yet even this censor is forced to allow that Woodstock displays certain excellences, not exemplified in all the author's fictions, and which attest, more remarkably than any others could have done, the complete self-possession of the mind when composing it. The success of the book was great: large as the price was, its publishers had no reason to repent their bargain; and of course the rapid receipt of such a sum as £8,000, the product of hardly three months' labour, highly gratified the body of creditors, whose debtor had devoted to them whatever labour his health should henceforth permit him to perform.

His Diary shews that he very soon began another work of fiction; and that he from the first designed the *Chronicles of the Canongate* to be published by Mr. Robert Cadell. That gentleman's connection with Constable was, from circumstances of which the reader may have traced various little indications, not likely to be renewed after the catastrophe of their old copartnership. They were now endeavouring to establish themselves in separate businesses; and each was, of course, eager to secure the countenance of Sir Walter. He did not hesitate a moment. In the prudence at least of the senior there could no longer be any confidence; and Cadell's frank conduct in warning him against Constable's last mad proposal about a guarantee for £20,000, had produced a strong impression.

The progress of the domestic story will be best given by a few more extracts from the Diary:—

"*April* 8.—We expect a *raid* of folks to visit us this morning, whom we must have *dined* before our misfortunes. Save time, wine, and money, these misfortunes—and so far are convenient things—Besides, there is a dignity about them when they come only like the gout in its mildest shape, to authorise diet and retirement, the night-gown and the velvet shoe:—when the one comes to chalk-stones and you go to prison through the other, it is the devil. Or compare the effects of Sieur Gout and absolute poverty upon the stomach—the necessity of a bottle of laudanum in the one case, the want of a morsel of meat in the other. Laidlaw's infant, which died on Wednesday, is buried to-day. The people coming to visit prevent my going—and I am glad of it. I hate funerals —always did;—there is such a mixture of mummery with real grief—the actual mourner perhaps heart-broken, and all the rest making solemn faces, and whispering observations on the weather and public news, and here and there a greedy fellow enjoying the cake and wine. I saw the poor child's funeral from a distance. Ah, that *Distance!* What a magician for conjuring up scenes of joy or sorrow, smoothing all asperities, reconciling all incongruities, veiling all absurdities, softening every coarseness, doubling every effect by the influence of the imagination. A Scottish wedding should be seen at a distance;—the gay band of dancers just distinguished amid the elderly group of the spectators—the glass held high, and the distant cheers as it is swallowed, should be only a sketch, not a finished Dutch picture, when it becomes brutal and boorish. Scotch psalmody, too, should be heard from a distance. The grunt and the snivel, and the whine and the scream, should all be blended in that deep and distant sound, which, rising and falling like the Eolian harp, may have some title to be called the praise of one's Maker. Even so the distant funeral : the few mourners on horseback, with their plaids wrapped around them—the father heading the procession as they enter the river, and pointing out the ford by which his darling is to be carried on the last long road—none of the subordinate figures in discord with the general tone of the incident, but seeming just accessions, and no more; this *is* affecting.

"*April* 24.—Constable is sorely broken down.

> ' Poor fool and knave, I have one part in my heart
> That's sorry yet for thee.'

His conduct has not been what I deserved at his hand; but I believe that, walking blindfold himself, he misled me without *malice prepense.* It is best to think so at least, until the contrary be demonstrated. To nourish angry passions against a man whom I really liked would be to lay a blister on my own heart.

"*May* 6.—The same scene of hopeless (almost) and unavailing anxiety. Still welcoming me with a smile, and asserting she is better. I fear the disease is too deeply entwined with the principles of life. I am a tolerable Stoic, but preach to myself in vain.

> ' Are these things, then, necessities?
> Then let us meet them like necessities.'

"*May* 11.—Charlotte was unable to take leave of me,

being in a sound sleep, after a very indifferent night.
Perhaps it was as well. Emotion might have hurt her;
and nothing I could have expressed would have been
worth the risk. I have foreseen, for two years and more,
that this menaced event could not be far distant. I have
seen plainly, within the last two months, that recovery was
hopeless. And yet to part with the companion of twenty-
nine years, when so very ill—that I did not, could not
foresee. It withers my heart to think of it, and to recollect that I can hardly hope again to seek confidence and
counsel from that ear to which all might be safely con-
fided.''

His niece Miss Anne Scott (daughter of Thomas) had
kindly arrived before he was thus forced to quit the scene,
and repair alone to his new lodgings in Edinburgh:—
''Diary—Mrs. Brown's Lodgings, North St. David
Street.—May 14.—A fair good-morrow to you, Mr. Sun,
who are shining so brightly on these dull walls. Methinks
you look as if you were looking as bright on the banks of
the Tweed; but look where you will, Sir Sun, you look
upon sorrow and suffering.—Hogg was here yesterday in
danger, from having obtained an accommodation of £100
from James Ballantyne, which he is now obliged to repay.
I am unable to help the poor fellow, being obliged to
borrow myself. But I long ago remonstrated against the
transaction at all, and gave him £50 out of my pocket to
avoid granting the accommodation,—but it did no good.

''May 15.—Received the melancholy intelligence that
all is over at Abbotsford.

''Abbotsford, May 16.—She died at nine in the morning, after being very ill for two days—easy at last. I
arrived here late last night. Anne is worn out, and has
had hysterics, which returned on my arrival. Her broken
accents were like those of a child—the language as well as
the tones broken, but in the most gentle voice of sub-
mission. 'Poor mamma—never return again—gone for
ever—a better place.' Then, when she came to herself,
she spoke with sense, freedom, and strength of mind, till
her weakness returned. It would have been inexpressibly
moving to me as a stranger—what was it then to the
father and the husband? For myself, I scarce know how
I feel—sometimes as firm as the Bass Rock, sometimes as
weak as the water that breaks on it. I am as alert at
thinking and deciding as I ever was in my life. Yet,

when I contrast what this place now is, with what it has
been not long since, I think my heart will break. Lonely,
aged, deprived of my family—all but poor Anne; an
impoverished, an embarrassed man, deprived of the sharer
of my thoughts and counsels, who could always talk down
my sense of the calamitous apprehensions which break the
heart that must bear them alone.—Even her foibles were
of service to me, by giving me things to think of beyond
my weary self-reflections.

"I have seen her. The figure I beheld is, and is not,
my Charlotte—my thirty years' companion. There is the
same symmetry of form, though those limbs are rigid
which were once so gracefully elastic—but that yellow
masque, with pinched features, which seems to mock life
rather than emulate it,—can it be the face that was once
so full of lively expression? I will not look on it again.
Anne thinks her little changed, because the latest idea she
had formed of her mother is as she appeared under circumstances of extreme pain—mine go back to a period of
comparative ease. If I write long in this way, I shall
write down my resolution, which I should rather write up
if I could. I wonder how I shall do with the large
portion of thoughts which were hers for thirty years. I
suspect they will be hers yet, for a long time at least.
But I will not blaze cambric and crape in the public eye
like a disconsolate widower, that most affected of all characters.

"_May_ 18.—Another day, and a bright one to the
external world, again opens on us; the air soft, and the
flowers smiling, and the leaves glittering. They cannot
refresh her to whom mild weather was a natural enjoyment. Cerements of lead and of wood already hold her—
cold earth must have her soon. But it is not my Charlotte
—it is not the bride of my youth, the mother of my
children, that will be laid among the ruins of Dryburgh,
which we have so often visited in gaiety and pastime—
No! no! She is sentient and conscious of my emotions
somewhere—somehow: _where_ we cannot tell; _how_ we
cannot tell; yet would I not at this moment renounce the
mysterious yet certain hope that I shall see her in a better
world for all that this world can give me. The necessity
of this separation—that necessity which rendered it even
a relief,—that and patience must be my comfort. I do
not experience those paroxysms of grief which others do

on the same occasion. I can exert myself, and speak even cheerfully with the poor girls. But alone, or if anything touches me,—the choking sensation. I have been to her room : there was no voice in it—no stirring; the pressure of the coffin was visible on the bed, but it had been removed elsewhere; all was neat, as she loved it, but all was calm—calm as death. I remembered the last sight of her : she raised herself in bed, and tried to turn her eyes after me, and said, with a sort of smile, ' You all have such melancholy faces.' These were the last words I ever heard her utter, and I hurried away, for she did not seem quite conscious of what she said; when I returned, immediately departing, she was in a deep sleep. It is deeper now. This was but seven days since.

"They are arranging the chamber of death—that which was long the apartment of connubial happiness, and of whose arrangements (better than in richer houses) she was so proud. They are treading fast and thick. For weeks you could have heard a foot-fall. Oh, my God !

"*May* 19.—Anne, poor love, is ill with her exertions and agitation—cannot walk—and is still hysterical, though less so. We speak freely of her whom we have lost, and mix her name with our ordinary conversation. This is the rule of nature. All primitive people speak of their dead, and I think virtuously and wisely. The idea of blotting the names of those who are gone out of the language and familiar discourse of those to whom they were dearest is one of the rules of ultra-civilisation, which in so many instances strangle natural feeling by way of avoiding a painful sensation. The Highlanders speak of their dead children as freely as of their living members— how poor Colin or Robert would have acted in such or such a situation. It is a generous and manly tone of feeling ; and so far as it may be adopted without affectation or contradicting the general habits of society, I reckon on observing it.

"*May* 20.—To-night, I trust, will bring Charles or Lockhart, or both. Sophia's baby was christened on Sunday 14th May, at Brighton, by the name of Walter Scott. May God give him life and health to wear it with credit to himself and those belonging to him ! Melancholy to think that the next morning after this ceremony deprived him of so near a relation !

"*May* 22.—Lockhart doubtful if Sophia's health will let

him be here.   Charles arrived last night, much affected, of
course.   Anne had a return of her fainting-fits on seeing
him, and again upon seeing Mr. Ramsay,[1] the gentleman
who performs the service.   I heard him do so with the
utmost propriety for my late friend, Lady Alvanley,[2] the
arrangement of whose funeral devolved upon me.   How
little I could guess when, where, and with respect to
whom, I should next hear those solemn words.   Well, I
am not apt to shrink from that which is my duty, merely
because it is painful; but I wish this day over.   A kind of
cloud of stupidity hangs about me, as if all were unreal
that men seem to be doing and talking about——

   " *May* 23.—About an hour before the mournful ceremony of yesterday, Walter arrived, having travelled
express from Ireland on receiving the news.   He was
much affected, poor fellow,—and no wonder.   Poor
Charlotte nursed him, and perhaps for that reason she
was over partial to him.   The whole scene floats as a sort
of dream before me—the beautiful day, the grey ruins
covered and hidden among clouds of foliage and flourish,
where the grave, even in the lap of beauty, lay lurking,
and gaped for its prey.   Then the grave looks, the hasty
important bustle of men with spades and mattocks—the
train of carriages—the coffin containing the creature that
was so long the dearest on earth to me, and whom I was
to consign to the very spot which in pleasure-parties we so
frequently visited.   It seems still as if this could not be
really so.   But it is so—and duty to God and to my
children must teach me patience.   Poor Anne has had
longer fits since our arrival from Dryburgh than before,
but yesterday was the crisis.   She desired to hear prayers
read by Mr. Ramsay, who performed the duty in the
most solemn manner.   But her strength could not
carry it through.   She fainted before the service was
concluded.

   " *May* 24.—Slept wretchedly, or rather waked
wretchedly all night, and was very sick and bilious in
consequence, and scarce able to hold up my head with
pain.   A walk, however, with my sons, did me a deal of
good;—indeed their society is the greatest support the
world can afford me.   Their ideas of everything are so
just and honourable, kind towards their sisters, and

----

[1] The Rev. E. B. Ramsay, now Dean of Edinburgh.
[2] Lady Alvanley died at Edinburgh, in January, 1825.

affectionate to me, that I must be grateful to God for sparing them to me, and continue to battle with the world for their sakes, if not for my own.

"*May* 25.—I had sound sleep to-night, and waked with little or nothing of the strange dreamy feeling which had made me for some days feel like one bewildered in a country where mist or snow has disguised those features of the landscape which are best known to him.—This evening Walter left us, being anxious to return to his wife as well as to his regiment.

"*May* 26.—A rough morning makes me think of St. George's Channel, which Walter must cross to-night or to-morrow to get to Athlone. His absence is a great blank in our circle, especially I think to his sister Anne, to whom he shews invariably much kindness. But indeed they do so without exception each towards the other; and in weal or woe have shewn themselves a family of love. I will go to town on Monday and resume my labours. Being now of a grave nature, they cannot go against the general temper of my feelings, and in other respects the exertion, as far as I am concerned, will do me good; besides I must re-establish my fortune for the sake of the children, and of my own character. I have not leisure to indulge the disabling and discouraging thoughts that press on me. Were an enemy coming upon my house, would I not do my best to fight, although oppressed in spirits? and shall a similar despondency prevent me from mental exertion? It shall not, by Heaven! This day and to-morrow I give to the currency of the ideas which have of late occupied my mind, and with Monday they shall be mingled at least with other thoughts and cares.——

"*Abbotsford, Saturday, June* 17.—Left Edinburgh to-day, after Parliament-House. My two girls met me at Torsonce, which was a pleasant surprise, and we returned in the sociable altogether. Found everything right and well at Abbotsford under the new *régime*. I again took possession of the family bedroom, and my widowed couch. This was a sore trial, but it was necessary not to blink such a resolution. Indeed, I did not like to have it thought that there is any way in which I can be beaten.

"*September* 12.—I begin to fear Nap. will swell of seven volumes.—As I slept for a few minutes in my chair, to which I am more addicted than I could wish, I heard, as I thought, my poor wife call me by the familiar name of fondness which she gave me.   My recollections on waking were melancholy enough.   These be

' The airy tongues that syllable men's names.'

" *September* 13.—Wrote my task in the morning, and thereafter had a letter from the sage Privy Councillor——. He proposes to me that I shall propose to the —— of ——, and offers his own right honourable intervention to bring so beautiful a business to bear.   I am struck dumb —absolutely mute and speechless—and how to prevent him making me farther a fool is not easy, for he has left me no time to assure him of the absurdity of what he proposes ; and if he should ever hint at such a piece of d——d impertinence, what must the lady think of my conceit or of my feelings !   I will write to his present quarters, however, that he may, if possible, have warning not to continue this absurdity." [1]

Lady Scott had not been quite four months dead, and the entry of the preceding days shews how extremely illtimed was this communication, from a gentleman with whom Sir Walter had never had any intimacy.   Nor will the next entry that I extract diminish this impression.   In October he resolved to make a journey to London and Paris, in both which capitals he had reason to expect important material would be submitted to him as the biographer of Napoleon.   At starting he writes :—— " *October* 11.—We are ingenious self-tormentors.   This journey annoys me more than anything of the kind in my life.   My wife's figure seems to stand before me, and her voice is in my ears—' Scott, do not go.'   It half frightens me.   Strange throbbing at my heart, and a disposition to be very sick.   It is just the effect of so many feelings which had been lulled asleep by the uniformity of my life, but which awaken on any new subject of agitation.   Poor, poor Charlotte ! !   I cannot daub it farther.   I get incapable of arranging my papers too.   I will go out for half an hour.   God relieve me !"

His expedition was a very seasonable relief ; nor was he disappointed as to its direct object.   By the kindness of Earl Bathurst, Colonial Secretary of State, and the Under-Secretaries, Mr. Wilmot Horton and Mr. Robert Hay (who were all attached friends of his), he had access to

---

[1] This was not the only proposition of the kind that reached him during his widowhood.   In the present case there was very high rank and an ample fortune.

many unpublished documents preserved in Downing Street, and copious extracts were prepared under his directions. The Duke of Wellington was good enough to give him a MS. commentary of his own on the Russian campaign, and many hours of confidential conversation respecting other parts of Buonaparte's military history. At Paris he was treated with equal kindness by Marshal Macdonald, with whom he had become acquainted a few years before, when the Marshal visited his paternal kindred in Scotland; among others, Sir Walter's constant friend, Hector M'Donald Buchanan. In both cities he was received with the most marked attention. The deep and respectful sympathy with which his misfortunes, and gallant behaviour under them, had been regarded by all classes of men at home and abroad, was brought home to his perception in a way not to be mistaken. Finally, he had the satisfaction of settling his son Charles's destiny : the King personally undertaking that as soon as he had graduated at Oxford, he should be launched in the diplomatic service. I must confine myself to a very few extracts from the Diary—which will illustrate, among other things, the range of his society on this occasion.

" *Windsor, October* 20.—Commanded down to pass a day at Windsor. The Lodge in the Forest, though ridiculed by connoisseurs, seems to be no bad specimen of a royal retirement, and is delightfully situated. A kind of cottage, too large perhaps for the style, but yet so managed that in the walks you only see parts of it at once, and these well composed and grouping with the immense trees. His Majesty received me with the same mixture of kindness and courtesy which has always distinguished his conduct towards me. There was no company besides the royal retinue—Lady Conyngham—her daughter—and two or three other ladies. After we left table, there was excellent music by the royal band, who lay ambushed in a green-house adjoining the apartment. The King made me sit beside him, and talk a great deal— *too much* perhaps—for he has the art of raising one's spirits, and making you forget the *retenue* which is prudent everywhere, especially at court. But he converses himself with so much ease and elegance, that you lose thoughts of the prince in admiring the well-bred and accomplished gentleman. He is in many respects the model of a British Monarch—has little inclination to try

530 Life of Sir Walter Scott

experiments on government otherwise than through his Ministers—sincerely, I believe, desires the good of his subjects—is kind towards the distressed, and moves and speaks 'every inch a king.' I am sure such a man is fitter for us than one who would long to head armies, or be perpetually intermeddling with *la grande politique.* A sort of reserve, which creeps on him daily, and prevents his going to places of public resort, is a disadvantage, and prevents his being so generally popular as is earnestly to be desired. This, I think, was much increased by the behaviour of the rabble in the brutal insanity of the Queen's trial, when John Bull, meaning the best in the world, made such a beastly figure.—*Pall-Mall, October* 21.—Walked in the morning with Sir William Knighton, and had much confidential chat, not fit to be here set down, in case of accidents. Returned to a hasty dinner at Lockhart's, and then hurried away to see honest Dan Terry's theatre, called the Adelphi. The heat was dreadful, and Anne so unwell that she was obliged to be carried into Terry's house,—a curious dwelling no larger than a squirrel's cage, which he has contrived to squeeze out of the vacant space of the theatre, and which is accessible by a most complicated combination of staircases and small passages. There we had rare good porter and oysters after the play."

Sir Walter returned from Paris about the middle of the ensuing month—and his progress from London homewards is indicated in the following entries :—"*Oxford, November* 21.—Breakfasted with Charles in his chambers at Brazen-nose, where he had everything very neat. How pleasant it is for a father to sit at his child's board ! It is like the aged man reclining under the shadow of the oak which he has planted. My poor plant has some storms to undergo, but were this expedition conducive to no more than his entrance into life under suitable auspices, I should consider the toil and the expense well bestowed.—*Nov.* 23. Slept at Macclesfield. As we came in between ten and eleven, the people of the inn expressed surprise at our travelling so late, as the general distress of the manufacturers had rendered many of the lower classes desperately outrageous.—*Nov.* 24. Breakfasted at Manchester;—pressed on—and by dint of exertion reached Kendal to sleep; thus getting out of the region of the stern, sullen, unwashed artificers, whom you see lounging sulkily along the streets in Lancashire. God's justice is requiting, and will yet farther requite, those who have blown up this country into a state of unsubstantial opulence, at the expense of the health and morals of the lower classes.—*Abbotsford, November* 26.—Naturally reflected how much expense has increased since I first travelled. My uncle's servant, during the jaunts we made together while I was a boy, used to have his option of a shilling per diem for board wages, and usually preferred it to having his charges borne. A servant now-a-days, to be comfortable on the road, should have 4s. or 4s. 6d. board wages, which before 1790 would have maintained his master. But if this be pitiful, it is still more so to find the alteration in my own temper. When young, on returning from such a trip as I have just had, my mind would have loved to dwell on all I had seen that was rich and rare, or have been placing, perhaps, in order, the various additions with which I had supplied my stock of information—and now, like a stupid boy blundering over an arithmetical question half obliterated on his slate, I go stumbling on upon the audit of pounds, shillings, and pence. Well,—the skirmish has cost me £200. I wished for information—and I have had to pay for it."——

On proceeding to Edinburgh to resume his official duties, Sir Walter established himself in a furnished house in Walker Street, it being impossible for him to leave his daughter alone in the country, and the aspect of his affairs being so much ameliorated that he did not think it necessary to carry the young lady to such a place as Mrs. Brown's lodgings. During the six ensuing months, however, he led much the same life of toil and seclusion from company which that of Abbotsford had been during the preceding autumn—very rarely dining abroad, except with one or two intimate friends, *en famille*—still more rarely receiving even a single guest at home : all the while, in fact, he suffered great pain (enough to have disturbed effectually any other man's labours, whether official or literary) from successive attacks of rheumatism, which seems to have been fixed on him by the wet sheets of one of his French inns; and his Diary contains, besides, various indications that his constitution was already shaking under the fatigue to which he had subjected it. Formerly, however great the quantity of work he put through his hands, his evenings were almost always reserved for the light reading of an elbow-chair, or the enjoyment of his family and friends. Now he seemed to grudge every minute that was not spent at the desk. The little that he read of new books, or for mere amusement, was done by snatches in the course of his meals; and to walk, when he could walk at all, to the Parliament-House, and back again, through the Prince's Street Gardens, was his only exercise and his only relaxation. Every ailment, of whatever sort, ended in aggravating his lameness; and, perhaps, the severest test his philosophy encountered was the feeling of bodily helplessness that from week to week crept upon him. The winter, to make bad worse, was a very cold and stormy one. The growing sluggishness of his blood shewed itself in chilblains, not only on the feet but the fingers, and his handwriting becomes more and more cramped and confused.

He spent a few days at Abbotsford at Christmas, and several weeks during the spring vacation; but the frequent Saturday excursions were now out of the question—if for no other reason, on account of the quantity of books which he must have by him while working at his Napoleon. He says on the 30th of December—" Wrote hard. Last day of an eventful year; much evil—and some good, but especially the courage to endure what Fortune sends, without becoming a pipe for her fingers. It is *not* the last day of the year; but to-morrow being Sunday, we hold our festival to-day. The Fergussons came, and we had the usual appliances of mirth and good cheer. Yet our party, like the chariot-wheels of Pharaoh in the Red Sea, dragged heavily.—It must be allowed that the regular recurrence of annual festivals among the same individuals has, as life advances, something in it that is melancholy. We meet like the survivors of some perilous expedition, wounded and weakened ourselves, and looking through diminished ranks to think of those who are no more. Or they are like the feasts of the Caribs, in which they held that the pale and speechless phantoms of the deceased appeared and mingled with the living. Yet where shall we fly from vain repining?—or why should we give up the comfort of seeing our friends, because they can no longer be to us, or we to them, what we once were to each other?"

On again quitting Tweedside after the spring holidays (1827), the Diary has:—" I never could help admiring the concatenation between Ahithophel's setting his house in order and hanging himself.[1]   The one seems to follow the other as a matter of course.   But what frightens and disgusts me is those fearful letters from those who have been long dead to those who linger on their wayfare through the valley of tears.   Those fine lines of Spencer came into my head—

> " The shade of youthful Hope is there,
>   That lingered long, and latest died;
> Ambition all dissolved to air,
>   With phantom Honours by his side,
> What empty shadows glimmer nigh?
>   They once were Friendship, Truth, and Love!
> Oh! die to thought, to memory die,
>   Since lifeless to my heart ye prove."[2]

Ay, and can I forget the author—the frightful moral of his own vision?   What is this world?—a dream within a dream: as we grow older, each step is an awakening. The youth awakes, as he thinks, from childhood—the full-grown man despises the pursuits of youth as visionary— the old man looks on manhood as a feverish dream.   The grave the last sleep?   No; it is the last and final awakening.

" *Edinburgh, May* 15.—It is impossible not to compare this return to Edinburgh with others in more happy times. But we should rather recollect under what distress of mind I took up my lodgings in Mrs. Brown's last summer.— Went to Court and resumed old habits.   Heard the true history of ——.[3]   Imagination renders us liable to be the victims of occasional low spirits.   All belonging to this gifted, as it is called, but often unhappy class, must have felt, that but for the dictates of religion, or the natural recoil of the mind from the idea of dissolution, there have been times when they would have been willing to throw away life as a child does a broken toy.   I am sure I know one who has often felt so.   O God! what are we?—Lords of nature?—Why, a tile drops from a house-top, which an elephant would not feel more than the fall of a sheet of paste-board, and there lies his lordship.   Or something of inconceivably minute origin—the pressure of a bone, or the inflammation of a particle of the brain—takes place, and

[1] 2d Samuel, xvii. 23.
[2] " Poems by the late Honourable W. R. Spencer," p. 45.
[3] Sir Walter had this morning heard of the suicide of a man of warm imagination, to whom, at an earlier period, he was much attached.

the emblem of the Deity destroys himself or some one else. We hold our health and our reason on terms slighter than one would desire, were it in their choice, to hold an Irish cabin."

These are melancholy entries. Most of those from which they have been selected begin with R. for Rheumatism or R.R. for Rheumatism redoubled, and then mark the number of leaves sent to Ballantyne—the proof-sheets corrected for press—or the calculations on which he reluctantly made up his mind to extend the Life of Buonaparte from six to seven, from seven to eight, and finally from eight to nine thick and closely-printed volumes.

During the early months of 1827, however, he executed various minor tracts also : for the Quarterly Review, an article on " Mackenzie's Life and Works of John Home, author of Douglas," which is, in fact, a rich chapter of Scott's own early reminiscences, and gives many interesting sketches of the literary society of Scotland in the age of which Mackenzie was the last honoured relic;—and for the Foreign Quarterly Review, then newly started under the editorship of Mr. R. P. Gillies, an ingenious and elaborate paper on the writings of the German novelist Hoffman. This article, it is proper to observe, was a benefaction to Mr. Gillies, whose pecuniary affairs rendered such assistance very desirable. Scott's generosity in this matter—for it was exactly giving a poor brother author £100 at the expense of considerable time and drudgery to himself—I think it necessary to mention; the date of the exertion requires it of me. But such, in fact, had been in numberless instances his method of serving literary persons who had little or no claim on him, except that they were of that class. I have not conceived it delicate to specify many things of this kind; but I am at liberty to state, that when he wrote his first article for the Encyclopædia Supplement, and the editor of that work, Mr. Macvey Napier (a Whig in politics, and with whom he had hardly any personal acquaintance), brought him £100 as his remuneration, Sir Walter said—" Now tell me frankly, if I don't take this money, does it go into your pocket or your publisher's? for it is impossible for me to accept a penny of it from a literary brother." Mr. Napier assured him that the arrangements of the work were such, that the editor had nothing to do with the fund destined for contributions. Scott then pocketed his due, with the observation, that "he had trees to plant, and no conscience as to the purse of his fat friend"—to wit, Constable.

At this period, the Edinburgh Diary very seldom mentions anything that could be called a dinner-party. Skene he often styles "his good Samaritan": he was now the usual companion of whatever walks he was willing or able to indulge in. He and his daughter partook generally once in every week the family meal of Mr. and Mrs. Skene; and they did the like occasionally with a few other old friends, chiefly those of the Clerk's table. When an exception occurs, it is easy to see that the scene of social gaiety was doubly grateful from its rarity. Thus one entry, referring to a party at Mr. J. A. Murray's,[1] says—"met Jeffrey, Cockburn, Rutherfurd, and others of that file. Very pleasant—capital good cheer and excellent wine —much laugh and fun. I do not know how it is, but when I am out with a party of my Opposition friends, the day is often merrier than when with our own set. Is it because they are cleverer? Jeffrey and Harry Cockburn are to be sure very extraordinary men; yet it is not owing to that entirely. I believe both parties meet with the feeling of something like novelty—we have not worn out our jests in daily contact. There is also a disposition on such occasions to be courteous, and of course to be pleased." Another evening, spent in Rose Court, seems to have given him especial delight. He says—"I wrote hard till dressing time, when I went to Will Clerk's to dinner. As a bachelor, and keeping a small establishment, he does not do these things often, but they are proportionally pleasant when they come round. He had trusted Sir Adam to bespeak his dinner, who did it *con amore*, so we had excellent cheer, and the wines were various and capital. As I before hinted, it is not every day that M'Nab mounts on horseback,[2] and so our landlord had a little of that solicitude that the party should go off well, which is very flattering to the guests. We had a very pleasant evening. The Chief-Commissioner was there, Admiral Adam, J. A. Murray, Tom Thomson, &c., &c.,—Sir Adam predominat-

[1] Afterwards Lord Advocate, and now a Judge of the Court of Session, by the title of Lord Murray.

[2] That singular personage, the late M'Nab of *that ilk*, spent his life almost entirely in a district where a boat was the usual conveyance. I suspect, however, that there is an allusion to some particular anecdote which I have not recovered.

ing at the head, and dancing what he calls his merry-and-rada in great style. In short, we really laughed, and real laughter is a thing as rare as real tears. I must say, too, there was a *heart*—a kindly feeling prevailed over the party. Can London give such a dinner?—it may, but I never saw one—they are too cold and critical to be easily pleased. ——I hope the Bannatyne Club will be really useful and creditable. Thomson is superintending a capital edition of Sir James Melville's Memoirs. It is brave to see how he wags his Scots tongue, and what a difference there is in the form and firmness of the language, compared to the mincing English edition in which he has hitherto been alone known.''

No wonder that it should be a sweet relief from Buonaparte and Blücher to see M'Nab on horseback, and Sir Adam Fergusson in his merry-andrada exaltation, and laugh over old Scotch stories with the Chief-Commissioner, and hear Mr. Thomas Thomson report progress as to the doings of the Bannatyne Club. But I apprehend every reader will see that Sir Walter was misled by his own modesty, when he doubted whether London could afford symposia of the same sort. He forgets that he had never mixed in the society of London except in the capacity of a stranger, a rare visitor, the unrivalled literary marvel of the time, and that every party at which he dined was got up expressly on his account, and constituted, whoever might be the landlord, on the natural principle of bringing together as many as the table could hold—to see and hear Sir Walter Scott. Hence, if he dined with a Minister of State, he was likely to find himself seated with half the Cabinet—if with a Bishop, half the Bench had been collected. As a matter of course, every man was anxious to gratify on so rare an occasion as many as he could of those who, in case they were uninvited, would be likely to reproach him for the omission. The result was a crowding together of too many rival eminences; and he very seldom indeed, witnessed the delightful result so constantly produced in London by the intermingling of distinguished persons of various classes, full of facts and views new to each other—and neither chilled nor perplexed by the pernicious and degrading trickery of lionising. But besides, it was unfair to institute any comparison between the society of comparative strangers and that of old friends dear from boyhood. He could not have his Clerks and

Fergussons both in Edinburgh and in London. Enough, however, of commentary on a very plain text.

That season was further enlivened by one public dinner, and this, though very briefly noticed in Scott's Diary, occupied a large space in public attention at the time, and, I believe I may add, several columns in every newspaper in Europe. His good friend William Murray, manager of the Edinburgh Theatre, invited him to preside at the first festival of a charitable fund for decayed performers. He agreed, and on Friday the 23rd February took the chair, being supported by the Earl of Fife, Lord Meadowbank, Sir John Hope of Pinkie, Admiral Adam, Robert Dundas of Arniston, *Peter* Robertson, and many other personal friends. Lord Meadowbank had come on short notice, and was asked abruptly on his arrival to take a toast which had been destined for a noble person who had not been able to appear. He knew that this was the first public dinner at which the object of the toast had appeared since his misfortunes, and taking him aside in the anteroom, asked him whether he would now consider it indelicate to hazard a distinct reference to the parentage of the Waverley Novels. Sir Walter smiled, and said, " Do just as you like—only don't say much about so old a story."—In the course of the evening the Judge rose accordingly, and said—

" I would beg leave to propose a toast—the health of one of the Patrons. The clouds have been dispelled—the *darkness visible* has been cleared away—and the Great Unknown—the minstrel of our native land—the mighty magician who has rolled back the current of time, and conjured up before our living senses the men and the manners of days which have long passed away, stands revealed to the eyes and hearts of his affectionate and admiring countrymen. We owe to him, as a people, a large and heavy debt of gratitude. He it is who has opened to foreigners the grand and characteristic beauties of our country ;—it is to him that we owe that our gallant ancestors and illustrious patriots have obtained a fame no longer confined to the boundaries of a remote and comparatively obscure country—he it is who has conferred a new reputation on our national character, and bestowed on Scotland an imperishable name, were it only by her having given birth to himself. I propose the health of Sir Walter Scott."

Long before Lord Meadowbank ceased speaking, the company had got upon chairs and tables, and the storm of applause that ensued was deafening. When they recovered from the first fever, Sir Walter spoke as follows :—

" I certainly did not think, in coming here to-day, that I should have the task of acknowledging before 300 gentlemen, a secret which, considering that it was communicated to more than twenty people, has been remarkably well kept. I am now at the bar of my country, and may be understood to be on trial before Lord Meadowbank as an offender; and so quietly did all who were *airt and pairt* conduct themselves, that I am sure that, were the *panel* now to stand on his defence, every impartial jury would bring in a verdict of *Not Proven*. I am willing, however, to plead *guilty*—nor shall I detain the Court by a long explanation why my confession has been so long deferred. Perhaps caprice might have a considerable share in the matter. I have now to say, however, that the merits of these works, if they had any, and their faults, are all entirely imputable to myself. Like another Scottish criminal of more consequence, one Macbeth,

> ' I am afraid to think what I have done ;
> Look on't again I dare not.'—

—I have thus far unbosomed myself, and I know that my confession will be reported to the public. I mean, then, seriously to state, that when I say I am the author, I mean the total and undivided author. With the exception of quotations, there is not a single word that was not derived from myself, or suggested in the course of my reading. The wand is now broken, and the book buried. You will allow me further to say, with Prospero, it is your breath that has filled my sails, and to crave one single toast in the capacity of the author of these novels. I would fain dedicate a bumper to the health of one who has represented several of those characters, of which I had en-deavoured to give the skeleton, with a truth and liveliness for which I may well be grateful. I beg leave to propose the health of my friend Bailie Nicol Jarvie—and I am sure, that when the author of Waverley and Rob Roy drinks to Nicol Jarvie, it will be received with the just applause to which that gentleman has always been accus-tomed,—nay, that you will take care that on the present occasion it shall be PRO—DI—GI—OUS ! " (Long and vehement applause.)

Mr. MACKAY.—" My conscience ! My worthy father the deacon could never have believed that his son would hae sic a compliment paid to him by the Great Unknown ! "

SIR WALTER SCOTT.—" The Small Known now, Mr. Bailie ! "

The reader may, perhaps, expect that I should en-deavour to name the " upwards of twenty persons " whom Sir Walter alluded to on this occasion as having been put into the secret of the Waverley Novels, previously, and without reference, to the catastrophe of 1826. I am by no means sure that I can give the complete list : but in addition to immediate members of the author's own family —(including his mother and his brother Thomas)—there were Constable, Cadell, the two Ballantynes—two persons employed in the printing-office, namely Daniel M'Corkin-dale and Daniel Robertson—Mr. Terry, Mr. Laidlaw, Mr. Train, and Mr. G. H. Gordon—Charles Duke of Buc-cleuch, Lady Louisa Stuart, Lord Montagu, Lord and

Lady Polwarth, Lord Kinnedder, Sir Adam Fergusson, Mr. Morritt, Mr. and Mrs. Skene, Mr. William Clerk, Mr. Rose, Mr. Hay Donaldson, Mr. Thomas Shortreed, Mr. John Richardson, and Mr. Thomas Moore.

We now reach the completion of that severe task—the *Life of Napoleon*: and following instantly, the commencement of the charming *Tales of a Grandfather*.

" *Diary.—June* 5.—Proofs. Parliament-House till two. Commenced the character of Buonaparte. To-morrow being a Treind-day, I may hope to get it finished—*June* 10.—Rose with the odd consciousness of being free of my daily task. I have heard that the fish-women go to church of a Sunday with their creels new washed, and a few stones in them for ballast, just because they cannot walk steadily without their usual load. I feel something like them, and rather inclined to take up some light task, than to be altogether idle. I have my proof-sheets, to be sure; but what are these to a whole day? A good thought came in my head to write Stories for little Johnnie Lockhart, from the History of Scotland, like those taken from the History of England. But I will not write mine quite so simply as Croker has done.[1] I am persuaded both children and the lower class of readers hate books which are written *down* to their capacity, and love those that are composed more for their elders and betters. I will make, if possible, a book that a child shall understand, yet a man will feel some temptation to peruse should he chance to take it up. It will require, however, a simplicity of style not quite my own. The grand and interesting consists in ideas, not in words. A clever thing of this kind might have a race."

I received, some years ago, from a very modest and intelligent young man, the late Mr. Robert Hogg (a nephew of the Ettrick Shepherd), employed in 1827 as a *reader* in Ballantyne's printing-office, a letter from which I must give an extract :—" Having been for a few days employed by Sir Walter Scott, when he was finishing his Life of Buonaparte, to copy papers connected with that

---

[1] The following note accompanied a copy of the First Series of the Tales of a Grandfather :—

" *To the Right Hon. J. W. Croker.*

" My Dear Croker,—I have been stealing from you, and as it seems the fashion to compound felony, I send you a sample of the *swag,* by way of stopping your mouth......Always yours,
" W. Scott."

work, and to write occasionally to his dictation, it may perhaps be in my power to mention some circumstances relative to Sir Walter's habits of composition, which could not fall under the observation of any one except a person in the same situation with myself. When I waited upon him to be informed of the business in which he needed my assistance, he asked me to attend him the next morning at six o'clock. I was punctual, and found Sir Walter already busy writing. He appointed my tasks, and again sat down at his own desk. We continued to write during the regular work hours till six o'clock in the evening, without interruption, except to take breakfast and dinner, which were served in the room beside us, so that no time was lost. I had no notion it was possible for any man to undergo the fatigue of composition for so long a time at once, and Sir Walter acknowledged he did not usually subject himself to so much exertion, though it seemed to be only the manual part of the operation that occasioned him any inconvenience. Once or twice he desired me to relieve him, and dictated while I wrote. I have performed the same service to several other persons, most of whom walked up and down the apartment while excogitating what was to be committed to writing; they sometimes stopped, too, and, like those who fail in a leap and return upon their course to take the advantage of an-other race, endeavoured to hit upon something additional by perusing over my shoulder what was already set down,—mending a phrase, perhaps, or recasting a sentence, till they should recover their wind. None of these aids were necessary to Sir Walter: his thoughts flowed easily and felicitously, without any difficulty to lay hold of them, or to find appropriate language; which was evident by the absence of all solicitude (*miseria cogitandi*) from his countenance. He sat in his chair, from which he rose now and then, took a volume from the bookcase, consulted it, and restored it to the shelf—all without intermission in the current of ideas, which continued to be delivered with no less readiness than if his mind had been wholly occupied with the words he was uttering. It soon became apparent to me, however, that he was carrying on two distinct trains of thought, one of which was already arranged, and in the act of being spoken, while at the same time he was in advance considering what was afterwards to be said. This I discovered by his sometimes introducing a

word which was wholly out of place—*entertained* instead
of *denied*, for example,—but which I presently found to
belong to the next sentence, perhaps four or five lines
farther on, which he had been preparing at the very
moment that he gave me the words of the one that preceded it. Extemporaneous orators of course, and no
doubt many writers, think as rapidly as was done by Sir
Walter; but the mind is wholly occupied with what the
lips are uttering or the pen is tracing. I do not remember any other instance in which it could be said that two
threads were kept hold of at once—connected with each
other indeed, but grasped at different points."

The *Life of Buonaparte,* then, was at last published
about the middle of June 1827. Two years had elapsed
since Scott began it; but, by a careful comparison of
dates, I have arrived at the conclusion that, his expeditions
to Ireland and Paris, and the composition of novels and
critical miscellanies, being duly allowed for, the historical
task occupied hardly more than twelve months. The
book was closely printed; in fact, if it had been printed
on the original model of his novels, the Life of Buonaparte
would have filled from thirteen to fourteen volumes: the
work of one twelvemonth—done in the midst of pain,
sorrow, and ruin.

The general curiosity with which it was expected, and
the satisfaction with which high and candid minds perused
it, cannot be better described than in the words of the
author's most illustrious literary contemporary.

" Walter Scott," says Goethe, " passed his childhood among the
stirring scenes of the American War, and was a youth of seventeen
or eighteen when the French Revolution broke out. Now well advanced in the fifties, having all along been favourably placed for
observation, he proposes to lay before us his views and recollections
of the important events through which he has lived. The richest,
the easiest, the most celebrated narrator of the century, undertakes
to write the history of his own time.

" What expectations the announcement of such a work must have
excited in me will be understood by any one who remembers that I,
twenty years older than Scott, conversed with Paoli in the twentieth
year of my age, and with Napoleon himself in the sixtieth.

" Through that long series of years, coming more or less into contact with the great doings of the world, I failed not to think
seriously of what was passing around me, and, after my own fashion,
to connect so many extraordinary mutations into something like
arrangement and interdependence.

" What could now be more delightful to me, than leisurely and
calmly to sit down and listen to the discourse of such a man, while

clearly, truly, and with all the skill of a great artist, he recalls to me
the incidents on which through life I have meditated, and the influence of which is still daily in operation? "—*Kunst und Altherthum*.

The lofty impartiality with which Scott treats the personal character of Buonaparte was of course sure to make
all ultra-politicians both at home and abroad condemn his
representation; and an equally general and better founded
exception was taken to the lavish imagery of his historical style. He despised the former clamour—to the latter
he bowed submissive. He could not, whatever character
he might wish to assume, cease to be one of the greatest
of poets. Metaphorical illustrations, which men born with
prose in their souls hunt for painfully, and find only to
murder, were to him the natural and necessary offspring
and playthings of ever-teeming fancy. He could not write
a note to his printer—he could not speak to himself in his
Diary—without introducing them. Few will say that his
historical style is, on the whole, excellent—none that it
is perfect; but it is completely unaffected, and therefore
excites nothing of the unpleasant feeling with which we
consider the elaborate artifices of a far greater historian—
the greatest that our literature can boast—Gibbon. The
rapidity of the execution infers many inaccuracies as to
minor matters of fact; but it is nevertheless true that no
inaccuracy affecting the character of the book as a fair
record of great events has to this hour been detected by
the malevolent ingenuity of Jacobin or Buonapartist.
Even the most hostile examiners were obliged to acknow-
ledge that the gigantic career of their idol had been
traced, in its leading features, with wonderful truth and
spirit. No civilian, it was universally admitted, had ever
before described modern battles and campaigns with any
approach to his daring and comprehensive felicity. The
public, ever unwilling to concede a new species of honour
to a name already covered with distinction, listened
eagerly for a while to the indignant reclamations of no-
bodies, whose share in mighty transactions had been
omitted, or slightly misrepresented; but, ere long, all
these pompous rectifications were summed up—and found
to constitute nothing but a contemptible monument of self-
deluding vanity. The work, devoured at first with breathless delight, had a shade thrown over it for a time by the
pertinacious blustering of these angry Lilliputians; but it
has now emerged, slowly and surely, from the mist of

suspicion—and few, whose opinions deserve much attention, hesitate to avow their conviction that, whoever may
be the Polybius of the modern Hannibal, posterity will
recognise his Livy in Scott.

Woodstock, as we have seen, placed upwards of £8,000
in the hands of Sir Walter's creditors. The Napoleon
(first and second editions) produced for them a sum which
it even now startles me to mention,—£18,000. As by
the time the historical work was published, nearly half of
the First Series of Chronicles of the Canongate had been
written, it is obvious that the amount to which Scott's
literary industry, from the close of 1825 to the 10th of
June 1827, had diminished his debt, cannot be stated at
less than £28,000. Had health been spared him, how
soon must he have freed himself from all his encumbrances!

CHAPTER XV

Death of Constable—Controversy with Gourgaud—Excursion to
Durham—Publication of the Chronicles of the Canongate and Tales
of a Grandfather—Religious Discourses—Fair Maid of Perth—
Anne of Geierstein—Threatening of Apoplexy—Death of Thomas
Purdie. 1827–1829.

My wife and I spent the summer of 1827, partly at a
sea-bathing place near Edinburgh, and partly in Roxburghshire. The arrival of his daughter and her children
at Portobello was a source of constant refreshment to
Scott during June; for every other day he came down and
dined there, and strolled about afterwards on the beach;
thus interrupting, beneficially for his health, and I doubt
not for the result of his labours also, the new custom of
regular night-work, or, as he called it, of serving double-
tides. When the Court released him, and he returned to
Abbotsford, his family did what they could to keep him
to his ancient evening habits; but nothing was so useful
as the presence of his invalid grandson. The poor child
was at this time so far restored as to be able to sit his
pony again; and Sir Walter, who had, as the reader has
observed, conceived, the very day he finished Napoleon,
the notion of putting together a series of Tales on the
history of Scotland, somewhat in the manner of Mr.
Croker's on that of England, rode daily among the woods

with his " Hugh Littlejohn," and told the story, and
ascertained that it suited the comprehension of boyhood,
before he reduced it to writing.　Sibyl Grey had been dismissed in consequence of the accident at the Catrail; and
he had now stooped his pride to a sober, steady creature,
of very humble blood; dun, with black mane and legs;
by name Douce Davie, *alias* the Covenanter.　This, the
last of his steeds, by the way, had been previously in the
possession of a jolly old laird near Peebles, and acquired
a distinguished reputation by its skill in carrying him
home safely when drunk.　Douce Davie, on such occasions, accommodated himself to the swerving balance of
his rider with such nice discrimination, that on the laird's
death the country people expected a vigorous competition
for the sagacious animal; but the club-companions of the
defunct stood off to a man when it was understood that
the Sheriff coveted the succession.

The Chronicles of the Canongate proceeded *pari passu*
with these historical tales; and both works were published
before the end of the year.　He also superintended, at the
same time, the first collection of his Prose Miscellanies, in
six volumes 8vo—several articles being remodelled and
extended to adapt them for a more permanent sort of existence than had been originally thought of.　Moreover,
he penned that autumn his beautiful and instructive
Article on the Planting of Waste Lands, which is indeed
no other than a precious chapter of his autobiography.
What he wrote of new matter between June and December fills from five to six volumes in the late uniform
edition of his works; but all this was light and easy after
the perilous drudgery of the preceding eighteen months.

On the 22nd of July, his Diary notes the death of Mr.
Constable:—" This might have been a most important
thing to me if it had happened some years ago, and I
should then have lamented it much.　He has lived to do
me some injury; yet, excepting the last £5,000, I think
most unintentionally.　He was a prince of booksellers.
Constable was a violent-tempered man with those he dared
use freedom with.　He was easily overawed by people of
consequence; but, as usual, took it out of those whom
poverty made subservient to him.　Yet he was generous,
and far from bad-hearted :—in person good-looking, but
very corpulent latterly; a large feeder, and deep drinker,
till his health became weak.　He died of water in the

chest, which the natural strength of his constitution set long at defiance. I have no great reason to regret him; yet I do. If he deceived me, he also deceived himself.''

Constable's spirit had been effectually broken by his downfall. To stoop from being *primus absque secundo* among the Edinburgh booksellers to be the occupant of an obscure closet of a shop, without capital, without credit, all his mighty undertakings abandoned or gone into other hands, except indeed his Miscellany, which he had now no resources for pushing on in the fashion he once contemplated,—this reverse was too much for that proud heart. He no longer opposed a determined mind to the ailments of the body, and sunk on the 21st of this month, having, as I am told, looked, long ere he took to his bed, at least ten years older than he was. He died in his 54th year; but into that space he had crowded vastly more than the usual average of zeal and energy, of hilarity and triumph, and perhaps of anxiety and misery.

Of the 10th of August—when the news of Mr. Canning's death reached Abbotsford—and the day following, are these entries : '' The death of the Premier is announced —late George Canning—the witty, the accomplished, the ambitious ;—he who had toiled thirty years, and involved himself in the most harassing discussions, to attain this dizzy height; he who had held it for three months of intrigue and obloquy—and now a heap of dust, and that is all.—No man possessed a gayer and more playful wit in society; no one, since Pitt's time, had more commanding sarcasm in debate; in the House of Commons he was the terror of that species of orators called the Yelpers. His lash fetched away both skin and flesh, and would have penetrated the hide of a rhinoceros. In his conduct as a statesman he had a great fault : he lent himself too willingly to intrigue. The last composition with the Whigs was a sacrifice of principle on both sides. To me Canning was always personally most kind. My nerves have for these two or three last days been susceptible of an acute excitement from the slightest causes : the beauty of the evening, the sighing of the summer breeze, bring the tears into my eyes not unpleasantly. But I must take exercise, and case-harden myself. There is no use in encouraging these moods of the mind.''

He received about this time a visit from Mr. J. L. Adolphus; who had not seen him since 1824—and says :—

" Calamity had borne heavily upon Sir Walter in the interval; but the painful and anxious feeling with which a friend is approached for the first time under such circumstances gave way at once to the unassumed serenity of his manner. There were some signs of age about him which the mere lapse of time would scarcely have accounted for; but his spirits were abated only, not broken; if they had sunk, they had sunk equably and gently. It was a declining, not a clouded sun. I do not remember any reference to the afflictions he had suffered, except once, when, speaking of his Life of Napoleon, he said in a quiet but affecting tone, ' I could have done it better, if I could have written at more leisure, and with a mind more at ease.' One morning a party was made to breakfast at Chiefswood; and any one who on that occasion looked at and heard Sir Walter Scott, in the midst of his children and grandchildren and friends, must have rejoiced to see that life still yielded him a store of pleasures, and that his heart was as open to their influence as ever. I was much struck by a few words which fell from him on this subject a short time afterwards. After mentioning an accident which had spoiled the promised pleasure of a visit to his daughter in London, he then added—' I have had as much happiness in my time as most men, and I must not complain now.' I said, that whatever had been his share of happiness, no man could have laboured better for it. He answered—' I consider the capacity to labour as part of the happiness I have enjoyed.'

" A substitute for walking, which he always very cheerfully used, and which at last became his only resource for any distant excursion, was a ride in a four-wheeled open carriage, holding four persons, but not absolutely limited to that number on an emergency. Tame as this exercise might be in comparison with riding on horseback, or with walking under propitious circumstances, yet as he was rolled along to Melrose, or Bowhill, or Yair, his spirits always freshened; the air, the sounds, the familiar yet romantic scenes, wakened up all the poetry of his thoughts, and happy were they who heard it resolve itself into words. At the sight of certain objects—for example, in passing the green foundations of the little chapel of Lindean, where the body of the ' Dark Knight of Liddesdale ' was deposited on its way to Melrose,—it would, I suppose, have been impossible for him, unless with a companion hopelessly unsusceptible or preoccupied, to forbear some passing comment, some harping (if the word may be favourably used) on the tradition of the place. This was, perhaps, what he called ' bestowing his tediousness '; but if any one could think these effusions tedious because they often broke forth, such a man might have objected against the rushing of the Tweed, or the stirring of the trees in the wind, or any other natural melody, that he had heard the same thing before.

" Some days of my visit were marked by an almost perpetual confinement to the house; the rain being incessant. But the evenings were as bright and cheerful as the atmosphere of the days was dreary. Not that the gloomiest morning could ever be wearisome where, independently of the resources in society which the house afforded, the visitor might ransack a library, unique, I suppose, in some of its collections, and in all its departments interesting and characteristic of the founder. So many of the volumes were enriched with anecdotes or comments in his own hand, that to look over his books was in some degree conversing with him. And sometimes this occupation was pleasantly interrupted by a snatch of actual conversation with himself, when he entered from his own room to consult or take away a book. How often have I heard with pleasure, after a long silence, the uneven step, the point of the stick striking against the floor, and then seen the poet himself emerge from his study, with a face of thought but yet of cheerfulness, followed perhaps by Nimrod, who stretched his limbs and yawned, as if tired out with some abstruse investigation.

" On one of the rainy days I have alluded to, when walking at the usual hour became hopeless, Sir Walter asked me to sit with him while he continued his morning occupation, giving me for my own employment the publications of the Bannatyne Club. His study, as I recollect it, was strictly a work-room, though an elegant one. It has been fancifully decked out in pictures, but it had, I think, very few articles of mere ornament. The chief of these was the print of Stothard's Canterbury Pilgrims, which hung over the chimney-piece, and from the place assigned to it must have been in great favour, though Sir Walter made the characteristic criticism upon it that, if the procession were to move, the young Squire who is prancing in the foreground would in another minute be over his horse's head. The shelves were stored with serviceable books; one door opened into the great library, and a hanging-stair within the room itself communicated with his bedroom. It would have been a good lesson to a desultory student, or even to a moderately active amanuensis, to see the unintermitted energy with which Sir Walter Scott applied himself to his work. I conjectured that he was at this time writing the Tales of a Grandfather. When we had sat down to our respective employments, the stillness of the room was unbroken, except by the light rattle of the rain against the windows, and the dashing trot of Sir Walter's pen over his paper; sounds not very unlike each other, and which seemed to vie together in rapidity and continuance. Sometimes, when he stopped to consult a book, a short dialogue would take place upon the subjects with which I was occupied—about Mary Queen of Scots, perhaps, or Viscount Dundee; or, again, the silence might be broken for a moment by some merry outcry in the hall, from one of the little grandchildren, which would half waken Nimrod, or Bran, or Spice, as they slept at Sir Walter's feet, and produce a growl or a stifled bark—not in anger, but by way of protest. For matters like these, work did not proceed the worse, nor, as it seemed to me, did Sir Walter feel at all discomposed by such interruptions as a message or the entrance of a visitor. One door of his study opened into the hall, and there did not appear to be any understanding that he should not be disturbed. At the end of our morning we attempted a sortie, but had made only a little way in the shrubbery-walks overlooking the Tweed, when the rain drove us back. The river, swollen and discoloured, swept by majestically, and the sight drew from Sir Walter his favourite lines—

' I've seen Tweed's silver streams, glittering in the sunny beams,
   Turn drumly and dark, as they rolled on their way.'

There could not have been a better moment for appreciating the imagery of the last line. I think it was in this short walk that he mentioned to me, with great satisfaction, the favourable prospects of his literary industry, and spoke sanguinely of retrieving his losses with the booksellers.''

    Towards the end of August, Sir Walter's Diary has a good deal about an affair which, however, annoyed his family much more than himself. Among the documents laid before him in the Colonial Office, when he visited London at the close of 1826, were some which represented one of Buonaparte's attendants at St. Helena, General Gourgaud, as having been guilty of gross unfairness, giving the English Government private information that the Emperor's complaints of ill-usage were utterly unfounded, and yet then, and afterwards, aiding and assisting the delusion in France as to the harshness of Sir Hudson Lowe's conduct towards his captive. Sir Walter, when using these remarkable documents, guessed that Gourgaud might be inclined to fix a personal quarrel on himself; and there now appeared in the newspapers a succession of hints that the General was seriously bent on this purpose. He applied, as *Colonel Grogg* would have done forty years before, to *The Baronet.*—He writes to William Clerk on the 27th:—" I am about to claim an especial service from you in the name of our long and intimate friendship. I understand that General Gourgaud has, or is about to set out for London, to *verify* the facts averred concerning him in my history of Napoleon. Now, in case of a personal appeal to me, I have to say that his confessions to Baron Sturmer, Count Balmain, and others at St. Helena—confirmed by him in various recorded conversations with Mr. Goulburn, then Under-Secretary of State—were documents of a historical nature which I found with others in the Colonial Office, and was therefore perfectly entitled to use. If his language has been misrepresented, he has certainly been very unfortunate; for it has been misrepresented by four or five different people to whom he said the same thing—true or false, he knows best. I also acted with delicacy towards him, leaving out whatever related to his private quarrels with Bertrand, &c., so that, in fact, he has no reason to complain of me, since it is ridiculous to suppose I was to suppress historical evidence, furnished by him voluntarily, because his present sentiments render it unpleasing for him that those which he formerly entertained should be known. Still, like a man who finds himself in a scrape, General Gourgaud may wish to fight himself out of it; and if the quarrel should be thrust on me—why, *I will not baulk him, Jackie.* He shall not dishonour the country through my sides, I can assure him. I have, of course, no wish to bring the thing to such an arbitrement. Now, in this case, I shall have occasion for a sensible and resolute friend, and I naturally look for him in the companion of my youth, on whose firmness and sagacity I can with such perfect confidence rely."

Clerk was ready for his part :—but the General, if he had ever meditated a direct call on Scott, did not persevere. The Diary of September 10th says—" Gourgaud's wrath has burst forth in a very distant clap of thunder, in which he accuses me of contriving, with the Ministry, to slander his rag of a reputation. He be d——d for a fool, to make his case worse by stirring. I shall only revenge myself by publishing the whole extracts I made from the records of the Colonial Office, in which he will find enough to make him bite his nails."—Scott accordingly printed a brief letter, with a crushing appendix of documents. This produced a blustering rejoinder from Gourgaud; but Scott declined to prolong the paper war, simply stating in Ballantyne's print, that " while leaving the question to the decision of the British public, he should have as little hesitation in referring it to the French nation, provided the documents he had produced were allowed to be printed in the French newspapers, *from which hitherto they had been excluded.*" And he would indeed have been idle had he said more than this, for his cause had been taken up on the instant by every English journal, of whatever politics ; and *The Times* thus summed up its review of the debate :—

" Sir Walter Scott did that which would have occurred to every honest man, whose fair-dealing had violent imputations cast upon it. He produced his authorities. In the General's reply there is enough, even to satiety, of declamation against the English Government,—of subterfuge and equivocation with regard to the words on record against himself,—and of gross abuse and Billingsgate against the historian who has placarded him ; but of direct and successful negative there is not one syllable. The Aide-de-camp of St. Helena shews himself to be nothing better than a cross between a blusterer and a sophist."

Before Gourgaud fell quite asleep, Sir Walter received an invitation from Lord and Lady Ravensworth to meet the Duke of Wellington at their castle near Durham. The Duke was then making a progress in the north of England, to which additional importance was given by the condition of politics ;—the chance of Lord Goderich's being able to maintain himself as Canning's successor seeming very precarious—and the opinion that his Grace must soon be called to the helm of State gaining ground every day. Sir Walter, who felt for the Great Captain the pure and exalted devotion that might have been expected from some honoured soldier of his banners, accepted this invitation, and witnessed a scene of enthusiasm with which its principal object could hardly have been more gratified than he was. The most remarkable feature was a grand dinner in the Episcopal Castle at Durham—that See being as yet unshorn of its Palatine magnificence. "On the 3rd October," says his Diary, "we dined about one hundred and forty or fifty men—a distinguished company—

> ' Lords and Dukes and noble Princes,
> All the pride and flower of Spain.'

We dined in the old baronial hall, impressive from its rude antiquity, and fortunately free from the plaster of former improvement, as I trust it will long be from the gingerbread taste of modern Gothicisers. The bright moon streaming in through the old Gothic windows contrasted strangely with the artificial lights within; spears, banners, and armour, were intermixed with the pictures of old bishops, and the whole had a singular mixture of baronial pomp with the grave and more chastened dignity of prelacy. The conduct of our reverend entertainer suited the character remarkably well. Amid the welcome of a Count Palatine he did not for an instant forget the gravity of the Church dignitary. All his toasts were gracefully given, and his little speeches well made, and the more affecting that the failing voice sometimes reminded us that our host laboured under the infirmities of advanced life." I was favoured at the time with a letter from Dr. Philpotts (now Bishop of Exeter), who said—" I never saw curiosity and enthusiasm so highly excited, and I may add, as to a great part of the company, so nearly balanced. Sometimes I doubted whether the hero or the poet was fixing most attention—the latter, I need hardly tell you, appeared unconscious that he was regarded differently from the others about him, until the good Bishop rose and proposed his health." Another friend, the Honourable Henry Liddell, says—" Bishop Van Mildert gave his health with peculiar felicity, remarking that he could reflect upon the labours of a long literary life, with the consciousness that everything he had written tended to the practice of virtue, and to the improvement of the human race. Sir Walter replied, ' that hereafter

he should always reflect with great pride upon that
moment of his existence, when his health had been given
in such terms, by the Bishop of Durham *in his own
baronial hall,* surrounded and supported by the assembled
aristocracy of the two northern counties, and *in the
presence of the Duke of Wellington.'* "

On the 8th Sir Walter reached Abbotsford, and forthwith resumed his Grandfather's Tales, which he composed
throughout with the ease and heartiness reflected in this
entry:—" This morning was damp, dripping, and unpleasant; so I even made a work of necessity, and set to
the Tales like a dragon.   I murdered Maclellan of Bomby
at the Thrieve Castle; stabbed the Black Douglas in the
town of Stirling; astonished King James before Roxburgh; and stifled the Earl of Mar in his bath in the
Canongate.   A wild world, my masters, this Scotland of
ours must have been.   No fear of want of interest; no
lassitude in those days for want of work—

> ' For treason, d'ye see,
>   Was to them a dish of tea,
>   And murder bread and butter.' "

Such was his life in autumn 1827.   Before I leave the
period, I must note how greatly I admired the manner in
which all his dependents appeared to have met the reverse
of his fortunes—a reverse which inferred very considerable
alteration in the circumstances of every one of them.   The
butler, Dalgleish, had been told, when the distress came,
that a servant of his class would no longer be required—
but the man burst into tears, and said, rather than go he
would stay without any wages.   So he remained—and
instead of being the easy chief of a large establishment,
was now doing half the work of the house, at probably
half his former salary.   Old Peter, who had been for
five-and-twenty years a dignified coachman, was now
ploughman in ordinary, only putting his horses to the carriage upon high and rare occasions; and so on with all the
rest that remained of the ancient train.   And all, to my
view, seemed happier than they had ever done before.
Their good conduct had given every one of them a new
elevation in his own mind—and yet their demeanour had
gained, in place of losing, in simple humility of observance.   The great loss was that of William Laidlaw, for
whom (the estate being all but a fragment in the hands of
the trustees and their agent) there was now no occupation

here. The cottage, which his taste had converted into a lovable retreat, had found a rent-paying tenant; and he was living a dozen miles off on the farm of a relation in the Vale of Yarrow. Every week, however, he came down to have a ramble with Sir Walter over their old haunts—to hear how the pecuniary atmosphere was darkening or brightening; and to read in every face at Abbotsford, that it could never be itself again until circumstances should permit his re-establishment at Kaeside.

All this warm and respectful solicitude must have had a salutary influence on the mind of Scott, who may be said to have lived upon love. No man cared less about popular admiration and applause; but for the least chill on the affection of any near and dear to him he had the sensitiveness of a maiden. I cannot forget, in particular, how his eyes sparkled when he first pointed out to me Peter Mathieson guiding the plough on the haugh: " Egad," said he, " auld *Pepe* " (this was the children's name for their good friend)—" auld *Pepe's* whistling at his darg. The honest fellow said, a yoking in a deep field would do baith him and the blackies good. If things get round with me, easy shall be Pepe's cushion. '' In general, during that autumn, I thought Sir Walter enjoyed much his usual spirits; and often, no doubt, he did so. His Diary, however, shews (what perhaps many of his intimates doubted during his lifetime) that, in spite of the dignified equanimity which characterised all his conversation with mankind, he had his full share of the delicate sensibilities, the mysterious ups and downs, the wayward melancholy, and fantastic sunbeams of the poetical temperament. It is only with imaginative minds, in truth, that sorrows of the spirit are enduring. Those he had encountered were veiled from the eye of the world, but they lasted with his life.

The first series of Chronicles of the Canongate—(which title supplanted that of *The Canongate Miscellany, or Traditions of the Sanctuary*)—was published early in the winter. The contents were, the Highland Widow, the Two Drovers, and the Surgeon's Daughter—all in their styles excellent, except that the Indian part of the last does not well harmonise with the rest; and certain preliminary chapters which were generally considered as still better than the stories they introduce. The portraiture of Mrs. Murray Keith, under the name of Mrs. Bethune

Baliol, and that of Chrystal Croftangry throughout, appear to me unsurpassed in Scott's writings. In the former, I am assured he has mixed up various features of his own beloved mother; and in the latter, there can be no doubt that a good deal was taken from nobody but himself. In fact, the choice of the hero's residence, the original title of the book, and a world of minor circumstances, were suggested by painful circumstances recorded in his Diary of 1827. He had, while toiling his life out for his creditors, received various threatenings of severe treatment from the London Jews formerly alluded to, Messrs. Abud and Co.; and, on at least one occasion, he made every preparation for taking shelter in the Sanctuary of Holyroodhouse. Although these people were well aware that at Christmas 1827 a very large dividend would be paid on the Ballantyne debt, they could not bring themselves to comprehend that their interest lay in allowing Scott the free use of his time; that by thwarting and harassing him personally nothing was likely to be achieved but the throwing up of the trust, and the settlement of the insolvent house's affairs on the usual terms of a sequestration. The Jews would understand nothing, but that the very unanimity of the other creditors as to the propriety of being gentle with him rendered it extremely probable that their own harshness might be rewarded by immediate payment of their whole demand. They fancied that the trustees would clear off any one debt, rather than disturb the arrangements generally adopted; they fancied that, in case they laid Sir Walter Scott in prison, there would be some extraordinary burst of feeling in Edinburgh—that private friends would interfere;—in short, that in one way or another, they should get hold, without farther delay, of their "pound of flesh."—Two paragraphs from the Diary will be enough as to this unpleasant subject :—

"*October* 31.—Just as I was merrily cutting away among my trees, arrives Mr. Gibson with a very melancholy look, and indeed the news he brought was shocking enough. It seems Mr. Abud had given positive orders to take out diligence against me for his debt. This breaks all the measures we had resolved on, and prevents the dividend from taking place, by which many poor persons will be great sufferers. For me—the alternative will be more painful to my feelings than prejudicial to my interests. To submit to a sequestration, and allow the creditors to take what they can get, will be the inevitable consequence. This will cut short my labour by several years, which I might spend, and spend in vain, in endeavouring to meet their demands. I suppose that I, the Chronicler of the Canongate, will have to take up my residence in the Sanctuary, unless I prefer the more airy residence of the Carlton Jail, or a trip to the Isle of Man.— *November 4.*—Put my papers in some order, and prepared for the journey. It is in the style of the Emperors of Abyssinia, who proclaim, 'Cut down the Kantuffa in the four quarters of the world, for I know not where I am going.' Yet, were it not for poor Anne's doleful looks, I would feel firm as a piece of granite. Even the poor dogs seem to fawn on me with anxious meaning, as if there were something going on they could not comprehend. Set off at twelve, firmly resolved in body and mind. But when I arrived in Edinburgh at my faithful friend Mr. Gibson's—lo! the scene had again changed, and a new hare is started.''

The '' new hare '' was this. It transpired in the very nick of time, that a suspicion of usury attached to these Israelites in a transaction with Hurst and Robinson, as to one or more of the bills for which the house of Ballantyne had become responsible. This suspicion assumed a shape sufficiently tangible to justify that house's trustees in carrying the point before the Court of Session. Thus, though the Court decided in favour of the Abuds, time was gained; and as soon as the decision was pronounced, Scott heard also that the Jews' debt was settled. In fact, Sir William Forbes, whose banking-house was one of Messrs. Ballantyne's chief creditors, had crowned his generous efforts for Scott's relief by privately paying the whole of Abud's demand (nearly £2,000) out of his own pocket—ranking as an ordinary creditor for the amount; and taking care at the same time that his old friend should be allowed to believe that the affair had merged quietly in the general measures of the trustees. It was not until some time after Sir William's death, that Sir Walter learned what had been done on this occasion; and I may as well add here, that he died in utter ignorance of some services of a like sort which he owed to the secret liberality of three of his brethren at the Clerks' table—Hector M'Donald Buchanan, Colin Mackenzie, and Sir Robert Dundas. I ought not to omit, that as soon as Sir Walter's eldest son heard of the Abud business, he left Ireland for Edinburgh; but before he reached his father, the alarm had blown over.

This vision of the real Canongate has drawn me away from the Chronicles of Mr. Croftangry. The scenery of his patrimonial inheritance was sketched from that of Carmichael, the ancient and now deserted mansion of the noble family of Hyndford; but for his strongly Scottish feelings about parting with his *land*, and stern efforts to suppress them, the author had not to go so far afield. Christie Steele's brief character of Croftangry's ancestry, too, appears to suit well all that we have on record concerning his own more immediate progenitors of the stubborn race of Raeburn:—" They werena ill to the poor folk, sir, and that is aye something; they were just decent bein bodies. Ony poor creature that had face to beg got an awmous, and welcome; they that were shamefaced gaed by, and twice as welcome. But they keepit an honest walk before God and man, the Croftangrys; and as I said before, if they did little good, they did as little ill. They lifted their rents and spent them; called in their kain and eat them; gaed to the kirk of a Sunday; bowed civilly if folk took aff their bannets as they gaed by, and lookit as black as sin at them that keepit them on." I shall give no offence by adding that many things in the character and manners of Mr. Gideon Gray of Middlemas, in the Tale of the Surgeon's Daughter, were considered at the time by Sir Walter's neighbours on Tweedside as copied from Dr. Ebenezer Clarkson of Selkirk. " He was," says the Chronicler, " of such reputation in the medical world, that he had been often advised to exchange the village and its meagre circle of practice for Edinburgh. There is no creature in Scotland that works harder, and is more poorly requited, than the country doctor, unless perhaps it may be his horse. Yet the horse is, and indeed must be, hardy, active, and indefatigable, in spite of a rough coat and indifferent condition; and so you will often find in his master, under a blunt exterior, professional skill and enthusiasm, intelligence, humanity, courage, and science." A true picture—a portrait from the life, of Scott's hard-riding, benevolent, and sagacious old friend, " to all the country dear."

These Chronicles were not received with exceeding favour at the time; and Sir Walter was a good deal discouraged. Indeed he seems to have been with some difficulty persuaded by Cadell and Ballantyne that it would not do for him to " lie fallow " as a novelist; and then, when he in compliance with their entreaties began a second Canongate Series, they were both disappointed with his MS., and told him their opinions so plainly that his good-nature was sharply tried. The Tales which they disapproved of were those of My Aunt Margaret's Mirror and the Laird's Jock; he consented to lay them aside, and began St. Valentine's Eve or the Fair Maid of Perth, which from the first pleased his critics. It was in the brief interval occasioned by these misgivings and debates, that his ever elastic mind threw off another charming paper for the Quarterly Review—that on Ornamental Gardening, by way of sequel to the Essay on Planting Waste Lands. Another fruit of his leisure was a sketch of the life of George Bannatyne, the collector of ancient Scottish poetry, for the Club which bears his name.

He had taken, for that winter, the house No. 6 Shandwick Place, which he occupied by the month during the remainder of his servitude as a Clerk of Session. Very near this house, he was told a few days after he took possession, dwelt the aged mother of his first love; and he expressed to his friend Mrs. Skene a wish that she should carry him to renew an acquaintance which seems to have been interrupted from the period of his youthful romance. Mrs. Skene complied with his desire, and she tells me that a very painful scene ensued. His Diary says:—" *November* 7.—Began to settle myself this morning after the hurry of mind and even of body which I have lately undergone.—I went to make a visit, and fairly softened myself, like an old fool, with recalling old stories, till I was fit for nothing but shedding tears and repeating verses for the whole night. This is sad work. The very grave gives up its dead, and time rolls back thirty years to add to my perplexities. I don't care. I begin to grow case-hardened, and, like a stag turning at bay, my naturally good temper grows fierce and dangerous. Yet what a romance to tell!—and told, I fear, it will one day be. And then my three years of dreaming, and my two years of wakening, will be chronicled, doubtless. But the dead will feel no pain.—*November* 10.—Wrote out my task and little more. At twelve o'clock I went again to poor Lady Jane to talk over old stories. I am not clear that it is a right or healthful indulgence to be ripping up old sores, but it seems to give her deep-rooted sorrow words, and that is a mental blood-letting. To me these things are now matter of calm and solemn recollection, never to be forgotten, yet scarce to be remembered with pain."

A few days afterwards arrived a very agreeable piece of intelligence. The King had not forgotten his promise with respect to the poet's second son; and Lord Dudley, then Secretary of State for the Foreign Department, was very well disposed to comply with the royal recommendation. Charles was appointed to a clerkship in the Foreign Office; and his settlement was rapidly followed by more than one fortunate incident in his father's literary and pecuniary history. The first Tales of a Grandfather appeared early in December, and their reception was more rapturous than that of any one of his works since Ivanhoe. He had solved for the first time the problem of narrating history, so as at once to excite and gratify the curiosity of youth, and please and instruct the wisest of mature minds. The popularity of the book has grown with every year that has since elapsed; it is equally prized in the library, the boudoir, the schoolroom, and the nursery; it is adopted as the happiest of manuals, not only in Scotland, but wherever the English tongue is spoken; nay, it is to be seen in the hands of old and young all over the civilised world, and has, I have little doubt, extended the knowledge of Scottish history in quarters where little or no interest had ever before been awakened as to any other parts of that subject, except those immediately connected with Mary Stuart and the Chevalier.

There had been serious doubts, in what proportions the copyright of the Novels, &c., was vested, at the moment of the common calamity, in Scott or in Constable. One of the ablest of the Scotch Judges, John Irving, Lord Newton, undertook the settlement of this complicated question, as private arbiter: and the result of his ultimate award was, that Scott had lost all hold on the copyright of the Novels from Waverley to Quentin Durward; but that Napoleon and Woodstock were wholly his. This decision, however, was not to be expected speedily: it had now become highly expedient to bring the body of copyrights to sale—and it was agreed to do so, the money to be deposited in bank until the award were given. This sale (on 19th December 1827) comprised all the Novels from Waverley to Quentin Durward inclusive, besides a majority of the shares of the Poetical Works. Mr. Cadell's family and private friends were extremely desirous to secure for him part at least of these copyrights; and Sir Walter's were not less so that he should seize this last opportunity of recovering a share in the prime fruits of his genius. The relations by this time established between him and Cadell were those of strict confidence and kindness; and both saw well that the property would be comparatively lost, were it not ensured that thenceforth the whole should be managed as one unbroken concern. The result was, that the copyrights exposed to sale were purchased, one-half for Sir Walter, the other half for Cadell, at the price of £8,500. Well might the " pockpuddings "—for so the Diary styles the English booksellers—rue their timidity on this day; but it was the most lucky one that ever came for Sir Walter's creditors. A dividend of six shillings in the pound was paid at this Christmas on their whole claims. The result of their high-hearted debtor's exertions, between January 1826 and January 1828, was in all very nearly £40,000. No literary biographer, in all likelihood, will ever have such another fact to record. The creditors unanimously passed a vote of thanks for the indefatigable industry which had achieved so much for their behoof.

On returning to Abbotsford at Christmas, after completing these transactions, he says in his Diary—" My reflections in entering my own gate to-day were of a very different and more pleasing cast than those with which I left this place about six weeks ago. I was then in doubt whether I should fly my country, or become avowedly bankrupt, and surrender up my library and household furniture, with the life rent of my estate, to sale. A man of the world will say I had better done so. No doubt, had I taken this course at once, I might have employed the money I have made since the insolvency of Constable and Robinson's houses in compounding my debts. But I could not have slept sound, as I now can under the comfortable impression of receiving the thanks of my creditors, and the conscious feeling of discharging my duty as a man of honour and honesty. I see before me a long, tedious, and dark path, but it leads to stainless reputation. If I die in the harrows, as is very likely, I shall die with honour; if I achieve my task, I shall have the thanks of all concerned, and the approbation of my own conscience."

He now took up in earnest two pieces of work, which promised and brought great ultimate advantage; namely, a complete collection of his Poems, with *biographical* prefaces; the other, an uniform edition of his Novels, each to be introduced by an account of the hints on which it had been founded, and illustrated throughout by historical and antiquarian annotations. On this last, commonly mentioned in the Diary as the *Magnum Opus*, Sir Walter bestowed pains commensurate with its importance;—and in the execution of the very delicate task which either scheme imposed, he has certainly displayed such a combination of frankness and modesty as entitles him to a high place in the short list of graceful autobiographers. True dignity is always simple; and perhaps true genius, of the highest class at least, is always humble. These operations took up much time; yet he laboured hard this year both as a novelist and a historian. He contributed, moreover, several articles to the Quarterly Review and the Bannatyne Club library; and to the Journal conducted by Mr. Gillies, an excellent Essay on Molière; this last being again a free gift to the editor.

But the first advertisement of 1828 was of a new order; and the announcement that the Author of Waverley had *Sermons* in the press was received perhaps with as much incredulity in the clerical world, as could have been excited among them by that of a romance from the Archbishop of Canterbury. A thin octavo volume, entitled " Religious Discourses by a Layman," and having " W.S." at the foot of a short preface, did, however, issue in the course of the spring, and from the shop, that all might be in perfect keeping, of Mr. Colburn, a bookseller then known almost exclusively as the standing purveyor of what is called light reading—novels of fashionable life and the like pretty ephemera. I am afraid that the Religious Discourses, too, would, but for the author's name, have had a brief existence; but the history of their composition, besides sufficiently explaining the humility of these tracts in a literary as well as a theological point of view, will, I hope, gratify most of my readers.—Sir Walter's cicerone over Waterloo, in August 1815, was a certain Major Pryse Gordon, then on half-pay, and resident at Brussels. The acquaintance, until they met at Sir Frederick Adam's table, had been slight; but the Major was exceedingly attentive during Scott's stay, and after-

wards took some pains about collecting reliques of the
field for Abbotsford. One evening the poet supped at his
house, and there happened to sit next him the host's eldest
son, then a lad of nineteen, whose appearance and situation much interested him. He had been destined for the
Church of Scotland, but, as he grew up, a deafness, which
had come on in him in boyhood, became worse and worse,
and at length his friends feared that it must incapacitate
him for the clerical function. He had gone to spend the
vacation with his father, and General Adam offered him
a temporary appointment as a clerk in the Commissariat,
which he hoped to convert into a permanent one, in case
the war continued. At the time of Scott's arrival that
prospect was well nigh gone, and the young man's infirmity, his embarrassment, and other things to which his
own memorandum makes no allusion, excited the visitor's
sympathy. Though there were lion-hunters of no small
consequence in the party, he directed most of his talk into
the poor clerk's ear-trumpet; and at parting, begged him
not to forget that he had a friend on Tweedside.

A couple of years elapsed before he heard anything more
of George Huntly Gordon, who then sent him his father's
little *spolia* of Waterloo, and accompanied them by a letter
explaining his situation, and asking advice, in a style
which renewed and increased Scott's favourable impression. He had been dismissed from the Commissariat at
the general reduction of our establishments, and was now
hesitating whether he had better take up again his views
as to the Kirk, or turn his eyes towards English orders;
and in the meantime he was anxious to find some way of
lightening to his parents, by his own industry, the completion of his professional education. There ensued a
copious correspondence between him and Scott, who gave
him on all points of his case most paternal advice, and
accompanied his counsels with offers of pecuniary assistance, of which the young man rarely availed himself. At
length he resolved on re-entering the Divinity Class at
Aberdeen, and in due time was licensed by the Presbytery
there as a Preacher of the Gospel; but though with good
connections, for he was "sprung of Scotia's gentler
blood," his deafness operated as a serious bar to his obtaining the incumbency of a parish. The provincial Synod
pronounced his deafness an insuperable objection, and the
case was referred to the General Assembly. That tribunal

heard the young man's cause maintained by all the skill and eloquence of Mr. Jeffrey, whose good offices had been secured by Scott's intervention, and they overruled the decision of the Synod. But Gordon, in the course of the discussion, gathered the conviction that a man almost literally stone deaf could *not* discharge some of the highest duties of a parish-priest in a satisfactory manner, and he with honourable firmness declined to take advantage of the judgment of the Supreme Court. Meantime he had been employed, from the failure of John Ballantyne's health downwards, as the transcriber of the Waverley MSS. for the press, in which capacity he displayed every quality that could endear an amanuensis to an author; and when the disasters of 1826 rendered it unnecessary for Scott to have his MS. copied, he exerted himself to procure employment for his young friend in one of the Government offices in London. Being backed by the kindness of the Duke of Gordon, his story found favour with the then Secretary of the Treasury, Mr. Lushington—and Mr. Gordon was named assistant private secretary to that gentleman. The appointment was temporary, but he so pleased his chief that there was hope of better things by and by.—Such was his situation at Christmas 1827; but that being his first Christmas in London, it was no wonder that he then discovered himself to have somewhat miscalculated about money matters. In a word, he knew not whither to look at the moment for extrication, until he bethought him of the following little incident of his life at Abbotsford.

He was spending the autumn of 1824 there, daily copying the MS. of Redgauntlet, and working at leisure hours on the Catalogue of the Library, when the family observed him to be labouring under some extraordinary depression of mind. It was just then that he had at length obtained the prospect of a living, and Sir Walter was surprised that this should not have exhilarated him. Gently sounding the trumpet, however, he discovered that the agitation of the question about the deafness had shaken his nerves—his scruples had been roused—his conscience was sensitive, —and he vowed that, though he thought, on the whole, he ought to go through with the business, he could not command his mind so as to prepare a couple of sermons, which, unless he summarily abandoned his object, must be produced on a certain day—then near at hand—before his

Presbytery. Sir Walter reminded him that his exercises when on trial for the Probationership had given satisfaction;—but nothing he could say was sufficient to re-brace Mr. Gordon's spirits, and he at length exclaimed, with tears, that his pen was powerless,—that he had made fifty attempts, and saw nothing but failure and disgrace before him. Scott answered—"My good young friend, leave this matter to me—do you work away at the Catalogue, and I'll write for you a couple of sermons, that shall pass muster well enough at Aberdeen." Gordon assented with a sigh; and next morning Sir Walter gave him the MS. of the "Religious Discourses." On reflection, Mr. Gordon considered it quite impossible to produce them at Aberdeen as his own: but they had remained in his hands; and it now occurred to him that, if Sir Walter would allow him to dispose of these to some bookseller, they might possibly bring a price that would float him over his little difficulties of Christmas.

The only entries in the Diary which relate to the business are the following:—"*December* 28. Huntly Gordon writes me in despair about £180 of debt which he has incurred. He wishes to publish two sermons which I wrote for him when he was taking orders; and he would get little money for them without my name. People may exclaim against the undesired and unwelcome zeal of him who stretched his hands to help the ark over, with the best intentions, and cry sacrilege. And yet they will do me gross injustice, for I would, if called upon, die a martyr for the Christian religion, so completely is (in my poor opinion) its divine origin proved by its beneficial effects on the state of society. Were we but to name the abolition of slavery and polygamy, how much has, in these two words, been granted to mankind in the lessons of our Saviour!—*January* 10, 1828. Huntly Gordon has disposed of the two sermons to the bookseller, Colburn, for £250; well sold, I think, and to go forth immediately. I would rather the thing had not gone there, and far rather that it had gone nowhere, yet hang it, if it makes the poor lad easy, what need I fret about it? After all, there would be little grace in doing a kind thing, if you did not suffer pain or inconvenience upon the score."

The next literary entry is this:—"Mr. Heath, the engraver, invites me to take charge of a yearly publication called the Keepsake, of which the plates are beyond comparison beautiful, but the letter-press indifferent enough. He proposes £800 a year if I would become editor, and £400 if I would contribute from seventy to one hundred pages. I declined both, but told him I might give him some trifling thing or other. To become the stipendiary editor of a New-Year's-Gift Book is not to be thought of, nor could I agree to work regularly, for any quantity of supply, at such a publication. Even the pecuniary view is not flattering, though Mr. Heath meant it should be so. One hundred of his close printed pages, for which he offers £400, are nearly equal to one volume of a novel. Each novel of three volumes brings £4,000, and I remain proprietor of the mine after the first ore is scooped out." The result was that Mr. Heath received, for £500, the liberty of printing in his Keepsake the long-forgotten juvenile drama of the House of Aspen, with Aunt Margaret's Mirror, and two other little tales, which had been omitted, at Ballantyne's entreaty, from the second Chronicles of Croftangry. But Sir Walter regretted having meddled in any way with the toyshop of literature, and would never do so again, though repeatedly offered very large sums—nor even when the motive of private regard was added, upon Mr. Allan Cunningham's lending his name to one of these painted bladders. In the same week that Mr. Heath made his proposition, Sir Walter received another, which he thus disposes of in his Diary:—" I have an invitation from Messrs. Saunders and Ottley, booksellers, offering me from £1,500 to £2,000 annually to conduct a journal; but I am their humble servant. I am too indolent to stand to that sort of work, and I must preserve the undisturbed use of my leisure, and possess my soul in quiet. A large income is not my object; I must clear my debts; and that is to be done by writing things of which I can retain the property."

He finished his novel by the end of March, and immediately set out for London, where the last budget of proofsheets reached him. The Fair Maid was, and continues to be, highly popular, and though never classed with his performances of the first file, it has undoubtedly several scenes equal to what the best of them can shew, and is on the whole a work of brilliant variety and most lively interest.

Though the Introduction of 1830 says a good deal on the most original character, that of Connachar, the reader may not be sorry to have one paragraph on that subject from

the Diary :—" *December* 5, 1827. The fellow that swam
the Tay, and escaped, would be a good ludicrous character. But I have a mind to try him in the serious line of
tragedy. Miss Baillie has made her Ethling a coward by
temperament, and a hero when touched by filial affection.
Suppose a man's nerves, supported by feelings of honour,
or say by the spur of jealousy, sustaining him against
constitutional timidity to a certain point, then suddenly
giving way, I think something tragic might be produced.
James Ballantyne's criticism is too much moulded upon
the general taste of novels to admit (I fear) this species
of reasoning. But what can one do? I am hard up as far
as imagination is concerned,—yet the world calls for
novelty. Well, I'll try my brave coward or cowardly
brave man. *Valeat quantum.*"

I alluded, in an early chapter, to a circumstance in Sir
Walter's conduct which it was painful to mention, and
added, that in advanced life he himself spoke of it with a
deep feeling of contrition. Talking over this character of
Connachar, just before the book appeared, he told me the
unhappy fate of his brother Daniel, and how he had declined to be present at his funeral or wear mourning for
him. He added—" My secret motive in this attempt was
to perform a sort of expiation to my poor brother's manes.
I have now learned to have more tolerance and compassion
than I had in those days." I said he put me in mind of
Samuel Johnson's standing bareheaded, in the last year of
his life, on the market-place of Uttoxeter, by way of penance for a piece of juvenile irreverence towards his father.
" Well, no matter," said he; " perhaps that's not the
worst thing in the Doctor's story." [1]

Sir Walter and Miss Scott remained at this time six
weeks in the Regent's Park. His eldest son's regiment
was stationed at Hampton Court; the second had recently
taken his desk at the Foreign Office, and was living in
my house; he had thus looked forward to a happy meeting
with all his family—but he encountered scenes of sickness
and distress, in consequence of which I saw but little of
him in general society. Nor is his Diary particularly interesting : with the exception of a few entries. That for
May 1st is :—" Breakfasted with Lord and Lady Francis
Gower, and enjoyed the splendid treat of hearing Mrs.
Arkwright sing her own music, which is of the highest

---

[1] See *Boswell* under August 1784.

order;—no forced vagaries of the voice, no caprices of tone, but all telling upon and increasing the feeling the words require. This is ' marrying music to immortal verse.' Most people place them on separate maintenance."— Among other songs, Mrs. Arkwright delighted Sir Walter with her own set of—

> " Farewell ! farewell !—The voice you hear
>   Has left its last soft tone with you ;
> Its next must join the seaward cheer,
>   And shout among the shouting crew," &c.

He was sitting by me, at some distance from the lady, and whispered as she closed—" Capital words—whose are they ? Byron's, I suppose, but I don't remember them." He was astonished when I told him that they were his own in The Pirate. He seemed pleased at the moment, but said next minute—" You have distressed me—if memory goes, all is up with me, for that was always my strong point."

" *May* 5.—Breakfasted with Haydon, and sat for my head. I hope this artist is on his legs again. The King has given him a lift, by buying his clever picture of the Mock Election in the King's Bench prison. Haydon was once a great admirer and companion of the champions of the Cockney school, and is now disposed to renounce them and their opinions. To this kind of conversation I did not give much way. A painter should have nothing to do with politics. He is certainly a clever fellow, but too enthusiastic, which, however, distress seems to have cured in some degree. His wife, a pretty woman, looked happy to see me, and that is something. Yet it was very little I could do to help them.[1]—*May* 8.—Dined with Mrs. Alexander of Ballochmyle :—Lord and Lady Meath, who were kind to us in Ireland, and a Scottish party, pleasant from having the broad accents and honest thoughts of my native land. A large circle in the evening. A gentleman came up to me and asked ' If I had seen The Casket, a curious work, the most beautiful, the most highly ornamented,— and then the editor or editress,—a female so interesting,— might he ask a very great favour ? ' and out he pulled a

---

[1] Sir Walter had shortly before been one of the contributors to a subscription for Mr. Haydon. The imprisonment from which this subscription relieved the artist produced, I need scarcely say, the picture mentioned in the Diary. This clever man concluded an unhappy history in the unhappiest manner in 1846.

piece of this picnic. I was really angry, and said,—for a subscription he might command me; for a contributor— No. This may be misrepresented, but I care not. Suppose this patron of the Muses gives five guineas to his distressed lady, he will think he does a great deal, yet he takes fifty from me with the calmest air in the world; for the communication is worth that if it be worth anything. There is no equalising in the proposal.—*May* 11.—Dined with his Majesty in a very private party, five or six only being present. It is impossible to conceive a more friendly manner than that his Majesty used towards me.—*May* 19. —Dined by command with the Duchess of Kent. I was very kindly recognised by Prince Leopold—and presented to the little Princess Victoria—I hope they will change her name—the heir-apparent to the crown as things now stand. How strange that so large and fine a family as that of his late Majesty should have died off, or decayed into old age, with so few descendants. Prince George of Cumberland is, they say, a fine boy about nine years old— a bit of a Pickle. This little lady is educating with much care, and watched so closely, that no busy maid has a moment to whisper, ' You are heir of England.' I suspect if we could dissect the little heart, we should find that some pigeon or other bird of the air had carried the matter. She is fair, like the royal family—the Duchess herself very pleasing and affable in her manners. I sat by Mr. Spring Rice, a very agreeable man. There were also Charles Wynn and his lady—and the evening, for a Court evening, went agreeably off. I am commanded for two days by Prince Leopold, but will send excuses.—*May* 25.—After a morning of letter-writing, leave-taking, papers-destroying, and God knows what trumpery, Sophia and I set out for Hampton Court, carrying with us the following lions and lionesses—Samuel Rogers, Tom Moore, Wordsworth, with wife and daughter. We were very kindly and properly received by Walter and his wife, and had a very pleasant day. At parting, Rogers gave me a gold-mounted pair of glasses, which I will not part with in a hurry. I really like S. R., and have always found him most friendly."

Breakfasting one morning with Allan Cunningham, (whose notes are before me) he looked round the table, and said, " What are you going to make of all these boys, Allan ? "—" I ask that question often at my own heart," said Allan, "and I cannot answer it."—"What does the eldest point to?"—"The callant would fain be a soldier, Sir Walter—and I have half a promise of a commission in the King's army for him; but I wish rather he could go to India, for there the pay is a maintenance, and one does not need interest at every step to get on." Scott dropped the subject; but went an hour afterwards to Lord Melville (who was now President of the Board of Control), and begged a cadetship for young Cunningham. Lord Melville promised to inquire if he had one at his disposal, in which case he would gladly serve the son of "honest Allan"; but the point being thus left doubtful, Scott meeting Mr. John Loch, one of the East-India Directors, at dinner the same evening, at Lord Stafford's, applied to him, and received an immediate assent. On reaching home at night, he found a note from Lord Melville, intimating that he had inquired, and was happy in complying with his request. Next morning, Sir Walter appeared at Sir F. Chantrey's breakfast-table, and greeted the sculptor (a brother of the angle) with—"I suppose it has sometimes happened to you to catch one trout (which was all you thought of) with the fly, and another with the bobber. I have done so, and I think I shall land them both. Don't you think Cunningham would like very well to have cadetships for two of those fine lads?"—"To be sure he would," said Chantrey, "and if you'll secure the commissions, I'll make the outfit easy." Great was the joy in Allan's household on this double good news; but I should add, that before the thing was done he had to thank another benefactor. Lord Melville, after all, went out of the Board of Control before he had been able to fulfil his promise; but his successor, Lord Ellenborough, on hearing the case, desired Cunningham to set his mind at rest; and both his young men are now prospering in the India service.

"*Rokeby, May* 30.—A mile from the house we met Morritt, looking for us. He is now one of my oldest, and I believe one of my most sincere friends;—a man unequalled in the mixture of sound good sense, high literary cultivation, and the kindest and sweetest temper that ever graced a human bosom. His nieces are much attached to him, and are deserving and elegant, as well as beautiful young women.—What there is in our partiality to female beauty that commands a species of temporary homage from

the aged, as well as ecstatic admiration from the young,
I cannot conceive; but it is certain that a very large portion of some other amiable quality is too little to counterbalance the absolute want of this advantage. I, to whom
beauty is, and shall henceforward be, a picture, still look
upon it with the quiet devotion of an old worshipper, who
no longer offers incense on the shrine, but peaceably presents his inch of taper, taking special care in doing so not
to burn his own fingers. Nothing in life can be more
ludicrous or contemptible than an old man aping the passions of his youth."

Next night Sir Walter rested at Carlisle,—" A sad
place," says the Diary, " in my domestic remembrances,
since here I married my poor Charlotte. She is gone, and
I am following—faster, perhaps, than I wot of. It is
something to have lived and loved; and our poor children
are so hopeful and affectionate, that it chastens the sadness
attending the thoughts of our separation." His feeling
and sprightly companion wrote thus a day or two afterwards to her sister :—" Early in the morning before we
started, papa took me with him to the Cathedral. This he
had often done before; but he said he must stand once
more on the spot where he married poor mamma. After
that we went to the Castle, where a new showman went
through the old trick of pointing out Fergus MacIvor's
very dungeon. Peveril said—' Indeed?—are you quite
sure, sir?' And on being told there could be no doubt,
was troubled with a fit of coughing, which ended in a
laugh. The man seemed exceeding indignant : so when
papa moved on, I whispered who it was. I wish you had
seen the man's start, and how he stared and bowed as he
parted from us ; and then rammed his keys into his pocket,
and went off at a hand-gallop to warn the rest of the garrison. But the carriage was ready, and we escaped a row."
They reached Abbotsford that night, and a day or two
afterwards Edinburgh ; where Sir Walter was greeted with
the satisfactory intelligence that his plans as to the *opus
magnum* had been considered at a meeting of his trustees,
and finally approved *in toto*. As the scheme inferred a
large outlay on drawings and engravings, and otherwise,
this decision had been looked for with much anxiety by
him and Mr. Cadell. He says—" I trust it will answer :
yet who can warrant the continuance of popularity? Old
Nattali Corri, who entered into many projects, and could

never set the sails of a windmill to catch the *aura populous*, used to say he believed that were he to turn baker, it would put bread out of fashion.   I have had the better luck to dress my sails to every wind; and so blow on, good wind, and spin round, whirligig."   The *Corri* here alluded to was an unfortunate adventurer, who, among many other wild schemes, tried to set up an Italian Opera at Edinburgh.

During the remainder of this year Sir Walter never opened his "locked book."   Whether in Edinburgh or the country, his life was such, that he describes himself, in several letters, as having become "a writing automaton." He had completed by Christmas the Second Series of Tales on Scottish History, and made considerable progress in another novel—Anne of Geierstein : he had also drawn up for the Quarterly Review his article on Hajji Baba in England ; and that delightful one on Davy's *Salmonia*— which, like those on Planting and Gardening, abounds in sweet episodes of personal reminiscence.   And, whenever he had not proof-sheets to press him, his hours were bestowed on the *opus magnum*.

About this time died Sir William Forbes of Pitsligo, the widower of his first love, and the most generous and efficient friend in the late crisis of distress.   On this event his letters have some very touching passages—but his feelings towards that admirable person have been sufficiently shewn in preceding extracts.

Visiting Abbotsford at Christmas, I found him apparently well in health (except that he suffered from rheumatism), and enjoying the society, as usual, of the Fergussons, with the welcome addition of Mr. Morritt and Sir James Steuart of Allanbank—a gentleman whose masterly pencil had often been employed on subjects from his poetry and novels, and whose conversation on art (like that of Sir George Beaumont and Mr. Scrope), being devoid of professional pedantries and jealousies, was always particularly delightful to him.   One snowy morning, he gave us sheets of *Anne of Geierstein*, extending to, I think, about a volume and a half ; and we read them together in the library, while he worked in the adjoining room, and occasionally dropped in upon us to hear how we were pleased. All were highly gratified with those vivid and picturesque pages,—and both Morritt and Steuart, being familiar with the scenery of Switzerland, could not sufficiently express

their astonishment at the felicity with which he had divined
its peculiar character, and outdone, by the force of imagination, all the efforts of a thousand actual tourists. Such
approbation was of course very acceptable. I had seldom
seen him more gently and tranquilly happy.

When these friends left him, he went with me to my
brother's in Clydesdale, and there enjoyed some days of
relaxation. It was then that he first saw the self-educated
sculptor, John Greenshields, who greatly interested him
from a certain resemblance to Burns, and took the first
sitting for a very remarkable statue in freestone, now in
Mr. Cadell's possession—the last work which this worthy
man was destined to complete.

Sir Walter's operations appear to have been interrupted
ever and anon, during January and February 1829, in
consequence of severe distress in the household of his
printer; whose warm affections were not, as in his own
case, subjected to the authority of a stoical will. On the
14th of February the Diary says :—" The letters I received
were numerous, and craved answers; yet the 3rd volume is
getting on *hooly and fairly*. I am twenty leaves before the
printer, but Ballantyne's wife is ill, and it is his nature to
indulge apprehensions of the worst, which incapacitates
him for labour. I cannot help regarding this amiable
weakness of the mind with something too nearly allied to
contempt." On the 17th, " I received the melancholy
news that James Ballantyne had lost his wife. With his
domestic habits the blow is irretrievable. What can he do,
poor fellow, at the head of such a family of children? I
should not be surprised if he were to give way to despair."
—James was not able to appear at his wife's funeral; and
this Scott viewed with something more than pity. Next
morning, however, says the Diary—" Ballantyne came in,
to my surprise, about twelve o'clock. He was very
serious, and spoke as if he had some idea of sudden and
speedy death. He has settled to go to the country, poor
fellow ! "—He retired accordingly to some sequestered
place near Jedburgh, and there indulged his grief in solitude. Scott regarded this as weakness, and in part at
least as wilful weakness, and addressed to him several letters of strong remonstrance and rebuke. In writing of
the case to myself, he says—" I have a sore grievance in
poor Ballantyne's increasing lowness of heart, and I fear
he is sinking rapidly into the condition of a religious

dreamer. His retirement from Edinburgh was the worst advised scheme in the world. I in vain reminded him, that when our Saviour himself was to be led into temptation, the first thing the Devil thought of was to get him into the wilderness.''—Ballantyne, after a few weeks, resumed his place in the printing-office; but he addicted himself more and more to what his friend considered as erroneous and extravagant notions of religious doctrine; and I regret to say that in this difference originated a certain alienation, not of affection, but of confidence, which was visible to every near observer of their subsequent intercourse. Towards the last, indeed, they saw but little of each other. I suppose, however, it is needless to add, that down to the very last, Scott watched over Ballantyne's interests with undiminished attention.

Many entries of his Diary during the Spring Session refer to the final carrying of the Roman Catholic Question. When the Duke of Wellington announced his intention of conceding those claims, there were meetings and petitions enough in Edinburgh as elsewhere; and though Scott felt considerable repugnance to acting in any such matter with Whigs and Radicals, in opposition to a great section of the Tories, he ultimately resolved not to shrink from doing his part in support of the Duke's Government on that critical experiment.[1] He wrote, I believe, several articles in favour of the measure for the Weekly Journal; he spoke, though shortly, at the principal meeting, and proposed one of its resolutions; and when the consequent petition was read in the House of Commons, his name among the subscribers was received with such enthusiasm, that Sir Robert Peel thought fit to address to him a special and very cordial letter of thanks on that occasion.

His novel was finished before breakfast on the 29th of April; and his Diary mentions that immediately after breakfast he began his compendium of Scottish history for Dr. Lardner's Cyclopædia. When the proprietors of that work, in July 1828, offered him £500 for an abstract of Scottish History in one volume, he declined the proposal. They subsequently offered £700, and this was accepted; but though he began the task under the impression that he should find it a heavy one, he soon warmed to the subject, and pursued it with cordial zeal and satisfaction. One volume, it by and by appeared, would never do,—in his

[1] See *ante*, pp. 476, 477.

own phrase, " he must have elbow-room "—and I believe
it was finally settled that he should have £1,500 for the
book in two volumes; of which the first was published before the end of this year.

Anne of Geierstein came out about the middle of May;
and this, which may be almost called the last work of his
imaginative genius, was received at least as well—(out of
Scotland, that is)—as the Fair Maid of Perth had been,
or indeed as any novel of his after the Crusaders. I partake very strongly, I am aware, in the feeling which most
of my own countrymen have little shame in avowing, that
no novel of his, where neither scenery nor character is
Scottish, belongs to the same pre-eminent class with those
in which he paints and peoples his native landscape. I
have confessed that I cannot rank even his best English
romances with such creations as Waverley and Old Mortality; far less can I believe that posterity will attach
similar value to this Maid of the Mist. Its pages, however, display in undiminished perfection all the skill and
grace of the mere artist, with occasional outbreaks of the
old poetic spirit, more than sufficient to remove the work
to an immeasurable distance from any of its order produced in this country in our own age. Indeed, the various
play of fancy in the combination of persons and events,
and the airy liveliness of both imagery and diction, may
well justify us in applying to the author what he beautifully says of his King René—

> " A mirthful man he was; the snows of age
> Fell, but they did not chill him. Gaiety,
> Even in life's closing, touch'd his teeming brain
> With such wild visions as the setting sun
> Raises in front of some hoar glacier,
> Painting the bleak ice with a thousand hues."

It is a common saying that there is nothing so distinctive of *genius* as the retention, in advanced years, of the
capacity to depict the feelings of youth with all their
original glow and purity. But I apprehend this blessed
distinction belongs to, and is the just reward of, virtuous
genius only. In the case of extraordinary force of
imagination, combined with the habitual indulgence of a
selfish mood—not combined, that is to say, with the genial
temper of mind and thought which God and Nature design
to be kept alive in man by those domestic charities out
of which the other social virtues so easily spring, and with

which they find such endless links of interdependence;—in this unhappy case, which none who has studied the biography of genius can pronounce to be a rare one, the very power which heaven bestowed seems to become, as old age darkens, the sternest avenger of its own misapplication. The retrospect of life is converted by its energy into one wide blackness of desolate regret; and whether this breaks out in the shape of a rueful contemptuousness, or a sarcastic mockery of tone, the least drop of the poison is enough to paralyse all attempts at awakening sympathy by fanciful delineations of love and friendship. Perhaps Scott has nowhere painted such feelings more deliciously than in those very scenes of Anne of Geierstein, which offer every now and then, in some incidental circumstance or reflection, the best evidence that they are drawn by a grey-headed man. The whole of his own life was too present to his wonderful memory to permit of his brooding with exclusive partiality, whether painfully or pleasurably, on any one portion or phasis of it; and besides, he was always living over again in his children, young at heart whenever he looked on them, and the world that was opening on them and their friends. But above all, he had a firm belief in the future reunion of those whom death has parted.

He lost two more of his old intimates about this time;—Mr. Terry in June, and Mr. Shortreed in the beginning of July. The Diary says:—" *July* 9. Heard of the death of poor Bob Shortreed, the companion of many a long ride among the hills in quest of old ballads. He was a merry companion, a good singer and mimic, and full of Scottish drollery. In his company, and under his guidance, I was able to see much of rural society in the mountains, which I could not otherwise have attained, and which I have made my use of. He was, in addition, a man of worth and character. I always burdened his hospitality while at Jedburgh on the circuit, and have been useful to some of his family. Poor fellow! So glide our friends from us. Many recollections die with him and with poor Terry."

His Diary has few more entries for this twelvemonth. Besides the volume of history for Lardner, he had ready by December the last of the *Scottish* Series of Tales of a Grandfather; and had made great progress in the prefaces and notes for Cadell's *opus magnum*. He had also overcome various difficulties which for a time interrupted the twin scheme of an illustrated edition of his Poems : and one of these in a manner honourably characteristic of the late John Murray of Albemarle Street, who had till now retained a share in the copyright of Marmion. Scott having requested him to *sell* that share, he generously replied :—" So highly do I estimate the honour of being, even in so small a degree, the publisher of the author of the poem, that no pecuniary consideration whatever can induce me to part with it. But there is a consideration of another kind, which until now I was not aware of, which would make it painful to me if I were to retain it a moment longer. I mean the knowledge of its being required by the author, into whose hands it was spontaneously resigned in the same instant that I read his request."

The success of the collective novels was far beyond what either Sir Walter or Mr. Cadell had ventured to anticipate. Before the close of 1829, eight volumes had been issued ; and the monthly sale had reached as high as 35,000. Should this go on, there was, indeed, every reason to hope that, coming in aid of undiminished industry in the preparation of new works, it would wipe off all his load of debt in the course of a very few years. And during the autumn (which I spent near him) it was most agreeable to observe the effects of the prosperous intelligence, which every succeeding month brought, upon his spirits.

This was the more needed, that his eldest son, who had gone to the south of France on account of some unpleasant symptoms in his health, did not at first seem to profit rapidly by the change of climate. He feared that the young man was not so obedient to his physicians as he ought to have been ; and in one of many letters on this subject, after mentioning some of Cadell's good news as to the great affair, he says—" I have wrought hard, and so far successfully. But I tell you plainly, my dear boy, that if you permit your health to decline from want of attention, I have not strength of mind enough to exert myself in these matters as I have hitherto been doing." Happily Major Scott was, ere long, restored to his usual state of health and activity.

Sir Walter himself, too, besides the usual allowance of rheumatism, and other lesser ailments, had an attack that season of a nature which gave his family great alarm, and which for several days he himself regarded with the darkest prognostications. After some weeks, during which he complained of headache and nervous irritation, certain hæmorrhages indicated the sort of relief required, and he obtained it from copious cupping. He says, in his Diary for June 3rd—"The ugly symptom still continues. Either way I am firmly resolved. I wrote in the morning. The Court kept me till near two. In the evening Dr. Ross ordered me to be cupped, an operation which I only knew from its being practised by those eminent medical practitioners the barbers of Bagdad. It is not painful; and, I think, resembles a giant twisting about your flesh between his finger and thumb." After this he felt better, he said, than he had done for years before; but there can be little doubt that the natural evacuation was a very serious symptom. It was, in fact, the precursor of apoplexy. In telling the Major of his recovery, he says— "The sale of the Novels is pro—di—gi—ous. If it last but a few years, it will clear my feet of old incumbrances, nay, perhaps, enable me to talk a word to our friend Nicol Milne.

'But old ships must expect to get out of commission,
   Nor again to weigh anchor with *yo heave ho!*'

However that may be, I should be happy to die a free man; and I am sure you will all be kind to poor Anne, who will miss me most. I don't intend to die a minute sooner than I can help for all this; but when a man takes to making blood instead of water, he is tempted to think on the possibility of his soon making earth."—Mr. Milne, be it observed, was the proprietor of a considerable estate conterminous with Abbotsford to the westward.

Among a few other friends from a distance, Sir Walter received this summer a short visit from Mr. Hallam, and made in his company several of the little excursions which had in former days been of constant recurrence. Mr. Hallam had with him his son, Arthur, a young gentleman of extraordinary abilities, and as modest as able, who not long afterwards was cut off in the very bloom of opening life and genius. His beautiful verses *on Melrose seen in company with Scott* have since been often printed.

The close of the autumn was embittered by a sudden and most unexpected deprivation. Apparently in the fullest enjoyment of health and vigour, Thomas Purdie leaned his head one evening on the table, and dropped asleep. This was nothing uncommon in a hard-working man; and his family went and came about him for several hours, without taking any notice. When supper was ready, they tried to awaken him, and found that life had been for some time extinct. Far different from other years, Sir Walter seemed impatient to get away from Abbotsford to Edinburgh. "I have lost," he writes (4th November) to Cadell, "my old and faithful servant—my factotum—and am so much shocked that I really wish to be quit of the country and safe in town. I have this day laid him in the grave. This has prevented my answering your letters."

The grave, close to the Abbey at Melrose, is surmounted by a modest monument, having on two sides these inscriptions :—

In grateful remembrance of the faithful and attached services of twenty-two years, and in sorrow for the loss of a humble but sincere friend; this stone was erected by Sir Walter Scott, Bart., of Abbotsford.

Here lies the body of Thomas Purdie, wood-forester at Abbotsford, who died 29th October, 1829, aged sixty-two years.—"*Thou hast been faithful over a few things, I will make thee ruler over many things.*"—St. Matthew, chap. xxv. ver. 21st.

CHAPTER XVI

Publication of the Ayrshire Tragedy, Letters on Demonology, Tales on the History of France, &c.—Apoplectic Seizure—Retirement from the Court of Session—Offers of a pension and of additional rank declined—Count Robert of Paris begun—Death of George IV.—Political Commotions—Fourth Epistle of Malagrowther—Speech on Reform at Jedburgh. 1830–1831.

AT this time, Mr. Pitcairn was editing for the Banna-tyne Club that curious collection of Ancient Scotch Criminal Trials, which Scott reviewed in the Quarterly of 1831. On his arrival in Edinburgh, Mr. Pitcairn sent him a new volume in proof, requesting his attention particularly to its details on the extraordinary case of Mure of Auchindraine, A.D. 1611. Scott was so much inter-

ested with these documents, that he resolved to found a
dramatic sketch on their terrible story; and the result was
a composition far superior to any of his previous attempts
of that nature.   Indeed, there are several passages in his
Ayrshire Tragedy—especially that where the murdered
corpse floats upright in the wake of the assassin's bark—
(an incident suggested by a lamentable chapter in Lord
Nelson's history)—which may bear comparison with anything but Shakespeare.   Yet I doubt whether the prose
narrative of the preface be not, on the whole, more
dramatic than the versified scenes.   It contains, by the
way, some very striking allusions to the recent murder of
Weare by Thurtell and others at Gill's Hill in Hertford-
shire, and the atrocities of Burke and Hare in the West
Port of Edinburgh.   This piece was published in a thin
octavo, early in 1830.

But he was now to pay the penalty of his unparalleled
toils.   On the 15th of February, about two o'clock in the
afternoon, he returned from the Parliament-House apparently in his usual state, and found an old acquaintance,
Miss Young of Hawick, waiting to shew him some MS.
memoirs of her father (a dissenting minister of great worth
and talents), which he had undertaken to revise and correct for the press.   The old lady sat by him for half an
hour while he seemed to be occupied with her papers; at
length he rose, as if to dismiss her, but sunk down again
—a slight convulsion agitated his features.   After a few
minutes he got up and staggered to the drawing-room,
where Anne Scott and my sister, Violet Lockhart, were
sitting.   They rushed to meet him, but he fell at all his
length on the floor ere they could reach him.   He remained speechless for about ten minutes, by which time a
surgeon had arrived and bled him.   He was cupped
again in the evening, and gradually recovered possession of speech, and of all his faculties, in so far that,
the occurrence being kept quiet, when he appeared
abroad again after a short interval, people in general
observed no serious change.   He submitted to the utmost
severity of regimen, tasting nothing but pulse and
water for some weeks, and the alarm of his family
and intimate friends subsided.   By and by he again
mingled in society much as usual, and seems to have
almost persuaded himself that the attack had proceeded merely from the stomach, though his letters

continued ever and anon to drop hints that the symptoms resembled apoplexy or paralysis. When we recollect that both his father and his elder brother died of paralysis, and consider the violences of agitation and exertion to which Sir Walter had been subjected during the four preceding years, the only wonder is that this blow (which had, I suspect, several indistinct harbingers) was deferred so long; there can be none that it was soon followed by others of the same description.

He struggled manfully, however, against his malady, and during 1830 covered almost as many sheets with his MS. as in 1829. About March I find, from his correspondence with Ballantyne, that he was working regularly at his *Letters on Demonology and Witchcraft* for Murray's Family Library, and also on a Fourth Series of the Tales of a Grandfather, the subject being French History. Both of these books were published by the end of the year; and the former contains many passages worthy of his best day —little snatches of picturesque narrative and the like—in fact, transcripts of his own familiar fireside stories. The shrewdness with which evidence is sifted on legal cases attests, too, that the main reasoning faculty remained unshaken. But, on the whole, these works can hardly be submitted to a strict ordeal of criticism. There is in both a cloudiness both of words and arrangement. Nor can I speak differently of the second volume of his Scottish History for Lardner, which was published in May. His very pretty reviewal of Mr. Southey's Life and Edition of Bunyan was done in August—about which time his recovery seems to have reached its *acmé*.

In the course of the Spring Session, circumstances rendered it highly probable that Sir Walter's resignation of his place as Clerk of Session might be acceptable to the Government; and it is not surprising that he should have, on the whole, been pleased to avail himself of this opportunity. He says, in his Diary—" *May* 27. I am agitating a proposed retirement from the Court. As they are only to have four instead of six Clerks of Session, it will be their interest to let me retire on a superannuation. Probably I shall make a bad bargain, and get only two-thirds of the salary, instead of three-fourths. This would be hard, but I could save between two or three hundred pounds by giving up town residence. At any rate, *jacta est alea*. I think the difference will be infinite in point of health and happiness. Yet I do not know. It is perhaps a violent change in the end of life to quit the walk one has trod so long, and the cursed splenetic temper which besets all men makes you value opportunities and circumstances when one enjoys them no longer."

On the 26th of June, he heard of the death of King George IV. with the regret of a devoted and obliged subject. He had received, almost immediately before, two marks of his Majesty's kind attention. Understanding that his retirement from the Court of Session was at hand, Sir William Knighton suggested that he might henceforth be more frequently in London, and that he might fitly be placed at the head of a new commission for examining and editing the MS. collections of the exiled Princes of the House of Stuart, which had come into the King's hands on the death of the Cardinal of York. This Sir Walter gladly accepted, and contemplated with pleasure spending the ensuing winter in London. But another proposition, that of elevating him to the rank of Privy Councillor, was unhesitatingly declined. He desired the Lord Chief-Commissioner, whom the King had desired to ascertain his feelings on the subject, to convey his grateful thanks, with his humble apology: and his reasons are thus stated in the Diary of the succeeding winter :—" I had also a kind communication about interfering to have me named a P. Councillor. But—besides that when one is old and poor, one should avoid taking rank—I would be much happier if I thought any act of kindness was done to help forward Charles; and having said so much, I made my bow, and declared my purpose of remaining satisfied with my knighthood. All this is rather pleasing. Yet much of it looks like winding up my bottom for the rest of my life."

In July came the formal intimation that he had ceased to be a Clerk of Session, and should henceforth have, in lieu of his salary, &c. (£1,300), an allowance of £800 per annum. This was accompanied by an intimation from the Home Secretary, that the Ministers were quite ready to grant him a pension covering the reduction of his income. Considering himself as the bond-slave of his creditors, he made known to them this proposition, and stated that it would be extremely painful to him to accept of it; and with the delicacy and generosity which through-out characterised their conduct towards him, they without

hesitation entreated him on no account to do injury to his
own feelings in such a matter as this. Few things gave
him more pleasure than this handsome communication.

Just after he had taken leave of Edinburgh, as he seems
to have thought for ever, he received a communication of
another sort, as inopportune as any that ever reached
him. His Diary for the 13th July says briefly—" I have
a letter from a certain young gentleman, announcing that
his sister had so far mistaken the intentions of a lame
baronet nigh sixty years old, as to suppose him only
prevented by modesty from stating certain wishes and
hopes, &c. The party is a woman of rank, so my vanity
may be satisfied. But I excused myself, with little picking
upon the terms."

During the rest of the summer and autumn his daughter
and I were at Chiefswood, and saw him of course daily.
Laidlaw, too, had been restored to the cottage at Kaeside;
and though Tom Purdie made a dismal blank, old habits
went on, and the course of life seemed little altered from
what it had used to be. He looked jaded and worn before
evening set in, yet very seldom departed from the strict
regimen of his doctors, and often brightened up to all his
former glee, though passing the bottle and sipping toast
and water. His grandchildren especially saw no change.
However languid, his spirits revived at the sight of them,
and the greatest pleasure he had was in pacing Douce
Davie through the green lanes among his woods, with
them clustered about him on ponies and donkeys, while
Laidlaw, the ladies, and myself, walked by, and obeyed
his directions about pruning and marking trees. After the
immediate alarms of the spring, it might have been even
agreeable to witness this placid twilight scene, but for our
knowledge that nothing could keep him from toiling many
hours daily at his desk, and alas! that he was no longer
sustained by the daily commendations of his printer. It
was obvious, as the season advanced, that the manner in
which Ballantyne communicated with him was sinking into
his spirits, and Laidlaw foresaw, as well as myself, that
some trying crisis of discussion could not be much longer
deferred. A nervous twitching about the muscles of the
mouth was always more or less discernible from the date
of the attack in February; but we could easily tell, by the
aggravation of that symptom, when he had received a
packet from the Canongate. It was distressing, indeed,

to think that he might, one of these days, sustain a second seizure, and be left still more helpless, yet with the same undiminished appetite for literary labour. And then, if he felt his printer's complaints so keenly, what was to be expected in the case of a plain and undeniable manifestation of disappointment on the part of the public, and consequently of the bookseller?

All this was for the inner circle. Country neighbours went and came, without, I believe, observing almost anything of what grieved the family. Nay, this autumn he was far more troubled with the invasions of strangers, than he had ever been since his calamities of 1826. The astonishing success of the new editions was, as usual, doubled or trebled by rumour. The notion that he had already all but cleared off his incumbrances seems to have been widely prevalent, and no doubt his refusal of a pension tended to confirm it. Abbotsford was, for some weeks at least, besieged much as it had used to be in the golden days of 1823 and 1824; and if sometimes his guests brought animation and pleasure with them, even then the result was a legacy of redoubled lassitude. The Diary, among a very few and far-separated entries, has this :—
"*September* 5.—In spite of Resolution, I have left my Diary for some weeks,—I cannot well tell why. We have had abundance of travelling Counts and Countesses, Yankees male and female, and a Yankee-Doodle-*Dandy* into the bargain—a smart young Virginia-man. But we have had friends of our own also—the Miss Ardens, young Mrs. Morritt and Anne Morritt, most agreeable visitors.—Cadell came out here yesterday with his horn filled with good news. He calculates that in October the debt will be reduced to £60,000. This makes me care less about the terms I retire upon. The efforts by which we have advanced thus far are new in literature, and what is gained is secure."

Mr. Cadell's great hope, when he offered this visit, had been that the good news of the *Magnum* might induce Sir Walter to content himself with working at notes and prefaces for its coming volumes, without straining at more difficult tasks. He found his friend, however, by no means disposed to adopt such views; and suggested very kindly, and ingeniously too, by way of *mezzo-termine*, that before entering upon any new novel, he should draw up a sort of *catalogue raisonné* of the most curious articles in his library and museum. Sir Walter grasped at this, and began next morning to dictate to Laidlaw what he designed to publish in the usual novel shape, under the title of " Reliquiæ Trottcosienses, or the Gabions of Jonathan Oldbuck." Nothing, as it seemed to all about him, could have suited the time better; but after a few days he said he found this was not sufficient—that he should proceed in it during *horæ subsecivæ*, but must bend himself to the composition of a romance, founded on a story which he had more than once told cursorily already, and for which he had been revolving the various titles of Robert of the Isle—Count Robert de L'Isle—and *Count Robert of Paris*. There was nothing to be said in reply to the decisive announcement of this purpose. The usual agreements were drawn out; and the Tale was begun.

In the ensuing month (Oct. 1830) the dethroned King of France, Charles X., was invited by the English Government to resume his old quarters at Holyrood; and among many other things that about this time mortified Scott, none gave him more pain than to hear that the popular feeling in Edinburgh had been so much exacerbated against the fallen monarch (especially by an ungenerous article in the great literary organ of the place), that his reception there was likely to be rough and insulting. Sir Walter thought that on such an occasion his voice might, perhaps, be listened to. He knew his countrymen well in their strength, as well as in their weakness, and put forth in Ballantyne's newspaper for the 20th of October, a manly appeal to their better feelings—closing in these words :—" The person who writes these few lines is leaving his native city, never to return as a permanent resident. He has some reason to be proud of distinctions received from his fellow-citizens; and he has not the slightest doubt that the taste and good feeling of those whom he will still term so will dictate to them the quiet, civil, and respectful tone of feeling, which will do honour both to their heads and their hearts, which have seldom been appealed to in vain.—The Frenchman Melinet, in mentioning the refuge afforded by Edinburgh to Henry VI. in his distress, records it as the most hospitable town in Europe. It is a testimony to be proud of, and sincerely do I hope there is little danger of forfeiting it upon the present occasion."

The effect of this admonition was even more complete than the writer had anticipated. The royal exiles were received with perfect decorum, which their modest bearing to all classes, and unobtrusive, though magnificent benevolence to the poor, ere long converted into a feeling of deep and affectionate respectfulness. During their stay in Scotland, the King took more than one opportunity of conveying to Sir Walter his gratitude for this salutary interference on his behalf. The ladies of the royal family had a curiosity to see Abbotsford, but being aware of his reduced health and wealth, took care to visit the place when he was known to be from home. Several French noblemen of the train, however, paid him their respects personally. I remember with particular pleasure a couple of days that the Duke of Laval-Montmorency spent with him: he was also gratified with a visit from Marshal Bourmont, though unfortunately that came after his ailments had much advanced. The Marshal was accompanied by the Baron d'Haussez, one of the Polignac Ministry, whose published account of his residence in this country contains no specimen of vain imbecility more pitiable than the page he gives to Abbotsford. So far from comprehending anything of his host's character or conversation, the Baron had not even eyes to observe that he was in a sorely dilapidated condition of bodily health.

The reader has already seen that he had many misgivings in contemplating his final retirement from the situation he had occupied for six-and-twenty years in the Court of Session. Such a breach in old habits is always a serious experiment; but in his case it was very particularly so, because it involved his losing during the winter months, when men most need society, the intercourse of almost all that remained to him of dear familiar friends. He had besides a love for the very stones of Edinburgh, and the thought that he was never again to sleep under a roof of his own in his native city cost him many a pang. But he never alludes either in his Diary or in his letters (nor do I remember that he ever did so in conversation) to the circumstance which, far more than all besides, occasioned care and regret in the bosom of his family. However he might cling to the notion that his recent ailments sprung merely from a disordered stomach, they had dismissed that dream, and the heaviest of their thoughts was, that he was fixing himself in the country

Life of Sir Walter Scott 585

just when his health, perhaps his life, might depend any given hour on the immediate presence of a surgical hand. They reflected that the only practitioner resident within several miles of him might, in case of another seizure, come too late, even although the messenger should find him at home; but that his practice extended over a wide range of thinly-peopled country, and that at the hour of need he might as probably be half a day's journey off as at Melrose. We would fain have persuaded him that his library-catalogues, and other papers, had fallen into such confusion, that he ought to have some clever young student in the house during the winter to arrange them; and had he taken the suggestion in good part, a medical student would of course have been selected. But, whether or not he suspected our real motive, he would listen to no such plan; and his friendly surgeon (Mr. James Clarkson) then did the best he could for us, by instructing a confidential domestic, privately, in the use of the lancet. This was John Nicolson—a name never to be mentioned by any of Scott's family without respect and gratitude. He had been in the household from his boyhood, and was about this time (poor Dalgleish retiring from weak health) advanced to the chief place in it. Early and continued kindness had made a very deep impression on this fine handsome young man's warm heart; he possessed intelligence, good sense, and a calm temper; and the courage and dexterity which Sir Walter had delighted to see him display in sports and pastimes, proved henceforth of inestimable service to the master whom he regarded, I verily believe, with the love and reverence of a son. Since I have reached the period at which human beings owe so much to ministrations of this class, I may as well name by the side of Nicolson, Miss Scott's maid, Mrs. Celia Street—a young person whose unwearied zeal, coupled with a modest tact that stamped her one of Nature's gentlewomen, contributed hardly less to the comfort of Sir Walter and his children during the brief remainder of his life.[1]

Affliction, as it happened, lay heavy at this time on the kind house of Huntley Burn also. The eldest Miss Fer-

[1] On Sir Walter's death, Nicolson passed into the service of Mr. Morritt at Rokeby. He died at Kelso in 1841. Mrs. Street remained in my house till 1836, when she married Mr. Griffiths, a respectable farmer at Ealing.

gusson was on her deathbed; and thus, when my wife and I were obliged to move southwards at the beginning of winter, Sir Walter was left almost entirely dependent on his daughter Anne, William Laidlaw, and the worthy domestics whom I have been naming. Laidlaw attended him as amanuensis, and often dined as well as breakfasted with him. A more delicate task never devolved upon any man's friend, than he had about this time to encounter. He could not watch Scott from hour to hour—above all, he could not write to his dictation, without gradually, slowly, most reluctantly taking home to his bosom the conviction that the mighty mind, which he had worshipped through more than thirty years of intimacy, had lost something, and was daily losing something more, of its energy. The faculties were there, and each of them was every now and then displaying itself in its full vigour; but the sagacious judgment, the brilliant fancy, the unrivalled memory, were all subject to occasional eclipse—

> " Amid the strings his fingers stray'd,
> And an uncertain warbling made."

Ever and anon he paused and looked around him, like one half-waking from a dream, mocked with shadows. The sad bewilderment of his gaze shewed a momentary consciousness that, like Samson in the lap of the Philistine, " his strength was passing from him, and he was becoming weak like unto other men." Then came the strong effort of aroused will—the cloud dispersed as if before an irresistible current of purer air—all was bright and serene as of old—and then it closed again in yet deeper darkness.

During the early part of this winter the situation of Cadell and Ballantyne was hardly less painful, and still more embarrassing. What doubly and trebly perplexed them was, that while the MS. sent for press seemed worse every budget, Sir Walter's letters continued as clear in thought, and almost so in expression, as formerly—full of the old shrewdness and firmness, and manly kindness, and even of the old good-humoured pleasantry. About them, except the staggering penmanship, and here and there one word put down obviously for another, there was scarcely anything to indicate decayed vigour. It is not surprising that poor Ballantyne, in particular, should have shrunk from the notion that anything was amiss,—except the choice of an unfortunate subject, and the indulgence of more than common carelessness and rapidity in composition. He seems to have done so as he would from some horrid suggestion of the Devil; and accordingly obeyed his natural sense of duty, by stating, in plain terms, that he considered the opening chapters of Count Robert as decidedly inferior to anything that had ever before come from that pen. James appears to have dwelt chiefly on the hopelessness of any Byzantine fable; and he might certainly have appealed to a long train of examples for the fatality which seems to hang over every attempt to awaken anything like a lively interest about the persons and manners of the generation in question; the childish forms and bigotries, the weak pomps and drivelling pretensions, the miserable plots and treacheries, the tame worn-out civilisation of those European Chinese. The epoch on which Scott had fixed was, however, one that brought these doomed slaves of vanity and superstition into contact with the vigorous barbarism both of western Christendom and the advancing Ottoman. Sir Walter had, years before, been struck with its capabilities;[1] and who dares to say that, had he executed the work when he sketched the outline of its plan, he might not have achieved as signal a triumph over all critical prejudices, as he had done when he rescued Scottish romance from the mawkish degradation in which Waverley found it?

In himself and his own affairs there was enough to alarm and perplex him and all who watched him; but the aspect of the political horizon also pressed more heavily upon his spirit than it had ever done before. All the evils which he had apprehended from the rupture among the Tory leaders in the beginning of 1827 were now, in his opinion, about to be consummated. The high Protestant party, blinded by their resentment of the abolition of the Test Act and the Roman Catholic disabilities, seemed willing to run any risk for the purpose of driving the Duke of Wellington from the helm. The general election, occasioned by the demise of the Crown, was held while the successful revolts in France and Belgium were uppermost in every mind, and furnished the Liberal candidates with captivating topics. The result had considerably strengthened the old opposition in the House of Commons; and a single vote, in which the ultra-Tories joined the Whigs, was considered by the Ministry as so ominous, that they immediately re-

[1] See his Essay on *Romance*, 1823.

tired from office. The succeeding cabinet of Earl Grey
included names identified, in Scott's view, with the wildest
rage of innovation. Their first step was to announce a
bill of Parliamentary Reform on a large scale, for which
it was soon known they had secured the warm personal
support of William IV. Great discontent prevailed, meanwhile, throughout the labouring classes of many districts,
both commercial and rural. Every newspaper teemed with
details of riot and incendiarism; and the selection of such
an epoch of impatience and turbulence for a legislative
experiment—more important than had ever before been
agitated within the forms of the constitution—was perhaps
regarded by most grave and retired men with feelings near
akin to those of the anxious and melancholy invalid at
Abbotsford. To annoy him additionally, he found many
eminent persons, who had hitherto avowed politics of his
own colour, renouncing all their old tenets, and joining the
cry of Reform, which to him sounded Revolution, as keenly
as the keenest of those who had been through life considered apostles of Republicanism. And I must also observe, that as, notwithstanding his own steady Toryism,
he had never allowed political differences to affect his
private feelings towards friends and companions, so it now
happened that among the few with whom he had daily
intercourse, there was hardly one he could look to for
sympathy in his present reflections and anticipations. The
affectionate Laidlaw had always been a stout Whig; he
hailed the coming changes as the beginning of a political
millennium. Ballantyne, influenced probably by his new
ghostly counsellors, was by degrees leaning to a similar
view of things. Cadell, his bookseller, and now the principal confidant and assistant from week to week in all his
plans and speculations, had always, I presume, considered
the Tory creed as a piece of weakness—to be pardoned, indeed, in a poet and an antiquary, but at best pitied in men
of any other class.

Towards the end of November, Sir Walter had another
slight touch of apoplexy. He recovered himself without
assistance; but again consulted his physicians in Edinburgh, and by their advice adopted a still greater severity
of regimen.

The reader will now understand what his frame and condition of health and spirits were, when he at length received from Ballantyne a decided protest against the novel

on which he was struggling to fix the shattered energies of his memory and fancy. He replied thus :

> "*Abbotsford, 8th Dec.* 1830.

"My Dear James,—If I were like other authors, as I flatter myself I am not, I should ' send you an order on my treasurer for a hundred ducats, wishing you all prosperity and a little more taste ';[1] but having never supposed that any abilities I ever had were of a perpetual texture, I am glad when friends tell me what I might be long in finding out myself. Mr. Cadell will shew you what I have written to him. My present idea is to go abroad for a few months, if I hold together as long. So ended the Fathers of the Novel—Fielding and Smollett—and it would be no unprofessional finish for yours—W. S."

This note to the printer, and a letter of the same date and strain to the publisher, "struck both," Mr. Cadell says, "with dismay." They resolved to go out to Abbotsford, but not for a few days, because a general meeting of the creditors was at hand, and there was reason to hope that its results would enable them to appear as the bearers of sundry pieces of good news. Meantime, Sir Walter himself rallied considerably, and resolved, by way of testing his powers, while the novel hung suspended, to write a fourth epistle of Malachi Malagrowther on the public affairs of the period. The announcement of a political dissertation, at such a moment of universal excitement, and from a hand already trembling under the misgivings of a fatal malady, might well have filled Cadell and Ballantyne with new "dismay," even had they both been prepared to adopt, in the fullest extent, such views of the dangers of our state, and the remedies for them, as their friend was likely to dwell upon. They agreed that whatever they could safely do to avert this experiment must be done. Indeed they were both equally anxious to find, if it could be found, the means of withdrawing him from all literary labour, save only that of annotating his former novels. But they were not the only persons who had been, and then were, exerting all their art for that same purpose. His kind and skilful physicians, Doctors Abercrombie and Ross of Edinburgh, had over and over preached the same doctrine, and assured him, that if he persisted in working his brain, nothing could prevent his malady from recurring ere long in redoubled severity. He answered—"As for

[1] Archbishop of Grenada, in *Gil Blas.*

bidding me not work, Molly might as well put the kettle on the fire and say, *Now, don't boil.*" To myself, when I ventured to address him in a similar strain, he replied—" I understand you, and I thank you from my heart, but I must tell you at once how it is with me. I am not sure that I am quite myself in all things; but I am sure that in one point there is no change. I mean, that I foresee distinctly that if I were to be idle I should go mad. In comparison to this, death is no risk to shrink from."

The meeting of trustees and creditors took place on the 17th—Mr. George Forbes (brother to the late Sir William) in the chair. There was then announced another dividend on the Ballantyne estate of three shillings in the pound— thus reducing the original amount of the debt to about £54,000. It had been not unnaturally apprehended that the convulsed state of politics might have checked the sale of the *magnum opus*; but this does not seem to have been the case to any extent worth notice. The meeting was numerous—and, not contented with a renewed vote of thanks to their debtor, they passed unanimously a resolu- tion, which was moved by Mr. (now Sir James) Gibson- Craig, and seconded by Mr. Thomas Allan—both, by the way, leading Whigs :—" That Sir Walter Scott be re- quested to accept of his furniture, plate, linens, paintings, library, and curiosities of every description, as the best means the creditors have of expressing their very high sense of his most honourable conduct, and in grateful ac- knowledgment for the unparalleled and most successful exertions he has made, and continues to make, for them."

On the 18th, Cadell and Ballantyne proceeded to Abbots- ford, and found Sir Walter in a placid state—having evidently been much soothed and gratified with the tidings from Mr. Forbes. His whole appearance was greatly better than they had ventured to anticipate; and deferring literary questions till the morning, he made this gift from his creditors the chief subject of his conversation. He said it had taken a heavy load off his mind; he appre- hended that, even if his future works should produce little money, the profits of the *Magnum,* during a limited num- ber of years, with the sum which had been insured on his life, would be sufficient to obliterate the remaining part of the Ballantyne debt : he considered the library and museum now conveyed to him as worth at the least

£10,000, and this would enable him to make some provision for his younger children.   He said that he designed
to execute his last will without delay, and detailed to his
friends all the particulars which the document ultimately
embraced.   He mentioned to them that he had recently
received through the Lord Chief-Commissioner Adam, a
message from the new King, intimating his Majesty's disposition to keep in mind his late brother's kind intentions
with regard to Charles Scott;—and altogether his talk,
though grave, and on grave topics, was the reverse of
melancholy.

Next morning, in Sir Walter's study, Ballantyne read
aloud the political essay—which had (after the old fashion)
grown to an extent far beyond what the author contemplated when he began his task.   To print it in the Weekly
Journal, as originally proposed, would now be hardly compatible with the limits of that paper : Sir Walter had resolved on a separate publication.

I believe no one ever saw this performance but the
bookseller, the printer, and William Laidlaw; and I cannot pretend to have gathered any clear notion of its contents,—except that the *panacea* was the reimposition of
the income-tax; and that after much reasoning in support
of this measure, Sir Walter attacked the principle of Parliamentary Reform *in toto*.   We need hardly suppose that
he advanced any objections which would seem new to the
students of the debates in both Houses during 1831 and
1832; his logic carried no conviction to the breast of his
faithful amanuensis; but Mr. Laidlaw assured me, nevertheless, that in his opinion no composition of Sir Walter's
happiest day contained anything more admirable than the
bursts of indignant and pathetic eloquence which here and
there " set off a halting argument."

The critical arbiters, however, concurred in condemning
the production.   Cadell spoke out.   He assured Sir Walter, that from not being in the habit of reading the
newspapers and periodical works of the day, he had fallen
behind the common rate of information on questions of
practical policy; that the views he was enforcing had been
already expounded by many Tories, and triumphantly answered by organs of the Liberal party; but that, be the
intrinsic value and merit of these political doctrines what
they might, he was quite certain that to put them forth at
that season would be a measure of extreme danger for the

author's personal interest; that it would throw a cloud over his general popularity, array a hundred active pens against any new work of another class that might soon follow, and perhaps even interrupt the hitherto splendid success of the Collection on which so much depended. On all these points Ballantyne, though with hesitation and diffidence, professed himself to be of Cadell's opinion. There ensued a scene of a very unpleasant sort; but by and by a kind of compromise was agreed to: the plan of a separate pamphlet, with the well-known *nom de guerre* of Malachi, was dropped; and Ballantyne was to stretch his columns so as to find room for the lucubration, adopting all possible means to mystify the public as to its parentage. This was the understanding when the conference broke up; but the unfortunate manuscript was soon afterwards committed to the flames. James Ballantyne accompanied the proof-sheet with many minute criticisms on the conduct as well as expression of the argument: the author's temper gave way; and the commentary shared the fate of the text.

Mr. Cadell opens a very brief account of this affair with expressing his opinion, that " Sir Walter never recovered it "; and he ends with an altogether needless apology for his own part in it. He did only what was his duty by his venerated friend; and he did it, I doubt not, as kindly in manner as in spirit. Even if the fourth epistle of Malachi had been more like its precursors than I can well suppose it to have been, nothing could have been more unfortunate for Sir Walter than to come forward at that moment as a prominent antagonist of Reform. Such an appearance might very possibly have had the consequences to which the bookseller pointed in his remonstrance; but at all events it must have involved him in a maze of replies and rejoinders; and I think it too probable, that some of the fiery disputants of the periodical press, if not of St. Stephen's Chapel, might have been ingenious enough to connect any real or fancied flaws in his argument with those circumstances in his personal condition which had for some time been darkening his own reflections with dim auguries of the fate of Swift and Marlborough. His reception of Ballantyne's affectionate candour may suggest what the effect of really hostile criticism would have been. The end was, that seeing how much he stood in need of some comfort, the printer and bookseller concurred in

urging him not to despair of Count Robert. They assured
him that he had attached too much importance to what
had formerly been said about the defects of its opening
chapters; and he agreed to resume the novel, which
neither of them ever expected he would live to finish.
" If we did wrong," says Cadell, " we did it for the best;
we felt that to have spoken out as fairly on this as we
had on the other subject would have been to make ourselves the bearers of a death-warrant." I hope there are
not many men who would have acted otherwise in their
painful situation.

The next entry of the Diary has these sentences :—
" Ever since my fall in February, it is very certain that I
have seemed to speak with an impediment. To add to
this, I have the constant increase of my lameness—the
thigh-joint, knee-joint, and ankle-joint. I move with
great pain in the whole limb, and am at every minute,
during an hour's walk, reminded of my mortality. I
should not care for all this, if I were sure of dying handsomely; and Cadell's calculations might be sufficiently
firm, though the author of Waverley had pulled on his
last night-cap. Nay, they might be even more trustworthy, if remains, and memoirs, and such like, were to
give a zest to the posthumous. But the fear is, lest the
blow be not sufficient to destroy life, and that I should
linger on, ' a driveller and a show.' "[1]

He says again—" *January* 18, 1831.—Dictated to Laidlaw till about one o'clock, during which time it was rainy.
Afterwards I walked, sliding about in the mud, and very
uncomfortable. In fact, there is no mistaking the Three
Sufficients,[2] and Fate is now straitening its circumvalla-
tions around me.—*January* 19.—Mr. Laidlaw came down
at ten, and we wrote till one. This is an important help
to me, as it saves both my eyesight and nerves, which last
are cruelly affected by finding those who look out of the
windows grow gradually darker and darker. Rode out,
or, more properly, was carried out into the woods to see
the course of a new road, which may serve to carry off the
thinnings of the trees, and for rides. It is very well
lined, and will serve both for beauty and convenience.
Mr. Laidlaw engages to come back to dinner, and finish
two or three more pages. Met my agreeable and lady-

---

[1] Johnson's *Vanity of Human Wishes*.
[2] See Piozzi's Tale of *The Three Sufficient Warnings*.

like neighbour, Mrs. Brewster, on my pony, and I was
actually ashamed to be seen by her.

' Sir Denis Brand ! and on so poor a steed ! ' [1]

I believe detestable folly of this kind is the very last
that leaves us.   One would have thought I ought to have
little vanity at this time o' day; but it is an abiding appurtenance of the old Adam, and I write for penance what,
like a fool, I actually felt.   I think the peep, real or
imaginary, at the gates of death, should have given me
firmness not to mind little afflictions.''

On the 31st of January, Miss Scott being too unwell
for a journey, Sir Walter went alone to Edinburgh for the
purpose of executing his last will.   He (for the first time
in his native town) took up his quarters at a hotel; but
the noise of the street disturbed him during the night (another evidence how much his nervous system had been
shattered), and next day he was persuaded to remove to
his bookseller's house in Athol Crescent.   In the apartment allotted to him, he found several little pieces
of furniture which some kind person had purchased for
him at the sale in Castle Street, and which he presented
to Mrs. Cadell.   '' Here,'' says his letter to Mrs. Lockhart, '' I saw various things that belonged to poor No. 39.
I had many sad thoughts on seeing and handling them—
but they are in kind keeping, and I was glad they had not
gone to strangers.''

There came on, next day, a storm of such severity that
he had to remain under this friendly roof until the 9th of
February.   His host perceived that he was unfit for any
company but the quietest, and had sometimes one old
friend, Mr. Thomson, Mr. Clerk, or Mr. Skene, to dinner
—but no more.   He seemed glad to see them—but they all
observed him with pain.   He never took the lead in conversation, and often remained altogether silent.   In the
mornings he wrote usually for several hours at Count
Robert; and Mr. Cadell remembers in particular, that on
Ballantyne's reminding him that a motto was wanted for
one of the chapters already finished, he looked out for a
moment at the gloomy weather, and penned these lines—

" The storm increases—'tis no sunny shower,
    Foster'd in the moist breast of March or April,
    Or such as parched Summer cools his lips with.

[1] Crabbe's *Borough*, Letter xiii.

Heaven's windows are flung wide; the inmost deeps
Call in hoarse greeting one upon another;
On comes the flood in all its foaming horrors,
And where's the dike shall stop it?

The Deluge: a Poem."

On the 4th February, the will was signed, and attested by Nicolson, to whom Sir Walter explained the nature of the document, adding, " I deposit it for safety in Mr. Cadell's hands, and I still hope it may be long before he has occasion to produce it." Poor Nicolson was much agitated, but stammered out a deep *amen*.

Another object of this journey was to consult, on the advice of Dr. Ebenezer Clarkson, a skilful mechanist, by name *Fortune*, about a contrivance for the support of the lame limb, which had of late given him much pain as well as inconvenience. Mr. Fortune produced a clever piece of handiwork, and Sir Walter felt at first great relief from the use of it: insomuch that his spirits rose to quite the old pitch, and his letter to me upon the occasion overflows with merry applications of sundry maxims and verses about *Fortune*: " *Fortes Fortuna adjuvat,*" &c., &c.

Of this excursion the Diary says—" *Abbotsford, February 9.*—The snow became impassable, and in Edinburgh I remained immovably fixed for ten days, never getting out of doors, save once or twice to dinner, when I went and returned in a sedan-chair. Cadell made a point of my coming to his excellent house, where I had no less excellent an apartment, and the most kind treatment; that is, no making a show of me, for which I was in but bad tune. Abercrombie and Ross had me bled with cupping-glasses, reduced me confoundedly, and restricted me of all creature comforts. But they did me good, as I am sure they sincerely meant to do; I got rid of a giddy feeling which I had been plagued with, and have certainly returned much better. I did not neglect my testamentary affairs. I executed my last will, leaving Walter burdened with £1,000 to Sophia, £2,000 to Anne, and the same to Charles. He is to advance them this money if they want it; if not, to pay them interest. All this is his own choice, otherwise I would have sold the books and rattle-traps. I have made provisions for clearing my estate by my publications, should it be possible; and should that prove possible, from the time of such clearance being effected, to be a fund available to all my children who shall be alive or leave representatives. My bequests must, many of them, seem hypothetical."

At the beginning of March, he was anew roused about political affairs; and bestowed four days in drawing up an address against the Reform Bill, which he designed to be adopted by the freeholders of the Forest. They, however, preferred a shorter one from the pen of a plain practical country gentleman (the late Mr. Elliott Lockhart of Borthwickbrae), who had often represented them in Parliament: and Sir Walter, it is probable, felt this disappointment more acutely than he has chosen to indicate in his Journal.

"*March* 11.—This day we had our meeting at Selkirk. I found Borthwickbrae had sent the frame of an address. It was the reverse of mine in every respect. As I saw that it met the ideas of the meeting (six in number) better by far than mine, I instantly put that in my pocket. It gives me a right to decline future interference, and let the world wag—'Transeat cum cæteris erroribus.'—I will make my opinion public at every place where I shall be called upon or expected to appear; but I will not thrust myself forward again. May the Lord have mercy upon us, and incline our hearts to keep this vow!"

He kept it in all parts. Though urged to take up his pen against the Reform Bill, by several persons of high consequence, who of course little knew his real condition of health, he resolutely refused to make any such experiment again. But he was equally resolved to be absent from no meeting at which, as Sheriff or Deputy-Lieutenant, he might naturally be expected to appear in his place, and record his aversion to the Bill. The first of these meetings was one of the freeholders of Roxburgh, held at Jedburgh on the 21st of March, and there, to the distress and alarm of his daughter, he insisted on being present, and proposing one of the Tory resolutions,—which he did in a speech of some length, but delivered in a tone so low, and with such hesitation in utterance, that only a few detached passages were intelligible to the bulk of the audience.

"We are told" (said he) "on high authority, that France is the model for us,—that we and all the other nations ought to put ourselves to school there,—and endeavour *to take out our degrees at the University of*

*Paris.*¹ The French are a very ingenious people; they have often tried to borrow from us, and now we should repay the obligation by borrowing a leaf from them. But I fear there is an incompatibility between the tastes and habits of France and Britain, and that we may succeed as ill in copying them, as they have hitherto done in copying us. We in this district are proud, and with reason, that the first chain-bridge was the work of a Scotchman. It still hangs where he erected it, a pretty long time ago. The French heard of our invention, and determined to introduce it, but with great improvements and embellishments. A friend of my own saw the thing tried. It was on the Seine, at Marly. The French chain-bridge looked lighter and airier than the prototype. Every Englishman present was disposed to confess that we had been beaten at our own trade. But by and by the gates were opened, and the multitude were to pass over. It began to swing rather formidably beneath the pressure of the good company; and by the time the architect, who led the procession in great pomp and glory, reached the middle, the whole gave way, and he—worthy, patriotic artist—was the first that got a ducking. They had forgot the great middle bolt—or rather, this ingenious person had conceived that to be a clumsy-looking feature, which might safely be dispensed with, while he put some invisible gimcrack of his own to supply its place."—Here Sir Walter was interrupted by violent hissing and hooting from the populace of the town, who had flocked in and occupied the greater part of the Court-House. He stood calmly till the storm subsided, and resumed; but the friend, whose notes are before me, could not catch what he said, until his voice rose with another illustration of the old style. "My friends," he said, "I am old and failing, and you think me full of very silly prejudices; but I have seen a good deal of public men, and thought a good deal of public affairs in my day, and I can't help suspecting that the manufacturers of this new constitution are like a parcel of schoolboys taking to pieces a watch which used to go tolerably well for all practical purposes, in the conceit that they can put it together again far better than the old watchmaker. I fear they will fail when they come to the reconstruction, and I should not, I confess, be much surprised if it were to turn out that their first step had been to break the main-spring."—Here he was again stopped by a Babel of contemptuous sounds, which seemed likely to render further attempts ineffectual. He, abruptly and unheard, proposed his Resolution, and then, turning to the riotous artisans, exclaimed—" I regard your gabble no more than the geese on the green." His countenance glowed with indignation, as he resumed his seat on the bench. But when, a few moments afterwards, the business being over, he rose to withdraw, every trace of passion was gone. He turned round at the door, and bowed to the assembly. Two or three, not more, renewed their hissing; he bowed again, and took leave in the words of the doomed gladiator, which I hope none who had joined in these insults understood—" MORITURUS VOS SALUTO."

CHAPTER XVII

Apoplectic Paralysis—Miss Ferrier—Election Scenes at Jedburgh and Selkirk—Castle Dangerous begun—Excursion to Douglasdale—Visits of Captain Burns and Wordsworth—Departure from Abbotsford—London—Voyage in the Barham—Malta—Naples—Rome—Notes by Mrs. Davy, Sir W. Gell, and Mr. E. Cheney—Publication of the last Tales of my Landlord. 1831–1832.

AFTER a pause of some days, the Diary has this entry for April 25, 1831 :—" From Saturday 16th April, to Saturday 24th of the same month, unpleasantly occupied by ill health and its consequences. A distinct stroke of paralysis affecting both my nerves and speech, though beginning only on Monday with a very bad cold. Doctor Abercrombie was brought out by the friendly care of Cadell—but young Clarkson had already done the needful, that is, had bled and blistered, and placed me on a very reduced diet. Whether precautions have been taken in time, I cannot tell. I think they have, though severe in themselves, beat the disease; but I am alike prepared."

The preceding paragraph has been deciphered with difficulty. The blow which it records was greatly more severe than any that had gone before it. Sir Walter's friend Lord Meadowbank had come to Abbotsford, as usual when on the Jedburgh circuit; and he would make an effort to receive the Judge in something of the old style of the place; he collected several of the neighbouring gentry to dinner, and tried to bear his wonted part in the conversation. Feeling his strength and spirits flagging, he was tempted to violate his physician's directions, and took two or three glasses of champagne, not having tasted wine for several months before. On retiring to his dressing-room he had this severe shock of apoplectic paralysis, and kept his bed under the surgeon's hands for several days.

Shortly afterwards his eldest son and his daughter Sophia arrived at Abbotsford. It may be supposed that they both would have been near him instantly, had that been possible; but Major Scott's regiment was stationed in a very disturbed district, and his sister was in a disabled state from the relics of a fever. I followed her a week later, when we established ourselves at Chiefswood for the rest of the season. Charles Scott had some months before this time gone to Naples, as an attaché to the British embassy there. During the next six months the Major was at Abbotsford every now and then—as often as circumstances could permit him to be absent from his Hussars.

On my arrival (May 10th), I found Sir Walter to have rallied considerably; yet his appearance, as I first saw him, was the most painful sight I had ever then seen. Knowing at what time I might be expected, he had been lifted on his pony, and advanced about half a mile on the Selkirk road to meet me. He moved at a foot-pace, with Laidlaw at one stirrup, and his forester Swanston (a fine fellow, who did all he could to replace Tom Purdie) at the other. Abreast was old Peter Mathieson on horseback, with one of my children astride before him on a pillion. Sir Walter had had his head shaved, and wore a black silk night-cap under his blue bonnet. All his garments hung loose about him; his countenance was thin and haggard, and there was an obvious distortion in the muscles of one cheek. His look, however, was placid—his eye as bright as ever—perhaps brighter than it ever was in health; he smiled with the same affectionate gentleness, and though at first it was not easy to understand everything he said, he spoke cheerfully and manfully.

He had resumed, and was trying to recast, his novel. All the medical men had urged him, by every argument, to abstain from any such attempts; but he smiled on them in silence, or answered with some jocular rhyme. One note has this postscript—a parody on a sweet lyric of Burns :—

> " Dour, dour, and eident was he,
>   Dour and eident but-and-ben—
>   Dour against their barley-water,
>   And eident on the Bramah pen."

He told me, that in the winter he had more than once tried
writing with his own hand, because he had no longer the
same " pith and birr " that formerly rendered dictation
easy to him; but that the experiment failed.   He was now
sensible he could do nothing without Laidlaw to hold the
Bramah pen; adding, " Willie is a kind clerk—I see by
his looks when I am pleasing him, and that pleases me."
And however the cool critic may now estimate *Count
Robert*, no one who then saw the author could wonder that
Laidlaw's prevalent feeling in writing those pages should
have been admiration.   Under the full consciousness that
he had sustained three or four strokes of apoplexy or
palsy, or both combined, and tortured by various attendant
ailments—cramp, rheumatism in half his joints, daily increasing lameness, and now of late gravel (which was,
though last, not least)—he retained all the energy of his
will, struggled manfully against this sea of troubles, and
might well have said seriously, as he more than once both
said and wrote playfully,

> " 'Tis not in mortals to command success,
>   But we'll do more, Sempronius, we'll deserve it." [1]

To assist them in amusing him in the hours which he
spent out of his study, and especially that he might be
tempted to make those hours more frequent, his daughters
had invited his friend the authoress of *Marriage* to come
out to Abbotsford; and her coming was serviceable.   For
she knew and loved him well, and she had seen enough of
affliction akin to his to be well skilled in dealing with it.
She could not be an hour in his company without observing what filled his children with more sorrow than all the
rest of the case.   He would begin a story as gaily as ever,
and go on, in spite of the hesitation in his speech, to
tell it with picturesque effect;—but before he reached
the point, it would seem as if some internal spring had
given way—he paused and gazed round him with the
blank anxiety of look that a blind man has when he has
dropped his staff.   Unthinking friends sometimes pained
him sadly by giving him the catchword abruptly.   I

---

[1] Addison's *Cato.*

noticed the delicacy of Miss Ferrier on such occasions. Her sight was bad, and she took care not to use her glasses when he was speaking; and she affected to be also troubled with deafness, and would say—" Well, I am getting as dull as a post—I have not heard a word since you said so and so ":—being sure to mention a circumstance behind that at which he had really halted. He then took up the thread with his habitual smile of courtesy—as if forgetting his case entirely in the consideration of the lady's infirmity.—He had also a visit from the learned and pious Dr. Macintosh Mackay, then minister of Laggan, but now at Dunoon—the chief author of the Gaelic Dictionary, then recently published under the auspices of the Highland Society; and this gentleman also accommodated himself, with the tact of genuine kindness, to the circumstances of the time.

In the family circle Sir Walter seldom spoke of his illness at all, and when he did, it was always in the hopeful strain. In private to Laidlaw and myself, his language corresponded exactly with the tone of the Diary— he expressed his belief that the chances of recovery were few—very few—but always added, that he considered it his duty to exert what faculties remained to him, for the sake of his creditors, to the very last. " I am very anxious," he repeatedly said to me, " to be done, one way or other, with this Count Robert, and a little story about the Castle Dangerous, which also I had long had in my head—but after that I will attempt nothing more—at least not until I have finished all the notes for the novels, &c. ; for, in case of my going off at the next slap, you would naturally have to take up that job,—and where could you get at all my old wives' stories? "

I felt the sincerest pity for Cadell and Ballantyne at this time ; and advised him to lay Count Robert aside for a few weeks at all events, until the general election now going on should be over. He consented—but immediately began another series of Tales on French History—which he never completed.

On the 18th of May, I witnessed a scene which must dwell painfully on many memories besides mine. The rumours of brick-bat and bludgeon work at the hustings of this month were so prevalent, that Sir Walter's family, and not less zealously the Tory candidate (Henry Scott, heir of Harden, now Lord Polwarth), tried every means to

dissuade him from attending the election for Roxburghshire. We thought overnight that we had succeeded,
and, indeed, as the result of the vote was not at all
doubtful, there could be no good reason for his appearing
on this occasion. About seven in the morning, however,
when I came down stairs intending to ride over to Jedburgh, I found he had countermanded my horse, ordered
his chariot to the door, and was already impatient to be
off for the scene of action. We found the town in a most
tempestuous state: in fact, it was almost wholly in the
hands of a disciplined rabble, chiefly weavers from
Hawick, who marched up and down with drums and
banners, and then, after filling the Court-hall, lined the
streets, grossly insulting every one who did not wear the
reforming colours. Sir Walter's carriage, as it advanced
towards the house of the Shortreed family, was pelted
with stones; one or two fell into it, but none touched
him. He breakfasted with the widow and children of his
old friend, and then walked to the Hall between me and
one of the young Shortreeds. He was saluted with
groans and blasphemies all the way—and I blush to
add that a woman spat upon him from a window;
but this last contumely I think he did not observe.
The scene within was much what has been described
under the date of March 21st, except that though
he attempted to speak from the Bench, not a word
was audible, such was the frenzy. Young Harden
was returned by a great majority, 40 to 19, and we
then with difficulty gained the inn where the carriage
had been put up. But the aspect of the street was by
that time such, that several of the gentlemen on the Whig
side came and entreated us not to attempt starting from
the front of our inn. One of them, Captain Russell
Eliott of the Royal Navy, lived in the town, or rather in a
villa adjoining it, to the rear of the Spread Eagle. Sir
Walter was at last persuaded to accept this courteous
adversary's invitation, and accompanied him through
some winding lanes to his residence. Peter Mathieson
by and by brought the carriage thither, in the same
clandestine method, and we escaped from Jedburgh—
with one shower more of stones at the Bridge. I believe
there would have been a determined onset at that spot,
but for the zeal of three or four sturdy Darnickers
(Joseph Shillinglaw, carpenter, being their Coryphæus),

who had, unobserved by us, clustered themselves beside the footman in the rumble. The Diary contains this brief notice :—" *May* 18.—Went to Jedburgh greatly against the wishes of my daughters. The mob were exceedingly vociferous and brutal, as they usually are nowadays. The population gathered in formidable numbers—a thousand from Hawick also—sad blackguards. The day passed with much clamour and no mischief. Henry Scott was re-elected—for the last time, I suppose. *Troja fuit.* I left the borough in the midst of abuse, and the gentle hint of *Burk Sir Walter.* Much obliged to the brave lads of Jeddart."

Sir Walter fully anticipated a scene of similar violence at the Selkirk election, which occurred a few days afterwards; but though here also, by help of weavers from a distance, there was a sufficiently formidable display of Radical power, there occurred hardly anything of what had been apprehended. Here the Sheriff was at home—known intimately to everybody, himself probably knowing almost all of man's estate by head mark, and, in spite of political fanaticism, all but universally beloved as well as feared. The only person who ventured actually to hustle a Tory elector on his way to the poll attracted Scott's observation at the moment when he was getting out of his carriage; he instantly seized the delinquent with his own hand—the man's spirit quailed, and no one coming to the rescue, he was safely committed to prison until the business of the day was over. Sir Walter had *ex officio* to preside at this election, and therefore his family would probably have made no attempt to dissuade him from attending it, even had he stayed away from Jedburgh. Among the exaggerated rumours of the time was one that Lord William Graham, the Tory candidate for Dumbartonshire, had been actually massacred by the rabble of his county town. He had been grievously maltreated, but escaped murder, though, I believe, narrowly. But I can never forget the high glow which suffused Sir Walter's countenance when he heard the overburdened story, and said calmly, in rather a clear voice, the trace of his calamitous affliction almost disappearing for the moment —" Well, Lord William died at his post—

' Non aliter cineres mando jacere meos.' " [1]

[1] Martial, i. 89.

I am well pleased that the ancient capital of the *Forest* did not stain its fair name upon this miserable occasion; and I am sorry for Jedburgh and Hawick. This last town stands almost within sight of Branksome Hall, overhanging, also, *sweet Teviot's silver tide.* The civilised American or Australian will curse these places, of which he would never have heard but for Scott, as he passes through them in some distant century, when perhaps all that remains of our national glories may be the high literature adopted and extended in new lands planted from our blood.

No doubt these disturbances of the general election had an unfavourable influence on the invalid. When they were over, he grew calmer and more collected; his speech became, after a little time, much clearer, and such were the symptoms of energy still about him, that I began to think a restoration not hopeless. Some business called me to London about the middle of June, and when I returned at the end of three weeks, I had the satisfaction to find that he had been gradually amending.

But, alas! the first use he made of this partial renovation had been to expose his brain once more to an imaginative task. He began his *Castle Dangerous*—the groundwork being again an old story which he had told in print, many years before, in a rapid manner.[1] And now, for the first time, he left Ballantyne out of his secret. He thus writes to Cadell on the 3rd of July:—"I intend to tell this little matter to nobody but Lockhart. Perhaps not even to him; certainly not to J. B., who having turned his back on his old political friends, will no longer have a claim to be a secretary in such matters, though I shall always be glad to befriend him." James's criticisms on *Count Robert* had wounded him—the Diary, already quoted, shows how severely. The last visit this old ally ever paid at Abbotsford occurred a week or two after. His newspaper had by this time espoused openly the cause of the Reform Bill—and some unpleasant conversation took place on that subject, which might well be a sore one for both parties—and not least, considering the whole of his personal history, for Mr. Ballantyne. Next morning, being Sunday, he disappeared abruptly, without saying farewell; and when Scott understood that he had

[1] See Essay on Chivalry—1814.

signified an opinion that the reading of the Church service, with a sermon from South or Barrow, would be a poor substitute for the mystical eloquence of some new idol down the vale, he expressed considerable disgust. They never met again in this world. In truth, Ballantyne's health also was already much broken; and if Scott had been entirely himself, he would not have failed to connect that circumstance in a charitable way with this never strong-minded man's recent abandonment of his own old *terra firma,* both religious and political. But this is a subject on which we have no title to dwell. Sir Walter's misgivings about himself, if I read him aright, now rendered him desirous of external support; but this his spirit would fain suppress and disguise even from itself. When I again saw him on the 13th of this month, he shewed me several sheets of the new romance, and told me how he had designed at first to have it printed by somebody else than Ballantyne, but that, on reflection, he had shrunk from hurting his feelings on so tender a point. I found, however, that he had neither invited nor received any opinion from James as to what he had written, but that he had taken an alarm lest he should fall into some blunder about the scenery fixed on (which he had never seen but once when a schoolboy), and had kept the sheets in proof until I should come back and accompany him in a short excursion to Lanarkshire. He was anxious in particular to see the tombs in the Church of St. Bride, adjoining the site of his "Castle Dangerous," of which Mr. Blore had shewn him drawings; and he hoped to pick up some of the minute traditions, in which he had always delighted, among the inhabitants of Douglasdale.

We set out early on the 18th, and ascended the Tweed, passing in succession Yair, Ashestiel, Innerleithen, Traquair, and many more scenes dear to his early life, and celebrated in his writings. The morning was still, but gloomy, and at length we had some thunder. It seemed to excite him vividly,—and on coming soon afterwards within view of that remarkable edifice (Drochel Castle) on the moorland ridge between Tweed and Clyde, which was begun, but never finished, by the Regent Morton—a gigantic ruin typical of his ambition—Sir Walter could hardly be restrained from making some effort to reach it. Morton, too, was a Douglas, and that name was at present his charm of charms. We pushed on to Biggar, however, and reaching it towards sunset, were detained there for some time by want of horses. It was soon discovered who he was; the population of the little town turned out; and he was evidently gratified with their respectful curiosity. It was the first time I observed him otherwise than annoyed upon such an occasion. Jedburgh, no doubt, hung on his mind, and he might be pleased to find that political differences did not interfere everywhere with his reception among his countrymen. But I fancy the cause lay deeper.

Another symptom that distressed me during this journey was, that he seemed constantly to be setting tasks to his memory. It was not as of old, when, if any one quoted a verse, he, from the fulness of his heart, could not help repeating the context. He was obviously in fear that this prodigious engine was losing its tenacity, and taking every occasion to rub and stretch it. He sometimes failed, and gave it up with *miseria cogitandi* in his eye. At other times he succeeded to admiration, and smiled as he closed his recital. About a mile beyond Biggar we overtook a parcel of carters, one of whom was maltreating his horse, and Sir Walter called to him from the carriage-window in great indignation. The man looked and spoke insolently; and as we drove on, he used some strong expressions about what he would have done had this happened within the bounds of his sheriffship. As he continued moved in an uncommon degree, I said, jokingly, that I wondered his porridge diet had left his blood so warm, and quoted Prior's

> " Was ever Tartar fierce or cruel
> Upon a mess of water-gruel? "

He smiled graciously, and extemporised this variation of the next couplet—

> " Yet who shall stand the Sheriff's force,
> If *Selkirk* carter beats his horse? "[1]

This seemed to put him into the train of Prior, and he repeated several striking passages both of the Alma and the Solomon. He was still at this when we reached a longish hill, and he got out to walk a little. As we climbed the ascent, he leaning heavily on my shoulder, we were met by a couple of beggars, who were, or professed to be, old

---

[1] " But who shall stand his rage and force,
　If first he rides, then eats his horse? "　　*Alma.*

soldiers both of Egypt and the Peninsula. One of them wanted a leg, which circumstance alone would have opened Scott's purse-strings, though for *ex facie* a sad old blackguard; but the fellow had recognised his person, as it happened, and in asking an alms, bade God bless him fervently by his name. The mendicants went on their way, and we stood breathing on the knoll. Sir Walter followed them with his eye, and planting his stick firmly on the sod, repeated without break or hesitation Prior's verses to the historian Mezeray. That he applied them to himself was touchingly obvious—

> " Whate'er thy countrymen have done,
>   By law and wit, by sword and gun,
>   In thee is faithfully recited;
>   And all the living world that view
>   Thy works, give thee the praises due—
>   At once instructed and delighted.
>
> " Yet for the fame of all these deeds,
>   What beggar in the Invalides,
>   With lameness broke, with blindness smitten,
>   Wished ever decently to die,
>   To have been either Mezeray—
>   Or any monarch he has written?
>
> " The man in graver tragic known,
>   Though his best part long since was done,
>   Still on the stage desires to tarry;
>   And he who play'd the harlequin,
>   After the jest, still loads the scene,
>   Unwilling to retire, though weary."

We spent the night at the Inn of Douglas Mill, and at an early hour next morning proceeded to inspect, under the care of one of Lord Douglas's tenants, Mr. Haddow, the Castle, the strange old *bourg*, the Church, long since deserted as a place of worship, and the very extraordinary monuments of the most heroic and powerful family in the annals of Scotland. That works of sculpture equal to any of the fourteenth century in Westminster Abbey (for such they certainly were, though much mutilated by Cromwell's soldiery) should be found in so remote an inland place attests strikingly the boundless resources of those haughty lords, " whose coronet," as Scott says, " so often counterpoised the crown." The effigy of the best friend of Bruce is among the number, and represents him cross-legged, as having fallen in battle with the Saracen, when on his way to Jerusalem with the heart of his king. The whole people of the barony gathered round the doors, and two persons of extreme old age,—one so old that he well remembered *Duke Willie*—that is to say, the Conqueror of Culloden—were introduced to tell all their local legends, while Sir Walter examined by torchlight these silent witnesses of past greatness. It was a strange and melancholy scene, and its recollection prompted some passages in Castle Dangerous, which might almost have been written at the same time with Lammermoor. The appearance of the village, too, is most truly transferred to the novel; and I may say the same of the surrounding landscape. We descended into a sort of crypt in which the Douglasses were buried until about a century ago, when there was room for no more; the leaden coffins around the wall being piled on each other, until the lower ones had been pressed flat as sheets of pasteboard, while the floor itself was entirely paved with others of comparatively modern date, on which coronets and inscriptions might be traced. Here the silver case that once held the noble heart of the Good Lord James himself is still pointed out. It is in the form of a heart, which, in memory of his glorious mission and fate, occupies ever since the chief place in the blazon of his posterity :—

> " The bloody heart blazed in the van,
> Announcing Douglas' dreaded name."

This charnel-house, too, will be recognised easily. Of the redoubted Castle itself, there remains but a small detached fragment, covered with ivy, close to the present mansion; but he hung over it long, or rather sat beside it, drawing outlines on the turf, and arranging in his fancy the sweep of the old precincts. Before the subjacent and surrounding lake and morass were drained, the position must indeed have been the perfect model of solitary strength. The crowd had followed us, and were lingering about to see him once more as he got into his carriage. They attended him to the spot where it was waiting, in perfect silence. It was not like a mob, but a procession. He was again obviously gratified, and saluted them with an earnest yet placid air, as he took his leave.

It was again a darkish cloudy day, with some occasional mutterings of distant thunder, and perhaps the state of the atmosphere told upon Sir Walter's nerves; but I had never before seen him so sensitive as he was all the morning after this inspection of Douglas. As we drove over the high table-land of Lesmahago, he repeated I know not how many verses from Winton, Barbour, and Blind Harry, with, I believe, almost every stanza of Dunbar's elegy on the deaths of the Makers (poets). It was now that I saw him, such as he paints himself in one or two passages of his Diary, but such as his companions in the meridian vigour of his life never saw him—"the rushing of a brook, or the sighing of the summer breeze, bringing the tears into his eyes not unpleasantly." Bodily weakness laid the delicacy of the organisation bare, over which he had prided himself in wearing a sort of half-stoical mask. High and exalted feelings, indeed, he had never been able to keep concealed, but he had shrunk from exhibiting to human eye the softer and gentler emotions which now trembled to the surface. He strove against it even now, and presently came back from the Lament of the Makers to his Douglasses, and chanted, rather than repeated, in a sort of deep and glowing, though not distinct recitative, his first favourite among all the ballads—

> "It was about the Lammas tide,
>   When husbandmen do win their day,
> That the Doughty Douglas bownde him to ride
>   To England to drive a prey,"—

—down to the closing stanzas, which again left him in tears—

> "My wound is deep—I fain would sleep—
>   Take thou the vanguard of the three,
> And hide me beneath the bracken-bush,
>   That grows on yonder lily lee."

We reached my brother's house on the Clyde some time before the dinner-hour, and Sir Walter appeared among the friends who received him there with much of his old graceful composure of courtesy. He walked about a little —was pleased with the progress made in some building operations, and especially commended my brother for having given his bridge "ribs like Bothwell." Greenshields was at hand, and he talked to him cheerfully, while the sculptor devoured his features, as under a solemn sense that they were before his eyes for the last time. My brother had taken care to have no company at dinner except two or three near neighbours, with whom

Sir Walter had been familiar through life, and whose entreaties it had been impossible to resist.   One of these was the late Mr. Elliott Lockhart of Cleghorn and Borthwickbrae—long Member of Parliament for Selkirkshire—the same whose anti-reform address had been preferred to the Sheriff's by the freeholders of that county in the preceding March.   But, alas ! very soon after that address was accepted, Borthwickbrae had a shock of paralysis as severe as any his old friend had as yet sustained.   He, too, had rallied beyond expectation, and his family were more hopeful, perhaps, than the others dared to be.   Sir Walter and he had not met for a few years—not since they rode side by side, as I well remember, on a merry day's sport at Bowhill; and I need not tell any one who knew Borthwickbrae, that a finer or more gallant specimen of the Border gentleman that he was in his prime never cheered a hunting-field.   When they now met (*heu quantum mutati !*) each saw his own case glassed in the other, and neither of their manly hearts could well contain itself as they embraced.   Each exerted himself to the utmost—indeed far too much, and they were both tempted to transgress the laws of their physicians.

At night Scott promised to visit Cleghorn on his way home, but next morning, at breakfast, came a messenger to inform us that the laird, on returning to his own house, fell down in another fit, and was now despaired of.   Immediately, although he had intended to remain two days, Sir Walter drew my brother aside, and besought him to lend him horses as far as Lanark, for that he must set off with the least possible delay.   He would listen to no persuasions.—" No, William," he said, " this is a sad warning.   I must home to work while it is called day; for the night cometh when no man can work.   I put that text, many a year ago, on my dial-stone; but it often preached in vain." [1]

We started accordingly, and, making rather a forced march, reached Abbotsford the same night.   During the journey, he was more silent than I ever before found him; he seemed to be rapt in thought, and was but seldom roused to take notice of any object we passed.   The little

---

[1] This dial-stone, which used to stand in front of the old cottage, and is now in the centre of the garden, is inscribed, ΝΥΞ ΓΑΡ ΕΡΧΕΤΑΙ. The same Greek words made the legend on Dr. Johnson's watch : and he had probably taken the hint from Boswell.

he said was mostly about Castle Dangerous, which he now seemed to feel sure he could finish in a fortnight, though his observation of the locality must needs cost the re-writing of several passages in the chapters already put into type.

For two or three weeks he bent himself sedulously to his task—and concluded both Castle Dangerous and the long-suspended Count Robert. By this time he had submitted to the recommendation of all his medical friends, and agreed to spend the coming winter away from Abbotsford, among new scenes, in a more genial climate, and above all (so he promised), in complete abstinence from all literary labour. When Captain Basil Hall understood that he had resolved on wintering at Naples (where, as has been mentioned, his son Charles was attached to the British Legation), it occurred to the zealous sailor that on such an occasion as this all thoughts of political difference ought to be dismissed,—and he, unknown to Scott, addressed a letter to Sir James Graham, then First Lord of the Admiralty, stating the condition of his friend's health, and his proposed plan, and suggesting that it would be a fit and graceful thing for the King's Government to place a frigate at his disposal. Sir James replied that it afforded his Royal Master, as well as himself, the sincerest satisfaction to comply with this hint; and that whenever Sir Walter found it convenient to come south-wards, a vessel should be prepared for his reception. Nothing could be handsomer than the way in which all this matter was arranged, and Scott, deeply gratified, ex-claimed that things were yet in the hands of gentlemen; but that he feared they had been undermining the state of society which required such persons as themselves to be at the head.

He had no wish, however, to leave Abbotsford until the approach of winter; and having dismissed his Tales, seemed to say to himself that he would enjoy his dear valley for the intervening weeks, draw friends about him, revisit all the familiar scenes in his neighbourhood once more; and if he were never to come back, store himself with the most agreeable recollections in his power, and so conduct himself as to bequeath to us who surrounded him a last stock of gentle impressions. He continued to work a little at his notes and prefaces, the *Reliquiæ* of Oldbuck, and a private tome entitled *Sylva Abbotsfordiensis*, but

did not fatigue himself; and when once all plans were
settled, and all cares in so far as possible set aside, his
health and spirits certainly rallied most wonderfully.   He
had settled that my wife and I should dine at Abbotsford,
and he and Anne at Chiefswood, day about; and this
rule was seldom departed from.   Both at home and in
the cottage he was willing to have a few guests, so they
were not strangers.   Mr. James (the accomplished and
popular novelist) and his lady, who this season lived at
Maxpoffle, and Mr. Archdeacon Williams,[1] who was
spending his vacation at Melrose, were welcome additions, and frequently so, to his accustomed circle of the
Scotts of Harden, the Pringles of Whytbank and Clifton,
the   Russels   of   Ashestiel,   the   Brewsters,   and   the
Fergussons.   Sir Walter observed the prescribed diet, on
the whole, pretty accurately; and seemed, when in the
midst of his family and friends, always tranquil—sometimes cheerful.   On one or two occasions he was even
gay; particularly, I think, when the weather was so fine
as to tempt us to dine in the marble hall at Abbotsford,
or at an early hour under the trees at Chiefswood.

He had the gratification of a visit from Mr. Adolphus,
and accompanied him one day as far as Oakwood and the
Linns of Ettrick.   He also received and made several little
excursions with the great artist, Turner, whose errand
to Scotland was connected with the collective edition of
his Poems.   One morning, in particular, he carried Mr.
Turner, with Mr. Skene and myself, to Smailholm Crags;
and it was in lounging about them, while the painter did
his sketch, that he told his " kind Samaritan " how the
habit of lying on the turf there among the sheep and
lambs, when a lame infant, had given his mind a peculiar
tenderness for those animals, which it had ever since
retained.   He seemed to enjoy the scene of his childhood
—yet there was many a touch of sadness both in his eye
and his voice.   He then carried us to Dryburgh, but
excused himself from attending Mr. Turner into the in-
closure.   Skene and I perceived that it would be better
for us to leave him alone, and we both accompanied
Turner.   Lastly, the painter must not omit Bemerside.
The good laird and lady were of course flattered, and
after walking about a little while among the huge old trees

[1] The Archdeacon, Charles Scott's early tutor, was at this time
Rector of the New Edinburgh Academy.

that surround their tower, we ascended to, I think, the
third tier of its vaulted apartments, and had luncheon in
a stately hall, arched also in stone, but with well-sized
windows (as being out of harm's way) duly blazoned with
shields and crests, and the time-honoured motto, BETIDE,
BETIDE—being the first words of a prophetic couplet
ascribed to Thomas the Rhymer :—

> " Betide, betide, whate'er betide,
> There shall be Haigs in Bemerside."

Mr. Turner's sketch of this picturesque Peel, and its
" brotherhood of venerable trees," is probably familiar
to most of my readers.

Mr. Cadell brought the artist to Abbotsford, and was
also of this Bemerside party. I must not omit to record
how gratefully all Sir Walter's family felt the delicate and
watchful tenderness of Mr. Cadell's conduct on this occasion. He so managed that the Novels just finished should
remain in types, but not thrown off until the author should
have departed ; so as to give opportunity for revising and
abridging them. He might well be the bearer of cheering
news as to their greater concerns, for the sale of the
Magnum had, in spite of political turbulences and distractions, gone on successfully. But he probably strained
a point to make things appear still better than they really
were. He certainly spoke so as to satisfy his friend that
he need give himself no sort of uneasiness about the
pecuniary results of idleness and travel. It was about
this time that we observed Sir Walter beginning to entertain the notion that his debts were paid off. By degrees,
dwelling on this fancy, he believed in it fully and implicitly. It was a gross delusion—but neither Cadell nor
any one else had the heart to disturb it by any formal
statement of figures. It contributed greatly more than
any circumstance besides to soothe Sir Walter's feelings
when it became at last necessary that he should tear himself from his land and his house, and the trees which he
had nursed. And with all that was done and forborne,
the hour when it came was a most heavy one.

Very near the end there came some unexpected things
to cast a sunset brilliancy over Abbotsford. His son, the
Major, arrived with tidings that he had obtained leave of
absence from his regiment, and should be in readiness to
sail with his father. This was a mighty relief to us all,

on Miss Scott's account as well as his, for my occupations
did not permit me to think of going with him, and there
was no other near connection at hand. But Sir Walter was
delighted—indeed, dearly as he loved all his children, he
had a pride in the Major that stood quite by itself, and
the hearty approbation which looked through his eyes
whenever turned on him sparkled brighter than ever as
his own physical strength decayed. Young Walter had
on this occasion sent down a horse or two to winter at
Abbotsford. One was a remarkably tall and handsome
animal, jet black all over, and when the Major appeared
on it one morning, equipped for a little sport with the
greyhounds Sir Walter insisted on being put upon Douce
Davie, and conducted as far as the Cauldshield's Loch to
see the day's work begun. He halted on the high bank to
the north of the lake, and I remained to hold his bridle, in
case of any frisk on the part of the Covenanter at the
" tumult great of dogs and men." We witnessed a very
pretty chase or two on the opposite side of the water—
but his eye followed always the tall black steed and his
rider. The father might well assure Lady Davy, that " a
handsomer fellow never put foot into stirrup." But when
he took a very high wall of loose stones, at which everybody else *craned*, as easily and elegantly as if it had been
a puddle in his stride, the old man's rapture was extreme.
" Look at him!" said he—" only look at him!   Now,
isn't he a fine fellow?"—This was the last time, I believe,
that Sir Walter mounted on horseback.

On the 17th of September the old splendour of Abbotsford was, after a long interval, and for the last time,
revived. Captain James Glencairn Burns, son of the
poet, had come home from India, and Sir Walter invited
him (with his wife, and their cicerones Mr. and Mrs.
M'Diarmid of Dumfries) to spend a day under his roof.
The neighbouring gentry were assembled, and having his
son to help him, Sir Walter did most gracefully the
honours of the table.

On the 20th Mrs. Lockhart set out for London to prepare for her father's reception there; and on the following
day Mr. Wordsworth and his daughter arrived from
Westmoreland to take farewell of him. This was a very
fortunate circumstance: nothing could have gratified Sir
Walter more, or sustained him better, if he needed any
support from without. On the 22nd—all his arrange-

ments being completed, and Laidlaw having received a paper of instructions, the last article of which repeats the caution to be " very careful of the dogs "—these two great poets, who had through life loved each other well, and, in spite of very different theories as to art, appreciated each other's genius more justly than inferior spirits ever did either of them, spent the morning together in a visit to Newark. Hence *Yarrow Revisited*—the last of the three poems by which Wordsworth has connected his name to all time with the most romantic of Scottish streams.

Sitting that evening in the library, Sir Walter said a good deal about the singularity that Fielding and Smollett had both been driven abroad by declining health, and never returned;—which circumstance, though his language was rather cheerful at this time, he had often before alluded to in a darker fashion; and Mr. Wordsworth expressed his regret that neither of those great masters of romance appeared to have been surrounded with any due marks of respect in the close of life. I happened to observe that Cervantes, on his last journey to Madrid, met with an incident which seemed to have given him no common satisfaction. Sir Walter did not remember the passage, and desired me to find it out in the life by Pellicer which was at hand, and translate it. I did so, and he listened with lively though pensive interest. Our friend Allan, the historical painter, had also come out that day from Edinburgh, and he since told me that he remembers nothing he ever saw with so much sad pleasure as the attitudes and aspect of Scott and Wordsworth as the story went on. Mr. Wordsworth was at that time, I should notice—though indeed his noble stanzas tell it—in but a feeble state of general health. He was, moreover, suffering so much from some malady in his eyes, that he wore a deep green shade over them. Thus he sat between Sir Walter and his daughter: *absit omen*—but it was no wonder that Allan thought as much of Milton as of Cervantes. The anecdote of the young student's raptures on discovering that he had been riding all day with the author of Don Quixote is introduced in the Preface to Count Robert and Castle Dangerous, which —(for I may not return to the subject)—came out at the close of November in four volumes, as the Fourth Series of Tales of My Landlord.

The following Sonnet was, no doubt, composed by Mr. Wordsworth that same evening :—

> " A trouble, not of clouds, or weeping rain,
> Nor of the setting sun's pathetic light
> Engendered, hangs o'er Eildon's triple height:
> Spirits of power assembled there complain
> For kindred power departing from their sight;
> While Tweed, best pleased in chanting a blithe strain,
> Saddens his voice again, and yet again.
> Lift up your hearts, ye mourners! for the might
> Of the whole world's good wishes with him goes;
> Blessings and prayers, in nobler retinue
> Than sceptred King or laurelled Conqueror knows,
> Follow this wondrous potentate. Be true,
> Ye winds of Ocean, and the Midland Sea,
> Wafting your charge to soft Parthenope."

Early on the 23rd of September 1831, Sir Walter left Abbotsford, attended by his daughter Anne and myself, and we reached London by easy stages on the 28th, having spent one day at Rokeby. I have nothing to mention of this journey except that, notwithstanding all his infirmities, he would not pass any object to which he had ever attached special interest, without getting out of the carriage to revisit it. His anxiety (for example) about the gigantic British or Danish effigy in the churchyard at Penrith, which we had all seen dozens of times before, seemed as great as if not a year had fled since 1797. It may be supposed that his parting with Mr. Morritt was a grave one. Finding that he had left the ring he then usually wore behind him at one of the inns on the road, he wrote to Morritt to make inquiries after it, as it had been dug out of the ruins of Hermitage Castle, and probably belonged of yore to one of the " Dark Knights of Liddesdale "; and if recovered, to keep it until he should come back to reclaim it, but, in the meantime, to wear it for his sake. The ring, which is a broad belt of silver with an angel holding the heart of Douglas, was found, and, having been worn to the end of his life by Mr. Morritt, was by him bequeathed to his friend's grandson.

Sir Walter arrived in London in the midst of the Lords' debates on the second Reform Bill, and the ferocious demonstrations of the populace on its rejection were in part witnessed by him. He saw the houses of several of the chief Tories, and above all, that of the Duke of Wellington, shattered and almost sacked. He heard of violence offered to the persons of some of his own noble friends; and having been invited to attend the christening of the infant heir of Buccleuch, whose godfather the King had proposed to be, he had the pain to understand that the ceremony must be adjourned, because it was not considered safe for his Majesty to visit, for such a purpose, the palace of one of his most amiable as well as illustrious peers.

During his stay, which was till 23rd of October, Sir Walter called on many of his old friends; but he accepted of no hospitalities except breakfasting once with Sir Robert Inglis on Clapham Common, and twice with Lady Gifford at Roehampton. Usually he worked a little in the morning at notes for the *Magnum*.

Dr. Robert Fergusson (now one of her Majesty's physicians), one of the family with which Sir Walter had lived all his days in such brother-like affection, saw him constantly while he remained in the Regent's Park; and though neither the invalid nor his children could fancy any other medical advice necessary, it was only due to Fergusson that some of his seniors should be called in occasionally with him. Sir Henry Halford (whom Scott reverenced as the friend of Baillie) and Dr. Henry Holland (an esteemed friend of his own) came accordingly; and all the three concurred in recognising evidence that there was incipient disease in the brain. There were still, however, such symptoms of remaining vigour, that they flattered themselves, if their patient would submit to a total intermission of all literary labour during some considerable space of time, the malady might yet be arrested. When they left him after the first inspection, they withdrew into an adjoining room, and on soon rejoining him found that in the interim he had wheeled his chair into a dark corner, so that he might see their faces without their being able to read his. When he was informed of the comparatively favourable views they entertained, he expressed great thankfulness; promised to obey all their directions as to diet and repose most scrupulously; and he did not conceal from them, that "he had feared insanity and feared *them*."

The following are extracts from his Diary:—" *London, October 2,* 1831.—I have been very ill, and if not quite unable to write, I have been unfit to do it. I have wrought, however, at two Waverley things, but not well.

A total prostration of bodily strength is my chief complaint. I cannot walk half a mile. There is, besides, some mental confusion, with the extent of which I am not, perhaps, fully acquainted. I am perhaps setting. I am myself inclined to think so, and like a day that has been admired as a fine one, the light of it sets down amid mists and storms. I neither regret nor fear the approach of death, if it is coming. I would compound for a little pain instead of this heartless muddiness of mind. The expense of this journey, &c., will be considerable; yet these heavy burdens could be easily borne if I were to be the Walter Scott I once was—but the change is great. And the ruin which I fear involves that of my country. I fancy the instances of Euthanasia are not in very serious cases very common. Instances there certainly are among the learned and the unlearned—Dr. Black, Tom Purdie. I should like, if it pleased God, to slip off in such a quiet way; but we must take what fate sends. I have not warm hopes of being myself again.''

Sir Walter seemed to enjoy having one or two friends to meet him at dinner—and a few more in the evenings. Among others he thus saw, more than once, Lord Montagu and his family, the Marchioness of Stafford (afterwards Duchess of Sutherland), the Macleods of Macleod, Lady Davy, Mr. Rogers, Lord Mahon, Mr. Murray, Lord Dudley, Lord Melville, the Bishop of Exeter, Lord Ashley, Sir David Wilkie, Mr. Thomas Moore, Mr. Milman, Mr. Washington Irving, and his three medical friends. At this time the Reform Bill for Scotland was in discussion in the House of Commons. Mr. Croker made a very brilliant speech in opposition to it, and was not sorry to have it said, that he had owed his inspiration, in no small degree, to having risen from the table at which Scott sat by his side. But the most regular of the evening visitors was, I think, Sir James Mackintosh. That master of every social charm and grace was himself in very feeble health; and whatever might have been the auguries of others, it struck me that there was uppermost with him at every parting the anticipation that they might never meet again. Sir James's kind assiduity was the more welcome, that his appearance banished the politics of the hour, on which his old friend's thoughts were too apt to brood. Their conversation, wherever it might begin, was sure to fasten ere long on Lochaber.

Before quitting home Scott had directed a humble monument to be prepared for the grave of Helen Walker, the original of Jeanie Deans, in the churchyard of Irongray. On the 18th he penned the epitaph now inscribed there—and also the pathetic farewell in the last page of the preface to *Count Robert of Paris*.

On the 19th, the Hon. Henry Duncan, R.N., storekeeper of the Ordnance, who had taken a great deal of trouble in arranging matters for the voyage, called on Sir Walter to introduce to him Captain, now Sir Hugh Pigot, the commanding officer of the Barham—who expected to sail on the 24th.

"*Oct.* 23.—Misty morning—looks like a yellow fog, which is the curse of London. I would hardly take my share of it for a share of its wealth and its curiosity—a vile double distilled fog, of the most intolerable kind. Children scarce stirring yet, but Baby and Macaw beginning their Macaw notes."—Dr. Fergusson, calling early, found Sir Walter with this page of his Diary before him. "As he was still working at his MS.," says the Doctor, "I offered to retire, but was not permitted. On my saying I had come to take leave of him before he quitted England, he exclaimed, with much excitement—' England is no longer a place for an honest man. I shall not live to find it so; you may.' He then broke out into the details of a very favourite superstition of his, that the middle of every century had always been marked by some great convulsion or calamity in this island. The alterations which had taken place in his mind and person since I had seen him, three years before, were very apparent. The expression of the countenance and the play of features were changed by slight palsy of one cheek. His utterance was so thick and indistinct as to make it very difficult for any but those accustomed to hear it to gather his meaning. His gait was less firm and assured than ever; but his power of self-command, his social tact, and his benevolent courtesy, the habits of a life, remained untouched by a malady which had obscured the higher powers of his intellect."

After breakfast, Sir Walter, accompanied by his son and both his daughters, set off for Portsmouth; and Captain Basil Hall had the kindness to precede them by an early coach, and prepare everything for their reception at the hotel. In changing horses at Guilford, Sir Walter got out of his carriage, and very narrowly escaped being run over by a stage-coach. Of all " the habits of a life," none clung longer to him than his extreme repugnance to being helped in anything. It was late before he came to lean, as a matter of course, when walking, upon any one but Tom Purdie; and, in the sequel, this proud feeling, coupled with increasing tendency to abstraction of mind, often exposed him to imminent hazard.

The Barham could not sail for a week. During this interval, Sir Walter scarcely stirred from his hotel, being unwilling to display his infirmities to the crowd of gazers who besieged him whenever he appeared. He received, however, deputations of the literary and scientific societies of the town, and all other visitors, with his usual ease and courtesy: and he might well be gratified with the extraordinary marks of deference paid him by the official persons who could in any way contribute to his comfort. The First Lord of the Admiralty, Sir James Graham, and the Secretary, Sir John Barrow, both appeared in person, to ascertain that nothing had been neglected for his accommodation on board the frigate. The Admiral, Sir Thomas Foley, placed his barge at his disposal; the Governor, Sir Colin Campbell, and all the chief officers, naval and military, seemed to strive with each other in attention to him and his companions. In Hall's Third Series of Fragments of Voyages, some interesting details have long since been made public:—it may be sufficient to say here that had Captain Pigot and his gallant shipmates been appointed to convey a Prince of the Blood, more anxious and delicate exertions could not have been made, either in altering the interior of the vessel, so as to meet the wants of the passengers, or afterwards, throughout the voyage, in rendering it easy, comfortable, and as far as might be, interesting and amusing.

On the 29th the wind changed, and the Barham got under weigh. After a few days, when they had passed the Bay of Biscay, Sir Walter ceased to be annoyed with sea-sickness, and sat most of his time on deck, enjoying apparently the air, the scenery, and above all the ship itself, the beautiful discipline practised in all things, and the martial exercises of the men. In Sir Hugh Pigot, Lieutenant (now Admiral Sir Baldwin) Walker, the physician, Dr. Liddell, and I believe in many others of the officers, he had highly intelligent as well as polished companions.

The course was often altered, for the express purpose of giving him a glimpse of some famous place; and it was only the temptation of a singularly propitious breeze that prevented a halt at Algiers.

On the 20th November, they came upon that remarkable phenomenon, the sudden creation of a submarine volcano, which bore, during its very brief date, the name of Graham's Island. Four months had elapsed since it " arose from out the azure main "—and in a few days more it disappeared. " Already," as Dr. Davy says, " its crumbling masses were falling to pieces from the pressure of the hand or foot." Yet nothing could prevent Sir Walter from landing on it—and in a letter of the following week he thus describes his adventure to Mr. Skene:—" Not being able to borrow your fingers, those of the Captain's clerk have been put in requisition for the inclosed sketch, and the notes adjoined are as accurate as can be expected from a hurried visit. You have a view of the island, very much as it shews at present; but nothing is more certain than that it is on the eve of a very important change, though in what respect is doubtful. I saw a portion of about five or six feet in height give way under the feet of one of our companions on the very ridge of the southern corner, and become completely annihilated, giving us some anxiety for the fate of our friend, till the dust and confusion of the dispersed pinnacle had subsided. You know my old talents for horsemanship. Finding the earth, or what seemed a substitute for it, sink at every step up to the knee, so as to make walking for an infirm and heavy man nearly impossible, I mounted the shoulders of an able and willing seaman, and by dint of his exertions, rode nearly to the top of the island. I would have given a great deal for you, my friend, the frequent and willing supplier of my defects; but on this journey, though undertaken late in life, I have found, from the benevolence of my companions, that when one man's strength was insufficient to supply my deficiencies, I had the willing aid of twenty if it could be useful. I have sent you one of the largest blocks of lava which I could find on the islet."

At Malta, which he reached on the 22nd, Sir Walter found several friends of former days. The Right Honourable John Hookham Frere had been resident there for several years, the captive of the enchanting climate and

the romantic monuments of the old chivalry.[1] Sir John
Stoddart, the Chief Judge, had known the Poet ever since
the days of Lasswade; and the Lieutenant-Governor,
Colonel Seymour Bathurst, had often met him under the
roof of his father, the late Earl Bathurst. Captain Dawson, husband to Lord Kinnedder's eldest daughter, was of
the garrison, and Sir Walter felt as if he were about to
meet a daughter of his own in the Euphemia Erskine who
had so often sat upon his knee. She immediately joined
him, and insisted on being allowed to partake his quarantine. Lastly, Dr. John Davy, the brother of his illustrious
friend, was at the head of the medical staff; and this
gentleman's presence was welcome indeed to the Major
and Miss Scott, as well as to their father, for he had
already begun to be more negligent as to his diet, and they
dreaded his removal from the skilful watch of Dr. Liddell.
     Nor less so was the society of Mrs. Davy—the daughter
of an old acquaintance and brother advocate, and indeed
almost a next-door neighbour in Edinburgh (Mr. Fletcher).
This lady's private journal, Sir Walter's own diary
(though hardly legible), and several letters to Laidlaw and
myself, tell of extraordinary honours lavished on him
throughout his stay. The Lieutenant-Governor had arranged that he should not be driven to the ordinary laza-
retto, but to Fort Manuel, where apartments were ready
for him and his party; and Mrs. Davy, accompanying
Colonel and Mrs. Bathurst on their first visit there, says,
the number of boats and the bustle about the sombre
landing-place of the Marsa Muscat "gave token even
then "—that is, in the midst of the terror for the cholera
—" of an illustrious arrival." The quarantine lasted
nine days, but Sir Walter, she says, " held a daily levee "
to receive the numerous visitors that flocked to converse
with him across the barrier—which Mr. Frere, notorious
for absence of mind, more than once all but transgressed.
On being set at liberty, Sir Walter removed to a hotel
close to Dr. Davy's residence in the Strada Ponente. He,
chiefly under Mrs. Davy's escort, visited the knightly antiquities of La Valetta, the Church of St. John and its rich
monuments, the deserted palaces and libraries of the heroic
brotherhood,—with especial interest the spot where the
famous pirate Dragut met his death, and the Via Stretta,

[1] Mr. Frere died there in 1846.

where the young knights of Malta used to fight their duels. " This town," he said to Mrs. Davy, " is quite like a dream—it will go hard but I make something of this " : —and in his letters he speaks repeatedly of his purpose to frame a new work connected with the Order. But the hospitalities of Malta were too much for him. The garrison officers got up a ball in his honour, and the dignitaries gave dinner after dinner. He, like most persons afflicted with paralytic disease, had begun to lose command over himself at table, and a very slight neglect of his physician's orders was now sure to infer a penalty. He seems to have escaped another fit of apoplexy only by the promptitude of Dr. Davy's lancet : and his children were well pleased when he consented to re-embark in the Barham for Naples on the 14th December. Mrs. Davy speaks much as Dr. Fergusson had done in London of the change in his appearance—and she gives some sad instances of his failing memory, especially that, when extolling certain novels, he could not bring out their writer's name, but only, after a painful pause, " that Irish lady." But Mrs. Davy, too, speaks, like Fergusson, of the unaltered courtesy of his demeanour on all occasions, and the warmth of affection that was evident in every allusion to old friends and ties. She told him, at their last meeting, that her husband was writing Sir Humphry's Life,—" I am glad of it," said Sir Walter; " I hope his mother lived to see his greatness."

On the 17th the Barham reached Naples, and Sir Walter found his son Charles ready to receive him. The quarantine was cut short by the courtesy of the King, and the travellers established themselves in an apartment of the Palazzo Caramanico. Here, again, the British Minister, Mr. Hill (now Lord Berwick), and the English nobility and gentry then residing in Naples, did whatever kindness and respect could suggest ; nor were the natives less attentive. The Marquis of Hertford, the Hon. Keppel Craven, the Hon. William Ashley and his lady, Sir George Talbot, the venerable Matthias (author of The Pursuits of Literature), Mr. Auldjo (celebrated for his ascent of Mont Blanc), and Dr. Hogg, who has since published an account of his travels in the East—appear to have, in their various ways, contributed whatever they could to his comfort and amusement. But the person of whom he saw most was the late Sir William Gell, who had long been condemned to live in Italy by ailments and infirmities not dissimilar to his own.

Though he remained here until the middle of April, the reader will pardon me for giving but few of the details to which I have had access. He was immediately elected into the chief literary societies of the place; and the king gave him unusual facilities in the use of all its libraries and museums. An ancient MS. of the Romance of Sir Bevis of Hampton being pointed out to him, he asked and obtained permission to have a transcript; and one was executed in his own apartments. He also expressed great curiosity as to the local ballads and popular tracts, chiefly occupied with the exploits of bandits, and collected enough of them to form about a dozen volumes, which he took a fancy to have bound in vellum. Sir William Gell was his cicerone to most of the celebrated spots in the city and its vicinity—but soon discovered that he felt comparatively little interest in anything that he saw, unless he could connect it somehow with traditions or legends of mediæval history or romance, or trace some resemblance to the scenery of familiar associations at home. Thus, amidst the chestnut forest near Pæstum, he was heard repeating *Jock of Hazeldean*—and again, in looking down on the Lucrine Lake, Baiæ, Misenum, and Averno, he suddenly pronounced, " in a grave tone and with great emphasis," some fragment of a Jacobite ditty—

> " 'Tis up the rocky mountain and down the mossy glen,
> We darena gang a milking for Charlie and his men."

At Pompeii alone did his thoughts seem to be wholly commanded by the realities before him. There he had himself carried from house to house, and examined everything leisurely; but said little, except ever and anon in an audible whisper, " The city of the dead—the city of the dead ! "

Meantime he more and more lost sight of the necessary restrictions—resumed too much of the usual habits in participating of splendid hospitalities, and, worst of all, resumed his pen. No persuasion could arrest him. He wrote several small tales, the subjects taken from the Newgate history of the Neapolitan banditti; and covered many quires with chapter after chapter of a romance connected with the Knights of St. John.

The MS. of these painful days is hardly to be deciphered by any effort; but he often spoke as well pleased with what he was doing, and confident that, on reaching Scotland again, he should have produced welcome materials for the press—though on many other occasions his conversation intimated apprehensions of a far different order, and he not only prognosticated that his end was near, but expressed alarm that he might not live to finish the journey homewards.

He continued, however, to be haunted with a mere delusion—on the origin of which I can offer no guess.—" In our morning drives " (writes Gell) " Sir Walter always noticed a favourite dog of mine, which was usually in the carriage, and generally patted the animal's head for some time, saying—' Poor boy—poor boy.' ' I have got at home,' said he, ' two very fine favourite dogs,—so large, that I am almost afraid they look too handsome and too feudal for my diminished income. I am very fond of them, but they are so large it was impossible to take them with me.'—He came one morning rather early to my house, to tell me he was sure I should be pleased at some good luck which had befallen him, and of which he had just received notice. This was, as he said, an account from his friends in England, that his last works, Robert of Paris and Castle Dangerous, had gone on to a second edition. He told me in the carriage that he felt quite relieved by his letters; ' for,' said he, ' I could have never slept straight in my coffin till I had satisfied every claim against me.' ' And now,' added he to the dog, ' my poor boy, I shall have my house, and my estate round it, free, and I may keep my dogs as big and as many as I choose, without fear of reproach.'—He told me, that, being relieved from debt, and no longer forced to write for money, he longed to turn to poetry again. I encouraged him, and asked him why he had ever relinquished poetry?—' Because Byron *bet* me, said he, pronouncing the word *beat* short. I rejoined, that I thought I could remember by heart as many passages of his poetry as of Byron's. He replied—' That may be, but he *bet* me out of the field in the description of the strong passions, and in deep-seated knowledge of the human heart; so I gave up poetry for the time.' He became extremely curious about Rhodes, and having chosen for his poetical subject the chivalrous story of the slaying of the dragon by De Gozon, and the stratagems and valour with which he conceived and executed his purpose, he was quite delighted to hear that I had seen the skeleton of this real or reported dragon, which yet remains secured by large iron staples to the vaulted roof of one of the gates of the city."

From this time, whoever was near him often heard, that when he reached Scotland, it would be to re-enter on the unfettered use and administration of his estate. He even wrote to Mrs. Scott of Harden bespeaking her presence at a little festival which he designed to hold within a few months at Abbotsford, in celebration of his release from all difficulties. All this while he sent letters frequently to his daughter Sophia, Mr. Cadell, Mr. Laidlaw, and myself. Some were of a very melancholy cast—for the dream about his debts was occasionally broken: in general, however, these his last letters tell the same story of delusive hopes both as to health and wealth, of satisfaction in the resumption of his pen, of eagerness to be once more at Abbotsford, and of affectionate anxiety about the friends he was there to rejoin. Every one of those to Laidlaw has something about the poor people and the dogs. One to myself conveyed his desire that he might be set down for " something as handsome as I liked " in a subscription then thought of for the Ettrick Shepherd; who that spring visited London, and was in no respect improved by his visit. Another to my wife bade her purchase a grand pianoforte which he wished to present to Miss Cadell, his bookseller's daughter. The same generous spirit was shewn in many other communications.

It had been his intention not to leave the Mediterranean without seeing Rhodes himself—but he suddenly dropped this scheme, on learning that his friend Sir Frederick Adam, Governor of the Ionian Islands, who had invited him to Corfu, was ordered to India. From that hour his whole thoughts were fixed on home—and his companions soon ceased from opposing his inclinations. Miss Scott was no doubt the more willing to yield, as having received intelligence of the death of her nephew, the " Hugh Littlejohn " of the Grandfather's Tales—which made her anxious about her sister. But indeed, since her father would again work, what good end could it serve to keep him from working at his own desk? And since all her entreaties, and the warnings of foreign doctors, proved alike unavailing as to the regulation of his diet, what remaining chance could there be on that score, unless from replacing him under the eye of the friendly physicians whose authority had formerly seemed to have due influence on his mind? He had wished to return by the route of the Tyrol and Germany, partly for the sake of the remarkable chapel and monuments of the old Austrian princes at Innsbruck, and the feudal ruins upon the Rhine, but chiefly that he might have an interview with Goethe at Weimar. That poet died on the 22nd of March, and the news seemed to act upon Scott exactly as the illness of Borthwickbrae had done in the August before. His impatience redoubled: all his fine dreams of recovery seemed to vanish at once—" Alas for Goethe! " he exclaimed: " but he at least died at home—Let us to Abbotsford." And he quotes more than once in his letters the first hemistich of the line from Politian with which he had closed his early memoir of Leyden—" *Grata quies patriæ.*"

When the season was sufficiently advanced, then, the party set out, Mr. Charles Scott having obtained leave to accompany his father; which was quite necessary, as his elder brother had already been obliged to rejoin his regiment. They quitted Naples on the 16th of April, in an open barouche, which could at pleasure be converted into a bed. Sir Walter was somewhat interested by a few of the objects presented to him in the earlier stages of his route. The certainty that he was on his way home for a time soothed and composed him; and amidst the agreeable society which again surrounded him on his arrival in Rome, he seemed perhaps as much of himself as he had ever been in Malta or in Naples. For a moment even his literary hope and ardour appear to have revived. But still his daughter entertained no doubt, that his consenting to pause for even a few days in Rome was dictated mainly by consideration of her natural curiosity. Gell went to Rome about the same time; and Sir Walter was introduced there to another accomplished countryman, who exerted himself no less than did Sir William, to render his stay agreeable to him. This was Mr. Edward Cheney—whose family had long been on terms of very strict intimacy with the Maclean Clephanes of Torloisk, so that Sir Walter was ready to regard him at first sight as a friend. Nor was it a small circumstance that the Cheney family had then in their occupancy the Villa Muti at Frascati, for many of his later years the favourite abode of the Cardinal York.

At Rome, Sir Walter partook of the hospitalities of the native nobility, many of whom had travelled into Scotland under the influence of his writings, and on one or two occasions was well enough to sustain their best impressions of him by his conversation. But, on the whole, his feebleness, and incapacity to be roused by objects which, in other days, would have appealed most powerfully to his imagination, were too painfully obvious : and, indeed, the only, or almost the only very lively curiosity he appeared to feel regarded the family pictures and other Stuart relics then preserved at the Villa Muti—but especially the monument to Charles Edward and his father in St. Peter's, the work of Canova, executed at the cost of George IV. Excepting his visits at Frascáti, the only excursion he made into the neighbouring country was one to the grand old castle of Bracciano : where he spent a night in the feudal halls of the Orsini, now included among the numberless possessions of the Banker Prince Torlonia.

" Walking on the battlements of this castle next morning " (10th May)—says Mr. Cheney—" he spoke of Goethe with regret ; he had been in correspondence with him before his death, and had purposed visiting him at Weimar. I told him I had been to see Goethe the year before, and that I had found him well, and though very old, in the perfect possession of all his faculties.—' Of all his faculties ! ' he replied ;—' it is much better to die than to survive them, and better still to die than live in the apprehension of it ; but the worst of all," he added, thoughtfully, ' would have been to have survived their partial loss, and yet to be conscious of his state.'—He did not seem to be, however, a great admirer of some of Goethe's works. Much of his popularity, he observed, was owing to pieces which, in his latter moments, he might have wished recalled. He spoke with much feeling. I answered, that *he* must derive great consolation in the reflection that his own popularity was owing to no such cause. He remained silent for a moment, with his eyes fixed on the ground ; when he raised them, as he shook me by the hand, I perceived the light-blue eye sparkled with unusual moisture. He added—' I am drawing near the close of my career ; I am fast shuffling off the stage. I have been perhaps the most voluminous author of the day ; and it *is* a comfort to me to think that I have tried to unsettle no man's faith, to corrupt no man's principle.' "

Next day, Friday, May 11, Sir Walter left Rome.— " During his stay there " (adds Mr. Cheney) " he had re-

ceived every mark of attention and respect from the
Italians, who, in not crowding to visit him, were deterred
only by their delicacy and their dread of intruding on an
invalid. The enthusiasm was by no means confined to the
higher orders. His fame, and even his works, are familiar
to all classes—the stalls are filled with translations of his
novels in the cheapest forms; and some of the most popular
plays and operas have been founded upon them. Some
time after he left Italy, when I was travelling in the mountains of Tuscany, it has more than once occurred to me to
be stopped in little villages, hardly accessible to carriages,
by an eager admirer of Sir Walter, to inquire after the
health of my illustrious countryman.''

CHAPTER XVIII

Return to England—Seizure at Nimeguen—Jermyn Street, London
—Edinburgh—Abbotsford—Death and funeral of Scott in Septem-
ber 1832—His Character—Monuments to his Memory—Pictures,
Busts, and Statues.

THE last jotting of Sir Walter Scott's Diary—perhaps
the last specimen of his handwriting—records his starting
from Naples on the 16th of April. After the 11th of May
the story can hardly be told too briefly.

The irritation of impatience, which had for a moment
been suspended by the aspect and society of Rome, returned the moment he found himself again on the road, and
seemed to increase hourly. His companions could with
difficulty prevail on him to see even the falls of Terni, or
the church of Santa Croce at Florence. On the 17th, a
cold and dreary day, they passed the Apennines, and dined
on the top of the mountains. The snow and the pines recalled Scotland, and he expressed pleasure at the sight of
them. That night they reached Bologna, but he would see
none of the interesting objects there :—and next day,
hurrying in like manner through Ferrara, he proceeded as
far as Monselice. On the 19th he arrived at Venice; and
he remained there till the 23rd; but shewed no curiosity
about anything except the Bridge of Sighs and the adjoining dungeons—down into which he would scramble, though
the exertion was exceedingly painful to him. On the other
historical features of that place—one so sure in other days

to have inexhaustible attractions for him—he would not
even look; and it was the same with all that he came within
reach of—even with the fondly anticipated chapel at
Innsbruck—as they proceeded through the Tyrol, and so
onwards, by Munich, Ulm, and Heidelberg, to Frankfort,
Here (June 5) he entered a bookseller's shop; and the
people, seeing an English party, brought out among the
first things a lithographed print of Abbotsford. He said
—" I know that already, sir," and hastened back to the
inn without being recognised. Though in some parts of
the journey they had very severe weather, he repeatedly
wished to travel all the night as well as all the day; and
the symptoms of an approaching fit were so obvious, that
he was more than once bled, ere they reached Mayence, by
the hand of his affectionate domestic.

At this town they embarked, on the 8th June, in the
Rhine steamboat; and while they descended the famous
river through its most picturesque region, he seemed to
enjoy, though he said nothing, the perhaps unrivalled
scenery it presented to him. His eye was fixed on the successive crags and castles, and ruined monasteries, each of
which had been celebrated in some German ballad familiar
to his ear, and all of them blended in the immortal panorama of Childe Harold. But so soon as they had passed
Cologne, and nothing but flat shores, and here and there
a grove of poplars and a village spire were offered to the
vision, the weight of misery sunk down again upon him. It
was near Nimeguen, on the evening of the 9th, that he sustained another serious attack of apoplexy, combined with
paralysis. Nicolson's lancet restored, after the lapse of
some minutes, the signs of animation; but this was the
crowning blow. Next day he insisted on resuming his
journey, and on the 11th was lifted into an English steam-
boat at Rotterdam.

He reached London about six o'clock on the evening of
Wednesday the 13th of June. Owing to the unexpected
rapidity of the journey, his eldest daughter had had no
notice when to expect him; and fearful of finding her either
out of town, or unprepared to receive him and his attendants under her roof, Charles Scott drove to the St.
James's Hotel in Jermyn Street, and established his quarters there before he set out in quest of his sister and
myself. When we reached the hotel, he recognised us with
many marks of tenderness, but signified that he was totally

exhausted; so no attempt was made to remove him further, and he was put to bed immediately. Dr. Fergusson saw him the same night, and next day Sir Henry Halford and Dr. Holland saw him also; and during the next three weeks the two latter visited him daily, while Fergusson was scarcely absent from his pillow. The Major was soon on the spot. To his children, all assembled once more about him, he repeatedly gave his blessing in a very solemn manner, as if expecting immediate death; but he was never in a condition for conversation, and sunk either into sleep or delirious stupor upon the slightest effort.

Mrs. Thomas Scott came to town as soon as she heard of his arrival, and remained to help us. She was more than once recognised and thanked. Mr. Cadell, too, arrived from Edinburgh, to render any assistance in his power. I think Sir Walter saw no other of his friends except Mr. John Richardson, and him only once. As usual, he woke up at the sound of a familiar voice, and made an attempt to put forth his hand, but it dropped powerless, and he said, with a smile—" Excuse my hand." Richardson made a struggle to suppress his emotion, and, after a moment, got out something about Abbotsford and the woods, which he had happened to see shortly before. The eye brightened, and he said—" How does Kirklands get on?" Mr. Richardson had lately purchased the estate so called in Teviotdale, and Sir Walter had left him busied with plans of building. His friend told him that his new house was begun, and that the Marquis of Lothian had very kindly lent him one of his own, meantime, in its vicinity. " Ay, Lord Lothian is a good man," said Sir Walter; " he is a man from whom one may receive a favour, and that's saying a good deal for any man in these days." The stupor then sank back upon him, and Richardson never heard his voice again. This state of things continued till the beginning of July.

During these melancholy weeks, great interest and sympathy were manifested. Allan Cunningham mentions that, walking home late one night, he found several working-men standing together at the corner of Jermyn Street, and one of them asked him—as if there was but one deathbed in London—" Do you know, sir, if this is the street where he is lying?" The inquiries both at the hotel and at my house were incessant; and I think there was hardly a member of the royal family who did not send every day.

The newspapers teemed with paragraphs about Sir Walter; and one of these, it appears, threw out a suggestion that his travels had exhausted his pecuniary resources, and that if he were capable of reflection at all, cares of that sort might probably harass his pillow. This paragraph came from a very ill-informed, but, I dare say, a well-meaning quarter. It caught the attention of some members of the Government; and, in consequence, I received a private communication, to the effect that, if the case were as stated, Sir Walter's family had only to say what sum would relieve him from embarrassment, and it would be immediately advanced by the Treasury. The then Paymaster of the Forces, Lord John Russell, had the delicacy to convey this message through a lady with whose friendship he knew us to be honoured—the Honourable Catherine Arden. We expressed our grateful sense of his politeness, and of the liberality of the Government, and I now beg leave to do so once more;—but his Lordship was of course informed that Sir Walter Scott was not situated as the journalist had represented.

Dr. Fergusson's Memorandum on Jermyn Street will be acceptable to the reader. He says—" When I saw Sir Walter, he was lying in the second floor back-room of the St. James's Hotel, in a state of stupor, from which, however, he could be roused for a moment by being addressed, and then he recognised those about him, but immediately relapsed. I think I never saw anything more magnificent than the symmetry of his colossal bust, as he lay on the pillow with his chest and neck exposed. During the time he was in Jermyn Street he was calm but never collected, and in general either in absolute stupor or in a waking dream. He never seemed to know where he was, but imagined himself to be still in the steam-boat. The rattling of carriages, and the noises of the street, sometimes disturbed this illusion—and then he fancied himself at the polling-booth of Jedburgh, where he had been insulted and stoned. During the whole of this period of apparent helplessness, the great features of his character could not be mistaken. He always exhibited great self-possession, and acted his part with wonderful power whenever visited, though he relapsed the next moment into the stupor from which strange voices had roused him. A gentleman [Mr. Richardson] stumbled over a chair in his dark room;—he immediately started up, and though unconscious that it was a friend, expressed as much concern and feeling as if he had never been labouring under the irritability of disease. It was impossible even for those who most constantly saw and waited on him in his then deplorable condition to relax from the habitual deference which he had always inspired. He expressed his will as determinedly as ever, and enforced it with the same apt and good-natured irony as he was wont to use.

" At length his constant yearning to return to Abbotsford induced his physicians to consent to his removal; and the moment this was notified to him, it seemed to infuse new vigour into his frame. It was on a calm, clear afternoon of the 7th July, that every preparation was made for his embarkation on board the steam-boat. He was placed on a chair by his faithful servant Nicolson, half-dressed, and loosely wrapped in a quilted dressing-gown. He requested Lockhart and myself to wheel him towards the light of the open window, and we both remarked the vigorous lustre of his eye. He sat there silently gazing on space for more than half an hour, apparently wholly occupied with his own thoughts, and having distinct perception of where he was, or how he came there. He suffered himself to be lifted into his carriage, which was surrounded by a crowd, among whom were many gentlemen on horseback, who had loitered about to gaze on the scene. His children were deeply affected, and Mrs. Lockhart trembled from head to foot, and wept bitterly. Thus surrounded by those nearest to him, he alone was unconscious of the cause or the depth of their grief, and while yet alive seemed to be carried to his grave.

On this his last journey, Sir Walter was attended by his two daughters, Mr. Cadell, and myself—and also by Dr. Thomas Watson, who (it being impossible for Dr. Fergusson to leave town at that moment) kindly undertook to see him safe at Abbotsford. We embarked in the James Watt steam-boat, the master of which (Captain John Jamieson), as well as the agents of the proprietors, made every arrangement in their power for the convenience of the invalid. The Captain gave up for Sir Walter's use his own private cabin, which was a separate erection—a sort of cottage on the deck; and he seemed unconscious, after being laid in bed there, that any new removal had occurred. On arriving at Newhaven, late on the 9th, we found careful preparations made for his landing by the manager of the

Shipping Company (Mr. Hamilton)—and Sir Walter, prostrate in his carriage, was slung on shore, and conveyed
from thence to Douglas's hotel, in St. Andrew's Square,
in the same complete apparent unconsciousness.   Mrs.
Douglas had in former days been the Duke of Buccleuch's
housekeeper at Bowhill, and she and her husband had also
made the most suitable provision.

At a very early hour on the morning of Wednesday
the 11th, we again placed him in his carriage, and he
lay in the same torpid state during the first two stages on
the road to Tweedside.   But as we descended the vale of
the Gala he began to gaze about him, and by degrees it
was obvious that he was recognising the features of that
familiar landscape.   Presently he murmured a name or two
—" Gala Water, surely—Buckholm—Torwoodlee."   As
we rounded the hill at Ladhope, and the outline of the
Eildons burst on him, he became greatly excited; and
when, turning himself on the couch, his eye caught at
length his own towers at the distance of a mile, he sprang
up with a cry of delight.   The river being in flood, we had
to go round a few miles by Melrose bridge; and during the
time this occupied, his woods and house being within prospect, it required occasionally both Dr. Watson's strength
and mine, in addition to Nicolson's, to keep him in the carriage.   After passing the bridge, the road for a couple of
miles loses sight of Abbotsford, and he relapsed into his
stupor; but on gaining the bank immediately above it, his
excitement became again ungovernable.

Mr. Laidlaw was waiting at the porch, and assisted us in
lifting him into the dining-room, where his bed had been
prepared.   He sat bewildered for a few moments, and then
resting his eye on Laidlaw, said—" Ha! Willie Laidlaw!
O man, how often have I thought of you!"   By this time
his dogs had assembled about his chair—they began to
fawn upon him and lick his hands, and he alternately
sobbed and smiled over them, until sleep oppressed him.

Dr. Watson having consulted on all things with Mr.
Clarkson of Melrose and his father, the good old " Country
Surgeon " of Selkirk, resigned the patient to them, and
returned to London.   None of them could have any hope
but that of soothing irritation.   Recovery was no longer to
be thought of : but there might be *Euthanasia*.

And yet something like a ray of hope did break in upon
us next morning.   Sir Walter awoke perfectly conscious

where he was, and expressed an ardent wish to be carried out into his garden. We procured a Bath chair from Huntley Burn, and Laidlaw and I wheeled him out before his door, and up and down for some time on the turf, and among the rose-beds then in full bloom. The grand-children admired the new vehicle, and would be helping in their way to push it about. He sat in silence, smiling placidly on them and the dogs their companions, and now and then admiring the house, the screen of the garden, and the flowers and trees. By and by he conversed a little, very composedly, with us—said he was happy to be at home—that he felt better than he had ever done since he left it, and would perhaps disappoint the doctors after all. He then desired to be wheeled through his rooms, and we moved him leisurely for an hour or more up and down the hall and the great library:—" I have seen much," he kept saying, " but nothing like my ain house—give me one turn more ! " He was gentle as an infant, and allowed himself to be put to bed again the moment we told him that we thought he had had enough for one day.

Next morning he was still better. After again enjoying the Bath chair for perhaps a couple of hours out of doors, he desired to be drawn into the library, and placed by the central window, that he might look down upon the Tweed. Here he expressed a wish that I should read to him, and when I asked from what book, he said—" Need you ask? There is but one." I chose the 14th chapter of St. John's Gospel; he listened with mild devotion, and said when I had done—" Well, this is a great comfort—I have followed you distinctly, and I feel as if I were yet to be myself again." In this placid frame he was again put to bed, and had many hours of soft slumber.

On the third day Mr. Laidlaw and I again wheeled him about the small piece of lawn and shrubbery in front of the house for some time ; and the weather being delightful, and all the richness of summer around him, he seemed to taste fully the balmy influences of nature. The sun getting very strong, we halted the chair in a shady corner, just within the verge of his verdant arcade around the court-wall; and breathing the coolness of the spot, he said, " Read me some amusing thing—read me a bit of Crabbe." I brought out the first volume of his old favourite that I could lay hand on, and turned to what I remembered as one of his most favourite passages in it—the description of the arrival

of the Players in the Borough. He listened with great
interest, and also, as I soon perceived, with great curiosity.
Every now and then he exclaimed, " Capital—excellent—
very good—Crabbe has lost nothing "—and we were too
well satisfied that he considered himself as hearing a new
production, when, chuckling over one couplet, he said,
" Better and better—but how will poor Terry endure these
cuts? " I went on with the poet's terrible sarcasms upon
the theatrical life, and he listened eagerly, muttering,
" Honest Dan ! "—" Dan won't like this." At length I
reached those lines—

> " Sad happy race ! soon raised, and soon depressed,
> Your days all passed in jeopardy and jest ;
> Poor without prudence, with afflictions vain,
> Not warned by misery, nor enriched by gain."

" Shut the book," said Sir Walter—" I can't stand more
of this—it will touch Terry to the very quick."

On the morning of Sunday the 15th, he was again taken
out into the little *pleasaunce*, and got as far as his favourite
terrace-walk between the garden and the river, from which
he seemed to survey the valley and the hills with much
satisfaction. On re-entering the house, he desired me to
read to him from the New Testament, and after that he
again called for a little of Crabbe ; but whatever I selected
from that poet seemed to be listened to as if it made part
of some new volume published while he was in Italy. He
attended with this sense of novelty even to the tale of
Phœbe Dawson, which not many months before he could
have repeated every line of, and which I chose for one of
these readings, because, as is known to every one, it had
formed the last solace of Mr. Fox's deathbed. On the
contrary, his recollection of whatever I read from the Bible
appeared to be lively ; and in the afternoon, when we made
his grandson, a child of six years, repeat some of Dr.
Watts' hymns by his chair, he seemed also to remember
them perfectly. That evening he heard the Church service,
and when I was about to close the book, said—" Why do
you omit the visitation for the sick? "—which I added accordingly.

On Monday he remained in bed, and seemed extremely
feeble ; but after breakfast on Tuesday the 17th he appeared revived somewhat, and was again wheeled about on
the turf. Presently he fell asleep in his chair, and after
dozing for perhaps half an hour, started awake, and shak-

ing the plaids we had put about him from off his shoulders, said—"This is sad idleness. I shall forget what I have been thinking of, if I don't set it down now. Take me into my own room, and fetch the keys of my desk." He repeated this so earnestly, that we could not refuse; his daughters went into his study, opened his writing-desk, and laid paper and pens in the usual order, and I then moved him through the hall and into the spot where he had always been accustomed to work. When the chair was placed at the desk, and he found himself in the old position, he smiled and thanked us, and said—"Now give me my pen, and leave me for a little to myself." Sophia put the pen into his hand, and he endeavoured to close his fingers upon it, but they refused their office—it dropped on the paper. He sank bank among his pillows, silent tears rolling down his cheeks; but composing himself by and by, motioned to me to wheel him out of doors again. Laidlaw met us at the porch, and took his turn of the chair. Sir Walter, after a little while, again dropped into slumber. When he was awaking, Laidlaw said to me—"Sir Walter has had a little repose."—"No, Willie," said he—"no repose for Sir Walter but in the grave." The tears again rushed from his eyes. "Friends," said he, "don't let me expose myself—get me to bed—that's the only place."

With this scene ended our glimpse of daylight. Sir Walter never, I think, left his room afterwards, and hardly his bed, except for an hour or two in the middle of the day; and after another week he was unable even for this. During a few days he was in a state of painful irritation—and I saw realised all that he had himself pre-figured in his description of the meeting between Chrystal Croftangry and his paralytic friend. Dr. Ross came out from Edinburgh, bring with him his wife, one of the dearest *nieces* of the Clerks' table. Sir Walter with some difficulty recognised the Doctor; but on hearing Mrs. Ross's voice, exclaimed at once—"Isn't that Kate Hume?" These kind friends remained for two or three days with us. Clarkson's lancet was pronounced necessary, and the relief it afforded was, I am happy to say, very effectual.

After this he declined daily, but still there was great strength to be wasted, and the process was long. He seemed, however, to suffer no bodily pain; and his mind, though hopelessly obscured, appeared, when there was

any symptom of consciousness, to be dwelling, with rare
exceptions, on serious and solemn things; the accent of
the voice grave, sometimes awful, but never querulous,
and very seldom indicative of any angry or resentful
thoughts. Now and then he imagined himself to be ad-
ministering justice as Sheriff; and once or twice he seemed
to be ordering Tom Purdie about trees. A few times also,
I am sorry to say, we could perceive that his fancy was at
Jedburgh—and *Burk Sir Walter* escaped him in a melancholy tone. But commonly whatever we could follow
him in was a fragment of the Bible (especially the Pro-
phecies of Isaiah and the Book of Job), or some petition
in the litany, or a verse of some psalm (in the old Scotch
metrical version), or of some of the magnificent hymns of
the Romish ritual, in which he had always delighted, but
which probably hung on his memory now in connection
with the Church services he had attended while in Italy.
We very often heard distinctly the cadence of the *Dies
Iræ*; and I think the very last *stanza* that we could make
out was the first of a still greater favourite:—

> " Stabat Mater dolorosa,
> Juxta crucem lachrymosa,
> Dum pendebat Filius."

All this time he continued to recognise his daughters,
Laidlaw, and myself, whenever we spoke to him—and received every attention with a most touching thankfulness.
Mr. Clarkson, too, was always saluted with the old
courtesy, though the cloud opened but a moment for him
to do so. Most truly might it be said that the gentleman
survived the genius.

After two or three weeks had passed in this way, I was
obliged to leave Sir Walter for a single day, and go into
Edinburgh to transact business, on his account, with Mr.
Henry Cockburn (now Lord Cockburn), then Solicitor-
General for Scotland. The Scotch Reform Bill threw a
great burden of new duties and responsibilities upon the
Sheriffs; and Scott's Sheriff-substitute, the Laird of Raeburn, not having been regularly educated for the law,
found himself unable to encounter these novelties, especially as regarded the registration of voters, and other
details connected with the recent enlargement of the elec-
toral franchise. Under such circumstances, as no one
but the Sheriff could appoint another substitute, it became necessary for Sir Walter's family to communicate

the state he was in in a formal manner to the Law Officers of the Crown; and the Lord Advocate (Mr. Jeffrey), in consequence, introduced and carried through Parliament a short bill (2 and 3 William IV. cap. 101), authorising the Government to appoint a new Sheriff of Selkirkshire, "during the incapacity or non-resignation of Sir Walter Scott." It was on this bill that the Solicitor-General had expressed a wish to converse with me: but there was little to be said, as the temporary nature of the new appointment gave no occasion for any pecuniary question; and, if that had been otherwise, the circumstances of the case would have rendered Sir Walter's family entirely indifferent upon such a subject. There can be no doubt, that if he had recovered in so far as to be capable of executing a resignation, the Government would have considered it just to reward thirty-two years' faithful services by a retired allowance equivalent to his salary—and as little, that the Government would have had sincere satisfaction in settling that matter in the shape most acceptable to himself. And perhaps (though I feel that it is scarcely worth while) I may as well here express my regret that a statement highly unjust and injurious should have found its way into the pages of some of Sir Walter's biographers. These writers have thought fit to insinuate that there was a want of courtesy and respect on the part of the Lord Advocate, and the other official persons connected with this arrangement. On the contrary, nothing could be more handsome and delicate than the whole of their conduct in it; Mr. Cockburn could not have entered into the case with greater feeling and tenderness, had it concerned a brother of his own; and when Mr. Jeffrey introduced his bill in the House of Commons, he used language so graceful and touching, that both Sir Robert Peel and Mr. Croker went across the House to thank him cordially for it.

Perceiving, towards the close of August, that the end was near, and thinking it very likely that Abbotsford might soon undergo many changes, and myself, at all events, never see it again, I felt a desire to have some image preserved of the interior apartments as occupied by their founder, and invited from Edinburgh for that purpose Sir Walter's dear friend, Sir William Allan—whose presence, I well knew, would even under the circumstances of that time be nowise troublesome to any of the family, but the contrary in all respects. Sir William willingly complied, and executed a series of beautiful drawings. He also shared our watchings, and witnessed all but the last moments. Sir Walter's cousins, the ladies of Ashestiel, came down frequently, for a day or two at a time, and did whatever sisterly affection could prompt, both for the sufferer and his daughters. Miss Mary Scott (daughter of his uncle Thomas), and Mrs. Scott of Harden, did the like.

As I was dressing on the morning of Monday the 17th of September, Nicolson came into my room, and told me that his master had awoke in a state of composure and consciousness, and wished to see me immediately. I found him entirely himself, though in the last extreme of feebleness. His eye was clear and calm—every trace of the wild fire of delirium extinguished. "Lockhart," he said, "I may have but a minute to speak to you. My dear, be a good man—be virtuous—be religious—be a good man. Nothing else will give you any comfort when you come to lie here."—He paused, and I said—"Shall I send for Sophia and Anne?"—"No," said he, "don't disturb them. Poor souls! I know they were up all night —God bless you all."—With this he sunk into a very tranquil sleep, and, indeed, he scarcely afterwards gave any sign of consciousness, except for an instant on the arrival of his sons.

They, on learning that the scene was about to close, obtained anew leave of absence from their posts, and both reached Abbotsford on the 19th. About half-past one p.m. on the 21st of September, Sir Walter breathed his last, in the presence of all his children. It was a beautiful day—so warm, that every window was wide open— and so perfectly still, that the sound of all others most delicious to his ear, the gentle ripple of the Tweed over its pebbles, was distinctly audible as we knelt around the bed, and his eldest son kissed and closed his eyes. No sculptor ever modelled a more majestic image of repose.

Almost every newspaper that announced this event in Scotland, and many in England, had the signs of mourning usual on the demise of a king. With hardly an exception, the voice was that of universal, unmixed grief and veneration.

It was considered due to Sir Walter's physicians, and to the public, that the nature of his malady should be distinctly ascertained. The result was, that there appeared the traces of a very slight mollification in one part of the substance of the brain.

His funeral was conducted in an unostentatious manner, but the attendance was very great. Few of his old friends then in Scotland were absent,—and many, both friends and strangers, came from a great distance. His domestics and foresters made it their petition that no hireling hand might assist in carrying his remains. They themselves bore the coffin to the hearse, and from the hearse to the grave. The pall-bearers were his sons, his son-in-law, and his little grandson; his cousins, Charles Scott of Nesbitt, James Scott of Jedburgh (sons to his uncle Thomas), William Scott of Raeburn, Robert Rutherford, Clerk to the Signet, Colonel (now Lieut.-General Sir James) Russell of Ashestiel, William Keith (brother to Sir Alexander Keith of Ravelstone); and the chief of his family, Hugh Scott of Harden, afterwards Lord Polwarth.

When the company were assembled, according to the usual Scotch fashion, prayers were offered up by the Very Reverend Dr. Baird, Principal of the University of Edinburgh, and by the Reverend Dr. David Dickson, Minister of St. Cuthbert's, who both expatiated in a very striking manner on the virtuous example of the deceased.

The court-yard and all the precincts of Abbotsford were crowded with uncovered spectators as the procession was arranged; and as it advanced through Darnick and Melrose, and the adjacent villages, the whole population appeared at their doors in like manner—almost all in black. The train of carriages extended, I understand, over more than a mile; the yeomanry followed in great numbers on horseback; and it was late in the day ere we reached Dryburgh. Some accident, it was observed, had caused the hearse to halt for several minutes on the summit of the hill at Bemerside—exactly where a prospect of remarkable richness opens, and where Sir Walter had always been accustomed to rein up his horse. The day was dark and lowering, and the wind high.

The wide enclosure at the Abbey of Dryburgh was thronged with old and young; and when the coffin was taken from the hearse, and again laid on the shoulders of the afflicted serving-men, one deep sob burst from a thousand lips. Mr. Archdeacon Williams read the Burial Service of the Church of England; and thus, about half-past five o'clock in the evening of Wednesday the 26th September 1832, the remains of SIR WALTER SCOTT were laid by the side of his wife in the sepulchre of his ancestors—"*in sure and certain hope of the resurrection to eternal life, through our Lord Jesus Christ: who shall change our vile body that it may be like unto his glorious body, according to the mighty working, whereby he is able to subdue all things to himself.*"

We read in Solomon—"The heart knoweth his own bitterness, and a stranger doth not intermeddle with his joy";—and a wise poet of our own time thus beautifully expands the saying:—

> "Why should we faint and fear to live alone,
>   Since all alone, so Heaven has willed, we die;
> Nor even the tenderest heart, and next our own,
>   Knows half the reasons why we smile and sigh?"[1]

Such considerations have always induced me to regard with small respect any attempt to delineate fully and exactly any human being's character. I distrust, even in very humble cases, our capacity for judging our neighbour fairly; and I cannot but pity the presumption that must swell in the heart and brain of any ordinary brother of the race, when he dares to pronounce *ex cathedrâ* on the whole structure and complexion of a great mind, from the comparatively narrow and scanty materials which can by possibility have been placed before him. Nor is the difficulty to my view lessened—perhaps it is rather increased—when the great man is a great artist. It is true, that many of the feelings common to our nature can only be expressed adequately, and that some of the finest of them can only be expressed at all, in the language of art; and more especially in the language of poetry. But it is equally true, that high and sane art never attempts to express that for which the artist does not claim and expect general sympathy; and however much of what we had thought to be our own secrets he ventures to give shape to, it becomes us, I can never help believing, to rest convinced that there remained a world of deeper mysteries to which the dignity of genius would refuse any utterance. I have therefore endeavoured to lay before the reader those parts of Sir Walter's character

[1] Keble's *Christian Year*, p. 261.

to which we have access, as they were indicated in his sayings and doings through the long series of his years; —but refrained from obtruding almost anything of comment. It was my wish to let the character develop itself: and now I am not going to "peep and botanise" upon his grave. But a few general observations will be forgiven—perhaps expected.

I believe that if the history of any one family in upper or middle life could be faithfully written, it might be as generally interesting, and as permanently useful, as that of any nation, however great and renowned. But literature has never produced any worthy book of this class, and probably it never will. The only lineages in which we can pretend to read personal character far back, with any distinctness, are those of kings and princes, and a few noble houses of the first eminence; and it hardly needed Swift's biting satire to satisfy the student of the past, that the very highest pedigrees are as uncertain as the very lowest. We flatter the reigning monarch, or his haughtier satellite, by tracing in their lineaments the conqueror or legislator of a former century. But call up the dead, according to the Dean's incantation, and we might have the real ancestor in some chamberlain, confessor, or musician. Scott himself delighted, perhaps above all other books, in such as approximate to the character of good family histories—as, for example, Godscroft's House of Douglas and Angus, and the Memorie of the Somervilles,—which last is, as far as I know, the best of its class in any language; and his reprint of the trivial "Memorials" of the Haliburtons, to whose dust he is now gathered, was but one of a thousand indications of his anxiety to realise his own ancestry to his imagination. No testamentary deed, instrument of contract, or entry in a parish register, seemed valueless to him, if it bore in any manner, however obscure or distant, on the personal history of any of his ascertainable predecessors. The chronicles of the race furnished the fire-side talk to which he listened in infancy at Smailholm, and his first rhymes were those of Satchels. His physical infirmity was reconciled to him, even dignified perhaps, by tracing it back to forefathers who acquired famousness in their own way, in spite of such disadvantages. These studies led by easy and inevitable links to those of the history of his province generally, and then of his native kingdom. The lamp of his zeal burnt on brighter and brighter amidst the dust of parchments; his love and pride vivified whatever he hung over in these dim records, and patient antiquarianism, long brooding and meditating, became gloriously transmuted into the winged spirit of national poetry.

Whatever he had in himself, he would fain have made out a hereditary claim for. He often spoke both seriously and sportively on the subject. He had assembled about him in his " own great parlour," as he called it—the room in which he died—all the pictures of his ancestors that he could come by; and in his most genial evening mood he seemed never to weary of perusing them. The Cavalier of Killiecrankie—brave, faithful, learned, and romantic old " Beardie," a determined but melancholy countenance— was often surveyed with a repetition of the solitary Latin rhyme of his Vow. He had, of course, no portraits of the elder heroes of Harden to lecture upon; but a skilful hand had supplied the same wall with a fanciful delineation of the rough wooing of " Meikle-mouthed Meg "; and the only historical picture, properly so called, that he ever bespoke, was to be taken (for it was never executed) from the Raid o' the Redswire, when

> " The Rutherfords with great renown,
> Convoyed the town o' Jedburgh out."

The ardent but sagacious " goodman of Sandyknowe," hangs by the side of his father, Bearded Wat; and when moralising in his latter day over the doubtful condition of his ultimate fortunes, Sir Walter would point to " Honest Robin," and say, " Blood will out:—my building and planting was but his buying the hunter before he stocked his sheep-walk over again." " And yet," I once heard him say, glancing to the likeness of his own staid calculating father, " it was a wonder, too—for I have a thread of the attorney in me." And so no doubt he had; for the " elements " were mingled in him curiously as well as " gently."

An imagination such as his, concentrating its day-dreams on things of this order, soon shaped out a world of its own—to which it would fain accommodate the real one. The love of his country became indeed a passion; no knight ever tilted for his mistress more willingly than he would have bled and died to preserve even the airiest surviving nothing of her antique pretensions for Scotland,

But the Scotland of his affections had the clan Scott for her kernel. Next, and almost equal to the throne, was Buccleuch. Fancy rebuilt and prodigally embellished the whole system of the social existence of the old time in which the clansman (wherever there were clans) acknowledged practically no sovereign but his chief. The author of "the Lay" would rather have seen his heir carry the Banner of Bellenden gallantly at a football match on Carterhaugh, than he would have heard that the boy had attained the highest honours of the first university in Europe. His original pride was to be an acknowledged member of one of the "honourable families" whose progenitors had been celebrated by Satchels for following this banner in blind obedience to the patriarchial leader; his first and last worldly ambition was to be himself the founder of a distinct branch; he desired to plant a lasting root, and dreamt not of personal fame, but of long distant generations rejoicing in the name of "Scott of Abbotsford." By this idea all his reveries—all his aspirations—all his plans and efforts, were overshadowed and controlled. The great object and end only rose into clearer daylight, and swelled into more substantial dimensions, as public applause strengthened his confidence in his own powers and faculties; and when he had reached the summit of universal and unrivalled honour, he clung to his first love with the faith of a Paladin. It is easy enough to smile at all this; many will not understand it, and some who do may pity it. But it was at least a different thing from the modern vulgar ambition of amassing a fortune and investing it in land. The lordliest vision of acres would have had little charm for him, unless they were situated on Ettrick or Yarrow, or in

> —— "Pleasant Tiviedale,
> Fast by the river Tweed"

—somewhere within the primeval territory of "the Rough Clan."

His worldly ambition was thus grafted on that ardent feeling for blood and kindred which was the great redeeming element in the social life of what we call the middle ages; and—though no man estimated the solid advantages of modern existence more justly than he did, when, restraining his fancy, he exercised his graver faculties on the comparison—it was the natural effect of the studies he devoted himself to and rose by, to indispose him for dwelling on the sober results of judgment and reason in all such matters. What a striking passage that is in one of his letters, where he declines to write a biography of Queen Mary, " because his opinion was contrary to his feeling ! " But he confesses the same of his Jacobitism; and yet how eagerly does he seem to have grasped at the shadow, however false and futile, under which he chose to see the means of reconciling his Jacobitism with loyalty to the reigning monarch who befriended him ! We find him, over and over again, alluding to George IV. as acquiring a title *de jure* on the death of the poor Cardinal of York ! Yet who could have known better that whatever rights the exiled males of the Stuart line ever possessed must have remained entire with their female descendants?

The same resolution to give imagination her scope, and always in favour of antiquity, is the ruling principle and charm of all his best writings. So also with all the details of his building at Abbotsford, and of his hospitable existence, when he had fairly completed his " romance in stone and lime ";—every outline copied from some old baronial edifice in Scotland—every roof and window blazoned with clan bearings, or the lion rampant gules, or the heads of the ancient Stuart kings. He wished to revive the interior life of the castles he had emulated— their wide open joyous reception of all comers, but especially of kinsmen and neighbours—ballads and pibrochs to enliven flowing bowls and *quaighs*—jolly hunting fields in which yeoman and gentleman might ride side by side— and mirthful dances, where no Sir Piercy Shafton need blush to lead out the miller's daughter. In the brightest meridian of his genius and fame, this was his *beau idéal*. There was much kindness surely in such ambition—in spite of the apparent contradiction in terms, was there not really much humility about it?

To this ambition we owe the gigantic monuments of Scott's genius; and to the kindly feelings out of which his ambition grew, grew also his connection with merchandise. I need not recur to that sad and complicated chapter. Nor, perhaps, need I offer any more speculations, by way of explaining, and reconciling to his previous and subsequent history and demeanour, either the mystery in which he had chosen to wrap his commercial connections from his most intimate friends, or the carelessness with which he abandoned these matters to the direction of inefficient colleagues. And yet I ought, I rather think, to have suggested to certain classes of my readers, at a much earlier stage, that no man could in former times be called either to the English or the Scottish Bar, who was known to have any direct interest in any commercial undertaking of any sort; and that the body of feelings or prejudices in which this regulation originated—(for though there might be sound reason for it besides, such undoubtedly was the main source)—prevailed in Scotland in Sir Walter's youth, to an extent of which the present generation may not easily form an adequate notion. In the minds of the " northern *noblesse de la robe*," as they are styled in Redgauntlet, such feelings had wide and potent authority; insomuch that I can understand perfectly how Scott, even after he ceased to practise at the Bar, being still a Sheriff, and a member of the Faculty of Advocates, should have shrunk sensitively from the idea of having his alliance with a trading firm revealed among his comrades of the gown. And, moreover, the practice of mystery is, perhaps, of all practices, the one most likely to grow into a habit : secret breeds secret; and I ascribe, after all, the long silence about Waverley to the matured influence of this habit, as much as to any of the motives which the author has thought fit to assign in his late confessions.

But was there not, in fact, something that lay far deeper than a mere professional prejudice? Among the many things in Scott's Diaries which cast strong light upon the previous part of his history, I must number the reluctance which he confesses himself to have felt towards the resumption of the day's proper appointed task—however willing, nay eager to labour sedulously on something else. We know how gallantly he combated it in the general—but these precious Diaries themselves are not the least pregnant proofs of the extent to which it very often prevailed—for an hour or two at least, if not for the day. I think this, if we were to go no farther, might help us somewhat in understanding the neglect about superintending ledgers and bill books; and, consequently, the rashness about buying land, building, and the like. But to what are we to ascribe the origin of this reluctance for accurate and minute investigation and transaction of business, so important to himself, in a man possessing such extraordinary sagacity, and exercising it every day with admirable regularity and precision, in the various capacities of the head of a family—the friend—the magistrate—the most distinguished citizen of Edinburgh—beyond all comparison the most distinguished member of society that figured in his time in his native kingdom?

The whole system of conceptions and aspirations, of which his early active life was the exponent, resolves itself into a romantic idealisation of Scottish aristocracy. He desired to secure for his descendants (for himself he had very soon acquired something infinitely more flattering to self-love and vanity) a decent and honourable middle station—in a scheme of life so constituted originally, and which his fancy pictured as capable of being so revived, as to admit of the kindliest personal contact between (almost) the peasant at the plough, and the magnate with revenues rivalling the monarch's. It was the patriarchal —the clan system, that he thought of ; one that never prevailed even in Scotland, within the historical period that is to say, except in the Highlands, and in his own dear Border-land. This system knew nothing of commerce—as little certainly of literature beyond the raid-ballad of the wandering harper,—

> "High placed in hall—a welcome guest."

His filial reverence of imagination shrunk from marring the antique, if barbarous, simplicity. I suspect that at the highest elevation of his literary renown—when princes bowed to his name, and nations thrilled at it—he would have considered losing all that at a change of the wind as nothing compared to parting with his place as the Cadet of Harden and Clansman of Buccleuch, who had, no matter by what means, reached such a position, that when a notion arose of embodying " a Buccleuch legion," not a Scott in the Forest would have thought it otherwise than natural for *Abbotsford* to be one of the field-officers. I can, therefore, understand that he may have, from the very first, exerted the dispensing power of imagination very liberally, in virtually absolving himself from dwelling on the wood of which his ladder was to be constructed. Enough was said in a preceding chapter of the obvious fact, that the author of such a series of romances as his must have, to all intents and purposes, lived more than half his life in worlds purely fantastic. In one of the last obscure and faltering pages of his Diary he says, that if any one asked him how much of his thought was occupied by the novel then in hand, the answer would have been, that in one sense it never occupied him except when the amanuensis sat before him, but that in another it was never five minutes out of his head. Such, I have no doubt, the case had always been. But I must be excused from doubting whether, when the substantive fiction actually in process of manufacture was absent from his mind, the space was often or voluntarily occupied (no positive external duty interposing) upon the real practical worldly position and business of the Clerk of Session—of the Sheriff,—least of all of the printer or the bookseller. The sum is, if I read him aright, that he was always willing, in his ruminative moods, to veil, if possible, from his own optics the kind of machinery by which alone he had found the means of attaining his darling objects. Having acquired a perhaps unparalleled power over the direction of scarcely paralleled faculties, he chose to exert his power in this manner. On no other supposition can I find his history intelligible;—I mean, of course, the great obvious and marking facts of his history; for I hope I have sufficiently disclaimed all pretension to a thoroughgoing analysis. He appears to have studiously escaped from whatever could have interfered with his own enjoyment—to have revelled in the fair results, and waved the wand of obliterating magic over all besides; and persisted so long, that (like the sorcerer he celebrates) he became the dupe of his own delusions. It is thus that (not forgetting the subsidiary influence of professional Edinburgh prejudices) I am inclined, on the whole, to account for his initiation in the practice of mystery—a thing, at first sight, so alien from the frank, open generous nature of a man, than whom none ever had or deserved to have more real friends.

The indulgence cost him very dear. It ruined his fortunes—but I can have no doubt that it did worse than that. I cannot suppose that a nature like his was fettered and shut up in this way without suffering very severely from the "cold obstruction." There must have been a continual "insurrection" in his "state of man"; and, above all, I doubt not that what gave him the bitterest pain in the hour of his calamities, was the feeling of compunction with which he then found himself obliged to stand before those with whom he had, through life, cultivated brotherly friendship, convicted of having kept his

heart closed to them on what they could not but suppose
to have been the chief subjects of his thought and anxiety,
in times when they withheld nothing from him. These,
perhaps, were the " written troubles " that had been cut
deepest into his brain. I think they were, and believe it
the more, because it was never acknowledged.

If he had erred in the primary indulgence out of which
this sprang, he at least made noble atonement. During
the most energetic years of manhood he laboured with
one prize in view; and he had just grasped it, as he
fancied, securely, when all at once the vision was dissi-
pated : he found himself naked and desolate as Job. How
he nerved himself against the storm—how he felt and
how he resisted it—how soberly, steadily, and resolvedly
he contemplated the possibility of yet, by redoubled exertions, in so far retrieving his fortunes, as that no man
should lose by having trusted those for whom he had
been pledged—how well he kept his vow, and what price
it cost him to do so—all this the reader, I doubt not,
appreciates fully. It seems to me that strength of character was never put to a severer test than when, for labours
of love, such as his had hitherto almost always been—the
pleasant exertion of genius for the attainment of ends that
owed all their dignity and beauty to a poetical fancy—
there came to be substituted the iron pertinacity of daily
and nightly toil, in the discharge of a duty which there
was nothing but the sense of chivalrous honour to make
stringent. It is the fond indulgence of gay fancy in all
the previous story that gives its true value and dignity
to the voluntary agony of the sequel, when, indeed, he
appears

> ——— " Sapiens, sibique imperiosus ;
> Quem neque pauperies, neque mors, neque vincula terrent ;
> Responsare cupidinibus, contemnere honores,
> Fortis ; et in seipso totus, teres atque rotundus,
> Externi ne quid valeat per læve morari ;
> In quem manca ruit semper Fortuna."

The attentive reader will not deny that every syllable of
this proud *ideal* has been justified to the letter. But
though he boasted of stoicism, his heroism was something far better than the stoic's; for it was not founded
on a haughty trampling down of all delicate and tender
thoughts and feelings. He lays his heart bare in his
Diary; and we there read, in characters that will never

die, how the sternest resolution of a philosopher may be
at once quickened and adorned by the gentlest impulses
of that spirit of love, which alone makes poetry the angel
of life.   This is the moment in which posterity will desire
to fix his portraiture.   But the noble exhibition was not a
fleeting one; it was not that a robust mind elevated itself
by a fierce effort for the crisis of an hour.   The martyr-
dom lasted with his days; and if it shortened them, let us
remember his own immortal words,—

> " Sound, sound the clarion, fill the fife,
>   To all the sensual world proclaim—
> One crowded hour of glorious life
>   Is worth an age without a name."

For the rest, I presume, it will be allowed that no
human character, which we have the opportunity of studying with equal minuteness, had fewer faults mixed up in
its texture.   The grand virtue of fortitude, the basis of all
others, was never displayed in higher perfection than in
him; and it was, as perhaps true courage always is, combined with an equally admirable spirit of kindness and
humanity.   His pride, if we must call it so, undebased by
the least tincture of mere vanity, was intertwined with a
most exquisite charity, and was not inconsistent with true
humility.   If ever the principle of kindliness was incar-
nated in a mere man, it was in him; and real kindliness can
never be but modest.   In the social relations of life, where
men are most effectually tried, no spot can be detected in
him.   He was a patient, dutiful, reverent son; a generous,
compassionate, tender husband; an honest, careful, and
most affectionate father.   Never was a more virtuous or a
happier fireside than his.   The influence of his mighty
genius shadowed it imperceptibly; his calm good sense,
and his angelic sweetness of heart and temper, regulated
and softened a strict but paternal discipline.   His children,
as they grew up, understood by degrees the high privilege
of their birth; but the profoundest sense of his greatness
never disturbed their confidence in his goodness.   The
buoyant play of his spirits made him sit young among the
young; parent and son seemed to live in brotherhood together; and the chivalry of his imagination threw a certain
air of courteous gallantry into his relations with his
daughters, which gave a very peculiar grace to the fondness
of their intercourse.   Though there could not be a gentler
mother than Lady Scott, on those delicate occasions most

interesting to young ladies, they always made their father the first confidant.

Perhaps the most touching evidence of the lasting tenderness of his early domestic feelings was exhibited to his executors, when they opened his repositories in search of his testament, the evening after his burial. On lifting up his desk, we found arranged in careful order a series of little objects, which had obviously been so placed there that his eye might rest on them every morning before he began his tasks. These were the old-fashioned boxes that had garnished his mother's toilet, when he, a sickly child, slept in her dressing-room—the silver taper-stand which the young advocate had bought for her with his first five-guinea fee—a row of small packets inscribed with her hand, and containing the hair of those of her offspring that had died before her—his father's snuff-box and étui-case—and more things of the like sort, recalling the " old familiar faces." The same feeling was apparent in all the arrangement of his private apartment. Pictures of his father and mother were the only ones in his dressing-room. The clumsy antique cabinets that stood there, things of a very different class from the beautiful and costly productions in the public rooms below, had all belonged to the furniture of George's Square. Even his father's rickety washing-stand, with all its cramped appurtenances, though exceedingly unlike what a man of his very scrupulous habits would have selected in these days, kept its ground. The whole place seemed fitted up like a little chapel of the lares.

Such a son and parent could hardly fail in any of the other social relations. No man was a firmer or more indefatigable friend. I knew not that he ever lost one; and a few, with whom, during the energetic middle stage of life, from political differences or other accidental circumstances, he lived less familiarly, had all gathered round him, and renewed the full warmth of early affection in his later days. There was enough to dignify the connection in their eyes; but nothing to chill it on either side. The imagination that so completely mastered him when he chose to give her the rein was kept under most determined control when any of the positive obligations of active life came into question. A high and pure sense of duty presided over whatever he had to do as a citizen and a magistrate; and as a landlord, he considered his estate as an extension of his hearth.

Of his political creed, the many who hold a different one will of course say that it was the natural fruit of his poetical devotion to the mere prejudice of antiquity; and I am quite willing to allow that this must have had a great share in the matter—and that he himself would have been as little ashamed of the word *prejudice* as of the word *antiquity*. Whenever Scotland could be considered as standing separate on any question from the rest of the empire, he was not only apt, but eager to embrace the opportunity of again rehoisting, as it were, the old signal of national independence; and I really doubt if any circumstance in his literary career gave him more personal satisfaction than the success of Malachi Malagrowther's Epistles. He confesses, however, in his Diary, that he was aware how much it became him to summon calm reason to battle imaginative prepossessions on this score; and I am not aware that they ever led him into any serious practical error. He delighted in letting his fancy run wild about ghosts and witches and horoscopes—but I venture to say, had he sat on the judicial bench a hundred years before he was born, no man would have been more certain to give juries sound direction in estimating the pretended evidence of supernatural occurrences of any sort; and I believe, in like manner, that had any Anti-English faction, civil or religious, sprung up in his own time in Scotland, he would have done more than other living man could have hoped to do, for putting it down. He was on all practical points a steady, conscientious Tory of the school of William Pitt; who, though an anti-revolutionist, was certainly anything but an anti-reformer. He rejected the innovations, in the midst of which he died, as a revival, under alarmingly authoritative auspices, of the doctrines which had endangered Britain in his youth, and desolated Europe throughout his prime of manhood. May the gloomy anticipations which hung over his closing years be unfulfilled! But should they be so, let posterity remember that the warnings, and the resistance of his and other powerful intellects, were probably in that event the appointed means for averting a catastrophe in which, had England fallen, the whole civilised world must have been involved.

Sir Walter received a strictly religious education under the eye of parents whose virtuous conduct was in unison with the principles they desired to instil into their children. From the great doctrines thus recommended he appears never to have swerved; but he must be numbered among the many who have incurred considerable risk of doing so, in consequence of the rigidity with which Presbyterian heads of families were used to enforce compliance with various relics of the puritanical observance. He took up, early in life, a repugnance to the mode in which public worship is conducted in the Scottish Establishment; and adhered to the sister Church, whose system of government and discipline he believed to be the fairest copy of the primitive polity, and whose litanies and collects he reverenced as having been transmitted to us from the age immediately succeeding that of the Apostles. The few passages in his Diaries in which he alludes to his own religious feelings and practices shew clearly the sober, serene, and elevated frame of mind in which he habitually contemplated man's relations with his Maker; the modesty with which he shrunk from indulging either the presumption of reason, or the extravagance of imagination, in the province of Faith; his humble reliance on the wisdom and mercy of God; and his firm belief that we are placed in this state of existence, not to speculate about another, but to prepare ourselves for it by active exertion of our intellectual faculties, and the constant cultivation of kindness and benevolence towards our fellow men.

But his moral, political, and religious character has sufficiently impressed itself upon the great body of his writings. He is indeed one of the few great authors of modern Europe who stand acquitted of having written a line that ought to have embittered the bed of death. His works teach the practical lessons of morality and Christianity in the most captivating form—unobtrusively and unaffectedly. And I think it is not refining too far to say, that in these works, as well as his whole demeanour as a man of letters, we may trace the happy effects—(enough has already been said as to some less fortunate and agreeable ones)—of his having written throughout with a view to something beyond the acquisition of personal fame. Perhaps no great poet ever made his literature so completely ancillary to the objects and purposes of practical life. However his imagination might expatiate, it was sure to rest over his home. The sanctities of domestic love and social duty were never forgotten; and the same circumstance that most ennobles all his triumphs affords also the best apology for his errors.

From the first, his possession of a strong and brilliant genius was acknowledged; and the extent of it seems to have been guessed by others, before he was able to persuade himself that he had claim to a place among the masters of literature. The ease with which he did everything deceived him; and he probably would never have done himself any measure of justice, even as compared with those of his own time, but for the fact, which no modesty could long veil, that whatever he did became immediately "*the fashion*,"—the object of all but universal imitation. Even as to this, he was often ready to surmise that the priority of his own movement might have been matter of accident; and certainly nothing can mark the humility of his mind more strikingly than the style in which he discusses, in his Diary, the pretensions of the pigmies that swarmed and fretted in the deep wake of his mighty vessel. To the really original writers among his contemporaries he did full justice; no differences of theory or taste had the least power to disturb his candour. In some cases he rejoiced in feeling and expressing a cordial admiration, where he was met by, at best, a cold and grudging reciprocity: and in others, his generosity was proof against not only the private belief but the public exposure of envious malignity. Lord Byron might well say that Scott could be jealous of no one; but the immeasurable distance did not prevent many from being jealous of him.

His propensity to think too well of other men's works sprung, of course, mainly, from his modesty and good-nature; but the brilliancy of his imagination greatly sustained the delusion. It unconsciously gave precision to the trembling outline, and life and warmth to the vapid colours before him. This was especially the case as to romances and novels; the scenes and characters in them were invested with so much of the "light within," that he would close with regret volumes which, perhaps, no other person, except the diseased glutton of the circulating library, ever could get half through. Where colder critics saw only a schoolboy's hollowed turnip with its inch of tallow, he looked through the dazzling spray of his own fancy, and sometimes the clumsy toy seems to have swelled almost into "the majesty of buried Denmark."

These servile imitators are already forgotten, or will soon be so; but it is to be hoped that the spirit which breathes through his works may continue to act on our literature,

and consequently on the character and manners of men.
The race that grew up under the influence of that intellect
can hardly be expected to appreciate fully their own obligations to it : and yet if we consider what were the tend-
encies of the minds and works that, but for his, must have
been unrivalled in the power and opportunity to mould
young ideas, we may picture to ourselves in some measure
the magnitude of the debt we owe to a perpetual succession, through thirty years, of publications unapproached in
charm, and all instilling a high and healthy code; a brac-
ing, invigorating spirit; a contempt of mean passions,
whether vindictive or voluptuous; humane charity, as
distinct from moral laxity as from unsympathising austerity; sagacity too deep for cynicism, and tenderness never
degenerating into sentimentality : animated throughout in
thought, opinion, feeling and style, by one and the same
pure energetic principle—a pith and savour of manhood;
appealing to whatever is good and loyal in our natures, and
rebuking whatever is low and selfish.

Had Sir Walter never taken a direct part in politics as
a writer, the visible bias of his mind on such subjects must
have had a great influence; nay, the mere fact that such
a man belonged to a particular side would have been a
very important weight in the balance. His services, direct
and indirect, towards repressing the revolutionary propensities of his age, were vast—far beyond the comprehension
of vulgar politicians.

On the whole, I have no doubt that, the more the details of his personal history are revealed and studied, the
more powerfully will that be found to inculcate the same
great lessons with his works. Where else shall we be
taught better how prosperity may be extended by beneficence, and adversity confronted by exertion? Where can
we see the " follies of the wise " more strikingly rebuked,
and a character more beautifully purified and exalted in
the passage through affliction to death? I have lingered
so long over the details, that I have, perhaps, become even
from that circumstance alone less qualified than more
rapid surveyors may be to seize the effect in the mass. But
who does not feel that there is something very invigorating
as well as elevating in the contemplation? His character
seems to belong to some elder and stronger period than
ours, and, indeed, I cannot help likening it to the archi-
tectural fabrics of other ages, which he most delighted in,

where there is such a congregation of imagery and tracery, such endless indulgence of whim and fancy, the sublime blending here with the beautiful, and there contrasted with the grotesque—half, perhaps, seen in the clear daylight, and half by rays tinged with the blazoned forms of the past—that one may be apt to get bewildered among the variety of particular impressions, and not feel either the unity of the grand design, or the height and solidity of the structure, until the door has been closed upon the labyrinth of aisles and shrines, and you survey it from a distance, but still within its shadow.

And yet as, with whatever admiration his friends could not but regard him constantly when among them, the prevailing feeling was still love and affection, so it is now, and so must ever it be, as to his memory. It is not the privilege of every reader to have partaken in the friendship of A GREAT AND GOOD MAN; but those who have not, may be assured that the sentiment, which the near homely contemplation of such a being inspires, is a thing entirely by itself.

And now to conclude.—In the year 1832, France and Germany, as well as Britain, had to mourn over their brightest intellects. Goethe shortly preceded Scott, and Cuvier followed him: and with these mighty lights were extinguished many others of no common order—among the rest, Crabbe and Mackintosh.

Of the persons closely connected with Sir Walter Scott, and often named accordingly in these pages, few remain. James Ballantyne was on his deathbed when he heard of his great friend and patron's death. The Ettrick Shepherd died in 1835; George Thomson, the happy "Dominie Thompson," of the happy days of Abbotsford, in 1838; William Laidlaw, after 1832, had the care first of the Seaforth, and then of the Balnagowan estates, in Ross-shire, as factor: but being struck with paralysis in August 1844, retired to the farm-house of his excellent brother James at Contin, and died there in May 1845. Mr. Morritt, to whom the larger Memoirs of his friend were inscribed, died at Rokeby on the 12th of July 1843: loved, venerated, never to be forgotten. William Clerk of Eldin, admired through life for talents and learning, of which he has left no monument, died at Edinburgh in January 1847.

But why extend this catalogue? Sixteen years have passed—the generation to which Scott belonged have been gathered to their fathers. Of his own children none now survive. Miss Anne Scott received at Christmas 1832 a grant of £200 per annum from the privy purse of King William IV. But her name did not long burden the pension list. Her constitution had been miserably shattered in the course of her long and painful attendance, first on her mother's illness, and then on her father's; and perhaps reverse of fortune, and disappointments of various sorts connected with that, had also heavy effect. From the day of Sir Walter's death, the strong stimulus of duty being lost, she too often looked and spoke like one

"Taking the measure of an unmade grave."

After a brief interval of disordered health, she contracted a brain fever, which carried her off abruptly. She died in my house in the Regent's Park on the 25th June 1833, and her remains are placed in the New Cemetery in the Harrow Road.

The adjoining grave holds those of her nephew John Hugh Lockhart, who died 15th December 1831; and also those of my wife Sophia, who expired after a long illness, which she bore with all possible meekness and fortitude, on the 17th of May 1837. Of all the race she most resembled her father in countenance, in temper, and in manners.

Charles Scott, whose spotless worth had tenderly endeared him to the few who knew him intimately, and whose industry and accuracy were warmly acknowledged by his professional superiors, on Lord Berwick's recall from the Neapolitan Embassy resumed his duties as a clerk in the Foreign Office, and continued in that situation until the summer of 1841. Sir John M'Neill, G.C.B., being then entrusted with a special mission to the Court of Persia, carried Charles with him as attaché and private secretary; but the journey on horseback through Asia Minor was trying for his never robust frame; and he contracted an inflammatory disorder, which cut him off at Teheran, almost immediately on his arrival there—October 28, 1841. He had reached his 36th year. His last hours had every help that kindness and skill could yield: for the Ambassador had for him the affection of an elder brother, and the physician, Dr. George Joseph Bell (now also gone), had been his schoolfellow, and through life his friend. His funeral in that remote place was so attended as to mark the world-wide reputation of his father. By Sir John M'Neill's care, a small monument with a suitable inscription was erected over his untimely grave.

Walter, who succeeded to the baronetcy, proceeded to Madras, in 1839, as Lieutenant-Colonel of the 15th Hussars; and subsequently commanded that regiment. He was beloved and esteemed in it by officers and men as much, I believe, as any gentleman ever was in any corps of the British army; and there was no officer of his rank who stood higher in the opinion of the heads of his profession. He had begun life with many advantages— a very handsome person, and great muscular strength— a sweet and even temper, and talents which in the son of any father but his would have been considered brilliant. His answers, when examined as a witness before a celebrated court-martial in Ireland in 1834, were indeed universally admired:—whoever had known his father, recognised the head and the heart: and in his letters from India, especially his descriptions of scenery and sport, there occur many passages which, for picturesque effect and easy playful humour, would have done no discredit even to his father's pen. Though neglectful of extraprofessional studies in his earlier days, he had in afterlife read extensively, and made himself, in every sense of the term, an accomplished man. The library for the soldiers of his corps was founded by him: the care of it was a principal occupation of his later years. His only legacy out of his family was one of £100 to this library; and his widow, well understanding what he felt towards it, directed that a similar sum should be added in her own name. Sir Walter having unwisely exposed himself in a tiger-hunt in August 1846, was, on his return to his quarters at Bangalore, smitten with fever, which ended in liver disease. He was ordered to proceed to England, and died near the Cape of Good Hope, on board the ship Wellesley, February the 8th, 1847. Lady Scott conveyed his remains to this country, and they were interred in the paternal aisle at Dryburgh on the 4th of May following, in the presence of the few survivors of his father's friends and many of his own. Three officers who had served under him, and were accidentally in Britain, arrived from great distances to pay him the last homage of their respect. He had never had any child; and with him the baronetcy expired.

The children of illustrious men begin the world with great advantages, if they know how to use them : but this is hard and rare. There is risk that in the flush of youth, favourable to all illusions, the filial pride may be twisted to personal vanity. When experience checks this mis-growth, it is apt to do so with a severity that shall reach the best sources of moral and intellectual development. The great sons of great fathers have been few. It is usual to see their progeny smiled at through life for stilted pretension, or despised, at best pitied, for an inactive inglorious humility. The shadow of the oak is broad, but noble plants seldom rise within that circle. It was for-tunate for the sons of Scott that his day darkened in the morning of theirs. The sudden calamity anticipated the natural effect of observation and the collisions of society and business. All weak unmanly folly was nipped in the bud, and soon withered to the root. They were both re-markably modest men, but in neither had the better stimulus of the blood been arrested. In aspect and manners they were unlike each other : the elder tall and athletic, the model of a cavalier, with a generous frank-ness : the other slender and delicate of frame, in bearing, of a womanly gentleness and reserve; but in heart and mind none more akin. The affection of all the family, but especially perhaps of the brothers, for each other, kept to the end all the warmth of undivided childhood. When Charles died, and Walter knew that he was left alone of all his father's house, he evidently began to droop in spirit. It appeared to me from his letters that he thenceforth dreaded rather than desired a return to Scotland and Abbotsford. His only anxiety was that his regiment might be marched towards the Punjaub.

The only descendants of the Poet now alive are my son Walter Scott Lockhart (a lieutenant in the army), who, as his uncle's heir of entail, has lately received permission to assume the additional surname of Scott;—and his sister, Charlotte Harriet Jane, married in August 1847 to James Robert Hope, Barrister, second son of the late General the Honourable Sir Alexander Hope, G.C.B.

In the winter succeeding the Poet's death, his sons and myself, as his executors, endeavoured to make such arrangements as were within our power for completing the great object of his own wishes and fatal exertions. We found the remaining principal sum of commercial debt to be nearly £54,000. £22,000 had been insured upon his life; there were some monies in the hands of the trustees, and Mr. Cadell very handsomely offered to advance to us the balance, about £30,000, that we might without further delay settle with the body of creditors. This was effected accordingly on the 2nd of February 1833; Mr. Cadell accepting as his only security, the right to the profits accruing from Sir Walter's copyright property and literary remains, until such time as this new and consolidated obligation should be discharged. Besides his commercial debt, Sir Walter left also one of £10,000, contracted by himself as an individual, when struggling to support Constable in December 1825, and secured by mortgage on the lands of Abbotsford. And, lastly, the library and museum, presented to him in free gift by his creditors in December 1830, were bequeathed to his eldest son with a burden to the extent of £5,000, which sum he designed to be divided between his younger children, as already explained in an extract from his Diary. His will provided that the produce of his literary property, in case of its proving sufficient to wipe out the remaining debt of the firm, should then be applied to the extinction of these mortgages; and thereafter, should this also be accomplished, divided equally among his surviving family.

Various meetings were held soon after his death with a view to the erection of Monuments to his memory; and the records of these meetings, and their results, are adorned by many of the noblest and most distinguished names both of England and of Scotland. In London, the Lord Bishop of Exeter, Sir Robert Peel, and Sir John Malcolm, took a prominent part as speakers : and the result was a subscription amounting to about £10,000; but a part of this was embezzled by a young person rashly appointed to the post of secretary, who carried it with him to America, where he soon afterwards died. The noblemen and gentlemen who subscribed to this fund adopted a suggestion—(which originated, I believe, with Lord Francis Egerton, now Earl of Ellesmere, and the Honourable John Stuart Wortley, now Lord Wharncliffe) —that, in place of erecting a cenotaph in Westminster Abbey, or a statue or pillar elsewhere, the most suitable and respectful tribute that could be paid to Sir Walter's memory would be to discharge all the encumbrances upon Abbotsford, and entail the House, with its library and other articles of curiosity collected by him, together with the lands which he had planted and embellished, upon the heirs of his name for ever. The sum produced by the subscription, however, proved inadequate to the realisation of such a scheme; and after much consultation, it was at length settled that the money in the hands of the committee (between £7,000 and £8,000) should be employed to liquidate the debt upon the library and museum, and whatever might be over, towards the mortgage on the lands. This arrangement enabled the late Lieutenant-Colonel Sir Walter Scott to secure, in the shape originally desired, the permanent preservation at least of the house and its immediate appurtenances, as a memorial of the tastes and habits of the founder.

Such was the state of matters when the Lieutenant-Colonel embarked for India : and in his absence no further steps could well be taken. Upon his death, it was found that, notwithstanding the very extensive demand for his father's writings, there still remained a considerable debt to Mr. Cadell and also the greater part of the old debt secured on the lands. Mr. Cadell then offered to relieve the guardians of the young inheritor of that great name from much anxiety and embarrassment by accepting, in full payment of the sum due to himself, and also in recompense for his taking on himself the final obliteration of the heritable bond, a transference to him of the remaining claims of the family over Sir Walter's writings, together with the result of some literary exertions of the only surviving executor. This arrangement was completed in May 1847; and the estate, as well as the house and its appendages, became at last unfettered. The rental is small : but I hope and trust that as long as any of the blood remains, reverent care will attend over the guardianship of a possession associated with so many high and noble recollections. On that subject the gallant soldier who executed the entail expressed also in his testament feelings of the devoutest anxiety : and it was, I am well assured, in order that no extraneous obstacle might thwart the fulfilment of his pious wishes, that Mr. Cadell crowned a long series of kind services to the cause and the memory of Sir Walter Scott, by the very handsome proposition of 1847.

Abbotsford, after his own immortal works, is the best monument of its founder. But at Edinburgh also, soon after his death, a meeting was held with a view to the erection of some visible memorial in his native city; the prominent speakers were the late Marquess of Lothian, the late Earl of Dalhousie, the Earl of Rosebery, Lord Jeffrey, and Professor Wilson : and the subscription then begun realised a sum of £8,000, which by subsequent exertions reached no less than £15,000. The result may now be seen in a truly magnificent monument, conspicuous to every visitor of Scott's " own romantic town "—a lofty Gothic cross, enclosing and surmounting a marble statue of the Poet, which, as well as many happy relievos on the exterior, does great honour to the chisel of Mr. Steele.

In Glasgow, also, there was a meeting in 1832 : the subscriptions there reached £1,200 : and in the chief square of that city, already graced with statues of two illustrious natives, James Watt and Sir John Moore, there is now a lofty pillar surmounted with a statue of Sir Walter Scott.

Finally, in the market-place of Selkirk there has been set up, at the cost of local friends and neighbours, a statue in freestone, by Mr. Alexander Ritchie of Musselburgh, with this inscription :—

" ERECTED IN AUGUST 1839,

IN PROUD AND AFFECTIONATE REMEMBRANCE

OF

SIR WALTER SCOTT, BARONET,

SHERIFF OF THIS COUNTY

FROM 1800 TO 1832.

By Yarrow's stream still let me stray,
Though none should guide my feeble way;
Still feel the breeze down Ettrick break,
Although it chill my withered cheek."

In what manner to cover the grave itself at Dryburgh required some consideration, in consequence of the state of the surrounding and overhanging ruins. Sir F. Chantrey recommended a block of Aberdeen granite, so solid as to resist even the fall of the ivied roof of the aisle, and kindly sketched the shape; in which he followed the stone coffin of the monastic ages—especially the " marble stone " on which Deloraine awaits the opening of the wizard's vault in the Lay. This drawing had just been given to Allan

Cunningham, when our great sculptor was smitten with a fatal apoplexy. As soon as pressing business allowed, " honest Allan " took up the instructions of his dying friend; the model was executed under his eye: and the letter in which he reported its completion was, I am informed, the very last that he penned. He also had within a few hours a paralytic seizure, from which he never rose. The inscriptions on this simple but graceful tomb are merely of name and date.

The authentic likenesses of Sir Walter Scott, as far as I have been enabled to trace them, are as follows :—

1. A very good miniature, done at Bath, when he was in the fifth or sixth year of his age, was given by him to his daughter Sophia, and is now in my possession—the artist's name unknown. The child appears with long flowing hair, the colour a light chestnut; a deep open collar, and scarlet dress. It is nearly a profile; the outline wonderfully like what it was to the last; the expression of the eyes and mouth very striking—grave and pensive.

2. A miniature sent by Scott to Miss Carpenter, shortly before their marriage in 1797—at Abbotsford. It is not a good work of art, and I know not who executed it. The hair is slightly powdered.

3. The first oil painting, done for Lady Scott in 1805, by Saxon, was, in consequence of repeated applications for the purpose of being engraved, transferred by her to Messrs. Longman & Co., and is now in their house in Paternoster Row. This is a very fine picture, representing, I have no doubt, most faithfully, the author of the Lay of the Last Minstrel. Length, three-quarters—dress black—hair nut-brown—the favourite bull-terrier Camp leaning his head on the knee of his master.

4. The first picture by Raeburn was done in 1808 for Constable, and passed, at the sale of his effects, into the hands of the Duke of Buccleuch. Scott is represented at full length, sitting by a ruined wall, with Camp at his feet —Hermitage Castle and the mountains of Liddesdale in the background. This noble portrait has been repeatedly engraved. Dress black—Hessian boots.—5. The second full-length by Raeburn (done a year later) is nearly a repetition; but the painter had some new sittings. Two greyhounds (Douglas and Percy) appear in addition to Camp, and the background gives the valley of the Yar-

row, marking the period of Ashestiel and Marmion. This piece is at Abbotsford.

6. A head in oil by Thomas Phillips, R.A., done in 1818 for Mr. Murray, and now in Albemarle Street. The costume was, I think, unfortunately selected—a tartan plaid and open collar. This gives a theatrical air to what would otherwise have been a very graceful representation of Scott in the 47th year of his age. Mr. Phillips (for whom Scott had a warm regard, and who often visited him at Abbotsford) has caught a true expression not hit upon by any of his brethren—a smile of gentle enthusiasm. The head has a vivid resemblance to Sir Walter's eldest daughter, and also to his grandson John Hugh Lockhart. A duplicate was added by the late Earl Whitworth to the collection at Knowle.

7. A head sketched in oil by Geddes—being one of his studies for a picture of the finding of the Scottish Regalia in 1818—is in the possession of Sir James Steuart of Allanbank, Baronet. It is nearly a profile—boldly drawn.

8. The unrivalled portrait (three-quarters) by Sir Thomas Lawrence, painted for King George IV. in 1820, and now in the Corridor at Windsor Castle. The engraving by Robinson is masterly.

9. A head by Sir Henry Raeburn—the last work of his hand—was done in 1822 for Lord Montagu, and is at Ditton Park : a massive strong likeness, heavy at first sight, but which grows into favour upon better acquaintance— the eyes very deep and fine. This picture has been well engraved in mezzotinto.

10. A small three-quarters, in oil, done at Chiefswood, in August 1824, by Gilbert Stewart Newton, R.A., and presented by him to Mrs. Lockhart. This pleasing picture gives Sir Walter in his usual country dress—a green jacket and black neckcloth, with a leathern belt for carrying the forester's axe round the shoulders. It is the best domestic portrait ever done. A duplicate, in Mr. Murray's possession, was engraved for Finden's " Illustrations of Byron."

11. A half-length, painted by C. R. Leslie, R.A., in 1824, for Mr. Ticknor of Boston, New England, is now in that gentleman's possession. I never saw this picture in its finished state, but the beginning promised well, and I am assured it is worthy of the artist's high reputation. It has not been engraved—in this country I mean—but a re-

duced copy of it furnished an indifferent print for one of the Annuals.

12. A small head was painted in 1826 by Mr. Knight, a young artist, patronised by Terry. This juvenile production, ill-drawn and feeble in expression, was engraved for Mr. Lodge's great work !

13. A half-length by Mr. Colvin Smith of Edinburgh, done in January 1828, for the artist's uncle, Lord Gillies. I never admired this picture; but it pleased many, perhaps better judges. Mr. Smith executed no less than fifteen copies for friends of Sir Walter; — among others, the Bishop of Llandaff (Coplestone), the Chief Commissioner Adam, and John Hope, now Lord Justice-Clerk of Scotland.

14. A half-length done by Mr. Graham Gilbert in 1829, for the Royal Society of Edinburgh.

15. An excellent half-length portrait, by John Watson Gordon, R.A., done in March 1830, for Mr. Cadell. Scott is represented sitting, with both hands resting on his staff —the stag-hound Bran on his left.

16. A cabinet picture done at Abbotsford in 1831 by Francis Grant, R.A.,—who had the advantage of a familiar knowledge of the subject, being an attached friend of the family. This interesting piece, which has armour and staghounds, was done for Lady Ruthven.

17. I am sorry to say that I cannot express much approbation of the representation of Sir Walter introduced by Sir David Wilkie in his "Abbotsford Family"; nor indeed are any of the likenesses in this graceful composition (1817) at all satisfactory to me, except only that of Sir Adam Fergusson, which is perfect. This is in Sir A.'s possession.—18, 19, 20. Nor can I speak more favourably either of the head of Scott in Wilkie's "Arrival of George IV. at Holyrood" (1822), or of that in Sir William Allan's picture of the "Ettrick Shepherd's Househeating" (1819). Allan has succeeded better in his picture of "The Author of Waverley in his Study"; this was done shortly before Sir Walter's death.

21. Mr. Edwin Landseer, R.A., has painted a full-length portrait, with the scenery of the Rhymer's Glen; and his familiarity with Scott renders this almost as valuable as if he had sat for it. This beautiful picture is in the gallery of Mr. Wells at Redleaf, Kent.

I have given better evidence than my own as to the inimitable bust done by Sir Francis Chantrey in 1820, and now in the library at Abbotsford. Previous to Sir Walter's death, the niche which this now occupies held a cast of the monumental effigy of Shakspeare, presented to him by George Bullock, with an elegant stand, having the letters W.S. in large relievo on its front. Anxiety to place the precious marble in the safest station induced the poet's son to make the existing arrangement on the day after his father's funeral. The propriety of the position is obvious; but in case of misrepresentation hereafter, it is proper to mention that it was not chosen by Sir Walter for an image of himself. As already stated, Chantrey sculptured, in 1828, for Sir Robert Peel, a bust possessing the character of a second original. Sir Walter's good nature induced him to sit, at various periods of his life, to other sculptors of inferior standing and reputation. I am not aware, however, that any of their performances but two ever reached the dignity of marble. One of these, a very tolerable work, was done by Mr. Joseph about 1822, and is in the gallery of Mr. Burn Callender, at Prestonhall, near Edinburgh. The other was modelled by Mr. Lawrence Macdonald, in the unhappy winter of 1830. The period of the artist's observation would alone have been sufficient to render his efforts fruitless.

The only statue executed during Sir Walter's lifetime is that by John Greenshields in freestone. On first seeing this, an early companion of the Poet, Mr. Thomas Thomson, D.C.S., exclaimed, "A petrifaction of Scott!" It is certainly a most meritorious work; and I am well pleased that it has its station in Mr. Cadell's premises in St. Andrew Square, Edinburgh. The proprietor has adopted the inscription for Bacon's effigy at St. Albans, and carved on the pedestal "SIC SEDEBAT."—Mr. Steele's noble marble statue for the Edinburgh Monument was erected in 1847.

INDEX

EVERYMAN'S LIBRARY: A Selected List

This List covers a selection of volumes available in Everyman's Library.

BIOGRAPHY

ESSAYS AND CRITICISM

FICTION

2

Defoe, Daniel (1661?–1731). THE FORTUNES AND MISFORTUNES OF MOLL FLANDERS, 1722. 837. JOURNAL OF THE PLAGUE YEAR, 1722. 289. THE LIFE, ADVENTURES AND PIRACIES OF THE FAMOUS CAPTAIN SINGLETON, 1720. 74. ROBINSON CRUSOE, and THE FARTHER ADVENTURES OF ROBINSON CRUSOE, 1719. Parts I and II complete. 59

De Rojas, Fernando (15th century). CELESTINA: OR THE TRAGI-COMEDY OF CALLISTO AND MELIBEA. Translation (1958) by *Phyllis Hartnoll*, M.A. 100

Dickens, Charles (1812–70). BARNABY RUDGE, 1841. 76. BLEAK HOUSE, 1852–3. 236. A CHRISTMAS CAROL and OTHER CHRISTMAS BOOKS, 1843–8. 239. CHRISTMAS STORIES, 1850–67. 414. DAVID COPPERFIELD, 1849–50. 242. DOMBEY AND SON, 1846–8. 240. EDWIN DROOD, 1870, and MASTER HUMPHREY'S CLOCK, 1840. 725. GREAT EXPECTATIONS, 1861. 234. HARD TIMES, 1854. 292. LITTLE DORRIT, 1857. 293. MARTIN CHUZZLEWIT, 1843–4. 241. NICHOLAS NICKLEBY, 1838–9, 238. THE OLD CURIOSITY SHOP, 1841. 173. OLIVER TWIST, 1838. 233. OUR MUTUAL FRIEND, 1864–5. 294. THE PICKWICK PAPERS, 1836–7. 235. A TALE OF TWO CITIES, 1859. 102. SKETCHES BY 'BOZ', 1835–6. 237

Dostoyevsky, Fyodor (1821–81). THE BROTHERS KARAMAZOV, 1879–80. Translated by *Constance Garnett*. 2 vols. 802–3. CRIME AND PUNISHMENT, 1866. Translated by *Constance Garnett*. 501. THE IDIOT, 1873. Translated by *Eva M. Martin*. 682. LETTERS FROM THE UNDERWORLD, 1864; and OTHER TALES. Translated by *C. J. Hogarth*. 654. POOR FOLK, 1845; and THE GAMBLER, 1867. Translated by *C. J. Hogarth*. 711. THE POSSESSED, 1871. Translated by *Constance Garnett*. 2 vols. 861–2

Dumas, Alexandre (1802–70). THE BLACK TULIP, 1850. The brothers De Witt in the Holland of 1672–5. 174. LE CHEVALIER DE MAISON ROUGE, 1846. 614. CHICOT THE JESTER, 1846. 421. THE COUNT OF MONTE CRISTO, 1844. Napoleon's later phase. 2 vols. 393–4. THE FORTY-FIVE, 1847–8. 420. MARGUERITE DE VALOIS, 1845. 326. THE THREE MUSKETEERS, 1844. The France of Cardinal Richelieu. 81. TWENTY YEARS AFTER, 1845. The Execution of Charles I. 175

Du Maurier, George Louis Palmella Busson (1834–96). TRILBY, 1894. 863

Edgeworth, Maria (1767–1849). CASTLE RACKRENT, 1800; and THE ABSENTEE, 1812. 410

Eliot, George. ADAM BEDE, 1859. 27. DANIEL DERONDA, 1876. 2 vols. 539–40. FELIX HOLT, 1866, 353. MIDDLEMARCH, 1872. 2 vols. 854–5. THE MILL ON THE FLOSS, 1860. 325. ROMOLA, 1863. The Florence of Savonarola. 231. SILAS MARNER, THE WEAVER OF RAVELOE, 1861. 121

English Short Stories. Thirty-six stories from Middle Ages to present time. 743

Fielding, Henry (1707–54). AMELIA, 1751. Amelia is drawn from Fielding's first wife. 2 vols. 852–3. JONATHAN WILD, 1743; and JOURNAL OF A VOYAGE TO LISBON, 1755. 877. JOSEPH ANDREWS, 1742. A skit on Richardson's *Pamela*. 467. TOM JONES, 1749. The first great English novel of humour. 2 vols. 355–6

Flaubert, Gustave (1821–80). MADAME BOVARY, 1857. Translated by *Eleanor Marx-Aveling*. 808. SALAMMBÔ, 1862. Translated by *J. C. Chartres*, 869. SENTIMENTAL EDUCATION, 1869. Translation by *Anthony Goldsmith*. 969

Forster, Edward Morgan (*b.* 1879). A PASSAGE TO INDIA, 1924. Notes by the author. 972

France, Anatole (1844–1924). AT THE SIGN OF THE REINE PÉDAUQUE, 1893, and THE REVOLT OF THE ANGELS, 1914. 967

Gaskell, Mrs Elizabeth (1810–65). CRANFORD, 1853. 83. MARY BARTON. 598

Ghost Stories. Eighteen stories. 952

Gogol, Nikolay (1809–52). DEAD SOULS, 1842. 726. TARAS BULBA. 740

Goldsmith, Oliver (1728–74). THE VICAR OF WAKEFIELD, 1766. 295

Goncharov, Ivan (1812–91). OBLOMOV, 1857. Translated by *Natalie Duddington*. 878

Gorky, Maxim (1868–1936). THROUGH RUSSIA. 741

Grossmith, George (1847–1912), and **Weedon** (1853–1919). THE DIARY OF A NOBODY, 1894. 963

Hardy, Thomas (1840–1928). STORIES AND POEMS. 708

Hawthorne, Nathaniel (1804–64). THE HOUSE OF THE SEVEN GABLES, 1851. 176. THE SCARLET LETTER, 1850. 122. TWICE-TOLD TALES, 1837–42. 531

Hugo, Victor Marie (1802–85). LES MISÉRABLES, 1862. 2 vols. 363–4. NOTRE DAME DE PARIS, 1831. 422. TOILERS OF THE SEA, 1866. 509

James, Henry (1843–1916). THE AMBASSADORS, 1903. 987. THE TURN OF THE SCREW, 1898; and THE ASPERN PAPERS, 1888. 912

Jerome, Jerome K. (1859–1927). THREE MEN IN A BOAT, 1889, and THREE MEN ON THE BUMMEL, 1900. 118

Kingsley, Charles (1819–75). HEREWARD THE WAKE, 1866. 296. WESTWARD HO!, 1855. 20. HYPATIA, 1853. 230

Kipling, Rudyard (1865–1936). STORIES AND POEMS. 690

Lamb, Charles (1775–1834), and **Mary** (1764–1847). TALES FROM SHAKESPEARE, 1807. Illustrated by *Arthur Rackham*. 8

Loti, Pierre (1850–1923). ICELAND FISHERMAN, 1886. 920

Lover, Samuel (1797–1868). HANDY ANDY, 1842. 178

Lytton, Edward Bulwer, Baron (1803–73). THE LAST DAYS OF POMPEII, 1834. 80

Manzoni, Alessandro (1785–1873). THE BETROTHED (*I Promessi Sposi*, 1840, rev. ed.). Translated (1951) by *Archibald Colquhoun*, with a Preface. 999

Marryat, Frederick (1792–1848). MR MIDSHIPMAN EASY. 82. THE SETTLERS IN CANADA, 1844. 370. PETER SIMPLE, 1834. 232

Maugham W. Somerset (1874–1965). CAKES AND ALE, 1930. 932

Maupassant, Guy de (1850–93). SHORT STORIES. Translated by *Marjorie Laurie.* 907

Melville, Herman (1819–91). MOBY DICK; OR THE WHITE WHALE, 1851. 179. TYPEE, 1846; and BILLY BUDD (*published* 1924). South Seas adventures. 180

Meredith, George (1828–1909). THE ORDEAL OF RICHARD FEVEREL, 1859. 916

Mickiewicz, Adam (1798–1855). PAN TADEUSZ. New translation in English verse. (*See* Poetry and Drama Section.)

Modern Short Stories. Selected by *John Hadfield.* Twenty stories. 954

Moore, George (1852–1933). ESTHER WATERS, 1894. 933

Mulock [Mrs Craik], Maria (1826–87). JOHN HALIFAX, GENTLEMAN, 1856. 123

Pater, Walter (1839–94). MARIUS THE EPICUREAN, 1885. 903

Poe, Edgar Allan (1809–49). TALES OF MYSTERY AND IMAGINATION. 336

Priestley, J. B. (*b.* 1894). ANGEL PAVEMENT, 1931. A finely conceived London novel. 938 BRIGHT DAY, 1946. The author's favourite novel. 671

Rabelais, François (1494?–1553). THE HEROIC DEEDS OF GARGANTUA AND PANTA-GRUEL, 1532–5. *Urquhart and Motteux's* unabridged translation, 1653–94.
2 vols. 826–7

Radcliffe, Mrs Ann (1764–1823). THE MYSTERIES OF UDOLPHO, 1794. 2 vols. 865–6

Reade, Charles (1814–84). THE CLOISTER AND THE HEARTH, 1861. 29

Richardson, Samuel (1689–1761). PAMELA, 1740. 2 vols. 683–4. CLARISSA, 1747–8. 4 vols. 882–5

Russian Short Stories. Translated by *Rochelle S. Townsend.* 758

Scott, Sir Walter (1771–1832). THE ABBOT, 1820. 124—sequel to THE MONASTERY, 1820. A sixteenth-century Border romance. 136. THE ANTIQUARY, 1816, 126. THE BRIDE OF LAMMERMOOR, 1819. A romance of life in East Lothian, 1695. 129. THE FAIR MAID OF PERTH, 1828. Scotland in the fifteenth century. 132. THE FORTUNES OF NIGEL, 1822. A romance of Jacobean London. 71. GUY MANNERING, 1815. A mystery story of the time of George III. 133. THE HEART OF MIDLOTHIAN, 1818. Period of the Porteous Riots, 1736. 134. IVANHOE, 1820. A romance of the days of Richard I. 16. KENILWORTH, 1821. The tragic story of Amy Robsart, in Elizabeth I's time. 135. OLD MORTALITY, 1817. Battle of Bothwell Bridge, 1679. 137. QUENTIN DURWARD, 1823. A tale of fifteenth-century France. 140. REDGAUNTLET, 1824. A tale of adventure in Cumberland, about 1763. 141. ROB ROY, 1818. A romance of the Rebellion of 1715. 142. THE TALISMAN, 1825. Richard Cœur-de-Lion and the Third Crusade, 1191. 144. WAVERLEY, 1814. 75. WOODSTOCK, 1826. England under Protector Oliver Cromwell. 72

Shchedrin (M. E. Saltykov, 1826–92). THE GOLOVLYOV FAMILY. Translated by *Natalie Duddington.* 908

Shelley, Mary Wollstonecraft (1797–1851). FRANKENSTEIN, 1818. 616

Shorter Novels. VOL. I: ELIZABETHAN. 824. VOL. II: SEVENTEENTH CENTURY, 841. VOL. III: EIGHTEENTH CENTURY. 856. All three volumes are edited by *Philip Henderson.*

Sienkiewicz, Henryk (1846–1916). QUO VADIS?, 1896. Translated by *C. J. Hogarth.* 970

Smollett, Tobias (1721–71). THE EXPEDITION OF HUMPHRY CLINKER, 1771. 975. PEREGRINE PICKLE, 1751. 2 vols. 838–9. RODERICK RANDOM, 1742. 790

Somerville, E. Œ. (1858–1949), and **Ross, Martin** (1862–1915). EXPERIENCES OF AN IRISH R.M., 1908. Containing *Some Experiences of an Irish R.M.*, 1897, and *Further Experiences of an Irish R.M.*, 1908. 978

Stendhal (pseudonym of Henri Beyle, 1783–1842). SCARLET AND BLACK, 1831. Translated by *C. K. Scott Moncrieff.* 2 vols. 945–6

Sterne, Laurence (1713–68). A SENTIMENTAL JOURNEY THROUGH FRANCE AND ITALY, 1768; JOURNAL TO ELIZA, written in 1767; and LETTERS TO ELIZA, 1766–7. 796. TRISTRAM SHANDY, 1760–7. 617

Stevenson, Robert Louis (1850–94). DR JEKYLL AND MR HYDE, 1886; THE MERRY MEN, 1887; WILL O' THE MILL, 1878; MARKHEIM, 1886; THRAWN JANET, 1881; OLALLA, 1885; THE TREASURE OF FRANCHARD. 767. KIDNAPPED, 1886; and CATRIONA, 1893. 762. THE MASTER OF BALLANTRAE, 1869; WEIR OF HERMISTON, 1896. 764. ST IVES, 1898. Completed by Sir Arthur Quiller-Couch. 904. TREASURE ISLAND, 1883; and NEW ARABIAN NIGHTS, 1882. 763

Story Book for Boys and Girls. Edited by *Guy Pocock.* 934

Swift, Jonathan (1667–1745). GULLIVER'S TRAVELS, 1726. An unabridged edition. 60

Tales of Detection. Nineteen stories. 928

Thackeray, William Makepeace (1811–63). HENRY ESMOND, 1852. 73. THE NEWCOMES, 1853–5. 2 vols. 465–6. PENDENNIS, 1848–50. 2 vols. 425–6. VANITY FAIR, 1847–8. 298. THE VIRGINIANS, 1857–9. 2 vols. 507–8

Tolstoy, Count Leo (1828–1910). ANNA KARENINA, 1873–7. Translated by *Rochelle S. Townsend.* 2 vols. 612–13. MASTER AND MAN, 1895; and OTHER PARABLES AND TALES. 469. WAR AND PEACE, 1864–9. 3 vols. 525–7

Trollope, Anthony (1815–82). THE WARDEN, 1855. 182. BARCHESTER TOWERS, 1857. 30. DOCTOR THORNE, 1858. 360. FRAMLEY PARSONAGE, 1861. 181. THE SMALL HOUSE AT ALLINGTON, 1864. 361. THE LAST CHRONICLE OF BARSET, 1867. 2 vols. 391–2

Byron, George Gordon Noel, Lord (1788–1824). THE POETICAL AND DRAMATIC WORKS. 3 vols. 486–8

Century. A CENTURY OF HUMOROUS VERSE, 1850–1950. 813

Chaucer, Geoffrey (c. 1343–1400). CANTERBURY TALES. Standard text edited by A. C. Cawley, M.A., PH.D. 307. TROILUS AND CRISEYDE. 992

Coleridge, Samuel Taylor (1772–1834). POEMS. 43

Cowper, William (1731–1800). POEMS. 872

Dante, Alighieri (1265–1321). THE DIVINE COMEDY. H. F. Cary's translation. 308

Donne, John (1573–1631). COMPLETE POEMS. Edited, with a revised Introduction, by Hugh I'Anson Fausset. 867

Dryden, John (1631–1700). POEMS. Edited by Bonamy Dobrée, O.B.E., M.A. 910

Eighteenth Century Plays. Edited by John Hampden. 818

Euripides (484?–407 B.C.). PLAYS. Translated by A. S. Way, D.LITT. 2 vols. 63, 271

Everyman, and Medieval Miracle Plays. Edited by A. C. Cawley, M.A., PH.D. 381

Goethe, Johann Wolfgang von (1749–1832). FAUST. Both parts of the tragedy, in the re-edited translation of Sir Theodore Martin. 335

Golden Treasury of English Songs and Lyrics, The, 1861. Compiled by Francis Turner Palgrave (1824–97). Enlarged edition, containing 88-page supplement. 96

Golden Treasury of Longer Poems, The. Revised edition (1954). 746

Goldsmith, Oliver (1728–74). POEMS AND PLAYS. Edited by Sir Sydney Roberts, M.A., HON.LLD. 415

Gray, Thomas (1716–71). POEMS: WITH A SELECTION OF LETTERS AND ESSAYS. 628

Heine, Heinrich (c. 1797–1856). PROSE AND POETRY. With Matthew Arnold's essay on Heine. 911

Homer (? ninth century B.C.). ILIAD. New verse translation by S. O. Andrew and Michael Oakley. 453. ODYSSEY. The new verse translation (first published 1953) by S. O. Andrew. 454

Ibsen, Henrik (1828–1906). BRAND, a poetic drama, 1866. Translated by F. C. Garrett. 716. A DOLL'S HOUSE, 1879; THE WILD DUCK, 1884, and THE LADY FROM THE SEA, 1888. Translated by R. Farquharson Sharp and Eleanor Marx-Aveling; revised by Torgrim and Linda Hånnas. 494. GHOSTS, 1881; THE WARRIORS AT HELGE-LAND, 1857; and AN ENEMY OF THE PEOPLE, 1882. Translated by R. Farquharson Sharp. 552. PEER GYNT, 1867. Translated by R. Farquharson Sharp. 747. THE PRETENDERS, 1864; PILLARS OF SOCIETY, 1877; and ROSMERSHOLM, 1887. Translated by R. Farquharson Sharp. 659. HEDDA GABLER, 1890: THE MASTER BUILDER, 1892 and JOHN GABRIEL BORKMAN, 1896. Translated by Eva Le Gallienne and Norman Ginsbury. 111

Ingoldsby Legends. Edited by D. C. Browning, M.A., B.LITT. 185

International Modern Plays. 989

Jonson, Ben (1573–1637). PLAYS. Complete collection. 2 vols. 489–90

Juvenal (c. A.D. 50–c. 130). SATIRES: with THE SATIRES OF PERSIUS. Introduction by Prof. H. J. Rose, M.A., F.B.A. William Gifford translation, 1802. Revised by John Warrington. 997

Keats, John (1795–1821). POEMS. Revised, reset edition (1944). Edited by Gerald Bullett. 101

La Fontaine, Jean de (1621–95). FABLES, 1668–74. Sir Edward Marsh translation. 991

'Langland, William' (1330?–1400?). PIERS PLOWMAN, 1362. 571

Longfellow, Henry Wadsworth (1807–82). POEMS, 1823–66. 382

Marlowe, Christopher (1564–93). PLAYS AND POEMS. New edition by M. R. Ridley, M.A. 383

Mickiewicz, Adam (1798–1855). PAN TADEUSZ, 1834. New verse translation, with Introduction by Kenneth Mackenzie. Napoleon and Poland. 842

Milton, John (1608–74). POEMS. New edition by Prof. B. A. Wright, M.A. 384

Minor Elizabethan Drama. 2 vols. Vol. I: Tragedy. Vol. II: Comedy. (With glossaries.) 491–2

Minor Poets of the Seventeenth Century. Edited and revised by R. G. Howarth, B.A., B.LITT., F.R.S.L. 873

Modern Plays. 942

Molière, Jean Baptiste de (1622–73). COMEDIES. 2 vols. 830–1

Persian Poems. Selected and edited by Prof. A. J. Arberry, M.A., LITT.D., F.B.A. 996

Poe, Edgar Allan (1809–49). POEMS AND ESSAYS. 791

Poems of our Time, 1900–60. An Anthology edited by Richard Church, C.B.E., M. M. Bozman and Edith Sitwell, D.LITT., D.B.E. Nearly 400 poems by about 130 poets. 981

Pope, Alexander (1688–1744). COLLECTED POEMS. Edited by Prof. Bonamy Dobrée, O.B.E., M.A. 760

Ramayana and Mahabharata. Condensed into English verse by Romesh Dutt, C.I.E. 403

Restoration Plays (Wycherley, Congreve, Dryden, etc.). 604

Rossetti, Dante Gabriel (1828–82). POEMS. 627

Shakespeare, William (1564–1616). A Complete Edition. Cambridge Text. Glossary. 3 vols.: Comedies, 153; Histories, Poems and Sonnets, 154; Tragedies, 155

Shaw, George Bernard (1856–1950). DEVIL'S DISCIPLE, MAJOR BARBARA and SAINT JOAN. 109

Shelley, Percy Bysshe (1792–1822). POETICAL WORKS. 2 vols. 257–8

Sheridan, Richard Brinsley (1751–1816). COMPLETE PLAYS. 95